Performativity and the Representation of Memory:

Resignification, Appropriation, and Embodiment

Frederico Dinis
Polytechnic University of Cávado and Ave, Portugal

IGI Global
PUBLISHER of TIMELY KNOWLEDGE

A volume in the Advances in Psychology, Mental Health, and Behavioral Studies (APMHBS) Book Series

Published in the United States of America by
  IGI Global
  Information Science Reference (an imprint of IGI Global)
  701 E. Chocolate Avenue
  Hershey PA, USA 17033
  Tel: 717-533-8845
  Fax: 717-533-8661
  E-mail: cust@igi-global.com
  Web site: http://www.igi-global.com

Library of Congress Cataloging-in-Publication Data

CIP Pending

Performativity and the Representation of Memory:
Frederico Dinis
2024 Information Science Reference

ISBN: 979-8-3693-2264-2
eISBN: 979-8-3693-2265-9

British Cataloguing in Publication Data
A Cataloguing in Publication record for this book is available from the British Library.

The views expressed in this book are those of the authors, but not necessarily of the publisher.

For electronic access to this publication, please contact: eresources@igi-global.com.

Advances in Psychology, Mental Health, and Behavioral Studies (APMHBS) Book Series

Harish C. Chandan
Argosy University, USA
Bryan Christiansen
Southern New Hampshire University, USA

ISSN:2475-6660
EISSN:2475-6679

Mission

The complexity of the human mind has puzzled researchers and physicians for centuries. While widely studied, the brain still remains largely misunderstood.

The **Advances in Psychology, Mental Health, and Behavioral Studies (APMHBS)** book series presents comprehensive research publications focusing on topics relating to the human psyche, cognition, psychiatric care, mental and developmental disorders, as well as human behavior and interaction. Featuring diverse and innovative research, publications within APMHBS are ideally designed for use by mental health professionals, academicians, researchers, and upper-level students.

Coverage

- Anxiety
- Human Behavior
- Neurological Disorders
- Personality Disorders
- Socialization
- Substance Abuse
- Treatment & Care

IGI Global is currently accepting manuscripts for publication within this series. To submit a proposal for a volume in this series, please contact our Acquisition Editors at Acquisitions@igi-global.com or visit: http://www.igi-global.com/publish/.

Titles in this Series

For a list of additional titles in this series, please visit: www.igi-global.com/book-series

Machine and Deep Learning Techniques for Emotion Detection
Mritunjay Rai (Department of Electrical and Electronics Engineering, Shri Ramswaroop Memorial University, India) and Jay Kumar Pandey (Department of Electrical and Electronics Engineering, Shri Ramswaroop Memorial University, India)
Medical Information Science Reference • copyright 2024 • 313pp • H/C (ISBN: 9798369341438) • US $265.00 (our price)

The Climate Change Crisis and Its Impact on Mental Health
Debabrata Samanta (Rochester Institute of Technology, Kosovo) and Muskan Garg (Mayo Clinic, USA)
Information Science Reference • copyright 2024 • 301pp • H/C (ISBN: 9798369332726) • US $245.00 (our price)

Using Machine Learning to Detect Emotions and Predict Human Psychology
Mritunjay Rai (Department of Electrical and Electronics Engineering, Shri Ramswaroop Memorial University, India) and Jay Kumar Pandey (Department of Electrical and Electronics Engineering, Shri Ramswaroop Memorial University, India)
Medical Information Science Reference • copyright 2024 • 313pp • H/C (ISBN: 9798369319109) • US $240.00 (our price)

Promoting Mindfulness and Well-Being with Indian Psychology
Anuradha Sathiyaseelan (Christ University, India) and Sathiyaseelan Balasundaram (Christ University, India)
Information Science Reference • copyright 2024 • 337pp • H/C (ISBN: 9798369326510) • US $245.00 (our price)

Impact of Climate Change on Mental Health and Well-Being
Debabrata Samanta (Rochester Institute of Technology, Kosovo) and Muskan Garg (Mayo Clinic, USA)
Information Science Reference • copyright 2024 • 282pp • H/C (ISBN: 9798369321775) • US $245.00 (our price)

African Womanhood and the Feminist Agenda
Maxwell Constantine Chando Musingafi (National University of Lesotho, Lesotho) and Chipo Hungwe (Midlands State University, Zimbabwe)
Information Science Reference • copyright 2024 • 280pp • H/C (ISBN: 9798369319994) • US $230.00 (our price)

IGI Global
PUBLISHER of TIMELY KNOWLEDGE

701 East Chocolate Avenue, Hershey, PA 17033, USA
Tel: 717-533-8845 x100 • Fax: 717-533-8661
E-Mail: cust@igi-global.com • www.igi-global.com

Table of Contents

Detailed Table of Contents

Chapter 1

Eleni Timplalexi, National and Kapodistrian University of Athens, Greece
Heidrun Führer, Lund University, Sweden

The media product is generally considered an "objectively" existing entity. Consequently, subjective notions have not found their special intermedial home. A brief historical overview of the shifting conceptualizations of these notions and their interplay highlights intermediality's key references to imagination, memory, and performativity, and calls upon their integration. The chapter questions established stereotypes and dualistic approaches in intermedial theory while suggesting a revision of adopted privileged frameworks. Delving into various incarnations of the intermediate stage, an alternate media product typology is proffered, where both "objectively" existing and subjectively experienced media products become cognitively assimilated on a performative basis. A new interpretation of the intermediate stage that discards the Cartesian knowledge divide thus emerges as a phase, space, time, and performative process, bound to memory and imagination, where subject and object, body and mind, perception and concept are intertwined with multiple agencies.

Chapter 2

Mayra E. García-Díaz, Georgia Southern University, USA

This chapter endeavors to illustrate how scholarly chapters that utilize Latin Testimonio as a methodological research approach drive the processes of shaping, preserving, transmitting, and validating collective memories. It also seeks to shed light on how collective recollections—as embodied and portrayed through the complexity of testimonios—contribute to a strong and cohesive sense of identity among the panethnicity of Latinxs in the U.S. This project inquires papers across four dimensions: 1) Research production and curriculum theorization, 2) intergenerational trauma and decolonial recovery, 3) transmission of cultural values and memories, and 4) external perspectives. The discussion features the conversations among testimonios and highlights its power to foster resilience, cultural richness, solidarity, healing, and the political representation of Latinx identity. Ultimately, the epistemology of the revolutionary act of collective recalling to mind, as exemplified by the embodiment of episodic memory in testimonios, is emphasized as a performative tool.

Chapter 3

Shrimoyee Chattopadhyay, University of Debrecen, Hungary

South Asian people migrate to the West, primarily to the US and the UK, in order to live a better life, full of opportunities. However, apart from fulfilling their desire, some of the diasporic immigrants, especially women, also move away from their home countries so as to escape from trauma. This chapter explores both individual and collective trauma, as portrayed in Monica Ali's *Brick Lane* (2003) and Bharati Mukherjee's *Jasmine* (1989). Relying on Cathy Caruth's notion, the chapter investigates trauma as an unclaimed experience. While Caruth's theory is Westocentric, theories of Jeffrey Alexander and Stef Craps will be useful in analysing the non-Western trauma as represented in the diasporic narratives. Furthermore, intergenerational trauma theories of Angela Connolly and Ana Dragojlovic will be particularly essential to explore the intergenerational haunting as experienced by the female protagonists.

Chapter 4

Saira Raza, Emory University, USA
Anicka Austin, Emory University, USA

Memory is explored as a currency of culture and power, reflecting both oppression and resistance within the United States' fragmented historical landscape. Exile narratives, exemplified in the works of a diverse array of activists, writers, and artists, illustrate memory's role in shaping political will. The chapter delves into the commodification of memory and the impact of displacement on cultural artifacts and archival material. Through participatory performance and creative interventions, archival silences are amplified, challenging dominant narratives. Speculative works highlight the transformative potential of composite memories, emphasizing the fluidity of meaning-making processes. The chapter engages a practice-based research methodology to propose a holistic approach to memory work through speculative participatory creative works, emphasizing embodied storytelling and collective expression in reclaiming cultural narratives.

Chapter 5

Siobhan Davies, London Metropolitan University, UK

Using a combination of qualitative research methods, the author documents her findings from the exploration of her recently acquired familial archive, a repository belonging to her step-aunt, from whom she has long been separated. Drawing upon her collected field notes, kept through the journey of reacquaintance, she links her personal, historical, and cultural observations. Steering between academic analysis and personal odyssey, the chapter reflects an inner dialogue provoked by the material discoveries of a half-remembered past. Within the chapter, "just" another family story unfolds, one that in its telling evokes the intricate interplay between objects, perception, memories, and culture through the experimental use of text, and narrative. Confessional endnotes contribute one final layer to the ethically modulated dance between truth, history, fiction, and power in a textual work that aims for a demonstration of the negotiated and performative construction of self.

This chapter considers the power of art to capture the dynamism of memory as it bounces between past, present and emergent future. In so doing, it focuses centrally on Rod Dickinson's *The Milgram Re-enactment*, 2002 – a performative and video re-enactment of Stanley Milgram's 'Obedience to Authority' experiments of 1962, in which "participants were asked to give apparently lethal electric shocks to an unwilling victim to test how far they would be prepared to obey an authoritative scientist and inflict pain on a protesting person" (Dickinson). What matters, the chapter argues, is less what memory 'remembers,' but how it is put to work as an inventive force in another time and context. Foreshadowing Weizman's interpretation of the Siege of Gaza, 2007 as an "inverse Milgram experiment," Dickinson's work is thus positioned as both re-enactment and pre-enactment of procedural Holocausts to come, and memory is explored as an active operant condition that continues to influence perspectives on as well as policy and conduct in the continuing and current conflict in the Gaza Strip.

This chapter aims to question the ontology of the audio-visual and the use of technology in multimedia performance, specifically in the use of sound and image as communicational and artistic means. Taking this objective into account a research methodology through the artistic practice was developed to analyze the site-specific projects developed by the author, which includes the process of approaching the site-specific and the (de)construction of a sense of place. A case study analysis of three site-specific projects was assessed through a process of continuous inquiry that involves assessing various levels of permanence and different modes of access to information. It has been observed that the performativity of memory can be strengthened through live audio-visual performances in specific places and performative moments can provide a platform for the community to shape its memory.

This chapter documents and discusses the musical piece titled A Cronulla si junceru, based on a text written in Sicilian, that narrates the events of the Cronulla riot. The incident took place in the eponymous South Sydney beach, on 11 March 2005. After criticising some of the media releases about Cronulla, the chapter author discusses various aspects related to the piece, ranging from its conceptual intents in terms of collective memory, to the circumstances of its composition (comprovisation) and performances, through to more technical considerations related to the Sicilian language and the use of text as compositional material.

This chapter explores how a collective memory of local jazz is constructed from a group interview designed as a record listening session. By bringing together mediators or agents who were in any way part of the jazz scene in Manila between 1946 and 1986, this ethnographic activity served as a space to observe how interactions emerging from individual and shared lived experiences can affect the way jazz memory is expressed and signified. The collective recollection was stimulated, navigated, and articulated from relevant media materials and from questions pertaining to agents' social, cultural, and economic negotiations. Aside from learning, emphasizing, or correcting ideas about the local scene during the conversation, this chapter brings forward multiple social and performative factors to observe how decolonial perspectives can affect the fabrication and circulation of memory and local music histories.

This chapter presents the results of a critical review of the scholarship surrounding Sámi women and the memories of the generational trauma and injustices, dispossession, and resilience of these women. Sámi women's feminism and activism are often left out of the scholarly discussions surrounding fairness and equity for this indigenous population, and little research has focused on the voice or vocality of this target population outside of arts-based research. The chapter presents the historical context that may be used for contemporary interpretations of transdisciplinary research findings for this target population. The systematic critical review involved recursivity for a systematically selected sample of current peer-reviewed articles filtered for memory, resilience, and voice constructs for Sámi women in Finnmark, Norway.

This chapter is a visual, aural, and written iteration of the performative walk "Where are we? Performing the city, slowing down time" developed and presented by the artists Beatriz Cantinho and Susana Mendes Silva in the context of the "Elia Academy 2023: exploring situatedness" that took place in the University of Évora in May. The aesthetic focus of this performative walk was a reflection on how one can create connections with the place where one is, and how one can look and unveil lost, forgotten, or erased stories of a given territory. The territory was the city of Évora, where Cantinho and Mendes Silva wanted participants to experience its history, landscape and soundscape, and their own bodies, their own presence from a situated perspective. The authors also wanted to trigger a conscious experience that contrasted with the touristic way of experiencing this World Heritage city and its water systems.

Narrating (fictitious) experience is a core element of political communication on environmental conflicts: To observe environmental change and to discern the ongoing redefinition of 'nature' in collective memory have accompanied the environmental movements from their beginning. This chapter takes an analytical look on the way pop music deals with tropes of a remembered ecology. Are there key topics and narrative strands when it comes to reflecting musically environmental change through memory? By examining selected songs that deal with ecological memory, the case studies of this chapter investigate "latent structures" of Western societies: partly unspoken or non-negotiated dynamics and aspects of environmental conflicts in the 'subconscious' streams of a society. Pop music is not just a sounding board for ecological crises; it popularizes historical concepts and provides an archive of environmental history and its inherent longing for forecasting the future.

In this chapter, the author re-thinks and reflects on the importance of the relationship and interconnection between the site-specific, the sense of place, the ambience and the performativity of memory, exploring and deepening the confluence between sound and image, relating concepts, purposes and coherence of site-specific artistic practices that mediate and reconfigure the memory of places. The chapter aims to study the confluence between sound and image in performative places, through a research methodology through the artistic practice used to analyse sound and visual performances and their representations of memory. Intermediate mediation, through sound and visual construction, promotes new interpretations, making use of the memory of the spectator. It is also observed that exploring intermediate forms of sound and visual representation of memory in live site-specific performances opens up new artistic possibilities, challenges traditional modes of storytelling, and facilitates deeper audience engagement with the artwork and its underlying themes.

In contemporary societies, the urgent acquisition of information is vital, reflecting in the (sub)(post) cultural dynamics of youth cultures. However, despite all these urgent needs, there are also attempts to preserve memory and heritage, especially in the Portuguese alternative and underground music scenes. Archives play an important role in structuring self-help projects for enthusiasts that challenge dominant notions of archiving. The democratisation of archives, facilitated by digital technologies, emphasises community-driven initiatives and challenges traditional notions of neutrality. This chapter explores the theoretical, methodological, and ethical dimensions surrounding the preservation of punk manifestations in Portugal, filling gaps in cultural and academic representation. The KISMIF archive represents a pioneering attempt to document Portuguese underground music scenes, revealing previously unknown cultural realities.

The modern human is performative. If we consider modernity as ritual process, a set of performance technologies that organize the intensive energies of the homo sapien into the extensive coordinates of the modern human, then perhaps altermodern rituals biogram something else. We might see the recent propositions of posthuman, metahuman, transhuman, and ahuman (amongst others) as a confirmation that the modern human is only one set of extensive coordinates for Homo sapien, and perhaps no longer even the most influential. This study folds ethnography, performance studies, and feminist technoscience in a developing cyborgraphic practice called CineWorlding, a mode of cinematic research-creation. The contribution of this chapter is to experiment with a method of transmedia study with emerging xhumans to investigate the role of technologically mobile transmemory in its biogrammatic formation.

This chapter investigates specific case studies of choreographic reenactment through memory considered both as a somatic embodied element and as a tool for reconstruction of choreographic pieces. Focusing primarily on British Gaby Agis, as a somatic movement educator and dancer, the author utilises embodied ethnography in the process of participant-observation and analysis of the case studies. The perspective of the inter-relationships between dancer and choreographer informs fieldwork analysis, delving into the direct and indirect impact of somatics on their works and creative approaches. The enquiry combines theoretical perspectives and fieldwork that acknowledges methodological interactions and parallels in different choreographic narratives.

Editorial Advisory Board

Preface

In the ever-evolving landscape of memory studies, the intersection of memory, representation, and performativity has emerged as a focal point for scholarly inquiry. *Performativity and the Representation of Memory: Resignification, Appropriation, and Embodiment*, delves into the intricate dynamics of memory, exploring its role in shaping individual and collective identities.

Memory is not a static entity confined to the past; rather, it is a dynamic and performative force that continually shapes our present realities. Concepts such as collective memory, places of memory, incorporated memory, post-memory and memory re-enactment, have helped to elucidate the complex interplay between past experiences and contemporary practices.

Central is also the notion of memory as a performative act—one that is enacted, contested, and reappropriated in various socio-cultural contexts. By examining the intersection of memory with history, heritage, and art, this book uncovers the multifaceted ways in which memory manifests in today's interconnected world.

Drawing on diverse examples from across Europe and beyond, the book illustrates how contemporary societies grapple with the politics of memory and the challenges of control, ownership, and transmission. Moreover, it sheds light on the unique features of contemporary digital culture, which not only exposes the processes of memory construction but also redefines the grammar and mediation of meaning-making.

Through thorough research and insightful analysis, the book invites readers to critically engage with the complexities of memory in contemporary society. Whether professionals, policymakers, or members of the scientific community, this book offers valuable insights into the evolving dynamics of memory, representation, and performativity in our interconnected world.

As editor, it is my privilege to present this volume, which promises to enrich our understanding of memory and its myriad manifestations in the modern age.

ORGANIZATION OF THE BOOK

In Chapter 1, "Claiming an Intermedial Home for Imagination, Memory and Performativity: A Subjective Approach to the Intermediate Stage of Communication", Eleni Timplalexi and Heidrun Führer embark on a journey to redefine the boundaries of intermediality. Through a historical lens, they challenge established notions of objectivity, advocating for the integration of subjective experiences within the intermediate stage. Their chapter proposes a new typology of media products, one that encompasses both objective existence and subjective perception, thus reshaping our understanding of memory, imagination, and performativity as intertwined processes.

Chapter 2, "Latinx Testimonio Methodology: Shaping the Collective Memory of an Identity" by Mayra García-Díaz, delves into the transformative power of testimonios in shaping Latinx collective memory. Through a multidimensional analysis, García-Díaz explores how testimonies contribute to a cohesive sense of identity among Latinxs in the U.S., shedding light on their role in research production, intergenerational trauma recovery, cultural transmission, and political representation.

Shrimoyee Chattopadhyay's Chapter 3, "Memory, Trauma, and Healing: Transformation of Identities of South Asian Diasporic Women", scrutinizes individual and collective trauma experiences of South Asian diasporic women, particularly in literary narratives. Drawing on theoretical frameworks from Western and non-Western perspectives, Chattopadhyay examines the intergenerational haunting portrayed in diasporic narratives, offering insights into the complexities of identity and trauma.

In Chapter 4 "Composite Harmonies: Reclaiming Memory Artifacts through Community Creative Practice", Saira Raza and Anicka Austin examine the commodification of memory and the impact of displacement on cultural artifacts, advocating for a feminist ethic of care in archival practices. Proposing a holistic approach to memory work through speculative participatory creative works Raza and Austin emphasize embodied storytelling and collective expression in reclaiming cultural narratives.

Siobhan Davies's Chapter 5, "Flowering Out: An Autoethnographic Study of My Stepfamily", presents a nuanced exploration of familial memory through autoethnography. Davies navigates between personal reflection and scholarly analysis, uncovering the intricate interplay between memory, perception, and culture within her stepfamily archive.

In Chapter 6, "Re-Echoing the Scream: Rod Dickinson's Shock Machine and the Re-Emergence of Milgram's 'Obedience to Authority' Experiments", Bernadette Buckley explores the performative dynamics of memory in art. Focusing on Rod Dickinson's re-enactment of Stanley Milgram's experiments, Buckley illuminates how memory operates as an inventive force, shaping perspectives and influencing conduct in contemporary society.

Frederico Dinis's Chapter 7, "Performativity of the Memory of the Place and Practices of Remembrance", investigates the role of technology in enhancing the performativity of memory in multimedia performance. Through site-specific projects and art-based research, Dinis examines how live performances amplify the performativity of memory, providing platforms for community engagement and the reshaping of collective memory.

In Chapter 8, "A Cronulla si junceru: Remembering Racial Violence through Text-Based Musical Composition", Marcello Messina documents the role of music in preserving collective memory. Focusing on a musical piece recounting the Cronulla riot, Messina delves into the conceptual intents, composition process, and socio-political implications of the work.

Krina Cayabyab's Chapter 9, "Lagáyan, Tengáhan, at Pakiramdáman: A Collective Recollection of Jazz in Metro Manila", explores the construction of collective memory through group interviews and record listening sessions. By observing interactions among mediators, Cayabyab examines how decolonial perspectives shape jazz memory and local music histories.

In Chapter 10, "A Critical Review of Voice, Memory, and Resilience among Finnmark Sámi Women", Robin Throne presents the results of a critical review of the scholarship surrounding Sámi women and the memories of the generational trauma and injustices, dispossession, and resilience of these women. By presenting the historical context Throne reinforces contemporary interpretations of transdisciplinary research findings for this target population.

"Where are we?: Performative Strategies of Encounter", Chapter 11, by Susana Mendes Silva and Beatriz Cantinho offers a visual and aural exploration of performative walks in the city of Évora. Through sensory experiences and historical reflections, the authors unveil forgotten narratives, inviting participants to engage with their surroundings from a situated perspective.

Thorsten Philipp's Chapter 12, "Sounds of Remembered Nature: Narrating Environmental Change Through Pop Music", examines the representation of ecological memory in pop music. By analyzing selected songs, Philipp uncovers latent structures of environmental conflicts, highlighting pop music's role in popularizing environmental history and forecasting the future.

In Chapter 13, "Exploring Intermediate Modes of Memory Representation and Resignification", Frederico Dinis delves into the confluence of sound and image in performative places. Through artistic practices and live performances, Dinis explores how intermediate forms of representation deepen audience engagement and offer new artistic possibilities.

Paula Guerra and Pedro Quintela's Chapter 14, "You Can Put Your Arms Around a Memory: Popular Music and Archives", explores the preservation of punk manifestations in Portugal. Through community-driven initiatives and digital technologies, they challenge traditional notions of archiving and documenting previously unknown cultural realities.

In Chapter 15, "Anarchist Erotica: Transmedia and Transmemory in Cyborgraphy" Michael MacDonald introduces CineWorlding, a cinematic research-creation practice. By folding ethnography and feminist technoscience, MacDonald investigates the role of transmedia in shaping transmemory and biogrammatic formations.

Elisa Frasson's Chapter 16, "Memory as a Tool for Choreographic Reenactment: Gaby Agis' Work as a Case Study", examines choreographic reenactment through the lens of memory. Focusing on Gaby Agis's works, Frasson explores the somatic and reconstructive aspects of memory in choreographic narratives.

IN CONCLUSION

As we conclude this exploration of memory, representation, and performativity across diverse cultural contexts, it becomes evident that memory is far from a passive recollection of the past; rather, it is a dynamic force that shapes our present realities and future aspirations. Through the insightful contributions of our esteemed authors, we have traversed through interdisciplinary landscapes, from the realms of literature and art to music, performance, and digital culture.

Each chapter has illuminated unique facets of memory, from its role in shaping collective identities to its power in fostering resilience, healing, and social transformation. We have witnessed how testimonies, literary narratives, artistic reenactments, and processes of construction of meaning serve as vehicles for preserving, transmitting, and resignifying memories across generations and communities.

Moreover, our exploration has underscored the importance of interdisciplinary dialogue in understanding the complex interplay between memory, imagination, and performativity. Whether through autoethnography, archival studies, art-based research or transmedia practices, scholars and practitioners alike have demonstrated the transformative potential of memory as a tool for cultural preservation, social critique, and artistic expression.

As editor, I am honored to have facilitated this journey through the intricate tapestry of memory studies. I am immensely grateful to our contributors for their scholarly rigor, creative insight, and dedication to advancing our understanding of memory in all its multifaceted dimensions. It is my sincere hope that this edited reference book will serve as a valuable resource for scholars, students, and practitioners across disciplines, inspiring further exploration and dialogue in the ever-evolving field of memory studies.

Frederico Dinis

Institute for Research in Design, Media and Culture ID +, Portugal & Polytechnic Institute of Cávado and Ave, Design School, Portugal

Acknowledgement

I would like to express my gratitude to everyone involved in this project, particularly the authors and reviewers who participated in the review process. Without their support, this book would not have become a reality.

Firstly, I extend my deepest thanks to each of the authors for their contributions. I'm deeply grateful to the chapter authors for dedicating their time and expertise to this book.

Secondly, I also wish to acknowledge the Editorial Advisory Board for their valuable input in enhancing the quality, coherence, and presentation of the chapters. Many authors also served as reviewers, and I greatly appreciate their dual role.

Frederico Dinis

Institute for Research in Design, Media and Culture ID +, Portugal & Polytechnic Institute of Cávado and Ave, Design School, Portugal

Chapter 1
Claiming an Intermedial Home for Imagination, Memory, and Performativity:
A Subjective Approach to the Intermediate Stage of Communication

Eleni Timplalexi
http://orcid.org/0000-0001-8120-8759
National and Kapodistrian University of Athens, Greece

Heidrun Führer
http://orcid.org/0000-0001-8456-365X
Lund University, Sweden

ABSTRACT

The media product is generally considered an "objectively" existing entity. Consequently, subjective notions have not found their special intermedial home. A brief historical overview of the shifting conceptualizations of these notions and their interplay highlights intermediality's key references to imagination, memory, and performativity, and calls upon their integration. The chapter questions established stereotypes and dualistic approaches in intermedial theory while suggesting a revision of adopted privileged frameworks. Delving into various incarnations of the intermediate stage, an alternate media product typology is proffered, where both "objectively" existing and subjectively experienced media products become cognitively assimilated on a performative basis. A new interpretation of the intermediate stage that discards the Cartesian knowledge divide thus emerges as a phase, space, time, and performative process, bound to memory and imagination, where subject and object, body and mind, perception and concept are intertwined with multiple agencies.

DOI: 10.4018/979-8-3693-2264-2.ch001

SETTING UP THE SCENE

Communication is usually seen as a technical and/or interpersonal exchange of information, messages and meaning. Consequently, the medium is considered to be an objectively existing entity, intentionally created by a producer, that enables the transfer of a message, or even meaning, through a channel to a receiver, under the condition of noise. Alternatively, the medium has been seen as attracting an active perceiver's selective attention, perception and meaning-making, without, however, any particular further questioning of the stereotypical constants of communication, nor evoking the space to encompass interaction with the self in the broader conceptual category of communication.

It becomes evident that, in such a state of affairs, more subjective understandings of the medium remain peripheral and find no fruitful terrain on which to come into full blossom, an orbit which, consequently, further marginalizes subjective notions such as imagination, memory and performativity, hampering their integration in communication discourses. Such is the case, we outline, with the intermedial perspective on the media product/intermediate stage duality and communication. Although phenomenally appearing as opening up towards more subjective paths, the main intermedial approach constitutes no special exception, because the same, more or less, objective stance has been assumed towards the media product. The lack of systematic references to memory, imagination and performativity at the core of intermedial theory pinpoint towards this direction.

It is our hypothesis that established stereotypes about the media product and communication divert attention away from the subjective dimension of the media product in intermedial theory - and possibly in general. Consequently, we explore and expand the understanding of the intermedial intermediate stage by integrating imagination, memory and performativity in intermedial communication theory, so that a more holistic picture emerges. The intermedial stage becomes a space, time and process that, although resisting a precise definition, discards the Cartesian knowledge divide (Alanen, 1989) by foregrounding the situated embeddedness of subject and object, body and mind, mind and matter, perception and concept with multiple agencies, where the exploration of both "objectively" existing and subjectively experienced media products in their performative assimilation processes becomes possible.

The chapter starts with a brief historical overview of the philosophical ruptures of imagination, memory and performativity, followed by a section dedicated to the intermedial field of inquiry and its theoretical framework. The theory of media modalities and qualifying aspects and the medium-centered model of communication are briefly sketched and situated within their multifaceted, multidisciplinary discursive landscape. Key intermedial references to imagination, memory and performativity are highlighted. Established stereotypes about communication pervading intermedial studies are traced and critically discussed, creating a context for engaging with the subjective dimension of the media product. The diachronic interplay between imagination, memory and performativity is considered as a basis for the intermediate stage, whereby its various "incarnations" are explored. A typology of the media product which also accommodates subjective media products is proffered, accumulating into a new interpretation of the intermediate stage as a phase, a space, time and performative process, bound to memory and imagination.

SUMMONING IMAGINATION, MEMORY, AND PERFORMATIVITY: A BRIEF HISTORICAL OVERVIEW

This section is dedicated to a brief historical overview of the key notions of imagination, memory and performativity and attempts to emphasize the nuances of their definitions, as well as help the reader traverse their diachronic constellations in models concerning human experience, so that the understanding of communication and the intermediate stage on more subjective grounds, beyond the subject/object dichotomy, is facilitated.

Imagination

Originating from the Latin word *imago*, the term "imagination" has an iconic or pictorial character, unfolding differently through times. In ancient ones, imagination overlapped with *phantasia*, which, according to Plato, is an experience of appearances. For Aristotle, imagination is a central animal cognitive function that provides images to the soul/mind, while the Epicureans and Stoics highlighted the connection between *phantasia* with impression (Barney, 1992, p. 283). The Middle Ages saw the transformation of a philosophical imagination into a spiritual one (Karnes, 2011), while the Renaissance period highlights imagination in its poetic dimension, grounded in rationality (Zuliani, 2022). Descartes claims that imagination is a special way of thinking of material things, the act of contemplating the figure or image of a bodily thing and the ways of conceiving (the idea of) a thing (Descartes in Lyons, 1999). During the eighteenth century, the focus shifted towards the human subject as an active creator, able to rationally control the process of *phantasia* (Mersch, 2009). Hume introduces imagination as a subjective matrix for causality in relation to the continual existence of objects (Klein et al., 1983). Kant subjugates imagination to the cognitive production of concepts, distinguishing between reproductive (mechanical) and productive (spontaneous) imagination in the process of apprehending an object in cognition. Coleridge, with one foot in the nineteenth century, rephrases the duality as "primary" and "secondary" imagination, but also calls it a "living power" (Hume, 1970), while Husserl denotes "imagination" or "imagining" as a sensory experience of something in its absence – a "quasi-perception" (Jansen, 2013).

The list of philosophers and authors negotiating imagination augments even more in the late nineteenth and twentieth centuries. Reichling (1990), in an attempt to systematize these various voices, demarcates four facets of imagination. First comes the facet of intuition, as outlined by Kant and preferred by Husserl and others. Then comes the facet of perception, which is grounded on the Kantian reproductive imagination and favored by Coleridge and Warnock. A third facet of imagination, that springs out from the writings of Hume, Warnock and Langer (among others), is thinking; here, the mind is seen as a faculty that produces ideas, hence imagination is attributed a cognitive function. Last is the facet of feeling, supported mostly by Langer, Ricoeur and Scheffler, to name but a few (p. 284-287).

Despite the enormous polyphony in conceptualizing imagination throughout times, its most influential concept today is the Romantic one that countered the positivistic, scientific and rational post Enlightenment approaches and shaped the *beaux arts* in opposition to crafts and performances (Munro, 1949). This ghost of imagination is the ground for aesthetic illusion and the dominance of "representation" or "content" that echoes the distinction between the real world and the highly valued "as-if" effect in all aesthetic media products, even when they are considered beyond the alleged sense of *mimesis* as "imitation" of reality. Nevertheless, reacting against the Romantic idealism of the autonomous subject, the subjective part linked to imagination is most often marginalized, as this historical review of the different positions shows. Still, we emphasize those voices that imagination integrates as the faculty "to represent possibilities other than the actual, to represent times other than the present, and to represent perspectives other than one's own" (Liao & Gendler, 2020), which includes dreams about a better world to come (Bottici, 2014).

Today, imagination is regarded as basis for all creative activities and is linked to cognitive and emotional processes (Vygotsky, 2004). As a medium, imagination is "a world where thought and images are nested in the mind to form a mental concept of what is not actually present to the senses" – "a form of mediation between what is considered "externalized" reality and internalized man" (Perdue, 2003).

Memory

Often a synonym of recollection or remembrance, memory refers to the processes of remembering past actions, events, thoughts and knowledge, as well as to rhetorical skill (*ars memorandi*). Memory grounds abstract thought and serves the performance of quotidian life practices. Lately, in the technical nuance of the term, memory becomes a device where data may be stored and retrieved, as in computers. However, the concept of media acting as memory devices is not new. As far back as Plato, writing was considered as a materialized record of past events. Memory may thus be understood as internal and external, natural and artificial, depending on the focus of attention, echoing dichotomies so much favored by Enlightenment thinkers or scientists; or, as an incredible, fundamental human capacity that blurs such distinctions.

Our sense of memory emerges from our understanding of time as one directional and going forward, attaching actions to past knowledge and future expectations. Hence, this "mundane" memory differs from the a-chronical *mneme*, personified in the divine *Mnemosyne* of ancient Greek mythology (Ganguly, 2002). Plato argued that memory, as in recollection, revived knowledge acquired in a life before birth and equals a trace of earlier experience, thus expanding the concept of memory beyond sensory experience of the present (Deutscher, 1998). Despite Plato's epistemological assumption of memory mechanisms focusing on the preservation and recollection of mental images, there was space for "the experience in the soul alone of things originally apprehended by the soul and body together" (Hochschild, 2012, p. 25), heralding his student's interest in such mechanisms. Indeed, Aristotle's perspective on memory has been more likened to that of the modern psychologist than that of a modern philosopher, more involved in demarcating different kinds of memory than discussing philosophical problems attached to it (Annas, 2003 [1995]), however informed by the insight that "nature refuses to conform to our cravings for clear lines of demarcation" (Lovejoy in Otte, 1998, p. 425). As if anticipating Kant's system of subjective thinking and the nature of time (Bobko, 2019), Saint Augustine grounds the sense of flow of time in the mind, that orders chronologically, thus engendering the linear understanding of time, claiming the present as an extensionless cut between the periods of past and future. By relying on reason and the newly acquired laws of physics, Descartes strives to define the senses, imagination, memory and intellect, as well as organize their interrelations. Memory was not included in his questioning of the senses; in fact, memory was not afforded Descartes' trust as a basis for reason. Locke did not challenge the view that all understanding of the past rested on personal memory (Deutscher, 1998). Hume proposed criteria for the distinction between memory and imagination (Urmson, 1967), while, for Kant, memory, as in "memorizing", comprises mechanical, ingenious and judicious memorizing and is also a compound of reproductive imagination. Sensitive memory, on the other hand, draws out sensuous stimuli (Acosta, 2020). Likewise, imagination is responsible for intuitive sensible representations of objects that are not immediately present to us, including ideas and concepts (Matherne, 2016). Thus, Kantian imagination becomes the basis for cognitive, aesthetic and morale experience. Russell (1915) invites us to inquire whether memory and imagination are distinguishable and on what grounds, although such distinction registers as a "universally" established one (Urmson, 1967, p. 83). Indeed, the very need for differentiation between memory and imagination has given rise to theories about various interrelations between the two. Memory, which provides impressions in their original temporal and spatial order, is one of the two elements of imagination, but also serves "as a store of material for the imagination in the sense of past experiences" (Klein et al., 1983). Husserl's phenomenology proposed that memory, integrated in the study of experience, is one of the ways to grasp the world and impact it – a position further explored by Heidegger, Sartre and Merleau-Ponty (Deutscher, 1998).

Mitchell (1994) considers memory beyond the disembodied, invisible spectrum, as both a material and semiotic process. Memory is also identified as a basis for the creation of identity and communication and as the starting point of media, since it is through memory that we learn how to create and comprehend (Ganguly, 2002). Memory is even called a medium itself, that combines "the same modalities (space and time), the same sensory channels (the visual and aural), and the same codes (image and word)" (Mitchell, 1994, p. 192).

Performativity

Performativity has come to signify actualization (emergence into being) and the process of the identity construction (including subject formation and subject-object relation), through processes and social practices linked to power. Initially, it was introduced by Austin (1962) as the power of language to effect change in the world beyond mere description. Austin's "performatives" inspired an expansion of the performative function beyond mere speech acts, with Butler (1999 [1990]) exploring the ascription and construction of gender identity as performance. Goffman's (1974) frame analysis offered the theoretical ground for performativity to pervade also social discourse and everyday life. Scholars such as Barad, Deleuze, Derrida, Callon, Lyotard and Kosofsky Sedgwick exploited the idea of performativity as discursive and material enactments that construct subjects and objects by rendering the concept an interdisciplinary tool, even beyond humanities and the social sciences (Suncana, 2020). Performativity is often discussed along with embodiment and embodied practices, agency, actualization (Jeanes, 2019) and politics. Barad's (2007) sociomaterial approach claims that the relationship between the human and the material is one of entanglement and of continuously performed intra-relations. In such an agential realist account of performativity, knowledge is not obtained from a distance, but from a material enmeshment with the world and cannot be separated from such practices (Hultin, 2019).

It is impossible to define performativity while neglecting its connections to performance, theatre and drama. Performativity draws its executional, agential and actualizational context from one of the definitions of performance as "doing" – other definitions being "being", "showing doing" and "explaining 'showing doing'" (Schechner, 2002, p. 28). A generally acclaimed definition of performance has been provided by Schechner (2002): a twice-behaved, restored behavior (p. 29) that is marked, framed, or heightened (p. 35) and publicly exhibited (p. 43). Performance Studies distinguished between drama – as in, verbal narratives, written texts, scripts, plans for events and material devolved from rehearsals or spontaneous improvisation – and performance, declaring the latter void of notions such as role and plot, removing the distance between the "real" and the metaphorical (Goldberg, 2001).

Mc Kenzie (2006) notes the "imperialistic" tendency of Performance Studies. The distinction between "is performance" and "as performance", as previously foretold by Schechner (2002, p. 38) all the more, empirically speaking, vanishes. However, much of what is considered "performative", is actually "theatrical". As Elam (1980) highlights, the term "theatrical" actually signifies the performer/audience transaction and meaning making production (p. 2). Féral (2002) proposes three scenarios of theatricality, from which emerges the attribution of a symbolic dimension via the perceiver's gaze on occurring events or representations/simulations of them (theatricality of the gaze). Theatricality partly coincides with spectacularity, as it is symbolically attached to the same sensorial path (vision), but it is not exhausted in/by it. It also contains a potential process of *θεωρείν* (theorein) (Πούχνερ, 2010), both sensorial and cognitive.

THE INTERMEDIAL FRAMEWORK: POSITIONING MEMORY, IMAGINATION, AND PERFORMATIVITY

This section considers the background of the intermedial field of inquiry and its theoretical framework - namely, theory on/of media modalities, qualifying aspects and the medium-centered model of communication.

Sketching the Intermedial Field of Inquiry: Media Modalities and the Medium-Centered Model of Communication

Despite different understandings of intermedial theory and multimedia (Müller, 1996; Rajewsky, 2008, indicatively), it is here Lars Elleström's (2010; 2018; 2021) systematic intermedial theory that attracts our focus of attention. The intermedial field of inquiry "has its historical roots in aesthetics, philosophy, semiotics, comparative literature, media studies and interart studies" (Elleström 2021a, p. 9) and is claimed to have assimilated multimodality, which derived from social semiotics, education, linguistics and communication studies (ibid). Intermediality studies the abstract relations between basic and qualified media, as well as the features of specific works, performances and media products, along with their interconnections (Elleström 2010, p. 30). Bruhn and Schirrmacher (2022) suggest that intermedial studies discuss the interactions of similarities and differences between media, the changes that occur when medial material is transported from one media type to another (p. 3) and "the ways in which objects and phenomena can function as media products" (p. 9).

The intermedial notion of media includes basic media types and qualified ones, media products and technical media of display (p. 8–9). "Basic media types" operate as "communicative building blocks", whereas "qualified media types" are defined by "context, convention and history and by our experience of many individual media products" (Bruhn & Schirrmacher, 2022, p. 4). Elleström (2021a) introduced the notion of the technical medium of display, comprising "any object, physical phenomenon or body that mediates sensory configurations in the context of communication" and "realizes and displays the entities that we construe as media products" (p. 34). The "media product" is "a single physical entity or phenomenon that enables inter-human communication" (Elleström, 2021a, p. 8) by interconnecting minds (p. 33). It is a delimited unit "formed by (often shared) selective attention to sensorially perceptible areas of communication" that depends on social praxis (p.15–16), as well as a specific communicative object, event or a material-based tool that grounds communication across time and space (Bruhn & Schirrmacher, 2022, p. 4).

Elleström considers the features of his overall intermedial media model on both an internal and an external basis. Elleström's media modalities model (2010; 2021a) and the medium-centered model of communication (2018; 2021a) describe the classifications of artifacts in their multimodal intertwinement as "qualified media products", thus systematize the diverse discourses that precede his work. Four abstract *modalities,* the material, the spatiotemporal, the sensorial and the semiotic, shape the mediality of each media product (Elleström, 2021a, p. 46-49).

The first is the material modality, which includes different states of matter, such as liquid, gas, plasma, organic and inorganic, is anchored in the physicality of all media products and "makes them perceptible and hence accessible to the perceiver's mind in various ways" (Elleström 2021a, p. 47).[1] Second, the spatiotemporal modality, which theorizes the spatiotemporal properties of media products as material entities, considers width, height, depth and time. Then, the sensorial modality is said to explain the properties stipulating the perceivers' senses regarding materiality. Finally, comes the semiotic modality, which creates a "frame for understanding representation", called the *semiosis* process. Two discrete apparatuses (operational and contextual aspects of public qualification) are involved in the process of intersubjective meaning-making. For instance, any theatre performance qualifies as belonging to a cluster of media products with which it shares similarities, whereas the operational qualifying aspect frames the general purpose, use and function of a medium (Elleström 2021a, 60–62).

Also, at play are tripartite interrelations between the sender and receiver through the media product, which regulate communication and present the media product as an intermediate stage between the subjects and the object. Thus, the media product emerges as a finite entity that enables the transfer of cognitive input in the communicative process (Elleström, 2018). In more detail, Elleström proposes three absolute essentials for communication to occur, three "indispensable and interconnected entities": something being transferred; two separate places between which the transfer occurs; and an intermediate stage that makes the transfer possible (p. 277). Furthermore, the essential relations that connect these entities include an act of production between the producer's mind and media product, an act of perception between the media product and the perceiver's mind, cognitive import inside the producer's mind and the perceiver's mind and, finally, transfer of cognitive import through the media product (p. 282).

Tracking the Position of Imagination, Memory, and Performativity in Intermediality

In Elleström's intermedial theory of multimodal media products and communication, the notions of memory, imagination and performativity might be tacitly deduced, but are not clearly integrated. Various intermedial discourses, such as the theatre/media studies perspective of theatre as the "hypermedium and home to all" (Chapple & Kattenbelt 2006, p. 24) and Bal's understanding of performativity as a "traveling concept" in the humanities (Bal, 2002), attempt to situate performativity within the realms of theatricality and interdisciplinarity respectfully. However, because in this chapter, the major Elleströmian intermedial models are adopted as tools for exploring memory, imagination and performativity in the intermediate stage, it is the intermedial perspective developed at Linnaeus University Centre for Intermedial and Multimodal Studies(IMS), Sweden, that we follow more closely.

The general tone of understanding the aforementioned terms (memory, imagination and performativity) is provided by Elleström (2021a) when he refers to dealing with the nature of the mind as "denoting (human) consciousness that originates in the brain and is particularly manifested in perception, emotion, thought, reasoning, will, judgment, memory and imagination" (p. 13). Hence, it becomes evident that Elleström primarily adopts the major scientific concept of cognition, which hosts imagination and memory, being situated in the brain. When contemplating communication, he seems to discard such cases of "pure thinking" and "perception of one's own media product", with memory receiving a mention here (p. 25) and later with regards to the concept of short and long-term memory (p. 27). Performativity receives some attention by Elleström (2021b) in relation to media borders. He refers to it as one of the two sub-facets of the qualifying aspects, the other being conventionality (p. 66). Finally, there is a closing remark on memory in relation to the sensorial modality as being a complex cognitive function (p. 223).

When it comes to the two volumes entitled *Beyond Media Borders,* edited by Elleström (2021a; 2021b), memory is explored in relation to media frames and truthfulness (Tseng, 2021a) and as "the art of memory technique" (Eide and Schubert 2021b, p. 190-191). More loose mentions of a performative context may be traced in Crossley's (2021a) recalibration of theatre's hypermediality and Lavender's (2021a) contribution on multimodal acting and performing.

More vivid intermedial interest in performativity appears in the *Intermedial Studies* book published a year later, edited by Bruhn and Schirrmacher (2022). There, a whole chapter is included, entitled "The Intermediality of Performance" (Bäckström et al., 2022, p. 198-224), providing a cultural-historical perspective to the concept of performativity as bound to performance, physicality and the body, with the cognitive performative dimension not attracting attention. Jensen et al. (2022) pick up the performative thread by adopting an intermedial performativity approach, which involves subtle references to cognition, regarding the posting of GIFs (p. 299-301). Perhaps the most "cognitive" aspect of performativity comes in Führer's and Schoene's (2022) "box" no. 14.2 entitled "the body as subject and object" (p. 260-61). Here, objectivity is considered as related to materiality and physicality, while subjectivity is considered as related to a more holistic understanding of being, which is relevant to experiencing, (dis)embodiment, agency and mediation (where, memory and imagination are also said to partake) (p. 261). An interesting "performative" reference to cognition passes rather unnoticed in Makai's proposed schema (p. 75), where both perception and cognition are considered as coming under the sensorial modality. Askander et al. refer to audience imagination with regards to transmedial storyworlds (p. 265-281). Memory receives only sporadic references in this edited book, especially in Atã's and Schirrmacher's (2022) chapter (p. 42-55), where memory seems to undertake a narrative tone, and Bruhn et al.'s (p. 162-193) chapter, where it is discussed in relation to embodied witnessing and visual representation.

The most systematic intermedial voice on memory belongs to Brunow, leader of the workgroup *Cultural Memory and Media* at NECS and initiator and co-chair of the regional workgroup MSA (Nordic in the Memory Studies Association). Brunow's significant publications revolve around media memory studies (2015), cultural memory and queerness (2017) and digitality and archiving (2018). This considerable contribution to intermedial memory, although invaluable, remains peripheral to our focus of interest, as it addresses collective socio-political nuances rather than cognitive ones.

Problematizing Objectivity in Intermediality: Discovering the Subjective Dimension

Intermedial theory offers an inspired, systematic, coherent and valuable framework for approaching media products and communication, and succeeds in suggesting its terrain, methodologies, tools and scope. As a rather new field of inquiry, it is probably more enthusiastically engaged in articulating already-existing knowledge and proposing its innovative framework than acknowledging the assumptions, metaphors and fallacies it inherits (Timplalexi, 2023; Timplalexi & Führer, 2023). However, a critical contemplation of emergent issues remains unexplored. Such issues involve the intermedial scientist's position in relation to the elements that are subjugated to analysis, as well as their adherence to specific pre-givens over others, implying a "view from nowhere" (Nagel, 1989). An objective approach is overall assumed and a spatiotemporal stance on hosting and materializing the media product is selected out of the perceptual continuum. The intended objectivity becomes evident through the universal materiality of the media product, the pre-semiotic character of the sensorial modality and *semiosis* occurring as an intersubjective process.

With regards to the mind's innate modes of processing sensorial phenomena, the intermedial framework takes on essential categories, or abstract principles, that point back to the separation of material and physical phenomena as a "pure given", and to Kantian idealistic transcendental aesthetics, thus echoing a dogmatic prerequisite also seen in the semiotic system of Peirce.[2] By adopting a formal approach, Elleström accounts for historically shifting and developing media technologies which proffer another medium, the technical medium of display, that incarnates a disembodied logic of the media product where the latter, although itself material, needs another body, as if it were a substance.

The media product is pictured as objectively and universally made up of elements, without exploring the relativity of any materiality to sensorial differentiations. A subjective account, on the other hand, would highlight the sensorial modality as pre-material. What is the materiality of a music piece to a deaf person or of a painting to a blind one? Furthermore, the pre-semiotic character of the sensorial modality suggested in the media modalities model may be challenged as it is the synergy between the sensorial and the semiotic that allows "automated" recognition of perceptual data, thus rendering the physical world into a habitable environment. Selective attention cannot afford to be constantly and intensely dedicated to perceptual data.

On the contrary, if the *semiosis* process does not depend on a universal sign system where objects-signs objectively exist in the physical world, the "wall" isolating the signifier and the signified *loci* could be removed and the distinction between things and signs could receive new light (Brandt, 2011). In presuming scientific objectivity, the media modalities model, with its clear and dynamic taxonomy, does not dethrone the certainty that the perceiver and the media product are spatially separate entities. Finally, other vulnerable aspects of the media modalities that may remain unnoticed include the Cartesian divide between *res extensa* and *res cogitans* or the assumption of a universal body, the sensorial capacities of which are subject to a specific hierarchy of the senses.

In terms of the medium-centered model of communication, previously established notions, such as "channel"/"medium", are echoed, allowing for the transfer of content or "message" (Shannon, 1948; Jakobson, 1960). Weaver's (1998 [1949]) irreversible validation of communication as a mind-to-mind phenomenon (p. 3) and Schramm's (1971) "intermediate stage" as another universal "collection of signs" (p. 15) indicate the capacity of an objective materiality to produce mental significance. Indeed, the medium-centered communication model, following Aristotle's alleged linear model interpretations,

Saussure's speech circuit and Shannon's and Weaver's model, adheres to communication constants inherited from the aforementioned theoretical mesh (Timplalexi & Führer, 2023, p. 105-106). Hence, the media product emerges at the central middle, constituted of a cluster of interacting medial properties that allows the transfer of a "sender's" cognitive import to a perceiver. These include psychical and mental symbols or information, ideas, and meaning, thus supporting that the interconnection of multiple minds is feasible (ibid.). As a result, and with the concepts of channel or semantic noise still applying (Narula, 2006, p. 5–6), the model accredits communication as successful or unsuccessful, not as a felicitous or infelicitous utterance (Austin, 1962).

This is the outcome of having established transfer as an objective literality, rather than a subjective metaphor, as already argued by Reddy (1979), Sapienza et al. (2017) and Craig (2020). Indeed, the act of transfer seems to be an unreliable process, as it takes for granted notions such as the channeling, storability and smart emission of cognitive import, as if all materialities are penetrable by "immaterial cognitive stuff". Elleström's proposal that cognitive import is transferred "through" a media product is based on such import's immateriality, selective embodimentability or disembodimentability, thus summoning into the conversation a cognitive import battery schema. All these axioms render the media product a vessel and the producer's cognitive import the content which fills the media product, emanating through it for possible perceivers. As for the "producer's mind", the term is revealed to be rather problematic, since it fails to capture this producing entity in its totality. Besides, the very entity of the objective and external producer has been empirically challenged (Timplalexi, 2023; Timplalexi & Führer, 2023).

The producer, we argue, is not an embedder of cognitive import to the empty vessel of a media product, nor does the perceiver decode any objectively transcribed cognitive import. The understanding of the perceiver as a distinct receiver of the producer's mind's cognitive import is clearly grounded in the unreliable aforementioned transfer principle. If, instead, transfer is understood in its metaphorical dimension, then it is revealed as a *millieu* role attributed to media products' making/perceiving processes by communication models. Also, cognitive import, rather than being a product of the mind – a content of some body – can be understood as a continuous, embodied activity, a life-span performance as opposed to an entity that is storable or transmittable. Instead, we propose that the media product should be acknowledged as a media product maker's performance (or trace of performance). What the perceiver perceives and interprets is an impact on materialities. Both producers and perceivers are unified, embodied subjects that act and perform on/with other subjects, objects, entities and events, thus performatively impacting materialities. Such logic shifts the focus from the obscure mind to embodied performances. The perceiver, by designing their own unique meaning-making sessions, could equally be seen as a media product maker, a performer organizing available data into the environment, entities and events.

ACCOMMODATING IMAGINATION, MEMORY, AND PERFORMATIVITY IN THE INTERMEDIAL SPACE

Intermedial studies, although providing cognitive references to imagination, memory and performativity, overall adopts these notions as parameters for discussion, rather than taking them into account in the core theory.[3] The medium-centered model of communication (Elleström, 2018) does not appear to cater for communicative events in which neither human producers, nor the spatiotemporal co-presence of the producer and receiver are provable, thus excluding a variety of possibilities in terms of less "normal" communicative scenarios (Timplalexi, 2023; Timplalexi & Führer, 2023). Despite the value of the medium-centered model of communication, generalizations of the sensorial and semiotic modalities "cut corners off" conceptual and empirical nuances and tend to establish neutral categories and formal classifications of scientific certainty. By so doing, this approach veils the rather indeterminate intermediate stage which correlates the subject and the media object.

Whereas the intermedial approach starts from different basic media (such as word, image and sound), that are further classified according to their operating systems of semiotic modes, media discourses overall circumvent the intermediate stage either by defining media pragmatically through technology or by integrating the materiality of signs (signifiers), within a broader concept of *techne*. The consideration of the latter in the established intermedial approach brings forth the separation between basic media entities and the technical medium of display, thus acceding to a law-like generalization from an assumed objective perspective.

The following section contributes to the theoretical background of the intermediate stage and proposed taxonomy of the media product. It considers deep philosophical issues that determine the stances of various disciplines, philosophers and scholars on the performative synergy between memory, imagination and media products. It appears that, by historically revisiting the interplay between imagination, memory and performativity, an intermedial revision of the nature of the media product becomes possible.

Foregrounding Imagination, Memory, and Performativity in the Intermediate Stage

Communication is interaction, both with ourselves and with others, as well as with our external and internal environments (Narula, 2006, p. 2). Often, we tend to neglect interaction with ourselves and internal environments and ground communication on solely an objective basis, thus understand the intermediate stage mostly, if not exclusively, *outside* ourselves. Our re-articulation of the producer-perceiver continuum has enriched and opened up possibilities for the producer and perceiver sub-roles to coincide within the same subjectivity (Timplalexi, 2023; Timplalexi & Führer, 2023). Hall's implicit idea that communication occurs between sites that are capable of holding "meaning" (Elleström, 2021a, p. 12) may suggest that meaning becomes cognitively anchored *within* the same subject: thus, two distinct *topoi* emerge as two poles within the same subjective space, which act like a trigger for the performative re-negotiation or re-contemplation of meaning.

Guillory (2010) claims that the concept of a medium of communication "was absent but wanted for several centuries prior to its appearance, a lacuna in the philosophical tradition that exerted a distinctive pressure, as if from the future, on early efforts to theorize communication" (p. 321). We thus deemed necessary to provide a more detailed outline of the trajectory of Ancient Greek epistemology on the performative interplay of imagination and memory in perception and cognition, followed by a brief mentioning of several key philosophical positions, also in upcoming fields of inquiry, such as cognitive semiotics and theory of mind.

For the Ancient Greeks and the Stoics, the interplay between imagination and performativity with regards to perception was evident. Barney (1992) reports that Plato associates what appears with i) judgement (*doxa*), "the internal version of assertion and denial"; ii) thought (*dianoia*), or "the inward, soundless dialogue carried on by the mind with itself"; and iii) imagination (*phantasia*), or appearance (p. 287). When judgement is said to occur through perception, "an experience of this sort" (*to toiouton pathos*) emerges, also called "appearance" (*phantasia*) (p. 287). Barney (1992) also mentions that Plato introduces two cognitive agential forces: an internal "scribe", who "records perceptual judgements in our soul, followed by an internal "painter" of "images", *eikones*, or, of the future, *phantasmata* (p. 287). As a result, the Platonic perspective establishes a blend of perception and judgement in the process of something "appearing" in thought: "to say that the stick appears bent to me is to say that my *phantasia* of the stick is that it is bent; and this is to say that I silently affirm the thought (which somehow involves perception) that it is so" (Barney, 1992, p. 288).

For Aristotle, perception is the reception of form without matter. Aristotle's sensible perspective on perception, grounded on the five senses with respect to the heterogeneity of the organs, does not operate through having a likeness to an idealist transcendental image, but through a mediative realm or intermediate stage, also termed the *diaphanês*: the "thing without name". This poses an effective distance between perceiving and the perceived (Mersch, 2016). This intermediate stage constitutes the visual medium, different from the auditory or olfactory medium, for which Aristotle assumes almost no distinction between senses of contact and senses of distance. According to this model, the medium represents what binds the soul to things (Aristotle, 1907). In short, there is a community of the perceiving and the perceived, not in spite of, but thanks to, the *metaxy*, i.e., the capacity of taking form. Therefore, the sensory *metaxy* indicates a mediacy that is less topological than it is operative.

More specifically, Aristotle distinguishes between judgement (*doxa*), said to involve conviction (*pistis*) as an outcome of persuasion (*to pepeisthai*) of reason (*logos*), and *phantasia*, a central animal cognitive function that provides images to the soul/mind, which derives from perception and is "invoked to account for memory, dreams and visual hallucinations" (Barney, 1992, p. 289). These images (*phantasia/phantasmata*), constructed by imagination (*phantasia)* are said to be of mental nature, hence *phantasia* "is the performance by which an image (*phantasia/phantasmata*) comes before the mind" (ibid.). A *phantasma* "must be 'combined' with the thought of something in the world, so that it is seen as an image of that something, and as making claims about it" (Barney, 1992, p. 292). Indeed, a notion of conversion of *hupolepsis* into *phantasia* (p. 290) that is allegedly performed by the subject is introduced here.

Epicureans' and Stoics' epistemologies echo the non-judgemental Aristotelian approach to *phantasia*, as they differentiate between an "impression" (*phantasia*) and a judgement (*doxa*) (Barney, 1992, p. 293-294). Sextus supports the idea that judgement (*doxa*) is distinct from and is additional to impression (*phantasia*), and that it seems to overlap considerably with the image received from the senses, as "sensation mechanically records the *eidola* received from an object" (p. 294). Furthermore, impression, according to the Stoics, occurs prior to appearance because the latter is said to affirm acts of judgement. In other words, appearance is "the component of the impression sustained in judgement" (p. 297).

For Saint Augustine, sense-knowledge is claimed to be a work "of the soul by means of the body", while the encounter between the bodily sense-organ and the object perceived is considered a necessary condition of sensation (Armstrong, 1967). Elaborating on vision as a metaphor for cognition, he distinguishes between three categories (Augustine of Hippo, 1841): corporeal vision (*visio corporalis*), said to allow the observation of physical objects; spiritual vision (*visio spiritualis*), which enables the vision of images in the mind in the form of memories or imaginations; and intellectual vision (*visio intellectualis*), which he claims includes *noesis* and intuition. Later, Descartes' Rule 12 explains that the sense organs transmit impressions to common sense (*sensus communis*) to then be further transmitted to the imagination (*phantasia*), from where impressions become available to the knowing force (*vis cognoscens*) (Sepper, 1996). Hume enhances the distinction between the sensations of objective states and subjective impressions (Jokornegay, 1993). He organizes conscious mental episodes, defined as "perceptions'", and distinguishes between "impressions", which include perceptual experiences and bodily sensations, and "basic" feelings and "ideas", which comprise of memories, occurrent beliefs and imaginings. "Ideas of the judgement" as well as "ideas of the fancy" belong to the domain of the ideas of imagination (Dorsch, 2016). Kant, overlapping ideas with notions of imagination, distinguishes between subjective sensation and conscious, objective representation (Janiak, 2022). Objective representations are said to include intuitions and concepts. Intuition is supposed to provide us with singular, immediate representations of particular things, while concepts are general, mediate representations (Engstrom, 2006). To connect a perceived phenomenon and a concept, Kant considers a judgment and a mediating representation in the concept of the transcendental schema (Kant, 1998 [1781]).

Perhaps the most difficult case here is Peirce. There are probably very few positions Peirce did not adopt in relation to representation and mediation. In simplifying terms, Peirce defines mediation as the main function of a sign or representation. Nöth (2011) writes that "after having abandoned *representation* for *representamen* in 1868 and *representamen* for sign in 1905, Peirce's intent was now to abandon sign for medium" (p. 467). For Peirce, the sign mediates between its object and its interpretant and the object is a mediator for it is a sign itself, while the interpretant mediates between the sign and its object (Nöth, 2011, p. 469).

Piaget's "genetic epistemology" is indeed a theory of knowledge (Kitchener, 1986). Learning, connected to the cognitive negotiation of new experiences, is not limited to early developmental stages, but refers to the life-long, general *genesis* of knowledge (Piaget, 1999). *Schemas* are knowledge categories that enable meaning-making and are enmeshed with their embodied processes (Scott & Cogburn, 2023). Any (new) information contributes to the modification or alteration of previously existing *schemas*. Assimilation allows for the incorporation of new information in an individual's cognition, thus modifying pre-existing *schemas*, while accommodation engenders the alteration of existing cognitive structures so that new information can be cognitively hosted. Finally, equilibration regulates assimilation and accommodation.

By relating imagination to actuality, Husserl coins the term "presentification", which opposes perception's "presentation". In perception, the object appears "in person"; in imagination, the object appears as a representation or as being possible, not actual (Husserl, 2005). Husserl viewed perception as the primary type of direct intuitive presentation, therefore determining it as immediate. With appearance and image being one, image consciousness is determined to have a mediating role, while its content (*phantasma*) has a doxically neutral interpretation (Aldea, 2013).

Gibson (2015), introducing an ecological approach to visual perception, forges a connection between performativity, perception and cognition. By rejecting the premise that information needs to be sent and received, thus questioning the need for a "channel" in communication, Gibson understands information for perception as available, like the information that can be extracted from ambient light (p. 56-57). It is exactly this availability of information that calls upon a performative agency in constructing the physical world into an environment. Most importantly, the distinctions between the abstracting mind and the embodied body become almost irrelevant, as the subject performatively composes its environment by discovering its affordances and what that offers (p. 119).

Klein et al. (1983) support the notion that the relation between impression and idea is one of the two elements of imagination, the other being memory (p. 16-17). Impression, one of the two elements of this relation, is said to be "constituted by sensations, passions and emotions", whereas "ideas are based on impressions in thinking and reasoning" and should rather be understood as *Gestalts*, "holistic entities of impressions", so as not to totally coincide with concepts (ibid.).

Grusin's (2015) concept of radical mediation attempts to significantly revise mediation as the process that generates the conditions for the individuation of entities within the world. It shifts the focus from a pre-existent subject and object to the generation of experiences and relations, a form of "premediation" (p. 142) that is said to "transform ontology into epistemology" (p. 144).

In conclusion, the field of inquiry of cognitive semiotics again drives us away from differentiated sensorial and semiotic abilities that may inform an understanding of the "real" and materiality. This is because it focuses on the co-relating concept of the sign as that which enables the appearance or presentation of phenomena in one proximal part of mind, space or time, which is separated from another part of mind, space or time. The separation between the signifying phenomenon and the signified phenomenon can thus be described as "a sort of phenomenal 'wall' isolating the signifier's proximal locus and the signified' s distal locus" (Brandt, 2011). This is claimed to be based upon the differentiated universal existence between things and signs. Thankfully, new voices (Pennisi & Falzone, 2019; Bickhard & Mirski, 2021) also ground performativity in cognitive processes. Pennisi & Falzone (2019) more specifically support the notion that the executive and motor component of cognitive behavior should be seen as an intrinsic part of the physiological functioning of the mind. In this respect, the interplay between performativity, performance, imagination and memory do receive some attention, like in Stern and Rotello's work (2000), where they confirm that performed event memories lose less information over time compared to imagined event memories.

Performing Subjectivity in the Intermediate Stage

As already outlined, Elleström's (2018) medium-centered model of communication introduces the concept of an intermediate stage as enabling "the transfer of cognitive import from a producer's to a perceiver's mind" (p. 281), but also "as a function rather than an essential property" as "virtually any material entity can be used as one" (ibid.). Hence, it remains rather obscure whether Elleström meant "stage" in its temporal, spatial or performative dimension.

In case this stage is thought of as temporal, what and whose time does it involve, the producer's, the perceiver's, or the time of the communication sequence? These times do not often coincide. As a result, we are prone to think that Elleström refers to the temporality of the communication sequence here. If, on the other hand, he meant the term "stage" spatially, the same issues apply; we deduce that the communication sequence is involved here as well. Finally, if the term "stage" is denoted in its theatrical/ performative dimension, the hypothesis that Elleström was probably referring to the communication sequence may be somehow articulated.

Let us now revisit the spatial dimension of the intermediate stage. If it coincides with the media product, then only the central circular formation referred to as "media product" (the entity or event which allows for the transfer of cognitive import though it) registers as the intermediate stage (Elleström, 2018, p. 282-fig. 5). Indeed, this appears to be a very material-oriented understanding of "stage". If, however, the intermediate stage also encompasses the act of production, the act of perception and the act of transfer, then the intermedial stage is not exhausted solely by the media product, but becomes therefore a synonym of communication. This latter understanding provides space for more performative, semiotic and discursive interpretations in communication. However, as Elleström clearly argues, the terms "intermediate stage" and "media product" may be used interchangeably, so the prospect of identifying the stage with the whole process remains partly an incomplete one.

There are at least three latent *oxymora* here. The first one concerns the materiality of the media product: if its materiality is determined *a priori* (media modalities model), it awaits to be perceived as such in, for example, surfaces and organic/inorganic matter. Accordingly, the sensorial modality does not partake in, let alone define, the formulation of the understanding of materiality which informs what the phenomenon *is*; but rather, what the phenomenon *is* prior to its sensorial and semiotic understanding. This is a principle that subjugates all the different sensorial and semiotic nuances to a rhetoric of right/wrong, with grades in between them. The second *oxymoron* is that, despite unique individual sensorial differentialities and sociocultural contexts being implied (Elleström, 2021a, p. 49), the media modalities model, by adhering to Peircean semiotics, recognizes universal materiality as invoking universal *semiosis*. However, both cannot be true: either universality is not phony *or* sensorial and contextual variations do invoke unique *semiosis* and determine the understanding of materiality. The third *oxymoron* arises from the opposing presuppositions that, on one hand, universal materiality is a pre-requisite for meaning-making, and, on the other, the alleged dematerialized cognitive import may be transferred through the media product in the medium-centered communication model; these two positions contradict each other. If materiality is penetrable by immaterial cognitive import in order for the latter to be transferred to a perceiver, the exact conceptions of this materiality and cognitive import remain questionable.

In our latest inquiry, when challenging cases of communication, we showed how relative this material objectivity might be in examples, such as Johnny's (Trumbo, 1971). Here is the extension of that initial argument: this relativity may actually expand beyond such border cases to *all* communicative instances. If we are unique, we are all different from one another. Hence, in a folk psychology of the soul's logic where we agree we are unique (Bering, 2006), materialities should be different as they are assimilated by our unique sensorial capacities and cognitive horizons. Indeed, just as a musical masterpiece cannot be tolerated when possibly played very loudly to a person with *misophonia*, or also a colour blind person sees a Velazquez hung on a museum wall. This shows how both the musical piece and the Velazquez are assimilated uniquely by anyone and therefore cause different *semioses*. The universal pre-sensorial understanding of materiality, in tune with *semiosis* and its internal universal signifieds, presupposes the latter are already present in cognition and are not perpetually formulated by the subject in a performative manner. Of course, the transfer metaphor leads to these sorts of fallacies. If we accept that there are people who lack sensorial capacities in some form, then those people would also lack semiotic ones. Until now, this established view is in favour of a lack and of noise in communication. It is time to reconsider this – and the instant way out is declaring a war on objectivity.

By now, it should have become clear that any attempt to ground communication on objectivity contradicts the communicational phenomenon. The fact that we negotiate with material entities to discover their affordances does not mean that these affordances are available to all of us in much the way: it is *our* negotiation with affordances that is performative. Human cognition does not have to be thought of as situated in a control room, where intended and fragmented immaterial and transferable cognitive import is produced; instead, cognition is a holistic, ongoing and continuous process within the subject, and, in its socio-political dimension, partakes in culture. The brain is not merely a small, detached center of a nervous system – the brain *is* a part of the nervous system.

Indeed, intermedial media products are burdened with the Cartesian divide between in/out, between knowledge within and outside of the self-*schemas*. Not only an objective reality is metaphysically assumed on a universal level, as, otherwise, the sensorial impact on the formulation of an understanding of the material as real would automatically dethrone objective certainty; also, the intermedial meaning making process (*semiosis*), following Peirce's semiotics, clearly posits that the material signs are outside of the subject, and therefore detached from their universal cognitive signified. If, for Peirce, a sign is supposed to create in the mind of a person an equivalent sign or a more developed sign (Peirce qtd. in Nöth, 2011, p. 464), the sign created in the mind should be understood as a sign *of a sign*. Furthermore, if the object is the referent of the *representamen*, then not only do signs refer to objects, but objects also *objectively* refer to signs.[4] This cannot be true, in light of the previous discussion. Put simply, it is one thing to say that perceiving a cat means you have a pre-installed universal understanding of what the cat indisputably is, and another thing to say that, by perceiving cats, you cognitively construct a schema that undergoes significant alterations through contact with new experiences, such as seeing a tailless Kurilian Bobtail cat. Furthermore, if an object remains unseen to a blind person, how may the *semiosis* process have any universal, objective character? How can it be possible that any physical sign actually exists in the world outside the self and that the "correct" meaning exists inside our heads? Any object assimilated by cognition certainly has to be sensorially processed. A physical object cannot be understood *unless* assimilated. This means that any object of the outside world metaphorically "appears" to cognition and so gets "recognized", categorized. Piaget (1999) discusses assimilation in children in his developmental psychology; however, this mechanism does not vanish as we grow up. Let us try and imagine classifying a mushroom the first time we see one: is there anyone who knows right from the start that a mushroom is not a plant but a fungus? As we assimilate a mushroom, its perceived appearance "appears" to our cognitive processes and demands recognition – demands categorizing. Peirce's example with the chair (Almeder, 1970, p. 101) is pretty comfortable, just like his chair is – it does not lie outside our comfort zone. However, if someone has never encountered a mushroom before, how can the signified mushroom and the knowledge of its fungal nature be pre-existing in their heads, despite all evidence (it springs out from the soil, it is reproduced with grains = plant) showing the opposite?

Hence, the Peircean approach presents half the story: the external object has to be internalized for meaning to be attributed to it. No sign exists objectively, let alone universally, but occurs within our cognition, because there is no spatial split between an external physical sign and an internal mental image. Signs and meanings are formed subjectively and perpetually, informing each other within cognition. In other words, a sign is an object-percept and not an object outside of the subject. What some may recognize as a sign, others may not. Some groups of people may agree on defining anything at all as a sign. There is no production of an *equivalent* sign to another sign that exists outside of us, but of a sign in cognition. Comparison and analogy are not between one sign outside and another one inside, but between object-percepts and unique, not universal and pre-existing cognitive schemas, with the negotiation between the two being a perpetual process that equals to Piagetian learning.

Hence, rather than a sign being something that evokes something for someone, something evokes a sign to someone. Rather than a sign pointing to an object, an object-percept cognitively points to sign. Thus, the intermediate stage, the in-between, is not just outside, occurring between a producer and a perceiver via a media product; it is perpetually inside – in us, in our cognitions. It is the cognitive space, time and function/performance that mediates between the assimilated perception of an object, regardless of its meaning, whether it is "objectively" available to perception to more than one entity, or whether it exists or not (we still perceive dreams, for example, even though they do not actually exist). Temporally speaking, it can last from milliseconds to a life-time. Spatially speaking, it is confined to each one of us within us. Performatively speaking, it equals to *theorein,* where an appearance appears in our thoughts; or, from a genetic epistemology perspective, a schema negotiating the process of assimilating and/or accommodating new information, regardless of in/out source.

SYSTEMATIZING ANEW THE MEDIA PRODUCT: TOWARDS AN EXPANDED TAXONOMY

Having shed light on the intermediate stage, we now address the notion of the media product, using nuances that we have encountered and have been implied in previous categories of media products, while also proposing further possible categories. The criterion for distinguishing between "objective" and "subjective" media products should be thought of as the interface of the subject, that renders plausible the distinction between in and out, thus perceivable by the self and perceivable by the self and the others.

"Objective" Media Products (Collectively Agreed as Such by a Majority)

"Objective" media products include all media products able to be perceived as such by the dominant majority of perceivers. The perceivers believe that their sensorial perceptions are correct. Hence, their data – their perception – feels objective and physically available in the world, when it is, in fact, contextually-framed. We have argued that this perception and cognition is not universal, but that it is implied by a lack of acknowledgement of differences and subjective perceptions involved in sensorial or semiotic modalities, which also affect a person's understanding of the material modality (Timplalexi, 2023; Timplalexi & Führer, 2023).

"Objective," Intentionally Produced Media Products

This category, usually taken as the exemplary prototype of the media product, encompasses media products – that is, objects or events – that have been intentionally created by their makers, such as books, films and theatre performances.[5] These media products offer "objective" physical perceptual data to their perceivers, as they are made by producers and are, in whatever form, exhibited to the multimodal perceivers' gaze. However, it must be noted that these "objectives" and produced media products become individually assimilated, subject to sensorial and cognitive-contextual differentialities in a perceiver/person.

Ambiguous "Objective" Media Products

Under this category come media products where the producers and production processes of which may be hypothesized, doubted or inquired.[6] In order to elaborate on such media products, an understanding of the process of framing/keying on the perceivers' behalf is required. During this process, the perceiver feels as if something is "missing" and has to fill in the gaps somewhat arbitrarily, without having full access to all information needed. These media products may not even be intended by their alleged producers;[7] they might not be intended at all, such as in the bone example (Elleström, 20921a, p. 16), where a bone becomes qualified as a media product because perceivers hypothesize scratches on it are human-made rather than being geological. These media products offer physical perceptual data to their perceivers which is perceived according to unique sensorial and cognitive capacities. However, they also retain a grade of mystery and a lack of full and indisputable access to their producers and production processes.

Subjective Media Products

These media products are not perceivable by others but solely by oneself, although their existence may be assumed by others. Their data may be of an objective source and mediated by cognition (although all data is cognitively processed, even in cases of "objective" media products). The perceiver, attempting to objectify them in order to render them available to others' multimodal gazes, creates new, intentional, "objective" media products.

Subjective Media Products of "Objective" Physical Objects or Events

Often, a physical object or phenomenon gains the status and quality of a media product in our cognition.[8] Objects, events, animals, plants, other humans, machines or even the self may feel somehow "heightened" in our cognitions. They may become sometimes arbitrarily "elevated", not because they do something or are somewhat deserving of our attention, but because we somehow qualify them differently, as Wilde suggests (1905). This is the realm of the theatricality of the gaze, the attribution of an aesthetic, a perspective, a cognitive product, keyed on metaphor. Féral (2002) introduces us to the vast virtuality that emerges by contemplating theatricality of perception, of attributing to perceptions a second-order level of attentive focus and projecting upon them some fictional layer from an "as if" perspective. These media products are produced in the perceivers' cognitions thanks to the interplay between objective physical perceptual data and subjective cognitive processes, and, although they can be described, those descriptions constitute new, "objective", intentionally-produced media products. The uniqueness of the sensorial and cognitive-contextual perceptual subjectivities in these cases holds a dominant role.

Dreams

Although we are not experts on dreaming, we cannot help but remark that dreams could be, in an extended understanding of the term, considered as media products, and dreaming itself a media type. Freud (2010), for example, discussed dreams in depth, as if they were actually films or VR experiences. The surrealists were also very tempted by the experience of dreaming. They highlighted the artistic qualities of dreams and drew inspiration from them, or even rendered them as methods for artistic production (Thompson, 2004). Dreams are framed by the process of sleep. Although objective environmental (i.e. sound) and personal (i.e. hunger) parameters are said to impact dreaming, their realm remains subjective: other people do not have access to our dream data; or, if we attempt to convey it, they experience data of our descriptions – new, "objective", intentionally-produced media products, such as narratives, paintings or poems, rather than of the dream itself. Memory and imagination play a crucial role in dreams, as the latter are often subject to reconstructions of experienced phenomena under the influence of imagination.

Second-Order Subjective Media Products

These media products may derive from objective physical encounters with agents, objects or events but always involve a subjective quality (bound to memory, imagination and possibly other cognitive parameters) in their formation. An old person sitting on bench, looking "in" rather than "out" while remembering their youth; an actor exploring the character they incarnate; a rebound thought of revenge after being bullied; scenarios explaining unrequited love or solving a mystery; even non-stated scientific hypotheses – they all fall in this category. These second-order subjective media products are similar to subjective media products of "objective" physical agents (objects or events) but the latter are distanced, spatiotemporally speaking, and no longer available as such to perception. Or, they just might not belong to the perceptual zone of the physical world. They are cognitive constructs of lived (memory) or potentially livable (imagination) experiences. In these constructs, the synergy of memory and imagination, as they constantly evoke one another, causes a destabilization of the rigid limits between the two.

A Brief Note on Media Products Categories

The aforementioned categories are rather schematic and cannot boast to fully demarcate the fluid and versatile nature of the media product. How often are there not subtle changes in our encounters with media products? From the perception of an objective media product, to questioning it as an ambiguous one; from the realm of the aesthetic and the poetic subjective media product to our dreams reflecting the same sun rays of that crisp February sunrise under an almond tree. This fluidity, in tune with so-called "stream of consciousness" (James, 1891), contradicts the notion of the cut. Indeed, when we categorize, we petrify; but this does not prevent us from revising, reforming and reconsidering. Nor does it exhaust our appetite to do so perpetually. Nevertheless, it is good to know that there is something unattainable that eludes Barad's (2007) agential cuts and coincides with the self-continuing to cognitively surf in its spatiotemporal continuum. Although the aforementioned categories derive from agential cuts and are organized around dualities (such as in/out, objective/subjective, perceivable/opaque) at the same time, it turns out that they all share a common feature: a cognitive assimilative process where both in and out become "in": "out" becomes "in", while "in" becomes a different "in". This is, we argue, the intermediate stage.

Having revised that media products are solely objective – man-made and intentionally created in the physical world's entities or processes – and presented an expanded taxonomy of the media product, we can claim we have grounded the function and properties of the intermediate stage beyond the schema of the ghost-in-the-machine (Ryle 1975 [1949]). The materiality of cognition, of course, does not exclude metaphysics; on the contrary, it empirically re-establishes the neglected connection of physics with metaphysics. In other words, philosophical, spiritual or even religious contemplation is not excluded as a potentiality, but an unmapped territory that pends for further exploration is acknowledged.

CONCLUSION

In this chapter, we have argued that in between any physical and/or conceptual media product and relevant meaning-making exists a subjective, personal assimilation of any objective or subjective objectivity and thus also of objective and subjective media products. We argue that this pervasive and perpetual, cognitive assimilative process is performative rather than representational. It is informed through, and informs, culture and the socio-political; it constructs meaning – it does not couple objective signs outside of the subject with subjective ones inside it. Memory and imagination are crucial during the assimilation process, since they provide both the schemas and categories while also bridging the gaps between the already known, remembered and imagined, and that which is under assimilation.

The subjectivity of perception, which contributes to the outcome of the meaning-making process, is in fact a remarkable tool to challenge the Cartesian divide between internal and external knowledge that is based on objectivity. It is also a tool for highlighting the importance of memory and imagination in the communication process. All out becomes in through/during an intermediate stage, and all in becomes meaningful through/during an intermediate stage. Instead of being understood as two separate things, they can be understood in relation to their common ground – a cognitive in-between phase. Even if they have differences, all of these in-between stages are subject to, and shaped by, performative processes and powers of memory and imagination.

The conceptual framework that wants performativity to be anchored in the body and memory and imagination anchored in the brain is the same that has fostered "transfer" and semantic "noise" in communication. Intermedial theory would benefit from a revision of such privileged, dualistic approaches, as already implied, but not fully explored, in the Elleströmian oeuvre, such as in the bone example (2021a, p. 16) and the dancer-dance continuum (2021a, p. 36). Our bodies partake in remembering and imagining and are activated accordingly; our brains in performing memory and imagination. We, as subjects, holistically perform, remember and imagine. Building upon previous contributions (Timplalexi 2023; Timplalexi and Führer, 2023), we augment our argument. Not only do we claim the co-occurrence of the sensorial and the semiotic as parallel to perception, we proffer the material as subject to the sensorial and the semiotic – not objectively existing as such, but depending on our perceptions and contexts of it. Those perceptions, subjective in their nature, do not couple an objective existing sign with a pool of equivalent universal meanings, but are themselves the signifiers performing a real-time formation of signifieds thanks to memory and imagination. As a result, the material modality celebrates no temporal primordiality over the sensorial.

Further suggestions may be made with regards to the problematic of terms widely used, such as embodiment, which implies an incarnation of some cognition (rather than cognition and body *being* a subject). Actualization is another example, which implies either intentionality or something forced, or an arbitrary emergence, not bare of hylomorphic conceptualizations. Intention is not always a pre-requisite for performance, but perception and meaning-making, on behalf of some perceiver, surely are.

It is naive to say an internal intermediate stage does not exist. Perceptual nuances do determine the assimilation of data into meaning, with data being in and outside the self. Per/sonare means to speak through a mask, and the only performative way to speak is through a first-person subjectivity. Such a subjectivity sees the construction of identity as an imaginary, ongoing, fluid process and is in the position not only to read what power does to it, or it to power – but to understand how it may be exercising power over other subjectivities by thinking that the same objective materiality exists on the same universal plane.

REFERENCES

Acosta, H. L. P. (2020). Kant on Empirical and Transcendental Functions of Memory. *Eidos*, 32, 103–134. 10.14482/eidos.32.193

Alanen, L. (1989). Descartes's Dualism and the Philosophy of Mind. *Revue de Metaphysique et de Morale*, 94(3), 391–413.

Aldea, A. S. (2013). Husserl's struggle with mental images: Imaging and imagining reconsidered. *Continental Philosophy Review*, 46(3), 371–394. 10.1007/s11007-013-9268-7

Almeder, R. F. (1970). Peirce's Theory of Perception. *Transactions of the Charles S. Peirce Society,* 6(2), 99–110. https://www.jstor.org/stable/40319589

Annas, J. (2003). Aristotle on Memory and the Self. In Nussbaum, M. C., & Rorty, A. O. (Eds.), *Essays on Aristotle's De Anima*. Oxford Academic. 10.1093/019823600X.003.0017

Aristotle, . (1907). *De anima* (Hicks, R. D., Trans.). Prometheus Books.

Askander, M., Gutowska, A., & Makai, P. K. (2022). Transmedial storyworlds. In Bruhn, J., & Schirrmacher, B. (Eds.), *Intermedial Studies: An introduction to meaning across media* (pp. 265–281). Routledge.

Atã, P., & Schirrmacher, B. (2022). Media and modalities – Literature. In Bruhn, J., & Schirrmacher, B. (Eds.), *Intermedial Studies: An introduction to meaning across media* (pp. 42–55). Routledge.

Augustine of Hippo. (1841). De Genesi ad litteram. *Patrologia Latina, 34,* 245–486. https://catholicgnosis .wordpress.com/2020/02/23/st-augustine-intellectual-vision/

Augustine. (1967). Sense and imagination. In Armstrong, A. H. (Ed.), *The Cambridge History of Later Greek and Early Medieval Philosophy* (pp. 374–379). Cambridge University Press.

Austin, J. L. (1962). *How to do things with words*. Clarendon Press.

Bäckström, P., Führer, H., & Schirrmacher, B. (2022). The intermediality of performance. In J.

Bal, M. (2002). *Travelling concepts in the humanities: A rough guide*. University of Toronto.

Barad, K. (2007). *Meeting the universe halfway: Quantum physics and the entanglement of matter and meaning*. Duke University Press. 10.2307/j.ctv12101zq

Barney, R. (1992). Appearances and Impressions. *Phronesis (Barcelona, Spain)*, 37(3), 283–313. https:// www.jstor.org/stable/4182417

Bering, J. M. (2006). The folk psychology of souls. *Behavioral and Brain Sciences*, 29(5), 453–498. 10.1017/S0140525X0600910117156519

Bobko, A. (2019). Augustinus and Kant – Two Founders of Modern Thinking. *Studies in the History of Philosophy*, 10(3), 27–38. 10.12775/szhf.2019.029

Bottici, C. (2014). *Imaginal Politics. Images Beyond Imagination and the Imaginary*. Columbia University Press.

Brandt, P. A. (2011). What is cognitive semiotics? A new paradigm in the study of meaning. *Signata*, 2(2), 49–60. 10.4000/signata.526

Bruhn, J., Lutas, L., Salmose, N., & Schirrmacher, B. (2022). Media representation: Film, music and painting in literature. In Bruhn, J., & Schirrmacher, B. (Eds.), *Intermedial Studies: An introduction to meaning across media* (pp. 162–193). Routledge.

Bruhn, J., & Schirrmacher, B. (2022). Intermedial studies. In Bruhn, J., & Schirrmacher, B. (Eds.), *Intermedial Studies: An introduction to meaning across media* (pp. 3–41). Routledge.

Brunow, D. (2015). *Remediating Transcultural Memory: Documentary Filmmaking as Archival Intervention.* De Gruyter. 10.1515/9783110436372

Brunow, D. (2017). Curating Access to Audiovisual Heritage: Cultural Memory and Diversity in European Film Archives. *Image and Narrative*, 1(18), 97–110.

Brunow, D. (2018). Naming, shaming, framing? Ambivalence of queer visibility in audiovisual archives. In A. Koivunen, K. Kyrölä & I. Ryberg (Eds.), *The Power of Vulnerability: Mobilizing Affect in Feminist, Queer and Anti-racist Media Cultures* (pp. 174-195). Manchester University Press.

Butler, J. (1999). *Gender Trouble: Feminism and the Subversion of Identity.* Routledge.

Chapple, F., & Kattenbelt, C. (2006). Key issues in internediality in theatre and performance. In F. Chapple & C.L. Kattenbelt (Eds.), *Intermediality in Theatre and Performance* (pp. 11–25). Rodopi.

Craig, R. T. (2020). Models of communication in and as metadiscourse. In M. Bergman, K. Kirtiklis & J. Siebers (Eds.), *Models of communication: Philosophical and theoretical approaches* (pp. 11–33). Routledge.

Crossley, M. (2021a). A recalibration of theatre's hypermediality. In L. Elleström (Ed.), *Beyond Media Borders, Volume 1: Intermedial relations among multimodal media* (pp. 95–112). Palgrave Macmillan. 10.1007/978-3-030-49679-1_2

Deutscher, M. (1998). History of the interest in memory. In Memory. In *The Routledge Encyclopedia of Philosophy.* Routledge. 10.4324/9780415249126-V020-1

Dorsch, F. (2016). Hume. In Kind, A. (Ed.), *The Routledge Handbook of Philosophy of Imagination* (pp. 40–54). Routledge.

Eide, Ø., & Schubert, Z. (2021). Seeing the Landscape Through Textual and Graphical Media Products. In L. Elleström (Ed.), *Beyond Media Borders, Volume 2: Intermedial Relations among Multimodal Media* (pp. 175–209). Palgrave Macmillan. 10.1007/978-3-030-49683-8_7

Elam, K. (1980). *The Semiotics of Theatre and Drama.* Routledge. 10.4324/9780203993309

Elleström, L. (Ed.). (2010). *Media Borders, Multimodality and Intermediality.* Palgrave MacMillan. 10.1057/9780230275201

Elleström, L. (2018). A medium-centered model of communication. *Semiotica*, 2018(224), 269–293. 10.1515/sem-2016-0024

Elleström, L. (2021a). The modalities of media II: An expanded model for understanding intermedial relations. In L. Elleström (Ed.), *Beyond Media Borders, Volume 1: Intermedial relations among multi-modal media* (pp. 3–91). Palgrave Macmillan.

Elleström, L. (2021b). Summary and Elaborations. In L. Elleström (Ed.), *Beyond Media Borders, Volume 2: Intermedial Relations among Multimodal Media* (pp. 213-233). Palgrave Macmillan. 10.1007/978-3-030-49683-8_8

Engstrom, S. (2006). Understanding and Sensibility. *Inquiry (Oslo, Norway)*, 49(1), 2–25. 10.1080/00201740500497225

Féral, J., & Bermingham, R. P. (2002). Theatricality: The specificity of theatrical language. *SubStance*, 31(2), 94–108. 10.1353/sub.2002.0026

Freud, S. (2010). *The Interpretation of Dreams. Translated from the German and* (Strachey, J., Ed.). Basic Books.

Führer, H., & Schoene, J. (2022). Media modalities of theatrical space. In Bruhn, J., & Schirrmacher, B. (Eds.), *Intermedial Studies: An introduction to meaning across media* (pp. 255–264). Routledge.

Ganguly, M. (2002). *Memory (2)*. CSMT. https://csmt.uchicago.edu/glossary2004/memory2.htm

Gibson, J. J. (2015). *The Ecological Approach to Visual Perception*. Psychology Press.

Goffman, E. (1974). *Frame Analysis: An essay on the organization of experience*. Northeastern University Press.

Goldberg, R. L. (2001). *Performance Art: From Futurism to the Present*. Thames & Hudson.

Grusin, R. (2015). Radical Mediation. *Critical Inquiry*, 42(1), 124–148. 10.1086/682998

Guillory, J. (2010). Genesis of the Media Concept. *Critical Inquiry*, 36(2), 321–362. 10.1086/648528

Hall, S. (1980). Encoding/decoding. In Hall, S. (Ed.), *Culture, media, language: Working papers in cultural studies, 1972–79* (pp. 128–138). Hutchinson.

Harviainen, T. J. (2008). Kaprow's Scions. In M. Montola & J. Stenros (Eds.), Playground Worlds: Creating and Evaluating Experiences of Role-Playing Games (pp. 216–231). Academic Press.

Hochschild, P. E. (2012). Plato. In P. E. Hochschild (Ed.), *Memory in Augustine's Theological Anthropology* (pp. 9-27). Oxford Academic. 10.1093/acprof:oso/9780199643028.003.0002

Hultin, L. (2019). On becoming a sociomaterial researcher: Exploring epistemological practices grounded in a relational, performative ontology. *Information and Organization*, 29(2), 91–104. 10.1016/j.infoandorg.2019.04.004

Hume, R. D. (1970). Kant and Coleridge on Imagination. *The Journal of Aesthetics and Art Criticism*, 28(4), 485–496. 10.2307/428488

Husserl, E. (2005). *Phantasy, image consciousness, and memory (1898–1925)* (Brough, J., Trans.). Springer.

Jakobson, R. (1960). Closing statement: Linguistics and poetics. In Sebeok, T. (Ed.), *Style in language* (pp. 350–377). Wiley.

James, W. (1891). *Principles of Psychology*. McMillan and Co.

Janiak, A. (2022). Kant's Views on Space and Time. In Zalta, E. (Ed.), *The Stanford Encyclopedia of Philosophy* (Summer 2022 Edition). https://plato.stanford.edu/archives/sum2022/entries/kant-spacetime/

Jansen, J. (2013). Imagination, Embodiment and Situatedness: Using Husserl to Dispel (Some) Notions of "Off-Line Thinking." In *Phenomenology of Embodied Subjectivity* (*Vol. 71*, pp. 63–79). Springer.

Jeanes, E. (2019). Performativity. In *A Dictionary of Organizational Behaviour*. Oxford University Press. https://www.oxfordreference.com/view/10.1093/acref/9780191843273.001.0001/acref-

Jensen, S. K., Mousavi, N., & Tornborg, E. (2022). Intermediality and social media. In Bruhn, J., & Schirrmacher, B. (Eds.), *Intermedial Studies: An introduction to meaning across media* (pp. 282–308). Routledge.

Jokornegay, R. (1993). Hume on the Ordinary Distinction between Objective and Subjective Impressions. *Canadian Journal of Philosophy*, 23(2), 241–269. 10.1080/00455091.1993.10717319

Kant, I. (1998). *Critique of Pure Reason*. Cambridge University Press. 10.1017/CBO9780511804649

Karnes, M. (2011). *Imagination, Meditation, and Cognition in the Middle Ages*. University of Chicago Press. 10.7208/chicago/9780226425337.001.0001

Kitchener, R. F. (1986). *Piaget's Theory of Knowledge: Genetic Epistemology and Scientific Reason*. Yale University Press. 10.2307/j.ctt1xp3sbd

Klein, J., Damm, V., & Giebeler, A. (1983). An Outline of a Theory of Imagination. *Zeitschrift für Allgemeine Wissenschaftstheorie*, 14(1), 15–23. 10.1007/BF01801172

Lavender, A. (2021a). Multimodal acting and performing. In L. Elleström (Ed.), *Beyond Media Borders, Volume 1: Intermedial relations among multimodal media* (pp. 113–40). Palgrave Macmillan. 10.1007/978-3-030-49679-1_3

Liao, S., & Gendler, T. (2020). Imagination. In E. N. Zalta (Ed.), *The Stanford Encyclopedia of Philosophy*. https://plato.stanford.edu/archives/sum2020/entries/imagination/

Lyons, J. D. (1999). Descartes and Modern Imagination. *Philosophy and Literature*, 23(2), 302–312. 10.1353/phl.1999.0043

Makai, P. K. (2022). Media and modalities - Computer games. In Bruhn, J., & Schirrmacher, B. (Eds.), *Intermedial Studies: An introduction to meaning across media* (pp. 69–85). Routledge.

Matherne, S. (2016). Kant's Theory of the Imagination. In Kind, A. (Ed.), *The Routledge Handbook of the Imagination* (1st ed.). Routledge., 10.4324/9781315657905

McKenzie, J. (2006). Is Performance Studies Imperialist? *The Drama Review*, 50(4), 5–8. 10.1162/dram.2006.50.4.5

McLuhan, M. (1994). *Understanding media: The extensions of man*. MIT Press.

Mersch, D. (2009). Imagination, Figurality and Creativity Conditions of Cultural Innovation. In Huppauf, B., & Wulf, C. (Eds.), *Dynamics and Performativity of Imagination: The Image between the Visible and the Invisible* (1st ed., pp. 56–64). Routledge.

Mersch, D. (2016). *Meta/dia* two different approaches to the medial. *Cultural Studies*, 30(4), 650 679. 10.1080/09502386.2016.1180751

Mirski, R., & Bickhard, M. H. (2021). Conventional minds: An interactivist perspective on social cognition and its enculturation. *New Ideas in Psychology*, 62, 100856. 10.1016/j.newideapsych.2021.100856

Mitchell, W. T. J. (1994). *Picture Theory: Essays on Verbal and Visual Representation*. The University of Chicago Press.

Müller, J. E. (1996). *Intermedialität. Formen moderner kultureller Kommunikation*. Nodus Publikationen.

Munro, T. (1949). *The Arts and their Interrelations*. The Liberal Arts Press.

Nagel, T. (1989). *The View from Nowhere*. Oxford University Press.

Narula, U. (2006). Handbook of Communication: Models, Perspectives, Strategies. Atlantic Publishers & Dist.

Nöth, W. (2011). From Representation to Thirdness and Representamen to Medium: Evolution of Peircean Key Terms and Topics. *Transactions of The Charles S.Peirce Society*, 47(4), 445–481. 10.2979/trancharpeirsoc.47.4.445

Otte, M. (1998). Limits of Constructivism: Kant, Piaget and Peirce. *Science & Education*, 7(5), 425–450. 10.1023/A:1008635517122

Pennisi, A., & Falzone, A. (Eds.). (2019). *The Extended Theory of Cognitive Creativity: Interdisciplinary Approaches to Performativity*. Springer Verlag.

Perdue, K. (2003). *Imagination*. https://csmt.uchicago.edu/glossary2004/imagination.htm

Piaget, J. (1999). *Play, Dreams and Imitation in Childhood*. Psychology Press.

Rajewsky, I. O. (2008). Intermedialität und remediation: Überlegungen zu einigen Problemfeldern der jüngeren Intermedialitätsforschung. In Paech, J., & Schröter, J. (Eds.), *Intermedialität Analog/Digital: Theorien—Methoden—Analysen* (pp. 47–60). Wilhelm Fink. 10.30965/9783846743744_005

Reddy, M. J. (1979). The conduit metaphor – A case off rame conflict in our language about language. In Ortony, A. (Ed.), *Metaphor and thought* (pp. 284–324). Cambridge University Press.

Reichling, M. J. (1990). Images of Imagination. *Journal of Research in Music Education*, 38(4), 282–293. 10.2307/3345225

Reinelt, J. (2017). Introduction. *Key Words: A Journal of Cultural Materialism*, *15*, 9-22.

Russell, B. (1915). Sensation and Imagination. *The Monist*, 25(1), 28–44. 10.5840/monist191525136

Ryle, G. (1975). *The Concept of Mind*. Hutchinsons's University Library.

Sapienza, Z., Veenstra, A., Kirtiklis, K., & Giannino, S. (2017). The Transmission Model of Communication: Toward a Multidisciplinary explication. *Researchgate*. https://www. researchgate.net/publication/323025486_The_Transmission_Model_of_Communication_

Schechner, R. (1976). Selective Inattention: A Traditional Way of Spectating Now Part of the Avant-Garde. *Performing Arts Journal*, 1(1), 8–19. 10.2307/3245182

Schechner, R. (2002). *Performance Studies: An Introduction*. Routledge.

Schramm, W. (1971). The nature of communication between humans. In Schramm, W., & Roberts, D. F. (Eds.), *The process and effects of mass communication* (pp. 3–53). University of Illinois Press.

Scott, H. K., & Cogburn, M. (2023). Piaget. In *StatPearls*. StatPearls Publishing. https://pubmed.ncbi.nlm.nih.gov/28846231/

Sepper, D. L. (1996). *Descartes's Imagination: Proportion, Images, and the Activity of Thinking*. University of California Press. http://ark.cdlib.org/ark:/13030/ft0d5n99fd/

Shannon, C. E. (1948). A mathematical theory of communication. *The Bell System Technical Journal*, 27(3), 379–423, 623–656. 10.1002/j.1538-7305.1948.tb01338.x

Sonesson, G. (2011). Semiotics Inside-Out and/or Outside-In. How to Understand Everything and (with Luck) Influence People. *Signata*, 2(2), 315–348. 10.4000/signata.742

Stern, E. R., & Rotello, C. M. (2000). Memory Characteristics of Recently Imagined Events and Real Events Experienced Previously. *The American Journal of Psychology*, 113(4), 569–590. 10.2307/142347311131743

Suncana, L. (2020). *Performativity*. Elsevier. https://www.unine.ch/files/live/sites/inst_geographie/files/shared/Agenda/ Performativity-encyclopedia.pdf

Thompson, R. L. (2004). The Automatic Hand: Spiritualism, Psychoanalysis, Surrealism. *Invisible Culture*, 7(Spring), 1–14. http://web.mit. edu/allanmc/www/Automatic_Hand.pdf

Timplalexi, E. (2022). Theatre Performance through the Intermedial Lens. *Performance Research*, 27(8), 22–34. 10.1080/13528165.2022.2224196

Timplalexi, E. (2023). Challenging key certainties in communication through Elleström's medium-centred model of communication: 'Transfer' and 'medium'. *Explorations in Media Ecology*, 22(4), 399–420. 10.1386/eme_00180_1

Timplalexi, E., & Führer, H. (2023). Reconsidering Elleström's medium-centered communication model: a critical inquiry. *EKPHRASIS*, 2, 93-114. https://www.ekphrasisjournal.ro/docs/R1/30e6.pdf

Trumbo, D. (dir.). (1971). *Johnny Got His Gun*. Cinemation Industries.

Tseng, C. I. (2021a). Truthfulness and Affect via Digital Mediation in Audiovisual Storytelling. In L. Elleström (Ed.), *Beyond Media Borders, Volume 1: Intermedial relations among multimodal media* (pp. 175–195). Palgrave Macmillan. 10.1007/978-3-030-49679-1_5

Turner, V. (1969). Liminality and Communitas. In *The Ritual Process: Structure and Anti Structure* (pp. 41-49). Cornell University Press.

Urmson, J. O. (1967). Memory and Imagination. *Mind, New Series*, 76(301), 83-91. https://www.jstor .org/stable/2252029

Vygotsky, L. S. (2004). Imagination and Creativity in Childhood. *Journal of Russian & East European Psychology*, 42(1), 7–97. 10.1080/10610405.2004.11059210

Warnock, M. (1978). *Imagination*. University of California Press.

Weaver, W. (1998). Recent contributions to the mathematical theory of communica tion. In *The mathematical theory of communication* (pp. 1–28). University of Illinois Press.

Wilde, O. (1905). The decay of lying. In *Intentions* (pp. 1–55). Brentano's.

Zemeckis, R. (dir.) (2002). *Cast Away*. 20th Century Fox, DreamWorks Pictures, ImageMovers and Playtone.

Zuliani, A. L. (2022). Imagination in Renaissance Literature. In Sgarbi, M. (Ed.), *Encyclopedia of Renaissance Philosophy*. Springer. 10.1007/978-3-319-14169-5_858

ENDNOTES

[1]   Elleström (2010) introduced the material modality as consisting of human bodies, flat surfaces and three-dimensional objects and waves (sound waves, for example).

[2]   "Semiotics must go beyond the standpoint of the user, to explain the workings of such operative, albeit tacit, knowledge that underlies the behaviour constitutive of any system of signification" (Sonesson, 2011, p. 326). See also Nagel's (1989) critique of objectivity.

[3]   For example, situating memory, imagination and judgement in brain-borne consciousness (Elleström, 2021a, p. 13) means adhering to a logic that equates the mind to the brain, whereas Makai's (2021a) speculation that cognition and perception are subject to the sensorial modality (p. 75) opens up a whole new potential to consider the interplay of these notions within a more phenomenological subjective perspective. A systematic intermedial attempt which unlocks the role of theatricality and performativity in communication perhaps comes with Timplalexi (2022), where the functional role of the performer acquires a key position in communication, along with the theatricality of the gaze.

[4]   For this reason, sometimes the arrows in Peirce's model afford to be read in a reverse orbit.

[5]   These media products are qualified as belonging to one or more media types, or may cause an intermedial disruptancy and bring forth the emergence of a new media type. For example, Kaprow's happenings (Harviainen, 2008) belongs to at least two media types, "installation" and "performance art"; whereas live action role-play, now a media type in its own right, conquered a discreet medial terrain despite initially being acknowledged as "games" or "performance".

6   In such cases, it may be unattainable to fully define who exactly was Homer or Shakespeare; whether that painting really is a Picasso or a fake, the scratches on this ancient bone (Ellestrom, 2021a, p. 16) are indeed the work of a human hand or Van Gogh's palette was intended by the painter to be exhibited.

7   Van Gogh's palette, for example, qualifies as a media product thanks to the museum curator exhibiting it, rather than Van Gogh himself (Timplalexi & Führer, 2023).

8   Picture a sunset on Santorini that would make any impressionist blush. Or the wrecked man's ball which becomes a companion in Zemeckis' (2002) film.

Chapter 2
Latinx Testimonio Methodology:
Shaping the Collective
Memory of an Identity

Mayra E. García-Díaz
Georgia Southern University, USA

ABSTRACT

This chapter endeavors to illustrate how scholarly chapters that utilize Latin Testimonio as a methodological research approach drive the processes of shaping, preserving, transmitting, and validating collective memories. It also seeks to shed light on how collective recollections—as embodied and portrayed through the complexity of testimonios—contribute to a strong and cohesive sense of identity among the panethnicity of Latinxs in the U.S. This project inquires papers across four dimensions: 1) Research production and curriculum theorization, 2) intergenerational trauma and decolonial recovery, 3) transmission of cultural values and memories, and 4) external perspectives. The discussion features the conversations among testimonios and highlights its power to foster resilience, cultural richness, solidarity, healing, and the political representation of Latinx identity. Ultimately, the epistemology of the revolutionary act of collective recalling to mind, as exemplified by the embodiment of episodic memory in testimonios, is emphasized as a performative tool.

INTRODUCTION

Latinx testimonios research and collective memory conceptions are interconnected in various ways, especially in shaping a new identity, preserving cultural heritage, and sharing historical and cultural memories of racialization within the Latinx community (DeRocher, 2018; Reyes & Rodríguez, 2012; Villa-Nichola, 2019). Testimonio encompasses personal accounts of experiences and collective involvements, transforming them into episodic collective memory containers (e.g. Burgos-Debray, 2009; Katyayani, 2023). These narratives and their theorization facilitate the processes of modeling combined rememberings, conveying memories to the community, and the intergenerational transmission of memories (Beverley, 1989; Flores-Carmona, 2010; Yúdice, 1991).

Huber (2010) claims "Scholarship highlights how testimonio is a process of collective memory, transcending a single experience and connected to a larger group struggle" (p. 83). These collective narratives contribute to restructuring identity and weaving the complexity of collective memory among

DOI: 10.4018/979-8-3693-2264-2.ch002

immigrants, facilitating the social construction of a new identity (Carmona, 2011; DeRocher, 2018; Hubert & Cueva, 2012; Reyes & Rodríguez, 2012). This identity construction is particularly evident with immigrants who, right from the start, learn what it means to identify themselves as Latinx in the U.S.

Therefore, to answer the questions, how do US-based critical scholarly articles that use Latinx testimonios contribute to our understanding of the processes involved in shaping, preserving, transmitting, and validating collective memory, and, what dialogue do these studies portray? The chapter begins by operationalizing key concepts such as Latinx and collective memory. Afterward, it historicizes the appearance of testimonios in academia and defines their methodology. Subsequently, it critically inquires academic articles across four dimensions: 1) Research Production and Curriculum Theorization, 2) Intergenerational Trauma and Decolonial Recovery, 3) Transmission of Cultural Values and Memories, and 4) External Perspectives. To end, the major insights and conversations are portrayed as a revolutionary act of collective remembering.

Operationalizing Key Concepts

This section aims to explore the historical and contextual nuances of defining Latinx. What does Latinx mean for Latinxs? What does it mean for white society? Is the correct term Latino or Latinx? Are Latinx and Hispanics the same? Thus, this section will delve into the complexity, context, and definitions of the pan-ethnic categorical boundary of "Latinx".

Latinx Category, From Census to Racialized Public Identity

Winker (2004) documents that the US census was the pioneer using the concept of Latino "The US government has defined race for its census takers, and for many years census takers then defined it for US residents" (p.1612). Making a historic approach, Winker encapsulates the milestones behind it beginning in the 1850 census when according to her, enumerators used a form that assumed a default race of white, with a checkmark indicating nonwhites as black or mulatto, with additional indications for free or slave. "The Indian category was added in 1860. Since 1960, individuals have been able to specify their own race and ethnicity, and by 2000 the census enumerated 126 racial and ethnic categories" (p.1612). The U.S. Census (2000) asked every individual living in the United States if they were Spanish, Hispanic, or Latino. The term Latino includes people who come from or have family roots coming from Mexicans, Puerto Ricans, Cubans, and people from the Dominican Republic, Central America (Costa Rica, Guatemala, Honduras, Nicaragua, Panama, Salvador, and other Central American countries), South America (Argentine, Bolivia, Columbia, Ecuador, Paraguay, Peru, Uruguay, Venezuela, and other South American countries), Spain, and other Latinos (Kayitsinga, 2015). "Historically, the Latino group included European or 'white' populations, Indigenous people, Asians, Africans, and people of mixed race. Therefore, as Lacomba (2020) documents, 'Latinos' view of their race is very different from the concept of race in the U.S." (p.25). Thus, the composition of the Latino category changes the traits in concordance with the times and laws. Lacomba (2020) emphasizes that Hispanic and Latino refer to an "identity that has always had a political component and has always brought together very disparate populations, which it continues to do today" (p. 1). In her definition of Latino as a *panethnic term*" she records that the term was first used in the Civil Rights Act mentioning the Hispanic as a minority group and "until 1980, censuses had referred Hispanics as being of Spanish origin or part of the "Spanish-speaking population" (p. 13). Okamoto and Mora (2014) state, "Panethnicity refers to the construction of a new categorical boundary through the consolidation of ethnic, tribal, religious, or national groups. It is often misunderstood as simply synonymous with race, ethnicity, or national identity" (p. 221). Consequently, Latino does not represent a single racial identity; instead, it encompasses diverse racial backgrounds. Machado (2023) expresses "The only place in the world where "Hispanics" exist is in the United States. And so, the Latino community lives with an ambiguous and imprecise externally imposed label" (p. 20). Villa-Nichola (2019) highlights that the term "Latinx" encompasses a cohort of individuals: "It's acknowledged that "Latinx" serves as an imperfect descriptor, homogenizing a diverse group of people" (p. 2). The author underscores that the utilization of "Latinx" is not a neutral or merely descriptive choice; rather, it sparks a politically charged debate regarding the standing of Latina/os as citizens or immigrants in the United States. Additionally, the Villa-Nichola (2019) clarifies that "Latinx" is introduced to address the gendered nature of terms like "Latina/o." By incorporating "Latinx," the language seeks to supplement the traditional gender signifiers of "a/o" neutralize the gendered identity, and offer resistance to gender binaries.

Hence, Latinx is observed here as a pan-ethnic categorical boundary since Latinxs are not a race, rather several ethnic groups constitute the Latinx category. It shapes identity through the amalgamation of various racial groups of immigrants and their descendants. Embracing hybridity, the letter 'x' emphasizes both indigenous inclusion and identity neutrality.

A Short History of Collective Memory

The objective of this section is to explore the historical and contextual nuances that define the complex concept of Collective Memory. Halbwachs (1992) emphasized that individual memories are intricately intertwined with pre-existing social frameworks. Human recollection inherently relies on collective contexts, drawing not only from traditions but also from contemporary images, ideas, and concrete experiences. These collective memories are not mere reflections of the past but rather active reconstructions (Vromen,1993). In this context, collective memory refers primarily to cultural practices, social knowledge, and past interactions that influence the appearance and transformation of social distinctiveness characteristics. Garagozov (2015) highlights the profound impact of collective memory on our behavior, emotions, and thoughts. Understanding collective memory and the processes that shape it is essential for interpreting the social aspects of ethnic identity. According to Korver-Glenn (2015) collective memories, which are focal points of intense conflict and debate, can function like institutions. They are shaped by influential elites in memory, overarching memory initiatives, ceremonial practices, and large-scale narratives or texts that can be conveyed and embraced by the general public. "Memory occurs in public and in private, at the tops of societies and at the bottoms, as reminiscence and as commemoration, as personal testimonial and as national narrative, and each of these forms is important" (Korver-Glenn, 2015, p. 426). As DeRocher 2018 asserts "The act of remembering becomes memorialized as an essential form of resistance that offers the possibility of a more profound sense of historical understanding" (p. 143). The concept of cultural memory is deeply connected with broader discourses and serves as a focal point for conflicts and discussions. Thus, collective memory could be observed as an act of resistance and defiance mechanism.

However, Vromen's critique of Halbwach's work proposes a shift from the notion of a fixed "pre-existing social framework" to a more fluid understanding of "collective frameworks of social reference points," which facilitate the coordination of memories across time and space" (Vromen, 1993, p. 510). In this view, Latinx identity, collective memory, and testimonios are not static categories or stable groups defined solely by victimization or mere ascription. Instead, they embody resistance and possess the potential for transformation.

A Short History of Testimonio in US Academia

This section aims to introduce the fluid concept of testimonio through a short historical evolution in the US academic inquiry. The interpretation of Latinx testimonios can be elucidated by exploring the interconnections among analogous works, by contrasting projects, or by being engaged in the criticism and contestation between detractors and supporters. However, the most comprehensive understanding may emerge when delving into their historical development.

The concept of testimonios has roots in Indigenous and oral storytelling Latin American traditions that date back centuries. This literary device became especially popular in the 20th century. One of the greatest recognized publications comes from the Nobel Peace Prize 1992, Rigoberta Menchú Tum. Her masterpiece, edited by Burgos-Debray, *Rigoberta Menchú: An Indian woman in Guatemala* (1984), tells her testimonio as a young Indigenous woman's growing up in Guatemala during political upheaval and violence. "My name is Rigoberta Menchu. This is my testimony... I would like to stress that it is not only my life, it is also the testimony of my people" (p. I).

In the U.S. academic publications and Chicana feminist literature, *Borderlands/la frontera: The new mestiza* (1987) by Gloria Anzaldúa is one of the most dominant tomes. "Perhaps no other author has influenced this body of literature more than Gloria Anzaldúa.... (she) set forth a groundbreaking path that has inspired, pushed, and created new ways to think about our multiple identities, lived/embodied experiences, and the work ahead of us" (Saavedra y Perez, 2013, p. 129). She has drawn from her own personal narrative and blended it with poetry. Additionally, Anzaldúa elaborated the notions of *Conocimiento, Embodied Knowledge, Nepantla, Hybridity* (as collective identities), and *Mestiza consciousness* to explore the life of women of color living on the US-Mexico border.

Gloria Anzaldúa's *theory in the Flesh* or *embodied knowledge* posits that true understanding arises from the lived experiences and physical realities of individuals. She illustrates how the body serves as a site of knowledge production, where cultural, social, and historical influences intersect. Anzaldúa argues that the body holds memories and insights that are often overlooked by traditional, disembodied academic approaches. Her work honors the wisdom inherent in diverse lived experiences. The essays in the book are genuinely personal and offer intimate glimpses into the lives and struggles of the authors: "We do this bridging by naming ourselves and by telling our stories in our own words" (Alzandua, 1981, p.19).

Gloria Anzaldúa's (1981, 1987) literary works are also political, Martinez (2005) describes them as the process of "Making oppositional culture". Her literary works generated social movements that sought to center the occurrences and perspectives of women of color in feminist and anti-oppression movements. According to Anzaldua "The coalition work attempts to balance power relations and undermine and subvert the system of domination-subordination that affects even our most unconscious thoughts" (p. 224). Her books emphasize solidarity, coalition-building, and activism. Her projects also introduced the testimonio tradition into a new scholarly dimension.

Defining Testimonio Methodology

Katyayani (2023) discusses that this genre provides a platform for individuals to share their stories, allowing marginalized voices to be heard and included in historical discourse. Accordingly, the first use of the world is to refer to a first-person narrative. Furthermore, in US-based academia, it is also allowed to describe the methods scholars use to gather personal narratives. According to Hubert (2009), testimonios move from method to methodology through their practice of collaborative reflexivity and co-creation of knowledge. This methodology is specially used within Chicana/Latina identity studies and Latin Curriculum Theorizing (Berry et al., 2019). Scholars follow Chicana/Latina Feminist Epistemologies (Delgado-Bernal 1998) to generate cultural understandings through the compendium of episodic collective remembrances.

Thus, testimonio is observed here not only as a first-person narrative but also, as a critical research method and methodology that follows a praxis of collective remembering and collaborative reflexivity. Its theorization is observed as cultural knowledge creators, as well as community memory media of preservation and diffuser. This method is fundamental in understanding how Latinx communities' collective memory makes sense of the experiences to not be set aside and vanish by malicious forgetfulness.

Encompassing the Heterogeneity of Testimonios

This segment aims to introduce the rich diversity inherent in this academic procedure and the pragmatic functions of testimonios. The multiplicity of narratives is presented here across four dimensions: 1) Research Production and Curriculum Theorization, 2) Intergenerational Trauma and Decolonial Recovery, 3) Transmission of Cultural Values and Memories, and 4) External Perspectives.

Research Production and Curriculum Theorization

As Reyes & Rodríguez (2012) argue "The term testimonio is deployed without necessarily reflecting a methodology" (p. 532). However, Hubert (2009) offers a significant approach using this methodology in education. She develops a procedure that encapsulates the sense of testimonios, using interviews and a three-step collaborative process. She provides insight into the use of LatCrit research using Chicana feminist epistemology. Hubert (2009) asserts "I describe how theory, method, and epistemology were bridged, and allowed for a methodology of testimonio to emerge" (p. 640). She documents that this process make available the co-construction of knowledge between the researcher and the participants and guides the strategies used throughout the inquiry process. Additionally, her methodology differs from traditional research methods by challenging the euro-centricity of traditional educational research, acknowledging and drawing from foundations of knowledge that exist outside of the academy and within Latinx communities.

In academic circles, the utilization of interviews has gained widespread popularity. According to Hubert (2010), "Testimonio interviews" that integrate elements from testimonio methodology and Latin Critics (LatCrit), serve various purposes for example, acknowledging and respecting the knowledge and life of marginalized groups as integral to the scholarly method; questioning prevailing ideologies influencing conventional epistemology and methodology; operating within a collective memory that extends beyond individual experiences to encompass diverse communities; and advancing racial justice by providing a platform within academia for the narratives of People of Color. Another example of this examination is described by Huante-Tzintzun (2016, 2020). She depicts *pláticas methodology* highlighting that it signifies two things "1) the researcher and contributor engage with self-reflexivity and 2) it allows for potential space(s) for healing. To be reflexive requires the researcher and contributor to listen with raw openness and be vulnerable" (Huante-Tzintzun, 2020, p. 52). According to her, the study engages in an informal conversation (plática) with participants to theorize their lived events together. A subsequent example is presented by Carmona et al. (2018) in *pláticas-testimonio*. The authors emphasize the use of feminist decolonizing methodologies within and beyond the borderlands to recount their experiences through various modes, including one-on-one interactions, collective discussions, and communal exchanges with conference attendees. As they initiate *platicando*, they participate in reflection and sharing. Throughout this process, they intersect positionalities, knowledges, pedagogies, and strategies for navigating the colonial and imperial borders within academia. The paper concludes by theorizing pláticas and testimonios as a reflective process grounded in trust, love, and solidarity.

Curriculum Theorization and Teaching Device

Berry (2019) describes that authors utilize testimonios as a methodological strategy to create alternative narratives that challenge deficit perspectives and emphasize educational frameworks that shift focus away from Whiteness, acknowledging the input of Latinx educators. One example of this asseveration is created by Saavedra (2011). She worked with third-grade students, who are first-generation immigrants and face the challenges of fitting into a new country. The author shares personal accounts and observations from the classroom, providing a qualitative and narrative-based approach to understanding the impact of using testimonios as pedagogies: "What follows are three testimonios from my life. They relate to the difficulties and challenges of being an immigrant second-language learner, a bicultural/bilingual teacher, and a Chicana/Latina feminist in a university's teacher education program" (p. 262). According to her, the children in the borderlands face unique challenges related to their cultural, linguistic, and socio-historical backgrounds. These challenges include navigating multiple identities, language barriers, and the impact of colonization on their communities. She documents how testimonio can help by empowering and promoting agency and providing children with a platform to share their personal narratives and struggles. According to her by expressing their narratives, children can connect with each other, recognize similarities in their stories, and build a sense of community and belonging. Saavedra (2011) asserts that another attribute is cultural and historical understanding. By engaging in this activity, children can gain a deeper understanding of their individual histories, traditions, and the impact of colonization on their communities as well as develop language and literacy. Children can use their testimonios to develop language skills, express themselves on their own terms, and engage in critical reflection on their events. Finally, she considers that this counter-narrative of marginalization and silencing of children's voices can liberate them because "Colonization has taught us well to hate ourselves- our brown, black skin, our brown eyes, our bodies" (Saavedra, 2001, p.264).

A second representative pedagogical tool comes from DeNicolo & Gónzalez (2015), *Testimoniando en Nepantla: Using testimonio as a pedagogical tool for exploring embodied literacies and bilingualism*. The authors describe a case study in which third-grade students read and responded to testimonios by writing their own. They chronicle their experiences with bilingualism and language learning. The paper discusses the sociopolitical contexts that shape the implementation of bilingual education programs and the non-traditional learning spaces where Latinx engage in language and literacy practices. The writers explain "We understand the process of giving testimonio, called testimoniando, as an embodied literacy practice that disrupts the notion of the mind-body split, and instead engages what Lara (2002) has conceptualized as the bodymindspirit" (p. 111). This ethnographic approach collected data through participant observation, written work, oral recordings, and interviews. A central concept here is drawn from Anzaldúa's (1987) conceptualization of Nepantla -the Nahuatl word meaning "in-between spaces"- the authors observe this concept "as a transitional and transformative space where those living on the margins are positioned and, thus, are open to experience multiple perspectives and forms of knowledge" (p.112).

A third example comes from Carmona & Delgado-Bernal (2012), who emphasizes the value of gathering testimonios from immigrants and sharing them with pre-service teachers to better prepare future teachers to address the needs of the growing immigrant population in communities where their presence has been unprecedented. The testimonialists, highlight "Adelante Oral Histories Project" as a vehicle to genuinely understand the assets that Latina/o students and their parents bring to school settings from their community. Using the theory of *pedagogies of home* (Delgado-Bernal, 2001) the project aims to incorporate the epistemologies of students of color by including their lives, their families, and community knowledge into the curriculum through the collection of family oral histories. The authors express "The students' and families' cultural assets, their bilingualism, their cross-cultural knowledge, and their experiences with transnationalism were drawn into the curriculum to teach culturally relevant pedagogies of the home" (p.9). They used interviews and organized the narration and images into a photo story. The project also involves teachers and community professionals who work with the students to help them learn about their family histories and cultural backgrounds. The last analysis in this section is *Reclaiming ourselves through Testimonio pedagogy: Reflections on a curriculum design lab in teacher education.* Sosa-Provencio et al. (2019) center attention on understanding and analyzing how testimonio pedagogy may be engaged in teacher preparation, especially for pre-service teachers of color. The article seeks to reveal how pedagogy can be utilized to reclaim dignity, resist oppression, and heal intergenerational trauma, particularly for pre-service Teachers of Color. The authors argue that this pedagogy can be incorporated into teacher education programs in several ways. One approach is to center testimonio narratives in the curriculum. Another approach is to create a safe and supportive space for pre-service teachers to share their personal narratives and to reflect on their own awareness of oppression and resilience.

Intergenerational Trauma and Decolonial Recovery

Shedding light on memoirs of challenges, as well as the impact of systemic inequalities and the process of recovery through sharing. Huber (2011) asserts "Racist nativist microaggressions are systemic, everyday forms of racist nativism that take the form of subtle, layered, and cumulative verbal and non-verbal assaults directed toward people of color that are committed automatically and unconsciously" (p. 156). This definition is also used by Huber and Cueva (2012), their research captures the educational experiences of ten immigrant students who were impacted by their immigration status, race, socioeconomic status, and gender. The author collected counternarratives of trauma and resilience that challenged deficit-oriented understandings of Latinx students. Writers placed the participants' individual testimonios within the context of "a larger collective memory" (p. 397) that illuminates shared Chicana subjectivities consisting of struggles against and resistance to oppression. The findings suggest that the female participants expressed perceptions of academic self-doubt and academic inferiority, which reveals the negative consequences of racist nativist microaggressions on the mind, body, and spirit of Latinx students. The authors also found that participants challenged microaggressions by seeking counterpaces of support and healing.

From a psychological perspective, Siham-Fernandez (2022) shares an article sustained by LatCrit theory and *mujerista* liberation. The source analyzes some excerpts from Latinx students' testimoniando essay assignments to engage with the themes in her online class. The writer considers that "The assignment provided students with an opportunity to engage in relationally critically reflexive dialogues through the process and method of testimonio" (p. 138). They also argue that this research is a *mujerista* strategy that communities have engaged to cultivate healing through revealing occurrences. The relational dialogic critical reflexivity of this activity facilitates and complements existing decolonial practices and healing therapies within and outside of the classroom space. "I purport that testimonio holds implications beyond pedagogy and methodology. Testimonio can be adapted and utilized as a strategy, tool, or resource to cultivate mutual recognition and radical hope that can help cultivate healing toward restored or sustained well-being" (Siham-Fernandez, 2022, p. 139). She argues that this instrument can be a healing, restorative, and therapeutic practice, as well as a political activism tool to support struggles for justice and emancipation.

On the importance of decoloniality praxis and pedagogies Silva et al. (2021), introduce an additional inquiry into the significance of decoloniality within psychology. This document features three contra-narratives from scholars who share their journeys toward decolonizing psychology and the impact of intersecting identities. Guided by the questions: "How do we resist forces of coloniality and colonialism in our work – teaching, research, and practice? How do our positionalities and identities inform our approach to epistemic decoloniality and decolonization?" (p. 389), the article explores the use of decolonial feminism in Critical Community Psychology (Kagan, 2019) and documents decoloniality and decolonization as well as their praxis and pedagogy. The authors argue that decoloniality includes the coloniality of power, which refers to how colonialism and imperialism continue to shape power relations and knowledge production in the present day. Decoloniality is observed as a process of disrupting colonial logic and centering marginalized perspectives and knowledge. And Decolonial Feminist Epistemology, which emphasizes the importance of situated and embodied knowledge and challenges the dominance of Western-Eurocentric ways of knowing.

As a healing action, many authors document that testimonios support recovery through catharsis, which can be therapeutic (e.g. Chavez-Diaz, 2015; Larios, 2020). Ramos & Torres-Fernandez (2020) contend that testimonios serve as a form of validation for doctoral students. This process allowed them to problematize and discuss their experiences in academia not as isolated incidents but as a reflection of a system that has oppressed and marginalized ethnic minorities, empowering them to examine their interactions through a more critical lens in hopes of creating more supportive spaces in which they can thrive and succeed. As stated by the authors, testimonios facilitate recovery from injustices, as it provides a platform for individuals to express their struggles and challenges, ensuring that their voices are not kept in the shadows. This act of remembering can be validating, necessary, and therapeutic, allowing individuals to feel fortified and empowered to continue their academic journeys.

Transmission of Cultural Values and Memories

This section emphasizes how testimonios as representation of community memories, serve as vehicles for communicating the multiplicity of cultural wealth and episodic memories within marginalized communities. One model of heritable memories, culture, and education is documented in the composition *Transgenerational education* by Flores-Carmona (2010). In her project she expresses "Latina mothers' stories and lessons are taught to their children through oral histories, their everyday rituals and practices, the stories that arise from interactions entre mujeres (among women), and in sharing their own testimonio" (p. iv). This critical ethnographic scholarly article utilized Chicana/Latina feminism, theory in the flesh (Moraga & Anzaldúa, 1983), and Latinx cultural citizenship to critically explore how Latina mothers share and collaboratively construct knowledge across generations with their children by using testimonio as a reciprocal progression. The primary emphasis of the research was to uncover how Latina mothers fulfill their obligation to advocate for essential social needs. According to the author, Latina mothers' bodies served as pedagogical tools as they navigated the decision of what knowledge to impart to their children and among themselves. Through pedagogies rooted in the home environment, Latina mothers instilled more comprehensive forms of education that she describes as "Educación of sobrevivencia and supervivencia through testimonio" (p. 32). The study revealed that cultural symbols and informal educational practices were transmitted through the actions of Latina mothers, showcasing how everyday teachings were conveyed to their children. The findings of this study recognize how the everyday cultural and familial communal practices of Latinas contribute to instilling survival lessons, memories, and transgenerational knowledge, thereby empowering their children to assert their rights and establish a sense of belonging.

Yosso (2005) developed the theory of Community Cultural Wealth (CCW) by outlining seven forms of capital that exist within communities of color: aspirational capital (the ability to maintain hope and dreams for the future in the face of real and perceived barriers), linguistic capital (bilingualism or multilingualism), familial capital (the support of extended family members and community), social capital (peers and other social contacts), resistant capital (historical legacy of resistance), and Spirituality. Using this frame, Hubert introduces ten critical race testimonios, from Chicana college students, highlighting their CCW. She states, the women drew on aspirational capital by setting high educational goals for themselves, as well as on familial capital by relying on the emotional and financial support of their families. They utilized social capital by building relationships with peers, professors, and community members who could provide them with information and resources, and navigational capital by developing strategies to navigate the educational system despite their undocumented status. Finally, according to the author, the women drew on resistant capital by challenging racist nativist discourses and advocating for their own rights and the rights of their communities. Hubert (2009b) claims a human rights background that recognizes the strengths and potential of undocumented students and ensures that all students have access to educational opportunities.

Another exemplary research using CCW is presented by Pérez (2016). Her study delves into the narratives of three sisters and their ties to community, family, and self-esteem through Mexican Folklore. Each testimonio is situated within a Latin Critical Race Theory (LatCrit) outline and further analyzed through CCW framework. The narratives within this paper enable each scholar to shape her story authentically, expressed through the voice, structure, and tone of each testimonio. They explore their connection to ethnic identity and cultural heritage. The testimonialist explores the distinctive ways in which their ethnicity intersects with other facets of their identities, such as gender, sexuality, and nationality. These narratives serve as examples of testimonio both as a product and a process. These works demonstrate how marginalized communities interpret the world around them in a manner that empowers and elevates the mind, body, and spirit.

Also, motherhood involvement in education has been strongly documented. Delgado-Bernal (2018) shares her critical race feminista parenting, drawing from her experiences growing up in a Mexican American family and her practices of mothering three Brown sons as a Chicana activist-scholar. She shared her mistakes, and (mis)understandings of parenting children of color, and to provide insights and strategies for other parents and educators interested in critical race feminist parenting. According to the essay, parenting includes the importance of employing pedagogies of the home that reinforce or deconstruct dominant narratives about race and other marginalized identities. She highlights a need for parents to help their children develop a meaningful racial identity within a society that devalues their history, culture, and customs, as well as the value of sharing knowledge with other parents of color to raise responsible, safe children in a world that continues to be shaped by white supremacy and growing racist nativism. She underlines the challenges of parenting children of color with an awareness of racism and its intersections with other oppressions, and the importance of recognizing that there is no unique right parenting way. Delgado-Bernal (2018) describes the potential of testimonio as a pedagogical tool for teaching and learning that brings the mind, body, spirit, and political urgency to the fore, and has the potential to connect people across social positions and build solidarity.

Against the deficit thinking framework and the blame of Latinx for not being involved in the children's education (Carmona & Delagado-Bernal, 2012, Davis & Museus, 2019; Solorzano & Yosso, 2001), García-Díaz (2024) proposes, *Multicultural identity challenge: An exploration of parental involvement in Latinx motherhood.* By positioning motherhood in parental involvement, the author offers insights into the intersection of Latinx identity and educational participation, shedding light on the diverse ways mothers navigate the educational landscape in the United States. The project delves into the life of three mothers, exploring their identity transformation as a consequence of immigration and its impact on their involvement in their children's education. The project examines the initial stage of parental involvement of Hoover-Dempsey and Sandler's theory (1995, 1997).

An example of artistic expression comes from Abril-Gonzalez (2018). She honors border-crossing Latinx knowledge, emerging from high school students' involvement and identities, through photography, drawing, poems, and other artistic expressions. She grounded her work in four combined conceptual frames of Chicana feminism, the concept *acompañamiento*, love and care, and the theory of *Nepantla*. For instance, her poem *Transformative Migrations*

Together again remembering
Relationships, experiences, joys, and pains
A border crossing journey, moving along together
Now and then, past, present, and future
See our potential?
For we started small, we awkwardly crawled
Opportunities to validate our language and culture
Reminiscing, nourished together, strangeness fades
Making a space, encompassed with love and care
A protective mask camouflages
The chrysalis protecting us
Identities trans/form – resisting, growing, and changing
Opening the windows and breaking through
New Knowledge emerges we fly forth to tell, write, and tell
Stories of our existence (Abril-Gonzalez, 2018, p. I)

External Perspectives

Centering the peripheral perspectives, both supportive and critical. Brabeck (2003), problematizes the concept of "otherness" and its role in perpetuating social injustice. She observes testimonios "as a feminist strategy of representing the other" (p. IV). The author argues that the construction of "otherness" is a social and political process used to justify the marginalization and oppression of certain groups. She also notes that "otherness" is often based on stereotypes and misconceptions. Otherness is used to create a sense of superiority among dominant groups. She suggests that testimonio is a powerful tool for challenging these constructions by giving voice to those who have been marginalized and challenging dominant narratives. The writer describes this method as a "first-person account of direct experience, where the narrator is a witness to social injustice and shares their story with a sense of urgency, and as an "alternative methodology for representing, privileging, and understanding the voice of the third world other" (Brabeck, 2023, p. IV). She emphasizes testimonios' collective nature as resistance, its power of building collective consciousness and mobilizing communities to challenge and transform oppressive social structures. Similarly, she argues that "Unlike official western history which is usually understood to be a history of a great individual... the speaker in testimonio gaining credibility not through being an exceptional member but thought being a part indistinguishable of the whole" (p. 253). Brabeck's position as an outsider researcher is an advocate and ally for marginalized communities. Brabeck (2003) invites Western intellectuals "to allow themself to remove their first-world blinkers that value individualism, objectivity, and linear relation, and hear Menchu's voice as finding strength in embeddedness in community" (p. 256). She stresses the need for Western intellectuals to engage in genuine dialogue that values and respects the knowledge of others: "Converse with otherness and learn about otherness in and through these conversations" (p. 256). Brabeck argues that testimonio can serve as a bridge between different forms of knowledge, allowing Western intellectuals to learn from the lived experiences of those who have been marginalized. This dialogue can lead to a more inclusive and equitable exchange of ideas, challenging traditional power dynamics and promoting a more collaborative approach to knowledge production and a more inclusive society.

In the politics of testimonios, Derek Willie (2015), explores the intersection of Western and subaltern feminist knowledge production. She observes how language and narrative shape political knowledge and reimagine discursive authority in terms of inclusivity and diversity. She argues that this approach re-politicizes the discursive sites of feminist epistemology in two ways: focalizing the inherent racialization of feminist discourses that feign to concern themselves purely with "gender". It works to reclaim the rights of political knowledge for the subaltern subject, particularly in the context of a (neo)colonially imposed gender system. The paper suggests that testimonio re-politicizes the discursive sites of feminist epistemology by explicitly de-centering the authority of theoretical discourse from the hegemony of white feminism and by reimagining this discursive authority in terms of the textual or literary production of a subaltern narrator. By highlighting the role of this genre in challenging the hegemony of white feminism and reimagining discursive authority, Willie (2015) positions testimonio as a narrative that contributes to the re-politicization of feminist epistemology.

Even though Brabeck (2003) and Willie (2015) call for Western intellectual openness and dialogue; as well as the documentation of testimonios as research methodology, some institutions still qualify those as quasifiction: "testimonios"—a quasi-fictional literary genre that involves re-enacting and re-imagining traumatic events as narrative or dramatic performances" (University of Georgia, 2011).

From another outsider's perspective, we find the book *The poetics of performance in testimonio* written by Brooks (2005). According to the author, the fundamental contradiction that threatens the credibility of testimonio as a genre lies in the tension between the insistence on the unimpeachability of the witness's testimony and the presence of obvious fabrications by witnesses and editors. Brooks (2005) maintains that detractors argue that the authenticity of the witness's testimony defines the genre, yet discrepancies between witness testimony and historical fact have raised concerns about the genre's credibility. According to her, this contradiction has led to debates about the genre's status as literature and how it should be taught and understood within the context of disciplines such as sociology, political science, anthropology, or history. "A fundamental contradiction looms over testimonio... its "authenticity," they argue, defines the genre; on the other, in the wake of Stoll's exposé of Menchú, they wrestle with obvious fabrications by witnesses (and editors), responding with vague concepts of subaltern "secrets" (Brooks 2005, p.181). She differentiates: it is not legal "testimony," nor a collection of verifiable facts, but rather a dialogical and reflexive genre that continually reminds itself and the reader of its polyphonic and constructed nature. The author compares it with performance and theaters because, according to her, it is seen as a performative genre that involves storytelling, staging, and acting: "Testimonio Staging" (p. 184), "Staging Witness Character and Background" (p.185), "Staging Liminality" (p.189), "Testimonio Acting" (p. 190). However, Brooks (2005) recognizes that testimonio has played a significant role in the development of identity politics by providing a platform for marginalized voices and challenging dominant narratives about identity and power.

Portraying the Dialogue of Collective Memories

In the echo of testimonio conversations, episodic collective memory unfurls to answer the question: what dialogue do these studies portray? And, despite being occasionally criticized, these written, recorded, artistic, or digitalized representations of memories, openly document and share memories of oppression, microaggression, deficit thinking accusations, stereotypes, marginalization, and dominant Western-Eurocentric perspectives, that consequently imply the politics of those. These projects, raise awareness about social issues in the educational context and institutional discrimination, which cannot be healed if kept silent.

Testimonios are observed, shared, and widely supported for collective healing and growth, amplifying the voices of the unheard. They foster dialogue, build bridges between communities, and promote understanding, and empathy. They serve as a catharsis as well as a decoloniality process. They are created as a tool for building collective consciousness. Through reader identification and solidarity, this genre promotes a strong sense of belonging to a collective and endorsed cohesion among Latinx.

As memory, culture, and knowledge containers and promoters, testimonios run through collective narratives that shape what it means to be part of the Latinx pan-ethnic category in the U.S. They highlight the panethnicity of a term that comprises a multiracial, multiethnic, multireligious, and multilingual group of people. Also, they documented the ethnic identity transformation of Latinx immigrants and the hybridity of the individuals.

This methodology supports the portrayal of memory by presenting a multiplicity of perspectives. Testimonio methodology allows for the inclusion of diverse voices, emotions, and viewpoints, offering a more comprehensive understanding of the past and present to change the future. By incorporating testimonios into the reconstruction of collective memory, alternative histories, and suppressed truths can be acknowledged, contributing to a more inclusive and nuanced understanding of societal interactions.

Testimonios speak out loud by themselves because of the authenticity of lived occurrences. They provide a platform for individuals to share their encounters. An enrichment of testimonios is that they convey factual information and embodied emotions. Readers likewise validate these narratives as part of their own involvements, such as personal experiences that often mirror many more. By valuing the emotional dimensions of experiences, these approaches enrich the fluid frameworks of collective remembrance, capturing the complexities of human existence beyond mere facts or statistics and documenting the profound impact of collective memory on our behavior, emotions, and thoughts.

Through the communal perspective and solidarity of sharing reflections of the past, individuals reclaim agency over their narratives and connect with others who often mirror similar occurrences, thereby strengthening social bonds and collective identity. These conversations, nurture and thrive cultural heritage recognition, promote pride in community cultural wealth, encourage wisdom, and allow the cycle of transgenerational memories. In this way, testimonios interrupt forgetfulness enabling the epistemological active reconstruction of collective memory.

The Academic Epistemic of Collective Memories

The struggle over the "legitimate and unique" knowledge is still alive. The apartheid of knowledge in academia does not openly recognize Latinx intellectual production and cultural theorizations (Delgado-Bernal & Villalpando, 2002; Hubert, 2009). However, testimonio has been strongly embraced by Latinx in academic circles, to define a space of embodied knowledge production, theorization, and cultural reproduction, uncovering the epistemology of community memory.

Testimonios allow cultural theorization and are observed and validated here as memory fluid frames, besides epistemological community memory portraits. Using testimonios as knowledge creators, they embrace the epistemic definition of Moraga and Anzaldúa (1981) *Embodied Knowledge* or the notion of *Theory in the Flesh* that describes knowledge as deeply intertwined with lived experiences and embodied perspectives. Furthermore, they infold Chicana Latina Feminist Epistemologies (Delgado-Bernal, 1998) and the philosophical assumptions of Critical Race Feminista Methodology (Delgado-Bernal et al., 2018).

Moving from method to methodology, the co-creation of knowledge and the practice of collaborative reflexivity of testimonios, assist the communications of communal memories. Following this research procedure, the academic rigor that adheres to high standards of accuracy, thoroughness, and intellectual integrity, ensures knowledge-making. The intellectual process of deconstructing memories by retrieving the information stored in their long-term memory and re-shaping those collaboratively to create cultural understandings, ensures the communal interpretation of memories, validating them to participate in the political discourse.

Following the methodology and method of testimonio, the epistemology of collective memory is supplemented through its emphasis on authenticity, diversity, resistance, embodiment, and solidarity to empower communities through representation. Thus, to answer the question, how do US-based critical scholarly articles that use Latinx testimonios contribute to our understanding of the processes involved in shaping, preserving, transmitting, and validating collective memory? This argumentation claims that not only but also through the methodology and epistemology of testimonios. These conversations, illustrate, perpetuate, and communicate the collective memory of a multicultural identity.

The Revolutionary Act of Collective Remembering

Drawing from diverse experiences, hybrid identities, and memories, this category, embracing multiracial and pan-ethnic perspectives, champions the acknowledgment and celebration of Latinx identity. The suppressed truths portrayed in testimonios emerge revitalized, proclaiming visibility as they strive for recognition. Within this discourse, memories become potent vessels of resistance, challenging the confines of marginalization and invisibility. Latinx testimonios purposefully confront the limitations imposed by societal boundaries, actively shaping the narrative to reflect the authentic multicultural and multiracial nuclear essence of the country.

Through testimonios discourse of collective memories, Latinx individuals engage in the politics of representation, by pushing away stereotypes, and oppressive power structures. It also fosters a deeper historical comprehension and dismantles the simplistic dichotomies that obscure reality. These narratives that refuse to remain silent possess the potential to forge connections and foster solidarity, empathy, and understanding, facilitating cross-cultural communication.

This academic and political instrument of representation stands as a potent testament to the revolutionary act of collective remembering. By embracing the power of collective memory, testimonios illuminate paths toward healing of intergenerational trauma, decolonial recovery, resilience, and social transformation. As we continue to listen, honor, and amplify these memories, we embark on a journey toward a more inclusive, empathetic, and just society, where every memory is valued, every story is heard, and every individual is seen.

REFERENCES

Abril-Gonzalez, P. (2018). *Recuerdos, expresiones y sueños en Nepantla: Identity journeys through spoken, written, and artistic testimonios* (Order No. 10840992). ProQuest Dissertations & Theses Global: The Humanities and Social Sciences Collection. (2113571081).

Anzaldúa, G. (1987). *Borderlands la frontera. The new mestiza.* Aunt Lute Book Company.

Bernal, D. D. (1998). Using a Chicana feminist epistemology in educational research. *Harvard Educational Review*, 68(4), 555–583. 10.17763/haer.68.4.5wv1034973g22q48

Bernal, D. D., & Villalpando, O. (2002). An apartheid of knowledge in academia: The struggle over the" legitimate" knowledge of faculty of color. *Equity & Excellence in Education*, 35(2), 169–180. 10.1080/713845282

Berry & Rodriguez. (2019). *Latinx Curriculum Theorizing.* Lexington Books.

Beverley, J. (1989). The margin at the center: On testimonio (testimonial narrative). *Modern Fiction Studies*, 35(1), 11–12. 10.1353/mfs.0.0923

Brabeck, K. (2003). IV. Testimonio: A strategy for collective resistance, cultural survival, and building solidarity. *Feminism & Psychology*, 13(2), 252–258. 10.1177/0959353503013002009

Brooks, L. M. (2005). Testimonio's poetics of performance. *Comparative Literature Studies*, 42(2), 181–202. 10.2307/40247475

Burgos-Debray, E. (Ed.). (2009). *Yo Rigoberta Menchu: Una mujer india en Guatemala.* Volver.

Carmona, J. F. (2010). *Transgenerational educación: Latina mothers' everyday pedagogies of cultural citizenship in Salt Lake City.* The University of Utah.

Cervantes-Soon, C. G. (2012). Testimonios of life and learning in the borderlands: Subaltern Juárez girls speak. *Equity & Excellence in Education*, 45(3), 373–391. 10.1080/10665684.2012.698182

Chavez-Diaz, M. (2015). *Social justice healing practitioners: Testimonios of transformative praxis and hope.* Academic Press.

Delgado-Bernal, D. (2001). Learning and living pedagogies of the home: The mestiza consciousness of Chicana students. *International Journal of Qualitative Studies in Education : QSE*, 14(5), 623–639. 10.1080/09518390110059838

Delgado-Bernal, D. (2002). Critical race theory, Latino critical theory, and critical raced-gendered epistemologies: Recognizing students of color as holders and creators of knowledge. *Qualitative Inquiry*, 1(8), 105–126. 10.1177/107780040200800107

Delgado Bernal, D. (2018). A testimonio of critical race feminista parenting: Snapshots from my childhood and my parenting. *International Journal of Qualitative Studies in Education : QSE*, 31(1), 25–35. 10.1080/09518398.2017.1379623

Delgado-Bernal, D., Huber, L. P., & Malagón, M. C. (2018). Bridging theories to name and claim a critical race feminista methodology. In *Understanding critical race research methods and methodologies* (pp. 109–121). Routledge. 10.4324/9781315100944-10

DeNicolo, C. P., & Gónzalez, M. (2015). Testimoniando en Nepantla: Using testimonio as a pedagogical tool for exploring embodied literacies and bilingualism. *Journal of Language & Literacy Education*, 11(1), 109–126.

DeRocher, P. (2018). *Transnational testimonios: the politics of collective knowledge production.* University of Washington Press.

Espino, M. M., Vega, I. I., Rendón, L. I., Ranero, J. J., & Muñiz, M. M. (2017). The Process of Reflexión in Bridging Testimonios Across Lived Experience: Michelle M. Espino Irene I. In *Chicana/Latina testimonios as pedagogical, methodological, and activist approaches to social justice* (pp. 93–108). Routledge.

Flores-Carmona, J. (2010). *Transgenerational Education: Latina mothers' everyday pedagogies of cultural citizenship in Salt Lake City, Utah.* [Unpublished dissertation, University of Utah].

Flores-Carmona, J., & Delgado Bernal, D. (2012). Oral histories in the classroom: Home and community pedagogies. In Sleeter, C. E., & Soriano Ayala, E. (Eds.), *Building solidarity between schools and marginalized communities: International perspectives.* Teachers College Press.

Flores-Carmona, J., Hamzeh, M., Bejarano, C. M., Hernandez, S. M., & El Ashmawi, P. Y. (2018). Platicas- Testimonio: Practicing Methodological Borderlands for Solidarity and Resilience in Academia. Chicana. *Latino Studies*, 18(1), 30–52.

Garagozov, R. (2015). *Collective Memory: How Collective Representations About the Past Are Created, Preserved and Reproduced.* Nova publisher.

Garcia-Diaz, M. (in press). Multicultural identity challenge: An exploration of parental involvement in Latinx motherhood. In M. Williams-Johnson & N. P. Rickert (Eds.), *Critical analysis of parental involvement in school: Working with families across sociocultural contexts.* Accademic Press.

Huante-Tzintzun. (2020). *The power of testimonio methodology: history, components, and resources.* Sociology Writing Manual.

Huante-Tzintzun, N. (2016). *The problematics of method: Decolonial strategies in education and Chicana/Latina testimonio/Platica.* ProQuest Dissertations. https://collections.lib.utah.edu/ark:/87278/s62n96dz

Huber, P. L. (2009). Challenging racist nativist framing: Acknowledging the community cultural wealth of undocumented Chicana college students to reframe the immigration debate. *Harvard Educational Review*, 79(4), 704–730. 10.17763/haer.79.4.r7j1xn011965w186

Huber, P. L. (2010). Using Latina/o critical race theory (LatCrit) and racist nativism to explore intersectionality in the educational experiences of undocumented Chicana college students. *Educational Foundations.*

Huber, P. L., Benavides-Lopez, C., Malagon, M., Velez, V., & Solorzano, D. (2008). Getting beyond the 'symptom,' acknowledging the 'disease': Theorizing racist nativism. *Contemporary Justice Review*, 11(1), 39–51. 10.1080/10282580701850397

Huber, P. L., & Cueva, B. M. (2012). Chicana/Latina testimonios on effects and responses to microaggressions. *Equity & Excellence in Education*, 45(3), 392–410. 10.1080/10665684.2012.698193

Kagan, C., Burton, M., Duckett, P., Lawthom, R., & Siddiquee, A. (2019). *Critical community psychology: Critical action and social change*. Routledge. 10.4324/9780429431500

Katyayani, S. (2023). Exploring the Role of Testimonio Method in Shaping Collective Memory of Indenture History: From Empathy to Empowerment. *Rupkatha Journal on Interdisciplinary Studies in Humanities, 15*(2).

Korver-Glenn, E. (2015). (Collective) memory of racial violence and the social construction of the Hispanic category among Houston Hispanics. *Sociology of Race and Ethnicity (Thousand Oaks, Calif.)*, 1(3), 424–438. 10.1177/2332649215576757

Lacomba, C. (2020). Hispanics and/or Latinos in the United States: The Social Construction of an Identity. *Observational Studies*. Advance online publication. 10.15427/OR065-11/2020EN

Larios, S. E. (2020). Digital Testimonios: A personal journey towards healing and empowerment. *Journal of Curriculum and Pedagogy*, 17(3), 318–322. 10.1080/15505170.2020.1808128

Latina Feminist Group. (2001). *Telling to Live: Latina Feminist Testimonios*. Duke University Press.

Machado, D. L. (2023). History and Latinx Identity: Mapping a Past That Leads to Our Future. *The Wiley Blackwell Companion to Latinoax Theology*, 25-43. Wiley.

Martinez, T. A. (2005). Making oppositional culture, making standpoints: A journey into Gloria Anzaldua borderlands. *Sociological Spectrum*, 25(5), 539–570. 10.1080/02732170500176021

Montoya, M. (2022). An introduction. In *LatCrit from critical legal theory to academic activism*. New York University Press. 10.7551/mitpress/12245.003.0003

Moraga, C., & Anzaldúa, G. (1981). *This bridge called my back. Writings by radical women of color* (4th ed.). SUNY Press.

Nora, P. (1989). Between memory and history: Les lieux de mémoire. *Representations (Berkeley, Calif.)*, 26, 7–24. 10.2307/2928520

Okamoto, D., & Mora, G. C. (2014). Panethnicity. *Annual Review of Sociology*, 40(1), 219–239. 10.1146/annurev-soc-071913-043201

Patton Davis, L., & Museus, S. (2019). What is deficit thinking? An analysis conceptualizations of deficit thinking and implications for scholarly research. *Currents*, 1(1), 117–130. 10.3998

Ramos, S. L., & Torres-Fernandez, I. (2020). Conociendo los caminos: Testimonios of Latina doctoral students. *Peace and Conflict*, 26(4), 379–389. 10.1037/pac0000450

Reyes, B. K., & Rodríguez, C. J. (2012). Testimonio: Origins, terms, and resources. *Equity & Excellence in Education*, 45(3), 525–538. 10.1080/10665684.2012.698571

Reyes, G. (2011). Latinx curriculum theorizing. *Oxford Research Encyclopedia of Education*. Oxford Press. https://oxfordre.com/education/view/10.1093/acrefore/9780190264093.001.0001/acrefore-9780190264093-e-1598

Reyes, K., & Rodríguez, J. (2012). Testimonio: Origins, terms, and resources. *Equity & Excellence in Education*, 45(3), 525–538. 10.1080/10665684.2012.698571

Reyes, V. D. (2017). Disparate lessons: Racial climates and identity-formation processes among Latino students. *Du Bois Review*, 14(2), 447–470. 10.1017/S1742058X17000054

Romero, O. (2022). *Why Indigenous people want you to stop labeling them as Latino*. TEDx Talks. https://www.ted.com/tedx

Rothe, E. M., Tzuang, D., & Pumariega, A. J. (2010, October). Acculturation, development, and adaptation. *Child and Adolescent Psychiatric Clinics of North America*, 19(4), 681–696. 10.1016/j.chc.2010.07.00221056341

Saavedra, C. M. (2011). Language and literacy in the borderlands: Acting upon the world through "Testimonios". *Language Arts*, 88(4), 261–269. 10.58680/la201113548

Siham-Fernández, J. (2022). A Mujerista Liberation Psychology Perspective on Testimonio to Cultivate Decolonial Healing. *Women & Therapy*, 45(2-3), 2–3, 131–156. 10.1080/02703149.2022.2095101

Silva, M. J., Fernández, J. S., & Nguyen, A. (2021). Three testimonios on the importance of decoloniality within psychology. *The Journal of Social Issues*, 77(2), 389–390.

Solorzano, D. G., & Yosso, T. J. (2001). From racial stereotyping and deficit discourse toward a critical race theory in teacher education. *Multicultural Education*, 9(1), 2–8.

Sosa-Provencio, M. A., Sheahan, A., Fuentes, R., Muñiz, S., & Prada-Vivas, R. (2019). Reclaiming ourselves through testimonio pedagogy: Reflections on a curriculum design lab in teacher education. *Race, Ethnicity and Education*, 22(2), 211–230. 10.1080/13613324.2017.1376637

University of Georgia. (2011). *Today's top news from University of Georgia. Obituary, Linda Brooks*. UGA. https://news.uga.edu/obituary-linda-brooks/

Valdes, F. (1999). Afterword - theorizing "OutCrit" theories: Coalitional method and comparative jurisprudential experience - RaceCrits, QueerCrits, and LatCrits'. *University of Miami Law Review*, 1265.

Villenas, S. (2001). Latina mothers and small-town racism: Creating narratives of dignity and moral education in North Carolina. *Anthropology & Education Quarterly*, 32(1), 3–28. 10.1525/aeq.2001.32.1.3

Vromen, S. (1993). [Review of *Maurice Halbwachs on Collective Memory.*, by L. A. Coser. *American Journal of Sociology*, 99(2), 510–512. 10.1086/230291

Willie, D. (2015). Testimonio and the discursive politics of feminist epistemology. *Journal of Feminist Scholarship*, 7, 1–15.

Winker, M. A. (2004). Measuring race and ethnicity: Why and how? *Journal of the American Medical Association*, 292(13), 1612–1614. 10.1001/jama.292.13.161215467065

Yosso, T. J. (2005). Whose culture has capital? A critical race theory discussion of community cultural wealth. *Race, Ethnicity and Education*, 8(1), 69–91. 10.1080/1361332052000341006

Yúdice, G. (1991). Testimonio and postmodernism. *Latin American Perspectives*, 18(3), 15–31. 10.1177/0094582X9101800302

Chapter 3
Memory, Trauma, and Healing:
Transformation of Identities of South Asian Diasporic Women

Shrimoyee Chattopadhyay
University of Debrecen, Hungary

ABSTRACT

South Asian people migrate to the West, primarily to the US and the UK, in order to live a better life, full of opportunities. However, apart from fulfilling their desire, some of the diasporic immigrants, especially women, also move away from their home countries so as to escape from trauma. This chapter explores both individual and collective trauma, as portrayed in Monica Ali's Brick Lane (2003) and Bharati Mukherjee's Jasmine (1989). Relying on Cathy Caruth's notion, the chapter investigates trauma as an unclaimed experience. While Caruth's theory is Westocentric, theories of Jeffrey Alexander and Stef Craps will be useful in analysing the non-Western trauma as represented in the diasporic narratives. Furthermore, intergenerational trauma theories of Angela Connolly and Ana Dragojlovic will be particularly essential to explore the intergenerational haunting as experienced by the female protagonists.

INTRODUCTION

One of the primary reasons why South Asian people migrate to the West is the "American Dream," which can be defined as a "dream of a land in which life should be better and richer and fuller for every man, with opportunity for each according to his ability or achievement...a dream of a social order in which each man and each woman shall be able to attain to the fullest stature of which they are innately capable" (Adams, 1931, p. 404). Similar to America, which is a popular destination for South Asian immigrants, Britain is also a dreamland for diasporic migrants. In this chapter, I will explore how America and London become sites for female empowerment, especially for the diasporic women as represented in Bharati Mukherjee's *Jasmine* (1989) and Monica Ali's *Brick Lane* (2003). In Ali's novel, the protagonist, Nazneen, moves from Bangladesh to London to accompany her husband who works there. On the

DOI: 10.4018/979-8-3693-2264-2.ch003

contrary, Mukherjee's narrative portrays the journey of the heroine, Jasmine, from Punjab to America after the death of her husband.

Many scholars have claimed that the American Dream is a myth. For instance, Neil ten Kortenaar criticises Bharati Mukherjee's *Jasmine* by claiming that the novel idealises "assimilation [as] thoroughly unrealistic in very problematic ways" (Kortenaar, 2016, p. 379). He poses the question, "[w]hat makes it possible for Jasmine to become so thoroughly American?" (Kortenaar, 2016, pp. 379-80). Kortenaar further argues that in Mukherjee's novel Jasmine "is the mouthpiece of an educated cosmopolitan writer who hides behind the mask of an uneducated, much victimized daughter of poverty" (Kortenaar, 2016, p. 380). In my view, however, the victimisation of Jasmine has a more complex role in the narrative than simply offering a safe mask for the writers to hide behind. As I argue in this chapter, apart from fulfilling their desire to live a better life in the US and the UK, diasporic immigrants such as Jasmine and Nazneen, also move away from their homelands in order to escape from trauma. This trauma can be both individual and collective. Relying on Kai Erikson's argument, I define individual trauma as "a blow to the psyche that breaks through one's defences so suddenly and with such brutal force that one cannot react to it effectively" (Erikson, 1976, p. 153), whereas collective trauma is "a blow to the basic tissues of social life that damages the bonds attaching people together and impairs the prevailing sense of communality" (Erikson, 1976, p. 154).

Furthermore, collective trauma can also be intergenerational, as I will showcase in my analysis of Ali's *Brick Lane*. In contrast to Mukherjee's heroine, Jasmine, who moves to America after the demise of her husband, Ali's protagonist, Nazneen, accompanies her husband to London. It is my contention that memories and traumas have a significant role in both Mukherjee's and Ali's narratives. Although I analyse individual trauma in both *Jasmine* and *Brick Lane*, I will show how Mukherjee's protagonist is traumatised by the political riot in Punjab, which is an example of collective trauma, while Ali's main character is haunted by intergenerational trauma inherited from her mother. Thus, I want to illuminate trauma and social identity in literature and not as a sociological and historical event.

In this chapter, I explore how traumatised characters, such as Jasmine and Nazneen, cope with their traumatic experiences in the West. Cathy Caruth has famously defined trauma as an "unclaimed experience," which is "not locatable in the simple violent or original event in an individual's past, but rather in the way that its very unassimilated nature – the way it was precisely not known in the first instance – returns to haunt the survivor later on" (Caruth, 1996, p. 4). My aim is to analyse trauma as such an unclaimed experience, which, due to its unassimilated nature, haunts the protagonists unconsciously. The journey from Jasmine's home country to the US, for instance, and her subsequent journeys within the host nation, reflect different stages of coping with trauma. My chapter will show that the protagonists, Jasmine and Nazneen, come to terms with their traumas to a certain extent. But it also needs to be foregrounded that the diasporic characters are further traumatised in the Western locations. Tracing Jasmine's journey from "city (Lahore, left by her father at Partition) to countryside (Hasnapur) to city (Jullundhar) to countryside (Florida) to city (New York) to countryside (Iowa)" (Kortenaar, 2016, p. 382), Kortenaar argues that the "geographical cycles correspond to a narrative pattern: the sequence of flight – confinement – escape – stability – flight is repeated over and over" (Kortenaar, 2016, p. 382) in the novel. In my reading, the geographical locations that she traverses in the West do not simply represent Jasmine's escape: they act both as sites where she experiences further traumatic events and grounds for her healing.

BHARATI MUKHERJEE'S *JASMINE*: **AN OVERVIEW**

Written in the first person, Mukherjee's novel explores the journey of a young woman, Jasmine, who moves to the US to fulfil her dead husband's dream of moving to a Western country in order to gain access to better educational opportunities and to escape from the political turmoil in India. Though the protagonist speaks of immigration as a "matter of duty and honor" (Mukherjee, 1989, p. 97), her husband, in fact, wanted her to move to America to have a "real life" (Mukherjee, 1989, p. 81). It is not clearly mentioned in the novel what Prakash, Jasmine's husband, has meant by "real life". He is an engineer and is not satisfied with his job as a repairman in India, so probably he desired to have a meaningful and successful life in America, where he could have made the best use of his engineering skills. His frustration is evident when he explains how he feels about his job to Jasmine: "You see how the mediocre are smart enough to get away? Only we, the best ones, let ourselves be hemmed in by bloodsuckers and dunderheads" (Mukherjee, 1989, p. 84). However, Prakash's dream of moving to the US and settling down there does not get fulfilled because of his untimely death. In contrast to the other female protagonists in the narratives I analyse, who move to the West primarily to accompany their husbands, Jasmine migrates to the US for socioeconomic reasons. Furthermore, and more importantly, she wants to leave due to the individual and collective trauma she has experienced in India: the loss of her husband and Sikh separatism, which led to armed conflicts between Hindus and Sikhs in Punjab.

In the West, the female characters help Jasmine cope with her traumatic experiences by offering her shelter and financial stability, which foster her healing since they listen to her stories and provide a sense of safety. These are Lillian Gordon, the first woman who helps her by giving her a place to stay after she migrates to America; Kate, Lillian's daughter, who finds her a job as a caregiver; Wylie, Taylor's wife, who appoints Jasmine to look after her daughter, Duff; Karin, Bud's ex-wife, who at the end of the narrative encourages Jasmine to walk out with the man of her choice; and Mother Ripplemeyer, Bud's mother, who helps her find a job at a bank in the US. Jasmine comes in contact with these women at different phases of her life and each of them has a significant impact on her: they not only help her to heal from her trauma but also encourage her to acquire a more empowered position in society. But it has to be foregrounded that although characters in the West extend their support, especially through empathy and understanding, they also impose American norms on her, which is indicated by the different names, such as "Jase" and "Jazzy," that these characters give to the protagonist. But before analysing the traumas the main character has experienced and her coping strategies, I would like to give a brief historical background of the political turmoil that resulted from the riot between the Hindus and the Sikhs in Hasnapur, as narrativised in the novel, and the role it has played in the emigration of the female protagonist. Though the riot, which is the collective trauma (albeit related to her individual trauma of the death of her husband), has begun in Hasnapur, India, it had a long-lasting impact on Jasmine's life: the impact of the event is haunting her, similar to the loss of her husband, even when she is in the Western cities, far away from her homeland.

SIKH SEPARATISM AND COLLECTIVE TRAUMA IN *JASMINE*

The main character of Jasmine is Jyoti, a Hindu girl from the village of Hasnapur, Punjab[1], India, who is also the narrator of the novel. Similar to Nazneen, a village girl in Brick Lane, who is portrayed as the representation of purity, Jasmine is also a "very special case" (Mukherjee, 1989, p. 135) as she is from a small village. In other words, she is also seen as an "uncorrupted," "pure" girl from the village, which is an identity that Jasmine, similar to Nazneen, comes to reject. Jasmine falls in love with Prakash Vijh, a friend of her brother, and they eventually get married. In contrast to Karim in Ali's narrative, who desires to possess the pure village girl whom he sees as authentic, however, Prakash wants to transform his wife, which is clearly expressed by his act of changing Jyoti's name to Jasmine: "He wanted to break down the Jyoti I'd been in Hasnapur and make me a new kind of city woman. To break off the past, he gave me a new name: Jasmine. He said, 'You are small and sweet and heady, my Jasmine. You'll quicken the whole world with your perfume'" (Mukherjee, 1989, p. 77). However, both gestures are possessive and patriarchal, though in different ways. Prakash's act of changing Jyoti's name can be read as a manifestation of his patriarchal authority, based on the idea that he can make decisions for Jasmine on her behalf. Furthermore, his desire to "make [her] a new kind of city woman" (Mukherjee, 1989, p. 77) suggests that he is trying to modernise Jasmine so that she can later fit into the Western society easily. However, it has to be foregrounded that Prakash is the only other person besides Masterji, her school teacher[2], who encourages Jasmine to study. He also desires a more comfortable future for both of them. Being frustrated with his mediocre job as a repairman and the growing unemployment in India, he plans to gain admission to the Florida's International Institute of Technology. He even contacts his one-time professor, Devinder Vadhera, in America, who promises to help him with the admission procedure. But his dreams remain unfulfilled: one day, when Prakash goes out shopping with Jasmine to buy her a new sari, he is attacked by Sukhinder (or Sukkhi), a member of the Sikh boys' gang, the Khalsa[3] Lions." Sukkhi places a bomb in a VCR, which instantly kills Prakash, but Jasmine survives the disaster. The death of Jasmine's husband, then, which is her individual trauma, needs to be understood in the larger context of Sikh separatism: the collective trauma Mukherjee's novel thematises.

Jasmine explores Sikh separatism[4] and the Khalistan Movement[5] in Punjab, which became dominant in the 1980s, the time when the novel is set. The root of the riot has been laid during the partition of India in 1947. The Sikhs wanted an independent state called Khalistan, which "spawned a militant wing that during the 1980s and 1990s involved thousands of individuals. The crackdown against insurgency by the Indian government was extreme; extrajudicial executions, 'disappearances,' custodial rapes, and ubiquitous torture earned India the condemnation of every major international human rights organization" (Mahmood, 2001, p. 528). During the same time, the Khalistan militants "moved beyond the international laws of armed conflict to commit atrocities against Punjabi civilians. Over the twenty years of conflict, tens of thousands of people...were killed, and Khalistan was not established" (Mahmood, 2001, p. 528). Even though Hasnapur, the setting of Mukherjee's narrative, had a Hindu majority, Hindu families, for instance, Jasmine's and Prakash's, among others, lived in fear because of the Sikhs[6]. In 1920, the Sikhs established the Akali Dal to promote the Sikh community. Subsequently, the Akali party failed[7] to "capitalise on its advantage of being the sole and effective champion of the Sikhs" (Jetly, 2008, p. 63). Although several military operations such as Operation Woodrose (1986-1987) and Operation Black Thunder (1988) were set up to control the growing violence, the force only aggravated the situation (Jetly, 2008, p. 69). Nevertheless, the movement for the formation of an independent Sikh state found support from the Sikh diaspora. Extremist organisations such as the "National Council of Khalistan, Babbar Khalsa International and Dal Khalsa flourished in different parts of the world, particularly in the US, Canada, Italy, Denmark, Holland, and the United Kingdom" (Jetly, 2008, p. 69). In New York City, Mukherjee's protagonist, Jasmine, meets Sukkhi, the member of the Khalistan group and murderer of her husband, and she is forced to run away to Iowa after the encounter.

Set in the 1980s, Mukherjee's narrative not only highlights the political turmoil in India, which is a result of the armed conflicts between the Hindus and the Sikhs, but it also traces the after effects of the riot by depicting the "collective psychological health" (Alexander, 2004, p. 7) of the characters. Exploring the notion of cultural trauma, Jeffrey Alexander points out that "[c]ultural trauma occurs when members of a collectivity feel they have been subjected to a horrendous event that leaves indelible marks upon their group consciousness, marking their memories forever and changing their future identity in fundamental and irrevocable ways" (Alexander, 2004, p. 1). A similar traumatic event is narrativised in Jasmine: the "horrendous event" (Alexander, 2004, p. 1) of armed conflicts "leaves [an] indelible" (Alexander, 2004, p. 1) mark on both Prakash and Jasmine. As a result, the couple decides to move away from India. But due to his sudden death, Jasmine travels to the US all by herself. She even plans to give him a proper funeral near the Florida university campus. I read her act of moving away from her home country as an attempt to resolve, or, at least to come to terms with her trauma, since, as Alexander argues, "[t]rauma will be resolved, not only by setting things right in the world, but by setting things right in the self" (Alexander, 2004, p. 5). Jasmine leaves India precisely for this reason: apart from the loss of her husband, she migrates due to the political turmoil in her home country. Therefore, Mukherjee's novel resonates with Alexander's claim that cultural trauma is "an empirical, scientific concept, suggesting new meaningful and casual relationships between previously unrelated events, structures, perceptions, and actions. But this new scientific concept also illuminates an emerging domain of social responsibility and political action" (Alexander, 2004, p. 1). As I argue in the next section, her journey both to the US and within the country reflects how she is trying to resolve the experience of these traumatic events.

THE IMPACT OF TRAUMATIC MEMORY ON JASMINE'S IDENTITY

Despite her emigration from Punjab, Jasmine is unable to get over her traumatic past easily. She oscillates between a *crisis of death* and the correlative *crisis of life*" (Caruth, 1996, p. 7) [italics in the original]. In other words, she suffers from the "unbearable nature of an event" (Caruth, 1996, p. 7), which is, in her case, the murder of her beloved husband, and the larger context of this trauma, which is collective. It is because of these traumatic experiences that she is forced to leave her homeland and search for a new place and identity for herself: "I was spiraling into depression behind the fortress of Punjabiness" (Mukherjee, 1989, p. 148). The collective trauma the narrative engages with, that is, the armed conflicts that result from Sikh separatism, is hardly known in the West. Therefore, in line with Alexander's argument that "[i]t would be a serious misunderstanding if trauma theory [were] restricted in its reference to Western social life" (Alexander, 2004, p. 24)[8], the novel sheds light on peripheralised historical events and explores their impact on the individual psyche. This way, Jasmine does not simply introduce hardly known historical events to Western readers but also contributes to non-Western conceptualisations of trauma.

Throughout the narrative, Jasmine takes up multiple names, which symbolise the protagonist's different "shapes" and "selves" (Mukherjee, 1989, p. 215). For each identity that she acquires, she has a different man in her life: "Prakash for Jasmine, Taylor for Jase, Bud for Jane. Half-Face for Kali" (Mukherjee, 1989, p. 197). However, Jasmine does not stick to one name and constantly sheds these identities in the novel. I would claim that this is a survival strategy of the protagonist to cope with her trauma: "We murder who we were so we can rebirth ourselves in the images of dreams" (Mukherjee, 1989, p. 29). Jasmine not only wants to discard her different names, but she also wants to forget her past experience, else "it will kill" (Mukherjee, 1989, p. 33) her. "Too much attachment" to her past memories will result in "too much disillusion" (Mukherjee, 1989, p. 200), she asserts. Furthermore, it can also be argued that Jasmine, similar to Nazneen, escapes from patriarchal oppression as she chooses to move from one place to another. The act of movement further echoes Freud's claim that even though the traumatic incident forces one to leave the home country, it also frees the person from the fear (Caruth, 1996, p. 23), which is based on his own experience of fleeing Vienna during Nazism. Jasmine's displacement, then, can be read as a coping strategy to deal with her traumatic experiences. In this chapter, I focus on Jasmine's journey to the West and within the United States, aiming to explore how she gradually comes to terms with her traumatic memories. Unlike other female protagonists, such as Ashima and Mrs. Sen, who long for the "good old days"[9] (Dragojlovic, 2018, p. 92) in their home country, Jasmine constantly struggles to forget her traumatic past, and, therefore, she distances herself from Indian cultural habits.

However, for Mukherjee's main character, trauma provides "the very link between cultures" (Craps, 2013, p. 2). The cultural linkage based on trauma is evident in the relationship between Jasmine and Lillian Gordon. Soon after her sexual assault in America, Lillian is the first person to take care of Jasmine. She provides her shelter and medical help. Similar to Jasmine, Lillian, too, distances herself from her past memories: she forbids all discussion of past events. She has a "low tolerance for reminiscence, bitterness or nostalgia" (Mukherjee, 1989, p. 131). This can also be read as Lillian's survival strategy. Highlighting an individual's response to trauma, Alexander points out that "[w]hen bad things happen to good people...they can become so frightened that they can actually repress the experience of trauma itself" (Alexander, 2004, p. 5). Although it is not mentioned in the narrative what Lillian has experienced, the readers can comprehend that by not remembering her past events she is likely to be repressing a traumatic experience. Furthermore, the protagonist is empathic towards Du, the adopted son of Jasmine and Bud, who also suffers from past traumas. As I have argued in the third chapter, however, the solidarity that exists between the characters in Mukherjee's novel seems to be rather idealistic. It is mostly their willingness to help that makes characters ready to listen to each other, but they often fail to connect on a deeper level since they find it difficult to imagine Jasmine's life outside America. Mukherjee's narrative, then, does not only engage with a non-Western collective trauma and its impact on the individual but also showcases the ways in which characters of different cultural backgrounds strive towards empathic connectedness and cross-cultural solidarity.

ON THE MOVE: JASMINE'S TRAUMATIC EXPERIENCES AND THE REINTEGRATION OF REPRESSED EMOTIONS

Mukherjee's narrative explores the instability of the protagonist. Focusing on the "mechanisms of psychological defense between the external shattering event and the actor's internal response" (Alexander, 2004, p. 5), Jeffrey Alexander argues that "[r]ather than activating direct cognition and rational understanding, the traumatizing event becomes distorted in the actor's imagination and memory" (Alexander, 2004, p. 5). Relying on Alexander's concept of trauma, I argue that in order to escape from the "external shattering event" (Alexander, 2004, p. 5) of armed conflicts due to Sikh separatism, Jasmine is constantly on the move. Not only the cultural trauma but also the loss of her husband "becomes distorted" (Alexander, 2004, p. 5) in her memory. Furthermore, because of her continuous displacement, Jasmine is similar to Bhabha's vernacular cosmopolitan[10] as she moves "in-between cultural traditions" and reveals "hybrid forms of life" (Bhabha, 2004, p. xiii). In contrast to James Clifford's argument that cosmopolitans are "necessarily elite" (Clifford, 1992, pp. 106-07), Jasmine belongs to the lower financial strata of the society. Thus, she can be read as a vernacular cosmopolitan, who is, by definition, outside this elite group. For instance, Jasmine is a "professional, like a school teacher or a nurse" (Mukherjee, 1989, p. 175). Though the narrative does not provide information about her financial status, it is clear that she has low-paid jobs in the United States. But despite her social status and her detestation[11] of American culture, she identifies herself more with the culture of the host nation. I would argue that this is due to the fact that Jasmine escapes from her homeland and the traumatic events experienced there. This is the very reason why she rather identifies with American cultural norms than with the traditions of her home country.

Even though Mukherjee's heroine thinks she has travelled "the world without ever leaving the familiar crops of Punjab" (Mukherjee, 1989, p. 128), in reality, she understands that her "home" is no longer in India. Jasmine represses memories of Punjab due to her trauma: "we're both a long way from home, aren't we? What'll we do?...There's no going back, is there?" (Mukherjee, 1989, p. 164). This echoes Brah's notion that home is a "mythical" place for the diasporic immigrants where they wish to return but, in fact, can never do so (Brah, 1996, p. 188). It is also to be foregrounded that there lies a contradiction in the protagonist's character. On the one hand, Jasmine relinquishes the cultural traditions of her home country; she distances herself from the "artificially maintained Indianness" (Mukherjee, 1989, p. 145) at the Professor's residence, and everything related to her past life in her homeland. But on the other hand, she depends on her traditional dishes, which help her challenge the American people's view of what good food is like. One explanation that can be provided for this detachment is the trauma that she has encountered and the "ongoing experience of having survived it" (Caruth, 1996, p. 7). Since her birth, Jasmine has endured several traumatic experiences. As she recalls, born as a girl-child she was not wanted by her parents and they decided to kill her: "When the midwife carried me out, my sisters tell me, I had a ruby-red choker of bruise around my throat and sapphire fingerprints on my collarbone...My mother was a sniper. She wanted to spare me the pain of a dowryless bride...I survived the sniping" (Mukherjee, 1989, p. 40). Later she witnessed the assassination of her husband. Therefore, her strong detestation of her home culture can be read as an "outer manifestation of childhood trauma" (Bhattacharya, 2021, p. 73). Her detachment from anything related to Indian culture and everything related to her past shows that she is in denial, not willing to face her past and her traumatic experiences.

Although Jasmine has primarily been traumatised in India, she experiences further traumatic events in the United States. This shows that America is not presented as an ideal country in the novel: Jasmine is both assisted in coping with her past and further traumatised there. The very first night in America is no less than a nightmare for her. The captain of the ship, Half Face[12], who has accompanied Jasmine to Florida, rapes her in a motel room. After the "hideous crime" (Mukherjee, 1989, p. 117), she murders her rapist:

I began to shiver. The blade need not be long, only sharp, and my hand not strong, only quick. His eyes fluttered open even before I felt the metal touch his throat, and his smile and panic were nearly instantaneous. I wanted that moment when he saw me above him as he had last seen me, naked, but now with my mouth open, pouring blood, my red tongue out. I wanted him to open his mouth and start to reach, I wanted that extra hundredth of a second when the blade bit deeper than any insect, when I jumped back as he jerked forward, slapping at his neck while blood, ribbons of bright blood, rushed between his fingers. (Mukherjee, 1989, p. 118)

In my reading, the above episode exposes the symptoms of the protagonist's repressed traumas: she experienced misogyny in India and witnessed the brutal killing of her husband, which is followed by sexual assault in the United States. These experiences are so severe that they push her to murder her molester. In the second chapter of my dissertation, I have read this episode as an example of empowerment. The protagonist's act of murder shows that she is able to defend herself, and similar to the goddess Kali, who slays demons to restore the order of the world, Jasmine murders her rapist to protest against the idea that women should suffer in silence. For her, Half-Face symbolically represents an extended version of her traumas and she does not regret her act of killing him: "Not illegal, not murderer, not widowed, raped, destitute, fearful" (Mukherjee, 1989, p. 171). Thus, the harshness of her act shows that she is becoming a fighter in the novel.

During Jasmine's journey, she meets several people, both male and female, who help her cope with her traumatic past to a certain extent. The first friend and guide in Jasmine's life is her husband, Prakash Vijh. He is clearly an open-minded person compared to other men in the village. He wants to be called by his first name, in contrast to the stereotypical belief in Indian households that women should not call their husbands by their first names. Prakash is against the idea of Jasmine getting pregnant at a young age, he rather encourages her to continue her studies. In India, Prakash helps her come to terms with the violent riot by encouraging her to read and write. Even though the protagonist experiences further traumatic events in the West, she also undergoes the process of healing, especially through "crosscultural solidarity" (Craps, 2013, p. 2). Lillian Gordon is the first woman in America who rescues Jasmine when she is lying semi-conscious on the highway after escaping from the motel room. By providing her a residence, Lillian not only rescues Jasmine physically, but her home symbolises a safe place for the protagonist; as she asserts: "I didn't tell Mrs. Gordon what she'd rescued me from" (Mukherjee, 1989, p. 131). Lillian calls her "Jazzy" and introduces her to American culture (Mukherjee, 1989, p. 133). She even allows Jasmine to borrow her daughter's clothes, which suggests that she supports, perhaps even loves Jasmine. Despite the helpful attitude of the American woman, however, renaming the protagonist shows that Lillian is imposing the norms of her own culture on Jasmine, suggesting that cross-cultural solidarity is rather an idealistic aim than a reality in this novel.

From Lillian's place, Jasmine goes to stay with Professor Ji, Prakash's teacher. Though she has a suffocating experience at the Professor's house because of the artificial Indianness in the apartment, the family treats her well. Thereafter, Jasmine contacts Kate, the daughter of Lillian Gordon, who helps her find a job as a professional caregiver for Taylor and Wylie's daughter, Duff. Taylor calls her Jase, and they fall for each other. Taylor's act of renaming suggests that he too, similar to Lillian, is trying to impose American cultural norms on Jasmine as a result of the unequal power relations between them. Nevertheless, this is Jasmine's first affair after the death of her husband, which helps her feel reborn: "Jyoti [is] now a *sati*-goddess; she [has] burned herself in a trash-can-funeral pyre behind a boarded-up motel in Florida" (Mukherjee, 1989, p. 176, italics in the original). Jasmine burns her old self, Jyoti, and engages in a love affair with Taylor, which may be seen as part of her healing process, as she is overcoming the loss of her husband. But the relationship does not last long, as Jasmine, after seeing Sukhinder, her husband's murderer in New York City, rushes to Baden in Iowa. In Iowa, she stays with Bud who calls her "Jane". Even though Jasmine gets pregnant with his child, she adopts a son, Du, a Vietnamese orphan. Being a child with a "past as troubled and erratic as Jasmine's" (Roberts, 1995, p. 91), Du symbolises the new life emerging from the "east-west encounter" (Ganaie, 2019, p. 180). Jasmine mourns when Du departs to live with his biological sister: "Blood is thick, I think. Du, my adopted son, is a mystery, but the prospect of losing him is like a miscarriage. I had relied on him, my silent ally against the bright lights, the rounded, genial landscape of Iowa" (Mukherjee, 1989, p. 221). Jasmine "views his adoption into their midWestern home as she does her own: as a tenuous rebirth of self" (Roberts, 1995, p. 91). Apart from Bud and Du, Bud's mother, Mother Ripplemeyer, also helps her by finding her a job at bank. Towards the end of the narrative, Bud's ex-wife, Karin, encourages Jasmine to leave Bud and move in with Taylor, the man of her love. These instances show that characters do their best to assist Jasmine in their own ways, yet genuine cross-cultural solidarity often fails in the novel due to the fact that they impose their own cultural norms on Jasmine by giving her different names.

Jasmine's journeys hint at how she is coming to terms with her traumatic past. Mukherjee's novel opens with an astrologer's prediction of her "widowhood and exile" (Mukherjee, 1989, p. 3): "What is to happen will happen" (Mukherjee, 1989, p. 3). But by the end, the female protagonist challenges the prophecy: "Watch me re-position the stars, I whisper to the astrologer who floats cross-legged above my kitchen stove" (Mukherjee, 1989, p. 240). Jasmine has the power to change her fate in Mukherjee's novel. Although it is not always clear whether she is indeed successful in overcoming her traumatic past or if she is simply deceiving herself by repressing her emotions as survivors of trauma tend to do, she becomes a "fighter and adapter" (Mukherjee, 1989, p. 40) in the novel. The narrative also shows that Jasmine is able to reintegrate her repressed emotions, which points towards her healing. She no longer feels the burden of her past, for instance, at the end of the novel the protagonist asserts: "It isn't guilt that I feel, it's relief" (Mukherjee, 1989, p. 240). In contrast to the protagonist's situation in India, where she has been forced to listen to her father and her two brothers, her journey to the US, despite the suffering and the difficulties, proves to be fruitful as it leads to the formation of an individual self who no longer lives at the mercy of others. The novel ends on a positive note: "there is nothing I can do. Time will tell if I am a tornado, rubble-maker, arising from nowhere and disappearing into a cloud. I am out the door and in the potholed and rutted driveway…greedy with wants and reckless from hope" (Mukherjee, 1989, p. 241). I would claim that by the end, Jasmine comes to terms with her traumatic past. She may not be able to get over her emotional anguish entirely, but she is definitely healing as she no longer seems to be in denial but portrays herself as a woman who has "seen the worst and survived. Like creatures in fairy tales, [she has] shrunk and [she has] swollen and [she has] swallowed the cosmos whole" (Mukherjee, 1989, p. 240). The narrative suggests that her repressed emotions are becoming integrated: "I…cry through all the lives I've given birth to, cry for all the dead" (Mukherjee, 1989, p. 241). This crying suggests that she is releasing emotions that were repressed earlier.

Narrating her story is the main experience that helps Jasmine overcome her traumatic past. Since Mukherjee's novel is retrospective, Jasmine remembers and narrates her past when she is twenty-four, which shows how she frames her story. This is how she comments on the astrologer's prediction, for instance: "That stench stays with me. I'm twenty-four now, I live in Baden, Elsa County, Iowa, but every time I lift a glass of water to my lips, fleetingly I smell it. I know what I don't want to become" (Mukherjee, 1989, p. 5). Although she receives love and support from the people in America, it is Jasmine's own efforts that enable her to reintegrate her repressed traumatic emotions, which she does by finding a narrative frame for her unacknowledged experiences.

MONICA ALI'S *BRICK LANE*: **AN OVERVIEW**

In contrast to Mukherjee's protagonist who moves to the US after the death of her husband and enters the host nation illegally, Ali's heroine is forced to move to London after her marriage. As the narrative portrays Nazneen finds it difficult to adjust in the host country: "Her new life, her enforced marriage, her loncliness in her new dwelling place and her husband's categorisation of her as a potential child-giver make her realise the truth about her situation and leaves her helpless" (Çelikel, 2022, p. 22). Moreover, Nazneen is constantly objectified by her husband, Chanu. She is described as "[n]ot beautiful, but not so ugly either. The face is broad, big forehead. Eyes are a bit too close together...Not tall. Not short. Around five foot two. Hips are a bit narrow but wide enough, I think to carry children. All things considered, I am satisfied" (Ali, 2003, pp. 22-23). She is described in terms of her bodily features as if measured like an animal to be bought.

However, similar to Mukherjee's novel in which the protagonist receives empathy from several male and female characters, in Ali's narrative there are some characters who encourage the female protagonist to fulfil her dreams and help her gain agency. Being constantly demeaned by her husband, Nazneen finds solace in Karim, the young boy who delivers sewing materials to her. In describing the physical and mental turmoil that Ali's main character undergoes, Sermet Melis Baysal relies on RoseMarie Perez Foster's argument that "immigration trauma consists of different parts that include 'premigration trauma' (that may be a probable reason for migration), 'traumatic events experienced during transit' along with resettlement period, 'substandard living conditions in the host country'" (Baysal, 2020, p. 32). Nazneen's situation is similar. She is depicted as a "depressed and suicidal woman due to her immigration trauma which is triggered not only by the act of migrancy but also her prolonged adaption to her newly changed environment" (Baysal, 2020, p. 33). Even though she moves away from her homeland, she is bounded by the rules of her patriarchal native cultures: Nazneen is not encouraged to go out of the house without her husband, her desire to learn English is discarded by Chanu, sometimes she is shy to eat in front of her husband and sneaks into the kitchen in the middle of the night to eat her dinner, and she has no right to participate in decision making in her family.

INTERGENERATIONAL TRAUMA IN MONICA ALI'S *BRICK LANE*

Besides focusing on non-Western or minority trauma in this chapter, I will also discuss intergenerational trauma in the diasporic context. Exploring the transmission of traumas, Angela Connolly points out that "the concept of intergenerational trauma was first used to describe the traumatic experiences transmitted by Holocaust survivors to their children, then it was applied to the traumas transmitted in repressive regimes" (Connolly, 2011, p. 610). Connolly further argues that "the presence of intergenerational trauma [is] not only in the children of Holocaust survivors but also in the children of repressive regimes" (Connolly, 2011, p. 610). In most cases, the individuals repress the memories of their traumatic past, which later seem to haunt them. Ana Dragojlovic uses the term "intergenerational haunting"[13] (Dragojlovic, 2018, p. 93) to highlight the negative impact of past events previous generations have experienced, which are passed on to the next generations unconsciously. The traumatic emotions are latently present in the unconscious of the subsequent generations: as Dragojlovic argues, the "unconscious" acts as a "crypt" for these generations, which is a space from where ancestral secrets are passed down" (Dragojlovic, 2018, p. 95) to them. Instances of intergenerational trauma are evident in Monica

Ali's *Brick Lane*. Both Nazneen and her sister are affected by their mother's tragic suicide, because the loss of their mother, Rupban, is "not only an individual childhood trauma. [Her] death has a social and cultural dimension which Nazneen and her sister, Hasina, inherit, as they were to adopt the life their mother had" (Györke, 2022, p. 180). However, Ali's novel does not shed much light on Rupban. It is from the exchange of letters between the sisters that the readers are informed about Rupban's oppressions and how she ended her life[14]:

> Amma always say we are women what can we do? If she here now I know what she say I know it too well. But I am not like her. Waiting around. Suffering around. She wrong. So many ways. At the end only she act. She who think all path is closed for her. She take the only one forbidden. Forgive me sister I must tell you now this secret so long held inside me...Amma go past kitchen. No one is there. She go into store room...She take spear and test on the finger. She take another and put it back. And third one she take before is happy. (Ali, 2003, pp. 434-35)

The above episode portrays how insignificant women's lives are especially in the rural parts of Bangladesh: as Györke points out, "Rupban's death is presented as an accident[15], which sounds improbable; the only thing that is clear is that Nazneen, and especially Hasina, who turns out to be a witness of this event later in the novel,...are escaping from this fate, at the heart of which is the feeling that women's lives have no significance and their death have no consequence" (Györke, 2022, p. 180). Even though Nazneen emigrates to London, the traumatic memories of her mother haunt her. In the beginning of the novel, she is not aware of her emotional agony regarding her mother's oppression, but gradually, it becomes an "active part of [her] present" (Dragojlovic, 2018, p. 104) life in the West. She imagines the presence of her mother in her Brick Lane apartment: "Nazneen dreamed of Gouripur. She sat cross-legged on a choki and Amma sat behind her and plaited her hair...' What shall I do now, Amma? Amma?' Nazneen turned around. There was no one there" (Ali, 2003, pp. 430-31). This is an example that reveals how the loss of her mother still haunts Nazneen in London. Hence, Nazneen's unconscious keeps the traces of her mother's tragic experiences even when she is away from her homeland.

GAPS AND SILENCES: THE REPRESENTATION OF TRAUMA IN *BRICK LANE*

Similar to Bharati Mukherjee's novel, Monica Ali's *Brick Lane* also highlights instances of trauma in the protagonist's home country as well as in the host nation. Though Nazneen is not the direct victim of violence, like Jasmine, both her mother's and her sister's fate suggest that abuse and patriarchal oppression would have been her lot had she stayed in Bangladesh. Through the exchange of letters between the sisters, the readers can see how Hasina, despite the fact that she is a strong woman, becomes a victim of sexual assaults: "Sometime when people see a beautiful thing they want to destroy it. The thing make them feel ugly so they act ugly" (Ali, 2003, p. 165). In contrast to Nazneen, who has married the man of her father's choice, has moved to London, and has mostly devoted herself to becoming a faithful wife and a caring mother, Hasina, at the tender age of sixteen, elopes with the man she loves. She also becomes financially independent, working in a garment factory in Dhaka. Although she is trying to avoid her mother's fate, there seems to be no viable option for her: "I thinking my life cursed. God have given me life but he has curse it" (Ali, 2003, p. 166). In comparison to Hasina's traumatic experiences, which are evident from the detailed information in the letters, the narrative does not shed much light on the tragic life[16] of Nazneen's mother, Rupban. It is suggested in the novel that she has committed suicide when she could no longer take the ill-treatment that has been inflicted upon her by the patriarchal society: "'God tests us,' she said. 'Don't you know this life is a test? Some He tests with riches and good fortune…or with jinn who come in the shape of men – or of husbands'" (Ali, 2003, p. 322). However, as the narrative does not reveal much about these traumas, the readers need to guess what is happening with Hasina and what causes Rupban's death.

Gaps are also evident in the narrative of Nazneen's traumatic experiences. Although the novel represents the struggle related to her birth and how the midwife, similar to Jasmine's parents, wanted to strangle her at birth (Ali, 2003, p. 13), and it is not disclosed how baby Nazneen survives without any medical help. Furthermore, she also becomes the victim of patriarchal oppression as she is forced to marry Chanu, who is much older than her, and was chosen by her father. Her emigration is left out from the narrative as well: the first chapter of Ali's novel, which is set in East Pakistan, describes her birth and childhood, and in the next, she is already in London. It is not clear how her first child, Raqib, dies either. The readers need to read between the lines to understand the tragic event:

> Open your eyes. Ruku! Ruku! What's wrong with him? Raqib! What's happened? Why does he not wake? Why doesn't he wake? The city shattered. Everything was in pieces. She knew it straight away, glimpsed it from the painful-white insides of the ambulance. Frantic neon signs. Headlights chasing the dark. An office block, cracked with light. These shards of the broken city. At the hospital she felt the panic…She ran with her son, carried him down long corridors while the walls fled before them. And then they took him out of her hands. (Ali, 2003, pp. 116-17)

Hence, the silences and gaps play a significant role in *Brick Lane*, which suggests that the narrative represses the unsayable. This is a common sign of traumatic experiences. Focusing on the "traumatic paradox" (Amir, 2019, p. 6) and the "inability to know it" (Amir, 2019, p. 7), Dana Amir argues that "[t]rauma is not only an experience, but also the failure to experience that experience; not merely the threat itself, but the fact that the threat was recognized as such only a moment too late" (Amir, 2019, p. 7). In other words, as traumatic events occur, the victim becomes "detached" (Amir, 2019, p. 6) from the experiences, which remain "powerful but frozen, untransformable by either circumstantial processes or the passing of time" (Amir, 2019, p. 7). This "traumatic paradox" (Amir, 2019, p. 6) is evident in Ali's narrative. The protagonist, when she moves from her home country, is not fully aware of her trauma, but later, she experiences emotional anxiety in London, which reveals that she is suffering from an unresolved traumatic experience. For instance, Nazneen, after imagining her mother's presence in her kitchen, faints "on the kitchen floor, vomit dried on the corners of her mouth, eyes open and unseeing" (Ali, 2003, p. 324). This episode clearly shows that the memories of her traumatic past still cause her emotional pain in London. Rupban's suicide has a significant impact on Nazneen, and probably this is one of the reasons why she refuses to return to Bangladesh with Chanu. In one episode, Nazneen hears her mother speak in her Brick Lane apartment: "Amma squatted on her haunches in the corner…When you were a little girl, you used to ask me, 'Amma why do you cry? My baby, do you know now?'…'This is what women have to bear. Once, when you were a little girl, you could hardly wait to find out'" (Ali, 2003, p. 322). Relying on Dragojlovic's notion of "intergenerational hauntings" (Dragojlovic, 2018, p. 93), I would claim that Nazneen's trauma is intergenerational: it is not only the loss of her mother that pains her, but also "what women have to bear" (Ali, 2003, p. 322), the very reason of her mother's suicide, which is transmitted from generation to generation in repressive, patriarchal societies. Throughout her life, Nazneen is exposed to patriarchal violence. This "continuous exposure" (Craps, 2013, p. 30) causes her to "develop feelings of inferiority, inadequacy, and self-hatred" (Craps, 2013, p. 30). Furthermore, the feelings that "[w]e are just women. What can we do?" (Ali, 2003, p. 103) and "[w]e will suffer in silence" (Ali, 2003, p. 302) also reveal that Nazneen's trauma is not simply an individual experience: it has intergeneration aspects that point beyond her individual suffering. These patriarchal ideologies are so ingrained in her that she encounters repetitive nightmares and suffers from depression and anxiety. Thus, even with the passing of time, she retains the memories of how her mother endured oppression and her own emotional pain partly stems from these memories.

Thus Ali, similar to Mukherjee, explores the impact of trauma on a diasporic female character. Both writers engage with non-Western conceptualisations of trauma and the ways in which these haunt the protagonists when they are in the West. Both Jasmine and Nazneen suffer from individual traumas. However, Jasmine has also been traumatised by the armed conflicts due to Sikh separatism, which is an example of collective trauma, while Nazneen is affected by an intergenerational trauma inherited from her mother. For both protagonists, "memories of trauma are not only rigid and concrete – but unmentalized" (Amir, 2019, p. 7). In other words, these traumatic experiences are not, and cannot, be represented in the narrative "properly." Nevertheless, it is significant how trauma is narrativised in the novels. This is because the narrativisation of trauma is part of the healing process: transforming the unspeakable events into coherent narratives already indicates that the traumatised individual is coping with the event successfully. In Mukherjee's *Jasmine*, which is a first-person narrative, the protagonist herself narrativises the traumatic experiences she has gone through, though her trauma is not accessible until the very end of the narrative, when her repressed emotions come to the surface. In contrast to *Jasmine*, *Brick Lane* is a third-person narrative. In Ali's novel, the readers do not get access to Nazneen's consciousness at all, nor do they have proper information about Rupban's or Hasina's traumatic experiences. Therefore, the letters between the sisters and the gaps and silences in the narrative become important elements which hint at the tragic events that are experienced by the female characters.

CONCLUSION

My chapter has analysed the traumatic experiences portrayed in *Jasmine* and in *Brick Lane*. I have explored different forms of trauma: collective trauma, such as the riot between the Hindus and the Sikhs in *Jasmine*; individual trauma, for instance, the loss of the protagonist's husband in Mukherjee's novel and the death of Nazneen's mother, and intergenerational trauma, which is transmitted to Nazneen as a result of patriarchal oppression. Relying on the theory of Caruth, I have analysed how unacknowledged traumatic events haunt the protagonists when they are away from their home countries. Alexander's theory has helped me distinguish between individual trauma and collective trauma. The theories of Alexander and Craps have enabled me to foreground the fact that these novels engage with non-Western experiences of trauma. Finally, to analyse the intergenerational trauma I have relied on the theories of Dragojlovic and Connolly.

In this chapter, I have not only explored the traumatic experiences of the diasporic female characters, but I have also probed into how these characters come to terms with their traumas. The journeys that Jasmine undertakes are not only symptoms of the traumatic events in her home country and in the host nation, rather, these journeys point towards her healing. For instance, even though Jasmine is a victim of sexual assault in America on the very first day of her arrival, by the end of the novel, she is able to reintegrate her repressed emotions. Although some of the people in America help her with love and financial support, they also impose Western norms on the protagonist by renaming her. Therefore, cross-cultural solidarity, though presented as an ideal in this novel, often fails, and it is the narrativisation of her own traumatic experiences that helps Jasmine heal.

Similar to the traumatic experiences of Mukherjee's protagonist, I have also analysed how Nazneen becomes a victim of trauma. Since her birth Nazneen has struggled, for instance, with the complications during her birth; the need to marry according to her father's choices, and later, in London, the loss of her first-born child. My chapter has also explored the traumatic experiences of Nazneen's mother and her sister. While Rupban suffers from patriarchal oppression, Hasina is a victim of both patriarchal as well as sexual violence. With the help of specific examples from the text I have shown that in Ali's novel traumatic events are hardly ever mentioned, and the reader needs to read between the lines. For example, Hasina writes about their mother's suicide, which was earlier presented as an accident, in a letter to Nazneen. I have also probed into how trauma is narrativised in the two novels and have shown that Mukherjee's novel, which is a first-person narrative, is able to reveal more about the protagonists' healing than Ali's third-person narrative, in which gaps and silences hint at the emotional agony of the characters.

REFERENCES

Adams, J. T. (1931). *The Epic of America*. Little, Brown, and Company.

Alexander, J. C. (2004). *Cultural Trauma and Collective Identity*. University of California Press.

Ali, M. (2003). *Brick Lane*. Black Swan.

Amir, D. (2019). *Bearing Witness to the Witness: A Psychoanalytic Perspective on Four Modes of Traumatic Testimony*. Routledge, Taylor and Francis.

Baysal, S. M. (2020). *Trauma, Survival, and Resistance: Possibilities of Recovery in Monica Ali's Brick Lane and Arundhati Roy's The God of Small Things*. [M.A. Thesis].

Bhabha, H. K. (2004). *The Location of Culture*. Routledge Classics.

Bhattacharya, R. (2021). Negotiating the Trauma of Displacement in Bharati Mukherjee's *Wife* and *Jasmine*. In *Understanding Women's Experiences of Displacement*. Taylors and Francis Group.

Brah, A. (1996). *Cartographies of Diaspora: Contesting Identities*. Routledge.

Caruth, C. (1996). *Unclaimed Experience: Trauma, Narrative, and History*. The Johns Hopkins University Press. 10.1353/book.20656

Çelikel, M. A. (2022). Traumatized Immigrant: Monica Ali's *Brick Lane*. *CUJHSS, 16*(2), 169-180. 10.47777/cankujhss.1160709

Chawla. (2017). The Khalistan Movement of 1984: A Critical Appreciation. *A Research Journal of South Asian Studies, 32*(1), 81-90.

Clifford, J. (1992). Travelling Cultures. In *Cultural Studies*. Routledge.

Connolly, A. (2011). Healing the Wounds of Our Fathers: Intergenerational Trauma, Memory, Symbolization and Narrative. *The Journal of Analytical Psychology*, 56(5), 607–626. 10.1111/j.1468-5922.2011.01936. x22039944

Craps, S. (2013). *Postcolonial Witnessing: Trauma Out of Bounds*. Palgrave Macmillan. 10.1057/9781137292117

Dragojlovic, A. (2018). Politics of Negative Affect: Intergenerational Haunting, Counter-archival Practices and the Queer Memory. *Subjectivity*, *11*, 91-107.

Erikson, K. (1976). *Everything in Its Path*. Simon and Schuster.

Ganaie, A. A. (2019). Multicultural Subjectivity and Cosmopolitan Identity: A Reading of Bharati Mukherjee's *Jasmine.Advances in Social Sciences Research Journal*, 6(7), 175–180. 10.14738/assrj.67.6175

Györke, Á. (2022). *From Transnational to Translocal: Space and Emotion in Contemporary Fiction*. [MS. Habilitation Thesis].

Jetly, R. (2008). The Khalistan Movement in India: The Interplay of Politics and State Power. *International Review of Modern Sociology*, 34(1), 61–75.

Mahmood, C. K. (2001). Terrorism, Myth, and the Power of Ethnographic Praxis. *Journal of Contemporary Ethnography*, 30(5), 520–545. 10.1177/089124101129024259

Mukherjee, B. (1989). *Jasmine*. Grove Press.

Roberts, J. (1995). Between Two 'Darknesses': The Adoptive Condition in *Ceremony* and *Jasmine*. *Modern Language Studies*, 25(3), 77–97. 10.2307/3195372

Tatla, D. S. (2004). Writing Prejudice: The Image of Sikhs in Bharati Mukherjee's Writings. In Singh, P., & Barrier, N. G. (Eds.), *Sikhs in History* (pp. 1–23). Oxford University Press.

ten Kortenaar, N. (2016). Bharati Mukherjee's *Jasmine*.*Cambridge Journal of Postcolonial Literary Inquiry*, 3(3), 379–385. 10.1017/pli.2016.26

ENDNOTES

[1]   Punjab is one of the smallest states located in the northwestern part of the Indian subcontinent. This state is also known as "The Land of Five Rivers". Though Punjabi is the official language of Punjab, Hindi is also widely spoken.

[2]   Masterji is the man who used to teach Jasmine in school. In India, the term "master" means teacher, and "ji" is used as an honorific suffix.

[3]   The Khalsa means "the Pure-Bodied and the Pure-Hearted," (Mukherjee, 1989, p. 65) referring to the Sikhs.

[4]   Sikh separatism is the "worst violence erupted in Punjab, where, ironically, the majority of the Sikh population had gained affluence in the wake of India's Green Revolution of the late 1960s. Yet bumper crops and higher per capita incomes brought all the gadgets and toys of modernity, which pulled or lured many younger Sikhs away from ingrained traditions and religious values that others considered sacred. This opened large gaps within Sikh society, almost as wide and deep as those that separated Punjab from the rest of India...By the early 1980s, some Sikhs were calling for more than mere separate provincial statehood, instead demanding nothing less than a nation-state of their own, an autonomous Sikh Khalistan, or "land of the Pure" ("Sikh separatism").

[5]   The Khalistan Movement is the "movement by Sikh leaders for a separate homeland and autonomy started to create serious problems when some rebellious Sikh elements started killings of gazetted officials, civil servants, and Hindu and Sikh citizens. The year 1984 became a turning point in the conflict and in June of that year, the Indian Army hit the Sikh's holiest place of worship, the Golden Temple in Amritsar, which had been converted into an armed camp by Sikh followers...In these attacks thousands of civilians were killed [and] most of them were Sikhs. This operation outraged the whole of the Sikh community at large and the demand for an independent state of Khalistan caught boom" (Chawla, 2017, p. 85).

[6]   Darshan S. Tatla argues that Mukherjee's portrayal of Sikhism and Sikh characters leads to a negative image of the community (Tatla, 2004, p. 1). According to him, as an upper-class Bengali Brahmin, Mukherjee's American neonationalist ideology changing migrants' exclusivity is evident from an Indian context and background (Tatla, 2004, p. 2). He further points out that "Mukherjee's American 'neo-nationalism,' her condemnation of 'cultural baggage' of immigrants, and their 'ex-

clusive reproduction in the first world'...arises partially from her understanding of the old world, and of India's multiethnic experiment in particular, where several minorities have graduated from seeking 'special position' to 'nationalist struggles' threatening its fragile unity" (Tatla, 2004, p. 2).

[7] The dilemma for the Akali party was that despite being a strong advocate of the Sikh culture and religion, it never enjoyed full support of the Sikhs (Jetly, 2008, p. 63). Sikhs had proven their loyalty to the British in the early years of "British Rule in Punjab," particularly as "members of the British Indian army" (Jetly, 2008, p. 62). "Their anger deepened as instead of the much-promised 33 percent representation that they expected as reward for their army services, they were given under the Government of India Act 1919, only 15 percent of a total of 93 seats in the Punjab's legislative council" (Jetly, 2008, p. 62).

[8] Alexander, similar to Stef Craps, points out that Caruth's trauma theory is Westocentric. He claims that "it has been Western societies that have recently provided the most dramatic apologias for traumatic episodes in their national histories. [...] it has been the non-Western regions of the world, and the most defenseless segments of the world's population, that have recently been subjected to the most terrifying traumatic injuries" (Alexander, 2004, p. 24). According to Craps, Caruth "[marginalises] or [ignores] traumatic experiences of non-Western or minority cultures" (Craps, 2013, p. 2). She provides a universal definition of trauma and in her work, she disregards the "connections between metropolitan and non-Western traumas" (Craps, 2013, p. 2).

[9] Ana Dragojlovic uses the term "tempo doeloe" to refer to the longing for the "good old days" (Dragojlovic, 2018, p. 92) in the diasporic context.

[10] Bhabha points out, diasporic immigrants can be divided into global and vernacular cosmopolitans. Global cosmopolitans, according to Bhabha, are privileged and frequently "inhabit 'imagined communities' that consist of silicon valleys and software campuses" (Bhabha, 2004, p. xiv). On the contrary, vernacular cosmopolitans move "in-between cultural traditions" and reveal "hybrid forms of life" (Bhabha, 2004, p. xiii).

[11] Jasmine finds American culture "humiliating" and "disappointing" (Mukherjee, 1989, p. 29): "I wish I'd known America before it got perverted" (Mukherjee, 1989, p. 201).

[12] Half-Face is the captain of the ship called The Gulf Shuttle, the ship which the protagonist boarded from at the Gulf Coast of Florida. Half-face "had lost an eye and ear and most of his cheek in a paddy field in Vietnam...Half-face was famous in the west Caribbean. Half-Face was a demolitions expert before he became a sea captain" (Mukherjee, 1989, pp. 104-05).

[13] Dragojlovic argues that "[haunting] always registers the harm inflicted or the loss sustained by a social violence done in the past or in the present....Haunting is precisely the domain of turmoil and trouble...But haunting, unlike trauma, is distinctive for producing something-to-be-done" (Dragojlovic, 2018, p. 96).

[14] There is a difference between the representation of Rupban's suicide in the novel and in the film: in Ali's novel, the protagonist's mother commits suicide by piercing herself with a spear, but, in the film (dir. Sarah Gavron), she drowns herself.

[15] Mumtaz, Nazneen's aunt, found Rupban, "leaning low over the sacks of rice in the store hut, staked through the heart by a spear. 'She had fallen,' said Mumtaz, 'and the spear was the only thing holding her up. It looked...It looked as if she was still falling.'" (Ali, 2003, p. 46).

[16] I have discussed Rupban's suicide and how it affects the protagonist's psyche in the subsection on intergenerational trauma in this chapter. See page 11.

Chapter 4
Composite Harmonies:
Reclaiming Memory Artifacts Through Community Creative Practice

Saira Raza
http://orcid.org/0000-0002-9931-7483
Emory University, USA

Anicka Austin
Emory University, USA

ABSTRACT

Memory is explored as a currency of culture and power, reflecting both oppression and resistance within the United States' fragmented historical landscape. Exile narratives, exemplified in the works of a diverse array of activists, writers, and artists, illustrate memory's role in shaping political will. The chapter delves into the commodification of memory and the impact of displacement on cultural artifacts and archival material. Through participatory performance and creative interventions, archival silences are amplified, challenging dominant narratives. Speculative works highlight the transformative potential of composite memories, emphasizing the fluidity of meaning-making processes. The chapter engages a practice-based research methodology to propose a holistic approach to memory work through speculative participatory creative works, emphasizing embodied storytelling and collective expression in reclaiming cultural narratives.

INTRODUCTION

Institutional cultural heritage collections are an ideal place to interrogate how and why systems of power appropriate memory. Historically, these institutions serve as an instrument of power to control the materials of memory and access to them. In recent years, activists have elevated the conversation about the role museums and archival collections play in dispossession to the public sphere, calling attention to objects and materials acquired by dubious means. Exiled, dispossessed, and displaced communities find ways to make space for, sustain, and amplify their authentic narratives through traditions, closed practices, artistic expression, activism, and storytelling. Take, for example, the recent successes of movements around the American South to remove Confederate memorials, flags, and names from public spaces or

DOI: 10.4018/979-8-3693-2264-2.ch004

the work of Native activists to repatriate remains of their ancestors, sacred objects, and cultural artifacts from prominent university collections. While many institutions are now cooperating with communities to return stolen items, there is still significant resistance and political obstacles to restoring objects to their rightful places.

Archivists and scholars call to attention intentional and unintentional silences in institutional collections and the settler-colonial policies and practices, including the destruction of records that do not serve the interest of the state, in use in acquisition, appraisal, and description of archival material. To counter these practices, archivists urge for a feminist ethic of care, one that includes non-custodial archival relationships, in which institutions do not own the material, but rather assist with its preservation and care while the material maintains its position, context, and home in the community from which it came. Although the dynamic of power still exists in many ways, ownership and authority over the *representation* of the records is in the hands of those who create them.

While institutions whose founding, legacy, public image, and asset value have benefited from the violence of colonialism and imperialism can be slow to acknowledge their role and embrace change, practitioners within those institutions can facilitate more immediate interventions that set the stage for marginalized communities to reclaim memory artifacts. In particular, archivists, librarians, and curators can engage in creative discourse with artists, elders, and willing participants, especially those whose histories are represented (or misrepresented) in institutional collections, to invoke liberatory praxis. In this chapter, we engage in a practice-based, intersectional, and interdisciplinary research methodology, grounded in our professions as artists, librarian, and archivist, to propose a holistic approach to memory work through speculative participatory creative works, emphasizing embodied storytelling and collective expression in reclaiming cultural narratives.

Power and Memory

Memory is the currency of culture and society and serves as a tool for defining identity and asserting power - who has won and who has lost. What we remember (or forget) is fluid in selection, retention, meaning, and recollection. Our perceptions of reality are constructed, composite projections of our memories, individual and collective. Memories are characterized by variable reliability, thus as the source material for meaning-making, our perceived reality is proportionately unreliable. Any attempt to understand or explain reality, history, the future, or anything else we would like to express is made up of these composite materials. The senses, space, time, and every measure of the real or imagined world offer materials to construct our perceptions and narratives. Historically, the cultures that come to dominate can manipulate the public narrative of events and experiences to benefit the ruling class. At the same time, memory inspires and motivates the rallying cry of the downtrodden and the conquered. Iconography, artistic expression, and stories of resistance provide a juxtaposed perception of historical events that overlays and disrupts the dominant narrative.

The ruling political, economic, and social class of the United States has a unique relationship with memory. A product of Europe's centuries-long colonial project, unreliable histories that center the European experience and its cultural hegemony are endemic to the present-day narrative of national identity embedded in primary education and the dominant political discourse. Consider the swell of challenges to collections in American public and school libraries. According to the American Library Association (ALA), in 2023, there were a record-breaking 1,247 attempts to censor books, including 4,240 unique titles of which 47% reflected LGBTQIA+ and BIPOC (Black, indigenous, people of color) experiences

(ALA, 2024). Add to this already complex picture the millions of stories of immigrants in the United States, pushed from their homelands to radically unfamiliar terrain due to war, poverty, hunger, fear of violence, and numerous other long term symptoms of the capitalist drive for self-expanding value, accumulation, and profit (Wood, 1999); or the ongoing impact of gentrification of neighborhoods that have provided affordable housing to the working class, immigrants, and other marginalized communities.

> "My turn to state an equation: colonization = 'thingification.'...*I am talking about societies drained of their essence, cultures trampled underfoot, institutions undermined, lands confiscated, religions smashed, magnificent artistic creations destroyed, extraordinary *possibilities* wiped out.*" (Césaire, 1972, pp. 42-3)

In the context of colonialism and imperialism, cultural objects, like land and people, become sources of extractive value for the ruling class. Items that once served a purpose in ceremony, ritual, cosmology, or even quotidian home life within their original context become commodities for exchange, exhibition, hoarding, and *possession*. For example, Christian ideology positions non-Christian practices as barbaric, justifying the theft and destruction of sacred objects, spaces, and practices and continued withholding of access to stolen objects and spaces (Césaire, 1972). As assets, the items appreciate in monetary value over time, giving institutions further leverage to fund self-congratulatory geographical and ideological expansion (see Table 1).

Table 1. Top U.S. universities' reported value of collections of art, historical treasures, or other assets from 2022 IRS form 990 filings (USD)

Institution	Reported Asset Value of Collections
Princeton University	$ 319,469,320
Duke University	$ 53,208,061
Cornell University	$ 109,199,239
Rice University	$ 14,151,902
University of North Carolina, Chapel Hill	$ 42,400,984
Carnegie Mellon University	$ 5,457,835
Emory University	$ 121,125,454

(Source: Guidestar)

Institutions that did not report asset value or revenue from collections: Harvard University, Yale University, Stanford University, Massachusetts Institute of Technology, University of Pennsylvania, California Institute of Technology, Brown University, Johns Hopkins University, Northwestern University, Columbia University, University of Chicago, University of California at Berkeley, University of California at Los Angeles, Dartmouth College, Vanderbilt University, University of Notre Dame, Georgetown University

While some collections are accessible for public viewing, objects in these collections that represent the experiences of displaced, dispossessed, or exiled people are themselves in exile from their own context and source of meaning. The further separation of these objects from their communities of origin or ancestry over time serves to estrange people from their histories, disrupting the ability to develop a sense of object permanence and alignment with cultural traditions, environmental markers of identity, and cosmologies.

Exile and Memory

> "... Memory had been there forever.
> We settled in around her;
> we brought the electricity
> of blues and baptized gospel,
> ancient adaptations of icons,
> spices, teas, fireworks, trestles,
> newly acquired techniques
> of conflict and healing, common
> concepts of collective survival. . ."

Excerpt from "Memory" in *Legends from Camp* (1993) by Lawson Fusao Inada

In *Legends from Camp* (1993), Lawson Fusao Inada shares his imprinted memories of life in Japanese American internment camps through a textured tapestry of poems, narratives, imagined conversations, and documentary materials (photos and ephemera). Framing the work as "legends," Inada captures the nuanced mechanics of reconstructing identity through memory after experiences of dispossession, displacement, and exile. Palestinian-American scholar Edward Said characterized exile as "a permanent state, where there's something that cannot be gotten over, cannot be restored" (Sykes, 1988). Inada and Said are members of a lengthy roster of great thinkers and artists whose ideas, talents, and identities were shaped by their experiences of exile, displacement, and dispossession. For many, these same ideas, talents, and identities were also the cause of their exile, displacement, and dispossession - making them easy targets within oppressive regimes and imperialist agendas.

For the exiled, memory becomes a tool of political will. Said (Sykes, 1988) continues,

> "...I think what the essential privilege of exile is to have not just one set of eyes, but half a dozen, each of them corresponding to the places you've been...And the more places you've been, the more displacements you've gone through, as every exile does, because every situation is new and you start out each day anew, the more experience seems to be multiple and complex and composite and interesting for that reason."

Memories can be harnessed and wielded through creative practice to reconstruct dispossessed histories and generate empowered narratives of survival and transformation. In *Ethics of Exile: A Political Theory of Diaspora* (2021), Ashwini Vasanthakumar suggests, "Any given case of exile usually multitasks: the same exile that iterates the absolute power of the sovereign also provides a site from which this power may be undone" (p. 29). Experiences of dispossession, displacement, and exile fundamentally shift the location of cultural artifacts from the physical world to performative works of memory.

For every person who rises to global prominence by sharing their story of exile and dispossession, there are countless more who start their lives from scratch in new, unfamiliar, and often unfriendly environments whose stories are not given a platform. In the public sphere, their stories are not heard. They are ignored. They are asked to forget. They are rewritten. The exiled must figure out how they will convince their new neighbors, politicians, and employers what they are "worth." People are thrust into communities with others who have vastly different backgrounds, lived experiences, perceptions, and interpretations of their shared environment. It is a volatile space in which *something* will inevitably be created through interactions – conflict, change, love, confusion, beauty, empathy, longing, loss. Memories from across so many times and places collide and vie for space in the collective consciousness – some more vulnerable to erasure than others. Thus, some memories must seek protection in the privacy of family traditions and community folklore, in an effort to preserve certain artifacts of "homeland," which resonate and adapt over generations. Memories become a closed practice of home and cultural communities (such as in places of worship, community centers, local businesses, and associations). Small, mundane objects and behaviors become imbued with the power of memory. When dispossessed, displaced, and exiled people seek healing through memory practice, memory becomes a tool of political will - constructed, deconstructed, and reconstructed to support a visionary narrative for how society should be now and in the future.

This phenomenon occurs in stark contrast to the monolithic aspirations by which policies, infrastructure, and economies are defined by the dominant settler, imperial, colonial culture, in which a person is measured by their productivity and consumer buying power. This phenomenon is most clearly enacted in the historical practices of archival collections by academic and cultural institutions, whose acquisition strategies signify a certain paternalism around memory and history.

Policy changes, reparative language initiatives, and person-centered archival practices at academic institutions are one part of a complex and layered process towards justice. The academic and cultural heritage institutions in the American South in which the authors work are monuments to histories of dispossession, forced exile, and enslavement. While institutions may be slow to change, archivists, librarians, community leaders, artists, etc., can design transformative experiences that are more immediately available and accessible. They can provide a forum for connection and imagination.

Educational and creative interventions invite communities to reflect on their relationship to these objects and documents and the stories they tell. Community art and personal creative practices provide critical means for preserving the integrity of cultural artifacts within their respective communities while providing a space to build intercultural relationships and momentary visions of harmonious connectedness to place, time, and each other. By inviting artists to engage with collections, archivists can call attention to and disrupt the colonialist imperialist trajectory of their institutions.

Art and Memory

Artists and archivists can help to rebalance the power dynamic of memory work through participatory performance and creative community practice. Archival material and the visual, oral, and kinesthetic documentation that results from archival research is a large part of how societies consume and construct public memory. Artists are often using "scenes of unbearable historical weight" present in the archive as a valuable space for "aesthetic, ethical, political, social, and cultural speculation." (Enwezor, 2008, p. 33) Artists are able to interrogate public understandings of history and complicate our constructed collective memories by bringing the instability and inconsistency of the archive to the fore. In order to create the conditions necessary for this type of work, artists and archivists can think critically about the harm inherent to institutional archival practices and the ways in which harm can be redressed, if any.

Postmodern archival theory supports artists' use of the archive as a liberatory practice space. For example, archivist-scholars Zakiya Collier and Tonia Sutherland's (2022) reflections on Black Archival Practice urge for testimony and witnessing (rituals of seeing and speaking to what one saw, grounded by being seen) as a way to counter further dispossession and silencing in the archive. Saidiya Hartman's groundbreaking book, *Scenes of Subjection: Terror, Slavery, and Self-Making in Nineteenth-Century*

America (1997) is a harmonious marriage of content and form regarding the nuance between witness and spectator and testimony and empathy when reading archival holdings related to enslavement. To attend to the nuance, archivists, researchers, scholars, and artists can read archival material "against the grain" (Hartman, 1997; Gross, 2021). That is, view the document and the document creator with a critical eye and look for evidence of a subjects' presence in the archive or historical narrative as one distinct from and not solely from their encounter with power. Hartman asserts that there is more harm in retelling a subject's story solely through the lens of power (the document creator's ledger, for example) and that there is potential retribution in exploring counterhistories. (Hartman, 2008 and 2019; Guilmette, 2023). Like Hartman, and later Collier and Sutherland suggest, artists in the archive can "break down the terms of order" imposed on these lives by way of archival acquisition, appraisal, and description and create sonic, visual, and textual landscapes that introduce radically new perspectives (Mckesson, 2017-present). Indigenous knowledge systems are also integral to countering silences, which are not only apparent in the stories in the archive and the stories of those who encounter the material, but also in the ways archival practices "diminish, downplay, and derail place-based and community-centered knowledge" (Christen, Pinkham, Hooee, and Wilson, 2022, p. 29). What does it mean to narrate with and alongside the voices in the archive through a community practice? This requires a nuanced reading of archival material that sees and visions experiences of dispossession and exile without restaging the suffering and violence inherent to those conditions. Artists can embody this practice through imagining new worlds and harnessing joy because the depiction and viewing of suffering alone is not enough to prevent further suffering (Mckesson, 2017-present).

Performance is a valuable space for bringing these complexities to the fore. Response to the archive through performance draws out nuance from the document and creates an embodied act of testimony and witness. One sort of dispossession widely experienced within American cities is due to gentrification and resource precarity, disabling a large part of the population from maintaining long term residence. Analysis of gentrification benefits from autoethnographic study, in which the researcher connects personal experience to a wider discourse (Bloch, 2022). Autoethnography allows the researcher to explore memory stored in the body, drawing from sensation and affect to understand displacement, a condition that exists in and of the body (Bloch, 2022). Combining this notion of the autoethnographic with performance, autobiographical performance allows for artists to make meaning of their own experiences, draw from the experiences of others, and create performance that is a proxy for something greater than the individual. By blurring the boundary between self and other, performance can offer a communal understanding of our collective memory without oversimplifying or negating individual experience (Albright, 1997). Autobiographical performance, as an embodied way of knowing, challenges the idea of total separation of self and other. In terms of remembering displacement and upheaval, two experiences that concern the body in place and space, embodied ethnography or autobiographical performance can lend more accuracy and legitimacy to generalized quantitative evidence around displacement. While quantitative evidence is necessary for breadth of study, it can also restage and downplay the effects of barbaric and violent systems at play in the same way as reading the archive without interrogation of those systems.

There is a broad conversation within performance studies around the ontology of performance, however many scholars have built off of the notion that performance comes into being through its disappearance (Phelan, 1993). While many approaches to and definitions of performance work in conversation with memory and the archive, the idea that performance resists commodification and the reproduction economy due to its ephemerality aligns with the propositions in this chapter. Thus, performance and memory share at least two qualities: their readiness to disappear and their mutability. Collectively created performances can offer a broad and more comprehensive understanding of the history of a place and people through embodiment by physically enacting the memories of the collective in a singular place and space, an experience that cannot be replicated and that is subject to change. Movement and the body present dynamic and numerous ways to remember a collective experience and can lend to improvisation and non-linear interpretations of memory that actively work against settler colonial recordkeeping practices designed to facilitate static, sometimes invented understandings of history and to promote destructive forgetting (Harris, 2012; Saha and Potdar, 2023). The ephemeral nature of performance can work with and against the document by engaging what Verne Harris (2012) calls an invagination between the archive and memory: one can't exist without the other and they fold into each other, prompt one another, and exist in tandem. Memory in the archives/memory nexus is not defined solely by its so-called unreliability (as opposed to the so-called reliability of the archive). The archive sparks memory and memory create an archive. Therefore, disappearance, change, variance, and dissection are all part of performance, memory, and the archive.

The performing artist's use of archival material highlights the necessity of a composite approach to meaning making and collective remembering around place and displacement. The dance company Sankofa Danzafro embodies the use of multiple tools across the Black diaspora to ground themselves in place and space.

> "Because Sankofa Danzafro specifically locates their aesthetic practices within a broader framework of Africanist diasporic expressive cultures, the boundaries between the different performance modes they use are often commingled…. For example, in any one dance piece audiences might witness Colombian Black popular dances such as the currulao, bullerengue, and mapale alongside North American krumping, South African gwara gwara, and Senegalese-inflected African contemporary dance. The corporeal eloquence the dancers demonstrate allows for "the lovely actuality of blackness" to assert its presence. They evidence a larger practice of Black life that draws meaning and value for itself from the multiple locations from which Black bodies were forcefully dispersed." (Borelli, 2022, p. 151)

In this example, music and dance performance is an emancipatory practice that privileges the body as a site of relearning and unlearning. The composite memories of the dancers and the diaspora are an essential feature of Sankofa Danzafro's choreographic storytelling.

Embodied memory is not limited to staged performance. Performance can be approached broadly, and can be social - the performance of gender, the performance of birth, the performance of a contractual agreement in the form of an utterance (ex: "I do") (Taylor, 2003). These performances, ones of identity or legal agreement, have an audience, are social and cultural markers of self and other, and are integral to how we understand space and place and how we are understood.

For example, while not devised for the stage, motherhood is a memory and meaning-making performance that engages the body and has the ability to ground the artist in place and space (Al-Adeeb, 2021). Alexis Pauline Gumbs' expansive view of motherhood, mothering, and ancestry broadens traditionally held notions of home. This view, which includes non-human relations, deepens our receptivity to ancestral memories and our ability to access human technologies beyond the institutional archive or when using the institutional archive. As an artist and scholar, Gumbs uses archival material from academic institutions and community archives, as well as in-person oral history, performance, and community artmaking to channel her work, giving the archive context and a sense of activeness. It is in discussion with community that her work manifests, as evidenced by the collection of essays she edited for *Revolutionary Mothering: Love on the Front Lines* (2016) and the ceremonial prose in *Dub* (2020), which also calls on the performance of language and the utterance as a memory gathering, meaning making tool.

Performance recordings accompanying archival documents are also powerful in their becoming a part of the historical record themselves. The performance lives on through this continued engagement and becomes part of and lives alongside the original record. The relationship between the original record and the record created from artistic engagement with the archive are powerful contrasts or compliments to each other. Together, they influence future scholarship and collective understandings of history. For example, in 2017, South Asian American Digital Archives (SAADA) co-creators Michelle Caswell and Samip Mallick initiated "Where We Belong: Artists in the Archive," in which composer Zain Alam created a soundtrack for silent home movies depicting the life of the Dhillon family. The home movies are revolutionary in that they depict the family during quotidian moments of their lives while also capturing, through subtle changes in ways of living, the cultural and social climate of Oklahoma in the 1950s and early 1960s (Caswell, 2021). The collaboration was so impactful to a live audience that SAADA created a toolkit for community members to view the film in their homes and discuss responses, which proved in the initial showing to bridge the personal and the political.

Performance Practices as Memory Work

The authors, having created performance based on archival material and local geographies, propose two speculative works that invoke the processional. Their history of performance and performance research in Atlanta, Georgia and a brief note on walking as art practice lays the groundwork for the proposal.

The Atlanta BeltLine is a 22-mile railroad corridor turned walking and biking trail, connecting several parts of Atlanta. It is home to Art on the Atlanta BeltLine, the largest public art exhibition and linear gallery in the United States. The BeltLine, and the housing displacement its creation has caused in Atlanta over the last decade, has been widely discussed and debated, especially as its success has become a template for other cities to mimic (Immergluck and Balan, 2017). Author, Anicka Austin, conducted research as 2021-2022 Art on the Atlanta BeltLine Scholar-in-Residence, resulting in an ongoing research project called *gaze, time-travel and the unknown: contemporary site-specific performance in Atlanta's public spaces* to explore how the moving body in outdoor space learns, makes meaning, shapes and abstracts time, and connects with story across generations. The research, in conversation with the themes of this chapter, speaks to methods artists employ when they create work for public space, engage collective histories, and consider the body as archive. Anicka organized a social art-influenced letter writing exchange between herself and seven artists, observed performances and behaviors along the trail, and conducted interviews. Some preliminary results of the research surfaced common themes used when artists create site-specific performances in Atlanta. Endurance, adornment, and improvisation as methods of storytelling and interacting with the public were main themes across all correspondents. Each of these tools contributed to forming an embodied archive (what we take with us) and an archive of a space (what we leave behind) while participating in a site-specific performance.

The improvisational aspects of the speculative works proposed in this chapter relate to the dynamic and mutable nature of the archive and of memory. Based on the BeltLine research, improvisation in site-specific work is a method to connect with other people and the environment. Collective improvisation can foster deep listening and awareness and an understanding of non-verbal communication tools.

Improvisation in public space offers artists and participants a way to navigate the unexpected and gather information even when conditions are unknown.

Based on the BeltLine research, Atlanta artists are interested in performing acts of care in public space, collaborative meaning-making, and working towards a goal together. Artists are open about the spectrum of viewers, witnesses, and audience members who might engage with their work. "Public space" often means that there is no filter for who is coming to or who happens upon a performance. There is no demarcation that delineates the performer space from audience space, an important distinction from works created for the stage. Overall, phase one the BeltLine research was a case study of how performance works as a method of engaging memory, in conversation with other people and with Atlanta's landscape and architecture. Continuation of the research is underscored by a hope that imaginative reconstructions of history, place, and autobiography through performance have the power to initiate radical social transformation.

For author Saira Raza, use of memory artifacts - both physical and ephemeral - informs the sounds and constructed environment created through improvisational music and interactive installations. In her site-specific installation, *You Are the Treasure*, at the Museum of Contemporary Art Atlanta in 2019, Raza created a life-size "walk-in" music box in which the visitors become the performers of the work. Touch-sensitive sensors in the floor activated light displays of soft violet and magenta hues, a unique array with each person and each step. Three music box elements containing three different but complementary original scores can be turned to create infinitely unique compositions. Having three music elements prevents one person from being able to turn them all at one time, requiring collaboration with another visitor and embracing the uncertainty of the outcomes. In the center of the three music box elements, three 3-D printed dolls of the traditional ballerina found in commercially mass-produced music boxes twirled on a turntable, but instead of holding the rigid pose of their commercial cast, they are bent and manipulated into different poses, problematizing the projection and performance of the feminine ideal that found its way into millions of young girls' bedrooms through these products. Most children who had these boxes used it to watch over their most precious memory objects - rocks, baubles, chains, secret notes. The small room, covered with reflective pink mirrors contained ephemeral objects with specific meaning to the artist from which visitors can construct their own narrative and meaning, but most importantly, they could see themselves in the work at every turn and have their own unique experience as a performer in the work.

Walking Art Practice and Memory

The speculative works proposed engage walking as a primary movement modality. Walking is a ritual monument that makes present our loss (Rosenberg, 2007). Artist and scholar Ernesto Pujol encourages an embrace of psychic lingering of the bodies that stepped along a path before us. They, and other energetic pulses of a space, mark the body of a landscape (Pujol, 2016) Sculpture and other material objects created by artists who mine the histories of a place and bring them to the surface can help us draw from those bodily remembrances, which may have even preceded our existence by generations (Solnit, 2001). Atlanta artist Iman Person, for example, recreated a lost body of water in Grant Park for Flux Projects that audiences could travel along and remember a long-forgotten landscape (Person, nd). Grant Park, the oldest park in the City of Atlanta, originally included a lake. The lake was drained in the 1960s under the guise of creating more parking for the nearby Grant Park Zoo. However, it is likely that the lake was drained to avoid racial integration (Lemos, 2018-present). By recreating a landscape that is no longer visible to us, Person makes a bridge between time, drawing the past into the present and asking us to consider what this means for the future. Person's work makes the memory of the landscape, as well as the memory of racial segregation, physical. A sinuous fabric map in which the contents of our collective history is made tangible.

Participants walk along the sculptural river in Person's work, but there is also the possibility for topographical variation during a walk, a rise and descent. Several artists have used this feature in their creation of memorial monuments such as Maya Lin and Dani Karavan (Rosenberg, 2007). The mythical descent into the underworld, or ascent to the heavens as a narrative device for meaning making works with the landscape and can create a sense of both choreography and guided improvisation to a participant's experience.

Whether the artist and participants use improvisational techniques, engage artifacts and adornments, or walk as performance, these practices can help us adopt a critical lens and challenge dominant collective narrative. Since the archive is lauded as a site of substantive proof, while memory and the body are seen as wavering and unreliable, employing an ephemeral communication tool like performance can entail its own risks and limitations such as vagueness, suspicion, and bias which are all natural responses to mystery and the unknown. Neither memory nor the archive can remedy these outcomes as they are inherently part of the formation of collective memory. Composite images and forms have "holes" - areas that are not filled in with data because it does not exist or is inaccessible. The work of remembering requires exercising the imagination, which inherently cannot be impartial - in this way the composite becomes a shared space for co-creation of realities, futures, and understandings of the past. The unstable and dynamic nature of performance is a feature of the work - changing positionality can impact what form the composite takes. Noticing the view from the side, the view from ahead or behind the composite acts in similar ways to "reading against" the archive.

Composite Harmonies: Two Variations on the Processional (Speculative Works)

Speculative works created with the composite memories gathered through and from displacement use artifacts, landscape, and movement to recreate something that no longer exists. By invoking memories through participatory performance, communities can add new layers of artifacts to the ever-evolving project of identity. Two works are proposed below. Readers are encouraged to develop performances of their own based on these proposals or ones they create themselves.

Variation #1: Moving Monument

Proposal. With collaborators, collect archival maps from cultural heritage institutions around your city. Identify trails near your home, place of work, or third spaces. Gather and review maps in small groups. Choose a trail and walk along it individually or in smaller groups or couples. Assign movement or song to one location along the trail. Note them on your archival map. Combine the songs and movements from each group member's map and create a compilation - a composite choreographic map. Perform in the sites on the trails from which the map was created.

The performance is purposefully open-ended. As a larger group, decisions are made about which trail to choose and how to note the movements on the map. Maps are also chosen with respect to group decisions. Is a map of the city appropriate? Is a map of the trail available? The movement itself can range from a single gesture to more complex and elaborate gestures and can utilize a range of tools including voice and prop, such as organic material collected along the trail. Movements can be written, illustrated, or recorded using audiovisual tools and maps can also take on various shapes and mediums. The original archival map can be altered. Each movement from the individual or small group can be taught to the rest of the group or performed as solos and duets along the trail. The moving monument can be performed as a memorial within the group (internal) or with an invited audience (external). Likely, an audience of passersbys on the trail will form. How much information is shared with this organic audience?

Location. Depends on where the collective is located. In Atlanta, for example, the Atlanta BeltLine or the Stone Mountain trail are both sites with their own geographical archival material from which to draw. Additionally, archival institutions such as the Atlanta History Center and Dekalb History Center house maps and other documents related to those trails.

Manifesto.*First, we make meaning through the body by walking the land. After, we make maps of significant locales and build paths and architectural structures that mark the symbolic and practical. The body dances the geometric measurements of the earth. The four directions of the world. The body maps where rivers run and where we ceremonialize the deaths of our loved ones (Careri, 2003). There would be no public brick-laid commons, no covered plazas, no temples to bridge heaven and earth without the meaning derived from our walking. Our pilgrimage is an echo of the godly, an effort to commune with the mysterious. Walking is the architectural plan for building a (new) home.*

Walking illuminates moments of timelessness, or no time, of subtle disappearances and mysteries unexplained by cognitive processes alone. We walk and reconstruct a place so that it becomes home. We build familiarity with organic material, previous bodies, and architecture. We reshape what those markers mean to us with our composite ancestral histories.

The archive is geography and landscape. The archive is the body.

Variation #2: Mending River

Proposal. A site-specific community performance in which groups of participants sing and play a single assigned note as they move in procession along a defined route. Along this route, they will encounter other groups singing and playing a different note to create momentary harmonies in these convergence points. At each convergence point, there are exhibits, musicians, dancers, and other expressions that improvise and interact with the converged harmonies.

Location. Select a site with a high concentration of cultural artifacts, historical materials, and artworks such as a museum, library, academic building, or cultural center. The space should have enough room and access for groups of people to traverse across several spaces (gallery rooms, wide hallways, outdoor paths, common areas). Select three or more separate starting points from which groups of participants can begin their procession. Select points of convergence for the groups along their procession routes.

Groups. Among participants, organize at least three groups. Invite community leaders and artists to help in planning and engaging with participants, particularly if their communities are (mis)represented in the collections. There should be one assigned conductor for each group that guides participants through the procession. Each member of the group can choose to sing or play their note using an instrument or other device (kazoo, phone app) - the only directive is to sing or play the same note throughout the procession. The conductor can encourage the participants to explore different rhythms, volume, or tone to add dimension, interest, or resonance with the objects and spaces they encounter on the journey.

Route. Consider the context of the routes through various spaces, what they hold, and how they are used. Be sure to use accessible pathways, avoiding narrow passages, stairs, elevators, or obstacles. Also mind relevant community guidelines and procedures, including permits and neighborhood announcements, related to public events (e.g., sound, traffic, safety, etc.). The route should be marked with clear signage or even markings on the ground. In addition to bringing clarity to the process for participants, the visual markings add another layer of meaning by representing a sort of darning or mending of a physical and psychological space that has been worn and damaged by the violence of oppressive political, economic, and social systems.

Convergence. As groups expressing different notes arrive at the same point, this is *convergence*. This is the moment to connect to the present with works by artists of different modalities from within the community. They will perform and participate within the composite harmony created by the converging groups. For example, if three groups produce an A minor chord as they converge into a space with an improvisational musician, the artist would riff on the harmony of the participants and engage in a collective creation of a brand new and ephemeral experience. The same effect could be produced with dancers, visual artists, or any medium as the result will be influenced by its response to the converged chord.

Manifesto. *Processions signify ritual contemplation of a journey from one state of being into another - known to unknown. It also can represent the journey of the exiled - one that never truly ends since the materials and environment that constitute a certain way of life no longer exist and cannot be returned to. The sounds created by participants are a conversation with those objects - an acknowledgement of the people, places, and the lived experiences they represent and an invitation for those memories to join this mending river.*

The experience can and should generate a range of positive emotions - joy, connection, surprise, fulfillment, introspection, love, elevation. It might also activate grief, pain, guilt, and sadness. Thus, the procession should be approached with reverence, respect, and empathy, keeping in mind that some of the objects and artifacts with which voices and sound will resonate represent painful and complicated histories. Like all memory work, the practitioner should engage in the process with humility, curiosity, care, and intention to bring healing and unity. It is easy to be swept into the trap of spectacle, reinforcing the imbalance of power the mending river is meant to disrupt.

Intentions and Outcomes

The proposed speculative works represent an intersectional practice that seeks to embrace the complexity of the composite materials and experiences that form identity - as individuals, institutions, and communities. Through creative and collective engagement with archival and historical collections, the exiled, dispossessed, and displaced can restore connective tissues to obscure histories. As liberatory praxis, these works invite participants to contribute to the practice of meaning-making, opening a pathway to more empowered personal narratives and a richer understanding of the human experience.

REFERENCES

Al-Adeeb, D. (2021). A Letter to My Daughter: An Archive of Future Memories. *Amerasia Journal*, 47(1), 144–149. 10.1080/00447471.2021.1993765

Bloch, S. (2022). For Autoethnographies of Displacement Beyond Gentrification: The Body as Archive, Memory as Data. *Annals of the American Association of Geographers*, 112(3), 706–714. 10.1080/24694452.2021.1985952

Book Ban Data. (2024, March 14). Banned & Challenged Books: Advocacy, Legislation & Issues; American Library Association. https://www.ala.org/advocacy/bbooks/book-ban-data

Borelli, M. B. (2022). Choreographing Displacement in Sankofa Danzafro's La Ciudad de los Otros. *Theatre History Studies*, 41(1), 148–165. 10.1353/ths.2022.0009

Careri, F. (2017). *Walkscapes: walking as an aesthetic practice*. Culicidae Architectural Press.

Caswell, M. (2021). *Urgent Archives: Enacting Liberatory Memory Work*. Taylor & Francis. 10.4324/9781003001355

Césaire, A. (1972). *Discourse on colonialism*. Monthly Review Press.

Collier, Z., & Sutherland, T. (2022). Witnessing, Testimony, and Transformation as Genres of Black Archival Practice. *The Black Scholar*, 52(2), 7–15. 10.1080/00064246.2022.2042666

Data from Form 990s for top 25 US Universities. (2022). Guidestar. https://www.guidestar.org/

Gross, A. J. (2021). Archives of the Dispossessed: Mourning, Memory, and Metahistory. *English Language Notes*, 59(1), 219–221. 10.1215/00138282-8815093

Guilmette, L. (2023). Wayward Fables, Poem-Life Experiments: Foucault and Hartman in the Archives. *The Journal of Speculative Philosophy*, 37(3), 437–446. 10.5325/jspecphil.37.3.0437

Gumbs, A. P. (2019). *Dub: Finding Ceremony*. Duke University Press. 10.1515/9781478007081

Gumbs, A. P., Martens, C., & Williams, M. (Eds.). (2016). *Revolutionary mothering: love on the front lines*. PM Press.

Harris, V. (2002). The archival sliver: Power, memory, and archives in South Africa. *Archival Science*, 2(1-2), 63–86. 10.1007/BF02435631

Harris, V. (2012). Genres of the trace: Memory, archives and trouble. *Archives & Manuscripts*, 40(3), 147–157. 10.1080/01576895.2012.735825

Hartman, S. (2008). Venus in Two Acts. *Small Axe*, 12(2), 1–14. 10.1215/-12-2-1

Hartman, S. V. (1997). *Scenes of subjection: terror, slavery, and self-making in nineteenth-century America*. Oxford University Press.

Hartman, S. V. (2019). *Wayward lives, beautiful experiments: intimate histories of social upheaval* (1st ed.). W.W. Norton & Company.

Immergluck, D., & Balan, T. (2018). Sustainable for whom? Green urban development, environmental gentrification, and the Atlanta Beltline. *Urban Geography*, 39(4), 546–562. 10.1080/02723638.2017.1360041

Inada, L. F. (1992). *Legends from camp: Poems*. Coffee House Press.

Mallick, S. (2016, June 6). *Where We Belong: Artists in the Archive*. South Asian American Digital Archive (SAADA). https://www.saada.org/wherewebelong

McKesson. (Host). (2017). *Pod Save the People* [audio podcast]. Crooked Media.

McKittrick, K. (2011). On plantations, prisons, and a black sense of place. *Social & Cultural Geography*, 12(8), 947–963. 10.1080/14649365.2011.624280

Pujol, E. (2018). *Walking art practice: reflections on socially engaged paths* (1st ed.). Triarchy Press.

Saha, S., & Potdar, A. (Eds.). (2023). *Performance making and the archive*. Routledge.

Said, E. W. (2000). Invention, Memory, and Place. *Critical Inquiry*, 26(2), 175–192. https://www.jstor.org/stable/1344120. 10.1086/448963

Solnit, R. (2001). *Wanderlust: a history of walking*. Penguin Books.

Sykes, C. (Director). (1988, June 23). Exiles: Edward Said (Season 1 Episode 4) [TV series episode]. In A. Yentob (Executive Producer) *Exiles*. BBC.

Vasanthakumar, A. (2021). *The Ethics of Exile: A Political Theory of Diaspora*. 10.1093/oso/9780198828938.001.0001

Wood, E. M. (1999). *The origin of capitalism*. Monthly Review Press.

Chapter 5
Flowering Out:
An Autoethnographic Study of My Stepfamily

Siobhan Davies
London Metropolitan University, UK

ABSTRACT

Using a combination of qualitative research methods, the author documents her findings from the exploration of her recently acquired familial archive, a repository belonging to her step-aunt, from whom she has long been separated. Drawing upon her collected field notes, kept through the journey of reacquaintance, she links her personal, historical, and cultural observations. Steering between academic analysis and personal odyssey, the chapter reflects an inner dialogue provoked by the material discoveries of a half-remembered past. Within the chapter, "just" another family story unfolds, one that in its telling evokes the intricate interplay between objects, perception, memories, and culture through the experimental use of text, and narrative. Confessional endnotes contribute one final layer to the ethically modulated dance between truth, history, fiction, and power in a textual work that aims for a demonstration of the negotiated and performative construction of self.

INTRODUCTION

Two years ago, I completed the task of clearing the house of my long-lost stepaunt upon her move to a residential care home. Although most of the property's contents were sold to subsidise her care, I retained the family's extensive collection of artefacts and documents.

I became engrossed with this archive, as it offered me reconnection with objects from which I had long been cut off and promised to verify memories that had dwelt only in my mind for over thirty years.

The archive was a mass of objects accrued by the women in the family over several generations; as I found it, the collection was unlabelled and grouped only by associative placement throughout the house.

DOI: 10.4018/979-8-3693-2264-2.ch005

My fascination with the archive was driven, in part, by the dissonance between my memories and the familial narrative "owned" by my stepfather. I wrote:

As I sort, order, and place this collection, I will find a way to take control of the narratives of self that have recently been as chaotic and disruptive as the large volume of "things" that arrived, and in doing so, I will create a new narrative that closes down some uncomfortable internal dialogues. (My notes, December 2022)

Identifying my hunger for ownership of the archive as, more correctly, ownership of the narrative led me in earlier work to structural theories of the archive. I found some useful answers there around the power the archive could confer upon its storytelling owner, but in looking for a beginning that would shed light on later events, the archive refused to yield any one absolute truth, providing, instead, clues as to a range of possibilities.

However, as per my reconnection with my aunt, the one thing it did incontrovertibly show me was that my stepfamily had regarded me as their own, as I had them. I and they had firmly believed that I was fully (and officially) adopted into the family.[1]

The discovery of their adherence to this belief is redemptive, and I retain this knowledge as one benign foundational "origin" or beginning. However, such a discovery has, in turn, posed me with other questions, so my attention has turned towards finding some other way to make sense of how and why things developed as they did.

Method and Practice

Using a combination of the materials from the archive, memories from the distant past, and memories of recent conversations with my late aunt, I am using the tools of memory work (Kuhn) and object analysis (Prown) with the practice of autoethnographic discovery-through-writing in which:

autoethnographers invoke and use the discovery available in the writing process, using writing as a research practice that drives inquiry rather than as a "mopping up" activity after research is conducted (Richardson, 2005)

Since re-meeting my aunt and gaining access to the archive, I have been keeping a journal in which I have been recording memories, associations, and emotional responses. As a meta-archive, this journal of field notes is a formal resource that I use as an evocative "bridging" layer that allows me to preserve cognitive and emotional responses, which I can then synthesise with findings in my wider research and reading. In this way, the discovery inherent in the writing has led my research, and I quote extensively from my notes throughout my essay.

Research Aims

From an academic perspective, I am setting out to investigate how a narrative can be formed and performed; at heart, my subject is an exploration of the intricate interplay between objects, perception, memories, and culture in eliciting and sustaining complex emotional individual and collective responses that can produce compelling and credible evocations of "history".

In writing of the profoundly personal to an external audience, there is, necessarily, a behind-the-scenes examination of the play between inclusion / exclusion, of content and revelation; in what is here demonstrated in a public negotiation of private self, I hope to have found a way to make this tangible to readers.

I believe the value of this research lies:

- As an addition to the canon, which Laurel Richardson calls the *creative analytic process of ethnography*, in which the construction of the reading experience is exposed within narratives of social science, allowing a richer understanding of others and self through the use of evocative writing and moving away from the passive adoption of an unsituated narration
- Exposing some of the mechanisms in identity-creation and memory-revision
- Understanding the importance of evocative objects, photographs and documents in confirming memories and evidencing the significance of their absence as an undermining barrier to the healthy development of personal identity

Approach

I will focus on one artefact from the archive that has become a dominant theme in my notes and thoughts—an early twentieth-century Dolls' House—and, via the methods described above, explore related themes and sub-texts that appear to be referenced recurringly by other materials in the archive.

I will write about this research journey and its outcomes in a way that explores the use of language, images, imagery, and typographical devices so that the reader's experience is directly and knowingly engaged, acknowledging this work as a creative academic endeavour.

Notes on Attributions From My Writings

I include quotes from my notes as unattributed; all other sources are cited as usual.

Similarly, all photographs from the archive are unattributed; those from other sources are credited in the captions.

BACKGROUND

My work synthesises multiple interdisciplinary threads and is grounded in my research using the primary source of my familial archive and the memories it provokes and confirms.

It is a piece of arts-based qualitative research. Qualitative approaches have become accepted within social science as a way to firstly — deal with the issue of narrative situation (following on from structuralist, post-structuralist, and feminist theories that gained mainstream acceptance from the 1960s to the early 2000s) and secondly — find some way to invigorate academic writing in the humanities by re-introducing the human, the very thing of which we write, but in so doing, often obscure.

Autoethnography is a discipline that arose out of the difficulty of authorial position within ethnographic research and writing; it is an autobiographical genre that draws on the lived experience of the author and researcher, enabling new insights at individual and societal levels. Hammersley and Atkinson's 2007 book *Ethnography: Principles and practice* was a seminal work in this field

Laurel Richardson's work *Writing: A method of inquiry*, which appeared in the *Handbook of qualitative research* in 1994, proposed that writing should be both a means of lively dissemination of research findings and also a research tool in and of itself. She proposes ways to write that she calls *Creative Analytic Practice (CAP) Ethnography*, in which literary devices are deployed to re-create lived experience and evoke emotional responses, "evocative representations." Also, in this vein, I have found the work of Christopher Poulos (*Essentials of autoethnography*, 2021) to be very clear and engaging.

This flow of thinking is echoed in the field of Material Culture. Jules Prown's method for interrogating objects to access their histories and meanings goes beyond observation and ventures into the world of the poetic (*Mind in matter: An introduction to material culture theory and method*, 1982). That paper posits that objects are more democratic means of understanding cultural history, being free of those difficult situated positions of privilege.

Judy Attfield's book, *Wild things: The material culture of everyday life* is what she calls "unashamedly hybrid", calling on the fields of social history, anthropology, archaeology, sociology, geography, psychoanalysis, and general cultural studies that veer out of her academic pigeonhole of design and art history to allow her free range to examine the more mundane objects that make up the texture and background of our lives.

Family secrets: Acts of memory and imagination (2002) by cultural theorist Annette Kuhn is a work in which she turns her critically dissective methods away from film and art and uses them to deconstruct images from her own family album, moving from the personal to the idea of collective acts of memory, examining how memory is used in shaping our identities and lives.

As I am engaged in ideas about narrative and the value of evocative writing, I find it helpful and illuminating to read fiction alongside non-fiction; books intersecting with my interests during this research have been Virginia Woolf's *To the lighthouse* (1927) and *A room of one's own (1928)*, Elizabeth Gilbert's *The signature of all things* (2021), and Charlotte Gilman's *The yellow wallpaper* (1892).

Figure 1. The Dolls' House

RE-MEETING KITTY

In 2022, I wrote:

I am on a train, returning from Weston-super-Mare, reading — alternately —

- a book in which the (female Victorian naturalist) protagonist posits there are four sorts of time *(Human Time, Divine Time, Geological Time and Moss Time) (Gilbert, 2013)*
- an essay in which the author seems to suggest that things don't happen in a linear time, i.e., one thing after another, because they are only experienced through the language needed to organise it for reflection and consumption, e.g., in a book.

I am getting a little cross with the ideas in Book 2 and revert to Book 1, but not before I read about the solitude of reading; of reading in public, on a train.

I am alone — on a train — reading about being alone and reading, reading about being alone on a train, arguing with the book and its idea of aloneness. Perfect.

***

I have just come from seeing my long-lost Aunt, Kitty. Kitty is 81; four-ish years ago she was made a Ward of Court and put in a dementia home by Social Services. The Home is in Weston-super-Mare; I live in London.

Three-ish years ago, I was reunited with Aunty Kitty — when my stepfather's own dementia reached the point that someone else gave me access to family papers.

I cut contact with my stepfather three-ish years ago.

Kitty cut contact with him 30-ish years ago.

Four-ish years ago, he became convinced that I was Kitty. Among Other Things.

Kitty was the nickname of my aunt, Eleanor Davies, who had been lost to me many years earlier when she and her brother (my stepfather) fell out.

In 2020, I was contacted by a team from Social Services, North Somerset, who were seeking her remaining family members. I welcomed the contact; I had long thought about what might, one day, happen, and wondered about Kitty:

Early in *Rift Time*, I barely knew it was there… (I was 28.) It was their business, not mine; I had my own business and that was very busy.

(Inklings of memories crossed my sleeping mind, nothing more.)

I had my second child (I was 35); I thought of Kitty; I thought of how I'd visited Kitty with my first child.

Then, I thought of Kitty on her own… of being alone and alone-ness.

I wrote to Kitty covertly via an old family friend. I received no reply.

The rift deepened. (I was 36, 37, 38….)

The inklings mustered, gathering themselves in drifts, accreting in Dr Freud's iceberg's underberg, poking their collected bulk above the waterline of my conscious.

Kitty-thoughts.

Then I tried online searches… Shrewsbury, I thought, for some reason. Antiques, Antiques in Shrewsbury? *The Cow Painting*. Auction houses and dealers of Specialist Dolls' Houses. Cards handmade from Victorian scraps. (Staffordshire. Herefordshire. Worcestershire. The Midlands.) Place-thoughts. Thing-thoughts.
A paisley carpet, a house made of shells, an owl looking surprised, a solid phone — *"Newton Abbot, five-two-oh-six-eight"*.
I gathered the Thing-thoughts and placed them in my House-thought. Then I thought-walked through the House-thought and visited the Things-thoughts in situ. (Jasmine and verbena at the front door, a barking dog, the door opens, the tiles are terracotta, the soap is *Pears*, the galoshes are under the macs …)

***

I was 40. My parents announced they were moving to Spain.
It was sudden: *Off They Went!*

***

Mum died (I was 53). In Spain. Suddenly.
(Hillocks now of Thing-thoughts; *Moving On (we Must. Move. On.)*; nostalgia, missing, missing-the-missing; inklings and darklings in the Underberg.)
Ted was dying (I was 55).
Kitty's (Court Order of) Protection Officer called.

From 2020 to 2023, I travelled between London and Weston-super-Mare; the first year, I cleared her house, the second, I "just" visited.
Kitty and I found a way to connect; for much of that time — *Finding Time* — she was on what the staff described as a "good plateau"; that is, a plateau of the illness where the losses were not so keenly felt, but the ability to live simply but well (with help) remained.
This meant we could talk a little about the past: she remembered her parents, her brother ("*darling Edward*"), my mother, many of the family's friends I had known, and a great deal about the house in Newton Abbot, Devon, where she had lived most of her life with her parents. While she did not recognise the older me, she knew who exactly who I was ("Shuv") and had a sense of my newer family — that I had a husband and two children.

I could always tell her my "news", and she was very keen to listen; she preferred it when I spoke. She could follow all I said while I was saying it. The next day, I could say it all again (if I liked), and it would still be well-received as new news.

During this time, there was a gradual decline, and Kitty lost everyone from her recollection except her parents (we had already found we preferred not to speak of Edward); the decline was gentle, and throughout, Kitty remained enamoured of news, and she could still follow quite complicated stories.

We spent much time looking at old photographs, and I would take her things from her own home, which always delighted her, so we never ran short of conversation. She was settled in the residential home but categorically maintained that her stay was temporary and that she would soon be going home.

Her decline came very suddenly as the year turned to autumn. My visits speeded up; I was back and forth bi-weekly, then weekly. I hurtled between homes, with time demonstrating all its elasticity… slow hours by the bedside were suddenly gone, and the void of missing her dulled by the busy blur of routine back in London. It seemed I was perpetually on a train…

The huge thing, for me, about finding Kitty was that not only did I find her — I also found the real objects behind those Thing-thought-memories that had grown so steadily in my mind:

Clearing through Kitty's house, I came face-to-face with confirmation of my remembered childhood… Going to her house for the first time — the smell of lemon verbena blossoming around the door, just as it had at my grandparents' house. The garden walled with West Country sandstone, the path paved with warm terracotta tiles up to a massive step of worn stone… the very gentle air — as it is there — promising drowsy evenings and the deepest sleep.

On entering… coal, coal dust, the smoke of many fires; wax polish. Coloured light from the glass of the door — yellow shafts, quiet motes hanging in that air. Some mustiness — old papers, furniture. Once a dog, perhaps. Such calm. Such a feeling of coming home.

And then there were *The Things*.

THE THINGS

Figure 2. Early in the house clearing, 2022

Some jumped out at me the minute I walked in the door, even though they were buried beneath layers of old post and papers... Others sparked recognitions that only emerged into my consciousness evenings or days later.

Some things I had been looking for and thinking of for some time; some things I had even bought myself on what I'd thought was a whim; some things I had drawn or sketched, sometimes knowing why, sometimes not.

Some things were revelations, long forgotten but entirely familiar.

Some things were missing, notably missing, but not much. (I still miss them. The Cow Painting. The Big Weird Doll. Sometimes I find a photo of them, in the papers I am still sorting, and even that is something.)

Now, this sounds not very nice — but — seeing the things again was at least as welcome as finding Kitty.

For, very sadly, Kitty is now in a place of just two times — a never-ending now and one of an amalgamated time somewhere in the middle of her past.

The things themselves are very much (almost) as they always have been and were (clearly, here and there, they have suffered that kind of consequential damage only afforded by linear, chronological time). Kitty, now, is the very essence of herself (and that is a very delightful self), but I feel I am much, much changed.

Kitty, her mother, her uncle, and her mother's mother were collectors of the everyday, the extraordinary and the antique. As the family's homes had gone from manor to villa to terrace, obviously some sorting, selling and throwing away had been necessary. Also, with each death, a similar process of whittling down for the new house-containers — and transition of ownership — had occurred.

***

Essentially, what I found was most of everything I'd remembered — and more (for, in truth, very little whittling down had been done).

Technically it was all Kitty's. While some of it definitely was precisely and only hers (that is, she had found, created, or bought it) much of it was inherited and, in that way, you could say some of it was her Mum's, her father's, her uncle's, her mother's parents', and many, many other predecessors. So yes, some of it was truly Kitty's, but at least as much of it had come through inheritance.

In truth, I have come to it more by expeditious circumstances[2].

Figure 3. Objects from the archive, clockwise from top left: An early Victorian hand painted "honey-comb" Valentine, A Note to a future finder, a child's Bear on Wheels c. 1910, A Stuffed Parrot in Glass Dome as found; late 19th century

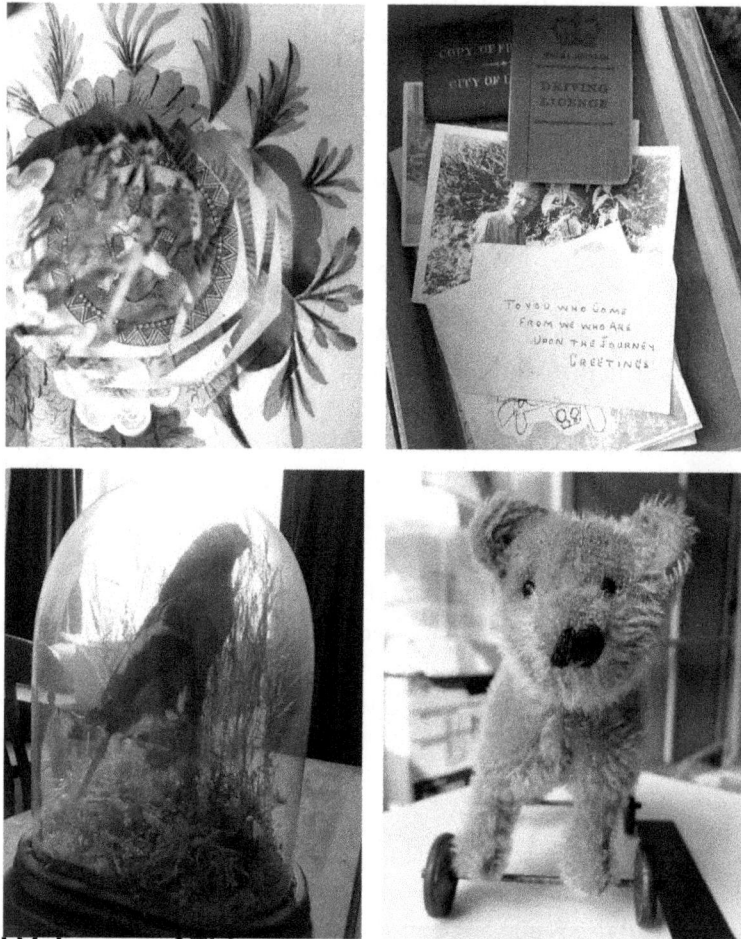

The Types and Volumes of Things

It would take too many words to adequately describe *The Types and Volumes of Things*, but suffice to say: there was a great deal, and here, indeed, were the real and actual things behind those *Thing-Thoughts*:

Figure 4. Excerpt from one of the insurance inventories of the Newton Abbot house, 1968

and cover.

The various ornaments and items of Victoriana, about the room of insufficient importance to enumerate individually.

An electric convector heater.

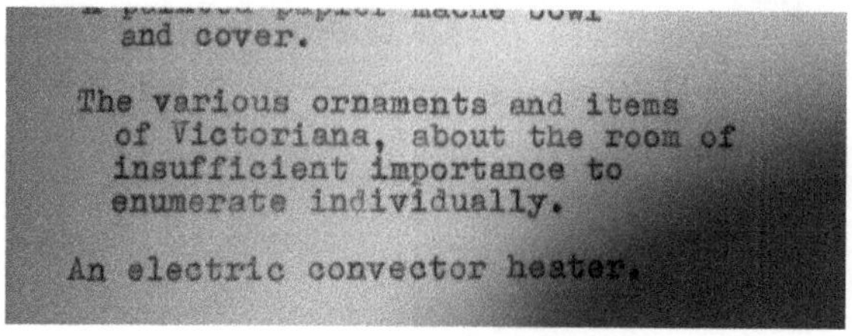

Antiques. A Dolls' House. Cards handmade from Victorian scraps. (Things from Staffordshire. Herefordshire. Worcestershire. The Midlands. Things of Staffordshire, Herefordshire, Worcestershire, and The Midlands.) A paisley carpet, a house made of shells, an "owl looking surprised", a solid Bakelite phone.

Figure 5. Sailor's shell house, late 19th century

Before really going through the objects and understanding their relevance, I had thought Kitty and my grandmother "just" collectors, and so — in letting so much go to the auction house — was a little careless of some objects that were, I later realised, heirlooms and family portraits.

But — happily for me — what was not wanted by the auctioneers at all was the large collection of Victorian "scraps" for scrapbooking, and of cards, often made with those scraps, and of images of flowers in competent watercolours, pages from sketchbooks. Items of beadwork, embroidery, one remaining intact scrapbook. Saccharine, ornate, floral. Gloriously unfashionable, deeply domestic — the antique flotsam of papery attachment and home.

Figure 6. One collection of cards as it was found (Victorian and Edwardian)

The Dolls' House

Figure 7. The inside of the Dolls' House today

If anyone had ever asked me which thing I missed or wanted most, I would have said the Dolls' House. Of course, it was an old and precious one, stuffed so full of collected miniature Victoriana that it was used more as a container than a playable or "habitable" set of rooms.

I remember that my playing, as a child, was, therefore, more of a dutiful attempt to organise than an immersive entry into a one-twelfth diminishment of historical reality. Nevertheless, given its prominent place in the real house and the reverence with which it was spoken, I always regarded such playing as a great honour, entrusted with not only the fragile house-container but the vast quantities of treasures within.

Inside, it was once all furniture and no space. Each childhood effort to make it more liveable (for its dolls) was spoilt by the sheer volume of its contents. This spoilage always occurred when I tried to re-insert its last twenty per cent; my heart came to expect this organisational failure, although I never lost heart for the endeavour.

Later that same visit, in the same room as the major cache of paintings, we unearthed the Dolls' House. One might think such a large object (almost a metre high) would be hard to overlook, but it was sandwiched between innocuous pieces of brown furniture, a sheet covering all, and all only made accessible by the recent removal of other items.

Sadly, it was empty:

In a Lilliputian reversal of scale, it ended up in a room similarly crowded [to its former furnished incarnation] — while the house itself was, by then, empty.

As I opened the doors, those five rooms were there, little changed, and:

…all exuding a perceptible smell of coal fires, must, and the West Country; I am back in Newton Abbot, dust hanging in the golden winter morning light before the fires are lit…

This vertiginous moment has taken on a memorial significance to me; it is *The Moment*, in *The Time of Finding*, a moment where:

that shitty familial rift and its consequences shifted towards a mending — as scale, memory, and time pulled together, and *Everything Was* (nearly) *Alright*.

***

The house now stands upstairs in our home. It has not moved from its temporary position in our bedroom. I put it there to see it as I went to sleep and when I awoke.

But it has been subject to great scrutiny.

This artefact, in particular, led me to J.D. Prown's work on *Material Culture* (1982), which provides a rigorous method for examining material artefacts.

Figure 8. Fireplace with soot, Dolls' House interior

There are many obvious things about the Dolls' House, but what I discovered then and later, through many such Prownian investigations, has been not only the homemade quality of the house, its rather dual identity of a Georgian townhouse / country pile, and its crumbling finishes — but three significant things:

1. The front steps are worn by the "feet" of the dolls
2. While the little lumps of real coal and wood sit in each fire grate, one chimney breast bears tell-tale soot where clearly once, one child succumbed to (what I can testify was) the overwhelming temptation to light it
3. By the opening catch of one front side there is an almost imperceptible graffiti that is hard not to read as saying "Kitty's"

While points one and two evidence only how well loved this toy once was, and that it was used (however delinquently) for its intended purpose, point three speaks to something else entirely:

… a possible source of conflict for Ted and Kitty — such a big, public toy; one more suited to the gendered play at that time (the 1940s) of a girl — and so filled with collected treasures it implies a parental treatment which bright children might perceive as preferential.
I think the graffiti is a surreptitious claim to ownership; barely noticeable to an adult but easily pointed out to a younger sibling. [3]

Figure 9. Gaffiti? Dolls' House exterior

Family Homes

Figure 10. Invitation to the children's birthday party, Hartlebury, c. late 1940s

Having noticed the specificity of its Georgian architecture (at odds with the vast array of Victoriana in the collection), I surmised that the appearance of the Dolls' House was iconic in the family's shared psyche of collective memories.

I went through the hundreds of photos in the archive, looking for houses. Often appearing as background to the family members, I sorted them by family groups and ages.

These photos of Ted and Kitty (see Figure 11) at ages that tally with the birthday invitation I found (see Figure 10) indicated one house. I remembered Ted talking of a place called *Goldenness* (which, in all of Ted's stories, had stood in Surrey). However, the invitation and some letters revealed to me a *Goldness* in Hartlebury, Kidderminster, and in finding the online photos, I recognised those distinctive elements of the Dolls' House architecture and saw that familiar red brick. This was the family home where Ted and Kitty lived from birth till their early adolescence.

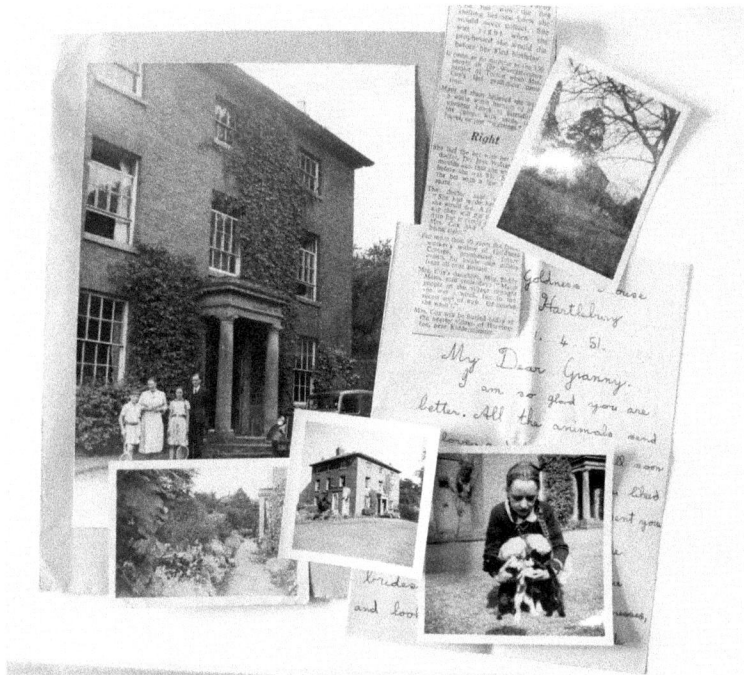

Then I tracked down two names of which I'd never heard:

Bleak House, Areley Kings

First, *Bleak House*, which I found from the correspondence of my great-grandfather, Dr Edward Stanley Robinson, at Areley Kings in Stourport.

Figure 12. Bleak House, early 20th century (demolished in the '60s). Image top right — public domain (this most clearly shows how the house matched the description in Dicken's novel)

Bought on their marriage near the end of the 19th century, it was a Victorian mansion perched on top of a small hill. They renamed it after Dickens' titular house, for reasons pointing both to the situational resemblance — their marriage, her inheritance, his profession — and the physical resemblance described so well in the book:

On the top of a hill… three peaks in the roof in front and a circular sweep leading to the porch... (Dickens, 1853)

This was the house where Kitty was born in 1941, shortly before her father rejoined the new family from his wartime service and they moved to Goldness.

York House, Stourport

Figure 13. Architectural background in the family photographs

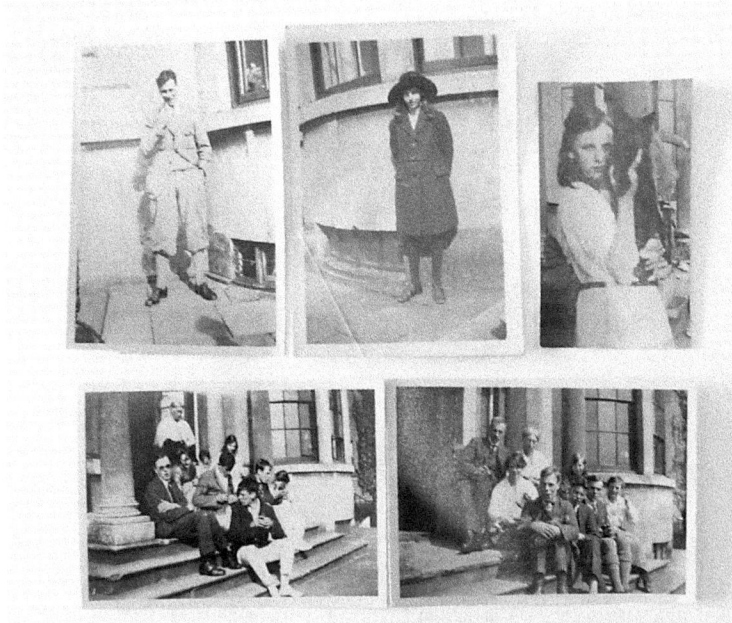

That left a pile of photographs of some less identifiable architecture. Knowing, by then, the close cast of the family from around 1900 on, I saw a great many of them that featured "Nor" (Kitty's namesake, Eleanor), my grandmother's sister who died in adolescence[4], and a set of arches and stretch of water, but also another frontage with large steps and curving bay windows. So, these photographs looked like another familial home in the early 1900s — but they were not Bleak House, and I was puzzled as to the seeming double occupancy.

From the house names in various archive documents, I found a *York House*. I looked it up:

…the first medical practice to use York House was that of Drs Robinson and Giles in approximately 1902. … it passed into the hands of Dr Robinson on his marriage to Miss Worth, a daughter of the carpet manufacturing family of that name…. (Practice Booklet, 2014)

Figure 14. York House, Country Life, *1951, from the archive, and the rear of York House as it is now*

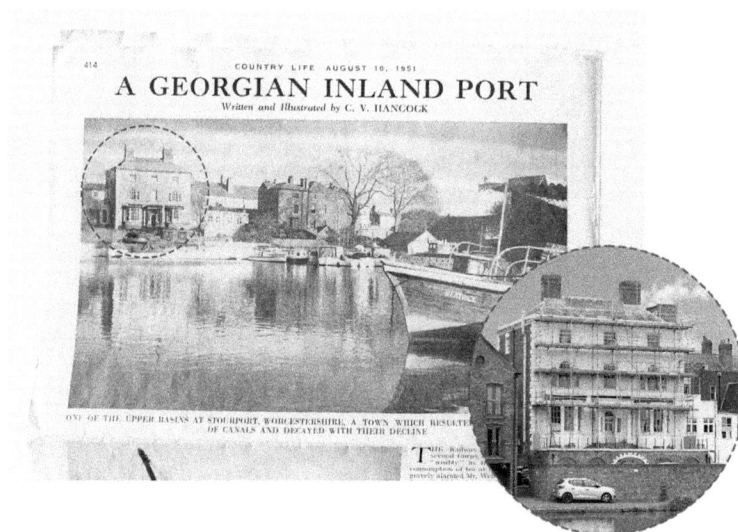

The practice leaflet included photographs, from which I was, finally, able to understand the particular architecture of York House and why it appeared so differently in the photos, for it is a house of three faces — the first, a red brick façade to the High Street at ground level, the second, the grander looking frontage of a white house looking over the canal basin, which is actually the rear of the house. The third, barely visible in the online resources — as it sits below the white building, at the level of the basin's water — is the set of colonnaded brick arches where Nor appears to have played so frequently.

All the family photographs are of the rear: the steps of the white house without the rest of it (perhaps not even painted white, then), and the arches below by the water.

Figure 15. The front of York House, 2024

The red brick façade on the High Street never features in those photographs — but here it is (see Figure 15), a Georgian townhouse that typifies the early merchants' houses of Stourport.

So, in my family's time, York House was intended to be used for medical practice, while the family home was Bleak House at Areley Kings. But, while Bleak House was being used as a hospital during the First World War, the family stayed at York House, accounting for its appearance in those family photographs.

Figure 16. Typical Stourport façade and fenestration

As the Historic England pamphlet tells me, most of Stourport is built in the Georgian vernacular, the town having sprung up quite suddenly on the arrival of the canals.

So, that odd duality of town/country house identity apparent in the Dolls' House makes perfect sense in terms of such a meaningful symbol to the later family; both York House (bought with my great-grandmother Eliza's inheritance) and Goldness (bought shortly after the Second World War with an inheritance of my grandmother's) were Georgian; one stood firmly in the town, the other, several acres of country, and both reflected the roots of the maternal line tying them back to Stourport and Kidderminster.

***

When I found Goldness, I was surprised by the size and opulence of the building. Bleak House — in all its horrible-loveliness was in keeping with my expectations of former family homes. But York House rather blew me away.

Historic England (English Heritage, 2007) calls it: "…perhaps the grandest house in Stourport."

I had known that there were some grander relatives in the family tree, but not of how wealthy the family had once been or from where the wealth came.

Ted used to keep a picture of Granny's great-uncle Stanley[5] upstairs when I lived at home; when my parents moved to Spain, this migrated — necessarily — downstairs (it being a bungalow[6]), and into the public space of their living/dining room, where it looked down over many get-togethers, inviting the curious to enquire about Ted's nugget of relation to greatness. [7] But that nugget did not divulge the roots of the Victorian industrialists Stanley had come from: the Wilden Ironworks in Worcestershire in the manor of Hartlebury, the place where Goldness still stands.

I can now see that the family's fortunes declined dramatically in less than two generations — and a little of how that happened. The Dolls' House and the research it provoked drew my attention to this aspect of the family history in a way that told me far more about them — what they had been, what they had lost, how they dealt with it — than any tale of grander relatives.

Figure 17. Wilden Ironworks, c. 1950s

BACK TO THE DOLLS' HOUSE

Figure 18. The Dolls' House in my grandparents' "drawing room" at Newton Abbot

I return repeatedly to the Dolls' House; it is compulsive — I am convinced that this object, more than the archive papers, holds some key to the later events within my family.

To open it is like physically opening the door on the past, and that feels so real it seems almost literal; the action of the opening invites one in, and

then one is inside — psychically, there is a trick, perhaps the *proscenium effect*? — the open doors letting one into the space; a space that for me, is still the space of my grandparents' house in which it played such a prominent role.

It is empty, and I have toyed with the idea of populating it again. I am not sure, though, that I want to fill it with random pieces collected without association; that would destroy meaning rather than augment it.

Instead, to keep it from the dejection of emptiness, I have placed there things that seem congruent, small things forming more of a reverent hideaway than an invitation to play.

Shut, the house is a vintage piece of furniture, a family heirloom, a decorative element, a thing of glorious decrepit beauty. But also, it remains slightly mysterious in the way that other people's houses are mysterious when viewed from the outside, especially when backlit glimpses of occupants and occupations are caught. Who knows what dramas are unfolding indoors?

But these people inside this house are mine and for me:

…they might be in there, my old family — getting on with things, uninterrupted and unobserved... safely tucked in the time of *Then*, in those unremarkable interstices between our visits.

All are, or become once again, benignly available upon arrangement…

Open, one has a god-like view; one is simultaneously inside the space as if participating, miniaturised but also — being aware of this miniaturising trick played by the framing proscenium, becoming more aware of one's corporeality on the outside — so by contrast, a giant:

...one is inside and outside all at once...

I think that is the trick of any Dolls' House, but this one clearly holds much more up its bricky sleeve.

***

As you can imagine, in so many conversations of and about the Dolls' House, I was urged to read Ibsen's play. It is an interesting piece, reflecting so much on gendered domesticity (Dolls' Houses were first a study aid to teach girls what would be expected of them as housekeepers), a time and culture in which women could not take out a loan or mortgage on their own behalf. The archive bears this out; it is Eliza Worth's (my great-grandmother) inherited wealth that enables the purchase of both Bleak House and York House (a fact sometimes lost in the online narratives).

Figure 19. Georgian silhouette (frame c. 1980s)

Later in the history, it is my grandmother's family wealth that enables the purchase of Goldness; a little later still, a mistake in the Will of Robert Worth (granny's uncle) leads to a contesting court case that goes right up to an Appeal in the Royal Court of Justice in 1955; won by my grandparents.[8] The cause of the mistake? Robert Worth appeared to have wanted to leave the money to his niece, whom he knew well, but bound by patriarchal convention, he bequeathed it via her husband. Unfortunately, as he barely knew her husband, he misremembered his name, leading to the money being diverted to another side of the family.

Figure 20. Correspondence and cuttings about the contestation of the Robert Worth's Will

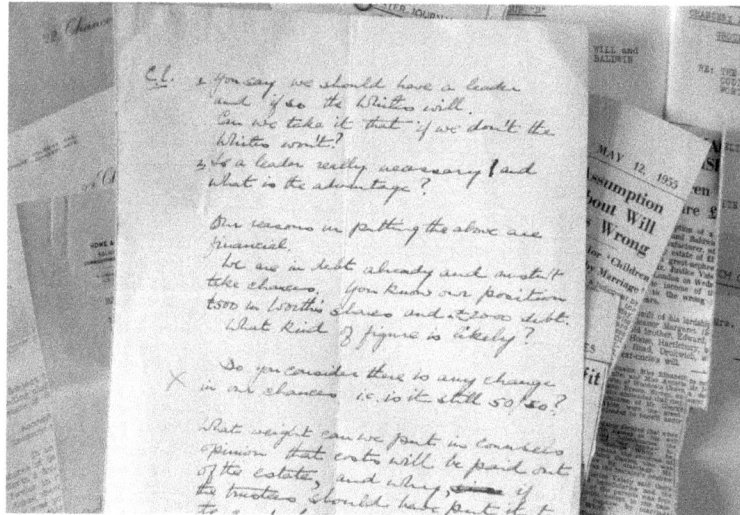

There is a great deal in the archive about this battle, which went on for several years, but nothing records my grandmother's feelings on the subject. Likewise, when the Bond Worth carpet firm collapses in the '70s[9], a letter to my grandmother telling her all her shares in the family business are now worthless exists — but I cannot find one word of her feelings on the subject in all the reams of paper there.[10]

Instead, there is the collection, which, in many ways, feels like a silent record of women's concerns. The women in my family collected women's work, and the work reflects not only what society was expecting of them but often a sense of thwarted ambition — or rather, re-directed energy, a low-level bubbling of subversive desire for a place in the external world of work, of exposure to the improving rigours of debate and critique. There is evidence of great industry in these pieces, of imagination, creativity, and determination.

Evidence of the very human desire to make a mark — all those beautiful watercolours, collages, sketches, embroideries, humbly unsigned. For to sign a piece of one's work is to envisage it finding its way in the world outside the home; the signature is the sign of its creator, a sign of their belief in the worth of their work, their self. The sign "says" that the thing should have value beyond that of a sentimental memento between two people known to each other, that the author believes the thing to be worthy of a place in public life, and that knowledge of the author's identity may, in fact, add greater value as the thing has the sign of authenticated provenance.

Figure 21. Unsigned watercolours

The lack of signatures on all of these works is remarkable. But they have survived, and here, in some way, they are in the world. Their longevity is a testament to their beauty, of their worth even without that precious sign, and that my female relatives collected them indicates to me a covert, long-term, collusive membership of a sisterhood whose roots were growing before such a thing emerged into the collective conscious, when it was only beginning to find the words to bring it into being.[11]

I remember (or I think I do), back in the '80s, hearing the word "just" applied to the collection/act of collecting. Granny and Kitty were always "just" doing something, and when I think about it now, while I feel a little sad that they spoke about it this way, I enjoy the thought that they were "just" busy with quite so much.

For now, we are back to my impression of so much going on for them, as per my Dolls' house reflections and Ibsen's Nora. At this point, I feel we are looking behind closed doors (as a Giant / Doll, trapped in domesticity) and can sense what they are flying under the radar, in the realm of underestimated "froth."

The house. The scraps. The flowers. The feminine.
The collecting of the feminine.
The Dolls' House.
The move, the missing, the collecting of the recollecting.
The squashing, the diminishment, the loss.
The Dolls' House.
Birmingham, Kidderminster, Bromsgrove.
Devon. Newton. Weston.
The train, from the Midlands, to the sea. From the canals, to the sea.
The sea, the shells, the Victoriana; the Victorian house. The Georgian house in the Victorian house; the Dolls' House in the new old house… all the houses in the one last house.

A NEW ROMANCE

Figure 22. Family photograph: Mum, me, "Dad," 1987

Back when all was well at Newton Abbot, the occupants fully occupied with their various preoccupations, and when I would visit with my father, it was the time of my adolescence and coming of age. That was a very particular time; one in which Thatcher "adjusted" Britain, getting beyond the post-war shadows, ushering in a version of modernity in which unions were thrashed, people got on their bikes to find work, Young Upwardly Mobile Professionals meritocratically transformed the City, phones became "mobile," and only the youth (some) was revolting.

The inhabitants at 19 College Road were stalwart refuseniks; while they all enjoyed discussing the changes in the world, those changes seemed not to touch them. My younger self saw them as belonging to a different time. Of my Aunt Kitty, separated by only two weeks in age from my mother, I wrote:

…I never thought of my aunt as a modern woman. That place I reserved for my mother, a fan of the new and the forward-looking; a hard-working professional, a wearer of pussy-bow blouses and electric satin blue, a paperer of orange-patterned walls, disciple of Tupperware and early adopter of microwaves.

A long dangling flex in our orange/brown kitchen connected our world up North to that of Newton Abbot's down South via the solid Bakelite at that end — *"Newton Abbot, five-two-oh-six-eight…."*

Those two worlds could not have been further apart.

And yet… my teenage self-found a great connection in the romanticism of late Victorian ideas and imagery that was the very stuff of Newton Abbot — the pre-Raphaelites, Poe, Shelley, Byron; the bohemian carpets, furniture, the paintings, the souvenirs of foreign travel; the rolling countryside visible from the windows; the House in its forms both miniature and human-size emerging as the backdrop of fictional transgression and the uncanny in my fond readings, at the time, but also, that "revolting" strand of youth culture, the one that emerged in opposition to the harsh new world of yuppies, avarice and big hair; one instead that embraced frilly shirts, romantic acts of selflessness and bohemian revelry. Tempting sirens, windswept moors with brigand highwaymen; social justice in velvet (for those not keen on spitting).

When I thought those two worlds were so different, perhaps they weren't. At that time of my remembrance, most women had, under their hair — however big or small — their own ways of negotiating issues of gender inequality. Mum in her pussy-bowed electric blue, part of the union asking for equal pay and access to the golf club; Granny sequestered with her memories of the fight for suffrage, sharing a closeted passion for women's work with her own "difficult" daughter — their unruly collection of unsigned women's work growing in every drawer, closet, nook, and cranny.

At the start of my homely investigations, I turned momentarily to Bachelard, remembering the writing I'd found so interesting back in those '80s days of my escape to art school and a new world of thinking, seeing and reading.

Here, in this favourite text of mine (at the time), "we" got to explore all kinds of dwellings and the spaces within them, and here "we" came, at last, to the drawers, chests and wardrobes: secret hiding places where I was told:

> …order reigns, or rather, this is the reign of order. Order is not merely geometrical, it can also remember the family history. A poet knew this:
> (Orderliness. Harmony.
> Piles of sheets in the wardrobe
> Lavender in the linen).
> (Bachelard, 1958/2014)

I see now that at that time, I had bought into that poetic vision of intimate space, of an ordered domesticity brought about by unmentioned hands, blind to the presumption, assumption and omission even while I puzzled at my mother's perpetual rage and was entranced by the eccentric contents of the drawers, chests, and wardrobes in Newton Abbot (of which very few housed linen).

For those hidden contents pointed to a far more interesting "reading" than the works of the (male) painters adorning the walls and the poppy songs of the day, and perhaps now, account for my impression that in those happy times I remember, surrounded by the hidden cultural clues populating the drawers, we (as a family) were actually segueing inexorably towards an ending that seems more like something from a gothic novel.

Figure 23. Page from my earlier writing, "Beginnings" — this one version of the beginning features Ted as he meets my mother, literally riding in on a horse, and sweeping us both back to England for a wedding befitting that to a divorcee-single-mother in the 1960s, held at "home" in Newton Abbot.[12]

The Feminine Gothic

With the sweetly sick feeling of those about to indulge in a guilty pleasure, I turned away from Derrida et al. and gave myself permission to investigate my first impression, that of being caught in the final few chapters of a Gothic novel[13].

I discover that this very particular strand of the gothic, of which I have been thinking, is already recognised as a distinct sub-genre of Gothic, and it is called *The Feminine Gothic*.

Narratives in this sub-genre contain a reliable set of ingredients, all bearing great resemblance to elements of the narrative that I am (not fully) telling here — the family house, some family secrets, a female protagonist whose mind is played upon by events that unfold in the house; an element of the uncanny.

Of course, as the story unfolds, the male protagonist's actions have sinister consequences for the woman/women at the heart of it—for it is told from the woman's perspective, and often in the first person. These narratives were written by women — those brave enough to "attempt the pen" — an implement perceived by many at that time and even through much of the twentieth century as being, by its very nature, inherently male.

Those stories' unfolding actions often reveal what we now call *toxic masculinity*; they generally appear under the guise of caring for the female (*infantilising*), which excuses such actions even while they amount to the diminishment of agency, the negation of personal narrative (*gaslighting*), coercive control; ultimately the annihilation of the (her) self's identity, by some means — either metaphorically or literally killing her entirely.

> The heroin of the marital Gothic… will always reawaken to the still-present actuality of her trauma because the gender expectations that deny her identity are woven in the very fabric of her culture, which perpetuates her trauma while denying its existence. (Masse, 1990)

Central to these stories is the family home and the container of all inside. The house-container's physical interior reflects the protagonists' mental interiority. As the one sphere in which women were allowed agency, even as they were confined to it, this is seen as inherently feminine. In these stories, the echoing reflection of self and mind takes us further into the realm of the uncanny, and it is worth pausing for a moment to contemplate, here, quite what *the uncanny* might be.

Most readers will have a residual memory of the meaning as per Freud's essay of 1919, which concludes, roughly, by defining the feeling of this particular sensation as something "off" within the familiar—something unknown lurking within the everyday, something unhomely in the home—and that was certainly my understanding.

Returning now to Freud's essay, I see his argument pursues two routes in his attempt to explain this perceptual phenomenon — the semantic route (in which uncanny = unhomely), and a series of examples from literature, of the uncanny. Here are dolls that come to life; later, the idea of the double, or doppelganger; here is omniscience, coincidence, and prescience, as well as common-or-garden ghosts and hauntings.

In all of these, he posits that the uncanny effect is caused by a repressed primitive or childlike belief that has been *surmounted* by the rational mind but is still being entertained by the unconscious. In certain moments, either the repressed or a memory of the repressed emerges, causing this particular feeling of dissonance in which the familiar is spookily "un"familiarised.

While I find great power in his central argument that the cause of this feeling is a clashing and simultaneous duality in which the familiar and unfamiliar meet, his list of etymological examples and literature largely takes us out of the home. This otherness of home (a place to go or think of going, not a place to be) is a masculine view:

> …if someone dreams of a certain place or a certain landscape and, while dreaming, thinks to himself, "I know this place, I've been here before", this place can be interpreted as representing his mother's genitals or her womb. Here too, then, the uncanny [the "unhomely"] is what was once familiar ["homely"]. (Freud, 1919/2003)

In this one paragraph, "someone" is, of course, "He." *His* mother, *His* mother's womb, *His* longing to go home. He is outside, and if he dreams of something familiar, he is not simply dreaming of the comfort of home's familiarity; he is dreaming of home's synonymity with the availability of feminine comfort (be that sexual or infantile).

This dominant construct, in which the home is a feminine gendered space for the enjoyment and sanctuary of the male (member), begs the question: where do women return or retreat to, then? Logically, it relegates women (those of the invisible hands, c.f. Bachelard's cupboard) to the status of metaphorical homelessness. It is not a place to which women go; it is simply a place where they are.

Figure 24. The Strand Magazine cover (1919)

[Photograph] (https://lmcc.web.unc.edu/wp-content/uploads/sites/3253/2023/03/Moberly_Inexplicable-Strand-Magazine-1917.pdf)

Similarly, women are largely invisible in the sources that Freud analyses in his essay, in which Freud's ideas of homeliness are largely illustrated by fictions unfolding outside the home. Although, on close reading, one story in his list stood out to me as it was of the home, and indeed, that turned out to be the sliver of an indication of the popular genre of horror / gothic and feminine gothic.

His summary and analysis of that piece, which appeared in the Strand Magazine in July 1917 and was by L. G. Moberly ("G" is for Gertrude) he gives less than a paragraph; he does not give the title or author's name, calling it a "naïve" story. Nevertheless, the tale has been sufficiently and uncannily memorable to him to slip into his roll call of "proper" literature (Goethe, Hoffman, Schiller, etc.).

It seems to me that Freud, blinkered by the cultural assumptions of his time, (almost) misses what to many now looks like one deep vein of uncanny demonstration — the one so readily available in the Feminine Gothic, in which women's desires to get out of the home, to operate, with agency, outside the realm of the domestic are both oppressed/repressed and emerge in twisted visions of domesticity gone awry.

In this type of fiction, the literature rarely confronts, directly, the difficult sexual politics of the time, as to do so would risk the precariously granted license to write at all; such tales need to creep about under the veil of romantic horror, appealing to an audience of women (and therefore readily dismissed in contemporaneous hegemonic critique).

Charlotte Gilman's "The Yellow Wallpaper" is a prime example of this metaphorical creeping, one of the most explicit in its depiction of a woman contained "for her own good" in one room of the home: ultimately, she, in her mind, escapes via the patterned wallpaper of the containing room:

I kept on creeping just the same, but I looked at him over my shoulder.
"I've got out at last," said I, "in spite of you...." (Gilman, 1892)

Figure 25. Watercolour from the collection

These repressions, as internalised cultural norms, seem to me to be the literary equivalents of what I see in that sign of the unsigned in the collected works in the archive.

It speaks to me of a disguise or mask. Cloaked in saccharine ornamentation, passed only as a sign of social ties — the level of accomplishment to reflect upon the "owning" patriarch — what is hidden or repressed becomes more visible by its repetition in the collection; the desire to make a mark, to transcend the confines of the parlour and participate in the world on a fair footing; the temerity to wield the brush or the pen in earnest.

I remember my grandmother telling me of the art classes she had taken, in which, as women, participating in a *life class* meant drawing animals, as it was not considered "seemly" for women to draw naked people. We both laughed at the enormity of the barrier to competence that such a restriction had imposed; she said, "The chickens were the worst."

(I have not heard of such a practice from any other source; I cannot corroborate it, but it remains a very clear memory.)

Figure 26. Page from a Victorian scrapbook/sketchbook, c. 1870s

Flowering Out

I will not discuss further how my story fulfils either the conditions of a gothic novel or those necessary for uncanny effect.

Instead, I would like to tell you about *Flowering Out*, a practice I developed in my earlier work to get around the difficulty I encounter in the development of my benign narrative, that of preserving the beloved and excising the "other":

I had been struggling for a while with my inclination to confide in these pages my father's poorer actions towards me, Kitty, my mother, and other women while at the same time wanting to unremember / not know / hide those realities. There is a guilt attached to speaking ill of others, especially once they are dead... There are profound societal pressures to edit the unpleasant from any account.[14]

It was something I found when contemplating the unpleasant cathexic effect upon me of images that contained my stepfather:

I considered the usual strategies for removals and obfuscations so often seen in dramas where scissors are wielded, or images are ripped. However, being loath to damage the photographs, I try some digital manipulations.

Through this experimentation, I arrived at an appealing solution — one in which I can get around the image of *Darling Edward* without obliterating or spoiling the image entirely, for there are members of his / my family that I adored in those pictures, all taken at a point as then untainted by what he would later go on to do.

I re-use — digitally — floral images from the archive. The effect, I find, is odd, but pleasant.

It has a visual equivalency to much that I do psychically, in my own thoughts, and socially — in how I am able to speak of my happy memories and my dear Aunt Kitty. It is remarkably effective, and in it, I find a great but subtle revisionary power, one in which all those ladies' hidden works now come to a fore, their polite compliance and humility pressed, perhaps, into something resembling — possibly —their own origins and determined, cheerful, survival.

Figure 27. Digitally altered photograph

CONCLUSION

Once, when I visited Kitty, an animatronic cat had been placed on the table in front of her. She devoted much of her time to the cat during that visit, more so than me; I was somewhat dismayed, of course, but I joined in with the petting. As I did, the unreality of the cat diminished and became convincing — soon, I was as convinced as Kitty. I entered the cat/Kitty world, crossing over via another proscenium-like trick, one in which we became part of the imaginary, the world of dreams and memories rather than that dim vestige of it that we all carry within us in our normal waking moments.

This strange morphing from reality to unreality, from imaginary to real, typifies what I will remember as this *Finding Time*, a time in which Kitty and the objects from my long-lost past emerged out of my imagination and placed themselves firmly back in reality.

These moments of emergence have, for me, stitched themselves together in a tapestry that I have tried to unpick by taking apart the textual/textural threads of time, context, history, and meaning, to make my own sense of it and a tellable story of it; a journey of remembering via the archive's objects.

As Annette Kuhn points out, this kind of remembering results in texts (even recounting with that inner voice is textual). These texts (my own being just more examples) have a characteristic temporal quality; time is cyclical (*repeating*), extended or contracted (*elastic*), fused together (*immutable*). This kind of time is illogical; its imagery snapshotted, *mise-en-scene*.

That recounting seeks an audience, starting — usually — with the family audience. That oral recounting between family members is a binding ritual, one that, itself, changes over time. The early recountings in a young family are light-hearted recitations of blunders and sweetness; anecdotal evidence of character, acceptance, belonging. Changing over time, they turn into — as Kuhn points out — mythical invocations of the past that carry with them (as the family ages) the heaviness of historical distance, longing and loss.

The social need to reclaim that kind of mythical narrative for myself was a key driver in both this work and previous work. My first attempt, in an earlier work, reflected my Derridean delight in becoming the new owner of the archive (*The Archon,* so grand), but it left me not fully satisfied, unable to identify the missing part or reason I felt it missing. It was this dissatisfaction that led to such a labyrinthine, thread-following approach here.

By following the most prescient of those threads from the archive — in truth, perhaps, better described as an assemblage with multitudinous rhizomatic possibilities — I have satisfied much of my desire to make a tellable story, one that not only harnesses that emergent imagery within its structure, but also one that explains the real-life culmination of the drama and includes the motivations behind the actions of the major *dramatis personae*; the "how" of "how things turned out as they did."

Although not all told here (and much never tellable in full), I have that tale now, one that is benign to my psyche, if not in all its contents. I can forget and obfuscate (Flower Out) as well as remember; I have achieved the kind of authorial omniscience a memory-teller is entitled to:

> Telling and retelling their memories is one of the strategies people use not only to make sense of the world, but to create their own world and to give themselves and others like them a place, a place of some dignity and worth, within it. (Kuhn, 1995/2002)

While we live, we continue to accrue memories, but the kind of mythical, oft-recounted tales of our stories of our *becoming* are now our origin stories, the foundational backdrop to whatever next-step memorial tales might arise. Because once one's identity has been laid down in the myth, what happens next will be, in part, shaped by one's reactions in line with that identity. Crucial to the satisfactory development of the original story is not just the factual evidence or memory; it is the social recounting and the memory of that accepted remembrance.

It seems to me nothing short of cannily providential that I had that short time, within the larger *Finding Time*, with Kitty, and even although she had become but *the very essence of herself,* we were able to perform that familial myth-building storytelling together, at last. And we did this many, many times: starting always at the front door (of 19 College Road), we soon got to the sitting room — an eternal, mythical sitting room where:

the dog is by the grate, the fire is down-to-embers, the air is hung with motes.
  verbena…
      honeysuckle…
          terracotta…
              coal…

Figure 28. The back of the Dolls' House

FUTURE RESEARCH DIRECTIONS

My next piece of research is to visit *Stourport, Kidderminster, Areley Kings* and *Hartlebury*. I want to see those red-brick houses, the canal basin, the common. How it is now, on the hill where Bleak House stood. How near or far is everything; what is the experience of getting from A to B there? It is always rewarding to identify the old in the new, and I have many old photographs to reference. I don't know what I will do with the knowledge I glean from this expedition; it may just reside in the next layer of memories.

I would like to look into future work that addresses the loss of access to memory objects for individuals, such as the recent MIRRA Project (Memory—Identity—Rights in Records—Access) at UCL (see https://blogs.ucl.ac.uk/mirra/about/). Perhaps the method I have developed can be used for others to develop their own narratives, which are vital in building one's idea of self.

I do have inklings of some ambition to move the mainstream narratives of interior design; currently, they seem to be either centred around images of aspirational interiors or the cult-like activity of "decluttering," while little attention is paid to the normal, the everyday. How a home is created through its contents and the stories it tells to all who enter or live in it; the very importance of cluttering. I think a book on this subject would sit well on a coffee table, at least in my own interior scheme.

REFERENCES

Attfield, J. (2005). *Wild things: The material culture of everyday life*. Berg.

Burns, S. (2012). 'Better for haunts': Victorian houses and the modern imagination *American Art*, 26(3), 2–25. 10.1086/669220

Chatman, S. (1974). Genette's analysis of narrative time relations. *L'Esprit Créateur*, 14(4), 353–368.

Derrida, J. (1996). *Archive fever: A Freudian impression* (Prenowitz, E., Trans.). University of Chicago Press.

Dickens, C. (1853). *Bleak house* (Bradbury, N., Ed.). Penguin.

Facebook. (n.d.). *Areley Kings Windmill and Bleak House*. We love Stourport-on-Severn past and present day. https://www.facebook.com/search/top?q=bleak%20house%20stourport

Freud, S. (2005). *Forgetting things*. Penguin. (Original work published 1901)

Freud, S., & McLintock, D. (2003). *The uncanny*. Penguin. (Original work published 1919)

Gibson, M. (2004). Melancholy objects. *Mortality*, 9(4), 365–376. 10.1080/13576270412331329812

Gilbert, E. (2021). *The signature of all things*. Bloomsbury Publishing.

Gilbert, S. M., & Gubar, S. (2000). *The Madwoman in the attic: The woman writer and the nineteenth-century literary imagination*. Yale University Press.

Gilman, C. P. (2012). *The yellow wallpaper*. Virago. (Original work published 1892)

Hammersley, M., & Atkinson, P. (2007). *Ethnography: Principles and practice*. Routledge.

Heller, T. (1997). Textual seductions: Women's reading and writing in Margaret Oliphant's "The library window.". *Victorian Literature and Culture*, 25(1), 23–37. 10.1017/S1060150300004605

Ibsen, H. (2010). *The works of Henrik Ibsen*. Kessinger Pub.

Kuhn, A. (2002). *Family secrets: Acts of memory and imagination*. Verso.

Massé, M. A. (1990). Gothic repetition: Husbands, horrors, and things that go bump in the night. *Signs (Chicago, Ill.)*, 15(4), 679–709. 10.1086/494624

Mayer, J. (2019). *Goldness House*. Fine & Country Stourbridge and Kidderminster. https://www.youtube.com/watch?v=duucCoPs8uk/

Moberly, L. G. (1917). Inexplicable. *The Strand*, 54(319), 572–581. https://lmcc.web.unc.edu/wp-content/uploads/sites/3253/2023/03/Moberly_Inexplicable-Strand-Magazine-1917.pdf

Murray, J. (n.d.). *History of Kidderminster Medical Society*. Kidderminister Medical Society. https://www.kidderminstermedicalsociety.co.uk/history_of_kms.htm

Poulos, C. N. (2021). *Essentials of autoethnography*. American Psychological Association. 10.1037/0000222-000

Prown, J. D. (1982). Mind in matter: An introduction to material culture theory and method. *Winterthur Portfolio*, 17(1), 1–19. 10.1086/496065

Ratekin, T. (2005). Allon White tracks down himself: Criticism as autobiography in "too close to the bone.". *CEA Critic*, 67(2), 62–75.

Richardson, L. (1994).Writing: A method of inquiry. In *Handbook of qualitative research* (pp. 923-948). N. K. Sage Publications, Inc.

Stewart, S. (2007). *On longing: Narratives of the miniature, the gigantic, the souvenir, the collection.* Duke University Press.

Watton, C. (2020, April 24). *Using scrapbooks as historical sources.* History Journal. https://historyjournal .org.uk/2019/12/16/using-scrapbooks-as-historical-sources/

Watton, C. (2022). Suffrage scrapbooks and emotional histories of women's activism. *Women's History Review*, 31(6), 1028–1048. 10.1080/09612025.2021.2012343

Watton, C. (n.d.). The radical history of scrapbooks – and why activists still use them today. *The Conversation.*https://theconversation.com/the-radical-history-of-scrapbooks-and-why-activists-still-use -them-today-172581

Woolf, V., & Minogue, S. (2012). *A room of one's own & The voyage out.* Wordsworth Classics. (Original work published 1928)

York House Medical Centre. (n.d.). *A Guide for Patients, Practice History.* My Surgery Website. www .mysurgerywebsite.co.uk. https://www.mysurgerywebsite.co.uk/website/M81040/files/PRACTICE _BOOKLET_13.11.14.pdf

KEY TERMS AND DEFINITIONS

Archon: In Derrida's discourse on the Archive as instrument of power, taken from an account of the Greek city state, the *Archon* is a magistrate, the owner of the *Arkhe* or Archive. In these theories, the Archive is the source of structural power, the resource of formal records for governance of the state; it is made, kept, and owned by the state.

Caxethis: A Freudian term for the psychic charge or emotional stimulus attached to objects that represent, in some way, a person. In the case of a photograph, this is the image of that person.

Inklings and Darklings: I use inkling in standard fashion, but in the creative note-writing, I invented *darklings*. They are the darker sort of inkling, obviously closely related to darlings, but on the more difficult side, as in memories of an aberrant family circumstance or event. They are often busy in the *underberg*.

Material Culture: The material objects and artefacts that surround us in the world and that can be used to understand a culture through various means of analysis. The term is most widely used in archaeology and anthropology; however it is also of interest within the context of design history.

Memory Work: The name Annette Kuhn gives to the act of conscious remembering undertaken in conjunction with contemplation of a photograph.

Rift Time and Finding Time: Following the precedent set in Elizabeth Gilbert's book, *The signature of all things*, I called the time of the rift between my parents and Kitty — and forced upon myself — *Rift Time*, while *Finding Time* is the time of our reacquaintance and my discovery of the familial archive.

Underberg: A word I invented to give metaphorical shape to the unconscious in my creative notes. Like Kitty, I took a course in counselling skills; Freud's concept of the psyche was explained to us as being like an iceberg, the top third above water being the conscious, the bottom two-thirds being the submerged unconscious. The Underberg, therefore, is the submerged part.

ENDNOTES

[1]   This was a lie. I found out, as a young adult, that I had not been adopted; my parents had changed my name by deed poll only. I do not think my grandparents or aunt ever knew that truth. Indeed, it was such an entrenched lie that my "father" included it in his eulogy [*lorem ipsum dolor sit amet, phasellus at consequat erat*].

[2]   I was not a blood-relative and had been cut-off from Kitty for so long, I felt at first that I was not really "family" and therefore was, possibly, intruding. But this changed; not only through the reconnection with Kitty, but also through that confirmation which I found in the archive, which gave me the secure knowledge that I had been considered a "real" grandchild / niece, just as per my childhood recollections.

[3]   When I, as a child, played with that Dolls' House, did I unwittingly trigger memories of that rivalry? Did that start the [*luctus lobortis*] of Kitty and myself in Ted's mind?

[4]   She died of an illness, something like 'flu.' This was a story Ted told me several times; she was at boarding school, no-one believed she was ailing badly except her sister, who escaped to alert their father, the doctor. Very sadly, he arrived too late. *Nor* had been my grandmother's closest sibling, and Nor, Granny, and Teddy (Edward's namesake) were the three "golden" children, Granny and Teddy remaining close throughout their lives. Philip fared badly in Ted's stories; having suffered the after-effects of mustard gas from his time in the War; he developed later-life fantasies towards his own [*lorem*], who, understandably, "rejected him" (verbatim), which led directly to his [*ipsum*]. The archive confirms his sudden death, in the '60s.

[5]   Stanley Baldwin, 1st Earl of Bewdley, former three times Prime Minister.

[6]   Although I now hear it was referred to as a "Villa".

[7]   And here is mine.

[8]   But I see they made a kind gift shortly after, sharing the inheritance 60:40 with the other family. Not that any of it mattered finally, the money was re-invested in Bond Worth shares and lost in the collapse.

[9]   This loss occurs at least a decade later than the one made visible by the downward trajectory apparent in the move from Goldness.

[10] Possibly, now I see how much paper over how many years, this had a profound effect upon Ted. He certainly played havoc with [*nascetur ridiculus mus. Mauris sed velit*] was safely dead and then we all saw what a [*consectetur adipiscing*] he really was.

[11] I was told, a long time ago, that Granny was on the fringes of the Bloomsbury Set, and also that she knew the Pankhursts. I do not know how much any of this, told to me in Ted's "humble brags", is true, but I do remember that in primary school or early secondary, I once sat down with Granny

and a tape recorder to capture her reminiscences for a school project, and that she corroborated at least some of these stories. What came of the resulting tape (Ted threw all of that and all of my childhood photographs away), I do not know, and all I remember is that yes, some of this was true, but then I think she went on to talk more about her involvement in the strikes of the '20s, a lot about bringing tea and sandwiches and fundraising efforts — only an impression remains (I imagine Uncle Stanley would not have been impressed by her participation, which, it seems might rather have spurred her on). I have not yet found anything in the archive to support these memories.

[12] Ted's letter sent from Africa announcing his marriage plans to his mother, reads: "...and I think you will like her very much. Unfortunately, however, there is a child..."

[13] Ted had prepared an extra surprise for me upon [*tempor in morbi*]. Unfortunately, even as I write, these [*sed velit hendrerit*] are still in train.

[14] It appears to me that the whole archive has been quite carefully edited by previous guardians, I imagine due to the very same pressures.

Chapter 6
Re–Echoing the Scream:
Rod Dickinson's Shock Machine and the Re-Emergence of Milgram's "Obedience to Authority" Experiments

Bernadette Buckley
Goldsmiths' University of London, UK

ABSTRACT

This chapter considers the power of art to capture the dynamism of memory as it bounces between past, present and emergent future. In so doing, it focuses centrally on Rod Dickinson's The Milgram Re-enactment, 2002 – a performative and video re-enactment of Stanley Milgram's 'Obedience to Authority' experiments of 1962, in which "participants were asked to give apparently lethal electric shocks to an unwilling victim to test how far they would be prepared to obey an authoritative scientist and inflict pain on a protesting person" (Dickinson). What matters, the chapter argues, is less what memory 'remembers,' but how it is put to work as an inventive force in another time and context. Foreshadowing Weizman's interpretation of the Siege of Gaza, 2007 as an "inverse Milgram experiment," Dickinson's work is thus positioned as both re-enactment and pre-enactment of procedural Holocausts to come, and memory is explored as an active operant condition that continues to influence perspectives on as well as policy and conduct in the continuing and current conflict in the Gaza Strip.

INTRODUCTION

Whilst 're-enactment' has long since existed in a myriad of forms (religious rituals, civil and world war re-enactments, courtroom and crime scene re-enactments; live action role-play, heritage and TV re-enactments etc.), it is only in relatively recent times that it has emerged as worthy of 'serious' scholarly attention. Having drawn interest as a legitimate object of concern for ethnographers and educationalists of all stripes, more recently, re-enactment has taken "a decisive shift" towards performative and artistic studies (Agnew et al, 2020, p. 7). Though it is beyond the scope of this chapter to track this development in any detail,[1] it is necessary to acknowledge that re-enactment – which remains relatively oblique as an epistemological object – has become increasingly characterised by "parallel processes and interdisciplinary entanglements" (Otto, 2019, p. 111). It now stretches across a shifting set of practices and

DOI: 10.4018/979-8-3693-2264-2.ch006

research studies that include art (of all kinds, including film, TV, theatre, performance and digital media), history and memory studies, political discourse, ritual, popular and narrative practices. Additionally, and importantly, re-enactment sits between 'the past' (from which we are necessarily distanced) and its creative, somatic or mediatised interpretation in the present (the latter of which is in a process of infinite regress). For these reasons, re-enactment is perfectly situated to stage an encounter between the scholarly insights of political, social and critical theory on the one hand and a plethora of performative, historical and activist concerns and practices, on the other.

For many years, Rod Dickinson's artwork, which is the main focus of this chapter, has been central to emerging practices and debates around re-enactment. Originally shown in Glasgow in 2002, *The Milgram Re-enactment*, Dickinson's work featured prominently in Inke Arns' and Gabriele Horn's major exhibition featuring artistic re-enactments. It was highlighted both in the exhibition at the KW Institute for Contemporary Art, Berlin, 2007, and in a subsequent publication entitled *History will repeat itself*. [2] Since then, Dickinson's work has been widely re-exhibited [3] and discussed by scholars from diverse fields including psychology, history, performance, politics and art. [4] Thanks to its rigorous reconstruction of the Milgram's original experiment, it is even frequently used as a primary resource for undergraduate programmes in Psychology wishing to introduce students to Milgram's work. [5]

However, and despite its widening interest to scholars of all kinds, questions remain as to how specifically, artistic re-enactments, as distinct from other forms, exist "in contradistinction to more conventional forms of re-enactment" (Arns, 2019, p. 198) and whilst it is often agreed that artistic re-enactments tend to expose the "constructedneess of mediation" (Benzaquen-Gautier, 2019, p. 17) in ways that open the past up to changing perspectives in the present (Verwoert, 2009, p. 31), the question of how this "transformative power" (Benzaquen-Gautier, 2019, p. 17) actually *operates* is seldom probed in detail. For this reason, the current chapter sets out to demonstrate not just that re-enactment necessarily differs from any (supposed to be) 'authentic' events of the past, but also to detail how artistic re-enactments can actively address and intervene into specific concerns in the present. The value of Dickinson's *The Milgram Re-enactment,* it is argued here, is that it offers a vital means by which to perform memory as a mode of immanent critique – to produce a form of 'anti-memory' that speaks to the present and the future, as well as the past.

The chapter responds to these questions in three distinct parts. First, it is necessary to outline Dickinson's re-enactment of Stanley Milgram's controversial 'Obedience to Authority' experiment of 1962, and in tandem with this, Milgram's 'original' test, which set out to explore obedience "as a determinant of behaviour" (Milgram 2010, p. 19). How far, Milgram wanted to know, were ordinary people prepared to go in compliance with authority? (Milgram, 2010, p. 23) Would they go so far as to administer (apparently) deadly electric shocks to other human beings? Milgram's experiments are therefore complicated by his own understanding of them as a kind of coded re-working (re-enactment) of the Holocaust relative to the production of present and future "malevolent systems of authority" and "destructive processes" (Milgram, 2010, pp. 205, 197). The relationship between Milgram's 'original' and Dickinson's 're-enacted' event is therefore not governed by any straightforward temporal sequencing but functions instead like a series of rebounding echoes, the origin and end points of which, are equally uncertain.

For this reason, the second part of the chapter moves on to pay close attention to the alterations and echoes that occur when Dickinson reconstructs Milgram's experiment for spectators in an art gallery. How does this shift in register from social psychology to artistic experiment trigger new 'echoes', not only of the past but of the becoming future? Here the discussion calls attention to the role of aesthetic devices in producing dehumanising effects *and* at the same time, paradoxically, opportunities for deeper self reflection about the "dilemma" of obedience to authority (Milgram, 2020, pp. 19-19) and how it can be resisted.

The third and final part of the chapter explores in detail how Dickinson's work provokes an active engagement with and a refraction of the performative nature of violence in larger cultural and geo-political contexts. In so doing, it speaks not only directly to the memory of the Holocaust, but to ongoing and repeated conflicts in Gaza. By re-situating Milgram's experiment at a different moment and context, Dickinson's work allows us to better understand the *imminence* of 'Holocaust memory' in ways that Milgram himself anticipated. Here we explore and expand on Eyal Weizman's notion of the Siege of Gaza (2007) as "an inverse Milgram experiment" (Weizman, 2012, p. 87) and finally, the implications of this move in relation to the current Israel-Hamas crisis (2023-). It is the deeply anarchic and anachronistic energy of artistic re-enactments, the chapter concludes, that allows us to see that re-enactment does not merely interrupt the temporal sequence but produces an active form of 'anti-memory' – a force that calls for our persistent intervention into and re-invention of the becoming future.

BACKGROUND

To unwind this knot of issues, it is necessary to briefly outline Dickinson's *The Milgram Re-enactment*, 2002 – a painstakingly reproduced live performance lasting three hours, forty-five minutes. Staging an exact facsimile of the layout, doors, windows, curtains, chairs, microphone and electro-shock equipment used in the Yale Interaction Laboratory where Milgram worked, Dickinson assiduously recreates one of the variants of Milgram's 'original' experiments, using archival documents and film. [6] Milgram's now-legendary experiment is thus re-built – part by part, lever by lever, word for word – to produce an iteration that is as true to the original undertaking as possible and by so doing, to re-stage Milgram's aim "to objectively monitor perceptions of human morality in the face of authoritative direction" (Gaskin, 2002, n. p.). Understanding that the experiment relies on aesthetic as well as scientific dimensions, Dickinson now executes, as an artwork, a real time reconstruction of the past that is read, necessarily, from the perspective of the present, thus demonstrating an involuting force that spins on and out in unpredictable echoes of itself.

However, the analysis of *how* Dickinson's artwork echoes, refracts and projects Milgram's 'original' experiment into new contexts, times and situations, itself requires a backstory, including a more detailed account of the mechanics and objectives of the original 'Obedience to Authority' experiments – which even today, remain some of the most widely cited and provocative experiments in social psychology. As already indicated and is now well known, Milgram's research was primarily designed to test levels of compliance and obedience in unsuspecting adult volunteers (subjects). Those recruited [7] were advised that they would be participating in an experiment, the purpose of which would be to help researchers determine the effects of punishment on memory and learning. The subjects were told that they would be playing the role of a 'teacher' in the experiment. They were introduced to other (perceived-to-be unbriefed) participants called 'learners', who unbeknownst to them, were in fact, Milgram's collaborators and not the trusting volunteer-subjects they *appeared* to be.

This set-up was 'explained' to the subjects by an authority figure known as 'the experimenter' who was present and observant at all times in the laboratory. Presenting himself as a 'scientific' specialist, complete with requisite lab-coat, the experimenter conveyed to the subjects of the experiment a strong sense of legitimacy, authority and credibility. For example, his expertise was quickly and credibly established via the provision of a research context for the experiment. He quickly explained that the expectation was that…

…a form of punishment will teach the child to remember better, will teach him to learn more effectively (Milgram, 2010, p. 35).

The experimenter then followed through by providing instructions as to how the experiments would proceed: subjects (teachers) would supply one half of a pre-determined word-pair. Sitting in an adjacent room (Figure 1) concealed by curtains, learners (Milgram's collaborators) would then need to correctly provide the other half of the word-pair.

Figure 1. Rod Dickinson, The Milgram Re-enactment, 2002

(Image reproduced by kind permission of the artist)

The experimenter explained that learners would communicate their answers by pressing one of four switches, which would light up on an 'answer box' located in the teacher's room, on top of the shock-machine (Figure 2).

Figure 2. The reconstructed shock machine

Rod Dickinson, The Milgram Re-enactment, 2002
(Image reproduced by kind permission of the artist)

If the learner (as the subject/ teacher unknowingly believed him to be) failed to supply the right answer, it was the subject's (teacher's) job to administer him/her with an electric shock.

Prior to the start of the experiment, the subject was taken into the adjacent room (Figure 3) and shown how 'learners' would be bound to an 'electric chair' using straps designed to "prevent excessive movement" (Milgram, 2010, p. 36). When the learner gave an incorrect answer, it would be the subject's job to administer an electric shock. To strengthen the subject's belief in the authenticity of the shock-generator, s/he was given a sample shock of 45 volts applied to the wrist.

Figure 3. The 'learner' being strapped into an electric chair by the 'scientist', whilst the subject/ teacher watches

Rod Dickinson, The Milgram Re-enactment, 2002 (Image reproduced by kind permission of the artist)

The teacher was then conveyed next door and instructed in the use of the shock-machine, the latter of which had 30 levers set in a horizontal line and clearly labelled with increasing intensity levels ranging from 'Slight Shock' (15 volts) to 'Danger: Severe Shock' (450 volts). (Figure 4) Two further switches were marked 'XXX'.

Figure 4. The reconstructed shock machine (detail)

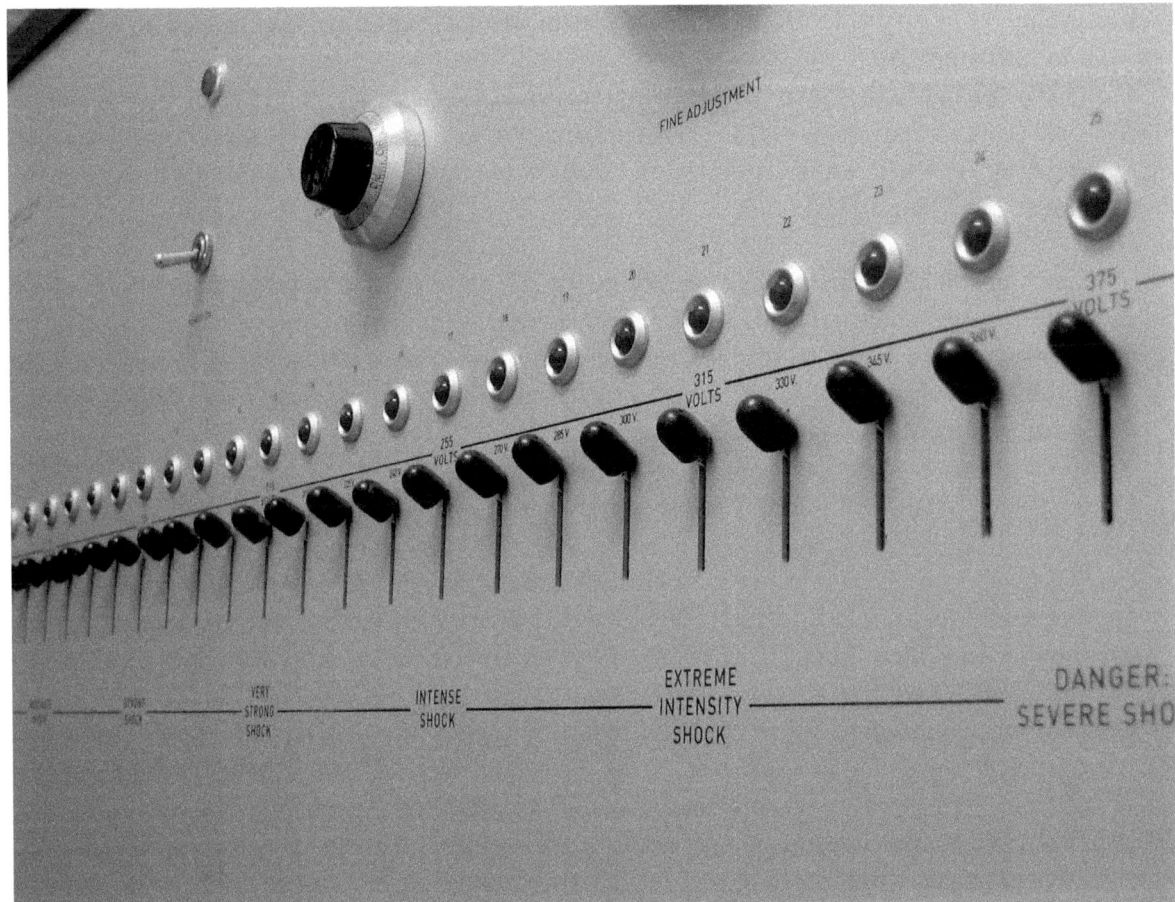

Rod Dickinson, The Milgram Re-enactment, 2002 (Image reproduced by kind permission of the artist)

When a switch was pulled, a corresponding red light was illuminated; an electric blue light labelled 'voltage energiser' flashed; the meter swung to the right and various relay clicks were sounded (Milgram, 2010, p. 37). The subject was instructed to announce the voltage level before administering the shock. As the intensity of shocks increased, s/he would hear the learner's whimpers, then cries, followed by shrieks of pain, pounding protests and sounds of agony, until eventually, after a voltage of 350 volts was delivered, only silence remained. If the subject questioned the wisdom of continuing, s/he would be urged by the scientist to proceed, using one of a number of pre-scripted prompts, including:

"Prod 1: Please continue, *or*, Please go on.
Prod 2: The experiment requires that you continue.
Prod 3: It is absolutely essential that you continue.
Prod 4: You have no other choice, you must go on" (Milgram, 2010, p. 38).

Of course, no electric shocks were actually delivered and the cries of pain that the subject/ teacher heard coming from the adjoining room whenever an incorrect answer was given, were in fact, the recorded screams of an affable Irish-American accountant who had been especially trained for his role as the 'victim' (Milgram, 2010, p. 33).

Prior to completion of these experiments, Milgram conducted a survey asking psychiatrists, graduate students and faculty in the behavioural sciences to predict how subjects of the experiment would respond. As subsequently reported, respondents expected that "virtually all subjects would refuse to obey the experimenter" (Milgram, 1973, p. 62):

"only a pathological fringe, not exceeding 1 or 2%, was expected to proceed to the end of the shockboard....[psychiatrists] predicted that most subjects would not go beyond the 10th shock level (150 volts, when the victim makes his first explicit demand to be freed); about 4% would reach the 20th shock level and about one subject in a thousand would administer the highest shock on the board." (Milgram, 2010, p. 48)

Contrary to expectations however, these predictions turned out to be entirely wrong:

"Of the forty subjects in the first experiment, twenty-five obeyed orders to the end, punishing the victim until they reached the most potent shock level available on the generator. After 450 volts were administered three times, the experimenter called a halt to the session." (Milgram, 1973, p. 62)

Clearly, some subjects did resist, or attempted to resist. Milgram describes how for example, Gretchen Brandt, a medical technician (in Experiment 8) who worked at the University Medical School and had emigrated from Germany five years previously, refused to administer the required 210 volts (Milgram, 2010, p. 102). Others demonstrated signs of strain, doubt or dissent, without being able, as Milgram put it, to galvanise the inner resources necessary to go beyond polite verbal exchanges and turn dissent into fully disobedient action (Milgram, 2010, p. 181).[8] Ultimately however, nearly two thirds of the subjects did as instructed and were "fully obedient". [9]

Milgram After Eichmann After Arendt After Milgram

Milgram, the son of Jewish immigrants from Hungary and Romania, had been profoundly impacted and shaped by his Jewish heritage and the atrocities of the Holocaust. He discussed this in later writings, acknowledging that:

"[My] laboratory paradigm . . . gave scientific expression to a more general concern about authority, a concern forced upon members of my generation, in particular upon Jews such as myself, by the atrocities of World War II " (Milgram, 2010, p. 119).

As Thomas Blass describes, at around the time Milgram was starting work on his experiments, he was profoundly aware of the fact that Adolf Eichmann – frequently referred to as 'the architect of the Holocaust' – had been captured in Argentina and was being flown to Israel for trial (Blass, 2004, p. 63).[10]

Milgram was also deeply influenced by Hannah Arendt's contention that the "prosecution's attempt to depict Eichmann as a sadistic monster was fundamentally wrong" (Milgram, 2010, p. 23). His book-length description of his experiments begins with an allusion to Hannah Arendt's *Eichmann in Jerusalem* in which he agrees with Arendt's conclusion that the "monstrous deeds carried out by Eichmann" were not so much those of a 'brutal, twisted...sadistic personality" but as Arendt claimed, that of "an uninspired bureaucrat who simply sat at his desk and did his job" (Milgram, 2010, p. 23).[11]

Of course Milgram openly acknowledged that the "authority system at work in the laboratory is less pervasive than the prepotent systems embodied in the totalitarian structures of Stalin and Hitler, in which sub-ordinates were profoundly submerged in their roles" (Lang, 2014, p. 173). Nevertheless, he insisted that his experiments demonstrated a similar 'agentic shift that caused otherwise "good people" to perform "harsh acts" (Lang, 2014, p. 141, 154).

In the intervening decades since Milgram's research, the contribution these experiments have made has been acknowledged as amongst the most significant and influential, prompting seminal changes to the practice and discipline of psychology and impacting on a variety of government, funding and military agencies (Nicholson, 2011b, p. 244). A staple of university programmes [12] and popular culture alike,[13] Milgram's experiments fuelled huge debate raising fundamental questions about ethical codes and moral conducts in war and ordinary life (Hale, 2020; Russell & Gregory, 2015; Nicholson, 2011a; Bauman, 2013; Benjamin & Simpson, 2009). This fact notwithstanding, Milgram's work has also been consistently criticised, going right back to Diana Baumrind's early critique of his methods in 1964, when she questioned the psychological distress caused to the subjects of Milgram's experiments, and his use of deception and lack of informed consent (Baumrind, 1964).

Other scholars have challenged the view that the Holocaust process was driven by obedient operators of a rigid hierarchical bureaucracy, pointing instead to the slave labour programmes operating in German-occupied territories and on the Eastern Front, where there was "a conscious and enthusiastic endorsement of the homicidal objectives of the Nazi regime" (Brannigan & Perry, 2016, p. 287; Allen, 2002; Bartov, 2001; Rothberg, 2019). The Holocaust they argue, required willing players committed to the use of 'human assets' in the dual task of war production and racial purification (Russell & Gregory, 2015). Still more scholars – Zygmunt Bauman for instance – follow Foucault in arguing that Milgram's work exemplifies the emergence of modern techniques of control: the "meticulous functional division of labour' in modern states, Bauman argues, has led to the "substitution of technical for a moral responsibility" (Bauman, 2007, p. 98).[14] This view is echoed by researchers who argue that Milgram's conclusions reflect "real processes" such as in Democratic Kampuchea (Cambodia during the Khmer Rouge years), when children were used by the regime, in a context of an already existing and deeply institutionalised culture of obedience, to fulfil its revolutionary mission (Pina e Cunha & Clegg, 2010).

Milgram After Dickinson: The Aesthetics of Dehumanisation and Affect

Despite the willingness of scholars to revisit Milgram's work from multiple perspectives, it is interesting that so much subsequent debate is concentrated in Psychology, the Social Sciences or historical research and, significant though these contributions may be, they have tended to ignore or occlude insights emerging from aesthetic and performative traditions. The echoes of Milgram's experiments that are gathered into Dickinson's *Re-enactment* however, allow us to take stock of important but overlooked issues, in ways that bear directly on the politics of memory, particularly in relation to traumatic 'limit events' (LaCapra, 2019).[15]

The first of these two neglected issues that *The Milgram Re-enactment* calls attention to, concerns the use of aesthetic devices that (paradoxically) on the one hand, help generate forms of estrangement linked with the processes of dehumanisation that frequently occur in conflict zones, but on the other, help generate affective experiences that prompt audiences to investigate something of (the pain of) their own potential compliance with societal controls and to ask searching questions about how resistant practices can be cultivated.

The second issue, explored towards the end of the essay, relates to the profoundly future-oriented qualities of Holocaust 'memory', which though often uncommented upon, Milgram himself clearly believed to be important. As I will show, Dickinson's work, by re-situating Milgram's experiment at a different moment and context, allows us to better understand the *imminence* of 'Holocaust memory' in ways that Milgram himself anticipated.[16] It thus allows us to see how in contemporary contexts, Milgram's experiments come to be inversed or scattered in spinning echoes of the 'originals'. To engage with *The Milgram Re-enactment* is not so much to 'remember' Milgram's work as it is to *transform* it. It is to accept that this transformation is in fact, the re-enactment's requisite task – the continued renewal of the past such that it remains vivid and meaningful in a new way. If, as Debarati Sanyal has it: "memory by definition entangles past with the present and fills the contemporary horizon with prior echoes," then re-enactment, as Dickinson's work shows, is memory on the move, taking us elsewhere, demanding new connections with the present (Sanyal, 2015, p. 17; Rothberg, 2009). *The Milgram Re-enactment*, as we shall see, is concerned, palpably and manifestly, with the transformation of the 'memory task'.

To explore the first of these two issues (the use of aesthetic devices in Milgram's and Dickinson's work) it is necessary to show how *The Milgram Re-enactment* foregrounds an *aesthetic* response to history and memory that is all too often bracketed off in advance, as if it is somehow less 'serious' than that which is *properly* 'political', historical, or 'scientific'. [17] It is sometimes difficult to fathom why this gnoseological pyramid persists, given that, as Fuller and Weizman observe (following Rancière) aesthetics is such a critical and influential epistemological space. As Fuller and Weizman note, sense-making itself depends on aesthetics, not as an philosophy of beauty, but as that which has "develop[ed] sensibilities of extremely careful looking" (Fuller, & Weizman, 2021, p. 14). As we shall see, Dickinson's *The Milgram Re-enactment* is sharply attuned to aspects of Milgram's work that remain foggy or entirely absent from most 'social scientific' discourse.

Consider for example, the fact that Milgram's experiment justifies itself *explicitly*, at least to the subjects of the experiments, in terms of 'memory'. Why then have scholarly discussions of the experiments so frequently glossed over the importance of this given 'pretext' beyond face value? By assuming that Milgram's 'memory-task' is simply a convenient subterfuge enabling him to justify the use of the shock machine in a 'scientific' context, scholars repeatedly fail to pay heed to what is after all, the experiment's central precept and framing device. Contrarily however, Dickinson's *The Milgram Re-enactment* makes it obvious to viewers that the 'memory task' is not incidentally but *literally*, part of the overall artistic artifice. It is never *not* exposed for what it is. We are never tricked (as Milgram's original subjects were) into thinking that memory failure can potentially be rectified through 'scientific' experiments that mete out punishment in increased measures (Rushton, 2003). Since the audience of the artwork can never confuse the performance with the 'original', Milgram's strategic use of 'memory' is, in Dickinson' re-enactment of it, immediately and self-evidently exposed as subject to (self-proclaimed) acts of aesthetic management and calculation. This is the whole basis on which Milgram is able to proceed. In *The*

Milgram Re-enactment however, Milgram's collusion with the managers of the 'memory task' is now literally displayed as an aesthetic event. Like all the other (fake) props deployed in the artwork, both memory and Milgram's mobilisation of it are *vaunted* as susceptible to modification.

In Twosome Twiminds: The Art of Memory-Echoes

It is worth remembering here that the ancient Greeks saw memory as one of the arts and sciences, as Frances Yates (1984) advises in her seminal work, *The Art of Memory* (p. 233).[18] The techniques of memory, like those of the arts, could be passed from practitioner to practitioner. One of the five parts of rhetoric, 'memory' was an 'art' that could be mastered, as Seneca did, to "repeat two thousand names in the order in which they had been given" (Yates, 1984, p. 2).[19] The analogy between Milgram's memory task and Seneca's is striking – in both cases, word series are meant to be memorised and repeated sequentially. In Seneca, as in Dickinson's treatment of Milgram's 'memory task', the *organisation* of 'memory' is entirely explicit. Memories can be stored, moved around, re-arranged. We can trick ourselves into remembering, depending on how we imagine particular memories being stored. The 'memory task' is therefore not merely the crooked mast to which Milgram's experiment is bound, but as *The Milgram Re-enactment* makes clear, it is also a kind of 'Chekhov's gun' – a plot device introduced early on in a drama, the significance of which does not become clear until presented to *audiences*. The 'memory task', we realise when encountering Dickinson's iteration of Milgram's experiment, is at once both *fictional* (fake) *and* necessary (a real device), but it can never aspire to anything more than an aesthetic investment in the forces of remembrance. Rather, it remains constantly responsive to the techniques through which it is recalled and imagined. For this reason, 'the memory task', as is the case with memory itself, remains unavoidably open to modelling.

Milgram's lab always *was*, as Dickinson's work now unequivocally *exhibits*, a mise en scène – complete with curtains, elaborately designed stage-set and actors with scripted, practiced lines. The experiments were *already* re-enactments – albeit coded ones – attempting to repeat something of the power and authority apparatuses of the 1930s. As Tom McCarthy had it:

> "Here was Milgram's artificiality both reproduced and elevated to another level: not only was Dickinson's laboratory not real, it was also not even properly fake. Nobody was expected to believe in the charade – and – to foreground this, Dickinson had given both the teacher's and the learner's rooms glass walls, so we could see the latter operating the machinery of deception, pressing the buttons that transmitted his pre-recorded cries" (McCarthy, 2003, p. 27).

Milgram's experimenter *dramatises* his power as a medical authority – by wearing a lab coat, or by pointing to a prominently positioned text that he declares, contains "the better-known theories" relevant to "our Memory Project" (Blass 2009, p. 77). But in Dickinson's re-enactment of the experiments, these dramatic devices are instantly recognisable as duplicitous – the sneaky set-dressing designed to underwrite the drama. What is (literally) exhibited to Dickinson's audience in other words, is 'artfulness' itself, in both senses of the term (both as cunning and as that of an aesthetic character).

Despite their being identical in every detail to Milgram's, Dickinson's props are now generating Joycean echoes: giving us "two thinks at a time", they put us in "twosome twiminds" (Joyce, 1999, pp. 583, 371). There is here an irreducible doubleness that again recalls those interfering echoes that clamour unharmoniously in some transitional state between existence and inexistence, before bouncing off in other directions. For not only are Dickinson's props exactly like Milgram's, they are also remarkably similar to the televised high drama of Eichmann's trial, when "the accused sat stoically in a bullet-proof glass enclosure, listening via headphones and translation to the accounts of horror for which he was responsible" (Benjamin & Simpson, 2009, p. 14).[20] Thus, as Dickinson' *Re-enactment* explicitly demonstrates, memory is that through which the aesthetic comes to be conflated with the historic. Here the circuit between memory, history, representation and event is radically porous, replete with inevitable, multidirectional anachronisms:

> "Not an event, or even an active interpretation of one, but rather a passive, anachronistic invocation of the very act of bearing witness – and an affirmation of our absolute, abject responsibility, to everything and everyone" (McCarthy, 2003, p. 32).

Echoes Over Time: 'Anachronising' Milgram

Anachronisms are, as Didi-Huberman (2007) well understood, 'images in motion' (pp. 7–19). Traditionally discredited, they are in fact, richly generative – operating at the interstices between memory and the imagining subject. They do not offer anchors against forgetting so much as they engender memory *effects* that constitute an active challenge to assumptions that memory and authenticity are necessarily linked. By accentuating the artfulness of Milgram's experiment, Dickinson's *Milgram Re-enactment* forces us to 'remember' our own ambiguous position as spectators: watching the test/performance unfold behind one-way glass windows, one 'think' oscillates with another (echo). Reflexively, one witnesses oneself watching, and with the increasingly painful awareness that we are only ever partly in control of what and how we see.

In Dickinson's handling of it, *seeing* has now become more complicated. Before our eyes, and without any alteration in design or appearance, the shock machine has become something other than it was. The alteration is not simply because, here in the performance space in Glasgow, a prop now stands in for a prop that once played a different role. But because, as Anne O' Byrne puts it, "appearance is always appearance *to*; seeing is always a seeing *of*" (O'Byrne, 2023, p. 26).

The Milgram Re-enactment forcefully demonstrates, in other words, that the operations of appearing, seeing and creating meaning from that which occurred in the past, are necessarily plural, variable and indeterminable, despite even the most scrupulous attempts at replication, authenticity and repetition. The past is not something we stumble upon and have to later make sense of – it is *instituted* within perspectives relative to our present and becoming world. This is how 're-enactment' induces investigation and interrogation rather than repetition or a literal reincarnation of the past. It is not a question of making real what has already occurred, but of holding open the space where we can start to work out what it is that we are 'seeing' when the 'facts' of the past appear to have been determined in advance by what appear to be definitive schema. If the operations of seeing are subject to manipulation by such 'arrangements', then *The Milgram Re-enactment* pressures us to ask how we can have knowledge of what appears, when what appears is always disrupted by time, or by the forceful perspectives of those who come before and after.

Welcome to the Heraclitean Fire Machine: Re-Enacting Procedural Holocausts to Come

This brings us to the second of the two neglected issues mentioned at the outset of the chapter, which Dickinson's *The Milgram Re-enactment* "draws attention to: i.e. the future-oriented qualities of Holocaust 'memory'. As we have seen, *The Milgram Re-enactment* does not so much *embed* memory as it *interrogates* it, by re-staging the experiments that, ostensibly at any rate, are contingent upon a 'memory task'. However, Dickinson's 're-enactment' conspicuously exceeds the epistemological framework within which 'memory' is situated. It releases the 'memory task' from a *particular* event and abstracts it in a way that ensures that that which has occurred can jump forward anachronistically into another time-frame and context. This shift facilitates and quickens the spectator's access to heterogeneous temporalities. It allows him/her to envisage 'memory' as that which is uncontrolledly restless and which therefore has the capacity to collide with the infinite ongoingness of the world. The echo does not reproduce sound but diffracts and unfastens it from its 'original' report, carrying it into future, still-unpredictable spaces of resonance and duration.

Dickinson's echoing of Milgram's echoing of the Holocaust thus offers a complex figure of repetition – incapable of duplication, it emits an itchy ricochet that bounces through multiple temporalities and vectors in an accelerated, infinitely regressing rejoinder. It energises and *activates* memory as an inventive, differentiating force, intensifying the shape of that which is yet to come. The screams resounding from Dickinson's re-enactors are no less frightening for the fact that the audience can clearly *see* the machinery of deception, the pressing of buttons that transmit the re-enactors' pre-recorded cries. But what troubles us most about *The Milgram Re-enactment* is that now the tension between the 'memory task' and punishment has become unambiguously *mechanised*. Shock, control, obedience have *literally* been arranged and regulated into repetitive sets of procedures that are plain to all. Not only this, but in a sly reiteration of Milgram's use of 'prods' to urge subjects to proceed with the experiment, Dickinson instructs invigilators that they should actively urge individual audience members *not* to leave the space until the end of the three hours and forty-five minutes' performance (R. Dickinson, personal communication, March 01, 2024). The doors have not been locked, but still, and of course, ironically, very few people challenge the invigilators' authority. Instead, confined to the installation space, which has been furnished with deliberately uncomfortable back-less benches, audiences resign themselves to watch the experiment being repeated over and over again for a full eight cycles, each iteration being played out in full, with different actors (Gaskin, 2003, p. 13).

In this context, the shock-machine is now operating in an entirely different way to Milgram's. It has been converted into a "Heraclitean fire machine" – as Deleuze once called Nietzsche's dream of a machine that would "release immense forces by small multiple manipulations" (Deleuze, 2006, p. 45). As audiences, we know for certain that no-one is being electrocuted in this re-enactment. Yet despite that knowledge, a terrifying shock is nonetheless produced, as it gradually dawns on us, at some stage during the eight cycles of *The Milgram Re-enactment*, that there are still more procedural Holocausts to come. In Dickinson's version of Milgram's version of the Holocaust, there is no Kantian-like, self-preservative step back to the safety of the secondary witness. The viewer is forced to play their role in what LaCapra calls the 'limit events' of history (LaCapra, 2009). "To remember, one must imagine", Didi-Huberman once said (Didi-Huberman, 2003, p. 30). And as audiences of Dickinson's *Re-enactment*, we slowly begin to recognise that this 'must' is a stipulation, not an opportunity. We cannot watch the experiment play out over and over again, without imagining ourselves in the teacher's shoes. For if "the executioners are our fellows" (as Robert Antelme once wrote) then we are compelled to see ourselves as potential arbiters and administrators of pain. Could we, in different circumstances, be the agents of annihilations to come? (Antelme, cited in Didi-Huberman, 2003, p. 28).

The Milgram Re-enactment implicates us. We are no longer merely spectators. We are *bystanders*. Having a front-row seat in Milgram's coded re-enactment of the Holocaust, we have long since been consumers of the spectacles that emerge from proceduralised, technologised forms of violence. We've been fascinated, seduced by it. As Peter Sloterdijk once pointed out, complicity is an inescapable existential predicament for all of us who sit transfixed by the 'shock-machines' in our living-rooms or on our phones:

> "To be modern, one must be touched by the awareness that, beside the inevitable fact of being a witness, one has been drawn into a sort of complicity with the newer form of the monstrous. If one asks a modern person, 'Where were you at the time of the crime?' the answer is 'I was at the scene of the crime' – that is to say, within that totality of the monstrous which as a complex of modern criminal circumstances encompasses its accomplices by knowledge. Modernity means dispensing with the possibility of having an alibi" (Sloterdijk, cited in Elden, p. 165).

For Sloterdijk, as for Dickinson's *Milgram*, everyone has a ring-side seat at the crime. Thanks to our ever-present digital devices, the war-media production cycle has been newly rejuvenated by the technological shock generators that, as Milgram realised, constitute "important buffer[s]" – reminding us constantly of the possibility of pain whilst at the same time delivering "dehumanising effects": "Distance, time, and physical barriers neutralize the moral sense" (Milgram, 2010, p. 175). The shock-machine makes pain seem spatially and affectively remote. Disconnected from hierarchical authority structures, it has increasingly become a free-floating, but structuring principle that catches us up in an age of 'surveillance capitalism' (Zuboff, 2019).[21] We have never been so connected to, nor complicit with the dystopian ecologies of contemporary conflict and violence. No longer just witnesses, now everyone can *participate* in the crime, whether by poring over the just-released dashcam footage on Telegram detailing the Hamas-led atrocities of October 7, 2023,[22] or, in the weeks that follow, by making TikToks mocking the living conditions of Palestinians amid the ongoing bombardment of Gaza.[23] Certainly the horror of such events, though they may have surprised Milgram, would surely not have shocked him. Once, in an interview with CBS News in 1979, he claimed that "if a system of death camps were set up in the United States of the sort we had seen in Nazi Germany, one would be able to find sufficient personnel for those camps in any medium-sized American town" (Milgram, cited in Blass, 1999, p. 955).

And so, the past comes to be set alight in the dystopian future that was Milgram's own, and in the future that came after that.

Gaza 2007: An 'Inverse Milgram Experiment'

We fast forward now to September 2007, twenty three years after Milgram's death. Hamas has become the de facto authority inside the Gaza Strip, after a violent takeover. The Israeli Government has declared Gaza a 'hostile entity' and "threatened to further cut fuel and electricity supplies if militants continue to fire Quassam rockets at Israel, a decision that was backed by the US" (Urguhart, 2007, September 20). Already under pressure after Israel has reduced to a minimum the amount of goods going in and out of Gaza, movement restrictions are now intensified. With few exceptions all of Gaza's crossing points have been closed to people and goods. Fuel and electricity supplies have been drastically reduced, culminating in total power outages and jeopardising essential medical and sanitation services. Unemployment levels are soaring. Those in employment are not receiving payment. Access to land, livelihoods, education and water resources have further been reduced. As Barakut puts it:

"The foisted isolation of Gaza is variously referred to as a 'blockade', 'siege', or 'closure', whereas 'Israel does not acknowledge its system of control as a siege' (Smith, 2016), referring instead to its 'separation policy' (Barakat et al., 2020, p. 481).

Effectively, Gazans are trapped in a world they cannot get out of [24] and the oppressive tactics of the Israeli government has made that world, as Eyal Weizman argues in *The Least of All Possible Evils*, into "an inverse Milgram experiment" (Weizman, 2012, p. 87).

In a section entitled 'Milgram in Gaza', Weizman draws a comparison between the experimenters in Milgram's obedience experiments and the actions of Israeli military personnel and policymakers in Gaza. Focussing on Israel's complete control over the supply of electricity to Gaza, he argues that

"In this inverted Milgram experiment, the authority figures are the scientists, engineers and humanitarian experts advising the Israeli High Court, which ultimately decides on the level of current. Although those administering the reduction guarantee to provide current at a threshold above that at which 'humanitarian crisis will be created', this threshold was constantly tested – much like the upper limits of the electric shock in the Milgram experiment" (Weizman, 2012, p. 88).

Weizman's argument is that "the ability to exercise control through the modulation of [electricity] flow – in which the checkpoints and terminals within the [separation] wall function as valves and switches" was analogous to Milgram's experiment, the crucial difference being that

"the response to bad political choices by the Hamas government was not to increase the current but rather to reduce it gradually – and thereby destroy the strip's life-sustaining infrastructure and eventually bring its population to the brink of physical existence" (Weizman, 2012, p. 87).

Pursuing this line of thought, Weizman goes on to give a detailed account of how the reduction of electricity by the Israeli High Court and operationalised by the Israeli military, combined with related policies and structural factors to produce detrimental effects in Gaza. Power cuts effected water provision, which effected irrigation, harvesting, sewage and the provision of emergency aid. Effectively, he argues, this produced a regime of control that was propped up by a "combination of legal technologies and complex institutional practices that are now often referred to as 'lawfare', the use of law as a weapon of war" (Weizman, 2012, pp. 91-92).

"Depending on the political calculation at any given time, the military reduced or increased the supply of diesel, seeking to achieve an optimum of maximum political impact with minimum intervention" (Weizman, 2012, p. 89).

If Milgram's question asked how otherwise decent people could, with "numbing regularity", "knuckle under to the demands of authority and perform actions that were callous and severe" (Milgram, 2010, p. 141), then Weizman, well aware of Dickinson's Milgram Re-enactment, [25] now migrates that question across multiple sites. A dialogue is created between Holocaust memory and the memory in Gaza of "collective punishment" as a "goal" that will later become the "new normal" (Barakat et al., 2020, p. 482). [26] In this way, the echo of 'memory work' recoils from Milgram to Dickinson to Weizman in a dynamic system of arousal and dissolution. Dickinson's work is thus positioned, not only as a re-enactment but also as a *pre*-enactment (Sasse, in Agnew et al, 2020, p. 153) of procedural Holocausts to come – it foreshadows Weizman's interpretation of the Siege of Gaza, 2007 as an "inverse Milgram experiment" that itself, as argued below, pre-enacts the current Israel-Hamas conflict (2023-).

The Now That Was After Comes Before: Before and After the Israel-Hamas War, 2023-

If Dickinson's work, for all its mimetic rigour, lays plain the discrepancy between the 'original' event and what it later *appears* or professes to be, then it also creates the very circumstances for such a shift to occur. It demonstrates, not only the difference between the (supposed to be) original and (assumed to be) copy, but on the contrary, the tendency of the re-enacted event, however faithfully it is reproduced, to produce differences that spin out in unpredictable directions, whilst at the same time conveying the *appearance* of faithfulness to a prior narrative. One paradox of Dickinson's *Re-enactment* is that it repeats an unrepeatable (Milgram's Obedience to Authority experiment) which itself repeats an unrepeatable (as Milgram saw it, the "code of obedience" behind the "Nazi extermination of European Jews", Milgram, 2010, p. 20). However, this apparent contradiction echoes a similar momentum at work in historical 'events' that also *appear* to repeat *as well as* to differ with the past. [27] The question is not 'where is the authentic original event?' but how do evental *series* operate? What are the permutating, circular structures at work in historical events and how or at what points do they diverge from one another?

Such questions seem particularly important in the current moment when a desperate humanitarian crisis is unfolding before our eyes in Gaza, with unparalleled scale and speed. At the time of writing, some 85% of Gaza's population are internally displaced amid a crippling blockade of food, water fuel and medicine (United Nations Population Fund, 2024, April 2). "Apocalyptic" consequences are predicted in the aftermath of aid shortages (Martin Griffiths, Secretary General, UN Office for Coordination of Humanitarian Affairs, cited in Tondo, 2024). The IDF operation on Rafah, where nearly 800,000 people are still crammed, is intensifying. [28] And yet, as Saree Makdisi suggests, to what extent do these recent events function as intensifications of previous Nakbas? And indeed, of the Nakbas before the Nakba of 1948, going back to the "planning for the Zionist settler-colonial project…in the 1920s and 1930s [which] were predicated on the transfer of the Palestinians from their land and their replacement by Jewish-Zionist settlers." (Makdisi, 2022, p. 88).[29] Here, Makdisi points not to an originary event but to ongoing series of events in which Palestinians were violently 'transferred' through Israeli military operations, which repeatedly destroyed villages, massacred civilians and expelled people from their homes, at gunpoint:

"Hundreds of Palestinian villages were erased from the maps—their very names wiped clear or "transferred," so to speak, into new, Hebrew place-names—as they were being wiped off the surface of the earth" (Makdisi, 2022, p. 22).

The emphasis here is on what *appears* and is therefore subject to being arranged – Palestinian land, like a theatrical re-enactment, can be re-staged in a different context. [30] As Dickinson's *Milgram Re-enactment* reminds us, our knowledge of what appears is always disrupted by time and by the forceful perspectives of those who come before *and* those who come after.

In such a context, Dickinson's work challenges us to come to terms with the apparent perspicuity of the present moment, but in a way that interrupts the linear necessity of cause and effect by producing an "*a priori* that denies *a prioris* their power of privilege" (Panagia, 2016, pp. 1-2). *The Milgram Re-enactment* reminds us not only of the enduring relevance of Milgram's work to contemporary affairs but of the anarchic and anachronistic *possibilities* of memory. For here, Dickinson's work offers a kind of 'repetition' that is unashamedly *interventionist* – not into any *particular* situation, but paradoxically perhaps, into *any* particular situation. It takes us back to that which has been, but via a forward movement that confuses the usual temporal sequence.

CONCLUSION

"… if you're in a forest, the quality of the echo is very strange because echoes back off so many surfaces of all those trees, that you get this strange itchy ricochet effect" (Brian Eno, 1979).

If the deep and thorny forest of Memory Studies has taught us anything, it is surely then that the past can never be contained or captured only to resurface, unscathed, in the present. We have seen the power of art re-enactments like that of Dickinson's, to peel back to the skin and sinews of the past, whilst always still recognising the *movement* of memory – its dynamism and energy as it rebounds in infinite recoil between the thorny surfaces of the past and the emergent, self-seeding spores of the future. Dickinson's *The Milgram Re-enactment* demonstrates the importance, not of the presentation of any notion of 'singular memory', but of understanding the strangely itchy 'ricochet' effects of memory. It demonstrates that, like Eno's echo, memory rouses and releases by (re)enacting the differentiating power of repetition *as* difference.

Yet in Dickinson's work, the 'echo' offers a complex figure of repetition: on the one hand it sets up an urgent and continuing response to the frayed wreckage of the past. But on the other, it is oriented (as Milgram's 'original' experiments were) [31] towards the inevitable flashing up of ever new 'moments of danger' (Benjamin, Eiland & Jennings, 2003, p. 391) in emergent conflicts and crises.

The pattern is there, but now refracted, expanded, *dispersed* by different operating forces. Like Erwin Hahn's 'spin echoes' – detected in nuclear magnetic resonance in 1950 – the first echo acts back on previous spins when a refocusing pulse is applied, leading to a train of self-stimulated secondary echoes (Hahn, 1950, pp. 580-594). Effectively, Hahn's echoes are echoes with active interference. In this context, 'memory' in *The Milgram Re-enactment* becomes a site of connective reading, capable of moving between geopolitical and artistic concerns and bringing different histories and contexts into contact without any ambition of merging them. This produces, as Sanyal once put it, "an alternative to the zero sum logic of competitive memory". It belies any "notion of memory as a closed economy in which the recognition of one history will necessarily diminish or displace that of another" (Sanyal, 2015, p. 7). Instead, memory becomes radically open to encounters that could not have been anticipated in advance.

In this way, chronological models of time and memory are entirely disrupted, opening space for complex 'memory work' that deliberately seeks to reconfigure or re-orientate the present-becoming-future.

As we have learned from Dickinson's work, artistic re-enactments, can offer not just an echo of that which has occurred, but the possibility of memory as a mode of immanent critique – an active engagement with and a refraction of the performative nature of violence as that which engages both political and aesthetic questions of agency, action, authority and embedded practices within much larger cultural and political contexts. These issues, as both Dickinson's and Milgram's work suggest, continue to resound in the present as well as in the times that are yet to come. *The Milgram Re-enactment* then, is important for the way that it speaks not only directly to the memory of the Holocaust, but as we have seen, to urgent questions at the forefront of major geo-political conflicts today – specifically and critically, as I have argued, to the (history of the) current conflict in Gaza.[32] By mobilising Milgram's insights about authority, power structures and dehumanisation, Dickinson's work demonstrates how re-enactment can take a future-oriented, searingly critical approach to violent conflicts in the present – indeed how it can press for the urgent need to rethink the relationship between past events and contemporary responses to them.

In one respect, Dickinson's work demonstrates that, as Kierkegaard once put it, "Repetition and recollection are the same movement, only in opposite directions, for what is recollected has been, is repeated backward; whereas the real repetition is recollected forward" (Kierkegaard & Mooney, 2009, p. 70).[33] But in another, as we have seen, *The Milgram Re-enactment* does more than merely drag the injuries of the past into the charged, unsettled present. Rather, it reminds us that, as Gavin Stevens famously articulated it in William Faulkner's *Requiem for a Nun,* "the past is never dead. It's not even past" (Faulkner, 1951/ 1996, p. 73).[34] Read through the current moment, when references to the Holocaust are constantly swirling in everyday political debate, mainstream and social media, and popular discourse, accompanied by an alarming rise in Islamophobia and antisemitism, [35] Dickinson's work indicates that memory of the Holocaust is more than a 'historical' legacy, or an open wound even (though it is both of these). But crucially, the Holocaust is an active operant condition – one that continues to influence policy, conduct and a range of national and international perspectives relevant to the continuing conflict in the Gaza Strip. In the forward rebounding echoes of the echoes of the past, earshot simultaneously travels backwards and forwards: in addition to the ear-piercing backfire that continues to startle us in the present, there are also the gathering vibrations of that which has not yet been heard but is already forming future reverberations: Holocaust memory has forward motion as well as backward force. It continues to be a vital point of comparison for Holocaust survivors, Israeli authorities, hostages' families, for all those who discuss whether a 'ceasefire' should be called in exchange for hostages, for those whose authorities regulate the memory of the Holocaust or oppose the BDS (Boycott, Divestment and Sanctions) movement, or object to terms that do not meet the IHRA definition of antisemitism, or insist or do not insist on the singularity of the Holocaust, or argue about the humanitarian catastrophe that is currently unfolding in Gaza.[36]

Gone is the injunction 'never again' – never has *already* occurred and cannot cease *recurring*, only differently, indefinitely, contrarily. Precisely because it is out of step with that which is re-enacted, *The Milgram Re-enactment* demonstrates that the present can never cease to reshape itself in its remembrance of the past, and that equally, the past will always remake itself in the presence of the current moment. The *now* that is always an *after* will come *before* and the now that is always *before* will come *later*. In this way then, as Dickinson's work demonstrates, 're-enactment' is not merely a technology for the production and enlivenment of the past but potentially a form of 'anti-memory' [37] that generates the echoes that *insist* on our intervention into and re-invention of the becoming-future.

REFERENCES

Agnew, V., Lamb, J., & Tomann, J. (2019). *The Routledge handbook of re-enactment studies*. Routledge. 10.4324/9780429445637

Allen, M. T. (2002). *The business of genocide: The SS, slave labour and the concentration camps*. University of North Carolina Press.

Arendt, H. (2006). *Eichmann in Jerusalem: A report on the banality of evil*. Penguin.

Arns, I., & Horn, G. (Eds.). (2007). *History will repeat itself: Strategies of re-enactment in contemporary (media) art and performance*. Revolver.

Bangma, A., Rushton, S., & Wüst, F. (Eds.). (2005). *Experience, memory, re-enactment*. Revolver.

Barakat, S., Milton, S., & Elkahlout, G. (2020). Reconstruction under siege: The Gaza Strip since 2007. *Disasters*, 44(3), 477–498. 10.1111/disa.1239431343753

Bartov, O. (2001). *The eastern front, 1941–45, German troops and the barbarisation of warfare*. Springer.

Bauman, Z. (2013). *Modernity and the Holocaust*. John Wiley & Sons.

Baumrind, D. (1964). Some thoughts on ethics of research: After reading Milgram's 'Behavioural study of obedience'. *The American Psychologist*, 19(6), 421–423. 10.1037/h0040128

BBC News. (2024, May 17). *Gaza war: UN defends casualty tally amid Israeli anger*. BBC. https://www.bbc.co.uk/news/world-middle-east-69025420

Benjamin, L. T.Jr, & Simpson, J. A. (2009). The power of the situation: The impact of Milgram's obedience studies on personality and social psychology. *The American Psychologist*, 64(1), 12–19. 10.1037/a001407719209959

Benjamin, W., Eiland, H., & Jennings, W. (1996). *Selected writings: 1938-1940* (Vol. 4). Harvard University Press.

Blass, T. (1999). The Milgram paradigm after 35 years: Some things we now know about Obedience to Authority. *Journal of Applied Social Psychology*, 29(5), 955–978. 10.1111/j.1559-1816.1999.tb00134.x

Blass, T. (2009). *The man who shocked the world: The life and legacy of Stanley Milgram*. Basic Books.

Brannigan, A., & Perry, G. (2016). Milgram, genocide and bureaucracy: A post-Weberian perspective. *State Crime*, 5(2), 287–305. 10.13169/statecrime.5.2.0287

Burger, M. (2009). Replicating Milgram: Would people still obey today? *The American Psychologist*, 64(1), 1–11. 10.1037/a001093219209958

Butt, K. M., & Butt, A. A. (2016). Blockade on Gaza strip: A living hell on earth. *Journal of Political Studies*, 23(1), 157–182.

Deleuze, G. (1987). Difference and repetition. *Continuum*.

Deleuze, G. (2006). *Nietzsche and philosophy*. Columbia UP.

Dettmer, J. (2024, February 2). How the Holocaust shapes Israel's war in Gaza. *Politico*. https://www.politico.eu/article/how-the-holocaust-shapes-israels-war-in-gaza/#:~:text=%E2%80%9CHamas'%20attack%20should%20never%20have,hostages%20alive%2C%E2%80%9D%20he%20added

Dickinson, R. (2024, March 01). *Personal communication [Personal interview]*.

Dickinson, R. (n.d). *The Milgram re-enactment*. R. Dickson. https://www.roddickinson.net/pages/milgram/project-synopsis.php.https://www.roddickinson.net/pages/milgram/project-synopsis.php

Didi-Huberman, G. (2007). Foreword: Knowledge-Movement. In Michaud, P. (Ed.), *Aby Warburg and the image in motion* (pp. 7–19). Zone.

Didi-Huberman, G. (2008). *Images in spite of all: Four photographs from Auschwitz*. University of Chicago Press.

Eilat, G., & Ilan, R. K. (2013). *Evil to the core*. Israeli Centre for Digital Art.

Erickson, R. (2009). The real movie: Re-enactment, spectacle and recovery in Pierre Huyghe's *The Third Memory*. In *Framework 50* (1-2), 107-24.

Farhat, T., Ibrahim, S., Abdul-Sater, Z., & Abu-Sittah, G. (2023). Responding to the humanitarian crisis in Gaza: Damned if you do… damned if you don't! *Annals of Global Health*, 89(1), 1–6. 10.5334/aogh.397537637468

Faulkner, W. (2011). *Requiem for a nun*. Vintage.

Fuller, M., & Weizman, E. (2021). *Investigative aesthetics: Conflicts and commons in the politics of truth*. Verso Books.

Gallanti, F. (2019). Forensic architecture. In *The Routledge Handbook of Re-enactment Studies* (pp. 79–83). Routledge. 10.4324/9780429445637-16

Gaskin, V. (2002). The tenth level. *Rod Dickinson: The power of persuasion*. [Exhibition catalogue]. Glasgow.

Gaskin, V. (2003). Subjects in search of an author. In Rushton, S. (Ed.), *The Milgram re-enactment: Essays on Rod Dickinson's re-enactment of Stanley Milgram's 'Obedience to Authority' experiments* (pp. 5–13). Jan van Eyck Academie.

Hahn, L. (1950). Spin echoes. *Physical Review*, 80(4), 580–594. 10.1103/PhysRev.80.580

Hale, R. (2020). They were just following orders': Relationships between Milgram's obedience experiments and conceptions of Holocaust perpetration. *Holocaust education: Contemporary challenges and controversies*, 74-94.

Joyce, J. (1999). *Finnegans Wake*. Penguin.

Kierkegaard, S., & Mooney, E. F. (2009). *Repetition and philosophical crumbs*. OUP Oxford.

LaCapra, D. (2011). *History and its limits: Human, animal, violence*. Cornell UP. 10.7591/9780801458927

LaCapra, D. (2019). *History and memory after Auschwitz*. Cornell University Press.

Lang, J. (2014). Against obedience: Hannah Arendt's overlooked challenge to social-psychological explanations of mass atrocity. *Theory & Psychology*, 24(5), 649–667. 10.1177/0959354314542368

Latour, B. (2011). Some experiments in art and politics. *e-flux, 23*, 1-7.

Lütticken, S. (2005a). *An arena in which to re-enact". Life once more: Forms of re-enactment in contemporary art*. Witte de With.

Lütticken, S. (2005b). *Life once more: Forms of re-enactment in contemporary art*. Witte de With.

Makdisi, S. (2022). *Tolerance is a wasteland: Palestine and the culture of denial*. University of California Press.

Masalha, N. (2002). The Palestinian Nakba: Zionism, 'transfer' and the 1948 exodus. *Global Dialogue*, 4(3), 77.

McCarthy, T. (2003). Between pain and nothing. In Rushton, S. (Ed.), *The Milgram re-enactment: Essays on Rod Dickinson's re-enactment of Stanley Milgram's 'Obedience to Authority' experiments* (pp. 16–32). Jan van Eyck Academie.

Michaud, P. (2007). *Aby Warburg and the image in motion*. Zone.

Milgram, S. (1973, December). The perils of obedience. *Harpers Magazine*.

Milgram, S. (2010). *Obedience to authority: An experimental view*. Pinter & Martin. (Original work published 1965.)

Nicholson, I. (2011a). 'Torture at Yale': Experimental subjects, laboratory torment and the 'rehabilitation' of Milgram's *Obedience to Authority.Theory & Psychology*, 21(6), 737–761. 10.1177/0959354311420199

Nicholson, I. (2011b). "Shocking" masculinity: Stanley Milgram, "obedience to authority," and the "crisis of manhood" in Cold War America. *Isis*, 102(2), 238–268. 10.1086/66012921874687

O'Byrne, A. (2023). *The genocide paradox: Democracy and generational Time*. Fordham UP.

Otto, U. (2019). History of the field. In V. Agnew, J. Lamb, & J. Tomann (Eds), The Routledge handbook of re-enactment studies (pp. 111–114). Routledge.

Panagia, D. (2016). *Ten theses for an aesthetics of politics*. University of Minnesota Press. 10.5749/9781452958514

Pappe, I. (2007). *The ethnic cleansing of Palestine*. Simon and Schuster.

Peschel, S. (2020, May 1). *Why Achille Mbembe was accused of anti-Semitism*. DW. https://www.dw.com/en/why-achille-mbembe-was-accused-of-anti-semitism/a-53293797

Pina e Cunha, M., Rego, A., & Clegg, S. R. (2010). Obedience and evil: From Milgram and Kampuchea to normal organizations. *Journal of Business Ethics*, 97(2), 291–309. 10.1007/s10551-010-0510-5

Quaranta, D. Caronia, A. & Janža, J. (Eds.). (2013) *RE:akt! Reconstruction, re-enactment, re-reporting*. Lulu.

Ramus, P. (1578). *Scholae in liberates artes. Scholae rhetoricae*. Lib. XIX (ed. of Bale, col. 309).

Rothberg, M. (2009). *Multidirectional memory: Remembering the Holocaust in the age of decolonization*. Stanford University Press.

Rothberg, M. (2019). *The implicated subject: Beyond victims and perpetrators*. Stanford University Press.

Rushton, S. (2003). Agentic states. In Rushton, S. (Ed.), *The Milgram re-enactment: Essays on Rod Dickinson's re-enactment of Stanley Milgram's 'Obedience to Authority' experiments* (pp. 49–63). Jan van Eyck Academie.

Russell, N., & Gregory, R. (2015). The Milgram-Holocaust linkage: Challenging the present consensus. *State Crime*, 4(2), 128–153. 10.13169/statecrime.4.2.0128

Sanyal, D. (2015). *Memory and complicity: Migrations of Holocaust remembrance*. Fordham UP.

Schechner, R. (2009). 9/11 as avant-garde art? *PMLA*, 124(5), 1820–1829. 10.1632/pmla.2009.124.5.1820

Schneider, R. (2011). *Performing remains: Art and war in times of theatrical re-enactment*. Routledge. 10.4324/9780203852873

Segal, S., & Weizman, E. (2003). The Mountain: Principles of building in heights. In Segal and Weizman (Eds.), *A civilian occupation: The politics of Israeli architecture* (pp. 79-99). Verso.

Sky News. (2024, March 4). More than 30,500 Palestinians now killed by Israeli strikes, Gaza health ministry says. *Sky News*. https://news.sky.com/story/gaza-hamas-israel-latest-30-000-deaths-sky-news-live-blog-12978800

Sloterdijk, P. (2012). The time of the crime of the monstrous: On the philosophical justification of the artificial. In Elden, S. (Ed.), *Sloterdijk Now* (pp. 166–181). Polity.

Tondo, L. (2024, May 19). UN humanitarian chief delivers 'apocalyptic' warning over Gaza aid. *The Guardian*. https://www.theguardian.com/world/article/2024/may/19/un-humanitarian-chief-delivers-apocalyptic-warning-over-gaza-aid

UN Office for the Co-ordination of Humanitarian Affairs ReliefWeb. (2023, November 13) *Initial reporting on the ongoing Israeli retaliatory attacks on Gaza: (Reporting Period, 7-28 October 2023) based on preliminary documentation [EN/AR] - occupied Palestinian territory*. Relief Web. https://reliefweb.int/report/occupied-palestinian-territory/initial-reporting-ongoing-israeli-retaliatory-attacks-gaza-reporting-period-7-28-october-2023-based-preliminary-documentation-enar

UN Office for the Co-ordination of Humanitarian Affairs ReliefWeb. (2024, March 14) *Hostilities at the Gaza Strip and Israel – reported humanitarian impact*. ReliefWeb. https://reliefweb.int/report/occupied-palestinian-territory/hostilities-gaza-strip-and-israel-reported-humanitarian-impact-14-march-2024-1500

United Nations Population Fund. (2024, April 2). *'Gaza is at breaking point': Health workers and patients describe an unfolding catastrophe in Rafah*. https://www.unfpa.org/news/%E2%80%9Cgaza-breaking-point%E2%80%9D-health-workers-and-patients-describe-unfolding-catastrophe-rafah

United Nations Population Fund. (2024, April 2). *Crisis in the occupied Palestinian territory*. UNPFA. https://www.unfpa.org/occupied-palestinian-territory

Urguhart, C. (2007, September 20). Israel declares Gaza Strip hostile territory. *The Guardian*. https://www.theguardian.com/world/2007/sep/20/israel1

Weizman, E. (2012). *The least of all possible evils: Humanitarian violence from Arendt to Gaza*. Verso.

Weizman, E. (2017). *Forensic architecture: Violence at the threshold of detectability*. Princeton UP. 10.2307/j.ctv14gphth

Winter, Y. (2016). The siege of Gaza: Spatial violence, humanitarian strategies, and the biopolitics of punishment. *Constellations (Oxford, England)*, 23(2), 308–319. 10.1111/1467-8675.12185

Yates, F. A. (1984). *Art of memory*.

Zuboff, S. (2019). *The age of surveillance capitalism: The fight for a human future at the new frontier of power*. Profile.

ENDNOTES

[1] For a recent, interdisciplinary overview of Re-enactment Studies, see Agnew, V., Lamb, J., & Tomann, J. (Eds.). (2019). *The Routledge handbook of re-enactment studies*. Routledge. For a now seminal study of the relationship between historical artifacts or 'remains' and performance, see Schneider, R. (2011). *Performing remains: Art and war in times of theatrical re-enactment*. Routledge. Amongst the most influential and cited texts on Art re-enactments are Lütticken, S. (2005b). *Life once more: Forms of re-enactment in contemporary art*. Rotterdam, Witte de With; Arns, I. & Horn, G. (Eds.). (2007). *History will repeat itself: Strategies of re-enactment in contemporary (media) art and performance*. Revolver; Bangma, A., Rushton, S. & Wüst. F. (Eds.). (2005). *Experience, memory, re-enactment*. Revolver; Quaranta, D. Caronia, A. & Janža, J. (Eds.). (2013) *RE:akt! Reconstruction, re-enactment, re-reporting*. Lulu.

[2] In addition to Rod Dickinson's work, the *History will repeat itself* 2005 exhibition also included seminal works by Guy Ben-Ner; Irina Botea; C-level (Team Waco); Daniela Comani; Jeremy Deller; Tom Mc Carthy (in collaboration with Rod Dickinson); Omer Fast; Forsyth & Pollard; Heike Gallmeier; Felix Gmelin; Pierre Huyghe; Korpys/Löffler; Zbigniew Libera. 2005 also saw the publication of Sven Lütticken's *Life, once more: Forms of re-enactment in contemporary art*, which discussed re-enactment works by Dickinson, along with those by Mike Bidlo, Bik Van der Pol, Omer Fast, Andrea Fraser, Robert Longo, Eran Schaerf, Catherine Sullivan and Barbara Visser.

[3] In addition to the venues listed above, the work has been shown regularly across the world. Though too numerous to list in full, these include Halle 15, Leipzig (2015); Dox Centre for Contemporary Art, Prague (2011-12); The Museum of Yugoslav History, Belgrade (2011); Haifa Museum of Art, Haifa (2011); The Israeli Centre for Digital Art, Tel Aviv (2009-10); Centre for Contemporary Art Ujazdowski Castle, Warsaw, (2008); HMKV Dortmund (2007); Witte de With, Rotterdam (2005); Australian Centre for the Moving Image, Melbourne, 2004; W139 Gallery, Amsterdam, 2003; Les Laboratoires d'aubervilliers, Paris, (2003); South London Gallery, London, 2002.

[4] By no means an exhaustive list, Dickinson's *The Milgram Re-enactment* has been discussed by scholars and curators including Bruno Latour (2011); Sven Lutticken (2005a and 2005b); Arns & Horn (2007); Steve Rushton (2003); Eilat & Ilan (2013); Rebecca Schneider (2011); Stephen

J. Scott-Bottoms, (2024). Ruth Erickson (2009) describes it as one of a "handful of seminal [re-enactment] works" that "crop up again and again".

5   ProQuest/ Ann Arbor distributes Dickinson's video of *The Milgram Re-Enactment* as an electronic resource for university libraries across the world.

6   By the time Milgram completed his research in 1962 he had processed 800 people through nineteen variations of the original design. Rod Dickinson's *The Milgram Re-enactment* created Variants Nos. 02 and 08.

7   Milgram tried to draw volunteers for his experiments from as wide a pool as possible. Having decided that undergraduates from an elite institution like Yale "did not seem wholly suitable" for his experiment, he instead advertised in a local newspaper and sent letters directly to several thousand residents in the New Haven area, to try to attract participants from a broad spectrum of backgrounds. Ultimately, his pool of subjects came from a range of age groups, occupational and educational backgrounds, genders and ethnicities (Milgram, 2010, pp. 31-34) See also, Burger (2009, pp. 5, 9).

8   Milgram describes how some subjects were severely strained – sweating, trembling, stuttering, biting lips, digging fingernails into flesh, or indeed, nervously laughing throughout. For several participants the number of 'prods' went into double figures – indeed in case, a woman was ordered to continue twenty-six times.

9   In the two variants of the experiment that Dickinson re-enacted, two thirds of the subjects were fully compliant. However in other variants of the experiment, compliance varied.

10   As is well known, Adolf Eichmann was not just a German-Austrian official in the Nazi Party and an SS officer but a participator in the January 1942 Wannsee Conference, at which the implementation of the genocidal Final Solution was planned. After Eichmann was captured by Israeli agents from his adopted home in Buenos Aires, he was flown to Israel to take part in a lengthy trial, and eventually executed for his role in the murder of six million Jews.

11   See also Arendt (2006). It should be mentioned that some critics argue that Milgram gets Arendt wrong and arrives at entirely different conclusions to hers. Johannes Lang, for example (2014) contends that while Arendt and Milgram agreed that obedience has a normative structure reliant on a political act of recognition, unlike Milgram, Arendt thought that 'obedience to authority' *alone* was an inadequate explanation of Nazi evildoing.

12   "Milgram's (1965) *Obedience* film was shown to more undergraduate students in psychology over the past 45 years than any other audio-visual resource in psychology" (Brannigan & Perry, 2016, p. 288).

13   Too numerous to mention in full, a variety of popular cultural spin-offs of Milgram's experiments include *The Tenth Level*, a film starring William Shatner and directed by Charles Dubin (1976); *The Heist*, a TV show made by Derren Brown and Channel 4 in 2006, in which four people were selected to hijack a security van at gun-point, unwittingly using a fake gun and confronted by a security guard who was an actor. The programme included references to and a mock-up of Milgram's experiment; *Experimenter: The Stanley Milgram Story*, 2015, directed by Michael Almereyda; *Game of Death*, 2010 – a French TV programme in which "…participants were instructed to pull levers to inflict electric shocks on their opponents…participants were unaware that contestants receiving shocks were actors and that there was no electrical current. Nevertheless 82% of people who played the *Game of Death* agreed to pull the lever." See Nicholson (2011a). One could also mention here,

Milgram's own frequent television appearances and contributions to popular magazines, including his infamous appearance on NBC's *60 Minutes* in 1979.

[14] Bauman further insists that "National Socialism is *the* definitive moment of modernity", akin to rationality and technocracy.

[15] Limit-events are traumatic events which, like the Holocaust are premised on their singularity and the unavailability to representation.

[16] In the epilogue to *Obedience to Authority*, Milgram (2010) discusses the relevance of his work to events that happen long after the end of WW2, such as the "internment of Japanese Americans, the use of napalm against civilians in Vietnam" (p. 196). He speaks specifically about 'war zone' training and indoctrination, where the maintenance of discipline is "an element of survival" and some transformation to the agentic stage" necessarily occurs, if only temporarily.

[17] Take for instance, Richard Schechner (2009) who claims in a discussion about the performative and aesthetic characteristics of mediated depictions of 9/11 that "art is not as serious as politics; art is play, secondary, a representation" (p. 1825).

[18] "The art of memory (says Quintilian) consists entirely in division and composition. If we seek then an art which will divide and compose things, we shall find the art of memory. Such a doctrine is expounded in our dialectical precepts…and method…For the true art of memory is one and the same as dialectics" (Ramus, cited in Yates 1984, p. 233).

[19] "The vivid story of how Simonides invented the art of memory is told by Cicero in his *De oratore* when he is discussing memory as one of the five parts of rhetoric; the story introduces a brief description of the mnemonic of places and images (loci and imagines) which was used by the Roman rhetors." The general principle of ancient (and later) memory practices, as described by Yates, involved a mnemonic device known as the 'method of loci', or the 'memory palace' technique. It was based on the idea of associating information with specific visual images placed in familiar locations, such as rooms in a house or landmarks in a familiar neighbourhood.

[20] As Benjamin & Simpson (2009) report, "The trial began in August 1961, the very month that Milgram's subjects began reporting to the basement laboratory in Linsly-Chittenden Hall. As Milgram ran his subjects, the three judges considering the evidence against Eichmann found him guilty on all counts. He was hanged on June 1, 1962, five days after Milgram completed the first of his obedience studies" (p. 14).

[21] While it is not within the scope of this chapter to develop this point in more detail, the connections between obedience and surveillance are apparent in Zuboff's book: 'surveillance capitalism' is envisaged as a new species of power capable of moulding human action by gently herding us down Google's interminable, hyperlinked paths.

[22] In the wake of Hamas's deadly attack on October 7, 2023, a slew of misinformation, disinformation and conspiracy theories about the ongoing conflict are percolating on social media. However, images showing heavily armed men breaching the fences separating Israel and Gaza, entering southern Israel and deliberately killing unarmed civilians, have been investigated and verified by HRW. https://www.youtube.com/watch?v=OlSybbUbPFA&rco=1

[23] This trend emerged shortly after the events of October 7, 2024 and shows prominent Israeli TikTokers wearing hijabs or keffiyehs, their teeth painted black, singing along to an Israeli song reportedly associated with Israel's 2005 disengagement plan that eventually saw it withdraw from Gaza and the northern occupied West Bank. https://www.youtube.com/watch?v=_mwcFEpAYkU

[24] As Butt and Butt (2016) describe, "Gaza has turned into a vast 'Human Cage' on the eastern Mediterranean where 1.8 million human beings have been trapped, seems, they have no chance of escaping from their grave condition" (pp. 157 ff.) See also, Farhat et al. (2023) and Winter (2016).

[25] Weizman and Dickinson are personal acquaintances and share many professional connections and platforms as well as an enduring interest in re-enactment, the exploitation of which is a consistent methodology for Forensic Architecture, of which Weizman is Founder and Director. Weizman's interest in criminal and legal re-enactments as well as in digital re-constructions, is apparent in his writings. For further discussion, see Gallanti (2019, p. 82) and Weizman (2017, 2012).

[26] Barakat analyses the damage caused to housing, water, social service sectors and agriculture caused by Operation Protective Edge (2014) and Operation Cast Lead (2008 – 2009). Rewinding further, one could mention also, Operation Summer Rains, Operation Autumn Clouds, Operation Breaking Dawn and Operation Guardian of the Walls.

[27] It is not for nothing for instance, that Deleuze speaks about the 'theatre of repetition' in the same breath as he puts into Marx's mouth, the idea that "history is theatre" (Deleuze, 1997, p.10).

[28] The collection of data and statistics in a war zone is of course, subject to incomplete information and unreliable sources, as well as to challenge and constant revision. At the time of writing, these figures from the UN's Office for the Coordination of Humanitarian Affairs (OCHA) are the most reliable currently available. They are based on information from the Hamas-run health ministry in Gaza, rather than, as was previously the case, from the Hamas-run Government Media Office (GMO). This switch in information source resulted in a recent reduction in UN estimates of killed Palestinian women and children. See Gaza war: UN defends casualty tally amid Israeli anger. BBC News. (2024, May 17). Gaza war: UN defends casualty tally amid Israeli anger. https://www.bbc.co.uk/news/world-middle-east-69025420

[29] For more on the concept of 'transfer' as a solution to the Zionist territorial/land, 'Arab demographic' and political problems in the period from 1882-1948, see Masalha (2002). For more on the 1948 Arab-Israeli War and the expulsion of more than 750,000 Palestinians from their homes, see Pappe (2006). Other works, most notably by Walid Khalidi, Simha Flapan, Nafez Nazzal, Benny Morris and Norman Finkelstein cover similar terrain.

[30] See also, Segal & Weizman's discussion of how planning and architecture were conscripted as tactical tools in Israeli state strategy, in accordance with national and geo-political objectives (2003, p. 92).

[31] In his 'Epilogue' Milgram describes the relevance of his experiments to all policies originating in the authority of a democratic nation, where "people lent themselves to the purposes of authority and bec[a]me instruments in its destructive processes." He lists a few of these: " the importation and enslavement of millions of black people, the destruction of the American Indian population, the internment of Japanese Americans, the use of napalm against civilians in Vietnam." All of these, he argues, originated in harsh policies of democratic national authority, and were responded to "with the expected obedience". (Milgram, 2010, pp. 196-206)

[32] As discussed above, suppression, expulsion and uneven, near constant war has been the story of the Palestinian territories, since its partition into three parts in 1947 and indeed prior to that, during the British Mandate of 1917-47. The structure that emerged in 1948 is still an incomplete one, despite significant force and the methodical demolition of Palestinian villages that continued right into the 1950s, 1960s and beyond. Whilst space prevents the development of a more extensive narrative here, in the sections above, I touch also, on more recent waves of destruction, as evidenced for example

by the Siege of Gaza in 2007. In addition to this, it is worth mentioning that in 2018-19, thousands of Palestinian demonstrators were shot, killed or injured in demonstrations at the Gaza-Israel buffer zone, where later, on October 7, 2023, paramilitary wings of several Palestinian groups, including Hamas, launched coordinated armed incursions. Here, the settlements previously established by military outposts stood, surrounded by fences, concrete walls, remote-control machine guns, surveillance equipment and more Israeli military bases. Thus the 'Israel–Hamas War' as it is now known, was sparked – almost exactly 50 years after Operation Badr and the Yom Kippur War of 1973. The Palestinian armed groups named the attacks 'Operation Al-Aqsa Flood', while in Israel, they are referred to as 'Black Saturday' or the 'Simchat Torah Massacre'. The attacks involved rocket barrages, paraglider incursions, and breaches of the Gaza–Israel barrier. Civilians in Israeli communities, including Be'eri, Kfar Aza, and Nir Oz, were targeted, resulting in significant casualties. The attacks led to 1,139 deaths, including Israeli civilians, foreign nationals and members of the security forces. Hostages were taken to the Gaza Strip and reports of rape and sexual assault emerged. Hamas claimed the attack was in response to the Israeli occupation, blockade of Gaza, settlement expansion, settler violence and recent escalations. The international response varied, with some countries denouncing the attack as 'terrorism' and others blaming Israel's occupation and settler colonialism as the root causes. The day was labelled the bloodiest in Israel's history and the deadliest for Jews since the Holocaust (UN Office for the Co-ordination of Humanitarian Affairs ReliefWeb, 2023, November 13).

Subsequently, Israel declared a state of war, tightened its existing blockade of Gaza and launched one of the most severe bombing campaigns in history, before commencing a ground invasion on 27 October and laying siege to Gaza City and later, Khan Yunis. At the time of writing, more than 85% of Palestinians in Gaza (approximately 1.9 million people) have been internally displaced (UN Population Fund, n.d.) and to date, at least 33,360 Palestinians have reportedly been killed and 75,993 others wounded in Israel's military offensive on Gaza since October 7, according to information collected from Gaza's health ministry . The latter figure given by the Palestinian Health Authority (PHA) in Gaza has been challenged on grounds that the source of the information is an organisation run by Hamas. According to Sky News however, the PHA's counts, "compared with the post-war United Nations analysis, shows that the initial data is largely accurate with at most, a 10-12% discrepancy." (Sky News, 2024; UN Office for the Co-ordination of Humanitarian Affairs ReliefWeb, 2024, March 14.)

[33]   The Danish title is *Gjentagelsen*, meaning literally "the taking back" and was originally published under the pseudonymous name of Constantine Constantius.

[34]   Frequently assumed to be Faulkner's own personal assertion, this oft-cited quotation is in fact, a line from Gavin Stevens, one of the characters in *Requiem for a Nun* (Act I, Scene III).

[35]   Dave Rich, Director of Policy at the Community Security Trust, UK, reported a global trend in Islamophobic and antisemitic sentiment since 7 October, 2023.

[36]   As Jamie Dettmer (2024, February 2) wrote in, 'How the Holocaust shapes Israel's war in Gaza': "Prime Minister Benjamin Netanyahu — joined by many other prominent Israelis — was quick to compare the Islamist militant group Hamas to the Nazis for the murderous assault of October 7, which killed 1,200 Jews in the worst pogrom since the Holocaust ". Additionally, the Cameroonian political philosopher Achille Mbembe had his invitation to a major festival questioned after the federal antisemitism commissioner accused him of supporting B.D.S. and "relativizing the Holocaust" (Peschel, 2020).

[37]   The term 'anti-memory' is referred to in Deleuze's *Difference and Repetition* (1987, p. 294): "becoming is an anti-memory". In this formulation, 'becoming' is a future-oriented process that overcomes memory in a shift with the past and orientates instead towards the future. Similarly, "History is made only by those who oppose history, not by those who insert themselves into it, or even reshape it." (p. 295). In this iteration, "anti-memory" is characterised not only the becoming but

also by the rhizome: "The rhizome is an anti-genealogy. It is a short-term memory, or anti-memory" (p. 21).

Chapter 7
Performativity of the Memory of the Place and Practices of Remembrance

Frederico Dinis
http://orcid.org/0000-0002-2178-5252
Research Institute in Design, Media, and Culture ID+, Portugal

ABSTRACT

This chapter aims to question the ontology of the audio-visual and the use of technology in multimedia performance, specifically in the use of sound and image as communicational and artistic means. Taking this objective into account a research methodology through the artistic practice was developed to analyze the site-specific projects developed by the author, which includes the process of approaching the site-specific and the (de)construction of a sense of place. A case study analysis of three site-specific projects was assessed through a process of continuous inquiry that involves assessing various levels of permanence and different modes of access to information. It has been observed that the performativity of memory can be strengthened through live audio-visual performances in specific places and performative moments can provide a platform for the community to shape its memory.

INTRODUCTION

Today's artistic reality, which comprises new media and their complex relationships, presents a challenge to established artistic currents and forms. Performance art has always stood out for breaking the rules of existing artistic movements. The concept of performance can be understood through different perceptions, resulting from different disciplinary approaches, artistic areas, or cultural contexts. Due to its conceptual openness and diverse creative procedures, performance has great potential for exploration, which we will explore in this personal reading, focused on the confluence between sound and visual mediums as a theme of creative recognition.

This chapter intends to identify and discuss artistic movements related to performance art. It contextualizes contemporary audio-visual performances within the history and dominant languages of performance art, as well as approaches centered on the use of sound and visual mediums.

DOI: 10.4018/979-8-3693-2264-2.ch007

To establish our approach, we assume Carlson's (2004) definition of performance as an action presented to an audience. However, the interpretation of this concept has varied among artists and contexts. Therefore, it is important to also refer to Alcázar's (2014) description of the concept to provide additional context for this chapter.

> *Performance is a hybrid form that draws on traditional arts (such as theatre, visual arts, music, poetry and dance), popular art (such as cabaret and circus) and new art forms (such as experimental cinema, video art, installation and digital art). But it also draws on extra-artistic sources, such as anthropology, journalism, sociology, semiotics and linguistics, as well as vernacular popular traditions (the preaching of street vendors, popular festivals, processions). Performance is, therefore, a borderline art, an art of the interstices, it is transdisciplinary art par excellence.* (Alcázar, 2014: 75)

Regarding the concept of multimedia, we adopt the definition proposed by Packer & Jordan (2001), which emphasizes the combination of different types of mediums. Multimedia performance is characterized by the incorporation of alternative aesthetics, technological innovations, and expansion to other mediums such as light, movement, sound, and image.

In this sense, this chapter aims to examine the ontology of the audio-visual and the use of technology in multimedia performance, specifically in the use of sound and image as communicational and artistic means by:

(i)   analyzing the role of sound and image as expressive processes in the production of the construction of meaning and the materiality of multimedia artworks;

(ii) reflecting on the impacts of performative moments in the promotion of new possibilities, recursive processes, repetitions, non-linear structures, simultaneous events and mixing of languages;

(iii) exploring the effects of how convergent expressive processes enhance the creation of new narratives, making them denser and more immersive in artistic representation, reflecting the complementarity of space and time.

Taking these objectives into account, this chapter has been divided into four sections. The first one, *Co-Constructed Interconnections*, identifies and discusses the importance of the backgrounds of multimedia performance practices assuming that theatre, dance, music and performance are interdisciplinary art forms that have always used various mediums. The second section, *Combinatory Contaminations*, reflects on performance and the ability it has to use different media simultaneously and the increase of creativity related to various ideological and cultural changes. The third one, *Methodological Process*, presents the research methodology through the artistic practice used to analyze the site-specific projects developed, which comprises the process of approaching the site-specific and the (de)construction of a sense of place. Finally, in the fourth and last section, *Case Study*, three site-specific projects are analyzed in a process of continuous inquiry that involves assessing various levels of permanence and different modes of access to information.

CO-CONSTRUCTED INTERCONNECTIONS

Theatre, dance, and performance are interdisciplinary art forms that have always used various mediums. The background of multimedia performance practices can be traced back to the late 19th and early 20th centuries. Theatre, from its classical origins to its more experimental forms, incorporates music, costumes, props, sets, lighting, the human voice, and text. Throughout history, theatre has used and incorporated the dramatic and aesthetic potential of emerging technologies, employing the most advanced knowledge of each era to enhance its productions. This is evident in the development of visual and sound effects in Ancient Greek theatre, advancements in perspective, the mechanical scenic devices of the 17th and 18th centuries, and the implementation of gas and electricity for lighting effects. This tendency persists in the digital era, especially with the use of computers to control sound, image, lighting, and scenery changes (Laurel, 1993).

Dance is closely linked to music and incorporates visual elements such as costumes, props, sets, and lighting to enhance the body's presence in space. As the most physical of the arts, dance has also been viewed as a practice that is constantly evolving technologically (Wesemann, 1997). The advent of electric light in 1889 is an example of the use of modern technology in dance. Choreographer Loie Fuller incorporated this technology in her pieces, including the use of large veils extended by poles, illuminated by several colored lights and a mirror on the floor. This pre-announced Oskar Schlemmer's *Slat Dance* (1927) and even later devices such as Stelarc's *Extended Arm* (2000). Fuller also incorporated film and projected shadows in her performances (Dixon, 2007). In his solo *Cyborg* (1995), Wayne McGregor, a pioneer of digital dance, used stage lights to fragment his body, creating the illusion of different shapes. This innovative use of older technology to achieve new effects has made Cyborg a reference in dance-technology (Dixon, 2007).

The history of theatre and dance reveals a continuous adoption and adaptation of technology, which has led to the development of multimedia performance. This evolution can be traced through various texts that have influenced the theory and practice of multimedia and new media. These texts have been published in numerous anthologies and publications at the turn of the millennium.

In addition to texts related to the history and theory of technology adoption in creation and on stage, it is important to acknowledge that a live performance is co-constructed by the bodily presence of performers and spectators. Performative moments can have a transformative effect, contingent on their occurrence (Fischer-Lichte, 2019).

The performativity universe involves the co-presence of actors and spectators in a physical space that encourages interaction. This deconstructs dichotomies, particularly the actor/spectator dichotomy that has dominated modern spectacle practices and theories. Spectators experience the materiality of a live performance, making it an ephemeral event. This differs from interpreting a work of art as an artistic object on an external plane (Fischer-Lichte, 2019).

The 'materiality of ephemerality' can also be achieved through the use of technology during the performative moment (Bay-Cheng et al., 2015). This establishes a potential path for later analysis of a performative moment that includes the materiality of its archive, such as photographs, videos, sketches, notes, and other writings created throughout the research-creation process (Bay-Cheng et al., 2015).

Thus, in the field of performance studies, action (research-creation process), document (archive), presentation (performative moment), and experiencing (materiality) are not treated as separate entities but as interconnected parts of a whole, by invoking not only the performative body but also image-centered identity (Harbison, 2019). Harbison draws on Butler's (2015) work on performativity and assumes an exercise in speculative genealogy, arguing that images can be created and produced in new media through the performativity of the image, which negotiates their meaning (Harbison, 2019). This transformative effect of the ephemeral materiality and performativity of the image is fundamental to the construction of an ontology of performance (Phelan, 1993) and the conceptualization of its broad disciplinary field.

It is essential in this chapter to analyze the contribution of Richard Wagner and his notion of Gesamtkunstwerk. This concept refers to the total work of art and was presented in Wagner's essay 'Das Kunstwerk der Zukunft' (Wagner, 1849). Wagner's concept is crucial to multimedia performance, not only because he advocates for spectacular theatre, but also as a convergence paradigm that anticipates the relationship between the total work of art and the contemporary understanding of the computer as a meta-medium capable of uniting all media (text, image, sound, video and others) in a single interface (Dixon, 2007). Wagner's music dramas aimed to achieve the same goal as many multimedia works today, namely audience immersion (Dixon, 2007). Wagner attempted to create an immersive experience for the audience by concealing the orchestra and using hypnotic, repetitive musical and sound leitmotifs with elongated chords (Lajosi, 2010; Vazsonyi, 2011). The Bayreuth Festspielhaus, Wagner's theatre, had a fan-shaped auditorium that aimed to eliminate distractions present in the sociability of theatres at the time, providing an unobstructed view of the stage (Bowman, 1966). The space was equipped with stage machinery and an original audio mixing system. The sound of the orchestra, which was placed under the stage, was directed first to the stage, where it was 'mixed' with the singers' voices, and only then to the audience. (Garai et al., 2015; D'Orazio et al., 2018).

Kurt Schwitters (1887-1948) advocated for the complete mobilization of all artistic forces to create a total work of art. This includes the inclusion of all materials. Schwitters also called for the overhaul of all theatres in the world (Richter, 1978:156; Dixon, 2007:42). Later, Vsevolod Meyerhold (1874-1940), a seminal force in modern international theatre, called for the destruction of the theatre box to create a spectacle without class divisions (Braun, 1979; Meyerhold et al., 1996; Pitches, 2004; Meyerhold, 2014; Schmidt, 2014).

The concept of the total work of art had a significant impact on various artists and theorists. For instance, Hugo Ball (1886-1927) incorporated it into his Cabaret Voltaire, Antonin Artaud (1896-1948) developed his theories of the theatre of cruelty based on it, Walter Gropius (1883-1969) explored it in his 'total theatre' concept, and the Bauhaus experimented with designs for multimedia immersive theatres (Smith, 2007; Roberts, 2011; Fischer-Lichte, 2013; Imhoof et al., 2016).

The Bauhaus artists deserve special mention in this context. Their first exhibition in 1923 had the motto 'Art and Technology - A New Unity'. The reconfiguration of dramatic forms and the experience of the spectacle were influenced by questions of space and space-time. Oskar Schlemmer (1888-1943) attempted to break the constraints of the stage, where elements were assembled, regrouped, amplified and gradually grew into something like a 'theatre play'.

These initial approaches to the total work of art formed the foundation for a series of contemporary approaches and remediation processes. For example, Anja Diefenbach and Christoph Rodatz's production Cyberstaging Parsifal (2000) remediates Wagner's Parsifal (1882) by combining split-screen projections, digital effects, several monitors, and recorded and live vocalizations. Commentators in the audience used microphones to further complicate the action. Sandy Stone referenced Wagner's opera Gotterdammerung (1876) in Cyberdammerung (1997), a rock'n'roll adaptation (Dixon, 2007).

It is important to note some significant contributions to the development of theatre performances that incorporate digital media and computer-generated projections. These have a long tradition (Dixon, 2007) that dates back to the first integration of film projection into a theatre performance during a revue in Berlin in 1911 (Billington, 1996). In 1914, Winsor McCay (1869-1934) toured the United States with Gertie the Dinosaur. Gertie was a mute animated character projected onto a cinema screen. McCay interacted with Gertie through verbal and gestural commands, creating a dialogical interactivity between the live performer and the projected images. This presentation is similar to countless multimedia performances today (Dixon, 2007).

The use of layers of form, content, and technology, typical of liminal (Broadhurst, 1999) and intermedial (Chapple & Kattenbelt, 2006) performance, as well as the notion of hybridity (Kaye, 1996), can be traced back to the experimental art movements of the 20th century. Particularly, the avant-gardes of the first decades, such as the Futurists, Dadaists, Constructivists, and Surrealists, refused the conventional boundaries between disciplines and employed any means that served their purposes (Jamieson, 2008).

Unlike theatre, dance, and performance, music was not always an interdisciplinary or multimedia art form. Some circumstantial factors prevented music and performance from coming together. According to Cook (2001), there are three distinct paths in the relationship between the semantic meaning of the word performance and musical performance itself:

(i)   the performance of music,
(ii) music and performance,
(iii) music as performance.

Cook (2001) argues that the first two formulations assume a distinction between performance and musical work, while the third aims to find a point of convergence between them. Cook (2001) argues that the fragmentation of the very concept of the word performance is implicit in the language itself, since

> *[...] in fact, the idea that performance is essentially reproduction and, consequently, is a subordinate and often redundant activity, is constructed within our language. Someone can "just play", but it's strange to talk about "just performing": the basic grammar of performance is that someone performs something, someone can realise a performance "of" something. In other words, language leads us to construct the process of performance as supplementary to the product that causes it or results from it; this is what leads us to naturally talk about music "and" its performance, in the same way that film theorists talk about film "and" music, as if the performance were no longer integrated into the music (and the music into the film). Language, in short, marginalises performance.* (Cook, 2001)

Based on this concept proposed by Cook (2001), musical meaning is created in the act of performance. Therefore, when we think of music as performance, we realize that its meaning is created in the act of performing it 'live' and also in the act of listening to it 'live' or in a recording. What's more, we can understand different meanings from what we hear, as these result from the different ways in which music is performed, for example in different contexts of periods and/or locations, and from the relationships created between artists, listeners and the musical work described in a score. In this way, the score acts as a script, which does not differentiate the result of the performance from the process, and is therefore not a consolidated 'text' (Cook, 2001).

In this understanding between music and performance, it is also important to emphasize the view of Frith (1996) who assumes that, in the limited shift between fiction and everyday reality, visual artists use their bodies as material and artistic support, and stage artists (actors, dancers and performers) assume themselves and their bodies as the objects and/or locations of narratives and feelings. From the objectification of the artist as the vehicle of art and the subjectification of the artist as the site of narratives, we have the configuration of a series of binary oppositions: subject/object, mind/body, interior/exterior, private/public.

Frith (1996) transfers the above propositions beyond the visual arts and the performing arts, relating them to the field of music, where the musician also acts as a performer. The context developed by Frith (1996) relates the term 'performance' as a social and communicative process that is dependent on an audience for its realization, following the chain "material-agent-work-public".

Performance is therefore a form of rhetoric, a rhetoric of gestures, where bodily and gestural movements generally dominate other forms of communicative signs, such as language and iconography. This rhetoric creates a relationship of interdependence between the performer and the audience, who act as interpreters of a composer/artist's work through their ability to apprehend the artist's performative elements, especially posture, gestures and body language. The audience understands the performative gesture, without the need for explanations, through a constant dialogue between inside and outside, projected by the body movement induced by the performer/artist's action.

Auslander (2006) proposes positioning musicians as social beings, not only in the sense that musical performances are interactions between them, as suggested earlier by Cook (2001), but in a broader sense, in which to be a musician it is necessary to perform an identity within a social context.

So, the material produced and perceived as music happens under its primary framing, that is, music is produced intentionally by a human agent acting concerning the comprehension and understanding of a particular social group. This concept of music can be extended beyond conventions, inserting it into any possible structure of sound action, such as the gestures of avant-garde and experimental musicians, namely the Italian futurists, musicians of concrete music and electronic music, musicians related to the Fluxus movement, among others.

COMBINATORY CONTAMINATIONS

Similar to political and social history, the history of performance has undergone gradual and incremental developments, punctuated by intense periods of more abrupt changes. Specifically, there have been three periods of more radical evolution: (i) a period related to futurism in the 1910s, (ii) another period linked with performance using different mediums in the 1960s, and (iii) a third period interconnected to experimentation with the use of computers in performance in the 1990s.

The first and third periods were influenced by the emergence of new technologies. The proliferation of multimedia performances in the 1960s, however, was related to the ability to use different mediums simultaneously and, more importantly, to greater artistic inspiration associated with various ideological and cultural changes (Dixon, 2007). It is important to reflect on experimentation using computers, interconnecting and relating the artists, the works and the associated purposes, to understand the development of multimedia performance and the advent of new media in the 90s.

The developments in contemporary artistic production that began in the 1990s, with the advent of digital culture, have influenced various combinations of mediums, including performance art, social practice, modular sculpture, painting on canvas, analogue film, design, and modernist architecture. New media art of the 1990s emerged as a response to the revolution in information technology and the digitalization of cultural forms.

Performance Art transformed from a transgressive function to an artistic genre among others between the mid-1980s and the early 1990s (Féral, 1992). This transformation was not solely due to changes in socio-cultural ambience, but also to evolving conceptions of the body resulting from contact with technology. This contact contributed to the consolidation of performance (Birringer, 1991). During the 1990s, computer technologies benefited from the digital revolution. Effective hardware and software with user-friendly features became increasingly prevalent. This decade saw the emergence of innovations such as digital cameras, portable computers, and the World Wide Web (Dixon, 2007).

The performance arts have always been interdisciplinary and have incorporated multimedia elements (Goldberg, 2001). At the beginning of the 20th century, Fuller was among the first choreographers to incorporate new technologies into her dances. She utilized film projections and shadow effects, among other techniques (Dixon, 2007). Her work served as a precursor for other artists in the 1990s, including Wayne McGregor with Cyborg (1995) and Bud Blumenthal & Fernando Martín with Rivermen (1999).

In 1995, Wayne McGregor choreographed and performed Cyborg at the Institute of Contemporary Arts in London. The performance utilized stage lights to fragment McGregor's body, creating the illusion of shape-shifting as parts of his body were cast into shadow and others illuminated. McGregor's use of old technology to generate new effects evokes the pioneering use of technology in dance.

The development of original software and hardware systems by dance artists was fragmented and individual, reflecting the development of dance and the technological movement. During the 1990s, digital dance works were mainly seen by aficionados, advertised on specialist e-lists or witnessed at specialist conference meetings. However, the use of software in dance saw significant growth in the last decade of the 20th century (Dixon, 2007).

The work *Merce Cunningham: Ciber Dances with Life Forms* (1997), developed by choreographer Merce Cunningham and programmer Thecla Schiphorst, became a seminal work for the implementation of multimedia in dance (Dixon, 2007). Cunningham also used motion-capture capabilities in the live show Biped (1999), where dancers interacted with the figurative forms, they have created which were projected in real-time onto a screen (Rush, 1999).

During this period, several innovative works incorporated technological and digital interaction on stage. For example, *the making of americans* (1991-) by The Gertrude Stein Repertory Theatre and *string* (1999) by Kunstwerk-Blend incorporated live videoconferences into the stage space, and The Builders Association's *IMPERIAL MOTEL (Faust)* (1996) and *JUMP CUT (Faust)* (1997-1998) allowed actors to manipulate images with digital projections.

The technological advancements of the 1990s not only encouraged experimentation with different media, languages, and techniques but also led to the expansion of multimedia performance through the emergence of new practices that emphasized the use of sound and visual media.

In recent years, there has been a further expansion of performance, with the emergence of new practices that focus on audio-visual performance, highlighting the importance of sound and visual media in a live context.

Mello (2008) argues that live audio-visual performances are not finished products, but rather proposals that involve a creative dialogue between various concepts such as improvisation, open-ended work, and the impermanence of artistic work. In other words, these approaches explore a procedural strategy that emphasizes the performative moment as a constitutive form of experience and the construction of meaning. Based on these observations, Mello (2008) highlights the concept of contamination in performative moments. He clarifies that manifestations that use live audio-visuals operate in a contaminated way with a diversity of mediums, ambiences, and artistic actions from both the visual arts and electronic music culture. The concept of contamination understands sound and image as a process in which other languages participate in the artistic experience without a hierarchical status. Thus, the audio-visual content is not limited to a single code, but rather enriched through dialogue with other languages, influencing them in the creation of a dialectical discourse.

Audio-visual performances are differentiated according to three vectors:

(i)   by history - by association with electronic music, multimedia performance and cinematic expression,
(ii) by context - by association with the moving image, expanded cinema and live cinema, and
(iii) by more or less multidisciplinary processes/procedural approaches - where the sound/visual are generated algorithmically, the visual is developed as a function of the sound, the sound is developed as a function of the visual, or based on independent sound and visual narratives.

Added to these intermediate practices is the context of 'live', an artistic expression that takes place in the moment and in front of an audience, which is present in a variety of other performance practices.

By situating the case studies of this chapter within the scope of performance and including sound and image in its practice, we implicitly assume that the sound and visual creations stimulate the senses of hearing and sight through the use of computer technologies, expanded through software and hardware (Wenger, 1998). Audio-visual performance in the context of 'live' combines in the form of a dialogue the performative contingency between two components - sound and image, to present a unique multisensory experience in front of an audience, in a defined time and space.

In this sense, the procedural approach to audio-visual performance is (i) based on programming, (ii) based on sound, (iii) based on images or (iv) based on independent sound and visual narratives. Below we highlight several works that have explored and consolidated these lines of creation in recent decades.

(i)   The use of programming for the production of images and/or sounds can be followed in its various modulations in the creations of:

   o   Adolfo Luxúria Canibal, João Martinho Moura and Miguel Pedro (*Câmara Neuronal*, 2011),
   o   António Rafael and João Martinho Moura (*NaN: Collider*, 2016),
   o   Boris Chimp 504 [Miguel Neto and Rodrigo Carvalho] (*MULTIVERSE*, 2016-2019; *VANISHING QUASARS*, 2019-),
   o   Chris Salter (*Chronopolis*, 2002; *Made in China: Return of the Soul*, 2007; *Chronotopia*, 2010; *N-Polytope*, 2012; *Other/Self*, 2017),
   o   cyclo [Ryoji Ikeda and Alva Noto] (*.id*, 2017),
   o   Daito Manabe (*YASKAWA × Rhizomatiks × ELEVENPLAY*, 2015; *phosphere*, 2017),
   o   Hiroaki Umeda (*Adapting for Distortion*, 2008; *Holistic Strata*, 2011; *split flow*, 2013; *Intensional Particle*, 2015; *Median*, 2018; *vaporising*, 2023),
   o   Hiroaki Umeda, Aoki Takamasa and Shuhei Matsuyama (*indivisible substance*, 2021),
   o   João Martinho Moura (*Nano Abstractions*, 2017; *Sci-fi Miners*, 2018-2019; *out > there*, 2020; *space~aprox*, 2022),
   o   Né Barros and João Martinho Moura (*CO: LATERAL*, 2016-2019; *UNA*, 2020),
   o   Ryoichi Kurokawa (*cm: av_c*, 2005; *celeritas*, 2009; *Rheo*, 2009; *syn_*, 2011; *mol*, 2012; *34°55'11"S 138°35'53"E*, 2015; *unfold.alt*, 2016; *ad/ab Atom*, 2017; *subassemblies*, 2019; *re-assembli*, 2022),

o   Ryoji Ikeda (*datamatics*, 2006; *test pattern*, 2008; *superposition*, 2012; *supercodex*, 2013; *ultratronics*, 2022).

(ii) As for the use of sound in the conception of visuals for soundscapes and electronic sonorities, we can emphasize the case of the work developed by:

o   @c and Lia Lia (2000-),
o   Alva Noto and Ryuichi Sakamoto (*Insen*, 2006; *utp_*, 2008),
o   Holy Other and Pedro Maia (2021-),
o   Jasmine Guffond and Ilan Katin (2021-),
o   John Kameel Farah and Ilan Katin (2021-),
o   Klara Lewis, Nik Colk Void and Pedro Maia (2021-),
o   Murcof and Roderick Maclachlan (*Océano*, 2008),
o   Murcof and Simon Geilfus (*Cosmos*, 2007),
o   Patti Smith, Soundwalk Collective and Pedro Maia (2022),
o   Robert Lippok and Pedro Maia (2018),
o   Shxcxchcxsh and Pedro Maia (2022),
o   Vitor Joaquim and Thr3hold (*Geography*, 2012),
o   XTRNGR and Desilence Studio (A/V, 2013).

(iii) The use of the image in the specific conception of sounds can be highlighted in the case of:

o   Dziga Vertov's film *Tchelovek s kinoapparatom* (*Man with a Movie Camera*) (1929), whose sound ambiences were developed by Biosphere (*Substrata2/Man with a Movie Camera*, 2001) and The Cinematic Orchestra (*Man with a Movie Camera*, 2001),
o   the film *Douro, Faina Fluvial* (1931) by Manoel de Oliveira, whose soundscapes were developed by Luís de Freitas Branco (*Douro, Faina Fluvial*, 1934) and Emmanuel Nunes (*Litaines du Feu et de la Mer*, 1996),
o   the trilogy of non-narrative films *Qatsi* (*Koyaanisqatsi: Life Out of Balance*, 1982; *Powaqqatsi: Life in Transformation*, 1988; *Naqoyqatsi: Life as War*, 2002) by Godfrey Reggio, whose soundscapes were developed by Philip Glass.

(iv) Creations based on independent sound and visual narratives in an experimentation in which the confluence of sound and visual medium capture two senses at the same time in a single sense, can be underlined the works of:

o   Bill Viola (Bodies of light, 2009),
o   Birgit Hein (La moderna poesia, 2000; Poesia', 2010; Abstrakter Film, 2013),
o   Carolee Schneemann (Devour, 2003-2004; SNAFU, 2004),
o   Frederico Dinis (peregrinatio perpetua, 2020; hollow murmurs, 2021; a morosidade da espera e do eco, 2022; o vagar que agrega e contém, 2023),
o   James Elaine and William Basinski (Iceland Celeste, 2022),
o   Keiichiro Shibuya and Shiro Takatani (live, 2009),
o   Loscil (Stases, 2006; Monument Builders, 2016; Adrift, 2023),
o   Lucy Railton and Pedro Maia (Janela do Inferno, 2021),
o   Rei Harakami and Shiro Takatani (red curb, 2005),
o   Robert Whitman (Antenna, 2004),

o   Ryuichi Sakamoto and Shiro Takatani (LIFE, 1999; Garden, 2007; collapsed, 2012; Forest Symphony, 2013; async, 2017; dis. play, 2018),

o   Shiro Takatani (La chambre claire, 2008; Chroma, 2012; ST/LL, 2015),

o   Shiro Takatani and Fujiko Nakaya (CLOUD FOREST, 2010),

o   William Basinski (The Disintegration Loops, 2004) and Yann Beauvais (Artificial Poetic, 2013; Schismes, 2014).

o   Also, in this line of creation based on independent sound and visual narratives can be referred the works a *morosidade da espera e do eco* [*the slowness of waiting and echo*] (2022), *o vagar que agrega e contém* [*the wandering that aggregates and contains*] (2023), *a demora na procura e no encontro* [*the delay in seeking and finding*] (2023) developed and which will be presented in the case studies analyses of this chapter.

These approaches and practices converge towards a performative moment of expression. The sound and image components are combined with other disciplines, expanding the live audio-visual performance conceptually. When sound and image capture both senses simultaneously, they create a single aesthetic-narrative sense. This not only captures the viewer's attention but also directs them towards new interpretations (Chion, 1999; Ricoeur, 2004, Chapple & Kattenbelt, 2006). In this sense, the dimension of performativity plays a role in producing effects of presence, which are extensions and intensifications of these emotions and senses (Fisher-Lichte, 2019).

METHODOLOGICAL PROCESS

Research through artistic practice, or practice-as-research, is a process of continuous inquiry. Unlike other academic research models, it is based on the experience and practice of artist-researchers. Therefore, it requires models that are suited to its unique and particular nature. Various discursive and presentation strategies can be employed to convey this singular practice. This makes the process of research through artistic practice challenging, as each proposed approach involves a form of productive uncertainty, creating a space for temporary 'constructions' of concepts and contingent thinking.

Projects developed using a hybrid methodology and executed as work in progress can be considered an alternative form of investigative practice. The approach is similar to the most recent dynamics of artistic practice but differs from traditional art. It drives the creation of new approaches and pushes boundaries. According to Witkin (2011),

In general, research is seen as providing important knowledge for practice, while practice can provide contextual relevance to research. However, differences in their aims, language, specialization, audience and ambience [among others] keep the two separate. Thus, the theme of "practice [as] research" as presented here refers to beliefs and values about practice and research that give rise to a perceived disparity between the current state of affairs and a more desirable outlook. (Witkin, 2011: 10)

In addition to the differences mentioned by this author, three other characteristics are presented as reasons for distinguishing practice from research. These are creativity, changeability, and presence. However, these characteristics can also be considered points of convergence, as they are present in both practice and research.

To confirm this convergence, the research approach presented in this chapter developed a set of projects using a process of research through artistic practice. The projects have their format and language of expression, and the purpose is to analyze and develop functional methods and strategies linked to the evolution of the site-specific projects themselves. Additionally, the research proposes ways of presenting them in performative moments. These were developed based on two main components: the process of contextualizing the place and approaching the site-specific and the deconstruction of the sense of place (Dinis, 2020).

The process of contextualizing the place starts with interacting with the location to apprehend and understand it. This is achieved by staying in the place (permanence) and exploring it (displacements). In this sense, site-specific projects developed in specific places are viewed as a means of representing memory through the construction of sound and visual narratives. These narratives are affective and contribute to foster corporeality for both the performers and the spectators. The use of performative moments enhances this experience.

Each site-specific project is the result of a systematic methodology that involves assessing the various levels of permanence and modes of access to information, as well as the relationship established with the place and the objectives defined for each project (Dinis, 2023).

The methodology employed in the site-specific projects we developed is part of a research process through artistic practice. This is because practice guides research and research that involves practical knowledge that can be demonstrated through practice. This knowledge is a matter of doing rather than being abstractly conceived and therefore cannot be articulated solely through a traditional proposition in words alone (Nelson, 2013: 9). According to Ingolds (2013: 6), knowledge is developed through the blending of practical and observational engagements with the beings and existences around us. Nevanlinna (2002) suggests that research involving artistic practice inevitably reflects an empirical dimension.

Rubidge (2005) argues that these processes favor the practice itself and do not require a systematic theoretical questioning of concepts that accompany this practice. Rubidge (2005:7) identifies a form of research practiced by professional artists such as Martha Graham, Merce Cunningham, Lloyd Newson, Ian Spink, William Forsythe, Hellen Sky and others. These artists have pushed the boundaries of their disciplines but have never engaged in articulating their reflections or practice in conventional theoretical terms.

Nelson (2013) supports the idea that research through artistic practice involves using practice as a key method of enquiry. In the arts, practice is presented as substantial evidence of an enquiry (Nelson, 2013: 8). Taylor (1985), emphasizes that these practices are 'semantic spaces' that cannot be distinguished from the language used to describe, invoke, or realize them (Taylor 1985: 33) and Gray (1996) defines practice-as-research, through practice, considering it to be

> *(...) firstly, (...) [a] research that is initiated in practice, where questions, problems and challenges are identified and shaped by the needs of practice and [its] practitioners; and secondly, (...) [a] research strategy that is conducted through practice, predominantly using specific methodologies and methods familiar to [its] practitioners (...).* (Gray, 1996: 3)

These research methods differ from traditional academic methodologies because they can address questions that are intrinsically linked to the research subject and follow various paths from hypothesis formulation to confirmation or refutation. They allow for more flexibility in exploring research questions. In this sense, Haseman (2006) argues that:

> (...) many practice-led researchers do not start a research project with a sense of 'a problem'. In fact, they may be guided by what is best described as 'an enthusiasm for practice': something that is exciting, something that may be anarchic, unruly, or even something that is just becoming possible as [a] new technology or new networks become available (but of which they cannot be certain). Practice-led researchers build experimental starting points from which practice follows. They tend to 'dive in', to start practicing to see what emerges. (Haseman, 2006: 3)

Bonenfent (2012) agrees with the idea of "exploring what emerges", adding that the process of research through artistic practice "transcends and interweaves 'body', 'experience', 'mind', 'sensation', 'analysis', 'articulation', 'memory' and 'argument', often in idiosyncratically created structures" (Bonenfent, 2012: 22).

This notion is also supported by authors such as Barret & Bold (2007), Kershaw & Nicholson (2011), Leavy (2015), and Bala et al. (2017). They argue that since artistic practice is individual, unique, and particular, research models through artistic practice can be adapted using different approaches. In an artistic research process, all aspects are often in motion and evolving (Arlander, 2012: 323). According to Arlander (2012), there is no universally accepted form of research for artist-researchers to follow, just as there is no universally accepted concept of art on which to base art-based research (Arlander, 2012: 332).

CASE STUDIES

In this section, we analyze three site-specific projects that follow a research approach through artistic practice following the methodology outlined in the previous section. The approach involves two components: the process of approaching the site-specific and the (de)construction of a sense of place (Dinis, 2020).

Interaction with the places initiated the process of approaching the site-specific, which was carried out through permanence and displacements at the chosen location. The slow speed of these two actions allowed for recording and assimilating the sensations of discovering the places. This emphasized the dimension of sensitive and affective experience, which were ordered from the memories of the places (Jackson, 1994). Upon reviewing the physical and digital records collected during the fieldwork we developed, it became apparent that the actions taken were not based on the subjective organization of the place, but rather an interference with the order of the elements present. The permanence and displacements were intended to reorder the place and create new narratives, infused with emotion, as part of a strategy to observe and assemble the locations (Dinis, 2023).

Each project focused on three specific locations: the Tree of Life Chapel in Braga, the Chapel of the Immaculate in Braga and the Church of Cedofeita in Porto, all of them in Portugal. The first step was to identify the contextual elements of each place that symbolized its unique characteristics, inventory its memories, and reconstruct experiences of the place. These memories and experiences were used as guiding elements for the performance moments of each site-specific project

The methodological approach of research through artistic practice assumes that the relationship between research, creation, performative moments (the live audio-visual performance), and residual artefacts circumscribe the dynamics of thought and the formulation of possibilities of meaning throughout the process. It provides a new point of view from which new relationships can be established (Dinis, 2020). Thus, the process of research through artistic practice is understood as part of the temporal cycle of artistic creation. This cycle involves a continuous iteration of enquiry and action, which is characteristic of the performativity that we wish to substantiate (Dinis, 2023).

To guide the audio-visual aesthetics of the site-specific projects, we adopted the concept of 'aesthetics of slowness' (Koepnick, 2014). This approach offers an alternative to the fast-paced culture of instant gratification, encouraging a more deliberate and thoughtful approach to artistic creation and appreciation. By embracing a slower pace, it is possible to explore the depth and complexity of the artistic experience. This promotes a greater understanding of the artwork, emotional resonance, and the transformative power of art (Dinis, 2024)

With the use of slowness, deliberate elements in sound and visual mediums create a particular artistic experience for the audience. These aesthetic challenges the fast-paced nature of contemporary culture and invites a more contemplative and immersive engagement through sound and image. Prolonged sound textures, elongated rhythm, and spacious harmonies are employed to achieve this aesthetic of slowness. Slow tempos and extended durations create a contemplative and introspective atmosphere, promoting a deeper connection with the auditory experience and deep listening. In moving images, slow-motion techniques emphasize visual detail and the passage of time. Image sequences can reveal hidden depths in ordinary actions or events, providing a new perspective and allowing for more attentive and reflective observation of visual elements. Therefore, the use of an aesthetic of slowness during performative moments invites the audience to pause, reflect, and engage in a sensory experience in a deeper and more contemplative way.

Next, the site-specific projects developed are presented providing information on each, organized into key elements related to their creation and presentation. Additional information, including recordings, images, and documentation related to the process of creation, research, presentation, and reception of each project, is also included and is an integral part of this chapter, available at a website [https://fredericodinis.wordpress.com/performance/lugares-religiosos/].

As a whole, these materials enhance and illustrate the research pathways through artistic practice, making them an important part of the reflective creative process. These projects ensure thematic and temporal heterogeneity in the fieldwork conducted as part of the research.

The meanings of the site-specific projects were discovered through the application of the conceptual model of approach to place (Dinis, 2020). The chosen places for the fieldwork were the Tree of Life Chapel in Braga, the Chapel of the Immaculate in Braga and the Church of Cedofeita in Porto. Each of these places represents a theme that activates performativity, namely 'shelter', 'humility', and 'fragility'. These places serve as 'shelters' for those seeking refuge, providing solace, peace, and a sense of spiritual connection. They create an atmosphere conducive to spiritual contemplation and inner reflection, reminding individuals of the importance of 'humility' in a spiritual approach. This fosters an attitude of openness, surrender, and willingness to learn and grow spiritually. Performance venues are often locations that inspire contemplation of the delicateness and impermanence of human life. They invite people to transcend their 'fragility' and connect with something greater and more lasting during performative moments.

A Morosidade da Espera e Do Eco [*The Slowness of Waiting and Echo*] (2022)

Inside the Conciliar Seminary of St Peter and St Paul in Braga is the Tree of Life Chapel, a place that appeals to the senses and emotions and is the result of the joint work of seminarians, teachers, architects, artists, sculptors, goldsmiths, painters, carpenters and masons.

The chapel's name comes from the triptych by Ilda David, located behind the altar and representing the Paschal mystery: The Passion, Death and Resurrection. The space is a detached volume, within a seminary space, which takes center stage. The design of this 'body' is intended to be a singular, balanced and visible structure, becoming a present and exceptional piece within the building.

This semi-compact body is distinguished from the existing one by its configuration and is completed by its symbolism. The space that surrounds it is assumed to be a moment of transition. The development of the project is intended to arouse the curiosity of those who wander through it, offering an invitation to walk towards it. The chapel's main characteristic is its simplicity. A wooden shelter where the various beams create a fascinating play of light and shadows. Figures 1, 2 and 3 are representative of the fieldwork carried out in the Tree of Life Chapel.

Inside the two renovated floors that guard the chapel, some daylight enters, which is very controlled and delicately used by the architects. The space around the chapel is quite dark, making the object appear almost transparent. Natural light is filtered through its walls, which are made of thin, horizontal wooden planks, giving the chapel a luminous appearance. The chapel's interior space, with its curved lines, conveys a sense of care and embrace. It evokes feelings of purity, of beauty; the presence of God. (Carvalho, 2013)

Figure 1. Fieldwork: Tree of Life Chapel in Braga

(Frederico Dinis, 2022)

Figure 2. Fieldwork: Tree of Life Chapel in Braga

(Frederico Dinis, 2022)

Figure 3. Fieldwork: Tree of Life Chapel in Braga

(Frederico Dinis, 2022)

With the 'shelter' (the theme and performativity activator of the site-specific project) and the memory linked to the Tree of Life Chapel, as the focal point, a phenomenological exercise of personal (re) interpretation of the identity characteristics of the place was used, selecting the keywords that guided the creation, and then choosing some specific contexts of the Tree of Life Chapel that figuratively symbolize these characteristics.

Considering 'shelter' as a metaphor for spirituality reinforces the idea of finding refuge, protection and inner peace within oneself. Just as a physical shelter offers protection and security from external elements, a spiritual shelter refers to an individual inner space where one finds solace, guidance and a sense of connection to something greater. A shelter also offers protection from external threats and spirituality provides a sense of safety and security, offering a refuge from everyday challenges and uncertainties.

Still, in a metaphorical sense, spirituality can serve as a foundation on which values, beliefs and worldviews are built, providing a stable structure for travelling through life's challenges, offering meaning, purpose and a sense of purpose. In this sense, the keywords that define the identity characteristics linked to 'shelter' are foundation, support, kindness, greatness, harmony, humility, perseverance, and endurance.

The artistic creation *a morosidade da espera e do eco* [*the slowness of waiting and echo*] (2022) is thus conceived based on these identity characteristics, taking into account a mapping between characteristics and local contexts in space. Having found the identity characteristics (keywords) associated with the Tree of Life Chapel and the theme of creation (shelter), it is important to unfold this mapping into the movements (sub-themes) of creation, thus producing the conceptual guide.

The audio and visual narratives of the audio-visual creation were developed taking this conceptual guide into account and are presented in the performative moment that takes place in the Tree of Life Chapel. The performer is not only an operator of the medium used, but also a real-time narrator, (re)constructing the sound and visual narratives, remembering and imagining other possible places. Time and space are thus altered, referring to so many other (re)invented and (un)known places, momentarily transforming the space of the Tree of Life Chapel into a space full of new meanings. The performance also seeks to portray sensations and emotions about a unique place, encompassing its identity, its memories and its history.

Figures 4, 5 and 6, are some of the residual artefacts produced as part of the public presentation of *a morosidade da espera e do eco* [*the slowness of waiting and echo*], which took place on 2022.12.20, in the Tree of Life Chapel of the Conciliar Seminary in Braga. More documentation about this site-specific project can be accessed at https://fredericodinis.wordpress.com/2022/12/21/capela-arvore-da-vida/.

Figure 4. a morosidade da espera e do eco [the slowness of waiting and echo] - Tree of Life Chapel, 2022.12.20

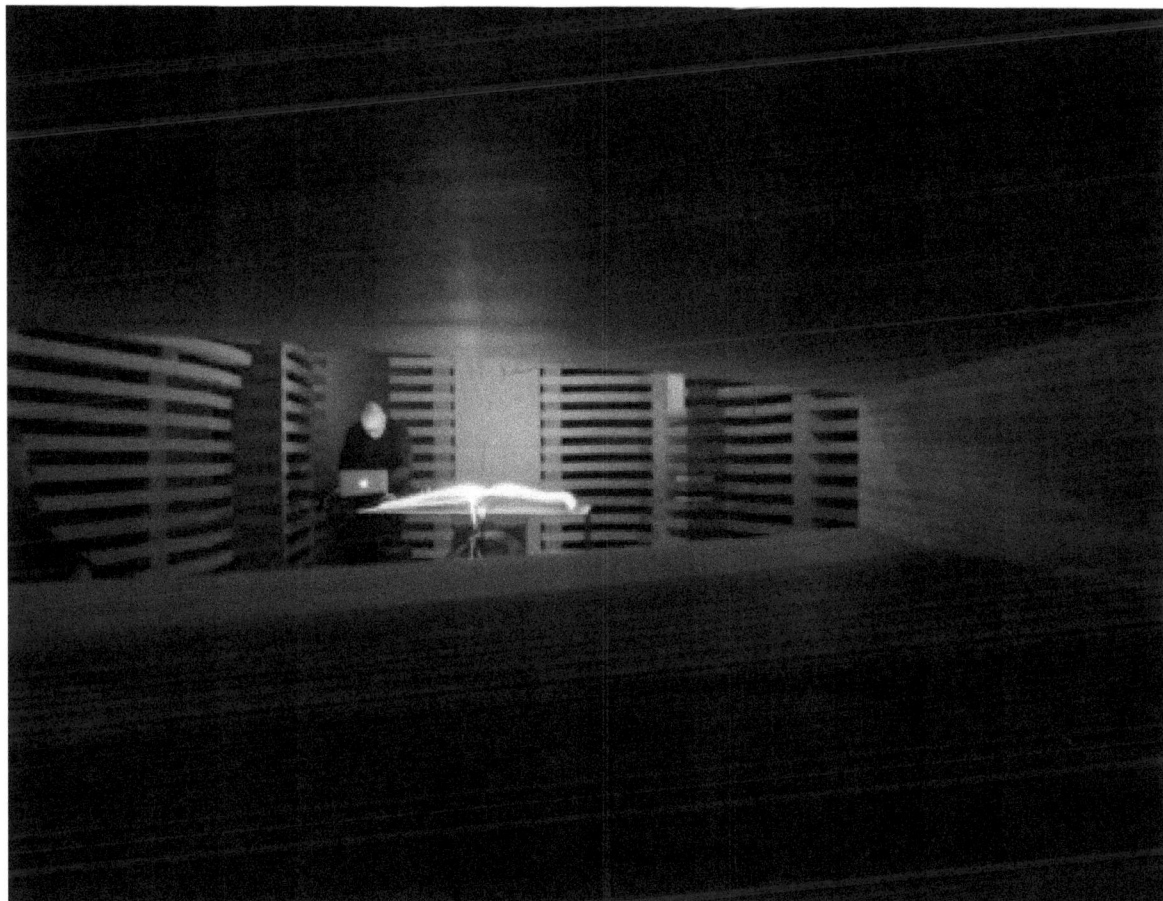

(Joaquim Félix de Carvalho, 2022)

Figure 5. a morosidade da espera e do eco [the slowness of waiting and echo] - Tree of Life Chapel, 2022.12.20

(Joaquim Félix de Carvalho, 2022)

Figure 6. a morosidade da espera e do eco [the slowness of waiting and echo] - Tree of Life Chapel, 2022.12.20

(Joaquim Félix de Carvalho, 2022)

o vagar que agrega e contém [*the wandering that aggregates and contains*] (2023)

A small wooden forest provides access to the Chapel of the Immaculate, located inside the Braga Minor Seminary. Passing through this forest, you reach a clearing that serves as the entrance to the assembly. This forest also serves as a support for the Full of Grace Chapel, which rises above the tree structure.

In addition to the forest, the entrance to the chapel features a granite pillar with a carved ear and an individual chair next to it, inviting listening and personal response. In the space, you can see a large concrete vault, apparently suspended thanks to a steel structure. Together with the other elements, this roof creates an atmosphere of humility, conducive to introspection. Essential aspects such as scale and light were approached with a more contemporary language.

With the same walls, the chapel (...) gained about four metres in height. And since they were made of masonry, they were stripped down, making the metaphorical constructive strength of the large granite and clay box visible. The space has become more harmonious in its proportions and with more luminosity. (Carvalho, 2021)

On the central axis of the nave, in front of the entrance, there is a 'body of light', a white marble panel suspended on a steel structure, crossed by an abundance of natural light that fills the space and gives it an extraordinary shine. Figures 7, 8 and 9 are representative of the fieldwork carried out.

Figure 7. Fieldwork: Chapel of the Immaculate in Braga

(Frederico Dinis, 2023)

Figure 8. Fieldwork: Chapel of the Immaculate in Braga

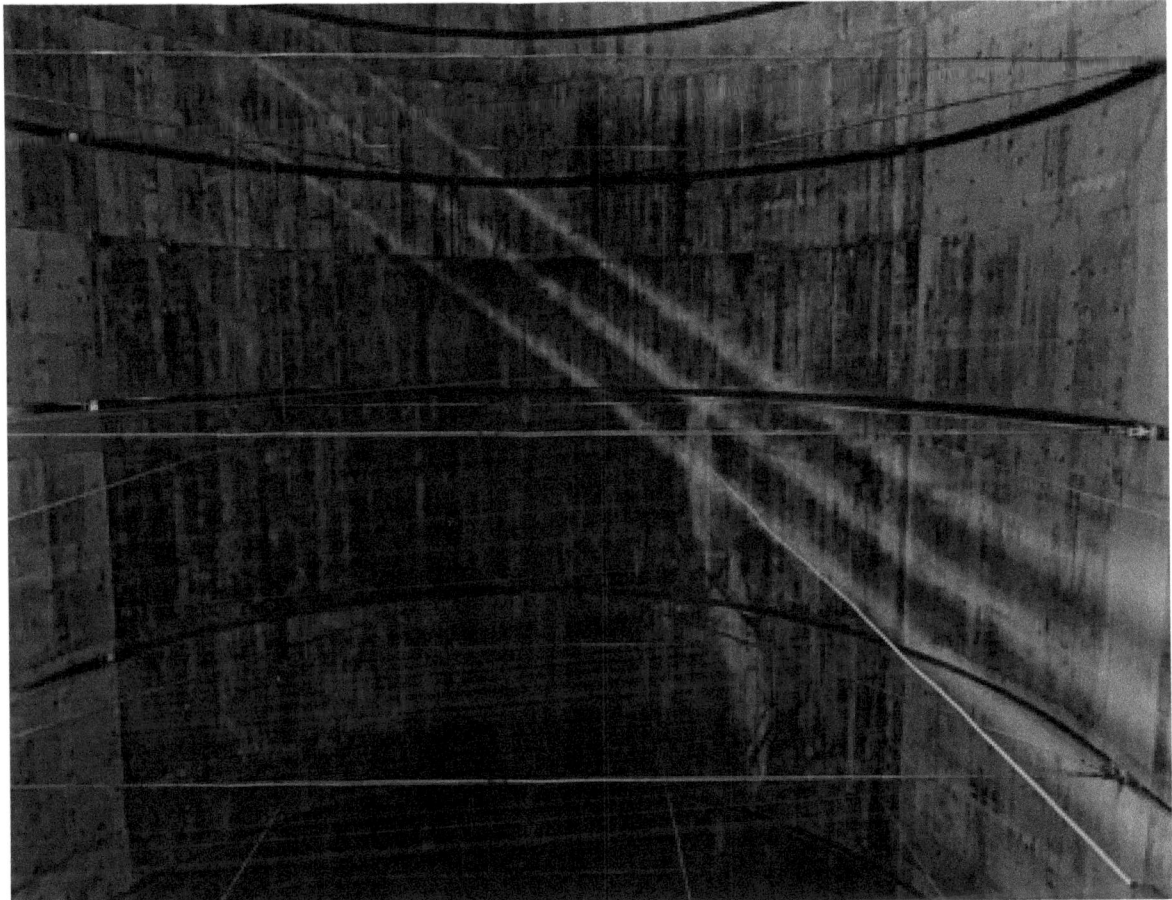

(Frederico Dinis, 2023)

Figure 9. Fieldwork: Chapel of the Immaculate in Braga

(Frederico Dinis, 2023)

With 'humility' (the theme and performativity activator of the site-specific project) and the memory linked to the Chapel of the Immaculate, as the focal point, we used a phenomenological exercise of personal (re)interpretation of the identity characteristics of the place, selecting the keywords that guided the creation, and then choosing some specific contexts in the Chapel of the Immaculate that figuratively symbolize these characteristics.

Humility can be seen as a metaphor for spirituality, representing a state of being that aligns with the fundamental principles and values of many spiritual traditions, involving recognizing that there is something greater than ourselves, adopting a sense of respect, acknowledging the limitations of personal knowledge and assuming a sense of openness and receptivity to spiritual teachings.

Encouraging self-reflection, self-awareness and the desire to learn from mistakes, promoting personal and spiritual development are other characteristics of humility, which seeks to maintain a balanced perspective and an attitude of openness and reverence for what surrounds us. In this sense, the keywords that define the identity characteristics linked to 'humility' are the following: body, ephemeral, fragility, equality, invisibility, luminosity, tranquility, and temporality.

The artistic creation, *o vagar que agrega e contém* [*the wandering that aggregates and contains*] (2023), is thus conceived based on these identity characteristics, taking into account a mapping between characteristics and local contexts in space. Having found the identity characteristics (keywords) associated with the Chapel of the Immaculate and the theme of creation (humility), it is important to unfold this mapping into the movements (sub-themes) of creation, thus producing the conceptual guide.

The audio and visual narratives of the creation were developed taking this conceptual script into account and are presented in the performative moment that takes place in the place. The performer is not only the operator of the media used, but also the real-time narrator, (re)constructing the sound and visual narratives, remembering and imagining other possible places. Time and space are thus altered, referring to so many other (re)invented and (un)known places, momentarily transforming the space of the Chapel of the Immaculate into a space full of new meanings. The performance also seeks to portray sensations and emotions about a unique place, encompassing its identity, its memories and its history.

Figures 10, 11 and 12, are some of the residual artefacts produced as part of the public presentation of *o vagar que agrega e contém* [*the wandering that aggregates and contains*], which took place on 2023.03.03 in the Chapel of the Immaculate at the Seminary of Our Lady of the Conception in Braga. More documentation about this site-specific project can be accessed at https://fredericodinis.wordpress .com/2023/03/06/capela-da-imaculada/

Figure 10. o vagar que agrega e contém [the wandering that aggregates and contains]

(Joaquim Félix de Carvalho, 2023) - Chapel of the Immaculate, 2023.03.03

Figure 11. o vagar que agrega e contém [the wandering that aggregates and contains]

(Joaquim Félix de Carvalho, 2023) - Chapel of the Immaculate, 2023.03.03

Figure 12. o vagar que agrega e contém [the wandering that aggregates and contains]

(Joaquim Félix de Carvalho, 2023) - Chapel of the Immaculate, 2023.03.03

a demora na procura e no encontro [*the delay in seeking and finding*] (2023)

The Cedofeita Church building is a monumental and brutal concrete structure. It is an example of the modernist architectural movement in Porto. In 2017, a fire inside precipitated the need to carry out an intervention to repair the church.

It was a simple, minimalist intervention that emphasized the use of primary materials such as stone and wood. A materialization that sought to highlight the plasticity and identity of these materials to the fullest, enabling visitors to the space not just to see the space, but to feel invited to perceive it in the space itself.

A space where time, silence and raw materials promote complementarity between authenticity and fragility, and which seeks to respond to the most important variables of space, time and silence, materialized in a space between the autonomous and the dialoguing. Figures 13, 14 and 15 are representative of the fieldwork carried out.

When you enter a church, you have to feel a different space, one that transports you to a different dimension and time scale, whether there are fifty or five hundred people there, or more. (...) it's a space that allows for smaller and larger celebrations. (Fontes, 2020)

Figure 13. Fieldwork: Church of Cedofeita in Porto

(Frederico Dinis, 2023)

Figure 14. Fieldwork: Church of Cedofeita in Porto

(Frederico Dinis, 2023)

Figure 15. Fieldwork: Church of Cedofeita in Porto

(Frederico Dinis, 2023)

With 'fragility' as the focal point (theme and performativity activator of the site-specific project) and the memory linked to the Church of Cedofeita, we implemented a phenomenological exercise of personal (re)interpretation of the identity characteristics of the place, selecting the keywords to guide the creation, and then choosing some specific contexts in the Church of Cedofeita that figuratively symbolize these characteristics.

Fragility insinuates a state of vulnerability, in which each person opens themselves up to the uncertainties and mysteries of the spiritual journey, and implies embracing vulnerability as a means of deepening the connection with the transcendent of existence. Fragility reminds the transitory nature of life and the impermanence of all things to find a deeper meaning beyond the ephemeral aspects of life.

Fragility can also be seen as an invitation to resilience and transformation, through perseverance and learning that can promote personal and spiritual growth. It also emphasizes the importance of compassion, empathy and mutual support, recognizing that each individual's spiritual journey is intertwined with the well-being of others. In this sense, the keywords that define the identity characteristics interconnected with 'fragility' are shelter, immanence, belonging, reminiscence, tension, transformation, transparency and trace.

Artistic creation, *a demora na procura e no encontro* [*the delay in seeking and finding*] (2023), is thus conceived based on these identity characteristics, taking into account a mapping between characteristics and local contexts in space. Having found the identity characteristics (keywords) associated with the Church of Cedofeita and the theme of creation (fragility), it is important to unfold this mapping into the movements (sub-themes) of creation, thus producing the conceptual guide.

The audio and visual narratives of the creation were developed taking this conceptual guide into account and are presented in the performative moment that takes place in the Church of Cedofeita. The performer is not only an operator of the media used, but also a real-time narrator, (re)constructing the sound and visual narratives, remembering and imagining other possible places. Time and space are thus altered, referring to so many other (re)invented and (un)known places, momentarily transforming the space of the Church of Cedofeita into a space full of new meanings. The performance also seeks to portray sensations and emotions about a unique place, encompassing its identity, its memories and its history.

Figures 16, 17 and 18, are some of the residual artefacts produced as part of the public presentation of a morosidade da espera e do eco, which took place on 2023.06.02 at the Church of Cedofeita in Porto. More documentation about this site-specific project can be accessed at https://fredericodinis.wordpress.com/2023/06/03/igreja-de-cedofeita/

Figure 16. A demora na procura e no encontro

Igreja de Cedofeita, 2023.06.02 (Ana Dinis, 2023)

Figure 17: A demora na procura e no encontro

Igreja de Cedofeita, 2023.06.02 (Ana Dinis, 2023)

Figure 18: A demora na procura e no encontro

Igreja de Cedofeita, 2023.06.02 (Ana Dinis, 2023)

These are artworks that are framed in the area of sound and visual performance, seeking to foster audio-visual processes that move between past and present, community and individual, and between specific types of performativity. Each audio-visual creation aimed to construct a representation of a space-time that explores the confluence between sound and visual narratives, places and the memory of those same places.

Inherent in this representation is a process of remembrance, which precedes a process of constructing sounds and images. Sounds that are imagined to have been heard, images that are thought to have already been visualized, and sounds and images that are understood as aids in the living experience of building memory, promoting a performativity of memory during the live performance moment (Dinis, 2024).

Considering that memory is a continuous performative act (Schneider, 2011), the purpose is not only to explore processes of audio-visual representation that confront medium, memory and place through a "repertoire in intermediate mode" (Bénichou, 2010) but also to discuss new intermediate forms of representing places using audio-visual performances.

In this sense, artistic practice related to sound and visual media is increasingly capable of creative experimentation, thus opening up endless relationships between sound and image. In the performative moment, the artist/performer is not only the operator of the media that makes it up, in this case, sound and image, but also the mediator, the creator and, consequently, the narrator, who constructs the sound and visual narratives.

CONCLUSION

This research, conducted through artistic practice examined the various phenomena, traditions, and grammar within the field of performance art, while also questioning the aesthetic significance of this discipline as an essential tool for understanding contemporary culture and our world.

The concept of performance has been understood through various perceptions resulting from different disciplinary approaches, artistic areas, or cultural contexts. Due to this conceptual openness and the diversity of creative procedures, performance, as an action in front of an audience, has great potential for experimentation through the confluence of sound and visual media.

In recent decades, performance has become a prominent creative practice due to technological advancements and its expansion to other media. This has led to a decentralization of the body/performer, allowing for the incorporation of other materialities such as sound or image. In the context of this decentralization, this chapter focuses on a set of artistic practices and audio-visual performance moments that were developed in three places and mediated by sound and image.

Performative moments promote new possibilities, recursive processes, repetitions, non-linear structures, simultaneous events and the mixing of languages, where time, performative space and the performativity developed between performer and spectator relate more freely and in cooperation with various means.

In these live audio-visual performances, sound and image converge as expressive processes, producing a sense of presence and enhancing the representation of memory. The relationship between sound and live image also stimulates the development of new narratives, resulting in more intricate and immersive artistic representations. This reflects the complementary nature of space and time and opens up new opportunities for live audio-visual performances to be explored and experimented with.

The site-specific projects developed and analysed here began with the theme of memory as a phenomenon that enables the present creation of an absence. We also emphasized that memory work involves representation. This representation work is also inherent in the process of remembrance, which precedes the construction of sounds and images. These sounds and images are considered tools to aid in the construction of memories, promoting a performative aspect of memory during live sound and visual performances.

The site-specific projects developed and presented in this chapter emphasize the performative aspects of memory, focusing on how it is represented, shaped, and influenced by various social, cultural, and spatial factors. These moments are crucial in the process of perception and apprehension. They take advantage of the spatial qualities of the places, stimulate multiple senses, evoke emotional and psychological responses, and encourage public involvement. Contextual significance is also taken into account.

The places selected for fieldwork have unique and intangible characteristics that could be uncovered, creating a sense of uniqueness. These are places that aspire to establish a spiritual connection, where one can experience an interaction with the sacred and where the meaning and significance of human existence are heightened. The performativity of memory creates an embodied perception of space in these places, which impacts the public by fostering a sense of belonging and identity. This evokes emotional and spiritual involvement, reinforces rituals and memories, and allows for a symbolic (re)interpretation, encouraging a deeper understanding of the formation of place, for the performer and the audience.

We observed that the performativity of memory can be strengthened through live audio-visual performances in specific places. This can be achieved by incorporating narratives and testimonies that are connected to the place and by integrating audio-visual media that evoke memories and autobiographical experiences. This emphasizes the individual and subjective nature of memory in the spatial context of the place itself.

Performative moments in specific places can provide a platform for the community to shape its collective memory. This can contribute to the reconfiguration of social dynamics within the community and promote the recognition of other perspectives, ultimately fostering feelings of belonging and cohesion. These moments involve artistic reconfigurations of practices, rituals, and artistic forms. They promote (re)interpretations, representations, or juxtapositions of narratives, symbolism, and spiritual aesthetics due to the contested, fluid, and uncertain nature of specific places. By restructuring artistic expressions, audio-visual performances encourage creativity, artistic exploration, and the development of new aesthetic approaches that reflect contemporary sensibilities while preserving the unique identity of specific places.

The aesthetic and performative configurations used in audio-visual artistic creations of a place can impact individual manifestations of belief. This can influence the interpretation and creation of meanings, evoke emotional and spiritual responses, facilitate embodied involvement, and promote personal transformation and transcendence.

REFERENCES

Alcázar, J. (2014). *Performance: un arte del yo: autobiografía, cuerpo e identidad.* Siglo XXI Editores.

Arlander, A. (2012). *Performing Landscape - Notes on Site-specific Work and Artistic Research (Texts 2001-2011).* Theatre Academy Helsinki, Performing Arts Research Centre.

Auslander, P. (2006). Musical Personae. *The Drama Review*, 50(1), 100–119. 10.1162/dram.2006.50.1.100

Bala, S., Gluhovic, M., Korsberg, H., & Röttger, K. (2017). *International Performance Research Pedagogies: Towards an Unconditional Discipline?* Palgrave Macmillan. 10.1007/978-3-319-53943-0

Barrett, E., & Bolt, B. (Eds.). (2007). *Practice as Research: Approaches to Creative Arts Enquiry.* I.B. Tauris. 10.5040/9780755604104

Bay-Cheng, S., Parker-Starbuck, J., & Saltz, D. Z. (2015). *Performance and media: Taxonomies for a changing field.* University of Michigan Press. 10.3998/mpub.5582757

Bénhichou, A. (2010). Ces documents qui sont aussi des oeuvres..... In Bénichou, A. (Ed.), *Ouvrir le Document: Enjeux et pratiques de la documentation dans les arts visuels contemporains.* Les Presses du Réel.

Billington, M. (1996). Footage and footlights. The Guardian.

Birringer, J. H. (1991). The postmodern body in performance. In *Theater: theory and postmodernism.* Indiana University Press.

Bonenfent, Y. (2012). A portrait of the current state of PaR: defining an (in)discipline. In Boyce-Tillman, J. (Ed.), *PaR for the Course: issues involved in the development of practice-based doctorates in the Performing Arts.* The Higher Education Academy Arts and Humanities.

Bowman, N. A. (1966). Investing a Theatrical Ideal: Wagner's Bayreuth "Festspielhaus". *Educational Theatre Journal*, 18(4), 429–438. 10.2307/3205270

Braun, E. (1979). *The Theatre of Meyerhold: revolution on the modern stage.* Eyre Methuen.

Broadwurst, S. (1999). *Liminal acts: a critical overview of contemporary performance and theory.* Cassel.

Butler, J. (2015). *Problemas de género: feminismo e subversão da identidade.* Civilização Brasileira.

Carlson, M. (2004). What is performance? In Bial, H., & Brady, S. (Eds.), *The Performance Studies Reader* (pp. 68–72). Routledge.

Carvalho, J.F. (2013). *A Capela Árvore da Vida: Arquitectura e Vida. COMMUNIO – Revista Internacional Católica, XXX (2013/2),* 201-214.

Carvalho, J. F. (2021). Arte Litúrgica: criações nas capelas de Braga. In Neto, M.J. & Cunha, J.A. (Coord.), *Arte e Igreja em Portugal - Histórias e protagonistas de diálogos recentes.* Casal de Cambra: Caleidoscópio.

Chapple, F., & Kattenbelt, C. (Eds.). (2006). *Intermediality in theatre and performance.* Rodopi. 10.1163/9789401210089

Chion, M. (1999). *The Voice in Cinema. Nova York*. Columbia University Press.

Cook, N. (2001). Between Process and Product: Music and/as Performance. *Music Theory Online, 7*(2).

D'Orazio, D., De Cesaris, S., Morandi, F., & Garai, M. (2018). The aesthetics of the Bayreuth Festspiel-haus explained by means of acoustic measurements and simulations. *Journal of Cultural Heritage*, 34, 151–158. 10.1016/j.culher.2018.03.003

Dinis, F. (2020). *Sinuous Sensations Hypnotic Emotions: Contemporary sound and visual performance* [PhD Thesis, Faculty of Arts and Humanities, University of Coimbra. Coimbra: Portugal].

Dinis, F. (2023). Performativity of the Memory of Religious Places through Sound and Image. *Religions*, 14(9), 1137. 10.3390/rel14091137

Dinis, F. (2024). *The Production of Effects of Presence in Live Audio-Visual Performances. Springer Series in Design and Innovation*. Springer. 10.1007/978-3-031-47281-7_72

Dixon, S. (2007). *Digital performance: a history of new media in theater, dance, performance art, and installation*. The MIT Press. 10.7551/mitpress/2429.001.0001

Féral, J. (1992). What is left of performance art? Autpsy of a function. *Birth of a genre. Discourse - Journal for theorical Studies in Media and Culture*. Springer.

Fischer-Lichte, E. (2013). The Transformative Aesthetics of the Gesamtkunstwerk/Total Work of Art as the Specter Haunting Modernism. *Theatre Journal*, 65(4), 593–603. 10.1353/tj.2013.0104

Fischer-Lichte, E. (2019). *Estética do Performativo*. Orfeu Negro.

Fontes, A. C. (2020). *Conversa com o arquiteto António Cerejeira Fontes*. Junho de 2020.

Frith, S. (1996). *Performing rites: on the value of popular music*. Havard University Press. 10.1093/oso/9780198163329.001.0001

Garai, M., Ito, K., D'Orazio, D., De Cesaris, S., & Morandi, F. (2015). The Acoustics of the Bayreuth Festspielhaus. *Proc. ICSV, 22*, 651.

Goldberg, R. L. (2001). *Performance Art: From Futurism to the Present*. Thames and Hudson.

Gray, C. (1996). Inquiry through practice: developing appropriate research strategies. In *No Guru, No Method?* UIAH.

Harbison, I. (2019). *Performing Image*. The MIT Press. 10.7551/mitpress/10973.001.0001

Haseman, B. (2006). A Manifest for Performative Research. International Australia Incorporating Culture and Policy, theme issue. *Practice-led Research*, 118, 98–106.

Imhoof, D., Menninger, M. E., & Steinhoff, A. J. (Eds.). (2016). *The Total Work of Art: Foundations, Articulations, Inspirations* (Vol. 12). Berghahn Books. 10.3167/9781785331848

Ingold, T. (2013). *Making: Anthropology, Archaeology, Art and Architecture*. Routledge. 10.4324/9780203559055

Jackson, J. B. (1994). *A sense of place, a sense of time*. Yale University Press.

Jamieson, H. V. (2008). Adventures in Cyberformance - Experiments at the interface of theatre and the internet. [Master Theasis, Drama, Creative Industries Faculty, Queensland Universty of Technology].

Kaye, N. (1996). *Art Into Theatre: Performance Interviews and Documents*. Psychology Press.

Kershaw, B. B., & Nicholson, H. (Eds.). (2011). *Research Methods in Theatre and Performance*. Edinburgh University Press. 10.1515/9780748646081

Koepnick, L. (2014). *On Slowness: Toward na Aesthetic of the Contemporary*. Columbia University Press. 10.7312/koep16832

Lajosi, K. (2010). *Wagner and the (Re)mediation of Art. Gesamtkunstwerk and Nineteenth-Century Theories of Media. Frame, 23*.

Laurel, B. (1993). *Computers as Theatre*. Addison-Wesley.

Leavy, P. (2015). *Method meets art: Arts-based research practice*. Guilford Publications.

Mello, C. (2008). *Extremidades do vídeo*. Editora Senac.

Meyerhold, V. (2014). *Meyerhold on theatre*. A&C Black.

Meyerhold, V., Gladkov, A., & Law, A. (1996). *Meyerhold speaks/Meyerhold Rehearses (Russian Theatre Archive)*. Routledge.

Nelson, R. (2013). *Practice as research in the arts: Principles, protocols, pedagogies, resistances*. Springer. 10.1057/9781137282910

Nevanlinna, T. (2002). Is 'Artistic Research' a meaningful concept? In Kiljunen, S., & Hannula, M. (Eds.), *Artistic Research* (pp. 61–71). Fine Art Academy.

Packer, R., & Jordan, K. (2001). *Multimedia: from Wagner to virtual reality*. New York: Norton & Company.

Phelan, P. (1993). *Unmarked: The Politics of Performance*. Routledge.

Pitches, J. (2004). *Vsevolod Meyerhold*. Routledge. 10.4324/9780203634172

Richter, H. (1978). *DADA: Kunst und Antikunst*. Dumont Verlag.

Ricoeur, P. (2004). *Memory, History, Forgetting*. The University of Chicago Press. 10.7208/chicago/9780226713465.001.0001

Roberts, D. (2011). *The total work of art in European modernism*. Cornell University Press. 10.7591/cornell/9780801450235.001.0001

Rubidge, S. (2005). Artists in the academy: Reflections on artistic practice as research. *Paper presented at Dance Rebooted: Initializing the Grid, Deakin University*. Deakin University.

Schmidt, P. (2014). *Meyerhold at work*. University of Texas Press.

Schneider, R. (2011). *Performing Remains: Art and War in Times of Theatrical Reenactment*. Routledge. 10.4324/9780203852873

Smith, M. W. (2007). *The total work of art: from Bayreuth to cyberspace*. Routledge. 10.4324/9780203963166

Taylor, C. (1985). *Philosophy and the Human Sciences: Collected Papers* (Vol. 2). Cambridge University Press. 10.1017/CBO9781139173490

Vazsonyi, N. (2011). The Total Work of Art: From Bayreuth to Cyberspace, and: Modernism after Wagner. *Modernism/Modernity*, 18(1), 196–199. 10.1353/mod.2011.0021

Wagner, R. (2001). The artwork of the future. In Packer, R., & Jordan, K. (Eds.), *Multimedia: from Wagner to virtual reality*. Norton & Company. (Original work published 1849)

Wenger, E. (1998). *Communities of Practice: Learning, Meaning and Identity*. Cambridge University Press. 10.1017/CBO9780511803932

Wesemann, A. (1997). Mirror Games with New Media: The Story of Dance has Always Been the Story of Technology. *International Ballet Tanz Aktuell*, 8/9.

Witkin, S. L. (2011). Why Do We Think Practice Research is a Good Idea? *Social Work & Society*, 9(1), 10–19.

ADDITIONAL READING

Ernst, W. (2017). *The Delayed Present: Media-induced Tempor(e)alities & Techno-traumatic Irritations of "the Contemporary"*. Sternberg Press.

Gaines, M. (2017). *Black Performance on the Outskirts of the Left*. NYU Press.

Ikoniadou, E. (2014). *The Rhythmic Event: Art, Media, and the Sonic*. The MIT Press. 10.7551/mitpress/9886.001.0001

Jarvis, L. (2019). *Immersive Embodiment: Theatres of Mislocalized Sensation*. Palgrave Macmillan. 10.1007/978-3-030-27971-4

Lavender, A. (2016). *Performance in the Twenty-First Century: Theatres of Engagement*. Routledge. 10.4324/9780203128176

Masura, N. (2020). *Digital Theatre: The Making and Meaning of Live Mediated Performance*. Palgrave Macmillan. 10.1007/978-3-030-55628-0

McMillan, U. (2015). *Embodied Avatars: Genealogies of Black Feminist Art and Performance*. NYU Press. 10.18574/nyu/9781479897766.001.0001

Reynolds, B. (2017). *Intermedial Theater: Performance Philosophy, Transversal Poetics, and the Future of Affect*. Palgrave Macmillan. 10.1057/978-1-137-50838-6

KEY TERMS AND DEFINITIONS

Identity: Is an articulation of one's social affiliation, both individually and as a group.

Materiality: Refers to the objects and substances that constitute matter - human and nonhuman bodies, nature, elements, and things. Performativity: In its broadest sense refers to the power of social and spatial practices to constitute subjects and objects. In other words, doings and sayings are performative when they construct the effects, they purportedly merely name.

Representation: Is a process of giving meaning to objects and things through linguistic signs and symbols.

Sense of Place: A vivid awareness of familiar surroundings, a ritual repetition, a sense of community-based on shared experience.

Site-specific Artworks: Practices in which exchanges are articulated between the artwork and the places in which its meanings are defined.

Spatiality: Signifies an attribute or a feature that is related to space. In human geography, the term refers to the way space is implicated in social life.

Chapter 8
A Cronulla si Junceru:
Remembering Racial Violence Through Text-Based Musical Composition

Marcello Messina
http://orcid.org/0000-0002-8822-3342
Southern Federal University, Russia

ABSTRACT

This chapter documents and discusses the musical piece titled A Cronulla si junceru, based on a text written in Sicilian, that narrates the events of the Cronulla riot. The incident took place in the eponymous South Sydney beach, on 11 March 2005. After criticising some of the media releases about Cronulla, the chapter author discusses various aspects related to the piece, ranging from its conceptual intents in terms of collective memory, to the circumstances of its composition (comprovisation) and performances, through to more technical considerations related to the Sicilian language and the use of text as compositional material.

INTRODUCTION

The aim of this chapter is to document and discuss the musical piece *A Cronulla si junceru*, composed by the chapter author Marcello Messina and performed in various occasions and locations throughout the year of 2018.[1] Between 2015 and 2016, the author of this chapter spent six months in Sydney as an "Endeavour Research Fellow" based at "Macquarie University". The fact that these institutional names and titles were written in quotation marks is not random or accidental, in that they both strongly and unmistakably celebrate Australia's histories of white settler colonial violence. To be more specific, Endeavour is the name of the British vessel, commanded by James Cook, that in 1770 reached the Australian coast, inaugurating a history of European pillage, genocide and ruthless conquest over the continent (Edwards, 2016; Rata, 2020; Fredericks and Bradfield, 2023). Macquarie, on the other hand, refers to Lachlan Macquarie, historical Governor of New South Wales (from 1810 to 1821) who also committed genocide against Aboriginal people — including the infamous Appin massacre of 1816 — and disguised his actions behind the unmistakably colonial curtain of a "civilising" mission (Howitt, Holt and Locke, 2016; Whittington, 2023). In other words, the present author's academic and personal journey in Australia has been, from the very beginning, marked by the experience of a continuous action

DOI: 10.4018/979-8-3693-2264-2.ch008

on collective memory, that seems to be shamelessly engaged in the effacement, naturalisation, or even worse, condonation of the continued colonial violence that inscribes the nation. In this same sense, Vanessa Whittington problematises the political agendas behind memorialisation in Australia, arguing that massacre memorials "that are conceived as shared heritage, and arise as acts of reconciliation, perpetuate a settler agenda of atonement, forgiveness and peacemaking intended to lay the past to rest: another form of silencing" (Whittington, 2023, p. 2).

The chapter author arrived in Australia at the end of November, 2015, just in time to witness the tenth anniversary of the Cronulla riots – or pogroms, as described by Suvendrini Perera (2009a). In line with what has been discussed so far, the 2005 Cronulla riots are yet another episode of settler colonial, racially charged collective violence, whose memory is perennially and periodically subjected to attempts at false reconciliations that are in fact aimed at the forgiveness, rehabilitation and acquittal of the ferocious and criminal violence committed by members of the Anglo-Celtic settler communities — this time, however, the day was nicknamed as "National Leb and Wog bashing day" (Al-Natour, 2017), in that the chosen victims were not Aboriginal people, but groups of people identified precisely as "Lebs" [as in "Leba-neses"], "wogs", or, in attempts to talk euphemistically, as people "Of Middle Eastern appearance". On this last expression, used *ad libitum* and *ad nauseam* by media releases when covering the Cronulla riot,[2] Joseph Pugliese had written an entire essay, a couple of years before the facts, in 2003:

> *This essay is an attempt to trace the racial fault-line designated by the sign "of Middle East-ern appearance." Seemingly bound by definable geopolitical borders, this fault-line is global in its topological reach, encompassing a heterogeneity of bodies, identities, locations and subjects. Of Middle Eastern appearance signs my face. This figure resonates with a double logic. I am of Middle Eastern appearance and I am not Middle Eastern. The racial fault-line that runs along this chiastic articulation shapes both the corporeal contours of this body and the textual corpus of this essay. It is a fault-line that enunciates the conditions of possibility of the post-foundational subject – conditions that mark the impossibility of securing for oneself an identity indissociably tied to place, origin or nation.* (Pugliese, 2003, n.p.)

Pugliese shares the same Southern Italian origins of the author of this chapter, who was also repeat-edly reminded, especially during those last days of 2015, that he is also a "wog" — again, not Middle Eastern, but still another specimen of (almost) the same racial debris that the Anglo-Celtic "Aussie" youths in Cronulla Beach were trying to expunge from their shores (and from existence) in 2005. The strong identification with the victims of the facts of Cronulla, the idea that *"had I been there, I might have been a victim, too"*, was decisive in giving the chapter author the idea of writing a musical/textual piece on the matter.

By relating his subjective experience of Australia (a decade post-Cronulla) and his consequent spec-ulations as someone who may have been subjected to violence if they were at Cronulla Beach that day, the author of this chapter is by no means attempting to diminish or invisibilise the massive implications of these terms for people who actually are of Middle Eastern descent, that is, those who both *appear to be* Middle Eastern and *are* Middle Eastern. Kabir (2015) documents the gradual tendency to unjustly associate Islam and Lebanese culture with gang rape crimes and suggests that this resulted in a violent demarcation within Cronulla beach, where racialised people from the Western suburbs were confined within a small portion at the southern end of the beach, and thus "excluded from the white imaginary spatiality" (Kabir, 2015, p. 275). Pugliese (2009) focusses on the "tacit knowledges", "compulsory visibilities" and "racially marked metonyms" that inscribe "Australian Muslim and/or Arabs" within "scopic economies of hyper-surveillance" and automatically marks them as "infralegal criminals who will breach the contract of the Western liberal state" (2009, p. 26).

In 2018, then, the chapter author finally got round to composing a musical piece titled *A Cronulla si junceru* ("In Cronulla they got together"). The piece is based on a text in Sicilian written by the same author, a text that narrates the events from the point of view of a Sydney-based Sicilian immigrant[3] — the text of *A Cronulla si junceru* is the only notated and fixed element of the composition, which otherwise relies on freely improvised instrumental accompaniment, performed by the chapter author (also acting as vocalist and composer/lyricist) and by his collaborators in various different capacities, instrumentations and setups. This particular configuration allows for a mixture of formal flexibility and fixed elements that is subsumable both under what Valério Fiel da Costa describes as the "invariance strategies" that make up the "morphology of the open work" (Costa, 2016), and under the concept of "comprovisation" (Hannan, 2006; Fujak, 2011), understood as a middle ground between composition and improvisation, but also as an ideal field for the interaction between self-regulating creative mechanisms (Aliel, Keller and Costa, 2018).

In this chapter, the discussion of *A Cronulla si junceru* is functional to a broader reflection on the conflation and complex interactions between historical reports, secondhand accounts and personal remembrances, under the umbrella of what Francesca Cappelletto has described as "mnemonic communities" (Cappelletto, 2003, p. 243). Paramount to the very concept of mnemonic community is language, and it could be argued that, in *A Cronulla si junceru*, the choice of using Sicilian within such an elitist and haute context as that of experimental music all the more significant (Messina, 2019), as it privileges the collective and subaltern dimension of remembrance over the orthodoxies of the musical genre. In this sense, while text-based music is by no means a total novelty within the experimental scene (cf. Redhead, 2016; Landy, 2010), *A Cronulla si junceru* can be understood in terms of what Simurra and co-authors (2023) define "radical creative semantic anchoring", i.e., an attempt to rethink the parameters and elements that inscribe music-making — with its acoustic-instrumental orthodoxies and attached social paraphernalia (cf. Keller et al. 2010) — by treating verbal material, with its recognisable and clear semantic content, not only as musical material, but also as the *only* fixated musical material.

After an outlining of the historico-critical background that inscribes the Cronulla riots, also in terms of media coverage and commentary on the facts, the chapter will focus on the conceptual foundations of *A Cronulla si junceru*, also detailing the creative, musicological and practical aspects of its composition and performance.

BACKGROUND

Cronulla Beach has been marked by a strong history of territorial demarcation that dates back to the 1950s and 1950s, and was initially predicated on the expungement of working-class "outsiders" by an increasingly dominant middle-class segment (Evers, 2009, p. 414). Concomitantly, Cronulla is also the most easily accessible beach from the working-class Western Suburbs of Sydney (Kabir, 2015, p. 275), whose population is also composed by relevant percentages of people with non-Anglo-Celtic backgrounds, including speakers of Arabic and, in particular, people with a Lebanese background (Kabir, 2015, p.

274). As Clifton Evers puts it, "by 2005, the Australian beach had been constructed as a place of racial purity for decades" (2009, p. 415).

The infamous Cronulla riots took place on 11 December 2005. On that occasion, a multitude of over five thousand Anglo-Celtic white youths concentrated on the beach premises since early morning, in order to "reclaim the beach" — that is, in order to to exert punitive violence — against an alleged Libanese "threat", declaiming and/or displaying various mottos such as "we grew here, you flew here", "wogs out of Nulla", "f*ck off Lebs!". The situation rapidly escalated, leading in various attempts at collective violence that were addressed at any passer-by who could only vaguely look as being of Middle-Eastern/Mediterranean background. The Cronulla riots have been described as "race riots" (Perera 2006), "ethnic cleansing" (Asquith and Poynting 2011) "pogroms" (Perera 2009a; Perera 2014), etc.

Problematic Documentaries

In her contundent essay, significantly titled *Terror Australis*, Maria Giannacoupulos (2006) considers the responses of the press and of the authorities to the Cronulla riots: she exposes the subtle workings of effacement of whiteness that newspapers such as the *Sydney Morning Herald* perform by counterposing, again, "men of Middle Eastern appearance" with non-racially characterised "mobs of youth chanting racist slogans" (Giannacoupulos, 2006). Furthermore, Giannacoupulos highlights the work of the local riot police, whereby law enforcement serves "to continue to naturalise the law's function as restoring order and not as being implicated in the ongoing project of white sovereignty which requires all locations to be treated unproblematically as legitimately white possessions" (Giannacoupulos, 2006).

Reflecting on the Australian Broadcasting Corporation (ABC) documentary — part of the *Four Corners* series — *Riot and Revenge* (2006), Kenta McGrath (2017) comments negatively on the fact that, by "focusing on the beach riot in the first half and the retaliatory attacks in the second half", the documentary "ultimately places equal emphasis on the two groups" (McGrath, 2017, p. 16). In other words, according to McGrath, the documentary puts on the same level the massive riot in Cronulla beach with the backlashes performed in the Western Suburbs of Sydney by groups of people who felt they might belong to the "wog" category summoned by the rioters and had to defend themselves. While sharing McGrath's negative impressions on the ABC documentary, the author of this chapter wants to argue that in fact *Riots and Revenge* seems directed, edited and structured in order to assign a much more questionable, shady and negative role to the second group, while the white "Aussies" that participated in the riots are almost explicitly forgiven and rehabilitated. Obvious visual elements contribute to this, such as the sunny settings when the young "Aussies" are interviewed, set against the dark and shady settings for the "Middle Eastern" subjects. The "Aussies" are filmed while playfully smiling and having fun on the beach, all of them claiming that they are "not racist [people] at all" and adding "nothing against them, but they [the "Lebs"] were always down there to cause fights". According to the documentary, the angry mobs of "Aussies" went down to the beach only "looking for a fight", in contraposition with the "smashing, bashing and stabbing" performed by the "Middle Eastern" dwellers of the western suburbs, acting "under the cover of darkness". The Aussie subjects' faces are shown, although their real names are not disclosed; the ME subjects are filmed in darkness, their faces are obscured: "Do you feel bad about going down there, at all?" the interviewer asks one of the ME subjects; "No, I don't feel bad", the subject replies, "got someone to get me a revenge". In general, the interviewer seems to question the ME subjects more than he does with Aussies, who, on the contrary, seem to be taken quite seriously when they express their racist concerns about the preposterous idea that "under Muslim law it's okay to rape" and about the equally absurd prediction that "they'll possibly outbreed us, and once they get their numbers they can vote their members into Parliament; and once their members are in Parliament they can pass laws, like they've already tried to get the Islamic law into Australia" (ABC, 2006). A policeman suddenly appears, to imply not-so-covertly that the MEs are in fact a law and order problem, while the Aussie mobbers are, after all, just confused but well-meaning, if highly alcohol-intoxicated, youth.

Other questionable TV shows resorted to condoning white violence while putting the most possible blame on "Middle Eastern" segments. A 2015 Channel 9 show, part of the *60 Minutes Australia* series, was titled *A Riotous Affair*, and tells the story of a couple of white Aussies who met in Cronulla during the riots, fell in love and went on to marry. Before introducing the Cronulla riots, the voiceover is very keen to point out that "the weekend before, local surf club volunteers had been attacked by a group of Middle Eastern beach goers from Sydney Southwest", while an interviewed police officer puts the blame for the burst of collective racial violence on the fact that "the place was just swimming with alcohol", and then adds "large crowds, a lot of emotion and then the heat, the build-up of the heat, when you bring all of those together it's almost like a perfect storm". While *A Riotous Affair* continues with pretty explicit descriptions of the violence at Cronulla, also pointing the attention on the racially marked connotation of the chasings, beatings and persecutions, it continues by then putting a lot more emphasis on the subsequent disorders in the western suburbs. The "romance rising out of the ashes of racism", as the anchorman puts it, emerges in reality as a reminder of the moral superiority of this white couple (again, keen to affirm that "we're not racist people" despite being there at the riots) over the "revenge" coming from the western suburbs. The graphic description of the stabbing undergone by the "him" of the couple, his asking her out while lying wounded in the ambulance, the lingering on the psychological scars left on him by the stabbing and on the perceived impunity of the offenders, the final healing provided by the love of his partner — everything is there to emerge as a narrative of the white settler-colonial nation that triumphs against any "foreign menace": it does so via its most typical minimal component, namely, the fertile couple that biologically reproduces the "legitimate" future components of the community (cf. Yuval-Davis, 1993; Weissman, 2017).

What these documentaries, as didscalic narratives of the afterwards, seem to propose is the idea that the Aussies have eventually left the riots behind, they are not racist anymore — in fact, they never were if one is to listen to the interviewees — and have now moved on to spend their days having fun on the beach or enjoying their romantic relationships while making an effort to build a family. At the same time, these documentaries seem to issue us with a warning about the persistence of the danger represented by the Middle Eastern communities: they show us that they do not regret their actions, and that they still linger there in the dark of their western suburbs, as "shadow-beasts" (Anzaldúa, 1987) that are still capable of leaving their peripheries at any time, harassing white women on the beach, imposing absurd rape-condoning "Muslim laws", stabbing people and getting out of prison too early, etc. What these documentaries seem to want to teach us is that the Aussie mobs in Cronulla might have been disproportionately violent, fuelled by excessive alcohol consumption, worryingly uncontrolled, but they were still part of a largely justified national reaction against an unbearable, irremediably different, ferally violent "foreign" community. It was largely in response to this unacceptable mystification that the chapter author wrote his musical piece.

THE PIECE *A CRONULLA SI JUNCERU*

Mnemonic Communities

The piece *A Cronulla si junceru*, with its verbal account of the 2005 violence in South Sydney, tries to extract a consistent narrative from the plethora of existing oral accounts of the facts. The role of these accounts is fundamental in the context of the formation and preservation of historical memory about the events, helping build what Francesca Cappelletto describes as "mnemonic communities" (Cappelletto, 2003) and establishing a public and shared dimension of the memory of the violence. Storytelling here is fundamental in the critical direction of the Benjaminian "narrator", whose task is to use both his own personal experience and the information at his disposal, to "give advice" and transmit "wisdom" for a community (Benjamin, 1987 [1936], p. 200). Storytelling signals involvement or proximity (both in spatial and temporal terms) to the community that suffered the massacre — reiteratively, as Pugliese puts it, "I am of Middle Eastern appearance and I am not Middle Eastern", but also, concretely, subjects of non-Middle Eastern background were subjected to the violence. A passage from *A Cronulla si junceru* reports the episode of an outburst of violence against a Spanish woman:

> Si lamintaunu, ricìunu ca ssi mussummani unn'arrispittavunu i fimmini, ccuttuttu ntrê primi ca ncagghiaru ci fu ggiustu ggiustu na fimmina, na carusiddha spagnola ca un ci traseva nenti ccù ttuttu stu schifiu. A vistunu mpocu cchiù niurinciola ri riddhi e accuminciaru a ssicutalla comu tanti cani.
>
> They complained and said that these Muslims did not respect women — however, among the first ones that they picked there was precisely a woman, a Spanish girl that had nothing to do with all that mess. They saw she was a bit darker than them and started chasing her like a pack of dogs.

Here the fears about the enforcement of a "Muslim law" under which is allegedly "okay to rape", and the preoccupations about "the way they're brought up" that allegedly does not contemplate any "respect for women" — externalised by the "Aussie" subjects depicted, for example, in the aforementioned documentary *Riots and Revenge* — clash with the fact that these "Aussie" defenders of the respect for women actually started harassing precisely a woman. The way in which they identify the woman as a member of the "Lebs" community has obviously to do with Pugliese's aforementioned remarks on being of Middle Eastern appearance and not being Middle Eastern — a "visual regime of racial profiling" (cf. Pugliese, 2006; Messina and Capogreco, 2021) that immediately interprets her darker completion as a threat and an authorisation to chase her. As suggested by bell hooks, Black – and, in general, racialised – women are deprived of both their humanity and womanhood, and "what this means in terms of the sexual politics of rape is that if one white woman is raped by a black man, it is seen as more important, more significant than if thousands of black women are raped by one white man" (hooks, 2015 [1981], p. 76). In other words, the "Aussie" mobsters' preoccupation with the "respect for women" needs to be interpreted as a preoccupation that is directed exclusively towards women that are understood as white Anglo-Celtic Australians.

A Cronulla si junceru narrates the facts in a way to avoid establishing any sympathy for the fierce perpetrators of the violence – contrary to what has been extensively done, as seen above, by Australian media. In this context, the narrator is the agent of a transformation of personal memories into historical accounts (cf. Bloch 1995; Cappelletto 2003). Within the storytelling, as Cappelletto (2003) puts it, the visual description of the violence functions to facilitate this transition from the personal to the collective dimension: the detailed description of events, with the use of vivid and detailed images, serves to give the community the impression of being "witnessing and re-witnessing" (Cappelletto, 2003, p. 248) the episodes of violence, and this also applies to situations in which neither the narrator nor the audience were personally witnessing the episodes. Cappelletto goes on to suggest that this use of vivid, gory visual descriptions allows the transition from a personal dimension of memory to a collective, shared dimension, to the point that, for some members of the community, it becomes difficult to distinguish events experienced personally from those heard from others (Cappelletto, 2003, p. 249). Trauma leaves the personal dimension and thus becomes collective trauma.

In the light of Cappelletto's useful insights, one could argue that, for example, the stabbing scene in the aforementioned documentary *A Riotous Affair* functions precisely to unite the white Aussie community reviving and fabricating the memory of an alleged threat, handing over, once and for all, the blame to the Middle Eastern communities for all the December 2005 events. In a completely symmetric and specular response, in *A Cronulla si junceru*, the chapter author intended to provide vivid, graphically detailed accounts of the episodes of violence committed by the Aussie beachgoers in Cronulla Beach. A small excerpt from the piece might help demonstrate that:

Quacchirunu rissi ca ni stava arrivannu n'autra para ri libbanisi, ccô ttrenu, e ntonsi lesti lesti ssi scattiati accumenzunu a curriri vessu a stazziuni, acchianunu nô ttrenu e ncagghiunu n-carusu: pugna na panza, pirati, buttigghiati n-capu, u scassunu rê coppa e picca cci manca c'u mmazzunu.

Someone said a bunch of Lebs was arriving by train, and so these psychos quickly started to run towards the station. They got on the train and threw themselves at a boy: punches in the belly, kicks, bottles smashed on the head, they beat him up and they almost killed him.

Avant-Garde Text-Setting Orthodoxies vs. Radical Creative Semantic Anchoring

By treating verbal material with recognisable and clear semantic content, not only as musical material, but also as the only notated musical material, the author attempted to rethink the parameters and elements that inscribe music-making with its acoustic-instrumental orthodoxies and attached social paraphernalia (Keller et al. 2010). Verbal language, in this sense, becomes avant-garde music in itself, contradicting established conceptions on music semiotics as lacking articulated meaning (cf. Monelle 2000). Post-1945 compositional aesthetics, especially those revolving around the *Internationale Ferienkurse für Neue Musik* hosted in the German city of Darmstadt, are predicated on a strongly delimited range of acceptable text-setting practices, and a famous, polemical debate between Karlheinz Stockhausen (1964, p. 49) and Luigi Nono (2007, p. 86-87), over the latter's piece *Il Canto Sospeso* (Nono, 1959), de facto crystallises the use of non-intelligible phonetic and syllabic fragments as perhaps the most preferable and appropriate practice in avant-garde or "New Music"[4] circles (cf. also Stoianova, 1987).

More recent compositional experiences have attempted to depart from this model, by proposing clarity and transparency in terms of the verbal signifiers used within avant-garde music forms. Emanuele Casale's *Conversazioni con Chomsky* (2010), for example, features "sonic interviews" and "musical debates" as contemporary operatic forms that privilege intelligible verbal discourses over the more manieristic use of "blows, noises and sighs" (Messina and Casale, 2014). Casale's solo voice piece *Composizione per voce* (1998), among other things, represents an almost unique precedent in terms of the setting of a Sicilian text in an avant-garde music context (cf. Messina, 2015).

Other text-setting experiences also explore creative solutions that diverge from the set terms of the Nono/Stockhausen dialectics: the aforementioned text-based works by Landy (2010) and Redhead (2016) are just some of the existing examples available. To describe this same creative situation, Ivan Simurra and coauthors have recently come up with the concept of Radical Creative Semantic Anchoring, or Radical ASC (acronym of the original Portuguese rubric *Ancoragem Semântica Criativa* - Simurra et al. 2023). Radical ASC addresses the operativity of semantics in shaping the musical and extra-musical (or epimusical) features of the creative processes, to an extent that transcends the pertinence of traditionally notated instructions (Simurra et al., 2023, p. 7) — in this sense, both the score/script of *A Cronulla si junceru* and the piece per se are subsumable to Radical ASC.

As pointed out above, the composer and chapter author did not compose, nor pre-plan, any part of the piece, except for the text to be declaimed. This means that all the instrumental and more strictly "musical" parts of the piece were totally improvised, making each performance significantly different from the others. This creative approach is obviously coextensive with Radical ASC, in that the semantic material literally drives all the other musical parameters of the piece, while also anchoring all the different manifestations of the piece to a determinate and fixed textual resource that represents the ontological core of the piece. Within the phenomenological sphere of Radical ASC – i.e., considering the written script as a legitimate and self-sufficient musical source –, the piece also subscribes to the concept of comprovisation, in that while the instrumental material is freely improvised from time to time, there is undoubtedly a pre-composed core that is invariable[5] from time to time.

Several previous pieces can be subsumed to Radical ASC and deal with issues such as memory, land, racial identity and social struggle exist across different genres and art forms. Victoria Santa Cruz's renown poem *Me Gritaron Negra!* (1978), for example, possesses undeniable performatic elements that situate it in an in-between that theatrical declamation with obvious musical elements. A recollection of the December 1968 police shooting on unarmed Sicilian peasants in Avola, Filippo Arriva and Carlo Muratori's *I fatti di Avola* (2008) also explores the intersection between song and theatrical monologues. In terms of works by more commercially prominent artists, spoken-word pieces such as *Giuanne Palestina* ('O Zulù, 2007) and *Famine* (O'Connor, 1994) were also extremely influential for the conception of *A Cronulla si junceru*.

Putting the Piece Together

Writing the script in Sicilian required different layers of successive negotiations, that regarded primarily a convincing linguistic and cultural adaptation, situated in the pursuit of a balance between a conventionalised English-language register, with its attached semantic protocols in terms of politeness, correctness, etc., and a more authentic and spontaneous Sicilian speech. A series of different narratives were used to put the script together, including: (1) material from the aforementioned documentaries; (2) stories taken from press items; (3) information from academic papers; (4) oral accounts heard from colleagues, friends and acquaintances in Sydney.

This last type of source was specifically important in order to extract pieces of information that may not have been otherwise at the forefront of sensation-based media releases such as the press stories and the documentaries. In particular, multiple contacts from different Mediterranean backgrounds (including Southern Europeans) told the author that, for a few days after the Cronulla beach riots, they decided to lock themselves down at home, avoiding any possible interaction in the streets, for fear of being caught in any further explosion of collective violence on the part of segments of the Anglo-Celtic "Aussie" community. Incidentally, this detail obviously clashes considerably with the narrative set by the aforementioned documentaries, where different innocent "Aussie" subjects are victimised in a context described as being primarily or exclusively characterised by a violent revenge from recalcitrant and bloodthirsty subjects "of Middle Eastern appearance". In the piece *A Cronulla si junceru*, these precious oral testimonies are condensed especially in the following passage:

> Ddhu jornu n-cafolu ri ggenti comu a nuatri, emigranti siciliani, napulitani, greci, marrucchini, palestinisi, si stesino ê casi rô scantu, nzemmula cchê só figghi e niputi, nanzamai cci puteva capitari quacchiccosa.
>
> On that day a lot of people like us, immigrants from Sicily, Naples, Greece, Morocco or Palestine, stayed home out of fear, together with their children and grandchildren, in case something bad could happen to them.

Overall, the final script is divided in seven paragraphs, corresponding to different chapters, or sections, of the narrative, and describable as follows: (1) the first gatherings in Cronulla in the morning; (2) a presentation of the "Aussie" mobsters and a description of their claims; (3) the first episode of violence against a Spanish girl; (4) other episodes of violence; (5) the train episode; (6) the fear and despair of the Mediterranean communities; (7) a polemical consideration on the claims for sovereignty of Anglo-Celtic settlers vis-à-vis the authentically legitimate sovereignty of Indigenous nations.

The narrative sections illustrated above deserve some important remarks. As mentioned above, the present author re-narrates the events from the point of view of an imaginary outsider (a Sicilian-speaking person) who witnessed the violence and attempts to describe it, lingering on the most brutal details in order to avoid establishing any sympathy for the fierce perpetrators of the violence – contrary to what, as abundantly demonstrated above, has been extensively done by Australian media. Since the incipit — described above as section (1) — the "Aussie" claims about an alleged lack of "respect" on the part of the "Leb" component (as abundantly claimed by the Anglo subjects interviewed in *Riot and Revenge*) is reverted — the detail of barbecuing pork produces in order to throw them at the "Lebs" in order to deliberately offend halal protocols is crucial here:

> A Cronulla si junceru, na ddhu jornu, cchiossai di cincumila chistiani. All'ottu e menza già ndrummavunu e cunsavanu i cuffulari. S'accupava rô cauru, e a cchissi ccà nzuppilu nzuppilu accuminciavanu a scattiari. A manziornu, mbriachi comu tanti signi, arrustevanu canni ri poccu e caddhozzi ri sasizza, ppì llassaricilli curriri ncoddu ê libbanisi.
>
> They gathered in Cronulla, on that day: more than five thousand people. At 8.30am they were already drinking and starting the barbecues. It was boiling hot, and these people, little by little, were starting to go bonkers. By midday, all drunk as skunks, they were roasting pork meat and sausages, in order to throw them at the Lebs.

Most of the episodes covered in sections 1 to 5 are also more or less detailedly mentioned by press stories and documentaries as well, although the chapter author has added several details taken from oral and academic sources — this is to say that, despite the needed criticism expressed in this chapter against the biases of the documentaries and media coverage of the events, an honest recognition of the valid aspects of these narratives has never been under review. In other words, the chapter author is happy to recognise that, however biased and partial, these documentaries and media items provide some important and valid insights on the facts of Cronulla. In particular, the car smashings at the early stages of the morning gatherings, as were abundantly covered by the documentaries and news items discussed above:

> Appoi accuminciaru a scassaricci i machini a cchiddi ca pareunu nnicchieddhu cchiù libbanisi ri l'autri. Scassunu ssi machini, e appoi ncagghiunu a dduj carusi mediurientali e ccuminciunu a ssuntumarili rê coppa. E mentri chissi ccà a munseddhu vastunaunu a ssi dduj carusi, na fuddha ri ggenti mbriachi taliava e arrireva. Ccu ll'occhi russi, assappanati ri sangu, si ciccaunu a malajucata, tiniunu u schifiu, ppì ffozza ddhu jornu cci'ava a nesciri u mottu.

> Later they started smashing the cars of those who looked a bit more "Lebs" than the others. They smash the cars, and then they bump into two Middle Eastern guys and start beating them up. And while the mob bashes these two guys, a crowd of drunk people stares at them laughing. With red eyes, soaked in blood, these mobsters were looking for trouble; they were making a mess, as if they wanted someone to end up dead on that day

Similarly, the beating of the Spanish girl quoted above, as described in section (3), is an element that was mainly extracted from the two documentaries discussed above.

Section 6, as suggested earlier, is the one that relies more on the oral accounts — this is the section when the present author identifies as a Sicilian and wonders what would have happened to him and his fellow Sicilians in that context: within the aforementioned dynamics of the mnemonic communities, this is precisely an attempt to share the memory of the trauma with communities and individuals who have not necessarily witnessed the violence.

Finally, section 7 has to do, first and foremost, with a judgement on the actual validity of the ethnic sovereignty imposed by Anglo-Celtic settlers in Australia — here, by no means, the present author intends to disqualify the idea of ethnic sovereignty altogether. On the contrary, taking a cue from Joseph Pugliese's critique of No Border activist rubrics, the present author is eager to avoid reproducing "*tabula rasa* effects that operate along two intersecting axes: the effacement of Indigenous nations that antedate the border regimes of settler states and the occlusion of the demarcated places of more-than-human entities that are a priori to settler border regimes" (Pugliese, 2021, pp. 1-2). Pugliese continues to argue that "despite its important contestatory charge", No Border claims tend to align to "the topological fold constituted by the settler colonial state, its racialised relations of power and its Euro-anthropocentric values" (Pugliese, 2021, p. 2). In *A Cronulla si junceru*, the idea of claiming sovereign rights over a specific piece of land is not contested in itself; what is contested is the self-proclaimed and usurped white Anglo-Celtic sovereignty over Australian land and, in particular, over Cronulla beach. The fact that multiple forms of Indigenous sovereignties predate the European colonisation and were, in fact, never ceded to the Anglo-Celtic settlers (Cf. Pugliese, 2015) is also suggested. Finally, the genocidal violence and the continued regimes of punishment, incarceration and abduction of Indigenous people that inscribe Anglo-Celtic Australia are also mentioned.

I nglisi ricìunu "nuatri nascemu ccà e vuatri vinisturu ccà", ma cu è ca nasciu ccà? L'inglisi na Australia cci'arrivaru no 1788, avantieri, cc'jerunu 52 nazzioni indigene na Australia, i mmazzaru a tutti pari, i misuru n galera, cci arrubbaru macari i picciriddhi. Cu è ca nasciu ccà? Tu nascisti ccà? Viautri nascisturu ccà? Ah! Mauopassu ca cc'jerunu autri ggenti ccà!

The Anglos said "we were born here, you flew here", but who was really born here? The Anglos arrived in Australia in 1788, the day before yesterday — there were 52 Indigenous nations in Australia, they killed them all, put them in jail, they even stole their children. Who was born here? You were born here? Oh, I thought there were other people here!

The spatial trajectory of the piece

The spatial trajectory of *A Cronulla si junceru* includes obviously its inception in Australia — where the piece was never performed or showcased so far — alongside its three different performances in other parts of the world — basically, Sicily and two different places in Brazil. The recording of a first rehearsal of the piece took place on 16 August, 2018 by the present author with the Grupo de Improvisação Livre – G.I.L. and presented in Sciacca, Sicily, as part of the *Ritrovarsi* Festival. On that occasion, G.I.L. was formed by its "core" musicians Arthur José "Miuda", Deivid de Menezes, João Araújo, Marcello Messina and Carlos Eduardo Silva, with the addition of Jehnny Lima, Joab Delfino and Bartholomeu Campos. Performed again with G.I.L. (with two other stable members Carlos Alberto Benjamin Tupinambá and Dyonnatan Silva Costa) in Rio Branco on 22 August 2018, at the Teatro Garibaldi Brasil on the campus of the Federal University of Acre. The piece was then performed one last time in João Pessoa, within the premises of the cultural association *Tamarindeira*, by Artesanato Furioso (Valério Fiel da Costa, Matteo Ciacchi, Luã Brito and Vitor Çó) on 23 October 2018. The last two versions included a part in Portuguese on the recent facts of Pacaraima, where the narrative of the Cronulla Riot is alternated with news excerpts on the then-recent Incidents of Pacaraima, at the border between Venezuela and the Brazilian state of Roraima, where in August, 2018, mobs of Brazilian residents violently attacked Venezuelan refugees, burned their belongings and forced them to the other side of the border while singing the Brazilian national anthem (Lopes, 2018; Messina et al, 2023). On both those occasions, the Portuguese script covering Pacaraima was declaimed by Teresa Di Somma.

FUTURE RESEARCH DIRECTIONS

Exploring the contribution to the consolidation of Mnemonic Communities via the composition — or better, comprovisation — of text-based musical pieces is definitely a path that the present author wishes to track extensively. In this sense, existing experiences by the same author pre-date *A Cronulla si junceru* — most notably, the piece *I saw them colours of your flag* (Messina, 2017) that was also included in Lauren Redhead's aforementioned album (2016). Later projects such as *Contracapas* (Messina and Mejía, 2020) have also explored the creative potential of the intersections between textual indications and Radical ASC. A current line of work explores the intersection between AI and the musical internet through the rubric of musical stuff (Messina and Aliel, 2023; Messina et al., 2024), and future endeavours in this sense will look at the potentialities of this existing research both in terms of textual instigators of musical creativity and in terms of the interactions with collective memory and the human/non-human binary: a preliminary paper in this sense was presented at the workshop *Bridging AI scholarship and Memory Studies* hosted by the University of Luxembourg in September 2023.

CONCLUSION

The piece *A Cronulla si junceru* represents an attempt to explore, recover and appropriate the memory of the 2005 Cronulla Riot in Sydney by imagining a Sicilian subject who re-narrates the events using Sicilian as a language. Despite its textual form, the script is understandable as a musical score, in that it is meant to investigate improvisative instrumental practices to be performed simultaneously with the declamation of the text.

The description lingers on graphic descriptions of various episodes of violence, with the precise intent of debunking media narratives on the facts — normally biased towards the victimisation and forgiveness towards the Anglo-Celtic youths that participated in the acts of violence. By using Sicilian as the language in which the story is declaimed, the chapter author attempts to achieve proximity to the members of the Southern Italian community in Australia (representing some 4% of the total population of the country), and, in general, to explore my identitarian contiguity with the victims of the Cronulla riots. As abundantly claimed throughout the chapter, this strategy also approximates the piece to the mechanism of creation and consolidation of "mnemonic communities", as described by Francesca Cappelletto (2003).

An element that has not been at the forefront of the analyses presented in this paper concerns the geopolitical and "geocorpographical" (cf. Pugliese, 2009) status of the beach as a traditional *locus* of whitewashing in settler-colonial Australia — a place where the sovereignty of white, normative bodies served precisely to disavow, exclude and remove other racialised bodies (Perera, 2009b). In this sense, *A Cronulla si junceru* — also with its usage of an unrecognised, disenfranchised and racialised language as Sicilian — concurs, together with a series of other, more significant manifestations, in a collective effort to symbolically reclaim the beach against the false sovereignty of the Anglo-Celtic settlers. In a spasm of ironic and derisive relief, typical of the sardonic and subversive attitude of Sicilian and Southern Italian comedy (cf. Tirino, 2017), *A Cronulla si junceru* ends in a sarcastic address to the "Aussie" mobs:

Allura siti vuatri i patruna ccà? Ah se? Siti vuatri? E nun v'affruntati a tèniri tuttu stu schifiu ppì'n pezz'i spiaggia??

Are you the ones in charge here, then? Really? Are you in charge? And aren't you ashamed of making all this fuss for a small piece of beach?

ACKNOWLEDGMENT

Many thanks to G.I.L., Artesanato Furioso, Ritrovarsi and NAP. This research received no specific grant from any funding agency in the public, commercial, or not-for-profit sectors.

REFERENCES

Adorno, T. W. (2006). *Philosophy of New Music*. University of Minnesota Press.

Al-Natour, R. (2017). 'Of Middle Eastern appearance'is a flawed racial profiling descriptor. *Current Issues in Criminal Justice*, 29(2), 107–122. 10.1080/10345329.2017.12036090

Aliel, L., Keller, D., & Costa, R. (2018). The Maxwell Demon: Comprovisation in ecologically grounded creative practice. *Musica Hodie*, 18(1), 103–116.

Anzaldua, G. (1987). *Borderlands: The new mestiza = La frontera* (1st ed.). Spinsters, Aunt Lute.

Arriva, F. (2008, December 2). *I Fatti di Avola. (C. Muratori, performer)*. Teatro Odeon, Avola. https://youtu.be/tsPhRpzGVCU?si=s5Q4VtnnVMP4VIh8.

Asquith, N., & Poynting, S. (2011). Anti-cosmopolitanism and 'ethnic cleansing' at Cronulla. In *Ocean to Outback: Cosmopolitanism in Contemporary Australia* (pp. 96–122). UWA Publishing.

Benjamin, W. (1987). O narrador: considerações sobre a obra de Nikolai Leskov. In: Benjamin, W. *Magia e técnica, arte e política: ensaios sobre literatura e história da cultura*. São Paulo: Brasiliense.

Bloch, M. (1995). *Mémoire autobiographique et mémoire historique du passé éloigné. Enquête*. Archives de la revue Enquête, (2), 59-76.

Cappelletto, F. (2003). Long-term memory of extreme events: From autobiography to history. *Journal of the Royal Anthropological Institute*, 9(2), 241–260. 10.1111/1467-9655.00148

Casale, E. (1998). *Composizione per voce. (B. Guerrera, Performer) Mappe*. Pescheria.

Casale, E. (2010). Conversazioni con Chomsky. (F. Micheli [Zavalloni, E. Ribatto, Icarus Ensemble, & MDI Ensemble, Performers) Teatro Cavallerizza, Reggio Emilia.]. *Director*, C.

Costa, V. F. D. (2016). *Morfologia da obra aberta*. Prismas.

Edmonds, P. (2016). Honourable Colonisation? Australia. In *Honourable Intentions?* (pp. 46-62). Routledge.

Edwards, E. (2016). The colonial archival imaginaire at home. Social Anthropology. *Anthropologie et Sociétés*, 24(1), 52–66.

Fredericks, B., & Bradfield, A. (2023). Asserting Indigenous Agencies: Constructions and Deconstructions of James Cook in Northern Queensland. In *The Palgrave Handbook on Rethinking Colonial Commemorations* (pp. 351–382). Springer International Publishing. 10.1007/978-3-031-28609-4_19

Fujak, J. (2011). Comprovisación–Notas para la discusión sobre la validez del concepto. *Oro Molido*, 33, 24–30.

Garigliano, C. (2009). *" L'Ottava Isola": Studies on Music, Heritage and Cultural Identity Between Sicily and Sydney* [Doctoral dissertation, Macquarie University].

Giannacopoulos, M. (2006). Terror Australis: white sovereignty and the violence of law. *Borderlands, 5*(1).

Hannan, M. (2006). *Interrogating comprovisation as practice-led research.* Queensland University of Technology.

hooks, b. (2015 [1981]). *Ain't I a Woman: Black Women and Feminism.* Routledge

Howitt, R., Holt, L., & Locke, M. L. (2022). Challenging the colonial legacy of/at Macquarie. *Geographical Research, 60*(1), 71–85. 10.1111/1745-5871.12496

Kabir, N. A. (2015). The Cronulla riots: Muslims' place in the white imaginary spatiality. *Contemporary Islam, 9*(3), 271–290. 10.1007/s11562-015-0347-x

Keller, D., Barreiro, D. L., Queiroz, M., & Pimenta, M. S. (2010). Anchoring in ubiquitous musical activities. In ICMC.

Landy, L. (2010). Rock's Music. In Lane, C. (org.) and Gruenrekorder (eds.) *Playing with Words: An Online Compilation.* Frankfurt: Gruenrekorder.

Lopes, R. C. (2018). Índios comunistas? Representações sociais dos imigrantes venezuelanos na cidade brasileira de Pacaraima. *PÓLEMOS–Revista de Estudantes de Filosofia da Universidade de Brasília, 7*(14), 152–171.

McGrath, K. (2017). *Riot and revenge: symmetry and the Cronulla riot in Abe Forsythe's Down Under.*

Messina, M., Keller, D., Freitas, B., Simurra, I., Gómez, C., & Aliel, L. (2024). Disruptions, technologically convergent factors and creative activities: Defining and delineating musical stuff. *Digital Creativity.* Advance online publication. 10.1080/14626268.2023.2301342

Messina, M., & Aliel, L. (2023). Things, objects, subjects and stuff: IoMuSt and ubimus perspectives on AI. In *2023 IEEE International Conference on Big Data (BigData)* (pp. 4503-4510). IEEE.

Messina, M., Bento da Silva, F., Porto Ribeiro, L., & de Araújo Souza, J. (2023). Towards Amazon-centred memory studies: Borders, dispossessions and massacres. *Memory Studies, 16*(6), 1407–1422.

Messina, M., & Capogreco, S. (2021). "Armato di carnagione": Chromatic Regimes of Racial Profiling in the Italian Press. In *Pesquisa em comunicação: jornalismo, raça e gênero.* Nepan Editora.

Messina, M., & Mejía, C. M. G. (2020). Contracapas for remote double bass and effects: Creative Semantic Anchoring, Corpus Linguistics and Remote Interaction. In *Proceedings of the 10th Workshop on Ubiquitous Music (UbiMus 2020)* (pp. 173-174).

Messina, M. (2017). I saw them colours of your flag–A Speech-Based Composition on Aboriginal Sovereignty. *Revista Vórtex, 5*(1), 1–8.

Messina, M. (2015). Contemporary Music, Unofficial Languages, Subaltern Voices: Composing Musical Pieces on Sicilian Texts. In *PERFORMA'15: Proceedings of the International Conference on Musical Performance.*

Messina, M., & Casale, E. (2014). Interview with Emanuele Casale. Síneris. Revista de Musicología, (16).

Nono, L. (2007). La nostalgia del futuro: Scritti scelti. Milan: Il Saggiatore.

O' Connor, S. (1994). *Famine. On: Universal Mother*. Chrysalis Records Limited.

Zulù, O. (2005). *Giuanne Palestina. On: Live in the Al Mukawama Experiment 3*. Novenove.

Perera, S. (2006). Race Terror, Sydney, December 2005. *borderlands, 5*(1).

Perera, S. (2009). A Pogrom on the Beach. In *Australia and the Insular Imagination: Beaches, Borders, Boats, and Bodies* (pp. 137–160). Palgrave Macmillan US. 10.1057/9780230103122_8

Perera, S. (2009b). *Australia and the Insular Imagination: Beaches*. Borders, Boats, and Bodies. New York. 10.1057/9780230103122

Perera, S. (2014). 'Aussie luck': The border politics of citizenship post-Cronulla Beach. *Critical Race & Whiteness Studies, 10*(2).

Pugliese, J. (2003). The Locus of the non: the racial fault-line of" of Middle-Eastern appearance". *Borderlands e-journal, 2*(3), 1-13.

Pugliese, J. (2006). *Asymmetries of terror: visual regimes of racial profiling and the shooting of Jean Charles de Menezes in the context of the war in Iraq. Borderlands, 5(1)*. NA-NA.

Pugliese, J. (2007). Geocorpographies of torture. *Australian Critical Race and Whiteness Studies Association Journal*, 3(1), 1–18.

Pugliese, J. (2009). Compulsory visibility and the infralegality of racial phantasmata. *Social Semiotics*, 19(1), 9–30. 10.1080/10350330802632758

Pugliese, J. (2015). Geopolitics of Aboriginal sovereignty: Colonial law as 'a species of excess of its own authority', aboriginal passport ceremonies and asylum seekers. *Law Text Culture*, 19, 84–115.

Pugliese, J. (2021). More-Than-Human Lifeworlds, Settler Modalities of Geno-ecocide and Border Questions. *Journal of Global Indigeneity*, 5(3), 1–34.

Rata, A. (2020). Dismantling Cook's legacy: Science, migration, and colonialism in Aotearoa. *New Zealand Science Review*, 76(1-2), 54–58. 10.26686/nzsr.v76i1-2.7834

Redhead, L. (2016). Solo speaking [Album]. Lauren Redhead. https://laurenredhead.bandcamp.com/album/solo-speaking (accessed 15 September 2020).

Santa Cruz, V. (1978). *Me Gritaron Negra* [video]. Youtube. https://www.youtube.com/watch?v=cHr8DTNRZdg

Simurra, I., Messina, M., Aliel, L., & Keller, D. (2023). Radical creative semantic anchoring: Creative-action metaphors and timbral interaction. *Organised Sound*, 28(1), 64–77. 10.1017/S1355771822000322

Stockhausen, K. (1964). Music and Speech. *Die Reihe*, 6, 40–64.

Stoianova, I. (1987). Testo-musica-senso. 'Il canto sospeso. In Restagno, E. (Ed.), *Nono* (pp. 126–141). EDT.

Tirino, M. (2017). Mi faccia il piacere! Totò e la sovversione dell'ipocrisia borghese: Un'analisi socio-culturale. H-ermes. *Journal of Communication*, 2017(9), 7–36.

Weissman, A. L. (2017). Repronormativity and the reproduction of the nation-state: The state and sexuality collide. *Journal of GLBT Family Studies*, 13(3), 277–305. 10.1080/1550428X.2016.1210065

Whittington, V. (2023). Memorialisation, Reconciliation and Truth-Speaking: The Role of Explorer and Massacre Memorials in Settler-Colonial Australia. *Journal of Australian Studies*, 1–19.

Yuval-Davis, N. (1993). Gender and nation. *Ethnic and Racial Studies*, 16(4), 621–632. 10.1080/01419870.1993.9993800

ENDNOTES

[1]   Two different recordings of the piece, which were recorded in Rio Branco and played back in Sciacca, are available at: <https://open.spotify.com/album/2ekG4Fh393InVyDpCMj3Vq?si=HR womEAuTAy5OKPb77tXwQ> [Accessed 19/05/2024].

[2]   Examples of more or less appropriate usage of this expression were found, for example, on Australian newspapers such as the Sydney Morning Herald <https://www.smh.com.au/national/ armed-gangs-on-rampage-20051213-gdmmg7.html> [Accessed 27/01/2024] and <https://www .smh.com.au/national/mob-violence-envelops-cronulla-20051212-gdmm4n.html> [Accessed 24/01/2024]; and on The Age <https://www.theage.com.au/national/violence-flares-at-cronulla -20051212-ge1eqi.html> [Accessed 24/01/2024]. Additionally, examples of this expression were found on the "World" sections of British media such as The Guardian <https://www.theguardian .com/world/2006/oct/20/australia> [Accessed 27/01/2024] and BBC News <http://news.bbc.co .uk/2/hi/asia-pacific/4525352.stm> [Accessed 24/01/2024].

[3]   On Sicilian immigration in Australia and New South Wales, cf. Garigliano (2009)

[4]   The present author takes this expression precisely from the Darmstadt Internationale Ferienkurse für Neue Musik (International summer courses for New Music) — this term can also be found in Adorno (e. g. Philosophy of New Music, 2006 [1949])

[5]   On the strategies of invariance associated to experimental pieces, that transcend the traditional role of the musical score, cf. Fiel da Costa (2016).

[6]   <https://www1.folha.uol.com.br/mundo/2018/08/refugiados-venezuelanos-sao-agredidos-e -expulsos-de-tendas-em-roraima.shtml> [Accessed 22/08/2018]

[7]   <https://www.papotv.com.br/posts/ao-som-do-hino-nacional-brasileiro-venezuelanos-sao -expulsos-do-brasil> [Accessed 22/08/2018]

[8]   <https://www1.folha.uol.com.br/mundo/2018/08/eles-nos-expulsaram-como-cachorro-diz -imigrante-venezuelana-em-roraima.shtml> [Accessed 22/08/2018]

[9]   <https://www1.folha.uol.com.br/mundo/2018/08/refugiados-venezuelanos-sao-agredidos-e -expulsos-de-tendas-em-roraima.shtml> [Accessed 22/08/2018]

[10]   *Ibid.*

[11] <https://www.brasil247.com/brasil/o-contexto-da-xenofobia-contra-os-venezuelanos-em-roraima> [Accessed 22/08/2018]

[12]   *Ibid.*

APPENDIX 1

"A Cronulla se junceru"
(Marcello Messina- August 2018)

A Cronulla si junceru, na ddhu jornu, cchiossai di cincumila chistiani. All'ottu e menza già ndrummavunu e cunsavanu i cuffulari. S'accupava rô cauru, e a cchissi ccà nzuppilu nzuppilu accuminciavanu a scattiari. A manziornu, mbriachi comu tanti signi, arrustevanu canni ri poccu e caddhozzi ri sasizza, ppì llassaricilli curriri ncoddu ê libbanisi.

Sti carusi australiani, janchi, ri razza nglisa, jerunu tutti cumminti ca s'avunu a arricupigghiari a sò praia contra ê furastera, sulu ca na sta praia ri Cronulla tutti sti picciotti janchi un s'avunu mai vistu, jerunu facci novi, ggenti ri autri quatteri. Vanniavunu comu tanti sciamuniti: "Tunnativinni nê vostri paìsi, nuatri nascemu ccà!".

Si lamintaunu, ricìunu ca ssi mussummani unn'arrispittavunu i fimmini, ccuttuttu ntrê primi ca ncagghiaru ci fu ggiustu ggiustu na fimmina, na carusiddha spagnola ca un ci traseva nenti ccù ttuttu stu schifiu. A vistunu mpocu cchiù niurinciola ri riddhi e accuminciaru a ssicutalla comu tanti cani.

Appoi accuminciaru a scassaricci i machini a cchiddi ca pareunu nnicchieddhu cchiù libbanisi ri l'autri. Scassunu ssi machini, e appoi ncagghiunu a dduj carusi mediurientali e ccuminciunu a ssuntumarili rê coppa. E mentri chissi ccà a munseddhu vastunaunu a ssi dduj carusi, na fuddha ri ggenti mbriachi taliava e arrireva. Ccu ll'occhi russi, assappanati ri sangu, si ciccaunu a malajucata, tiniunu u schifiu, ppì ffozza ddhu jornu cci'ava a nesciri u mottu.

Quacchirunu rissi ca ni stava arrivannu n'autra para ri libbanisi, ccô ttrenu, e ntonsi lesti lesti ssi scattiati accumenzunu a curriri vessu a stazziuni, acchianunu nô ttrenu e ncagghiunu n-carusu: pugna na panza, pirati, buttigghiati n-capu, u scassunu rê coppa e picca cci manca c'u mmazzunu. Tannu arriva nu vaddia, e i cunsuma a vastunati a tutti pari: chissi allura s'alluntananu, e nesciunu râ stazziuni.

Ju pensu ca su ppì ddiri cc'jera ju ddhu jornu, sti scattiati m'avissunu scassatu a lignati macari a mmia, a mmia ccu tutti i me cumpagni catanisi, palemmitani, sciacchitani. Ddhu jornu n-cafolu ri ggenti comu a nuatri, emigranti siciliani, napulitani, greci, marrucchini, palestinisi, si stesino ê casi rô scantu, nzemmula cchê só figghi e niputi, nanzamai cci puteva capitari quacchiccosa. Sydney addivintau n-campu ri battagghia, ccù scerri a tutti i banni.

I nglisi ricìunu "nuatri nascemu ccà e vuatri vinisturu ccà", ma cu è ca nasciu ccà? L'inglisi na Australia cci'arrivaru no 1788, avantieri, cc'jerunu 52 nazzioni indigene na Australia, i mmazzaru a tutti pari, i misuru n galera, cci arrubbaru macari i picciriddhi. Cu è ca nasciu ccà? Tu nascisti ccà? Viautri nascisturu ccà? Ah! Mauopassu ca cc'jerunu autri ggenti ccà! M'a scusari! Allura siti vuatri i patruna ccà? Ah se? Siti vuatri? E nun v'affruntati a tèniri tuttu stu schifiu ppì'n pezz'i spiaggia??

APPENDIX 2

"A Cronulla si junceru / Em Pacaraima se juntaram"
(Marcello Messina+ excerpts from Brazilian newspapers - August 2018)
A Cronulla si junceru, na ddhu jornu, cchiossai di cincumila chistiani. All'ottu e menza già ndrummavunu e cunsavanu i cuffulari. S'accupava rô cauru, e cchissi ccà nzuppilu nzuppilu accumminciavanu a scattiari. A man-ziornu, mbriachi comu tanti signi, arrustevanu canni ri poccu e caddhozzi ri sasizza, ppì llassaricilli curriri ncoddu ê libbanisi.

"Grupos de brasileiros estão perseguindo refugiados venezuelanos que vivem na cidade de [Pacaraima, no estado de] Roraima, e queimando seus pertences. [...] Agredidos com pedaços de pau, os refugiados foram expulsos das tendas que ocupavam na região, na fronteira do Brasil com a Venezuela. As autoridades brasileiras no local não intervieram".[6]

Sti carusi australiani, janchi, ri razza nglisa, jerunu tutti cumminti ca s'avunu a arricupigghiari a sò praia contra ê furastera, sulu ca na sta praia ri Cronulla tutti sti picciotti janchi un s'avunu mai vistu, jerunu facci novi, ggenti ri autri quatteri. Vanniavunu comu tanti sciamuniti: "Tunnativinni nê vostri pàisi, nuatri nascemu ccà!".

"Os moradores da cidade chegaram a bloquear a BR-174, na entrada da cidade, por cerca de 5 horas. Enquanto os venezuelanos atravessavam a fronteira de volta para a Venezuela, os moradores de Pacaraima cantavam o Hino Nacional Brasileiro".[7]

Si lamintaunu, ricìunu ca ssi mussummani unn'arrispittavunu i fimmini, ccuttuttu ntrê primi ca ncagghiaru ci fu ggiustu ggiustu na fimmina, na carusiddha spagnola ca un ci traseva nenti ccù ttuttu stu schifiu. A vistunu mpocu cchiù niurinciola ri riddhi e accumminciaru a ssicutalla comu tanti cani.

"Agarravam os meninos e os agrediam. Batiam nos pais. Atiravam pedras, telhas. Batiam na cabeça. [...] Pegaram nossa comida e nos expulsaram como se fôssemos cachorro. Quem estava no banheiro [e não podia fugir] ficou sem nada [...]. Queimaram a tenda, as coisas que a gente guarda, não deixaram nada".[8]

Appoi accumminciaru a scassaricci i machini a cchiddi ca pareunu nnicchieddhu cchiù libbanisi ri l'autri. Scassunu ssi machini, e appoi ncagghiunu a dduj carusi mediurientali e ccuminciunu a ssuntumarili rê coppa. E mentri chissi ccà a munseddhu vastunaunu a ssi dduj carusi, na fuddha ri ggenti mbriachi taliava e arrireva. Ccu ll'occhi russi, assappanati ri sangu, si ciccaunu a malajucata, tiniunu u schifiu, ppì ffozza ddhu jornu cci'ava a nesciri u mottu.

"Moradores da cidade passaram a andar em bandos pelas ruas da cidade, [...] procurando per-tences de venezuelanos e queimando. Uma tenda que abrigava venezuelanos foi destruída com um trator. Bombas improvisadas de gás e pedras foram usadas como munição contra os refugiados".[9]

Quacchirunu rissi ca ni stava arrivannu n'autra para ri libbanisi, ccô ttrenu, e ntonsi lesti lesti ssi scattiati accumenzunu a currirí vessu a stazziuni, acchianunu nô ttrenu e ncagghiunu n-carusu: pugna na panza, pirati, buttigghiati n-capu, u scassunu rê coppa e picca cci manca c'u mmazzunu. Tannu arriva nu vaddia, e i cunsuma a vastunati a tutti pari: chissi allura s'alluntananunu, e nesciunu râ stazziuni.

"Das ruas da cidade, o confronto avançou para a fronteira. Com pedradas, um grupo fez venezuelanos recuarem para dentro de seu território, até que membros da guarda venezuelana no local, disparassem tiros de advertência para evitar a DETERIORAÇÃO da situação".[10]

Ju pensu ca su ppì ddiri cc'jera ju ddhu jornu, sti scattiati m'avissunu scassatu a lignati macari a mmia, a mmia ccu tutti i me cumpagni catanisi, palemmitani, sciacchitani. Ddhu jornu n-cafolu ri ggenti comu a nuatri, emigranti siciliani, napulitani, greci, marrucchini, palestinesi, si stesino ê casi rô scantu, nzemmula cchê só figghi e niputi, nanzamai cci puteva capitari quacchiccosa. Sydney addivintau ncampu ri battagghia, ccù scerri a tutti i banni.

"As lideranças que provocaram este ataque violento contra os venezuelanos, já comandaram um ataque à sede da Funái, já formaram bandos de pistoleiros para ataque contra os índios, e fazem enorme lobby no Congresso Nacional para a extinção da reserva indígena de São Marcos, com a intenção de remarcar o Município, invadindo mais terras indígenas e desmatando a região, para ampliação do cultivo de arroz".[11]

I nglisi riciunu "nuatri nascemu ccà e vuatri vinisturu ccà", ma cu è ca nasciu ccà? L'inglisi na Australia arrivaru no 1788, avantieri, c'jerunu 52 nazzioni indigene na Australia, i mmazzaru a tutti pari, i misuru n galera, ci arrubbaru macari i picciriddhi. Cu è ca nasciu ccà? Tu nascisti ccà? Viautri nascisturu ccà? Ah! Mauopassu ca cc'jerunu autri ggenti ccà! M'a scusari! Allura siti vuatri i patruna ccà? Ah se? Siti vuatri? E nun v'affruntati a teniri tuttu stu schifiu ppì'n pezz'i spiaggia??

"Pacaraima foi emancipada em 1995. O Município, fronteiriço com a Venezuela, [...] é uma invasão de comerciantes, dentro de uma reserva indígena, a reserva de São Marcos. [...] A energia elétrica de Pacaraima vem da Venezuela. O único posto de abastecimento de combustíveis, vem da Venezuela. Os moradores da cidade de Pacaraima, para aquecer o comércio do município e para consumo de energia, dependem da Venezuela. Sem gasolina, o comércio e o trânsito de Pacaraima param. Sem compradores venezuelanos, o comércio de Pacaraima para".[12]

Chapter 9
Lagáyan, Tengáhan, at Pakiramdáman:
A Collective Recollection of Jazz in Metro Manila

Krina Cayabyab
http://orcid.org/0000-0002-9266-1054
University of Edinburgh, UK

ABSTRACT

This chapter explores how a collective memory of local jazz is constructed from a group interview designed as a record listening session. By bringing together mediators or agents who were in any way part of the jazz scene in Manila between 1946 and 1986, this ethnographic activity served as a space to observe how interactions emerging from individual and shared lived experiences can affect the way jazz memory is expressed and signified. The collective recollection was stimulated, navigated, and articulated from relevant media materials and from questions pertaining to agents' social, cultural, and economic negotiations. Aside from learning, emphasizing, or correcting ideas about the local scene during the conversation, this chapter brings forward multiple social and performative factors to observe how decolonial perspectives can affect the fabrication and circulation of memory and local music histories.

INTRODUCTION

Jazz scene histories are constructed by an entangled variety of mediators or agents. From a jazz lover's personal archives and newspaper articles to testimonies and prompted oral stories; the associations attached to the idea of "jazz"; the kind of music played in various spaces; the forces that sustained memories with it through time – these and more have sketched how jazz was situated in Manila from 1946 to 1986.[1] As it takes different kinds of mediators across time and space to shape a jazz narrative, this chapter explores the prospect of several mediators, participants, or agents to come together and engage in a *collective*

DOI: 10.4018/979-8-3693-2264-2.ch009

recollection. By agents, I mean anyone who has mobilized the scene of jazz such as musicians, relatives of musicians, club owners, producers, and record collectors, to name a few (Jackson, T.A., 2012, p.42).

Taking place in Quezon City on May 15, 2023, this gathering was engaged around the act of *listening* as if being in a record listening party, jam session, or a backstage downtime where a conversation developed, drawing from one thought to another. The dialogue of memories and shared experiences was stimulated by recordings and images from the past. Designed as a group interview, *Jazz ng Inyong Buhay* (Jazz of Your Lives) was a venture in reconditioning history, using a method motivated by a decolonial perspective through collaborating with and listening to hidden voices that embodied, signified, and shaped the culture of jazz in Manila, post-World War II. The stories that emerged further contextualized newspaper articles and individual interviews. At the same time, archival materials and other correspondences were cross-checked to validate information. Setting the collective recollection as an organic "open horizon," memories of the past flowed as a "history in motion" (Quijano A. et al, 2024, p. 25) by recognizing diverse views, observing recurring myths, contradicting ideas, and verifying facts on the spot.

This collective recollection is part of a research project that explores the scene construction of jazz that was situated in a place and time of post-colonial urban impact that altered notions of identity, race, gender, and class lines in Manila during the wake of "Americanization" complexities and post-world war cultural politics. Specific information gathered from the activity will not be the focus of this chapter, but will be included to expound on crucial observations in conducting the group interview; and to highlight key arguments that will be discussed in the overall research. This chapter will present the following: 1) relevant literature in collective listening, memory, and decoloniality; 2) the procedure in conducting the collective recollection; 3) observations on interactive cues that motivated the recollection process; 4) emergent stories relevant to the overall research; 5) reflections and recommendations from the activity; and 6) future research directions and conclusion.

BACKGROUND

The primary aim of this ethnographic activity is to describe how jazz was signified and embodied in Manila based on individual responses, interlinked stories, and observed interactions evoked by selected media materials (audio recordings, photographs, other primary sources) from 1946 to 1986. To enable the emergence of a collective recollection and to address the certainty that "memories are not only disparate among individuals in the group but within a single person who may remember an event in the past in different ways on different occasions" (Schaft, G.E. 2019, p. 7), I draw from Nicole M. Ardoin et al's collaborative research approach of 'community listening sessions' (2022). Their method is grounded from sociocultural learning theory to "promote efficient and effective group talk," while "participants learn from each other" as a result of centering the voice and experience of jazz agents (Ardoin et al., 2022, pp. 470-471). Much like a discursive approach, this "talk" among players of the interview mobilized individual and collective identity constructions (Wilson and MacDonald, 2005, p. 344).

By being in a space with peers of varying degrees of social proximity but strung together by a concurrent set of pathways (Finnegan, R. 2007, pp. 305-306), the authority in the oral history of jazz in Manila becomes mutual. Pathways can be thought of as interwoven experiences that have "established routines of musical practice which people could choose to follow" and that emphatically, can be "taken in the company of others" (Ibid., p. 305). These pathways can consequently be thought of as vestiges of *agency* that shaped and operated within the scene. In understanding agency, recognition is given to the multivalence of social and cultural tensions juxtaposed with a person's commitments, intentionality, and aspirations. In this sense, with all these in one space – an active jazz musician from the 1960s, a daughter of a jazz player from the period, a 1970s club owner, a musician who spent much of his active years in cruiseships, a grandson of a jazz journalist, a record collector, and a singer who began her career at the tail end of period of study – a collective memory can be captured in the way scenes are constructed. With these agents carrying with them their unbroken associations and social negotiations from the past, a scene's cultural meanings and memory are shaped (Jackson, T., 2012, pp. 38-39; Bennett and Rogers, 2016, p. 2). Thus, following M. Halbwachs, this recollection is structured to interpret a collective memory of jazz, where it is conditioned within the social pathways of scene players; where it continues to be reconstructed; and is persisted by artefacts that sustain meaningful prompts (as cited in Dinter, 2023, p. 2). J. Assman develops this further as 'communicative memory' by underscoring the "interaction between a remembering mind and a reminding object," the embodiment of memory, and the informality of conveying individual reflections with contemporaries (Assman, 2011, p. 16-22).

This brings me to a decolonial perspective of constructing local histories where agency, collective memory, spatial and temporal elements, and everyday life subjectivities are perceived while acknowledging the persistence of what Aníbal Quijano describes as the "coloniality of power" (2024, pp. 2-11). Recognizing the intersecting repercussions of race, gender, class, and ethnicity, decolonization calls for pluriversality and autonomy (Escobar, A., 2018, p.4, 181) such that the modernity of the people involved in the scene are brought forward (Mignolo, 2009, p.169; Quijano, 2024, p.18). By highlighting agents' lived experiences and memories of their habits of living and thinking, their alterity in the context of jazz in Manila emerge (Dussel, E., 2000, p.473). Providing a space for multiple and unfamiliar voices in the scene to be heard makes alternative and relative encounters to be resonant. I thus apply the act of curating and playing records from the past to arouse memories and experiences that set in motion the group's shared recollection. I employed the following Filipino musicking terms to approach the activity: *lagáyan, tengáhan, pakiramdáman.*

Jazz jam sessions and performance practices carry out the interactive play of this triumvirate. Lagáyan is used to describe how a band musically converses during improvisatory and arranged instances of technical skills, musical utterances, and dynamic intuition which all aim to stir elation among band members and listeners. As if filling a container with tricks and possessions of trade (lagáyan in its most literal meaning, is a "container"), the musicians pitch in impressive musical chops. Consequently, this jazz dialogue emerges as a musical experience that is assembled from collectively-charged sensibilities of adapting, adjusting, and repositioning musical ideas – all to achieve a group's aesthetic sonic impact. Tengáhan is synchronising all listening sensitivities to piece together individual gestures of producing musical elements like melodies, harmonies, and rhythms to fabricate the group's ideal performance. In a way, tengáhan concocts the interplay of lagáyan as the players "fill the container" of performance. Related to this, but further probing into one's social consciousness, is pakiramdáman. This can be described as the coordinated set of intuitions and sensibilities, where musical responses are produced by how the players perceive and react to the playing dynamic of the group. Building through this concurrent set of jazz musicking not different at all from any type of group performance, "lagáyan, tengáhan and pakiramdáman" is a constant social exercise of adapting and shaping a band's collective perception of the music.

As this group construction of history is stimulated by the act of listening, I delved into the challenge of "listening to listening" (Eidhseim, 2019, pp. 27-29) as a fellow agent being the researcher. I listened more closely to the implications reflected in the flow of the conversation. Although this practice of observation may be relevant to music psychological and neurosciences analyses, the collective recollection was not intended for obtaining quantitative or qualitative results for these fields of study. Instead, in the course of the group's dialogue, I tuned into the sonorous reactions and engagement that emerged. Echoing Aaron A. Fox, I "listen[ed] carefully to these 'real' sounds and the relationships and memories they signified" in discerning jazz experiences (2004, p.17). Furthermore, these intentions call on a more discursive approach, wherein the agents' "opinions and identities are understood as fluid and context-dependent" thus encouraging "disagreement, challenges, and resistances" in their construction of the jazz scene (Smithson, 2019, p. 12). Subsequently, I picked up reinforced orientations (Ahmed, 2006, pp. 12-21), positions, and dispositions (Bourdieu, 1983, p. 341) that the agents of the jazz scene negotiated with which reflected social and cultural conditions of the place and time of their experiences (Jago, 2018, pp. 19-30). By giving attention to *how* they were listening and how they were responding to the music and to the interactions in the space, what were *chosen* to be said, supported, emphasized, or corrected became amplified.

As in conducting ethnographic activities, the balance of performing flexibility, sensitivity, assertiveness, and strategy was vital for me as the event organizer and moderator. Immediately functioning as an agent myself, my "role and positioning... [are] understood to make a difference to the group dynamic as well as to the data obtained" (Smithson, 2019, p. 16). In the following section, I discuss the procedures planned for *Jazz Ng Inyong Buhay*. Observations and reflections on the activity come after.

JAZZ NG INYONG BUHAY

The Invitation

Invitations were sent out digitally or by courier to individuals whom I was able to interview or was directed to connect with during my three month fieldwork in Manila from March to May 2023. The date was based on my preference and was invariable. Though the overall research project involves interviewing people who now live overseas but were active during the period of study, this collective recollection was limited to those residing in Manila. Figure 1.1 shows the cover page and Figure 1.2 contains the invitation in Filipino poetry.

Figure 1. Page one of the invitation

Figure 2. Page two of the invitation in poetry

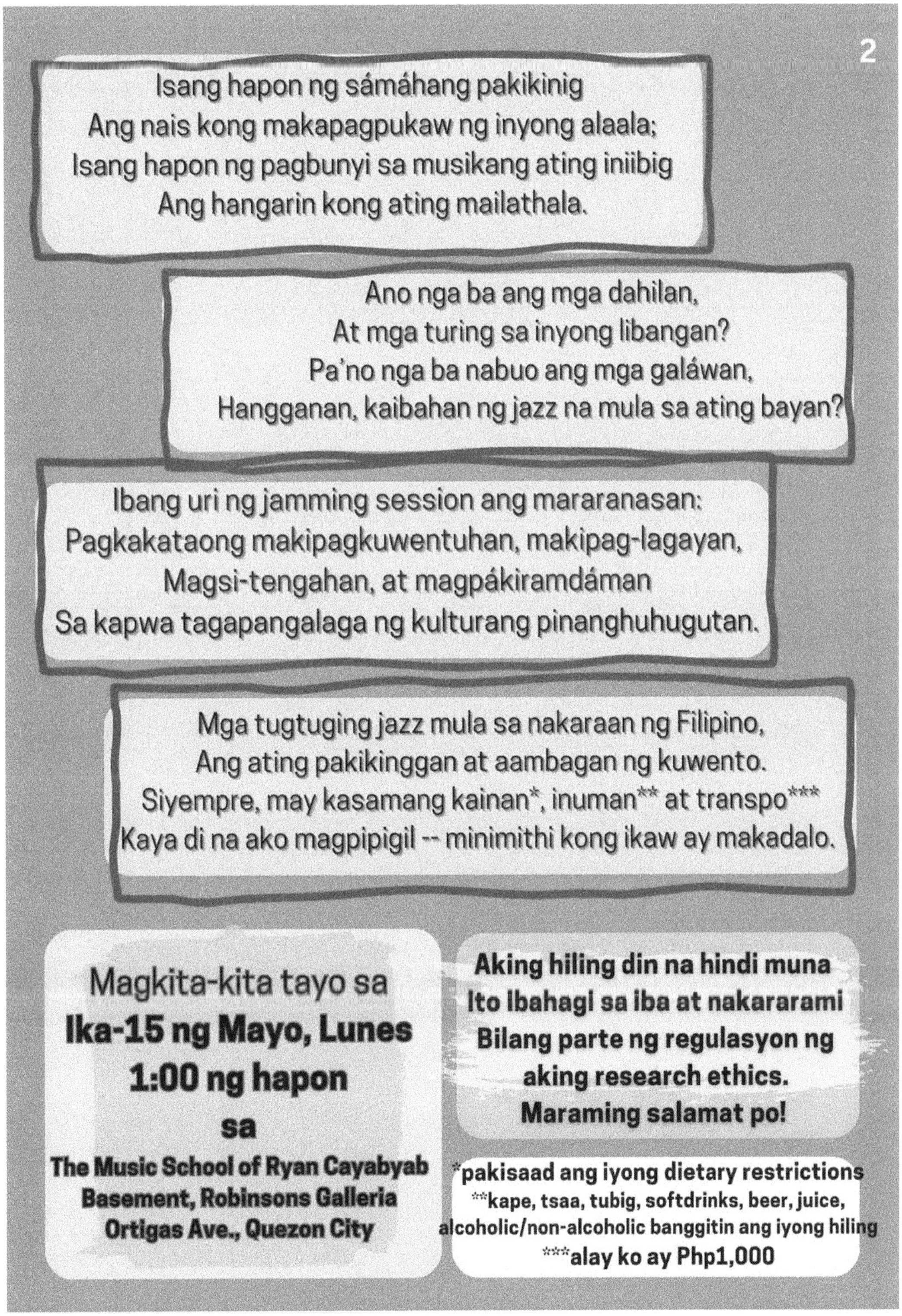

2

Isang hapon ng sámáhang pakikinig
Ang nais kong makapagpukaw ng inyong alaala;
Isang hapon ng pagbunyi sa musikang ating iniibig
Ang hangarin kong ating mailathala.

Ano nga ba ang mga dahilan,
At mga turing sa inyong libangan?
Pa'no nga ba nabuo ang mga galáwan,
Hangganan, kaibahan ng jazz na mula sa ating bayan?

Ibang uri ng jamming session ang mararanasan:
Pagkakataong makipagkuwentuhan, makipag-lagayan,
Magsi-tengahan, at magpákiramdáman
Sa kapwa tagapangalaga ng kulturang pinanghuhugutan.

Mga tugtuging jazz mula sa nakaraan ng Filipino,
Ang ating pakikinggan at aambagan ng kuwento.
Siyempre, may kasamang kainan*, inuman** at transpo***
Kaya di na ako magpipigil -- minimithi kong ikaw ay makadalo.

Magkita-kita tayo sa
**Ika-15 ng Mayo, Lunes
1:00 ng hapon**
sa
**The Music School of Ryan Cayabyab
Basement, Robinsons Galleria
Ortigas Ave., Quezon City**

**Aking hiling din na hindi muna
Ito Ibahagi sa iba at nakararami
Bilang parte ng regulasyon ng
aking research ethics.
Maraming salamat po!**

*pakisaad ang iyong dietary restrictions
**kape, tsaa, tubig, softdrinks, beer, juice,
alcoholic/non-alcoholic banggitin ang iyong hiling
***alay ko ay Php1,000

Figure 3 briefly lays out the expectations for the collective recollection: lágáyan of memories, tengáhan of shared experiences, and pákiramdáman with fellow storytellers. This page also informally articulates pertinent content from the participant information sheet, namely, the possible benefits of taking part; and what happens with the proceedings of the activity. As part of the research ethics procedures, the participants were asked to read and fill out the information sheet and the consent form at the beginning of the session.

Figure 3. Page three of the invitation containing a brief background and expectations of the study

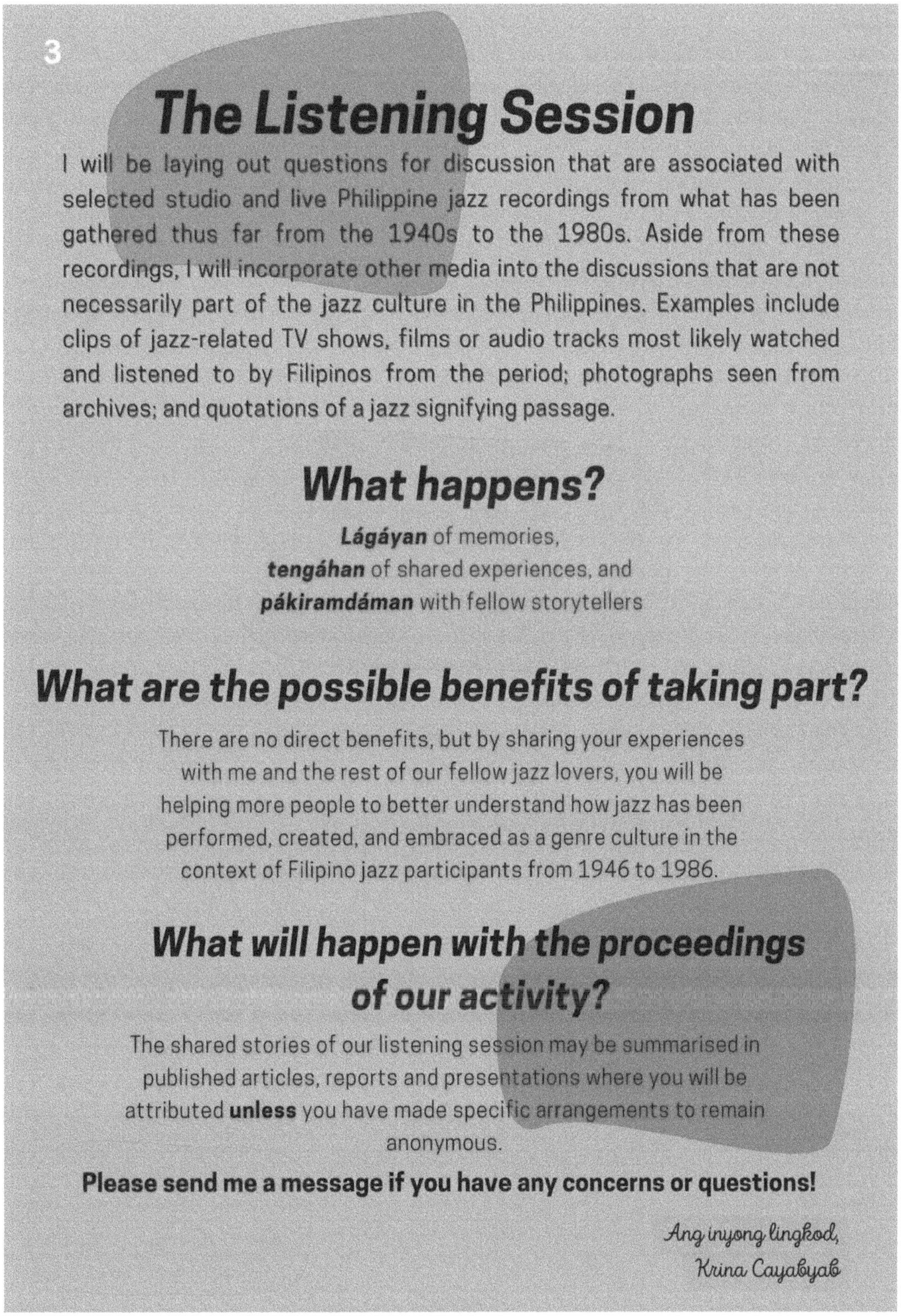

3

The Listening Session

I will be laying out questions for discussion that are associated with selected studio and live Philippine jazz recordings from what has been gathered thus far from the 1940s to the 1980s. Aside from these recordings, I will incorporate other media into the discussions that are not necessarily part of the jazz culture in the Philippines. Examples include clips of jazz-related TV shows, films or audio tracks most likely watched and listened to by Filipinos from the period; photographs seen from archives; and quotations of a jazz signifying passage.

What happens?

Lágáyan of memories,
tengáhan of shared experiences, and
pákiramdáman with fellow storytellers

What are the possible benefits of taking part?

There are no direct benefits, but by sharing your experiences with me and the rest of our fellow jazz lovers, you will be helping more people to better understand how jazz has been performed, created, and embraced as a genre culture in the context of Filipino jazz participants from 1946 to 1986.

What will happen with the proceedings of our activity?

The shared stories of our listening session may be summarised in published articles, reports and presentations where you will be attributed **unless** you have made specific arrangements to remain anonymous.

Please send me a message if you have any concerns or questions!

Ang inyong lingkod,
Krina Cayabyab

217

The Agents

Out of 37 invitees, 20 accepted the invitation, however one got exposed to COVID so unfortunately had to back out. One interviewee also could not make it, but proposed for his son to participate in his stead. With the large size, it was considered to conduct two sets of group interviews to attain balance in the frequency, duration, and depth of insight across all agents. However, aside from the logistical reason to have all participants in one go, I wanted everyone to see and spend time with possibly everyone that they had not seen for a very long time, and even meet others for the first time. I was also interested on how bringing as many mediators as possible altogether at one time might give an enthusiastic and nostalgic air not only to stimulate more memories, but also to perhaps uplift and kindle their spirits. I did wonder if there might be any case of rough relationships that needed avoiding, and so I sent each invitee a list of the possible attendees for consideration, which also served as a form of encouragement.

Table 1 provides an overview of the group demographics, illustrating the jazz roles and the years each one was most active in the scene during the period of study. Out of 19, there were 5 female participants (including me), and 15 males. The group was homogeneous, in the view that their pathways were in one way or another connected with the jazz scene from the 1950s to the 1980s. At the same time, the combination was heterogeneous in terms of tenure and role in the scene, which allows both for diversity of views and gravity of validation in significant points of discussion. Most were active in the scene during the 1970s and the 1980s with half of this number productive in the 1960s. One began playing in the 1950s but focused on a different career path by the 1980s; while one's father was active in the scene in all decades. The jazz roles represented include singer; instrument players of keyboard, trumpet, trombone, guitar, percussions, alto saxophone; music director; composer; jazz joint owner; and relatives such as daughter, son, grandson, and husband of jazz scene players. All have consented for their names to be disclosed if necessary for any research output such as this chapter.

Table 1. Jazz players who participated in the collective recollection

Name	Years Most Active During the Period of Study				Jazz Role
	50s	60s	70s	80s	
1. Megan Herrera		X	X		Singer, husband of Roger Herrera (bass)
2. Ronnie Marqueses		X	X	X	Trombone
3. Butch Silverio		X	X	X	Trumpet, The Executives
4. Jun Regalado		X	X	X	Drums
5. Florencio Gonzaga			X	X	Trumpet
6. Jun Cadiz		X	X		Piano
7. Johnny Alegre			X	X	Guitar
8. Ramon Guevarra	X	X	X		Percussions
9. Richie Quirino			X	X	Percussions, writer
10. Ryan Cayabyab			X	X	Piano, composer, arranger, music director
11. Mel Villena			X	X	Baritone Sax, arranger, music director
12. Serafin Pua			X	X	Birds of the Same Feather owner

continued on following page

Table 1. Continued

Name	Years Most Active During the Period of Study				Jazz Role
	50s	60s	70s	80s	
13. Tina Salustiano*	X	X	X	X	Daughter of Doming Salustiano
14. Vivian Valdez*		X	X	X	Daughter of Doming Valdez
15. Richard Merk		X	X	X	Singer, son of Annie Brazil (vocals)
16. Eddie Sangcap		X	X	X	Alto Sax, flute, arranger
17. Henry Katindig				X	Piano, son of Eddie Katindig (saxophone, vibraphone)
18. Jeannie Tiongco				X	Singer
19. Carlo Lopez*		X	X	X	Husband of Pilita Corrales

*family member representative of jazz players

The Recollection Flow

Jazz ng Inyong Buhay was held on March 15, 2023 from 1:00pm to 5:30pm, including settling in, late arrivals and interruptions, at the rehearsal space of The Music School of Ryan Cayabyab. Materials, seating arrangement, audiovisual and recording equipment were set up in the morning. For transcribing purposes, recordings were made on three sets of iPhone devices for video recording from different angles in the room; one Garage Band audio recording; and one Zoom H2N audio recording. A slide presentation with the various media materials was prepared. The following subsections illustrate the segments of the collective recollection.

Introduction and Guidelines

I opened the session by reiterating what the research was about, including the ethnographic activities I was doing. After this background, I had them introduce themselves by saying their name, a few sentences about when they began playing jazz or their first encounter with jazz; and what they were doing at present. I then proceeded to explaining our guidelines for the activity:

1. **Pagpaparinig at Kuwentuhan** (*Playing a Record and Conversation*)

Treat this as a *kuwentuhan* (conversation or storytelling) session where everyone can just jump in to share thoughts based on the questions and the music you will be listening to. I'm sure everyone is interested to listen to each other, hear one's thoughts, and even say something related to that. You are given a notepad to jot down thoughts that you can probably pull from while listening to the music for 2-3 minutes, and share to the group later if you choose to.

2. **Pakiramdáman at Respeto**(*Feeling and Doing Based On Group Dynamics and Respect*)

Please be mindful that we all have diverse ideas with different levels of acquaintance with the group participants.

3. **Tapat at Bukás na Lagáyan**(*Honest and Open Fill Ins*)

As there are no wrong or right answers, this is a safe space for you to share your views and experiences openly and honestly, every time you choose to say something.

4. **Malinaw na Dokumentasyon***(Clear Documentation)*

Please speak clearly. This session will be audio and video recorded for personal documentation. If in the future there will be events where this research will be shared, photos and audio/video snippets from this get together will be included. Quotes that may be used in the dissertation and forthcoming projects that might be published will automatically be attributed to you. However, you can remain anonymous if you wish, and for certain writing contexts if necessary.

5. **Pag-iba ng Daloy***(Changes in Flow)*

I may call on you if I haven't heard from you in a while. I may also ask the group to move on to a question or re-visit a question if deemed necessary.

Materials For Listening, Viewing, and Recollecting

After discussing the expectations, the recollection and conversation kicked off. Curated from archival research, the prompts presented were a blend of audio and visual media, which were associated with corresponding questions. Below is a list of these prompts with their questions. However, not all prompts were utilized as expected, mainly due to time constraints. I will return to this matter in the reflections and recommendations section.

Prompt 1: "This Can't Be Love." Recorded in a jam session at Tony Martin's residence in 1968. IndiRa Records. From the CD collection of Richie Quirino. 2002.

Do you recognize the players in the recording? Any guesses? How did a jam session roll? What common words, phrases, or standard rehearsal practices did you do or know about from these sessions?

Prompt 2: Mixtape of artists listed on newspaper radio program listings and the *Make Mine Music (MMM)* section of *Sunday Times*: "Dardanella" Ray Bloch, DZPI 1947; "Perfidia" Jimmy Dorsey and his Orchestra, KZPI 1947; "Peanut Vendor" Stan Kenton and his Orchestra, DZBB, April 1950; "Where's Prez" Les Brown and his Orchestra, DZBB, April 1950; "The Gypsy" Anita Boyer, *Make Mine Music,* 1946; "Give Me The Simple Life" Benny Goodman, *MMM,* 1947; "Two Silhouettes" Dinah Shore, *MMM,* 1947; "Dig You Later Hubba Hubba" Perry Como and the Satisfyers, *MMM,* 1947.

What songs or artists do you recall hearing on the radio?

Prompt 3: "Body and Soul," (Entry to VOA Jazz Clinic July '61). From the Digitised Collection of Lito Molina at the UP Center for Ethnomusicology.

What were jazz tunes that were often included in the local show repertoire? May mga mas sumikat ba dito sa bansa kaysa sa Amerika? (Were there tunes that surprisingly became more popular here than in America?)

Prompt 4: "Desafinado," Narding Aristoreñas (tenor), Manny Semana (gtr), Nilo Aristoreñas (bass), Bert Tiambeng (drums). Recorded live on a cruise ship, the Rasa Siam on December 23, 1976. IndiRa Records. 2002. From the CD collection of Richie Quirino.

What were memorable encounters you had performing outside the country playing jazz at hotels, military bases, night clubs, cruiseships, recording studios?

Prompt 5: Image of a word map of venues where jazz was played.

Which ones played mostly jazz? What was the ambience of bars along Dewey Blvd? What kinds of jazz tunes were being played?

Prompts 6 to 8 were not discussed due to time constraints.
Prompt 9: Photo of Doming Valdez and the Manila Studio Jazz Band in Antipolo Festival. Photo courtesy of Ronnie Valdez.

What Filipino-composed or arranged tunes have become part of the local jazz standards or repertoire?

Closing Media: Photo Slideshow of photos from various library and personal archives accompanied by Angel Peña's *Ugaling Pilipino*, performed by the Jazz Friends Big Band for the UP Jazz Concert. 1961. From the digitized collection of Lito Molina c/o Bong Molina and the UP Center for Ethnomusicology.

While the participants had a 30-minute break, they were given Prompt 5 that contained a word map of venues for them to reflect on. It is in these breaks, as well as the arrival and departure of the participants, that a backstage downtime kind of chatter, reminiscing, and catching up took place. In the next section, I discuss interactive cues that can be considered to have motivated the direction, flow, and dynamics of the collective recollection.

Listening to Interactive Cues

Aside from the conversation's content, I was listening to interactive cues that served as performative gestures in the recollection process. This enumeration of cues unfolded and became more apparent to me while listening to and transcribing the recording. As significant with the information learned, these cues contributed in enhancing the direction of the collective process of lagáyan, tengáhan, at pakiramdáman.

"Accidental Unfocus"

In the context of focus group methods, Nancy Franz (2011) describes how having "unfocus" in a group "can result in personal reflection, discovery of new things… can introduce new themes related to the goals of the project." Though the interview was structurally designed to attain these results, responses and questions were raised that brought about moments of crucial accidental unfocus of the conversation. For example, the first question from the group came from one who did not want to be identified as a jazz musician, yet some of his musical output were considered by the agents to be part of the scene. Right after Prompt 1 was presented, he directed a question to the group:

Ah, can I start asking lang? How did you, kasi I never did a banda na kasama ako. How did you know… was it a tacit agreement kung ikaw na yung assigned na mag-iimprovise, chorus and verse ba.. I never never knew kung ano yung routine.

Ah, can I just start asking? How did you, because I never became part of a band. How did you know… was it a tacit agreement that when you are assigned to improvise, is it a chorus, a verse… I never knew what the routine was.

This query was beneficial to the research for a number of reasons. First, it became a demonstration for the participants to perceive the activity as a space of confidence and openness, that we were all interested in what everyone wanted to share, with no judgment. Second, consequently, it portrayed at first instance the action of lagáyan, as players took turns in building up an elaborate answer to this question. Third, the question covered how the agents collectively defined how jazz jamming and improvisation operate – the foundations of jazz performance.

Elaboration

Much of the personal accounts were articulated with moving emotions and curious details. Because of the familiarity and common perceptions of shared experiences, a group or an individual would eventually engage in elaborating stories. One instance was when the group began discussing the consternation of musicians when show producers, such as those during a Tony Bennett concert in Manila, would decide to reduce the number of rehearsals. The consequence was the musicians' loss of income in the end (A is for "Agent" followed by an identifying number; not necessarily the same identifying number in succeeding sets of dialogues)

A1: Oo, puro mga session musician magkakasama, pero meron silang kasamang rhythm section saka may kasama silang lead alto tsaka yung MD nila. Meron kaming i-schedule ng 3 or 4 rehearsals sa kanya. Pagkatapos yung first rehearsal, nag-usap yung musical director atsaka si Tony Bennett. Sabi nila 'I don't think they need another rehearsal.'

Yes, it was all [local] session musicians, but they had a rhythm section, a lead alto and their MD [or music director]. We were scheduled to have 3 or 4 rehearsals with him. After the first rehearsal, the musical director and Tony Bennett talked, and said 'I don't think they need another rehearsal.'

(group applause)

A1: Eh yun ang ayaw naming mangyari!

But that was exactly what we did not want to happen!

A2: Sayang ang budget!

It would be a waste to lose that budget!

A1: Sayang ang kikitain, diba? Per session ang bayad ng rehearsals eh.

It would be a waste to lose that income, right? Fees were given each rehearsal.

(laughter)

A3: So dapat hindi niyo pinagbutihan. Dapat binitin niyo nang kaunti.

(with sarcasm) Then you should not have played well. You should have shortchanged them a bit.

(laughter)

A1: Nakakahiya naman kung ikaw ay nakakaabala, hindi ba? At saka yun na talaga ang ano namin, talagang first sight reading, andun na kami. So sabi nila wala na.. Nagsisisihan ngayon yung grupo… (laughter) Eh ang hirap satin sabi nila eh di hindi tayo kikita.

(with sarcasm) It would be shameful if you were causing such inconvenience, right? And that was how we'd really be, just on first sight reading, we're already there. And so they said "no more"… That got the group blaming one another… (laughter) That's just it, that's what they said and so unfortunately we'd end up not earning.

Such storytelling enabled related anecdotes about economic negotations among the musicians later on. The semi-soliloquy was dynamically played out, engaging others to pile one quip after another, amusing the whole group toward emphasizing a point about the cultural and musical positionalities of Filipino musicians in the concert industry standards during the 1970s.

Ensemble Storytelling and Masayáng Bangayán

The previous example demonstrated the impact of an ensemble storytelling. As with all responses and manners of expressing during the recollection, the ensemble storytelling was an improvised form of saying something as a group. This observation reflects the importance given by Wilson and Mac-Donald (2005) to "a range of structural features in discourse" during their group interview among jazz musicians which shaped subjective identities based on "patterns of accounting and justification or the use of humor." And so listening to these in the conversations has enhanced the candor of a story, as well as sharpens the collaborative act of decolonizing history. Furthermore, as the storytelling became impassioned and they focused on elaborating a musician's amusing experience, the sound of rapturous and friendly bangayán resounded in the room – when the musician being bantered about had already passed on, was absent, or was even present in the room.

A4: Yan [to A2], nilagay niya yung areglo niya, yun ang kumpas, tuloy yung tugtog namin. Ano yan ah, malaking ano, ilang saxes yun, kamado kami talaga. Bumabaligtad yung tiyempo namin. Tapos ito (sings in tempo), si [Absent Reference] cu-cue. Pam pam pam pam… (laughter) baliktad. Mamaya huminto siya. O isa pa nga. (demonstrates again)

This guy [to A2], he placed his arrangement, started conducting, then we played. That's a huge section, how many saxes, we were playing very tight. We were playing the beat in reverse. And then (sings in tempo) [Absent Reference] cues. Pam pam pam pam… (laughter) in reverse. Then [A2] stops. One more time.

(laughter)

A4: Lahat kami. Teka sandali, tinignan yung pyesa ni [A5]. Tama naman (laughter). Nung ano na, hagikhik, tawa kami nang tawa, nakahalata na siya kamado kami na tumatalon yung tugtog.

All of us. Wait (as if miming A2's actions), and he checked the piece of [A5]. Looks correct [so it should sound in correct time] (laughter). There, we were chuckling, we kept laughing. He noticed that we were very tight, as if playing like a record skipping.

A2: Eh ang nangyari non kasi gusto kong isipin na baka ako yung mali ah? (sings)… Ako na yung nag-adjust. Your husband talaga [to A6] prankster eh! Anyway yung take namin na yun, pag take namin yun, kung anuman yun, tama lahat! …That's what they call good time. Ginu-good time ka.

What happened then was I wanted to know, maybe I was wrong. (sings)... I adjusted. Your husband [to A6] was such a prankster! Anyway on the next take, whatever that was, everyone was already correct!... That's what they call good time.

A5: Maraming storya.

So many stories.

A4: Tsaka yung mga burado, diba? Yung mga bura tinutugtog namin eh.

Also those erasures, right? We also played what were already crossed out from the score.

A5: Meron kaming singer, magre-rehearse dala yung piyesa niya.. Si [Absent Reference], yun nag-umpisa eh. Saxes, one up. Trumpet, one down. Rhythm section, as is.

We had a singer, she was going to rehearse, she brought in her piece... [Absent Reference] started it all. Saxes, one [key] up. Trumpet, one[key] down. Rhythm section, as is.

A7: Nako clash na clash.

Oh dear, very clashed.

A5: Yun na yung singer, pagtugtog namin ang sama ng tugtog... Ulit na naman, yun din. Sabi ni [Absent Reference] pagtingin sa pyesa ng singer, "kaya naman pala eh, xerox ito eh, yung original yung dalhin mo dito. (A5 gestures that looked like the singer brought in the original, then musicians play) o tuloy na kami, [tapos sabi ng singer] "Ay kaya pala..."

Singer is there, when we started playing the sound was terrible... we repeated the same thing. [Absent Reference] said, after looking at the singer's piece,"That explains it, this is a xerox copy (photocopy), you should bring the original here (A5 gestures what looked like the singer brought in the original, then musicians began playing correctly)... We then continued, [then singer said] "Oh, so that's why..."

(laughter)

Reminder

When participants blanked out or trailed off trying to recall a name of a person, term or place, someone else would utter the right word being searched for – quite like the call-a-friend advantage of a group interview. In other cases, one would be reminded that they had done something that they thought otherwise or had forgotten. As such, this recollection disclosed new memories emerging from a shared situation. It is instances like this when the group seemingly combined their energies to pluck from a stream of memories, aligning and voicing out ideas, until they reached an agreement of who or what they were describing.

Confirmation

Nods, reactions of agreement, and bringing out additional details were gestures of confirmation. These were especially crucial in taking personal accounts as evidence of what happened in the jazz scene.

A8: ...Anita O'Day, Sarah Vaughn. And my job for my dad was to pick them up from the airport. But there were no pictures so I don't know if you wanna believe me.

(laughter)

A6: But it's true!

A8: Thank you! May witness!

Thank you! There's a witness!

Correction

Likewise, players also spoke out details that needed correction.

A9: Then in the 70s I think there was one that they called themselves a jazz station but was it 88.3?

Ensemble: Ah 80s na yan... Citylite...

Ah that's already the 80s... Citylite...

Turns and Contrary Views

Related to accidental unfocus, turns were more confrontational and took a more insinuating drift as a one steered another participant to eventually elaborate on another relevant matter.

A11: You know, people ask me in different places, what's happening to the Philippines, music in general. Well of course eventually, it goes down to, how's the jazz scene. But in general they would go, how's the music scene in Manila?

A12: [A11], may I cut?

A11: Go ahead.

A12: How are you in gigs now?

A11: I'm doing very well actually.

A12: How many gigs do you have now?

A11: Me? I get grants kasi eh, I go institutional. I don't rely on...

A13: Wise guy.

A11: [...] but it's different, that's beside the point...

Jazz Vernacular

Colloquial terms emerged as participants communicated, understood, and performed terms and phrases known in the local scene, such as:

"aalarga": when a player goes ahead to do a solo, often confidently

"ang lakas ng loob": to describe the confidence of a novice jazz player who performs a challenging piece among more senior players or for a critical audience

"ang linis": to describe an aesthetically flawless performance "kamado": when ensemble players perform impressively tight (melodically, harmonically, rhythmically, dynamically, etc.)

"cifra-do": when a tune is learned by ear then transcribed in music notation or instantly in performance

"dikit na dikit": related to "kamado," and can also mean to play very close harmonies

"hindi bara-bara": when one does not play indiscriminately or randomly

"lagari": literally translated as the construction equipment "saw," this term is used when a musician has to work excessively – i.e., performing numerous, non-stop, consecutive gigs in a day

"pasada": when instructing an ensemble to play a run through of a whole piece or of a part, often preceded by the number of times

"puwesto": when one describes playing regularly at a particular venue

"sabit": to describe a disruptive sound produced by a player's lack of control, often an unintentional crack (for blown instruments), an off pitch, or an out-of-sync rhythm

"signal-an" or "senyas-an": when one gives physical cues or gestures for directions while playing

"sutil": a prankster or a jaunty player of a band

"tukador": to describe a "hitman," often for brass or wind musicians – especially trumpet players – who hit notes excellently by execution and/or sight-reading (M. Villena, clarified through personal communication, February 23, 2024)

"tugtugan": a noun that means collective music-making, often paired with an adjective or a description to express the aesthetic effect of a group performance to the listeners and to the players

These terms, as mentioned and contextualized in the agents' experiences, demonstrate the local interpretations and the conversation palette that circulated in the local jazz scene. These can also be presumed to still be of use at present.

Recognition

A number of times, agents could not resist speaking so highly about their fellow participants, both present during the session and the deceased. There were no prompts for such testimonials to emerge. In different times of the recollection, one would recall particular memories with another to describe how they changed their lives in and out of the jazz scene. The generosity, camaraderie, and inspiring rapport among all the agents overflowed throughout the collective recollection.

Emergent Key Stories

Aside from elucidating cultural markers such as jazz tunes, venues, musicians and vernacular terms, the interactive cues reinforced the sociocultural negotiations experienced by jazz agents in Manila from 1946 to 1986. As this collective memory depicts how Halbwachs describes as "the shared representation of the past common to a group of people who identified with one another" (as cited in Schafft, 2019, p. 8), this section discusses significant implications about Manila's jazz scene emerging from interactions.

"I'm Not a Jazz Player. I Just Play Music" (Eddie Sangcap, 2023)

Musicians Eddie Sangcap (alto sax, flute, arranger), Ryan Cayabyab (composer, music director, pianist) and Onioc Gonzaga (trumpet) expressed straight away that they didn't consider themselves as jazz musicians. Despite being recognized as being part of the scene, they asserted their positionality of being a musician who worked/s with flexibility. And so some pertinent questions, in the context of Manila include: How did a musician become labelled with jazz? What were mediators that mythologized the perception and sound of jazz? What did being a jazz musician *exclude?* The quote above was an indicator of the complex layers involved in narrating history, such as how players negotiated their musical identity; the mobility of musicians from one genre or music-cultural space to another; and the impact of the multiple meanings that different agents individually came to remember more resonantly.

Sustaining a Jazz Life

This combination of embracing a jazz identity in varying degrees contributed to the questions raised. As one asked, "Can a jazz musician, a Filipino musician live with what we have here?" He continued on,

> Kunwari I dedicate myself to being purely jazz musician, do not crossover to pop. Kunwari hindi ako kilala as a pop musician, so hindi mo kukunin… knowing there are other jazz musicians in the country, how do they cope, meron bang kabuhayan ang pagiging jazz musician dito sa Pilipinas?
>
> What if I dedicate myself to being purely a jazz musician, that I do not crossover to pop. What if I wasn't known as a pop musician, so you don't hire me… knowing there are other jazz musicians in the country, how do they cope, is there a livelihood for being a jazz musician here in the Philippines?

Mel Villena (sax, music director, arranger) answered point-blank, "Wala (*None).*" He adds, "You must be a rich guy to be just doing that all your life. Dapat may iba kayong takbuhan, ibang sasandalan (*You should have another job to run to, to hang on to*). That's the reality." Butch Silverio (trumpet) adds that it happens elsewhere, that a jazz musician having no other job would not survive. Villena pointed out immediately that it depends on one's lifestyle and where they play, for example when one plays in the jazz clubs on New York's 48th street, you'd earn for a living, "huwag ka nang mamili ng lifestyle na mataas (*just don't choose a high lifestyle)*" and "kung isa ka lang, mabubuhay ka naman (*if you're earning just for yourself, you can live)."*

Richard Merk (singer) reinterpreted the question to highlight the importance of venues, "if we have many jazz clubs in the Philippines, a jazz musician will survive," to which Villena supplied a response that leads back to the question of jazz identity:

> The people who are playing sa mga (*in*) jazz clubs are not only doing jazz. Yung mga (*The*) musicians who are playing in those jazz clubs are also pop musicians (group responds in agreement). Meaning to say, nakakapagpabahay talaga nung 1970s ang mga musiko (*musicians could really have houses built in the 1970s*) 'cause they can work in clubs, at times they do jingle… the recording of albums that time was really flourishing…

Sustaining a jazz life did not mean only doing jazz. Not unique to the scene in Manila then and now, it is beneficial and often conventional for a jazz musician to be a session player. Looking at it in another way, playing jazz becomes an asset or cultural capital which can be sustainable for a session musician.

Live Music Economy Shifts

Threading from the subject of livelihood, work conventions from the past and the present came into dialogue. In the 1960s to the early 1970s, Megan Herrera (singer) toured the hotel circuit in Southeast Asia and the Intercon hotels in Lebanon, Afghanistan and Iran with her husband Roger Herrera (bass, bandleader). She observed the absence of certain conventions at present,

> Roger would sign contracts for years. We would play 6 nights a week, and the contracts were one year with one year option. With Intercon. And now, it's by night! I mean, the poor singers [now], they never know when they're going to sing. You know, one night here, one night there. But years ago, we had comfortable lives because we had contracts by the year. It's a big, big difference. And 6 nights a week in the same place. So you would build the following.

As contract practices may be different from one venue to another, the changes in economic conventions and the decline on the number of performances through the years must be given further research and socioeconomic analysis. The music being played in these hotels and various joints advertised as jazz venues, also brings to light how jazz as a label took on different meanings and functions. Thinking about the local scene of jazz as having its own economic structure built on ideas about jazz musicking perceptions will also be more meaningful when contextualized within the larger local live music economy.

Keeping It Intact

While their loved ones played music, Vivian Valdez and Monina Regalado assisted by taking care of business. Valdez described how she was put in charge by her father Domeng Valdez (sax, music director, arranger) in distributing and organizing the fees of the band musicians:

> "…at that time mga 1970s I was very young. For example in one week's time, naglalagay ako sa (*I would place in an*) envelope ng 500 pesos [per musician]…"

This was a considerable amount at that time, comparable to about Php10,000 a week at present. And so Valdez continued,

> "I could attest to the fact that my father and my mother, they raised us through the music talaga eh (*really*), from the fruits of their labor. They were able to afford us a good home… So yun yung mga nare-remember ko na I think totoo na if you're really good and you're ano, you can pay well. And masipag. (*So that's what I remember which I believe is true, that if you're really good and you're hardworking, you can be paid well.*)

Jun Regalado's wife Monina, whom the participants regarded as superior when it came to doing business since the 1970s, also chimed in,

My husband is a musician, ang bisyo niya noon, manigarilyo (*his vice before was smoking*). Other than that, wala (*nothing else*). And all his earnings honestly he gives to me, and I try to manage it. Ayun, sinasabi ko sa kanila, masarap ang buhay namin because my husband is a musician… (*So there I would tell others, we live a comfortable life because my husband is a musician…*) they cannot believe that we have a good life… And also we have this business. Siguro maganda rin yun. (*Maybe that is also good*) If you have any other profession and you have a business, it will add up to your income.

The Regalado couple was described by Johnny Alegre (guitarist) as enterprising, having provided jobs for other musicians and electronic instruments for rent. Also taking the role of *numbrador* (hiring agent or nominator), Jun Regalado was also described as part of the session musician mafia.

Mentorship and Jazz Traditions

Singer Jeannie Tiongco shared that she began performing popular songs from Barbra Streisand, Diana Ross and Dionne Warwick. She was then brought in by Bert Nievera to his music lounge in 1981, where she started singing standard tunes such as "The Nearness of You," "As Time Goes By," and "Someone To Watch Over Me." From here she was able to work with more senior musicians who would give her music sheets and cassette tapes to study. Her interactions with drummer Tony Velarde were significant for her growth in singing jazz:

> One time sinabihan ako ni Mang Tony, pag-aralan mo 'tong pyesang ito, 'It's Alright With Me.' It's a fast swing so bago pa lang ako noon. Pinag-aralan ko, I listened to it… maraming beses. Sum-alang ako… Pagkanta ko, pagbaba ko ng stage, kinausap ako ni Mang Tony. 'Huwag mo munang kantahin 'yan ah.' Okay po! 'Hindi ka nagsiswing, parang ballad pa rin ang dating mo'
> One time I was told by Mang Tony to study this piece, 'It's Alright With Me.' It's a fast swing and I was just new then. I studied it, listened to it… so many times. I finally sang it… when I came down the stage, Mang Tony talked to me. 'Don't sing that first, okay.' Okay! 'You're not swinging, you're still singing it as a ballad'
> (laughter)
> …So ginawa ko talaga.. Dun ko nasabi sa sarili ko na, kung ito yung gusto ko talaga – jazz – hindi na muna ako makikinig ng pop…Simula noon, pagkagising ko sa umaga, jazz na yung pinapakinggan ko para makuha ko talaga yung pakiramdam. Otherwise, kung hindi ko makukuha, huwag na lang.
> So I really did it… That's when I told myself, if this is what I really want – jazz – I won't listen to pop first. Since then, when I woke up in the morning, jazz would be what I'd listen to so I could really get the feeling. Otherwise, if I don't get it, I should just not do it.

For Mel Villena, Doming Valdez (sax, music director, arranger) was very instrumental to his development as a big band arranger. Villena also recalled the responses to his first arrangements for television shows in the 1970s as an apprentice to Valdez. An elaborate story-telling ensued:

> Jun Regalado: May sinulat si Mel, talagang matataas ang nota sa trumpet.
> Mel wrote something with really high notes for the trumpet.
> (group chuckles)
> Mel Villena: Kayo yung mga sutil noon!

You were all the naughty ones then (referring to the senior players)!
(laughter)

With much animation and repartee, Villena continued to share how during rehearsals and in recording the takes for the television show *Pilita and Jackie,* it was unavoidable for the highest trumpet sound to crack or break everytime because it was just beyond the range. They were already going overtime, but the musicians kept it professional until the trumpet player and others had enough, leaving the rehearsal.

> Mel Villena: Nandun ako, yung bata. I was like 18. I was in the corner, tatay mo (to Vivian Valdez) nakatungong ganun. Nag-aaway yata sila ng dahil sa ginawa ko. Sabi ng tatay mo nung umalis na sila, pinabayaang umalis. But the gracious dad that you had.. "Totoy halika. Hindi porket kami tumutugtog pag-practisan mo kami.
>
> There I was, the kid. I was like 18. I was in the corner, your father (to Vivian Valdez) had his head down. They must have been arguing because of what I did. He let them go. But the gracious dad that you had... "Son, come here. It doesn't mean that if we were going to play your piece you'd make us your practice band.
>
> (laughter)
>
> Villena: If there is ever going to be one word na sinabi ng daddy mo na sinabi sa'kin na I still carry until today, sabi niya, 'Iho, ganto lang yun. Gagawa ka maski anong bagay. Isipin mo, economy. Ekonomiya.' ... 'Wag lahat banat. Kung sinong kasama, gano katagal gagawin, sino yung tutugtugan, ano yung appropriate. It's the appropriateness of it all.' So everytime I do arrangements now... I always think of that...
>
> If there is ever going to be one word that your daddy told me that I still carry until today, it's, 'Son, it's just like this. In anything that you do, always think of economy. Economy.'... 'Not everything should be given it all or strong or stretched out. Whoever is involved, how long the event is, who you are playing for, what is appropriate. It's the appropriateness of it all.'

Having Valdez's daughter Vivian in the recollection has made it even more poignant, as Villena reflected on the legacy of her father. He described his mentor as an inspiring and outstanding arranger and composer who had a big heart and a charisma who knew how to get in touch with and talk to the right musicians.

As mentioned earlier, agents voiced out memories to recognize musicians who have for them influenced the jazz scene in Manila. Ramon Guevarra (Latin jazz percussionist) considered Eddie Katindig as

> ...the first conga player in the Philippines. At his prime years, I consider him the best conga player. That's why Emil [Mijares] taught me to follow the style of Eddie... And Eddie told me, a good percussionist, a good conga player, must be very good in adaptation... hindi yung bara-bara (*not randomly or being careless in playing*).

Guevarra also described the perfectionist type of leadership and musicianship of pianist Emil Mijares, to which Johnny Alegre also echoes, "I love Emil, very supportive. Very strict."

Birds of the Same Feather club owner Serafin Pua recalled the time when Ramsey Lewis visited the club and witnessed Romy Katindig (piano), and described Lewis' reaction:

Nakita niya maliit na tao, maikli lang yung mga daliri niya, pumunta siya sa likod ni Romy. Tinitignan yung hand work niya. Tapos manghang-mangha. After that, breaktime… he was looking for him. "Where's that piano player? I'm gonna cut his fingers." Oo bumilib talaga.

He observed [Romy] having a small frame, with short fingers, and so he went behind Romy. He was watching his hand work. He was so astonished. After that, breaktime… he was looking for him. "Where's that piano player? I'm gonna cut his fingers." Yes he was really impressed.

Learning jazz conventions and practices from nurturing veteran players of the scene are indeed imperative in continuing the traditions of jazz musicking in the local setting. The valuable chain of insights and the pakikitungo (*inspiring engagement*) of the players in the afternoon's interaction shaped the collective memory of jazz in Manila. These stories played out a collaborative construction of ideas, opinions, and a shared past that illustrated the local scene's histories. I close this chapter with thoughts to consider based on the limitations, procedures, and outcome of the collective recollection.

REFLECTIONS AND RECOMMENDATIONS

Jazz ng Inyong Buhay (*Jazz Of Your Lives*) was one of the ethnographic activities conducted for my dissertation project of narrating post-colonial significations in a decolonial attempt to construct a jazz scene history in Manila from 1946 to 1986. While gathering and validating information were intended, I was more interested to witness and understand how the entanglement of voices and memories in one space and on the spot can be a decolonizing exercise, and if taken without caution, a colonizing process to the meaning making of jazz in Manila, Philippines. It was also realized that, aside from my questions and the structure of the recollection, "the degree of shared experiences among participants, the nature of pre-existing relationships, the sensitivity or privacy of the subject matter, the positions opened up and closed down by other participants' contributions, and the developing dynamic of the interaction itself" (Palmer et al, 2010, p. 100-101) were all variables to the construction of a jazz scene narrative based on the afternoon's assembled collective memory. Although I was at first concerned about keeping an equitable opportunity for everyone to express themselves, it soon became the least of my worries when the conversation began to play. With the ground rules set; a planned structure loose and controllable enough; participants knowing why they were there; and with a vigilant sense of lagáyan, tengáhan at pakiramdáman to keep up with, the recollection of a local jazz scene's diverse agents flowed as organically as possible.

However from the outset, I was not able to hold a mock or a rehearsal interview. So out of the ten prompts, questions six to eight were not tackled. It was indeed a big number to begin with, so 5 to 6 most crucial prompts should have been enough, especially as the breadth of elaboration and ensemble storytelling was effervescent. As I was transcribing the audio and video recordings, a number of side comments was captured which the whole group could have heard and responded to as well. I could then just imagine the turn of the conversation if these missed sounds were addressed. Other limitations came up, such as: the barrier effect of facemasks worn by others restricted a clearer comprehension of words; and participants with stronger vocal frequencies and clearer enunciations tended to dominate the flow of conversation.

For these reasons, having more than one group interview with a different set of individuals, especially ones sharing a different but still correlated set of social and cultural experiences, will contribute alternative perceptions about the local jazz scene. In particular, agents who were active in Manila during the period of study but by the 1980s decided to migrate to the US, Canada or another country in Asia would indeed have much to say about position-takings and dispositions raised in relation to the local scene economic culture. Particularly significant to learn would be encounters in playing at hotels, military bases, night clubs, cruise ships and recording studios abroad; how musicians learned about jobs abroad and how they were recruited; and how musicians endured in different socioeconomic environments. If this were to be pursued, an online meeting may be organized, however other social variables will certainly arise in the process of engaging, remembering, and communicating.

FUTURE RESEARCH DIRECTIONS

The framework of decolonizing scene histories as practiced in the exploration of collective recollection contributes to the growing discourse of memory as a fluid, interactive, and culturally based performative act. This is crucial to the local significations of a genre, in this case jazz, in the context of agents who belonged to Manila's scene after the Second World War to 1986. The exercise of sharing lived experiences in a corporeal space at a particular time using a combined method of group interview and listening session contributes to the book's research on how memory signifies and in turn is signified by sounds, images, and narratives that construct a generational collective identity based on a music culture of a genre. This process then of (re)constructing and decolonizing the knowledge about modernities in jazz from the perspective of the activity's participants can provide compounded, if not alternative interpretations of the past. By highlighting the intermingling and the relativity of these voices, we can contemplate on the entangled processes of how jazz might be understood, placed, controlled, authenticated and colonized crucially by cultural institutions, music industries, media, and other groups in power, particularly in Southeast Asia.

CONCLUSION

This chapter has explored the method of constructing the memory of jazz in Manila through a collective recollection. Agents whose pathways shaped the scene in any way and anytime between 1946 to 1986 were gathered for a group interview and a listening session. This ethnographic method provided a space to share experiences and collaborate on narratives that were evoked by selected media materials and questions that sought to understand the ways that jazz unfolded from multiple and collective perspectives. At the same time the interactions, when viewed as performative responses, affected the meanings, directions and dispositions that were uttered by other group participants. In effect, the social exercise of "lagáyan, tengáhan, and pakiramdáman" developed a collective memory of jazz built upon relative stimuli and generational factors. Thus, aside from learning, emphasizing or correcting ideas about the local scene as expressed from lived experiences, the activity demonstrates how a multitude of social and performative factors can affect how memory and history can be mediated, constructed, fabricated, and transmitted. Looking forward, an awareness of such intermediations allows scene stakeholders of the present music industry to explore ways on how to navigate their socioeconomic and cultural positionalities in the larger local music economy.

ACKNOWLEDGMENT

My deepest gratitude to the Tweedie Research Fellowship 2023 and the University of Edinburgh's Postgraduate Research Expenses Grant 2022-2023 for supporting my travel and other ethnographic activities in Manila; The Music School of Ryan Cayabyab for its space, facilities and staff assistance; and the Department of Musicology of the University of the Philippines College of Music for its continued support.

REFERENCES

Ahmed, S. (2006). *Queer phenomenology: Orientations, objects, others*. Duke University Press.

Ardoin, N. M., Gould, R. K., Wojcik, D., Roth, N. W., & Biggar, M. (2022). Community listening sessions: An approach for facilitating collective reflection on environmental learning and behavior in everyday life. *Ecosystems and People (Abingdon, England)*, 1(18), 469–477. 10.1080/26395916.2022.2101531

Assmann, J. (2011). Communicative and cultural memory. In Meusburger, P., Heffernan, M., & Wunder, E. (Eds.), *Cultural Memories. Knowledge and Space* (Vol. 4). Springer., 10.1007/978-90-481-8945-8_2

Bourdieu, P. (1983). The field of cultural production, or: The economic world reversed. *Poetics*, 12(4), 311–356. 10.1016/0304-422X(83)90012-8

Dinter, M. T. (2023). *Introduction: what is cultural memory? Cultural Memory in Republican and Augustan Rome*. Cambridge University Press.

Dussel, E. D., Krauel, J., & Tuma, V. C. (2000). Europe, modernity, and eurocentrism. *Nepantla*, 1(3), 465–478. https://www.muse.jhu.edu/article/23901

Eidsheim, N. S. (2019). *The race of sound*. Duke University Press.

Emms, R., & Crossley, N. (2018). Translocality, network structure, and music worlds: Underground metal in the United Kingdom. *Canadian Review of Sociology, 55*(1), 111+. https://link-gale-com.eux.idm.oclc.org/apps/doc/A530106505/AONE?u=ed_itw&sid=bookmark-AONE&xid=247f3b7d

Escobar, A. (2018). *Designs for the pluriverse: Radical interdependence, autonomy, and the making of world*. Duke University Press. 10.1215/9780822371816

Finnegan, R. H. (2007). *The Hidden Musicians: Music-Making in An English Town*. Wesleyan University Press.

Franz, N. K. (2011). The unfocused focus group: Benefit or bane? *The Qualitative Report*, 16(5), 1380–1388. 10.46743/2160-3715/2011.1304

Jackson, T. A. (2012). *Blowin' the blues away: Performance and meaning on the New York jazz scene* (1st ed., Vol. 16). University of California Press. 10.1525/california/9780520270442.001.0001

Jago, M. (2018). *Live at the cellar: Vancouver's iconic jazz club and the Canadian co-operative jazz scene in the 1950s and '60s*. UBC Press. 10.59962/9780774837705

Mignolo, W. D. (2009). Epistemic disobedience, independent thought and decolonial freedom. *Theory, Culture & Society*, 26(7–8), 159–181. 10.1177/0263276409349275

Palmer, M., Larkin, M., de Visser, R., & Fadden, G. (2010). Developing an interpretative phenomenological approach to focus group data. *Qualitative Research in Psychology*, 7(2), 99–121. 10.1080/14780880802513194

Quijano, A., Mignolo, W. D., Segato, R., & Walsh, C. E. (2024). *Aníbal Quijano: Foundational essays on the coloniality of power* (1st ed.). Duke University Press., 10.1215/9781478059356

Schafft, G. E. (2019). *Memory research. Sage Research Methods Foundations*. Sage Publications. 10.4135/9781526421036842523

Wilson, G. B., & MacDonald, R. A. R. (2005). The meaning of the blues: Musical identities in talk about jazz. *Qualitative Research in Psychology*, 2(4), 341–363. 10.1191/1478088705qp044oa

ADDITIONAL READING

Berish, A. (2019). Space and place in Jazz. In *The Routledge Companion to Jazz Studies* (1st ed., pp. 153–162). Routledge. 10.4324/9781315315805-15

Jago, M. (2019). Sitting in and subbing out: The gig economy of 1960s New York. In *The Routledge Companion to Jazz Studies* (1st ed., pp. 251–260). Routledge. 10.4324/9781315315805-24

Macdonald, R., & Wilson, G. (2005). Musical identities of professional jazz musicians: A focus group investigation. *Psychology of Music*, 33(4), 395–417. 10.1177/0305735605056151

Mahon, M. (2019). Constructing race and engaging power through music: Ethnomusicology and critical approaches to race. In *Theory for Ethnomusicology* (2nd ed., pp. 99–113). Routledge. 10.4324/9781315408583-5

Monson, I. T. (1996). *Saying something: Jazz improvisation and interaction*. University of Chicago Press.

Stoever, J. L. (2016). *The sonic color line: Race and cultural politics of listening*. New York Press. 10.18574/nyu/9781479899081.001.0001

Taylor, I. A. (2020). 'Well-worn grooves': Music, materiality and biographical memory. In *Popular Music History*, 12(3), 256–74. 10.1558/pomh.41832

Waldock, J., & Cohen, S. (2020). Music, memory and wellbeing: A pilot project in Liverpool. In *Movies, Music and Memory* (pp. 73–107). Emerald Publishing Limited. 10.1108/978-1-83909-199-520201004

Zembrzycki, S. (2014). *According to Baba : a collaborative oral history of Sudbury's Ukrainian community*. UBC Press. 10.59962/9780774826976

KEY TERMS AND DEFINITIONS

Collective Recollection: The act of remembering and articulating experiences with other people that in the process of construction becomes part of the group's collective memory.

Decoloniality: A perspective of constructing local histories where agency, collective memory, spatial and temporal elements, pluriversality, autonomy, and everyday life subjectivities are perceived while acknowledging the persistence of what Aníbal Quijano describes as the "coloniality of power".

Genre Culture: A collective identity of a music category that is shaped by changing conventions, cultural and musical values, significations, and practices.

Listening: The multiple layered process of aurally and orally approaching knowledge, communication and observation to signify ideas and sounds.

Mediator: An object, person, event, place, sound, or any active agent that motivates an idea, a gesture and any engagement during a collective recollection; and in constructing a culture or scene's collective memory.

Music Scene: A socially and culturally constructed notion shaped by musical practices, passed-on meanings, local traditions, relationships, mediators, and shared experiences.

Pathways: A concurrent set of people's trajectories that are socially interwoven, forming a circuit of interrelated experiences that shape a music scene.

ENDNOTE

[1] In this research, "Manila" will be used to connote the scope of Metro Manila or the National Capital Region, one of the twelve regions that was instituted between 1972 to 1986 formed of sixteen cities and one municipality, including the city of Manila.

Chapter 10
A Critical Review of Voice, Memory, and Resilience Among Finnmark Sámi Women

Robin Throne
http://orcid.org/0000-0002-3015-9587
University of the Cumberlands, USA

ABSTRACT

This chapter presents the results of a critical review of the scholarship surrounding Sámi women and the memories of the generational trauma and injustices, dispossession, and resilience of these women. Sámi women's feminism and activism are often left out of the scholarly discussions surrounding fairness and equity for this indigenous population, and little research has focused on the voice or vocality of this target population outside of arts-based research. The chapter presents the historical context that may be used for contemporary interpretations of transdisciplinary research findings for this target population. The systematic critical review involved recursivity for a systematically selected sample of current peer-reviewed articles filtered for memory, resilience, and voice constructs for Sámi women in Finnmark, Norway.

INTRODUCTION

How I respect old Sápmi
How could they have lived for ten thousand years
without the right
to call the Sámiland Sápmi
without the right to Sápmi
to be Sámi
~Nils-Aslak Valkeapä[1]

DOI: 10.4018/979-8-3693-2264-2.ch010

Figure 1. Artist rendering by Elvira Dana that includes Sámi land along the Arctic region

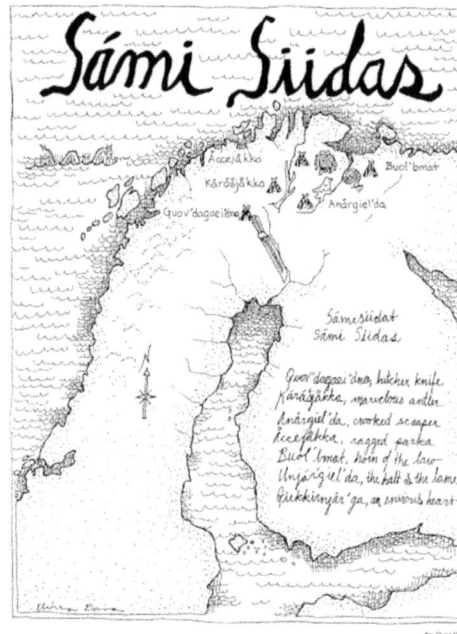

(Dana, 1997)

Over the past several decades, the scholarship has expanded to women's time- and space-bound experiences within land-based cultures, especially among indigenous cultures. Memory, with memory as a means to explore resilience and resulting voice dispossession, is a necessary concept to consider to understand best the experiences of Northern Sámi women, especially those residing in Finnmark along the Arctic Circle, boundaries now defined by national law after years of struggle to retain the culture (see Figure 1). This critical review evaluated the current research since 2019 into the experiences of Sámi women with the three constructs of memory, resilience, and voice dispossession.[2]

BACKGROUND

The research into the experiences of Sámi women within Finnmark (from *finn* meaning Sámi and *mork* meaning borderland) has expanded since the awareness raising of the 1970s to 1990s (Halsaa, 2020; Minton & Lile, 2018), and others have documented these efforts since the early 1900s (Bladow, 2019). Dana (1997) reported on the observational experiences of the Northern Sámi in the 1970s when they had begun to claim their culture, identity, and indigeneity. Likewise, Graver and Ulfstein (2004) described the challenges in achieving the Finnmark Act (2005), a landmark legislation that granted the

Sámi their right to manage their land and culture and has since been amended. The Northern Sámi have faced many hurdles to attain and protect their rights as partial sovereignty in their regions (Akhtar, 2022).[3]

Resilience, as a salutogenic concept, has been under-researched, especially in indigenous populations of older women (Alex, 2016). Pooley and Cohen (2010) noted that resilience develops over a lifetime and defined resilience as "the potential to exhibit resourcefulness by using available internal and external recourses in response to different contextual and developmental challenges" (p. 30). Alex (2016) reported that the lack of resilience among older Sámi women had decreased feelings of wellbeing. This lack was expressed as

> …experiences of discrimination, lack of connectedness, and living on the border of the dominant society. Analysis of the Sámi women's narratives can give broader perspectives on women's health deepen the perspectives on human resilience and increase the understanding of minority groups in a multicultural world. (Alex 2016, p. 30)

Thus, family and cultural connectedness were essential to feelings of resilience and well-being, which were further enhanced by experiences of gender equality and economic security (Alex, 2016).

While the debate over the meaning and scientific definition of memory continues among scholars, memory is broadly defined as a phenomenon of experience whereby one will alter the way an individual may respond to stimuli in the future as a function of the past (Colaço, 2020). In addition, memory is a critical concept in understanding the experiences of indigenous cultures. As Chahine (2021) noted, when it comes to indigenous research, memory is not about the past but very much informing the present and, often, the future of the culture. Further, Sámi scholar Porsanger (2022), an expert in indigenous research, noted that repatriation of historical and cultural objects can serve as an advancement of indigenous decolonization and positive transformation for the culture by its rescue of values and reality of the past transgressions perpetuated upon the culture and as representative of these experiences by the artifacts themselves. The author further noted, "In the Sámi context, repatriation and provenance research are of crucial importance because most of the objects related to the cultural heritage of the Sámi people have been stored and displayed outside the Sámi region" (Porsanger, 2022, p. 74).

Similarly, Minde (2017) noted the cultural distinctiveness of the Sámi in the Arctic region, whereby memories held by older Sámi women may be best retained by proximity to the land, its creatures, and the connections to the ancient culture and time that assist in identity preservation. Carstens (2016) asserted that explorations of land rights have resulted in Sámi self-determination, which may illustrate cultural and individual resilience. Indigenous self-determination for land-based cultures necessitates rights to traditional land use and natural resources, and future assurances may sustain or even restore memory in the indigenous, not dominant, context (Carstens, 2016; Minde, 2017).

Still, other scholars have reported that the historical marginalization of the Sámi has often led to a degradation of wellbeing as demonstrated by depression or addiction. Kvaløy et al. (2017) noted that the inculturation or "Norwegianization" of the Sámi as marginalization has not been well-researched. Thus, the impact of these aspects on memory and resilience may not yet be known. In addition, Burman (2017) found that intimate partner violence (IPV) is underreported within Finnmark, so causes of patriarchy, including historical and contemporary cultural beliefs, may foster this. In such cases, memory and resilience may be further complicated by sociocultural oppression, cultural beliefs, and taboos, and further research is needed to explore these complexities (Burman, 2017; Kvaløy et al., 2017). Further, these aspects may contribute to voice dispossession among the target population, but more research is needed to understand this phenomenon better.

More recently, Brustad (2018) described the historical impact of eugenics on the Northern Sámi, similar to the 19th- and even 20th-century egregious acts of *othering* among North America, Australia, and other continents, where measurement of skull length and width were to be indicative of evolution by race with the ulterior motive to "safeguard the purity of the Nordic race" (p. 2). Eugenics medical research was conducted extensively throughout Norway and in Northern Norway. The past research focused extensively on the Sámi and Kvens,[4] resulting in a "negative collective historical memory" that adversely impacts contemporary Sámi healthcare (Brustad, 2018).

The intentional colonization of Sámi into nomad schools has also been widely reported across the scholarship to have contributed to the trauma of this indigenous nation.[5] Finally, Eriksen et al. (2018) purported recollection bias may lead Sámi adults to underreport childhood trauma, and current anxiety and depression may distort or repress memory and recollection, which may reduce the individual's awareness of resilience. "These disparities have often been linked to colonisation, forced assimilation, violence and discrimination" (Eriksen et al., 2018, p. 1). While much remains unknown regarding memory, resilience, and voice dispossession (and their layered and complex meanings) among Northern Sámi women, the gap in the research supports the need for continued work into these constructs.

METHOD, SOURCING, AND POSITIONALITY

The critical approach to reviewing the current scholarship since 2019 surrounding the experiences of Sámi women was employed. Article sourcing was conducted using a systematic procedure, and article filtering was conducted by deploying recursivity over time (Leech & Onwuegbuzie, 2008). Four sourcing databases were used for EBSCO, ProQuest, Web of Science, and Google Scholar. One hundred and ninety-four sources were identified since 2019 for Sámi women in Finnmark, Norway, and narrowed to 71 to reference Finnmark. Sixty-three books/book chapters/book reviews, organizational/association reports, dissertations/theses, white papers, and other grey literature were excluded. The sample was further filtered for memory/memories, resilient/resilience, and voice/vocal/vocality, resulting in a final peer-reviewed journal article sample of eight for critical analysis.

Further, recursivity incorporated indigenous research strategies to allow for systematic reasoning of time and space to consider the constructs of memory and resilience as experiential in context and nonlinear in meaning and interpretation (Leech & Onwuegbuzie, 2008; Porsanger et al., 2021). This nonlinear approach to the analysis provided a lens by which to critically consider the sources from a deconstructed perspective by a non-indigenous researcher of Norwegian emigrant-settler descent. Transparency and fidelity of researcher positionality (Throne, 2018) allowed for an understanding of the researcher's non-indigenous viewpoint in the articles' context. They necessitated the recursive approach as the experiences of Sámi women remain incomplete within the scholarship and warrant close inspection of the work conducted.

The researcher, as a descendant of Scandinavian immigrant groups involved in the 19th century U.S. migration, required rigorous outsider reflexivity with recursivity to ensure retrospective distance from settler-society inculturation to reduce researcher bias, privilege, and unconscious perspective (Throne, 2021a) as introspection of the researcher positionality has been shown to demonstrate researcher fidelity and data trustworthiness (Throne, 2021b). As Mellor (2022) concluded, "Non-Indigenous positionality may draw on Indigenous standpoints to better understand Indigeneity but cannot claim Indigenous epistemological and/or ontological authority" (p. 27). However, the contributions of researcher descendancy from settler-colonizers may foster reconciliation and deepen understanding (Mellor, 2022).

RESULTS

The critical review analysis resulted in 79 occurrences of the three constructs across the eight sources (see Table 1). Excerpting resulted in the capture of 23 segments that included a systematic review of the three constructs in proximity to Sámi woman/women/girl/female for content analysis and identification of patterns for the lived experiences of the target population. Three other excerpts of phrases were gathered from non-gendered perspectives.

Table 1. Sources by construct frequency

Memory/Memories	Resilience/Resilient	Voice/Vocal/Vocality
Bladow (2019) 2	Bladow (2019) 1	Bladow (2019) 5
Eriksen et al. (2021) 2		
	Damsgård et al. (2020) 5	
Friborg et al. (2020) 1	Friborg et al. (2020) 24	Friborg et al. (2020) 1
Halsaa (2020) 2		Halsaa (2020) 5
		Normann (2019) 6
	Nystad et al. (2020) 23	
	Webber (2021) 2	

Note: N=8.

Memory

Four sources within the sample included a discussion on memory. Bladow (2019) reported on the use of the Sámi *joik*, a traditional form of song, as an arts-based activism vehicle for memory. The *joik* connected to Valkeapää's poetry as a replicated sentiment to promote climate justice for Mother Earth and broader awareness of the Sámi land claims and land dispossession. The author purported that Sámi's collective memory can be used to instill indigenous feminist values and advance the concept of "artivism" to do so (Bladow, 2019, p. 325). In a study of IPV, Eriksen et al. (2021) noted that the intrusiveness of memory associated with post-traumatic stress (PTS) existed within a sample that included Sámi women from five municipalities within Finnmark, as defined as Sámi majority regions. Friborg et al. (2020) also used a pre-validated scale to measure intrusive memories as related to PTS with a sample of Sámi men and women placed in boarding schools in the 20th century and noted by 1955, 50 boarding schools were established within Finnmark to expedite inculcation of "*Norwegianization*" (p. 851). Despite the boarding school experience 40-50 years prior, participants reported a robust Sámi identity. However, results generally disfavored "boarding school participants [who] reported more discrimination, violence, unhealthier lifestyle behavior (smoking), less education and household income compared to non-boarding participants" (Friborg et al., 2020, p. 848). Finally, Halsaa (2020) reported on the challenges in documenting Sámi women's memories of their 1980-1990s activism and commented on the additional challenges of insider/outsider perspectives and researcher positionality for qualitative Sámi research.

Resilience

Five sources within the sample reported on some aspects of resilience. Webber (2021) and Nystad et al. (2020) reported non-gendered perspectives as indicative of Sámi resilience as depicted within "Sámi indigenous theology, which emphasizes the circle of life, creation, and humanity's relationship within the creation and its Creator" (Webber, 2021, p. 155) and resilience via place attachment (Nystad et al., 2020). Damsgård et al. (2020) noted the connections between chronic pain and resilience to emphasize how the importance of family within Sámi culture may lead women with chronic pain to foster resilience. The authors also cited Friborg et al. (2020) to report how discrimination experiences result in a solid Sámi identity as a component of resilience. Lastly, Bladow (2019) claimed that a resilient, committed perspective promoted artistic confidence for Sámi women artist-activists.

Voice Dispossession

Four sources within the sample commented on voice and vocality. Normann (2019) reported on the power of collective Sámi women's voices within Sápmi fostered "collective listening and multiple dialogues" delivered to broad audiences, likely reducing Sámi women's voice dispossession (p. 9). The collective listening was conducted within a circle that reflected Sámi historical culture, whereby participants reported closing their eyes to enhance a sensorial experience to expand the listening (Normann, 2019). Halsaa (2020) reported on the conflicts between non-indigenous Sámi researchers and the Sámi women participants themselves, who desired to have their "own voice" in the process (p. 128). According to one participant, "Sámi women's rights to represent and speak for themselves were not respected... We want to influence, have our own voice" due to imbalances between non-indigenous researchers and Sámi participants in the past (Halsaa, 2020, p. 128). Bladow (2019) shared contemporary Sámi women who gained a reduction in voice dispossession via electronic and hip-hop music and enhanced political consciousness. In contrast, Friborg et al. (2020) found that Sámi adults could voice positive insights from youth experiences from the systematic inculcation of Norwegianization despite the trauma and harm.

DISCUSSION

Memory as a means to resilience and voice as a means to empowerment and self-reliance continue as compelling constructs within current research. Yet, the deeper meaning of these constructs, specifically for Sámi women in Finnmark, deserves further examination and interpretation amidst past trauma and discrimination. Activism, arts-based research, and artistic activism may reduce voice dispossession and allow Sámi women to describe their individual experiences with these constructs (Greiner, 2015; Normann, 2019). The Sámi storytelling traditions "reflect a rich and vital wellspring of cultural knowledge and memory" (Greiner, 2015, p. 21).

Guttorm et al. (2021) called for those presenting decolonized research storying must expand our way of thinking about storying as moments that can inform an emergent politics of memory and enact landscapes of remembrance" (p. 132). In this review, it was reported that when Sámi participants were considered research participants, they were hesitant to voice their experiences (Halsaa, 2020). Yet, when evaluated for their art and activism, they were forthcoming with memory and illustrations of resilience and self-empowerment through arts-based means (Bladow, 2019; Normann, 2019). These experiences of past researchers may hold the answer to better understanding the lived experiences of these participants and providing platforms to facilitate the "collective memory" to be shared over the individual. Yet, this work can be challenging within cultures that experienced past trauma, and the culture has a negative historical collective memory (Brustad, 2018) and can be connected to PTS, which requires additional care in sharing individual experiences (Eriksen et al., 2021).

The resilience fostered by place attachment and the land parallels the research into resilience with other indigenous land-based cultures, whereby land curation is a means to reflections of self-determination and freedom and a necessary generational source of sustainability and resilience (Versey & Throne, 2021). However, when a culture has been subject to assimilation and inculturation from a dominant culture, these memories and resulting resilience have been diminished; however, connections to family and place protect them from discontinuity despite the negative impact on wellbeing (Nystad et al., 2020). This fact alone may be representative of Sámi cultural capacity for resilience.

The chapter author, among others, has noted the voice dispossession and attributional accommodation women, even women in leadership roles, often make to survive within imbalanced power structures (Stewart et al., 2022). In other research, differences in how older and younger women react to these imbalanced power structures may provide answers to the metaphoric silencing of Sámi women's voices in the past and today (Burkinshaw & White, 2020). For example, the comparison of systematic inculturation via boarding schools in the likeness of internment camps may foster vocalization of the experiences of Sámi women and the reflective experiences of younger Sami women of this generational trauma (Friborg et al., 2020). "As the Norwegian national ambition was to suppress Sámi and Kven languages and cultures, the policy was clearly negative and suppressive of cultural pride" (Friborg et al., 2020, p. 850). Thus, the ability of Sámi women to vocalize their cultural pride today demonstrates the dominant culture's failure of such historical policies.

Junka-Aikio et al. (2021) noted that by the 1960s and 1970s, a new generation of Sámi began to link their history and traditions to the latest information systems and said:

> In this context, Sámi access to knowledge production became one of the key pillars of the Sámi ethnopolitical project. If research, until then, had advanced the interests of the dominant society and excluded Sámi voices and perspectives, now time was ripe for the Sámi themselves to become researchers, and to do research which would emanate from the needs of the Sámi society, and build on Sámi experiences, epistemologies and worldviews. (p. 6).

Thus, the non-indigenous researcher positionality and the limitations of commercial and open-access source databases for article sourcing may have limited results (Langham-Putrow et al., 2021). Perhaps dissertations and theses contributed to the scholarship should be considered or used for analysis as a means to bring a new generation of Sámi researchers into the discussion.

FUTURE RESEARCH RECOMMENDATIONS

Future research is necessary to extend the findings of the articles systematically sourced and reviewed in this chapter, as well as the background sources. Alex (2016) called for ongoing research into this target population that involves perspectives of culture, gender, intersectionality, and narrative to deepen understanding of the complexities of Sámi culture, gender, age, economic status, and place. In addition, Eriksen et al. (2018) called for more research into Sámi mental health, including IPV. Nystad et al., 2020) recommended further research into Sámi school-age children's wellbeing and health within educational environments, and Webber (2021) called for a consideration of the Sámi context, specifically this unique Scandinavian creation theology, as a contribution to contemporary vocabulary to address the ongoing sociocultural challenges within the context of natural resources for this land-based culture and as a defense against historical dehumanization. Perhaps, the specific construct of resilience deserves further analysis from these many perspectives for an enduring land-based culture. Nystad et al. (2020) called for more research into Sámi youth wellbeing in contemporary educational settings, especially within environments that promote culturally sensitive programming.

Future research is also needed to extend Friborg et al. (2020) and Eriksen et al. (2021) to examine relationships between Sámi boarding school and other discriminatory experiences with IPV and PTS for the impact on memory, resilience, and voice dispossession. The findings of Damsgård et al. (2020) and Friborg et al. (2020) should also be continued to examine further relationships among resilience, family connections, and discriminatory experiences. Ultimately, future critical inquiry is needed to establish standards for indigenous research with this target population to foster more research to address these gaps within the scholarship. In the following study, the grey literature must be incorporated, especially for the scholarship of Sámi indigenous researchers. Last, the definitions and distinctions for memory, resilience, and voice dispossession contextually with their unique land-based culture and the interactions between these constructs warrant further inquiry and specificity for Sámi women, and regional limitations may unnecessarily bind sourcing for an already incomplete realm of research.

CONCLUSION

This critical review utilized systematic means to filter the research into measurable constructs of memory, resilience, and voice for a critical analysis of the experiences of Sámi women within a specific geographic region where the culture is most populous. The systematic critical review involved recursivity for a systematically selected sample of 8 current peer-reviewed articles filtered for memory, resilience, and voice constructs for Sámi women in Finnmark, Norway. The current research into these constructs for this population since 2019, both research into past and present considerations, remains extremely limited for the experiences of Sámi women. The paucity of research into these constructs for Sámi women in Finnmark is evident. While ongoing research continues, it may be necessary to consider the grey literature due to these gaps in the peer-reviewed scholarship to ensure that the scholarship of Sámi scholars entering the academy is incorporated. Further, due to the authenticity found within arts-based or activist-based research, these sources must continually be curated to ensure inclusion in future studies to best understand the experiences of Sámi women in this segment of Norway.

REFERENCES

Akhtar, Z. (2022). Sámi peoples land claims in Norway, Finnmark Act and providing legal title. *The Indigenous Peoples' Journal of Law, Culture & Resistance, 7*(1).

Aléx, L. (2016). Resilience among old Sámi women. *Ageing and Society*, 36(8), 1738–1756. 10.1017/S0144686X15000719

Bladow, K. (2019). "Never shut up my native": Indigenous feminist protest art in Sápmi. *Feminist Studies*, 45(2), 312–332. 10.1353/fem.2019.0029

Brustad, M. (2018). *Sámi health: A summary of published results of population studies in Norway*. Sámi Statistics Speak. https://samilogutmuitalit.no/sites/default/files/publications/3sami_health.pdf

Burkinshaw, P., & White, K. (2020). Generation, gender, and leadership: Metaphors and images. *Frontiers in Education*, 5, 517497. 10.3389/feduc.2020.517497

Burman, M. (2017). Men's intimate partner violence against Sámi women: A Swedish blind spot. *Nordic Journal on Law and Society, 1*(01-02), 194-215.

Carstens, M. (2016). Sámi land rights: The Anaya report and the Nordic Sámi Convention. *ECMI Journal of Ethnopolitics and Minority Issues in Europe*, 15(1), 75–116.

Chahine. (2021). Memory is not about the past. *Journal of Anthropological Films, 5*(1). 10.15845/jaf.v5i01.3189

Colaço, D. (2022). What counts as a memory? Definitions, hypotheses, and "kinding in progress". *Philosophy of Science*, 89(1), 89–106. 10.1017/psa.2021.14

Damsgård, E., Thrane, G., Fleten, N., Bagge, J., Sørlie, T., Anke, A., & Broderstad, A. R. (2020). Persistent pain associated with socioeconomic and personal factors in a Sámi and Non-Sámi population in Norway: An analysis of SAMINOR 2 survey data. *International Journal of Circumpolar Health*, 79(1), 1787022. 10.1080/22423982.2020.178702232780007

Dana, K. O. (1997). Sámi literature in the Twentieth Century. *World Literature Today*, 71(1), 22–28. 10.2307/40152555

Eriksen, A. M., Hansen, K. L., Schei, B., Sørlie, T., Stigum, H., Bjertness, E., & Javo, C. (2018). Childhood violence and mental health among indigenous Sámi and non-Sámi populations in Norway: A SAMINOR 2 questionnaire study. *International Journal of Circumpolar Health*, 77(1), 1508320. 10.1080/22423982.2018.150832030112962

Eriksen, A. M., Melhus, M., Jacobsen, B. K., Schei, B., & Broderstad, A. R. (2021). Intimate partner violence and its association with mental health problems: The importance of childhood violence–The SAMINOR 2 Questionnaire Survey. *Scandinavian Journal of Public Health*, 1–3.34192982

Finnmark Act. (2005). Ministry of Justice and Public Security. LOV-2005–06–17–85.

Friborg, O., Sørlie, T., Schei, B., Javo, C., Sørbye, Ø., & Hansen, K. L. (2020). Do childhood boarding school experiences predict health, well-being and disability pension in adults? A SAMINOR study. *Journal of Cross-Cultural Psychology*, 51(10), 848–875. 10.1177/0022022120962571

Graver, H. P., & Ulfstein, G. (2004). The Sámi people's right to land in Norway. *International Journal on Minority and Group Rights*, 11(4), 337–377. 10.1163/1571811042791175

Greiner, C. (2015). "The North chose us": Selected poems by Nils-Aslak Valkeapää as expressions of Sámi cultural ecology and indigenous rights concerns. *IK: Other Ways of Knowing*, 21-32.

Guttorm, H., Kantonen, L., Kramvig, B., & Pyhälä, A. (2021). Decolonized research-storying: Bringing Indigenous ontologies and care into the practices of research writing. In *Indigenous research methodologies in Sámi and global contexts* (pp. 113–143). Brill. 10.1163/9789004463097_006

Halsaa, B. (2020). The (trans) national mobilisation of Sámi women in Norway. *Le Mouvement Social*, 63, 119–145.

International Work Group for Indigenous Affairs (IWGIA). (2022). *Indigenous peoples in Sápmi*. IWGIA. https://www.iwgia.org/en/sapmi.html

Junka-Aikio, L., Nyyssönen, J., & Lehtola, V. P. (Eds.). (2021). *Sámi research in transition: Knowledge, politics and social change*. Routledge. 10.4324/9781003090830

Kristiina Virtanen, P., Keskitalo, P., & Olsen, T. (2021). *Indigenous research methodologies in Sámi and global contexts*. Brill. 10.1163/9789004463097

Kvaløy, K., Melhus, M., Silviken, A., Brustad, M., Sørlie, T., & Broderstad, A. R. (2018). Disordered eating in Sámi and non-Sámi Norwegian populations: The SAMINOR 2 clinical survey. *Public Health Nutrition*, 21(6), 1094–1105. 10.1017/S1368980017003597729223188

Langham-Putrow, A., Bakker, C., & Riegelman, A. (2021). Is the open access citation advantage real? A systematic review of the citation of open access and subscription-based articles. *PLoS One*, 16(6), e0253129. 10.1371/journal.pone.025312934161369

Leech, N. L., & Onwuegbuzie, A. J. (2008). Recursivity. In *The Sage encyclopedia of qualitative research methods*. SAGE.

Mellor, K. (2022). Developing a decolonial gaze: Articulating research/er positionality and relationship to colonial power. *Access: Critical explorations of equity in higher education, 10*(1), 26-41.

Minde, G. (2017). Older Sámi women living in the Arctic: A cultural background that breaks with western conventions. *Journal of Community & Public Health Nursing*, 3(1). 10.4172/2471-9846.1000155

Minton, S. J., & Lile, H. S. (2018, May). A conversation about the proposed truth commission in Norway for the Sámi and Kven peoples: What can be learnt from truth and reconciliation processes elsewhere. In *14th International Congress of Qualitative Inquiry*. University of Illinois in Urbana-Champaign.

Normann, S. (2019). Constructing dialogues and solidarity through "Radio-Cinema" in the Sámi-Norwegian colonial context. *Community Psychology in Global Perspective*, 5(2), 1–18.

Nystad, K., Ingstad, B., & Spein, A. R. (2020). How academic experiences and educational aspirations relate to well-being and health among Indigenous Sámi youth in Northern Norway: A qualitative approach. *Journal of Northern Studies*, 14(1), 35–61. 10.36368/jns.v14i1.975

Pooley, J. A., & Cohen, L. (2010). Resilience: A definition in context. *Australian Community Psychologist*, 22(1), 30–37.

Porsanger, J. (2022). An Indigenous Sámi museum and repatriation on a Sámi drum from the XVII century. *Dutkansearvvi dieđalaš áigečála*, 6(1).

Porsanger, J., Seurujärvi-Kari, I., & Nystad, R. L. (2021). *'Shared remembering' as a relational Indigenous method in conceptualization of Sámi women's leadership. Indigenous research methodologies in Sámi and global contexts*. Brill Sense.

Stewart, T. J., Throne, R., & Evans, L. A. (2022). Voice dispossession and attributional accommodation for career persistence: A systematic review of gender parity in US higher education leadership. *Policy and Practice Challenges for Equality in Education*, 39-54.

Throne, R. (2018). The letter: Fidelity in researcher positionality to exhume dispossessed voices for Leavy's concept of coherence in feminist narrative research. *Gender and Women's Studies*, 2(1). 10.31532/GendWomensStud.2.1.003

Throne, R. (2021a). Land as agency: A critical autoethnography of Scandinavian acquisition of dispossessed land in the Iowa Territory. In *Indigenous research of land, self, and spirit* (pp. 118–131). IGI Global.

Throne, R. (2021b). New investigator fidelity: Fostering doctoral practitioner researcher positionality. In *Practice-based and practice-led research for dissertation development* (pp. 165-187). IGI Global.

Versey, H. S., & Throne, R. (2021). A critical review of Gullah Geechee midlife women and heirs' property challenges along the Gullah Geechee Cultural Heritage Corridor. *Examining international land use policies, changes, and conflicts*, 46-64.

Webber, T. B. (2021). Creation and relations—A Sámi perspective on Scandinavian creation theology. *Dialog*, 60(2), 155–160. 10.1111/dial.12666

ADDITIONAL READING

Allard, C., & Skogvang, S. F. (Eds.). (2015). *Indigenous rights in Scandinavia: Autonomous Sámi law.* Ashgate Publishing.

Doria, A., & Udén, M. (2006). Indigenous women in Scandinavia and a potential role for ICT. In *Encyclopedia of gender and information technology* (pp. 802–807). IGI Global. 10.4018/978-1-59140-815-4.ch125

Helander, H., Aikio, H., Keskitalo, P., & Turunen, T. (2022). Land-based participatory pedagogical experiment in Sámi language distance teaching: Maintaining children's relationships with land and nature. In *Handbook of research on teaching in multicultural and multilingual contexts* (pp. 369–390). IGI Global. 10.4018/978-1-6684-5034-5.ch021

Kent, N. (2019). *The Sámi peoples of the North: A social and cultural history.* Oxford University Press.

Kuokkanen, R. J. (2008). Sámi higher education and research: Toward building a vision for future. In *Indigenous peoples: Self-determination-knowledge-Indigeneity* (pp. 267-286). Eburon.

Lehtola, V. P. (2004). *The Sámi people: Traditions in transition.* University of Alaska Press.

Parahakaran, S. (2022). Digital ethnography within Indigenous contexts: An exploratory perspective. In *Practices, challenges, and prospects of digital ethnography as a multidisciplinary method* (pp. 138–147). IGI Global. 10.4018/978-1-6684-4190-9.ch010

Roman, R. B. (2021). Between religious identity and national identity? Pentecostal Finnish Roma in Lutheran Finland. *Finnish Studies*, 136.

Sand, S. (2022). Dealing with racism: Colonial history and colonization of the mind in the autoethnographic and Indigenous film *Sámi Blood. Journal of International and Intercultural Communication*, 1–15.

Ween, G. B., & Lien, M. E. (2012). Decolonialisation in the Arctic? Nature practices and land rights in Sub-arctic Norway. *Journal of Rural and Community Development*, 7(1).

ENDNOTES

[1]   Valkeapää, N. (1994). *Trekways of the wind.* DAT.

[2]   A portion of this chapter was previously presented as a conference paper at the 5th Memory, Affects, and Emotions International Interdisciplinary Conference, April 2023.

[3]   The scholarship surrounding the challenges overcome by the Northern Sámi has been widely published. Thorough accounts have been provided by Akhtar (2022), Carstens (2016), and Ween and Lien (2012), as well as in the work by Allard and Skogvang (2015) and many other indigenous and non-indigenous scholars.

[4]   Kvens are currently known as a national minority within Norway, sometimes referred to as "Norwegian Finns." Other scholars have tracked Kvens as ancient settlers within the Arctic region and credited them for the introduction of agriculture to the region.

[5]   A poignant autoethnographic account of these experiences is depicted in Amanda Kernell's film, *Sámi Blood.*

Chapter 11
Where Are We?
Performative Strategies of Encounter

Susana Mendes Silva
http://orcid.org/0000-0003-3647-0189
University of Évora, Portugal

Beatriz Cantinho
http://orcid.org/0000-0002-1627-1441
University of Évora, Portugal

ABSTRACT

This chapter is a visual, aural, and written iteration of the performative walk "Where are we? Performing the city, slowing down time" developed and presented by the artists Beatriz Cantinho and Susana Mendes Silva in the context of the "Elia Academy 2023: exploring situatedness" that took place in the University of Évora in May. The aesthetic focus of this performative walk was a reflection on how one can create connections with the place where one is, and how one can look and unveil lost, forgotten, or erased stories of a given territory. The territory was the city of Évora, where Cantinho and Mendes Silva wanted participants to experience its history, landscape and soundscape, and their own bodies, their own presence from a situated perspective. The authors also wanted to trigger a conscious experience that contrasted with the touristic way of experiencing this World Heritage city and its water systems.

INTRODUCTION

Every environment, every place is shaped by water: by the way it is situated and used; by how it is protected, managed, and distributed; by the conditions of its accessibility; by its quality, and by its quantity.

Water can be both a protector and a threat, and the struggles over water can be both for and against it (Garcia et al., n.d.)

DOI: 10.4018/979-8-3693-2264-2.ch011

This chapter is a visual, aural and written iteration of the performative walk "Where are we? Performing the city, slowing down time" developed and presented by the artists Beatriz Cantinho and Susana Mendes Silva in the context of the "Elia Academy 2023: exploring situatedness" that took place in the University of Évora in May.

The aesthetic focus of this performative walk was a reflection on how one can create connections with the place where one is, and how you can look and unveil lost, forgotten, or erased stories of a given territory. The territory was the city of Évora, where we wanted participants to experience its history, landscape and soundscape, and their own bodies, their own presence from a situated perspective. We also wanted to trigger a conscious experience that contrasted with the touristic way of experiencing this World Heritage city and its water systems.

To develop this experience we applied different conceptual and compositional strategies shared with the participants such as written instructions, deep listening, audio narratives, sound files, and human landscapes/formations, created together with a group of students from the Visual Arts and Multimedia BA. These strategies aimed at creating a choreographic and performative *modus operandi* that had the potential to change both the collective experience of the group as well as the individual.

CONTEXT

Drawing from choreography, performance, and visual arts, in our practice we explore ways in which one relates to the movement of the bodies and their sensorial experience in a poetic and affective relationship with visible and invisible spaces of given territories.

Our practice also draws inspiration from the situationist legacy (Debord, 1958) and the way in which it informs our compositional strategies. An aesthetic analysis of the transformative power of movement and performance, inside and outside the artistic realm, is a way to reconfigure modes of experiencing and living the territory. Situationist drift and psychogeography — in particular their cartographic, abstract and poetic visual representations and mapping — have largely contributed to a new perception of space. Thus, we wanted to question multiple qualities of space, such as duration, speed and their intertwined relations expressed through the movement of bodies.

By sharing our compositional strategies and methodology we hope to challenge our own perception in the scope of these practices and to explore different possibilities with other artists and researchers.

The Alentejo region in Portugal, where the city of Évora is situated, is frequently exposed to drought where the levels of pluviosity have been very scarce in the last decade. In 2023 we were particularly under the designation of **severe drought**. This aspect in relation to the thematic of ELIA's encounter — **exploring situatedness** — played an inevitable role in our artistic and thematic choices, regarding the route for the walk and our research on specific sites.

Within the landscape of the city, the XVI century water aqueduct prevails as a major landmark of Évora, connecting past and present in the lives of its inhabitants. Another aspect that we wanted to imprint in our walk was **contemplation** and the attention to other dimensions of life, being those synesthetic or kinesthetics, through an embodied experience of site and cityscape. **Silence** seemed fundamental to enhance other ways of seeing and listening. For that reason, we felt compelled to include The Santa Maria Coeli Monastery in the route. The monastery was built for Carthusian monks from 1587 to 1598. Those who know the Carthusian Order, associate it with silence, contemplation and solitude. It is renowned for being the strictest Catholic religious order. The austerity of the rules of the Carthusians is due to the emphasis on silence rather than the practice of penance. It is as if silence alone would draw us closer to God rather than speech itself. The monastery was supplied with water by the Aqueduct which we followed along in our walk until it enters the city and intertwines with it, culminating in the fountain of the main square of the city.

Another aspect that permeated our research is the fact that Évora has recently won the competition for the European Capital of Culture in 2027, under the theme *Vagar,* which can be translated in English as 'slow pace'. This *vagar* characterizes the modes of living in Alentejo and it is imprinted in the culture of the region. Thus, becoming an intangible legacy that reverberates and contrasts with the increasing velocity that characterizes our contemporary lifes, and that, in the perspective of our work, brings into the discussion major contemporary issues, such as the ones of ecological sustainability and degrowth.

METHODOLOGY

When we proposed to develop a performative walk for the 2023 ELIA's program — under the thematic of **situatedness** — we decided that our walk would be a reflection on how one can create connections with the place where one is, and how we can unveil lost, forgotten, or erased stories of a given territory. Our territory was the city of Évora, where we wanted our participants to experience its history, *genius loci*, landscape and soundscape, and their own bodies, their own presence from a situated perspective. But all that should be done through considering a specific pace: there was a desire for slowing down time and giving space for contemplation, *vagar*. We wanted to connect with specific aspects of the **art of walking** as a reflexive practice that is both a relationship with the visible as well as the invisible places and landscapes of the city.

To develop this experience, we started with intense conceptual, historical and embodied research which included walking with a group of students of the Visual Arts and Multimedia BA. There was the need to test, rehearse and discuss the coherence of different conceptual and compositional strategies that were being created by us and also together with our students. There were constraints that we considered like the time of the day for the walk because of the heat; the coherence of the starting point, the route and the final stop; on how we could create the appropriate conditions for our participants regarding their physical resistance, senses and perception.

We then decided to start the walk at Santa Maria Coeli Monastery, where silent religious orders have been living since late sixteenth century, and follow along the Aqueduct of Água da Prata until the fountain at Praça do Giraldo which is the central square of the city. This relation to the water circuits of the ancient city was intended to underline the relevance of **water** in a territory which is at risk of desertification. We also decided that the walk should be made in **silence** in order to enhance the attention and the physical experience of the participants with the landscape, its visual and sound singularities as well as conveying a **bodily connection** between the participants and the performers.

THE PERFORMATIVE WALK

The group of participants arrived at the Santa Maria Coeli Monastery. We and our students were waiting for them at the entrance gate.

1.

We lowered our voices and spoke slowly:

"Hi, welcome everyone!

We are Beatriz and Susana.

Where are we? is a performative walk and it will be important to keep as silent as possible, to slow your breathing and to enjoy every minute.

You will be briefly blindfolded and guided by one of us.

If you feel uncomfortable you can silently opt out at any time.

We are going to give you a sound file that we will hear later on".

2. Our group of students blindfolded the participants and guided them inside the church for a **deep listening** moment.

Beatriz and Susana remained silently inside the church with them.

Meanwhile the group of students positioned themselves in the garden.

After some minutes, we gently touched our participants in the shoulder and whispered to their ears to please remove their blindfold.

We handed them card 1:

Santa Maria Coeli Monastery

Dom Teotónio de Bragança, Archbishop of Évora from 1578 to 1602, built a monastery for the Carthusian monks in the archiepiscopal city from 1587 to 1598. The monastery was gradually improved and embellished: in the 17th century King Pedro II had the magnificent portico and marble facade of the monastery church constructed and in the 18th century João V installed the majestic altarpiece in gilded wood, and the building was recognized as a national monument in 1910.

The monastery's noble standing derives from its role as providing a place for contemplation and spiritual development, in accordance with the ways of St Bruno. The beautiful habit of early-morning prayer for all, without exception, was seen by local people as a motherly gesture of caring for, watching over and praying for their children during the night.

Those who know what the Carthusian Order, associate it with silence, contemplation and solitude. It is renowned for being the strictest Catholic religious order.

The austerity of the rules of the Carthusians is due to the emphasis on silence rather than the practice of penance. It is as if silence alone draws us closer to God rather than speech itself. It is not easy to explain the mystery (CMÉ, n.d.).

3.

We left the church and let them enjoy the garden and view the group of students in the space.

They left the space behind Susana and passed the gate of the Monastery.
We made a circle.
We gave the card 2:

Solvitur Ambulando

= an appeal to practical experience for a solution or proof, Latin, literally "(the problem) is solved by walking"
Follow your breathing
Dwell mindfully on your steps, soon you will find your balance
Visualise a tiger walking slowly, and you will find that your steps become as majestic as hers
Convert your ears
your feet
your whole body
into a radar
You are now detecting, locating, tracking, and recognizing
what is around you
Meanwhile the group of students left towards the city.

From this moment on we walked in complete silence.

The participants formed a straight line behind Susana. We waited for her sign to begin walking and followed her pace. Beatriz was at the end of the line.

We ask them to put the sound file as soon as we are on the road.

Once on the road into the city everyone was hearing the sound file we gave them previously — the poem "Beyond the bend in the road" by Alberto Caeiro, who was an heteronym of Fernando Pessoa:

We walked towards the city at a slow pace with the Aqueduct always on sight and crossed the city wall.
4.

As we entered Rua do Cano we gave card 3:

Rua do Cano = Pipe Street

The Aqueduto da Água da Prata [Silver Water Aqueduct] is an immense work of Renaissance hydraulic engineering, which involved, at the time of construction (1533-1537), apart from a heavy financial load, an unprecedented use of technical and human resources.

It was praised by chroniclers and poets like Luís Vaz de Camões in *The Lusiad* (1572):

Two hundred arches, stretch'd in length, sustain

The marble duct, where, glistening to the sun,

Of silver hue the shining waters run.

Evora's frowning walls now shake with fear,

And yield, obedient to Giraldo's spear.

Nor rests the monarch while his servants toil,

Around him still increasing trophies smile,

And deathless fame repays the hapless fate

That gives to human life so short a date.

It was King Dom João III — sensitive to the precarious conditions in Évora concerning the public water supply, as well as its frequent shortage, particularly in the months of summer — to make the decision to order the construction of such a grandiose project. The contract was conferred to the Architect Francisco de Arruda, who directed it with notable speed and efficiency, achieving a distance of 18,000 metres, from a drop of a little more than 20 metres between Fontes da Prata, in Graça do Divor, and the fountain of the Praça do Giraldo.

5. After one minute, the straight line of students passed us by walking faster than our group and disappeared into Largo do Chão das Covas and positioned themselves.

6. When we entered Largo do Chão das Covas the students were already positioned in the space. We approached the dry fountain and listened to the sound of water dripping:

We gave card 4:

Your brain has 92% of water, your muscles 83%, your lungs 70%, your kidneys 60%, your blood 50%, your bones 48% of water

"Be water my friend"

Bruce Lee

Following Susana's lead the participants looked at the students in formation on the square.
After a while the students left following the first of their group.
7. We left.

Before passing through a very low arch of the Aqueduct we gave card 5:

Free yourself from expectations; get ready to be surprised and take your time. Expect the unexpected and be ready to capture the nuances and emotions of the environment. Try to absorb the mood of the city, the emotional charge transmitted by the spaces we cross.

Retain in your memory anything that surprises or strikes you, unknown places that you discover, accidents or happenings that attract your attention.

[Adapted from *City of Situations* by OginoKnaus]

We all had to bend ourselves and pass under the arch.

8. We walked silently.

We turned right to Rua de Pedro Simões, always following the Aqueduct.

We arrived at Caixa de Visita — a small building that allows one to enter or repair some parts of the Aqueduct.

We gave card 6:

Every environment, every place is shaped by **water**: by the way it is situated and used; by how it is protected, managed, and distributed; by the conditions of its accessibility; by its quality, and by its quantity. **Water** can be both a protector and a threat, and the struggles over **water** can be both for and against it. [In *Hydroreflexivity* by Andreia Garcia, Ana Neiva, Diogo Aguiar, and e-flux Architecture]

9. We headed to Praça do Giraldo where students were sitting on the benches in the circle of the fountain facing us.

10. After a while we invited everyone to sit on the stairs of the church just in front of the fountain and asked the group some **questions**.

We just stayed there for a while talking and enjoying the end of afternoon sun.

Have you ever been on a silent walk?
What was it like?
When have you experienced a prolonged
amount of silence?
How did you feel?
What did you retain in your memory?
How hard was it to stay silent?
Why do you think it was so hard?
Did the silence make you uncomfortable?
If so, what made it uncomfortable?
What was one sound that you heard that
surprised you? What made it surprising?
What distracted you from listening?
What did you do about it?
What did this teach you about listening?
How is listening directional?
What did you notice about your awareness the
longer you were on the walk?
What invisible landscapes did you create
in your mind?
How did your own memories relate to the
landscape's visible and invisible aspects?
What synesthetic and kinesthetic affects
did you feel in relation to the landscape?
How has this experience changed your
relationship with the city?

"Where are we? Performing the city, slowing down time"
Beatriz Cantinho and Susana Mendes Silva with the students of Drawing IV - Class B

[Adriana Rico, Ana Carol, Andria Caseiro, Beatriz Duarte, Beatriz Mira, Berry Cheta, Francisco Bandola, joão vidinha, Jubas Barreto, Kay, Liam L. and Ruben Silva]

Images: Himi rLc

Production: BErTO, Production Assistants: Bruna de Oliveira and Margarida Peneirol

Partner: Fundação Eugénio de Almeida

Breakout Session 1: Wed 10 May, 5-7 pm, Elia Academy 2023, Exploring Situatedness, Seen & Heard sessions overview, University of Évora, Portugal

The authors would like to thank the amazing collaboration of Fundação Eugénio de Almeida and especially to Maria José Barril, to Janja Škerget from ELIA to the School of Arts, Department of Theater, Department of Landscape, Environment and Planning of the University of Évora, to our participants, and last but not least to our talented students.

REFERENCES

Caeiro, A. (2020). Beyond the bend in the road. In *The complete works of Alberto Caeiro*. New Directions Publishing. CMÉ. http://www.evora.net/percursos/PercursoAguaPrata.pdf

Debord, G. (1958). Theory of the Dérive. *Internationale Situationniste #2*.

Garcia, A., Neiva, A., Aguiar, D., & e-flux Architecture. (n.d.). *Hydroreflexivity. e-flux Architecture*. e-Flux. https://www.e-flux.com/architecture/hydroreflexivity/535262/editorial/

Chapter 12
Sounds of Remembered Nature:
Narrating Environmental Change Through Pop Music

Thorsten Philipp
http://orcid.org/0000-0003-3497-7170
Technische Universität Berlin, Germany

ABSTRACT

Narrating (fictitious) experience is a core element of political communication on environmental conflicts: To observe environmental change and to discern the ongoing redefinition of 'nature' in collective memory have accompanied the environmental movements from their beginning. This chapter takes an analytical look on the way pop music deals with tropes of a remembered ecology. Are there key topics and narrative strands when it comes to reflecting musically environmental change through memory? By examining selected songs that deal with ecological memory, the case studies of this chapter investigate "latent structures" of Western societies: partly unspoken or non-negotiated dynamics and aspects of environmental conflicts in the 'subconscious' streams of a society. Pop music is not just a sounding board for ecological crises; it popularizes historical concepts and provides an archive of environmental history and its inherent longing for forecasting the future.

INTRODUCTION

Constructing, remembering and forgetting a (fictitious) past is a core element of crises dynamics and political communication on environmental conflicts: The perception of ecological degradation, the communicative exchange of it, and the comparison of 'then' and 'now' are decisive factors of environmental action (Luhmann, 1989, p. 28). Narrating the ecological past and showcasing losses, guilt, and responsibility is part of a continuous knowledge production in the age of global environmental crises. Although pop music has long since been analyzed as a cultural practice to deal with environmentalism, the interrelatedness of memory, pop music performativity, and environmentalism still poses questions: How is the fictive past of a remembered ecology represented in pop music? Are there musical key topics

DOI: 10.4018/979-8-3693-2264-2.ch012

and narrative strands when it comes to reflect environmental change through memory? In which way do pop music narratives of historical environmental conflicts indicate social norms and societal change?

Academic contributions on the interplay of pop music culture and sustainability have emerged from various disciplinary perspectives in recent years. These contributions belong to a broad discussion about the cultural dimension of the idea of sustainability (Birkeland et al. 2018) and the role of cultural production and cultural policy in the age of global environmental change (Boykoff 2010). However, coherent analyses of ecological issues in pop music are rare (e.g., Braun et al. 2014) and, for the most part, have remained genre-specific (Müller and Durand 2022; Nocella et al. 2017; Rosenthal 2006). Occasionally, the ecological commitment of selected pop music representatives and communities has gained academic interest (Taylor 2019; Ingram 2008; Kahn 2013). In recent years, the question of the concrete environmental impact of music production has attracted greater attention: In fact, both the production and consumption of music (sound carriers, streaming servers, distribution chains) are associated with high environmental impact (Brennan 2020, 2021; Brennan and Devine 2020; Devine 2019). In line with this development, scientific contributions are increasingly examining how music festivals and music concert practice can be used to promote ecological goals and support social transformation (e.g., Klöckner 2015: 213-234; Brennan et al. 2019). In the emerging sub-discipline of ethnomusicology and its research field of ecomusicology (Allen 2013; Titon 2019), a growing number of contributions deals with the pedagogic functions of pop music in the context of education for sustainable development (Prior 2022; Arnold 2009), e.g., with regard to the interplay between music, natural sounds and culture (Dawe and Allen 2016; Pedelty 2012; Rehding 2011). In his comprehensive study on the impact of ecocriticism on US popular music, Ingram (2010: 16) has pointed out that the act of listening to music can play a prominent role in shaping ecological awareness. He further explored that music has effective potential to promote ecological reflection and overcome the Western dualistic juxtaposition of humans and nature (similar arguments: Glahn 2014; Gilmurray 2017). Comparative case studies developed from anthropological and cultural-geographical research design have shown how local understandings and conceptions of nature find performative expression in music cultures (McDowell et al. 2021). Ethnomusicological research on the materiality of popular music has highlighted that artists are not only inspired by environmental issues in their work for musical or activist purposes, they are also materially and physically implicated in the environmental crisis, for example through the musical instruments they rely on (Gibson 2019; Gibson and Warren 2016; Reid and Petocz 2021). Contributions from sociology and communication studies have focused on the way pop music narrates conceptions of nature (Philipp, 2023) and processes sustainability tropes in pre-political pop music contexts (Ingram, 2010; Mounsey, 2023; Philipp, 2019, 2022). The examination of environmental issues in pop music is part of a much broader debate of the musician's role in political participation and social engagement (Street et al. 2008, Street 2007, Street 2013) and discussions on the societal impact of pop aesthetics (Frith 2002) and political activism through street music (McKay 2007) and musical-bodily experiences (Feixa/Guerra 2017). Rather than contributing to these multiple and lively research tracks, this article attempts to trace techniques of historicisation and fictional memory work in pop music with a particular focus on environmental conflicts. It analyzes ways of communicating sustainability theories and ecological norms in response to phenomena such as water irrigation, soil degradation, biodiversity loss, and the danger of a lethal catastrophe in the age of climate change.

By exploring pop music as a sounding board of environmental debate, this study approaches pop music lyrics and sound regimes as an expression of Western societies' *latent structures*: their unspoken and under-the-ground conflicts, insufficiently processed through communication. According to system theorist Nicolas Luhmann, the challenge of *latency* succinctly concerns the "observation of what other observers *cannot* observe" (Luhmann, 2000, p. 94, emphasis in original). Luhmann argues that all societies experience conflicts and problems that are not addressed or insufficiently addressed through communication. They remain hidden for lacking knowledge, for intended prevention of communication or for unconscious social dynamics that serve to protect existing hierarchies. At the same time, modern societies develop cultural and scientific techniques of observation, e.g. through psychoanalysis or fiction novel: analytic practices with particular interest for the observed actors' unknown decision mechanisms and emotions.

Developing Luhman's diagnosis further, to observe others and to focus them with particular interest for what they themselves are possibly unable to perceive may provide insight into the hidden, subconscious streams of a society and thereby offer a diagnosis of political and, in particular, environmental communication. Even if it is true that ecological and climate topics are openly discussed in public today, some aspects such as unequal vulnerability, gender aspects, colonial heritage, etc. still flow under the surface, at least partially hidden behind the facades of institutionalized environmental politics. The aim therefore is to use pop music as a communication practice that opens a path toward 'subconscious' streams of a society. It is an everyday forum of hidden, partly unspoken social conflicts that might demand stronger attention or public negotiation.

Looking at pop music as an artistic code to deal with latent structures and their inherent unresolved conflicts around ecology, the following considerations focus on the manifold ways of communicating environmental remembrance and narrations on a fictive ecological past through pop music. In a first step, it showcases musical contributions that deal with environmental conflicts on (1) *land, soil, and sceneries* from the 1960's singer-songwriter culture and later decennia. A second productive item to observe how memory designs narrations of environmental conflicts are pop music contributions on (2) *water streams and river valleys*. Apart from these forms of indicating the change of ecosystems, a third investigation is dedicated to attempts of communicating (3) *ideas on the future* through prophetic speech and remembrance of a fictive past. Finally, a (4) *summary analysis* will reflect the communicative potential of these different ways of dealing with memory by arguing about their latency aspects.

The selection of music on which the articles are based covers a broad spectrum and represents a variety of pop music genres and subcultures. Nonetheless, it is not representative of the colorful interplay of sustainability communication and pop music. In view of the breadth and complexity of the field, boundaries had to be drawn. For the special interest in latency, only text music was included. Although artists such as Pantha du Prince and Dominik Eulberg have shown ways to process environmental issues and experiences of nature through textless sound experiences and (techno-)musical nature writing, their analysis requires a more musicologically oriented methodology. In these cases, the lack of song lyrics does not permit to focus the latency problems. The selection was based on comprehensive research in which over 700 pop music songs were identified that explicitly addressed nature and the environment in their lyrics, title design or music videos. The production period of the works examined ranged from 1961 to 2023. In addition, numerous songs were considered that allow for a possible ecological interpretation in terms of lyrical ambivalence and semantic openness. Macy Gray's *All I Want For Christmas* (2015), for example, promotes in its lyrics a peaceful world and can be implicitly understood as a plea in favor of sustainable development; however it does not contain any explicit lyrical reference to environment and ecology. Greg Graffin's *Time of Need* (2017), like John Mayer's *Waiting On The World To Change* (2006), deal with social change and mobilization, but both songs remain ambivalent and open in their significance. Such and similar musical works, in which a clear lyrical relation to environmental, nature and sustainability issues could not be identified, were not included in the study. In view of the popularity and market value of Anglo-Saxon pop music, mainly pop music works with English-language lyrics were focused in the analysis. The further selection from the broad corpus is primarily due to the author's experiences in academic teaching and numerous discussions with experts and students. The aim of these analyses is not to cover the entire spectrum of sustainability communication through pop music, but to test and differentiate a methodological approach in which the remembered environmental conflicts through pop music can be analyzed without focusing the question of intentionality. In the end, this research is based on the conviction that the overdue "Great Transformation" (Polanyi 2010) requires the full use of all available communication forums and that pop music with its capabilities to entertain, provides profound insights into social perceptions, feelings, hopes and fears. The political and communicative handling of ecological crises is unlikely to succeed without a sound knowledge of these societal resources.

REMEMBERING LAND, SOIL, AND SCENERIES

Early examples of critically evaluating ecological change by exploring a fictive past appear during the late 1960s in US folk music, a major forum for environmental protest. While jazz was increasingly perceived as complex, and rock-and-roll never had developed any visible political appeal, folk music succeeded in conveying meaning, and political purpose (Rodnitzky, 1999, p. 105). Changes in land use and conflicts around soil ecosystems form a major discourse line that is fueled by arguments from the land ethic (Leopold, 1949/2013) and the wilderness conversation debates (cf. Callicott, 1998; Cronon, 1996; Nash, 2014). Narrative patterns from the romantics and from the nationalist folk movements, that intentionally connected folk and land by producing imagined communities to represent the true foundation of the nation, were among the inspiring sources. Author-composer Billy Edd Wheeler from West Virginia is one of the first musicians to champion for ecological topics by applying memory. *The Coming of the Roads*, poignantly performed by Judy Collins to guitar accompaniment in 1965, thematizes changing environment, conflicts of land use, societal transition and the loss of home through mining: "Once I had you and the wild wood / Now, it's just dusty roads." Whereas the conquest and exploitation of the US-West had been a result of the railway expansions, it is now the asphalted highway that industrializes the countryside and ties the rural population to the city. The arising social conflicts are processed in country music (Gaillard, 2004, p. 52; Peterson, 1994, p. 52). Both the former beauty of nature and the values of the countryside are replaced by mining, taverns, and greed. Roads come, soil changes, people leave their homes, and a remembered scenery is all that is left.

Further processing this collective experience, Tom Paxton's folk standard *Whose Garden Was This* from 1970, combines memory with present exhaustion through a melancholic environmental ballad that reflects the loss of the natural world. Musically inspired by Woody Guthrie and Pete Seeger, the song was originally written for an ecological teach-in at Northwestern University Illinois on the occasion of the first Earth Day in 1970 (Ingram, 2008, p. 34). With this day, the support for environmental protection became socially institutionalized, and the ecological movements were given a visible landmark in the public eye. Evoking the past and a sense of nostalgia for a once-thriving garden, Paxton describes a world devastated by human intervention. The song does not deal with nature, but with its remains from the past: "Whose garden was this? It must have been lovely / Did it have flowers? I've seen pictures of flowers / And I'd love to have smelled one." Accompanied by minor chords of the acoustic guitar and a lively classical piano, evoking a pastoral and introspective atmosphere, the narrator's remembrance displays the beauty of the world, though the world is lost. The narrator is a representative from the future who has no knowledge of nature other than memories: "Tell me again, I need to know / The forests had trees, the meadows were green / […] Can you swear that was true?"

Among the most successful examples of processing changes in soil related environmental conflicts and evaluating them through memory, folk rock musician Joni Mitchel's *Big Yellow Taxi*, released in 1970 and certified Platinum in Canada, describes a seemingly everyday process of rural development: the conversion of natural land into commercial space. The song is a fast-paced diagnosis of the remodeling of social environments: In the past, trees grew in wilderness, but now they be could be marveled for an entrance fee: "They took all the trees / Put 'em in a tree museum / And they charged the people / A dollar and a half just to see 'em", the lyrics say. Behind the story of losing wild nature, Mitchell's song is a far more fundamental reflection on the historical disappearance of things. Seemingly, only through its extinction did people realize the value of nature: "Don't it always seem to go / That you don't know what you've got / Till it's gone." With her top-seller song, frequently covered and sampled by artists such as Amy Grant, Janet Jackson, and Harry Styles, Mitchell contributed to the discourse against insecticides and environmental toxins, which Rachel Carson's *Silent Spring* in 1962 (Carson, 1962/2000) had already set a metaphorical monument to.

In contrast to these general observations on a non-located nature, US country folk musician John Prine opts for communicating personal memory on a spatially determined location in rural Kentucky. *Paradise* from 1971 stages a fictive dialogue between a father and his son on a changing environment. The boy articulates his wish to return to Muhlenberg County, an industrial area that is crossed by the Green River and gained economic importance through coal-mining. However, it is industrial activity that makes the trip obsolete: "Well, I'm sorry my son, but you're too late in asking / Mister Peabody's coal train has hauled it away." Paradise, in this case, is not just a metaphor, but a true story of the artist's childhood memory. Prine's song refers to a historical conflict in Paradise, a town on the banks of the Green River. In 1963, the Tennessee Valley Authority had commissioned a new coal-fired power plant and contracted the Peabody Coal Company to strip-mine the area: the surface layers of soil and rock were removed with heavy machinery to exploit coal. The facility's cooling water poured into the Green River and killed its fish stocks (Osmon, 2021, p. 20). In 1967, four years before the song's release, the town was closed down and demolished by the Authority. The conflict was a classical struggle of environmental justice: The coal mining and the power-plant promised jobs and income to a structurally weak region. Born in the suburbs of Chicago, Prine never lived in Kentucky, but Muhlenberg was his ancestral homeland, the longtime home of his parents (Baxter-Moore, 2021, p. 93). An article in *Penthouse* in December 1973 quoted the testimonial of a former habitant who lamented the loss of forests and farms in his homeland: "A lot of people can grow older and go back home and say, 'Well, here's where I played as a boy.' I can't go back. There's not even any ground that I can walk over" (Huffman, 2015, p. 80). Memorializing the land and its struggle, Prine articulated a personal last will in the final verse: "When I die, let my ashes float down the Green River." After his death, Prine's family spread his ashes from the Rochester Ferry, which crosses the river in Kentucky, turning the landscape into a nature monument for the artist and for the environmental conflicts around Paradise. In 2022, even a memorial park was dedicated to the songwriter at the upper river (Hines, 2023, p. 122). The song became a reminiscence not just to an environmental conflict that happened similarly in various places around the globe, but also to the poor and exploited rural population of the Upper South (Osmon, 2021, p. 110). Among the most influential cover versions, Jim & Jesse's arrangement from 1974 provoked a whole series of small-label bluegrass interpretations and contributed essentially to further the song's memorial work.

REMEMBERING WATER STREAMS AND RIVER VALLEYS

Conflicts around river ecosystems and their history constitute a common tradition in the singer-songwriter milieu and their topical strand of reconstructing nature. Monument and symbol for a lost nature, the remembered stream both metaphorically and ecologically has many applications in country music and its (neo)traditional appraisal of rural life, home, resilience, and national pride. Pete Seeger's *My Dirty Stream (The Hudson River Song)* from 1961 is one of the first examples to advocate watershed conservation in the US. Accompanied by the swinging rhythm of Seeger's 5-string long-neck banjo fingerpicking, the lilting melody's lyrics represent the opposition between past and present by the narrator's story of sailing down the waterway. Seeger's journey goes from the river spring in the Adirondack mountains and leads to the estuary in the Upper New York bay. With every mile, the singer experiences the river more and more littered through industry and cities. The stream is not only about water and flow direction, but also about the flow of time, downfall and longing for societal renewal: "Well it's Sailing up my dirty stream / Still I love it and I'll dream / That some day […] / My Hudson and my country will run clear." Seeger's Clearwater Foundation, founded in 1969 to protect the Hudson River water reservoirs through research, education, and advocacy, was a way of institutionalizing this engagement politically.

Different in style and degree of activism, the British singer-songwriter Albert Hammond's *Down by the river* from 1972 also deals with the environmental changes of a river. The first-person narrator and his girlfriend go swimming at an unnamed watercourse in the countryside and fall ill as a result. The next day they realize that the water is full of dead fish. A doctor explains that "Only foolish people go […] / Down by the river." Hammond situates the confrontation with environmental toxins in a youthful situation of light-heartedness, naiveté and inexperience. The song begins ponderously in a steady four-on-the-floor beat with alternating basses, orchestrated with banjo, guitar, piano and sparse percussion. The chorus, which follows the short, four-line verse, has ear-catching quality. The easy memorability of the appealing melody allows the environmental subject matter to be ignored, and is likely to be one of the key factors in the commercial success of the song, which topped the charts in German-speaking countries as well as in Belgium and the Netherlands. The numerous performances in which Hammond has played his song up to this day, many of them available on YouTube, show the artist in front of an ageing TV audience, who clap to the beat and enjoy the light-hearted character of the melody. In Hammond's case, it is not the remembered environmental destruction, but rather the cheerful teenage love that creates a bridge to the past.

With *Don't go near the water* from 1974, US country singer Johnny Cash also stages the remembered past as an experience of a river environment while the nature of the present opens up as a poisoned landscape. Here, too, the narrative framework is the fictive dialog between father and son. Both go fishing at the river, but the prey makes the son wonder whether the fish is safe to eat. The father's gloomy answer refers to a happier time in history: "I said, 'Well there was a time son / This water's bad now and I might not be safe to eat the fish / But there was a time' / There was a time the air was clean." The father's statement concludes with a general warning to the audience: "Don't go near the water." Cash's argumentation works comparatively, addressing the relationship between generations and referring implicitly to the principle of intergenerational justice.

Among the most prominent examples of interlinking the river landscape with memorial culture is the particular case of the Cuyahoga River, an 80-mile long stream that runs through Cleveland, Ohio, and became known as one of the most polluted rivers of the US, due to its heavy industrial use. Randy Newman's *Burn On* from 1972 as well as R.E.M.'s *Cuyahoga* from 1985, and Adam Again's meditative and mournful *River on Fire* from 1992 address the uncontrolled discharge of industrial wastewater from the mid-19th century onwards. Oil, flammable chemicals, animal waste from slaughterhouses and other litter had turned the river into a cesspool. The flammable substances floated on the water, repeatedly causing fires on its surface. In 1936, for example, a spark from a blowtorch set fire to floating debris and oil; in 1952, a fire on the river caused more than 500,000 US dollars of damage, and in 1969, the burning water became a poster motif of mass appeal in *Time* magazine's new environment section (Steinberg, 2002, p. 232). Randy Newman processes the topic within a poetic depiction at the interface between remembrance and nightmare. Accompanied by plaintive, overtone-rich piano chords that hand over to full orchestral sounds, Newman sings: "Cleveland, city of light, you're calling me / Cleveland, even now I can remember / 'Cause the Cuyahoga River goes smoking through my dreams." The stream is not just a watercourse, but metaphorically a stream of consciousness: an ever-recurring nightmare. Thirteen years later, R.E.M.'s *Cuyahoga*, though never released as a single, has been the economically most successful example in this series: the album *Life's Rich Pageant* was a Gold record (Henderson & Stacy, 2013, p. 532). The song comments the scandal from a post-colonial perspective and interlinks the environmental disaster with the fate of the indigenous communities, addressing their historical loss: "This land is the land of ours / This river runs red over it / We are not your allies / We cannot defend." – an inversion of Woody Guthrie's political folk song *This Land is Your Land*, numerously performed and recorded by artists such as Bob Dylan and Pete Seeger. According to band guitarist Peter Buck, *Cuyahoga* was "a metaphor for America and its lost promises" (Rosen, 1997, p. 63). As R.E.M. multi-instrumentalist Ken Stringfellow put it in retrospect, the song was an "anti-anthem" (Buckley, 2003, p. 165) in the sense that it addressed historical injustice around the environmental conflict and provided a musical monument to it.

In James Keelaghan's *River Run* from 1993, the imagined river stands metaphorically for the flow of memory and the narrator's life story. To the plain sound of his acoustic guitar, the Canadian singer-songwriter narrates the episodes of a blue river of his childhood, the valley, and the precious moments of memory. The place is unconcreted. Now, decennia later, the narrator turns back from the city to the place of his childhood and sees the river tamed by human intervention: "There's a dam there restricting the flow."

REMEMBERANCE AND PROPHECY: CONTRUCTING PAST AND FUTURE

Besides the stories around soil and water ecosystems, a further strand of remembered landscapes questions the time ahead: what emotions do ecological remembrance and future vision provoke in constellations of global environmental crises? How does society escape from doom and downfall scenarios? At this point, pop music merges with a particularly productive form of environmental communication that has intensively accompanied the development of Western ecological movements: Major representatives of environmentalism such as John Muir, Donella Meadows, Al Gore, and nowadays Greta Thunberg have frequently been criticized as "prophets of pessimism" (Herman, 1997, p. 9) and communicators of doom (Boucher, 2019; Radkau, 2014, 182 f.; Skrimshire, 2014).

The combination of catastrophic prophecy and remembrance in ecological contexts covers a broad spectrum of examples in pop music. Pink Floyd's *Sorrow* from 1987, the last track on the thirteenth studio album *A Momentary Lapse to Reason*, focuses on grief and pain over the total loss of a remembered nature. The sound gains monumental character through its minute-long, massive solo guitar performance, that songwriter, guitarist and co-lead vocalist David Gilmour plays on his Steinberger GL. The guitar track was recorded in a complex way, with two studio amplifiers, in the stadium of Los

Angeles in which the band set up a mobile 24-track studio (Guesdon & Margotin, 2017, § 1724). The result was a multi-amplified, idiosyncratic, and inimitable guitar sound, supplemented by a programmed drum machine. The narration starts intermedially by addressing olfactory senses: "The sweet smell of a great sorrow lies over the land," an intertextual reference to Nobel laureate John Steinbeck, who literally wrote the sentence in his novel *The Grapes of Wrath* in 1939. Steinbeck's socio-critical work showcases the fate of impoverished farmers of Oklahoma during the mid-1930s. The memory of a past nature and a lost future is no longer a nostalgic act, but a hidden prison from which there is no escape: "A man lies and dreams of green fields and rivers [...] / He's haunted by the memory of a lost paradise / [...] He's chained forever to a world that's departed." In the end, the narrator sinks into a river of dark waters that flow into an oily sea. A spherical two-and-a-half-minute solo concludes the song.

Memories on a post-catastrophic setting also characterize US rock musician Warren Zevon's *Run Straight Down* from 1998. The song features David Gilmour from Pink Floyd as a guest guitarist. Hissing corona discharge noise from high voltage power lines create the sonic opening. The first-person speaker revives a brownfield area, "walking in the wasted city", musing about downfall, and smelling "the wind from the ruined river." In the background, a constant spoken-word tapestry of sound incessantly serializes chemical compounds: "Four, aminobiphenyl, hexachlorobenzene / Dimethyl sulfate, chloromethyl methylether". The linguistic cocktail echoes the debate on ozone depletion, which took on panic overtones in the 1990s – with a US president suffering from skin cancer (Radkau, 2014, p. 384). Comparing the remembered past and the presence, the narrator finds himself in an infinite nightmare that progresses relentlessly: "And it's worse when I try to remember [...] / When I think about then and now." The music video features Zevon with his electric guitar performing his song in the middle of an industrial plant, while workers in white protective suits do their hazardous jobs.

However, ecological remembrance in times of a lethal catastrophe can also turn out to be a tribute to the inherent goodness of humanity. In 2008, the Canadian songwriter Ian Kelly has in *Wonderful Humans* a final sonic monument for the whole human species soon to be extinct. The intro consists of a seemingly psychedelic mesh of piano, strings, and acoustic guitar. The lyrics memorialize the Last Human: "Here comes the last of the wonderful humans / They're pushed to the edge, so don't be ashamed to be one of them." Further backed by synthesizer, xylophone, background voices and drums, the narrator remembers the lost wealth: "We have destroyed what was beautiful / [...] Now there is no, there is no remedy." Though the future is blocked and the final day is unavoidable, remembrance provides access to praise and gratitude.

In a comparable way, the Berlin-based Indian singer-songwriter Aditi Veena, known as Ditty, has shown in a full series of songs a culture of ecological reminiscence that not just mourns the losses, but reflects splendor and gratitude. Ditty's debut album *Poetry Ceylon* from 2019, largely created in her living room (Rodrigo, 2019), is a set of eight folk-tinged, ecology-inspired tracks that process impressions from her stay in Sri Lanka, where she worked as a conservation architect. In her song *Eulogy to a sparrow*, Ditty sings with a calm, clear voice about nature and its beauty, switching from reciting to singing lyrics. The sound consists of a fingerpicked acoustic guitar along with restrained keyboard and nature sounds such as birdsong and the ocean. The title indicates what the song is all about, a grief tribute for what is lost and continues to live in memory: "What was the name / Of that little birdie / Singing songs to me / What was the fate / Surrounding her end [...] / Oh she's gone." *Eulogy for the Sparrow* was written on the sparrow's entry to the Red List of endangered species in Sri Lanka (Vargese, 2019). Though still alive, the bird is introduced as the last representative of its species, an "endling" (Jørgensen, 2017).

CONCLUSION

The overview shows that the remembrance of nature experience and environmental conflicts constitute a continuous narrative in pop music. Folk music, a major forum of political activism and environmental protest, is particularly relevant in communicating ecological knowledge from the past when it comes to deal with degradation of soil and water ecosystems. Despite their variety, all these songs are manifestations of a culture of environmental preservation that gleams subtly to the surface of the entertainment industry. But how do these songs help to observe latent structures? To summarize their communicative potential, three aspects may appear relevant.

First, ecological remembrance is implemented in pop music as a narrative trope, a story to communicate knowledge and to evaluate the present. All the songs discussed above tell us stories about *how people remember a fictive past*. The return to a river (Keelaghan), the dialogue between father and son (Prine, Hammond), or the imagination of a sparrow (Ditty) can serve as narrative frames. When Cash, Hammond, Seeger or R.E.M. tell us about their alleged memories, their songs constitute performative knowledge (van den Berg & Schmidt-Wulffen, 2023) as they provide experience from a fictive past through musical practice. They offer ways to understand the world and its crises, and *make sense of past events*.

Second, the songs themselves form an archive of environmental history and contribute in their variety to *document environmental change*: from the social consequences of mining, the pollution of freshwaters to the fires of the Cuyahoga River and the entry of the sparrow to the Red List – in all these cases we see pop music acting as a cultural memory of environmental conflicts. As a major knowledge resource of the "age of ecology" (Radkau 2011), these songs can help us not only to remember, but also to perceive ourselves in ongoing environmental questions: how do we experience (industrial) progress? How do we process our losses? In contrast to other forms of political communication, these songs permit experience in nature through public narrations that address emotions rather than reason. The local determination in songs of Prine (the town of Paradise), Seeger (the Hudson River) and R.E.M. (the Cuyahoga River) also shows the specific significance of concrete spaces as an expression of ''critically aware place-connectedness'' (Buell, 2001, p. 66). Relics of continuity in the face of modern progress, their tropes offer learning opportunities. At the same time, they permit spatial transfer through memory: Paradise, the Hudson river, Ohio, and the Cuyahoga River are everywhere. As an element of social memory on environmental change, the songs bridge between generations, implicitly advocating intergenerational justice; they indicate environmental ruptures and conflictive chapters of environmental history. Additionally, they reveal power constellations: As Paradise, the Hudson River, and the sparrow show, exploitation prevails in situations of progress. These songs also remind us of historical shifts in Western ways in defining and perceiving 'nature' through concepts such as wilderness. Memory, as research has shown, is always socially and culturally determined. Among many other symbols, these songs serve as a *aides-mémoires* or monument sites in which the memory of a whole group is condensed (cf. Assmann, 2006, pp. 8-9; Long & Gebhardt, 2020).

Third, several of these musical attempts of dealing with the past offer moments of *prophecy and prognoses of the future*, inherent promises, doom scenarios, risks and dangers in times of major environmental challenges. While their artists do not yet know what will happen, the songs' first-person narrators *claim to know*. In this way, they contribute to communicate the options ahead (Horn, 2018, p. 178), addressing the most crucial point of all environmental debates: the future (Warde et al., 2018, p. 14). The comparative figuration of 'then' and 'now' through memory turns into a prophetic plot of 'before' and 'after' the catastrophe, implying that as long as we are still talking about the apocalypse, it has yet taken place. On the one hand, these narrations' latent function is *prevention* by providing a counter-discourse to the Western idea of progress and human ingenuity. The pop musical remembrance of nature is a way of dealing with the modern malaise that apocalyptical futures are communicated soberly through numerous environmental studies, but an effective transformation is not in sight: The catastrophe is ongoing through daily actions such as mobility and consumption, and the pop-musical fiction provides an emotional artistic code to it. On the other hand, the musical examples that explicitly highlight the future are just the most evident examples of the hidden connection between memory and a vision of the future. A further latent function of looking back is a means of *gaining foresight*: Reaching out from the past, the songs latently depict a *story of the future* people are longing for. The idea that species are only recognized in their value through their disappearance, as Mitchel suggests, reveals a core tragedy in the apocalyptic story: by then it is too late.

In this setting of societal disruption, stories of the garden, the soil, and the river offer continuity and familiarity despite gloomy prospects for the future. Consistently, Paxton conceptualizes the remembered nature as a garden: a space that only takes its shape through human activity. Created by and for humans, the garden is not just an ecological, but above all a *social* concept in which well-being, relaxation and enjoyment needs are given expression. The musically constructed garden, the watershed, and the soil latently express human desires: the need for a safe environment, for fresh air, clean water, healthy sleep, etc. Articulating ecological needs through musical remembrance, the songs reveal a human nature, caught between destruction and conservation: Nature, aesthetically sublimated through the tropes of the river, the land, or the sparrow, turns out to be a space of social renewal.

In this way, the selected songs also make the case for a musical politics of *ecological commemoration* that might help a wounded society to depathologize their losses. The commemoration of degradation and ecological disaster through music can offer a way to reform social norms, as it valorizes negative emotions and acknowledges grief. At the same time, it teaches those who are not yet affected, to feel compassion, solidarity, and care (Mihai & Thaler, 2023). As Ditty shows, attentiveness toward the loss of a species can be a way to communicate care for those who are threatened with extinction (cf. Barnett, 2022, p. 14). To no coincidence, her musical *Eulogy* had a prominent predecessor in the historical conservation movements: when in 1914, the last specimen of the passenger pigeon died in Cincinnati Zoo in Ohio, a monument was erected by the Wisconsin Society of Ornithology, and US conservationist Aldo Leopold gave a notable eulogy, addressing the impending loss of memory:

> "Men still live who, in their youth, remember pigeons. Trees still live who, in their youth, were shaken by a living wind. But a decade hence only the oldest oaks will remember, and at long last only the hills will know. There will always be pigeons in books and in museums, but these are effigies and images, dead to all hardships and to all delights" (Leopold, 1949/2013, p. 108).

Pop songs write history in multiple functions: Firstly, they *accompany* environmental events and make history visible; at the same time, they *define history* and popularize historical concepts; thirdly, as Seeger's and Prine's examples show, they themselves *initiate history* by stimulating activism. With this communicative potential, pop music reveals the fictional and remembered nature not only as a part of medial politainment (Nieland, 2008), but also as a monumental ecotope itself, a temporally extended and interconnected system in which varying images of nature are cultivated, abandoned and remembered: a resource that at times nourishes grief and anger, at times comfort and longing, offering orientation and a chance of societal renewal – and in all of this always leads back to an allegedly original and authentic fiction of nature.

REFERENCES

Allen, A. S. (2013). Ecomusicology. In Oxford University Press (Hrsg.), *Oxford Music Online*. Oxford University Press. 10.1093/gmo/9781561592630.article.A2240765

Arnold, E. (2009). The Greening of Hip Hop: The Greening of Hip-Hop: Urban Youth Address Climate Change and Sustainability. *Reimagine! Race Poverty and the Environment, 16*(2). https://www.reimaginerpe.org/files/Arnold.Climate.%2016-2-29.pdf

Assmann, J. (2006). *Religion and cultural memory: Ten studies*. Stanford University Press.

Barnett, J. T. (2022). Vigilant mourning and the future of earthly coexistence. In C. V. Fletcher (Ed.), Communicating in the Anthropocene: Intimate relations (pp. 13–34). Lanham.

Baxter-Moore, N. (2021). John Prine, 1946–2020. *Rock Music Studies*, 8(1), 92–96. 10.1080/19401159.2020.1852765

Birkeland, I., Burton, R., Parra, C., & Siivonen, K. (2018). *Cultural Sustainability and the Nature-Culture Interface: Livelihoods, Policies, and Methodologies*. Routledge. 10.4324/9781315625294

Boucher, E. (2019). The dangers of depicting Greta Thunberg as a prophet.*The Conversation*. https://theconversation.com/the-dangers-of-depicting-greta-thunberg-as-a-prophet-128813

Boykoff, M. T. (Ed.). (2010). *The politics of climate change: A survey*. Routledge. 10.4324/9780203819234

Braun, J., Lengel, L., & Johnson, J. (2014). Environmental Causes and Campaigns. In Thompson, W. F., Lamont, A., Parncutt, R., & Russo, F. A. (Eds.), *Music in the social and behavioral sciences: An encyclopedia* (pp. 401–406). SAGE.

Brennan, M. (2020). The Environmental Sustainability of the Music Industries. In Oakley, K., & Banks, M. (Eds.), *Cultural industries and the environmental crisis: New approaches for policy* (pp. 37–49). Springer. 10.1007/978-3-030-49384-4_4

Brennan, M. (2021). The infrastructure and environmental consequences of live music. In Devine, K., & Boudreault-Fournier, A. (Eds.), *Oxford scholarship online. Audible infrastructures: Music, Sound, Media*. Oxford University Press. 10.1093/oso/9780190932633.003.0006

Brennan, M., & Devine, K. (2020). The cost of music. *Popular Music*, 39(1), 43–65. 10.1017/S0261143019000552

Brennan, M., Scott, J. C., Connelly, A., & Lawrence, G. (2019). Do music festival communities address environmental sustainability and how? A Scottish case study. *Popular Music*, 38(2), 252–275. 10.1017/S0261143019000035

Buckley, D. (2003). *R.E.M. fiction: An alternative biography*. Virgin.

Buell, L. (2001). *Writing for an endangered world: Literature, culture, and environment in the U.S. And beyond*. Harvard University Press. 10.4159/9780674029057

Callicott, J. B. (Ed.). (1998). *The great new wilderness debate*. University of Georgia Press.

Carson, R. (2000). *Silent spring*. Penguin. (Original work published 1962)

Collins, J. (1965). The Coming Of The Roads. *Judy Collins' Fifth Album*. Elektra EKS-7300.

Cronon, W. (1996). The Trouble with Wilderness: Or, Getting Back to the Wrong Nature. *Environmental History*, 1(1), 7–28. 10.2307/3985059

Dawe, K., & Allen, A. S. (Eds.). (2016). *Current directions in ecomusicology: Music, culture, nature*. Routledge.

Ditty. (2019). Eulogy For A Sparrow. *Poetry Ceylon*. Pagal Haina.

Dylan, B. (1979). This Land Is Your Land. *The Hurricane Carter Benefit*. Phoenix Records 44777.

Feixa, C., & Guerra, P. (2017). Unidos por el mismo sueño en una canción: On music, gangs and flows. *Portuguese Journal of Social Science*, 16(3), 305–322. 10.1386/pjss.16.3.305_1

Frith, S. (1996). *Performing rites: Evaluating popular music*. Oxford University Press. 10.1093/oso/9780198163329.001.0001

Gaillard, F. (2004). *Watermelon wine: Remembering the golden years of country music*. NewSouth.

Gibson, C., & Warren, A. (2016). Resource-Sensitive Global Production Networks: Reconfigured Geographies of Timber and Acoustic Guitar Manufacturing. *Economic Geography*, 92(4), 430–454. 10.1080/00130095.2016.1178569

Gilmurray, J. (2017). Ecological Sound Art: Steps towards a new field. *Organised Sound*, 22(1), 32–41. 10.1017/S1355771816000315

Glahn, D. (2014). *Music and the skillful listener: American women compose the natural world*. Indiana University Press.

Grant, A. (1994). Big Yellow Taxi. *House Of Love*. A&M Records.

Guesdon, J.-M., & Margotin, P. (2017). *Pink Floyd All the Songs: The Story Behind Every Track*. Running Press.

Headrick, D. R. (2020). *Humans versus nature: A global environmental history*. Oxford University Press.

Henderson, L., & Stacy, L. (2013). *Encyclopedia of Music in the 20th Century*. Routledge.

Herman, A. (1997). *The idea of decline in Western history*. Free Press.

Hines, R. (2023). *Kentucky's Green River*. Arcadia.

Horn, E. (2018). *The future as catastrophe: Imagining disaster in the modern age*. Columbia University Press. 10.7312/horn18862

Huffman, E. (2015). *John Prine: In spite of himself*. University of Texas Press.

Ingram, D. (2008). "My Dirty Stream": Pete Seeger, American Folk Music, and Environmental Protest. *Popular Music and Society*, 31(1), 21–36. 10.1080/03007760601061456

Ingram, D. (2010). *The jukebox in the garden: Ecocriticism and American popular music since 1960. Nature, culture and literature*. Rodopi. 10.1163/9789042032101

Janet [Jackson] featuring Q-Tip and Joni Mitchell. (1997). *Got 'Til It's Gone*. Virgin VSTX1666.

Jim & Jesse. 1974. *Paradise*. Opryland Records P-3842.

Johnny Cash. (1974). Don't Go Near The Water. *Ragged Old Flag*. CBS S80113.

Jørgensen, D. (2017). Endling, the Power of the Last in an Extinction-Prone World. *Environmental Philosophy*, 14(1), 119–138. 10.5840/envirophil201612542

Kahn, R. (2013). Environmental Activism in Music. In Edmondson, J. (Ed.), *Music in American life: An encyclopedia of the songs, styles, stars and stories that shaped our culture* (pp. 412–417). Greenwood.

Keelaghan, J. (1993). River Run. *My Skies*. JTR 8455-2.

Kelly, I. (2008). Wonderful Humans. *Speak Your Mind*. Audiogram ADCD 10225.

Klöckner, C. A. (2015). *The psychology of pro-environmental communication: Beyond standard information strategies*. Palgrave Macmillan. 10.1057/9781137348326

Leopold, A. (2013). *A sand county almanac & other writings on ecology and conservation* (Meine, C., Ed.). Library of America. (Original work published 1949)

Long, P. L., & Gebhardt, N. (2020). Listening again to popular music as history. *Popular Music History*, 12(2), 147–151. 10.1558/pomh.41400

Luhmann, N. (1989). *Ecological communication*. Polity.

Luhmann, N. (2000). *Art as a social system*. Stanford University Press. 10.1515/9781503618763

Macy Gray. 2017. All I Want For Christmas. *Ultimate Chrismas Hits*. Sony 88985430942.

Mayer, J. (2006). Waiting On The World To Change. *Continuum*. Columbia 8276 79019 1.

McDowell, J. H., Borland, K., Dirksen, R., & Tuohy, S. (Eds.). (2021). *Performing environmentalisms: Expressive culture and ecological change*. University of Illinois Press. 10.5622/illinois/9780252044038.001.0001

McKay, G. (2007). A soundtrack to the insurrection: Street music, marching bands and popular protest. *Parallax*, 13(1), 20–31. 10.1080/13534640601094817

Mihai, M., & Thaler, M. (2023). Environmental commemoration: Guiding principles and real-world cases. *Memory Studies*, 1–18. 10.1177/17506980231176037

Mitchell, J. (1970). *Big Yellow Taxi*. Ladies Of The Canyon.

Mounsey, C. (2023). Frost or Fire? Popular Music Responses to Climate Change, from Woodstock to Glastonbury. In Fosbraey, G. (Ed.), *Coastal environments in popular song: Lost horizons* (pp. 44–57). Routledge.

Müller, T., & Durand, A.-P. (2022). Hip Hop Ecologies: Mapping the Field(s). An introduction. *Ecozon@: European Journal of Literature. Culture and Environment*, 13(1), 1–7.

Nash, R. F. (2014). *Wilderness and the American mind* (5th ed.). Yale University Press.

Newman, R. (1972). Burn On. *Sail Away*. Reprise Records REP 44185.

Nieland, J.-U. (2008). Politainment. In Donsbach, W. (Ed.), *The international encyclopedia of communication* (pp. 3659–3661). Blackwell. 10.1002/9781405186407.wbiecp047

Nocella, A. J., Parmar, P., Sawyer, D. C., & Cermak, M. (2017). Hip Hop, Food Justice, and Environmental Justice. In Nocella, A. J., Ducre, K. A., & Lupinacci, J. (Eds.), *Addressing Environmental and Food Justice toward Dismantling the School-to-Prison Pipeline: Poisoning and Imprisoning Youth* (pp. 177–192). Palgrave Macmillan. 10.1057/978-1-137-50822-5_10

Osmon, E. (2021). *John Prine's John Prine*. Bloomsbury.

Pedelty, M. (2012). *Ecomusicology: Rock, folk, and the environment*. Temple University Press., 10.2307/j.ctt14bt8qd

Peterson, R. A. (1994). Class Unconsciousness in Country Music. In MacLaurin, M. A. (Ed.), *You wrote my life: Lyrical themes in country music* (2nd ed., pp. 35–62). Gordon and Breach.

Philipp, T. (2019). Popmusikforschung. In Zemanek, E., & Kluwick, U. (Eds.), *Nachhaltigkeit interdisziplinär: Konzepte, Diskurse, Praktiken* (pp. 330–346). Böhlau.

Philipp, T. (2021). Der Sound der Katastrophe. Popmusik als Resonanzraum ökologischer Krisen. *Forschungsjournal Soziale Bewegungen*, 2. https://forschungsjournal.de/fjsb-plus_2021-2_philipp/

Philipp, T. (2022). Spaceship Earth and its Soundscapes: Latency Problems of International Ecological Conflicts in Pop Music. In Flath, B., Jacke, C., & Troike, M. (Eds.), *Transformational POP: Transitions, Breaks, and Crises in Popular Music (Studies)* (pp. 117–134). IASPM. http://www.vibes-theseries.org/philipp-spaceship-earth

Philipp, T. (2023). Simply Longing for Wilderness: Fictions of Nature Preservation in Western Pop Music. *Todas as Artes: Revista Luso-Brasileira De Artes E Cultura*, 6(1), 12–25. 10.21747/21843805/tav6n1a1

Pink Floyd. (1987). Sorrow. *A Momentary Lapse Of Reason*. EMI 7 48068 1.

Polanyi, K. (2010). *The great transformation: The political and economic origins of our time* (2nd ed.). Beacon.

Prine, J. (1971). *Paradise*. John Prine.

Prior, H. M. (2022). How Can Music Help Us to Address the Climate Crisis? *Music & Science*, 5, 205920432210757. 10.1177/20592043221075725

Radkau, J. (2008). *Nature and power: A global history of the environment*. Cambridge University Press.

Radkau, J. (2014). *The Age of Ecology*. Wiley.

Rehding, A. (2011). Ecomusicology between Apocalypse and Nostalgia. *Journal of the American Musicological Society*, 64(2), 409–414. 10.1525/jams.2011.64.2.409

Reid, A., & Petocz, P. (2021). *Educating Musicians for Sustainability*. Routledge., 10.4324/9781003044642

R.E.M. (1986). Cuyahoga. *Lifes Rich Pageant*. I.R.S. Records IRS-5783.

Rodnitzky, J. L. (1999). The sixties between the microgrooves: Using folk and protest music to understand American history, 1963-1973. *Popular Music and Society*, 23(4), 105–122. 10.1080/03007769908591755

Rodrigo, J. (2019). *Poetry Ceylon: When a girl from Goa fell in love with all that is Sri Lanka*. The Morning. https://www.themorning.lk/articles/40232

Rosen, C. (1997). *R.E.M. inside out: The stories behind every song*. Thunder's Mouth.

Rosenthal, D. J. (2006). „Hoods and the Woods": Rap Music as Environmental Literature. *Journal of Popular Culture*, 39(4), 661–676. 10.1111/j.1540-5931.2006.00284.x

Seeger, P. (1966). My Dirty Stream. *God Bless the Grass*. CBS 62618.

Seeger, P. (1972). This Land Is Your Land. *The World Of Pete Seeger*. Columbia CG 31949.

Skrimshire, S. (2014). Climate change and apocalyptic faith. *Wiley Interdisciplinary Reviews: Climate Change*, 5(2), 233–246. 10.1002/wcc.264

Steinberg, T. (2002). *Down to earth: Nature's role in American history*. Oxford University Press. 10.1093/oso/9780195140095.001.0001

Street, J. (2007). *Politics and popular culture*. Polity Press.

Street, J. (2013). *Music and Politics*. John Wiley & Sons.

Street, J., Hague, S., & Savingy, H. (2007). Playing to the crowd: The role of music and musicians in political participation. *British Journal of Politics and International Relations*, 10(2), 269–285. 10.1111/j.1467-856x.2007.00299.x

Styles, H. (2024). *Big Yellow Taxi. Live Sessions Duets And Cover Versions. Not On Label*. Harry Styles.

Taylor, S. M. (2019). *Ecopiety: Green media and the dilemma of environmental virtue*. NYU Press.

van den Berg, K., & Schmidt-Wulffen, S. (2023). Performative Knowledge. In T. Philipp & T. Schmohl (Eds.), *Handbook Transdisciplinary Learning* (pp. 267–276). transcript. 10.14361/9783839463475-028

Vargese, R. (2019). *Ditty's debut album, Poetry Ceylon is a memoir of her life in Sri Lanka*. New Indian Express. https://www.indulgexpress.com/culture/music/2019/jun/07/-15504.html

Warde, P., Sörlin, S., & Robin, L. (2018). *The Environment: A History of the Idea*. John Hopkins University Press.

Zamalin, A. (2019). *Black utopia: The history of an idea from black nationalism to Afrofuturism*. Columbia University Press. 10.7312/zama18740

Zevon, W. (1989). Run Straight Down. *Transverse City*. Virgin America 210253.

Chapter 13
Exploring Intermediate Modes of Memory Representation and Resignification

Frederico Dinis
https://orcid.org/0000-0002-2178-5252

Research Institute in Design, Media, and Culture (ID+), Polytechnic University of Cávado and Ave, Portugal

ABSTRACT

In this chapter, the author re-thinks and reflects on the importance of the relationship and interconnection between the site-specific, the sense of place, the ambience and the performativity of memory, exploring and deepening the confluence between sound and image, relating concepts, purposes and coherence of site-specific artistic practices that mediate and reconfigure the memory of places. The chapter aims to study the confluence between sound and image in performative places, through a research methodology through the artistic practice used to analyse sound and visual performances and their representations of memory. Intermediate mediation, through sound and visual construction, promotes new interpretations, making use of the memory of the spectator. It is also observed that exploring intermediate forms of sound and visual representation of memory in live site-specific performances opens up new artistic possibilities, challenges traditional modes of storytelling, and facilitates deeper audience engagement with the artwork and its underlying themes.

INTRODUCTION

The concept of performance can be understood through different perceptions, resulting from different disciplinary approaches, artistic areas or cultural contexts (Wardrip-Fruin, 2006). It is due to this conceptual openness and the diversity of creative procedures that performance, as an action in front of an audience (Carlson, 2004), presents a great potential for exploration on which this chapter is based,

DOI: 10.4018/979-8-3693-2264-2.ch013

especially focussed on the confluence between sound and visual, mnemonic and sensory media, as a theme of theoretical and creative recognition.

Performance has become a meeting point between the arts, in which unconventional forms of dialogue converge, in a desire to develop fusion experimentation by artists with an intertextual, multisensory, technological and experiential approach to the event (Dinis, 2023). In this sense, sound and visual performances stand out because they involve alternative aesthetics and are technologically innovative because they move away from the body/performer and expand into other media, namely sound and image.

In addition to this expansion to other media, live performance is co-constructed by the bodily presence of performers and spectators and performative moments can have a transformative effect since spectators experience the materiality of a live performance as an ephemeral event (Fischer-Lichte, 2019). This materiality of the ephemeral can also be achieved with the inclusion of technological means during the performative moment (Bay-Cheng et al., 2015), thus enhancing a performativity of sound and image, where sounds and images negotiate their meaning (Harbison, 2019). These experiences with sounds and images remain fundamental in the contemporary framework as they are linked to the concept of synaesthesia as a relationship between the senses, a concept that is even more present in audio-visual practices due to technology's ability to simultaneously produce stimuli for the various senses.

The interrelationship between sound and visual media thus emerges as an artifice for weaving new possibilities for constructing meanings where dialogical connections can emerge through rereadings and reinterpretations that induce the audience to move to other contexts through the manipulation of sounds and images, where the sound follows the image or vice versa, not mixing homogeneously in fruition. Sound and image, in confluence, provide a wider range of possibilities for interrelation, constructing other narratives which, in the performative moment, are no longer either sound or visual, but both, in a materialisation of an ephemerality that is achieved through the use of technological means.

Sound and visual media develop in combinatory potential, thus conceptually expanding the live sound and visual performance. When sound and image capture both senses at the same time in a single aesthetic-narrative sense, there is an articulation that not only captures the viewer's attention but also directs them towards new interpretations. This discussion about the capacity of live sound and visual performances to promote new interpretations and poetic readings of the works raises a new set of questions about the technological mediation of the materiality of interactions between works of art, sounds, images, place, memory, and the public. It is therefore necessary to analyse these territories and processes associated with intermediate forms of memory representation and the construction of re-significations in sound and visual performance.

In this sense, this chapter aims to study the confluence between sound and image in performative places, through a process of research through artistic practice in the context of contemporary performance that (i) reflects on the impacts of sense of place and the site-specific in reinforcing and blurring the boundaries between place, memory and art; (ii) analyses the role of ambience and the importance of remembering in the process of perception and apprehension of site-specific sound and visual performances; (iii) investigates the effects that aesthetic and audiovisuality configurations have on the construction of re-significations in site-specific sound and visual artistic creations.

To meet these objectives, a methodology of research through artistic practice is used which assumes that the performativity of memory and the construction of a narrative as a temporal text reinforce the role of sound and visual media in the context of sound and visual performances and during performative moments. The involvement of the audience thus escapes the commonplace of everyday corporeality, blurring permanent boundaries and starting from bodily experience as a motto for spatial transgression.

Taking the stated objectives into account, this chapter has been divided into four parts. The first part identifies and discusses the importance of the concepts of the site-specific and sense of place, assuming that to ensure effective appropriation of space, it is important to have a better understanding of the place and its context, in which the work of art will be incorporated. The second part reflects on the aesthetics related to the notion of ambience and the importance of remembering through performativity, a performativity that acts through sounds and images in the materiality of interactions between memories of the place and the audience. The third part analyses the construction of audiovisuality as an element that promotes new interpretations mediated by sound and image, making use of the memory of the spectator. Finally, the fourth and last part presents the research methodology through the artistic practice used to analyse sound and visual performances and their representations of memory.

Taking as a starting point this set of artistic practices and performative moments that were developed as part of this chapter, the confluence of sound and image is explored and deepened, linking and relating concepts, purposes and coherence of artistic practices that use these two media, in the reformulation of performative places and how individual and community memories are mediated and reconfigured. Performative places are spaces that seek to produce a place of connection and interaction, where the meaning and significance of human existence are intensified.

SENSE OF PLACE AND THE SITE-SPECIFIC

It is important to acknowledge the impact of a sense of place and the site-specific in reinforcing and blurring the boundaries between place, memory and art. The term 'site-specific' originated in the late 1960s and early 1970s to categorise a series of artistic works that were intrinsically linked to their location. Artists such as Nancy Holt, Robert Smithson, and Walter de Maria are associated with the first productions of this genre, as are other artists linked to other artistic genres, particularly land art, such as Dennis Oppenheim, Mary Miss, Michael Heizer, and Robert Morris.

Although the creations related to land art were mostly realized on a large scale at the time, this did not stop the artists from moving towards minimalism. The artists' primary aim in this context was to distance themselves from what O'Doherty (1986) referred to as the 'white cube' - a self-contained space with no connection to the outside world, where "the work is isolated from everything that would jeopardise its own evaluation of itself" (O'Doherty, 1986: 14). Crimp (1986) argues that artists began to look for external spaces to create their art due to "the implausibility of works for enclosed spaces, which were presented as if they were in a clean white room" (Crimp, 1986: 46). Kaye (2000) suggests that site-specific works describe "practices in which exchanges are articulated between the artwork and the places in which its meanings are defined" (Kaye, 2000: 1). This proposition assumes that a site-specific creation cannot be viewed in isolation from its context. The artists were interested in demystifying the modernist paradigm of the tabula rasa, rather than questioning the concept of the 'white cube' of exhibition spaces and their "closed system of values" (O'Doherty, 1986: 14). Kwon (2002) defends this departure from modernism:

> *If modern sculpture absorbed its pedestal/base to break its connection with/or express its indif-*
> *ference to the site (...) site-specific works, when they emerged in the wake of minimalism in the late*
> *1960s and early 2000s, forced a dramatic reversal of this modernist paradigm.* (Kwon, 2002:11)

The purpose of site-specific practice is for the place to directly influence the outcome of artistic creation. This approach moves away from the "sterile and idealistic pure art space of the dominant modernisms" and "is no longer understood as a gap, but as a real space" (Kwon, 2002: 11). According to Crimp (1986), the introduction of specificity of place into contemporary art by minimalist artists in the mid-1960s challenged the idealism of modern sculpture. For these artists, the work needed to be physically integrated into the place. Vaz-Pinheiro (2005) defends that the concept of 'site' is an integral part of the work itself. Even works designed for traditional exhibition spaces have a strong and undeniable connection with the architectural layout of the exhibition space. In minimal art, objects redirect consciousness towards themselves and the real space that houses them. In contrast, site-specific art projects itself into a concrete space, respecting its physical and visual qualities, and relating to the specificity of a particular place, whether built or natural.

It is important to the discussion in this chapter to define the concept of 'place'. Therefore, it is crucial to understand the subjective experience of place to fully understand its significance. As Lippard (1997: 7) explains, 'place' refers to "a portion of land, city, or urban landscape that is seen from the inside and resonates with a specific known and familiar experience". Heidegger (1971) also emphasizes this resonance, stating that the relationship between man and space is not one of opposition, but rather a coexistence. According to Harrison (2008), the fusion of place and soul involves neither an external object nor an inner experience. Harrison (2008) emphasizes that the soul is as much a container of the place as the place is a container of the soul, and both are sensitive to the same forces of destruction. Lippard (1997: 7) supports this concept by arguing that a sense of place is "the geographical component of the psychological need to belong somewhere [space], [and] an antidote to a prevailing alienation" or, as Jackson (1994: 159) claims, "a vivid awareness of familiar surroundings, a ritual repetition, a sense of community-based on shared experience".

Kwon (2002) observes that the relationship between the site-specific and sense of place can cause some confusion due to the number of related terms: as 'site-determined', 'site-oriented', 'site-referenced', 'site-conscious', 'site-responsive', and 'site-related', that have emerged among artists and critics to describe various modifications of site-specific art. These are some of the terms that have emerged in recent years among artists and critics to describe modifications of site-specific art (Kwon, 2002). These variations have arisen due to site-specificity, that is, the specificities of each place where the work is located. Smithson (1996: 182) defines 'site-specificity' as the conflict between the artist and the chosen place. The artist cannot ignore this dialectical relationship as each place has its particularities and challenges. Therefore, the artist may need to make adaptations and incorporate physical, cultural, and/or social aspects of the place. In some situations, the place itself or the people who inhabit it may indicate to the artist which direction the art creation should take.

According to Kaye (2000: 2), "site-specificity challenges notions of 'original' or 'fixed' location, [thus] problematising the relationship between work and place". The artist's approach to this relationship determines the development of their work. Kaye also argues that the specificity of place is "best thought of in terms of the relationship that emerges as a disturbing unease, the opposition between 'ideal' space and 'real' space" (Kaye, 2000: 46). The 'ideal' space is the one that the artist imagines beforehand and considers appropriate for realizing the work, while the 'real' space is the actual place with all its imperfections and unforeseen events. The work's specificity lies in this difference, where the dialectical relationship creates tensions and changes that manifest in the place's specificity and, consequently, in the artwork.

The "specificity of place (...) can be understood (...) when a site-specific work must articulate and define itself in terms of properties, qualities or meanings produced in specific relationships between an 'object' or 'event' and the position it occupies" (Kaye, 2000: 1). Kaye refers to the art object itself as the 'object' and the act of intervention, such as a performance or other artistic language that presupposes an action for a given time, as the 'event'. In site-specific art, the artist's choices are considered less important than the sense of place. Kwon (2002) claims in this context that "in an effort to integrate art more directly into the realm of the social, (...) manifestations of site-specificity tend to treat aesthetic and historical concerns [of art] as secondary issues" (Kwon, 2002: 1). When considering the specificity of a place, the chosen artistic language plays a secondary role. The focus must lie on the relationship that the artist develops with the location and the solutions found to the tensions between the work and the place. While aesthetic factors are important, they remain in the background. The main focus is on the connections that the work creates with the location and the people who inhabit it.

Toft (2016: 53-54) suggests that site-specific artworks are related to two aesthetic ideals that go hand in hand: pragmatism and aestheticism. This aesthetic-pragmatic ideal is connected to "the paradigm of site-specific art, which was institutionalised as a practice between the 1980s and 1990s and used to reaffirm the cultural valorisation of places" (Toft, 2016: 54). The purpose of site-specific art is determined by the specificity of the place, which directs the choices of the artist/creator. Pragmatism is concerned with 'what' and aestheticism with 'how', which is a secondary issue since the place will determine 'how' the work will be developed.

According to Kwon (2002), the new experiments suggest that the place of art is not solely a physical space, but is also shaped by social, economic, and political processes. As a result, artists naturally desire to occupy these new spaces and the appropriation of space allows for the exercise of dominion, control, and power, as Segaud (2016) explains. The statement that the space belongs to the artist is a form of appropriation. This proposition assumes an approximation between art and the sense of place, as the socio-cultural context of a place is determined by its inhabitants. To ensure effective appropriation of space, it is important to have a better understanding of the place and its context, in which the work of art will be incorporated. The process is complex, as it involves various factors,

> *appropriating space means establishing a relationship between that space and the "self" [making it one's own] through a set of practices. It's about attributing meaning to a place: this can be done at the level of semantics, through words and the objects and symbols that are linked to them.* (Segaud, 2016: 126-127)

For an artist to carry out an 'appropriation', they must first understand the codes of the place and establish an interaction with the inhabitants. Kaye (2000) argues that a "prior reading of the space" must be undertaken, as elements such as "political, aesthetic, geographical or institutional discourses inform everything that can be said by the artist about that place" (Kaye, 2000: 1). This spatial reading deepens the understanding of the place, since "space says something about the society, group or individual that occupies it, indicating (...) [the] state of social relations, [and] 'communicates', as long as we know the code to be able to read what it tells us" (Segaud, 2016: 106). Artistic creations can also be considered a form of spatial occupation. The artist appropriates the place through their artistic process and the work directed towards it. This proposition has been the focal point of the selected audio-visual performances developed by the author and that exemplify intermediate forms of memory representation and resignifications, explored in the last part of this chapter.

Over the last few years, technological advancements have made recording, production, and projection equipment more portable. This has led to the development of site-specific works using such equipment, expanding the possibilities for other media, particularly sound and image, to be used in art created for a specific place and in the sound and visual representation of the memories of that place (Dinis, 2024).

AMBIENCE AND THE PERFORMATIVITY OF THE MEMORY

It is important to consider the aesthetics related to the notion of ambience and the importance of remembering through performativity, both of which are related to the previously discussed concepts of the site-specific and sense of place.

Aesthetics is central to the notion of ambience as it explicitly addresses the issue of human sensorial experience. Two elements frame aesthetics in terms of ambience. Firstly, the ambience evokes an 'ambient aesthetic' that cannot be reduced to an aesthetic of the plastic arts. The aesthetic at the centre of this chapter is focused on nature in its broadest sense. While it has both a narrative and an ambient facet, the previous has largely dominated until now (Foster, 1998). Secondly, another important element is that ambience allows us to return to the original meaning of aesthetics, which is a theory of sensory perception.

So, the following discussion tries to broaden the understanding of aesthetics beyond subjective evaluations and to emphasize the importance of the body, sensitivity, and emotion. It also intends to reduce the significance of semiotics and language in aesthetics, as proposed by Böhme (1997).

Jean-François Augoyard and Gernot Böhme coined the terms 'ambience' and 'atmosphere' respectively[1]. Although these two concepts were developed independently, they share several similarities. Both seek to return to a theory of sensory perception and emphasise the architectural and spatial dimensions of ambience. In both cases, the objective was to create an ambience aesthetic for constructing space [place]. An aesthetic of ambience that encompasses everyday situations, rather than just monumental architecture or landmark buildings. This approach opposes a 'museum-like' view of art and refuses to combine artistic and aesthetic experiences, providing an escape hatch for the analysis of the most common situations.

The contextual nature of ambience is highly valued, which encourages the development of ecological aesthetics. Augoyard (1998) proposes in situ approaches and interdisciplinary tools that operate perceptible physical signs, norms, rules, codes, references, instruments, characteristics and uses to build forms. According to Böhme (2000), the matter at hand involves observing the relationship between environmental qualities and human sensitivity to gain a better understanding of how individuals experience their surroundings. Despite the differing terminology used by both, they address the complexity of situations, suggesting that heterogeneous contextual components are interconnected. This logic of articulation is present at every level of their thinking, emerging as though the ambience serves as the foundation from which different components or polarities must be linked together into a cohesive dynamic.

Although Augoyard and Böhme share a great affinity, particularly in their use of phenomenology, each has unique characteristics. It is important to note that they do not treat the material and objective aspects of ambience in the same terms. Augoyard links these aspects to physical signs and built space, while Böhme links them more closely to the world of things.

Additionally, Augoyard and Böhme are based on markedly different categories. The concept of ambience is crucial for the previous, consisting of six complementary elements: physical signs, spatio-temporal forms, perceptions, representations, codes, and norms, as well as social interaction. As for the last, the idea of atmosphere revolves around the notion of presence, which has three main components: the thing, the environment, and the senses.

Thus, the aesthetics of ambience in spaces [places]offers three main contributions. Firstly, it provides a new perspective on sensory perception by highlighting its contextual nature and including it in everyday social life. This approach considers all senses and emphasizes the significance of physical and material factors. Furthermore, the focus on the phenomenology of built space helps to develop the idea of urban and architectural ambience. Secondly, the focus on the phenomenology of built space helps to develop the concept of urban and architectural ambiences. Secondly, the phenomenological aesthetic emphasises the complexity of ambiences and encourages a modal and interdisciplinary approach. Instead of dissociating the terms of an ambience and isolating its elements, the aim is to connect them. Although each follows a different path, the goal is to establish links and continuity that give body to an ambience. Finally, the aesthetics of ambience involves a dynamic approach. The purpose is to envision locations not as a given or a static state, but as an ongoing process that involves both the permanent activity and the actions of those who create the ambience (Dinis, 2020).

As previously acknowledged by the author, the artist's creative process and resulting artwork can be viewed as a form of spatial occupation, as they appropriate the space through a sensory perception of the ambience. This is accomplished through the performativity of memory during the interaction with the space and the presentation of the artwork, especially in sound and visual performances.

According to Féral (2015), performance artists are primarily responsible for generating energy flows and are not limited to the notion of representation. As forms of art, performing arts, including sound and visual performances, have the potential to influence the artistic proposal and shift the focus of the artist throughout the spatial occupation (the narrator-performer).

Consequently, interferences or contaminations from external factors, such as space, light, sound, or observer-performer (the artist after the spatial reading), mediate the narrator-performer's (the artist throughout the spatial occupation) experience in the space. This can unfold the process of performing the artwork live, prioritising the process over the notion of a finished product. Unlike a completed work, the performer's body in the space seeks to raise questions from the fragments left by the artwork that is (being) constructed, formulating a kind of question and then inviting the observer-receiver (the audience) to find the answers.

In this way, performative creations present themselves as forms in constant process, since they are not exhausted, in other words, the performing arts do not arrive at a specific place, they do not lend themselves to an end and they reject the formalistic outcomes of the work (Dinis 2020).

Performativity values what happens outside of structuralist schemes, what appears as an unstable place during the performer's action, and what simply occurs on stage. It enhances the performer's ability to perceive and offer the spectator an experience of the real. An experience of reality is a complex set of actions performed by the actor that balances interpretation with pure presence on stage. This creates a game with the audience, full of tension, uncertainty, and gaps (Dinis, 2023).

Like ambience, performativity transcends the design of traditional aesthetic theory because it resists the hermeneutical disputes of understanding the artwork. According to Fischer-Lichte (2007), experiencing the artist's actions is more important than comprehending them, and moving through the proposed event.

Participating in the experience can evoke a wide range of sensations that may be difficult to interpret or assign meaning to. However, this does not imply that there is nothing for the spectator to interpret. It is important to note that the actions of the narrator-performer (the artist) may have multiple meanings and interpretations.

Performativity is characterised by the dissolution of physical and/or imaginary barriers between the narrator-performer and the observer-receiver. It proposes a series of sound or visual stimuli, among others, for those who take part in its event (Dinis 2020).

The space created by performativity becomes a shelter for an open, procedural work in the artistic creation of a politics of the senses. Politics that should not solely rely on verbal, analytical, and rational messages. It should also move beyond the rigidity of formal and institutionalized discourses and explore other subjectivities and ways of constructing scenes. A performativity that moves between verb and action, between logical understanding and synaesthetic understanding, between the power of a formal narrative and the narrative of fragmented, simultaneous or successive images.

The concept of performativity is versatile, as it can be influenced by different disciplines, media, and ideas from the art world. It prioritises autonomous and creative experimentation, placing value on the act of artistic creation rather than the final product.

Thus, performativity avoids the limitations of everyday physicality by creating mechanisms of continuous movement, blurring boundaries, and seeking to destabilise previously clear differences in everyday life. This is achieved by using bodily experience as a means of spatial transgression (Fernandes 2011) during live sound and visual performances. Therefore, performativity appears to favour open works that aim to generate participation through physical or mediated influence, rather than finished works. Performativity operates through sounds, images, and embodiment, in the materiality of interactions between audience, space, and memory (Dinis, 2023).

Memory serves as a means of interpreting the past, providing a voice, sound, and image of past events. As Le Goff (1996) argues, the concept of memory materializes when it refers to the ability to preserve certain information, allowing individuals to recall past impressions or information. These sounds and images, configurations and representations of the past, belong to the field of memory. However, they are rarely utilized in the reconstruction of the history of a place.

Memory, in its ephemeral and unfinished expression, finds its corporeal material in language. The creator-narrator's voice is welcomed in memory and language, as they search for what is remembered, select it, and present it in their recorded and preserved archives. This reception process is based on the premise that history serves as a vehicle for memory, as it emphasizes the events experienced in specific places (Dinis, 2020).

According to Lévinas (2012: 65), the concept of the "trace" delineates temporality within space by unveiling the existence of something that has vanished. The trace embodies the presence of absence, wherein absence encapsulates a form of presence. It engenders a silence, representing an "intense resistance and attentiveness [...] of the artist, and, in the truest sense, a nurturing of silence. [...] the artwork nurtures silence, allowing it to become the essence of existence, akin to how a shepherd tends to his flock" (Lévinas 2012: 96). Concerning the interplay between memory and place, this chapter follows Salomão's (2014: 272-273) assertion that "memory acts as an island of editing" and Tiberghien's (2012: 180) argument that "place possesses a fundamental relational dimension, rather than being a mere object".

The issue of memory and the tendency to expand its scope, considering the role of the performance of bodily and non-bodily practices (Hoelscher and Alderman 2004), means that there is a diversity of approaches and that memory is observed from different areas, which "look at memory and the memory of place remodelled by its collective forms, to give itself a coherent identity, a narrative (...), a place in the world" (Said 2000: 179).

This act of remembering will interfere with two human domains of dismemberment: one, remembering the memory, and the other about the memory that is remembered. These two components are not necessarily distinct, but the disjunction of one from the other is difficult to act upon since it interferes with the action of reformulating thought about the memory that is remembered and the meaning that is given to it (Wood and Byatt 2008).

These theoretical perspectives that examine the relationship between memory, representation, and sound and visual performances were explored by the author in the analysis of specific sound and visual elements, their interplay, and their contribution to memory narratives. To support this in-depth analysis, the author developed several sound and visual site-specific performances that exemplify intermediate forms of memory representation and resignifications. This research through artistic practice started with the theme of memory as a phenomenon that allows for the present creation of an absence (Ricoeur 2006). It is also assumed that all memory work involves representation work.

This work of representation is also inherent in a process of remembrance, which precedes a process of constructing sounds and images. Sounds that are imagined to have been heard, images that are thought to have already been visualized, and sounds and images that are understood as aids in the living experience of memory construction, promoting a performativity of memory during live audio-visual performances (Dinis, 2023)

A performativity that acts through sounds and images, through flexibility, in the materiality of interactions between memories, individual and collective, of place and audience, in performances where the most important thing is not what the work seeks to signify or symbolize, but rather the traversal of the experience, which transcends the possibility and effort of interpretation and production of meaning, going beyond pure reflection or rational interpretation (Dinis, 2024).

AUDIOVISUALITY

The previous reflection on the site-specific, the sense of place, the ambience and the performativity of memory can be combined with a sound and visual construction as an element that promotes new interpretations mediated by sound and image, making use of the memory of the spectator. This memory allows for the presence of an absence, so it can be said that all memory involves a work of representation. According to Ricoeur (2006), the process of representation is inherent in both remembering and constructing sounds and images. This involves imagining sounds that were heard, visualising images that were seen, and using sounds and images as aids in building memory. To this process of representation is added another level of reading with the interference of the sense of place since, as D'Annunzio (1983) argues, the richest experiences [in places] happen long before the soul realises it since, by the time we begin to open our eyes to the visible, we have already been advocates of the invisible for a long time.

It can be assumed that the unique character and identity of a place is derived from the importance of its 'atmosphere' (Böhme, 1993), as supported by Pallasmaa (2005). These dimensions of reading, place, sounds, and images can also be linked to 'audiovisuality' (Chion, 2011). Chion (2011) proposed the concept of 'audiovisuality' as a "place of images and sounds", which can be analysed from two perspectives: (i) the definition of the field of sound and its relationship with the field of the visual image, showing that although audiovisuality is presented as a project of sound valorisation, the centrality of the image is not questioned, but rather reinforced; (ii) the limits of the concept of listening, considering possible openings based on the concept of 'trans-sensoriality', also proposed by Chion (2011).

Chion (1999) argues that sound is divided into visible and invisible, according to what is being represented on screen, thus dividing the sound universe into two and placing the visual medium as the structuring element of the sound field, suggesting that there is no such thing as a soundtrack, as sound is an integral part of the audio-visual experience and defining that the image's characteristic of 'pulling' sounds towards itself and organising them as the magnetisation of sound by the image. This concept is fundamental to Chion's understanding of cinema, proposing an 'ontologically visual' definition of cinema (Chion, 2011: 114). Later, Chion (2002) expands this concept to move beyond the specific domain of cinema, presenting a broader theory of sound and associating it with music and literature. Chion (2002: 182) argues that the notion of a soundtrack is unfeasible due to the variety of sound types, that consist of music, language, and noise. Chion (2011) identifies and separates language and music within the sound universe, leaving what he calls noise. The distinction between music and language from the universe of noise is based on culturally specific 'values' (Chion, 2002: 175). The audible universe is a continuous field where the ear distinguishes between different types of sounds according to known linguistic or musical codes (Chion, 2002: 169). Chion (2002) argues that the varied field of sounds cannot be unified by any totalising structure, making it impossible to refer to it as a soundtrack, which requires the image to give it structure and be apprehended by viewers.

Chion (2006) argues for a stronger ontological status of the image, assuming that the screen provides a unifying structure to the set of images, regardless of their variety. The screen, as a perceived structure, exists independently of the images and persists even after the projection is over. In contrast, Chion (2006) contends that there is no comparable unifying structure for sound, highlighting a fundamental difference between sound and image.

Contrary to the idea of sound and image being separate entities, Bayle (1993) suggests the concept of 'image-of-sound', where sound is considered an image as soon as it is recorded and played back through speakers,

> *(...) comparing it to the image visible on the surface of the photographic support, i-sound [or image-of-sound] lends itself to designating any sound heard thanks to reproduction by loudspeakers, subtracted from its original space of creation (and, at the same time, also from its time), with "repro- duction" being understood as something other than mere repetition.* (Caesar, 2016: 171)

Caesar (2012, 2013) argues that sound possesses a materiality that is often overlooked, despite its abil- ity to function as an image even when not recorded on a medium. The existence of other types of media, such as air and the brain, is frequently disregarded. This challenges the common perception of sound as elusive and obscure, potentially offering a solution to the sound/image dichotomy (Caesar, 2012, 2013).

It is important to revisit Chion's (2002) concept of 'trans-sensoriality' due to its relevance to this discussion:

> *We call trans-sensory those perceptions that are not of any particular sense, but can seek the channel of one or the other, without their content or effect being restricted to the limits of that sense. (...) In other words, to speak of trans-sensoriality is to remember that it would be wrong to think that everything that is auditory is only auditory, and to say that the senses are entities closed in on themselves.* (Chion, 2002: 56-57)

Trans-sensory perceptions are an exception to the traditional five-senses model. According to Chion (2002, 2011), new 'fields' are formed through processes related to sight and hearing, including rhythmic, textural, spatial, and language fields. Chion suggests that sound serves as a metaphor for a broader perception:

> *What matters is that sound is the metaphor of a continuous and borderless perception that presents a field of verifiable objects, those that are offered to the auditory window, but that overflows it. Sound is the symbol of a perception that crosses all our senses, surpassing their limits, and gives us the impression of continuing somewhere beyond (...).* (Chion, 2002: 62)

Also important is the concept of 'haptic visuality', as proposed by Marks (2000). It is based on the homonymous concept coined by Riegl ({1901} 1985) and is defined by an attitude of vision that prioritises touch-like qualities.

> *(...) the eyes themselves function as organs of touch. (...) Haptic vision tends to move over the surface of its object rather than plunge into an illusionistic depth, seeks less to distinguish form and more to discern texture. It is more inclined to move than to focus, more inclined to scratch than to contemplate.* (Marks, 2000: 162)

According to Marks, a 'haptic image' is one that invites a view that moves over the surface of the plane and is the result of a gradual figuration. In other words, haptic cinema,

> *does not invite identification with a figure - a sensory-motor reaction - as much as it encourages a bodily relationship between the viewer and the image. Consequently, as in the mimetic relationship, it is not appropriate to speak of the object of a haptic gaze, but of a dynamic subjectivity between the gazer and the image.* (Marks, 2000: 164)

Marks (2000) argues that cinema can be understood as multisensory due to the prevalence of haptic visuality and synaesthesia in perception, challenging that the term 'image' encompasses all sensory impressions conveyed by a perceived object at a given moment. Marks also argues that the audio-visual apparatus provokes sensations beyond sight and hearing through sensory memory, starting from the idea of a multisensory image (Marks, 2000: 210). This understanding can be expanded to other media, including exclusively sound media, as Marks also suggests (2000: 182-183).

For this debate related to the sensory mediation capacity of sound and visual media, it is also important to emphasise the understanding of sound as an image, valuing the materiality of other sensory vehicles, such as air,

> *this kind of buffer that we humans tend to ignore as such, because we confuse invisibility with non-existence. Air is not solid, however (...) it is also matter, and as such it carries images, dynamised as in the buffer memory of computers. The materiality of air is contrary to any notion of instant: what exists is a sequence of pseudo-instants perceived as such, all separated from the moment of their creation. What is perceived is perceived after it has occurred. Everything ends - at its moment - so that it can, once space has been crossed, at the cost of time, be born in perception.* (Caesar, 2013: 7)

Sound is linked to the support of the gaseous or liquid matter of the ambience in which it propagates. Bayle's (1993) concept of image-of-sound generalises the idea of 'support' beyond the technological, developing an understanding of sound as an image.

> *Sound is already an image even when the only support available is the brain, and when its transmission is from mouth to ear, or in the direct path of things that sound to the ear (...). Just like seeing, listening is always about forming images. Of course, the formation of the image depends on the medium. Why wouldn't it be possible to think that, before being a "technological support" [occurring thanks to extracorporeal means], the support can also be that of the body itself: memory?* (Caesar, 2016: 172)

This chapter assumes Caesar's (2016) proposition that listening always involves forming mental images, starting from memory as a support that allows for the present creation of an absence, and integrating sound and visual representations.

After reviewing the theoretical framework and integrating these theoretical perspectives into the analysis of the relations between site-specific, sense of place, ambience, performativity of memory, and audiovisuality, it is necessary to explain the methodology used to analyse sound and visual performances and their representations of memory.

METHODOLOGICAL APPROACH

The author developed a personal proposal for re-signification in sound and visual performances to examine the challenges in studying intermediate forms of memory representation. This was achieved through sound and visual site-specific performances that exemplify intermediate forms of memory representation and resignifications. Considering that listening involves forming mental images from memory, this search for the sound and visual representation of memory extends the idea of the medium beyond technology, reinforcing the understanding of sound as an image.

The previous discussion has shown that site-specific sound and visual performance mediate the materiality of interactions between works of art, sounds, images, place, memory, and the public through plasticity. This is supported by Scruton (1976), Fuchs (1985), Auslander (2006), Godlovitch (2008), Siepmann (2010), Caesar (2016), and Dinis (2023). By using bodily experience as a motto for spatial transgression, mechanisms of continuous movement are created, blurring seemingly permanent boundaries and allowing the audience's involvement to escape the commonplace of everyday corporeality. This follows the propositions of Augoyard (1995), Böhme (2000), Chion (2002, 2011), Fernandes (2011), Lima & Caldeira (2006), Segaud (2016) and Dinis (2023).

As Spielmann (2004) argues, there is an unprecedented affinity and coherence between (electronic) sound and image, since the frequencies, voltages and instruments that organise them are identical. To Pareyson (1993)

> *(...) the artist studies his material with love, scrutinises it to the core, observes its behaviour and reactions, questions it so that he can direct it, interprets it so that he can take it, obeys it so that he can overcome it, delves into it so that it reveals latent possibilities adapted to his intentions, excavate it so that it itself suggests new and unprecedented possibilities, follow it so that its natural movements can*

coincide with the demands of the work to be realised, investigate the ways in which a long tradition has taught us to manipulate it in order to bring out new and original aspects or to extend them in new progressions, and if the tradition of which the material is laden seems to compromise its own ductility and make it severe, slow and opaque, he seeks to recover its virgin freshness, which is all the more fruitful the more unexplored it is, and if the material is new, He will not allow himself to be impressed by the audacity of certain suggestions that seem to come out of it spontaneously, and he will not refuse the courage of certain experiments or shirk the duty of penetrating it in order to better highlight the possibilities It is not a question of saying that the artist's humanity and spirituality are configured in a material, becoming a whole, made up of sounds, colours and words, because art is not the figuration and formation of a person's life. Art is not the figuration and formation of a matter, but the matter is formed according to an unrepeatable way of forming that is the artist's own spirituality made up entirely of style. (Pareyson, 1993: 98)

Matter, including sound and image, serves as an obstacle to inventive activity, which transforms the obstacle's needs into laws of artistic creation. The aim is to find new dynamic configurations between sound and image, creating new narratives and recreating sensations and emotions. Sound and image are expressive processes that significantly contribute to the meaning and manifestation of artistic work (Wardrip-Fruin, 2006). This personal research through an artistic practice approach uses sound (electronic ambient music) and visual media (back and white videos) to transmit sensations and emotions.

The aim of creating electronic ambient music is to establish an ambience that transports the audience to unknown places where the narrative unfolds. The creation of electronic ambient music to evoke sensations is founded on the creation of atmospheres that engage the listener's consciousness, immersing them in the sound and encouraging active listening. This is achieved through the use of site-specific field recordings and sound textures developed specifically for the space. The soundscapes were produced, by the author, using pieces with extended durations, with no indication of when each piece begins or ends. This feature enables the observer-receiver (the audience) to further engage with the immersive sound and experience a true sound narrative.

The visual medium employs video to represent sensations and emotions, creating an interplay between the senses and perception. This medium is closely interrelated to the idea that video merges memory and imagination, serving as a channel for giving shape to remembered and imagined objects. Black and white images are used because they have a timeless quality and can convey emotions effectively. Additionally, the absence of colour allows for a greater focus on form, texture, and pattern, as noted by Hedgecoe (2006: 118). Westgeest (2008) highlights the analysis of the image as a medium, focusing on the concepts of fragment and memory. This refers to the idea of image transparency as a window into reality, the sense of place through the recognition of reality, and the potential for social documentary intervention. These ideas provide clues to the narrative being conveyed. The videos created, also by the author, depend on a prior analysis and study of the presentation space and its ambience. It is also necessary to evaluate the approach and methodologies used to produce them, to reinforce the site-specific and sense of place conveyed by these media.

The sound and visual narratives are prepared in advance and manipulated in real-time to guide the construction of the narrative. This approach is experimental and differentiated, adapting the performativity of each space and creating unique sound and visual narratives.

The author's artistic approach combines sound and visual media to create an emotive experience for the spectator. The approach involves the spectator in the creation of their narrative, using their memories and the present moment as a starting point. The presence of the viewer, both spatially and temporally, creates a relational and emotional experience with the visual and sonic events so that the viewer is contingent on the performativity associated with the site-specific projects developed through a personal process of artistic research.

Artistic research is a distinct questioning process that differs from conventional academic models. It derives knowledge from the experiences and practices of artists. To align with its unique characteristics, this form of research requires models that employ various discursive and representational strategies (Dinis, 2023).

Artistic research insists that outcomes and knowledge must be conveyed through symbolic language and the researcher-artist's practice. This adds complexity to the research process, making the development of any proposed approach a realm of productive uncertainty - a space for the temporary 'construction' of concepts and contingent thinking (Dinis, 2023).

Projects within this framework often employ a hybrid methodology and are presented as works in progress. They can be seen as an alternative form of investigative practice, aligning with the evolving dynamics of practice-as-research. This approach diverges from traditional art contexts, fosters the creation of new methodologies, and pushes the boundaries of artistic exploration.

Research is widely recognised for providing valuable knowledge to inform practice, and conversely, practice can offer contextual relevance to research. However, despite the potential for synergy, differences in goals, language, expertise, audience, and environment, among other factors, often maintain a separation between the two realms. The concept of practice-as-research, as used in this context, involves beliefs and values about both practice and research. It highlights the acknowledged gap between the current state of affairs and a more desirable situation (Witkin, 2011).

In addition to the differences highlighted by Witkin (2011), this argument suggests three other characteristics - creativity, mutability, and presence – that can also serve as points of convergence, as they are inherent in both practice and research.

To support this convergence, site-specific research through artistic practice projects has been conducted by the author in spaces, using a unique format and language of expression (Table 1.). These projects aim to examine and develop effective methods and strategies for creating and presenting art forms. This research, which employs artistic practice, focuses on two central elements: engaging with the context of the place and (de)constructing the sense of place, following the approach developed by Dinis (2020).

Table 1. List of site-specific projects developed by the author

Date	Title	Place
2023.09.22	passamos pelas coisas sem as habitar…	Fort of St John the Baptist, Esposende
2022.10.14	peregrinatio perpetua	House of Recoleta, Barcelos
2022.07.09	reminiscências corporalizadas	Alto' Factory, Pevidém, Guimarães
2022.06.11	um aguçar dos sentidos	Municipal Theatre, Covilhã
2022.02.23	fonte interminável de simbolismo	Municipal Museum, Póvoa de Varzim
2021.11.06	a vivacidade dos instantes	Andresen' House, Porto

continued on following page

Table 1. Continued

Date	Title	Place
2021.08.27	onde ser é estar	Neiva River Ecomuseum, Viana do Castelo
2021.08.06	the mists of time	Maritime Museum, Ílhavo
2021.07.18	hollow murmurs	St Francis Convent, Coimbra
2020.11.26	an indelible testimony	Neighbourhood of Couros, Guimarães

Source: Frederico Dinis, 2024

The method of observing the contextual elements of each location began with engaging with the places, seeking to understand them through extended presence and varied movements within. This approach is particularly evident in the site-specific projects carried out in spaces, which are characterized as a practice of memory. This practice involves the creation of sound and visual narratives, which contribute to the formation of corporeality and influence those who witness them during performative moments.

The site-specific projects result from a systematic methodology, functioning as both a practice of memory and a tangible representation of it. This methodology comprises several stages, including approaching the location, assessing different levels of permanence and information access modalities, establishing a relationship with the place, and outlining specific objectives for each project (Dinis, 2020).

These site-specific projects are essential components in the methodology used to analyse sound and visual performances and their representation of memory and to review the theoretical perspectives presented in this chapter that relate the site-specific, sense of place, ambience, performativity of memory, and audiovisuality.

It is important to note that additional information plays a crucial role in this chapter[2]. In addition to providing access to recordings and images associated with each creation, consulting these materials offers supplementary documentation on the design process, research efforts, presentation aspects, and the reception of each project. These materials deepen understanding and illustrate the pathways of practice-as-research, constituting inherent components of the reflective creative process. The projects ensure the thematic, temporal, and spatial heterogeneity of the practical work conducted within the conceptual framework of this research. They promote the analysis of specific sound and visual elements, their interplay, and their contribution to memory narratives.

FUTURE RESEARCH DIRECTIONS

This research sought to add another sketch to the territory of performance, taking into account the importance of the performativity of memory and the materialisation of experienced ephemerality, through a sound and visual confluence. To pursue this reflection future research opportunities should include the incorporation of other aspects such as storytelling and digital re-enactment processes related to sound and visual representation of memory and practices of remembrance.

CONCLUSION

The concept of performance has been understood through different perceptions resulting from different disciplinary approaches, artistic fields or cultural contexts. Due to this conceptual openness and the diversity of creative practices, performance, as an action before an audience, offers great potential for experimentation through the confluence of sound and visual media.

With its technological appropriation and expansion into other media, performance has stood out among the creative practices of recent decades, allowing a decentralization of the body/performer and thus opening up to other media and other materialities, such as sound or image. In the context of this decentralization, throughout this chapter, the author has sought to re-think and reflect on the importance of the relationship and interconnection between the site-specific, the sense of place, the ambience and the performativity of memory.

The author also observed that intermediate mediation, through sound and visual construction, can promote new interpretations mediated by sound and image, making use of the memory of the spectator. In this way, intermediate forms of memory representation should be seen as a bridge between places, memories and artworks, allowing dialogue and communication between different artistic realities.

Exploring these intermediate forms of memory representation in sound and visual performances has profound implications because the use of intermediate forms allows narrators-performers to access and reinterpret memories in real time. This involves manipulating sound and visual elements to reconstruct memories in ways that evoke specific emotions or narratives, creating a dynamic and immersive experience for the audience.

Intermediate forms of representation also enable performers to convey complex narratives through sound and visuals. By layering different memory representations, performers can create multi-dimensional storytelling experiences that engage the audience on intellectual, emotional, and sensory levels. It also invites audience members to participate actively in the interpretation of the performance. By presenting sound and visual memories in abstract or fragmented forms, performers encourage spectators to construct their meanings and connections, fostering a deeper engagement with the artwork.

Exploring sound and visual representations of memories allows performers to manipulate the temporal aspects of memory, using techniques such as time dilation, compression, or fragmentation to create non-linear narratives that challenge traditional notions of time. Integrating sound and visual representations of memory in live performances can also induce synesthetic experiences, where auditory stimuli evoke visual sensations and vice versa. By synchronizing and intertwining sound and visual elements, performers can create immersive environments that stimulate multiple sensory modalities simultaneously. Sound and visual representations of memory also have the power to evoke strong emotional responses by modulating the intensity and texture of these representations, heightening emotional resonance and creating moments of catharsis or introspection for the audience.

Exploring intermediate representations often involves leveraging cutting-edge technologies, driving innovation in both artistic expression and technological development, and pushing the boundaries of what is possible in live performance. Finally, memory representations can serve as a vehicle for exploring cultural and social themes. By incorporating elements of collective memory or personal experience, performers can engage with issues such as identity, nostalgia, trauma, or cultural heritage, fostering dialogue and reflection within the audience.

So, exploring intermediate forms of sound and visual representation of memory in live performances opens up new artistic possibilities, challenges traditional modes of storytelling, and facilitates deeper audience engagement with the artwork and its underlying themes.

REFERENCES

Augoyard, J.-F. (1995). L'environnement sensible et les ambiances architecturales. *L'Espace Geographique*, 4(4), 302–318. 10.3406/spgeo.1995.3409

Augoyard, J.-F. (1998). Eléments pour une théorie des ambiances architecturales et urbaines. *Les Cahiers de la Recherche Architecturale*, 42/43, 13–23.

Auslander, P. (2006, Spring). Musical Personae. *The Drama Review*, 50(1), 100–119. 10.1162/dram.2006.50.1.100

Bay-Cheng, S., Parker-Starbuck, J., & Saltz, D. Z. (2015). *Performance and media: Taxonomies for a changing field*. University of Michigan Press. 10.3998/mpub.5582757

Bayle, F. (1993). *Musique acousmatique: propositions... positions*. Buchet/Chastel.

Böhme, G. (1993). Atmosphere as the Fundamental Concept of a New Aesthetics. *Thesis Eleven, 36*, 113-126.

Böhme, G. (1997). Aesthetics Knowledge of Nature. *Issues in Contemporary Culture and Aesthetics*, 5, 27–37.

Böhme, G. (2000). Acoustic Atmospheres. A Contribution to the Study of Ecological Aesthetics, Soundscape. *The Journal of Acoustic Ecology*, I(1), 14–18.

Caesar, R. (2012). O som como imagem. In *III SMCT, 2012, São Paulo. Anais do III SMCT*. ECA-USP.

Caesar, R. (2013). A espessura da sonoridade: entre som e imagem. In: *XXIII Anppom, 2013, Natal*. Anais do XXIII Congresso da Anppom. Natal: UFRN.

Caesar, R. (2016). *O enigma de lupe*. Zazie Edições.

Carlson, M. (2004). What is performance? In H. Bial & S. Brady (eds.) *The Performance Studies Reader*. London and New York: Routledge.

Chion, M. (1999). *The Voice in Cinema. Nova York*. Columbia University Press.

Chion, M. (2002). *Le son: traité d'acoulogie*. Nathan/VUEF.

Chion, M. (2006). Le son et l'image. In Soulages, F. (Ed.), *Les Cahiers du Collège iconique: communications et débats*. INA.

Chion, M. (2011). *A Audiovisão: som e imagem no cinema*. Texto & Grafia.

Crimp, D. (1995). *Redening Site Specicity in On the Museum's Ruins*. The MIT Press.

D'Annunzio, G. (1983). *Contemplazioni della morte {1912}. As quoted in G. Bachelard, Water and Dreams: An Essay on the Imagination of Matter*. The Pegasus Foundation.

Dinis, F. (2020). Sinuous Sensations Hypnotic Emotions: Contemporary sound and visual performance [PhD Thesis, Faculty of Arts and Humanities, University of Coimbra. Coimbra: Portugal].

Dinis, F. (2023). Performativity of the Memory of Religious Places through Sound and Image. *Religions*, 14(9), 1137. 10.3390/rel14091137

Dinis, F. (2024). The Production of Effects of Presence in Live Audio-Visual Performances. *Springer Series in Design and Innovation*. Springer. 10.1007/978-3-031-47281-7_72

Féral, J. (2015). Além dos limites: Teoria e prática do teatro. *São Paulo em Perspectiva*, 2015.

Fernandes, S. (2011). Teatralidades e performatividade na cena contemporânea. Repertório. *Teatro & Dança, Salvador*, 16, 11–21.

Fischer-Lichte, E. (2019). *Estética do Performativo*. Orfeu Negro.

Foster, C. (1998). The Narrative and the Ambient in Environmental Aesthetics. *The Journal of Aesthetics and Art Criticism*, 56(2), 127–137. 10.1111/1540_6245.jaac56.2.0127

Fuchs, E. (1985). Presence and the revenge of writing. *Performing Arts Journal*, 9(2/3), 163–173. 10.2307/3245520

Godlovitch, S. (2008). *Musical performance: a philosophical study*. Routledge.

Harbison, I. (2019). *Performing Image*. The MIT Press. 10.7551/mitpress/10973.001.0001

Harrison, R. P. (2008). *Gardens: An Essay on the Human Condition*. The University of Chicago Press. 10.7208/chicago/9780226317861.001.0001

Hedgecoe, J. (2006). *The art of digital photography*. Dorling Kindersley.

Heidegger, M. (1971). *Poetry, language, thought*. Harper and Row.

Hoelscher, S., & Alderman, D. H. (2004). Memory and place: Geographies of a critical Relationship. *Social & Cultural Geography*, 5(3), 347–355. 10.1080/1464936042000252769

Jackson, J. B. (1994). *A sense of place, a sense of time*. Yale University Press.

Kaye, N. (2000). *Site-specic Art: Performance, Place and Documentation*. Routledge.

Kwon, M. (2002). *One Place After Another - Site-Specic Art and Location Identity*. The MIT Press. 10.7551/mitpress/5138.001.0001

Le Goff, J. (1996). *História e Memória*. Editora da UNICAMP.

Lévinas, E. (2012). *Humanismo do outro homem*. Editora Vozes.

Lima, E., & Caldeira, S. (2006). Em busca de novos paradigmas: concepções inusitadas no teatro europeu. In *Das vanguardas à tradição* (17-34). Rio de Janeiro: 7 Letras.

Lippard, L. (1997). *The Lure of the Local: Senses of Place in a Multicultural Society*. The New Press.

Marks, L. U. (2000). *The Skin of the Film: Intercultural Cinema, Embodiment*. Duke University Press.

O'Doherty, B. (1986). *Inside the White Cube – The Ideology of the Gallery Space. São Francisco*. The Lapis Press.

Pallasmaa, J. (2005). *The Eyes of the Skin: Architecture and the Senses.* John Wiley & Sons.

Pareyson, L. (1993). *Estética da Formatividade.* Vozes.

Ricoeur, P. (2006). *Memory, History, Forgetting.* The University of Chicago Press.

Ricgl, A. ({1901} 1985). Die spätrömische Kunstindustrie (Late Roman Art Industry). Roma: Giorgio Bretschneider

Said, E. W. (2000). Invention, memory, and place. *Critical Inquiry,* 26(2), 175–192. 10.1086/448963

Salomão, W. (2014). *Poesia Total.* Companhia das Letras.

Scruton, R. (1976). Representation in Music. [Cambridge: Cambridge University Press.]. *Philosophy (London, England),* 51(197), 197. 10.1017/S0031819100019331

Segaud, M. (2016). *Antropologia do espaço: habitar, fundar, distribuir, transformar.* Edições Sesc São Paulo.

Siepmann, D. (2010). A Slight Delay: Agency and Improvisation in, the Ambient Sound World. *Perspectives of New Music,* 48(1), 174. 10.1353/pnm.2010.0011

Smithson, R. (1996). *Robert Smithson: the collected writings.* University of California Press.

Spielmann, Y. (2004). *Video and Computer: The Aesthetics of Steina and Woody Vasulka.* The Daniel Langlois Foundation.

Tiberghien, G. (2012). Dossiê - Trajetória e interesses: entrevista com Gilles A. Tiberghien. *Revista-Valise,* 2 (3), Porto Alegre.

Toft, T. (2016). *What Urban Media Art Can Do. What Urban Media Art Can Do: Why When Where and How.* Munique: av edition.

Vaz-Pinheiro, G. (2005). *Curadoria do local: algumas abordagens da prática e da crítica.* Torres Vedras: ArtinSite.

Wardrip-Fruin, N. (2006). *Expressive processing: on process-intensive literature and digital media.* [PhD Thesis. Brown University, Providence, Rhode Island].

Westgeest, H. (2008). The Changeability of Photography in Multimedia Artworks. Belfast: Leuven University Press.

Witkin, S. L. (2011). Why Do We Think Practice Research is a Good Idea? *Social Work & Society,* 9(1), 10–19.

Wood, H. H., & Byatt, A. S. (2008). *Memory an anthology.* Chatto & Windus.

ADDITIONAL READING

Auslander, P. (1999). *Liveness: Performance in a Mediatized Culture.* Routledge.

Bolter, J. D., Grusin, R., & Grusin, R. A. (2000). *Remediation: Understanding new media*. The MIT Press.

Chapple, F., & Kattenbelt, C. (Eds.). (2006). *Intermediality in theatre and performance*. Rodopi. 10.1163/9789401210089

Connerton, P. (1989). *How Societies Remember*. Cambridge University Press. 10.1017/CBO9780511628061

Daniels, D. (2016). *Silence and Void. The Oxford Handbook of Sound and Image in Western Art*, 315. Oxford Press.

Dixon, S. (2007). *Digital performance: a history of new media in theater, dance, performance art, and installation*. The MIT Press. 10.7551/mitpress/2429.001.0001

Giannachi, G., & Kaye, N. (2011). *Performing Presence: Between the live and the simulated*. Manchester University Press.

Kaye, N. (2007). *Multi-Media: video–installation–performance*. Routledge. 10.4324/9780203964897

Nelson, R. (2013). *Practice as research in the arts: Principles, protocols, pedagogies, resistances*. Springer. 10.1057/9781137282910

KEY TERMS AND DEFINITIONS

Appropriating Space: Establishing a relationship between that space and the 'self' (making it one's own) through a set of practices.

Audiovisuality: A place of images and sounds.

Narrator-Performer: The artist throughout the spatial occupation.

Observer-Performer: The artist after the spatial reading.

Observer-Receiver: The audience.

Sense of Place: A vivid awareness of familiar surroundings, a ritual repetition, a sense of community-based on shared experience.

Site-Specific Artworks: Practices in which exchanges are articulated between the artwork and the places in which its meanings are defined.

ENDNOTES

[1]   Other authors have also addressed the aesthetics of ambience, including Martin Seel, Yuriko Saito, Pierre Sansot, Henri Maldiney, Herman Schmitz and Michael Hauskeller.

[2]   Available at: https://fredericodinis.wordpress.com/performance/p-a-r/

Chapter 14
You Can Put Your Arms Around a Memory:
Popular Music and Archives

Paula Guerra
http://orcid.org/0000-0003-2377-8045
Institute of Sociology, University of Porto, Portugal

Pedro Quintela
http://orcid.org/0000-0003-2383-342X
Institute of Sociology, University of Porto, Portugal

ABSTRACT

In contemporary societies, the urgent acquisition of information is vital, reflecting in the (sub)(post) cultural dynamics of youth cultures. However, despite all these urgent needs, there are also attempts to preserve memory and heritage, especially in the Portuguese alternative and underground music scenes. Archives play an important role in structuring self-help projects for enthusiasts that challenge dominant notions of archiving. The democratisation of archives, facilitated by digital technologies, emphasises community-driven initiatives and challenges traditional notions of neutrality. This chapter explores the theoretical, methodological, and ethical dimensions surrounding the preservation of punk manifestations in Portugal, filling gaps in cultural and academic representation. The KISMIF archive represents a pioneering attempt to document Portuguese underground music scenes, revealing previously unknown cultural realities.

THE MEMORY TURN: INTRODUCTION

In contemporary societies, the instantaneous attainment of information has closely become a demand. This is no less true in the (sub)(post)cultural dynamics of youth cultures (Muggleton and Weinzierl, 2003). Paradoxically, that same informational urgency is accompanied by an interest in the preservation of memory, past experiences, and a search for 'territories' of ontological safety, return to roots and heritage, as well as community participation (Loff, Piedade and Soutelo, 2015). It is precisely in this context that archives on alternative and underground manifestations, which are being built on the Portuguese

DOI: 10.4018/979-8-3693-2264-2.ch014

contemporary music scenes, on a more or less formal way, are explicitly important. Serving as memory deposits (objects and recordings, both audio and video graphic), kept with a tremendous 'love of art and music', they structure many of the self-improvement projects of lovers and *connoisseurs* of these music scenes (Bennett, 2014). Much like Featherstone (2006) said 'today, the desire to archive is a powerful impulse of contemporary culture'. In this article, we seek to approach the importance of archives to a sociological analysis of (sub)(post)cultural expressions. We will focus on the various forms that compose the modern archives: photography, record covers, concert tickets, posters, documentaries, newspapers and magazine clippings, fanzines and other independent, self-edited and self-distributed DIY publications.

Indeed, there has been a growing interest in these (sub)(post)cultural expressions, something which has been reflected by the increase in the production, exposition and acquisition of these DIY objects: fanzines, 'artist books', photos, album covers, memorabilia, author editions and other self-edited publications. These are produced in bordering on artisanal way, distributed independently, and are nowadays beginning to be seen in record and book shops, art galleries and museums, as well as in several other non-conventional places both online and offline (Dale, 2010). In an interesting approach to the systems of legitimacy of mainstream art (Marcus, 2000), this in turn has led to a growing investment by some academic and cultural institutions in the recollection, analysis and preservation of production efforts associated with an underground (sub) culture.

In this paper, we start by offering a brief review of the process that has led the (growing) interest of social scientists towards the importance of recollection, analysis and preservation of sub cultural productions, restructuring deeply the notions of archive, heritage and memory. From here, we seek to approach some of the challenges and questions posed to those who have attempted to build these types of archives (Guerra and Quintela, 2020). In this sense, we focus on the development of an archive of punk manifestations in Portugal in the last 40 years. The Portuguese case has an almost endless myriad of specificities. It emerged in a post-revolutionary period of political demobilization after politically intense years. In a country crystallized in time – socially, politically, and culturally –, the 'punk movement' came to shake the political and social environment. It signalled a possible path of modernity and cosmopolitanism, an opening of Portuguese society to the aesthetic-cultural experiments that were taking place in the United Kingdom. All this did not fail to influence the Portuguese process of transition to democracy, in the sense that it provided an opening in the universe of possibilities for a youth eager to experience new sonorities and aesthetic sensibilities in line with what was happening in the rest of Europe (and in the United States of America). Despite this social, political, and cultural importance, a veil of invisibility by a part of academic and cultural institutions, fell on the punk movement. In fact, so far very few academic studies in Portugal have dealt with the depth and complexity of punk (Guerra, 2013).

Hence the relevance of the research project 'Keep it Simple, Make it Fast! (KISMIF)' can be seen. The aim of the KISMIF[1] investigation project was to contribute to the social knowledge, by taking into consideration the changes in Portuguese society between 1978 and 2013. We sought to systematically study the diverse contexts where the various expressions of punk took place, listening to different social actors associated with this 'movement' in Portugal, while choosing a synchronic and diachronic posture, blending time and space. It was then, of utmost importance that there should be a systematic gathering of empirical data. This included: (i) interviews with key-elements who are or related to punk scenes in Portugal in different historic periods; (ii) ethnographic observation of punk events; and (iii) recollection and cataloguing of various materials related to punk manifestations in Portugal, including sound recordings, videos, flyers, and posters. For the purpose of this article, we approach the process of constructing and making public such an archive of punk productions in Portugal, which is one of the aspects that we consider of utmost relevance.

This is taking into considerations that, as aforementioned, expressions of punk were – and still are, to some respect missing from the social science investigation agenda. They are equally missing from the mainstream media, who when depicting punk, limit themselves to stereotypes and clichéd notions. The construction of an archive, dedicated to the memory of this urban culture is then, a relevant instrument of research for the construction of a counter-history in Portugal, shedding light on a socio-historical reality that, despite its strong dynamics, remains largely unknown and invisible in Portuguese society[2].

The *corpus* of the KISMIF archive, with a website, which emerged in 2013 – has until now, a wide array of artefacts and entries. It has 177 fanzine editions; a database with 788 Portuguese punk bands; a database with 1,429 phonographic records; 800 covers of phonographic records; the lyrics of 400 Portuguese punk songs; over a thousand photographs; and 760 newspaper and magazine articles related to punk in Portugal, amongst a myriad of other things[3].

AND POPULAR MUSIC GOES TO MUSEUM: MEMORY, ARCHIVES, AND HERITAGE

Increasingly, history is dispersed in several spheres: popular culture, community archivism, etc – a form of public history that has faced, and shaped, the traditional practices of historians, marked by a fetishization of archives. Likewise, it endeavours to facilitate more democratic, personal and localized forms of knowledge - particularly since baby boomers now need to present all the memorabilia that have been accompanying them as music lovers, a condition of reaffirmation and identity belonging, which cannot be dissociated from the important phenomenon of *retromania* (Reynolds, 2011). This movement of 'public history' was further boosted by the emergence and diffusion of digital technologies, with we-blogs, websites, digital archives emerged and maintained by crowdfunding, for example. If archives are the essence from which we build our stories, we must agree that this means that various social groups have plenty of reasons to be dissatisfied with the ways their stories are represented. Hence the impor-tance of community (Flinn, 2007) or DIY (Baker and Huber, 2013) archives, that exist to document and explore local and community histories without 'institutional filters'. In addition to the advantages of a local archival work for communities, including the empowerment that goes with it, we must consider the importance that these projects have for a thick description of the reality studied – a more detailed way of knowing the corporate reality, whether British, Portuguese or European. To do this, it is necessary to make the archives more representative of the cultural, artistic, ethnic, racial and political diversity that permeates contemporary societies. This critical positioning of the way in which archives are constituted has led to the questioning of the traditional vision of the archivist as a neutral actor, a mere facilitator of historic research. As Flinn defends, the archivist is 'a central conspirator of the way through which investigations are led, as well as a conspirator of the histories that archives tell'. (Flinn, 2012, p. 24) In this way, a first and decisive step would be the acceptance of the ever partial, intentional, and contingent, process of the creation and development of an archive and of the role of the archivist.

In this context of profound questioning – how archives were built, who built them and why, what perspectives were represented, and which were excluded – there is yet another important question re-lated to the user-friendliness. The accessibility of the different segments of audiences to archives is a crucial aspect for those who study the 'counter-history', with frequent tensions between, on one side, archivists and historians who claim to rigorously record, preserve, and treat the materials, and on the other, all those who defend the need of these archives for public access (Featherstone, 2006: 593). This counter-history, fomented by the democratic potential of online culture, aims to objectify the multiple voices, minority groups or underground aesthetic-cultural movements, omitted in the traditional archival process. It is therefore a question of facing the archives as a political issue: that is, they are containers of democratic plurality, allowing the expression of new stories, and reversing what Hoyle calls 'symbolic annihilation' of the social differences and cultural particularities carried out by the institutional archives (Hoyle, 2017, p.2).

All these positions and perspectives have led to a profound process of transformation and reconfiguration of the archives, with new approaches steadily rising. Particularly, the processes of gathering and archiving of information developed autonomously and independently – be it on an individual or a communitary/institutional level (Baker and Huber, 2013) – have growingly become more relevant. We can see this through the recent development of new conceptual approaches that focus on interpreting emerging archivist practices, giving emphasis to community-driven projects concerning memory and heritage, the latter being seen as vital for the preserving of history. Important concepts in this respect include, namely, the ones of 'independent or communitary archives', (Flinn, 2012) 'autonomous archives', (Moore and Pell, 2010) 'archivistic activism' (Rosenzweig and Thelen, 1998),'domestic archives' (Moran, 2010), 'popular archives' (Mckee, 2011) and 'DIY archives' (Bennett, 2014).

Moreover, it is precisely in this context that there has been a growing debate over the need to widen the participation in archival practices, going beyond just the archivists and similar specialists (which include, namely, social scientists). Recent technological developments, and the affirmation of the Web 2.0 paradigm, are crucial in this process, offering new opportunities for the gathering, storage, cataloguing and accessibility of these archives. In this sense, we can talk about a digital presence that has served to shift the notions of the conventional archive, whilst revealing its potential (Geiger, Moore, and Savage, 2010). This new digital environment has also allowed the implementation of communitarian and collaborative practices, namely allowing members of certain communities to upload new materials and memories, as well as introducing commentary over pre-existent materials, widening, and enriching the information present in these structures (Flinn, 2012, pp. 17-19; Huvila, 2008). This is once again a matter of accepting multiple points of view, incorporating them in the archives, as well as stimulating the participation of all the people to their own development. This means that archives should be open to specialists (archivists, historians, sociologists, and other social scientists), in the same way as to other users who, though lacking in technical or academic knowledge, have a different know-how as well as different expectations which need to be considered (Huvila, 2008).

Finally, it should be noted that interest in these archive-related issues lies above all in the Anglo-Saxon reality, as can be seen from a set of conferences, newspapers, books and, most importantly, community museums and DIY, as well as examples of DIY preservationist. Likewise, if we analyse these concerns historically, we can trace their genesis in the antiquarianism of the 17th century to the movements in the 1960s and 1970s of the History Workshop and the recovery of oral history, essentially aimed at recording and disseminating the stories of working-class communities (Flinn, 2007).

However, for all that has been mentioned, ethical dilemmas are more pressing in this archival process. How will the collection, selection, organization and dissemination take place? In the background, these are issues that affect all archives, but which here, due to their characteristics, are even more relevant and complex. As Duncombe stated, 'alternative culture has already been discovered—the more important question is who will represent it and how?' (Duncombe, 1997, p.20).

Let's look at the case of the fanzines. Given its reduced circulation, a good way to ensure their preservation would be through scanning. However, Woodbrook and Lazzaro speak about the possibility of this disclosure provoking contradictory reactions in their authors, namely the exposure of their ideas and art. Likewise, given that fanzines are made for a very small audience, and sometimes just for a small circle of friends, when they are made available online for anyone wishing to consult, this can cause friction with the authors.

On the other hand, considering that we are dealing with documents that express emotions, this accentuates the problems in the organization and systematization of the archive. That is, there is the desire to operationalize and create a coherence in the archive, looking for continuities between the different fanzines, characterize them according to certain components, etc. (Woodbrok and Lazzaro, 2013).

Additionally, there are specific issues pertaining to digital archives. For example, many of the individuals who manage and maintain these files do not have copyright law concerns. This has led, for example, to some blogs and websites being closed by Google for infringement against the Digital Millennium Copyright Act (DMCA). This closure, in many cases, entails the total loss of all stored material. Thus, in addition to the subsequent lack of motivation to recover all the work done, since we cannot forget the high investment of free time (Arvidsson, 2008) by individuals, there may also be the dissolution of communities that sometimes form around such archives (Collins and Long, 2014). Therefore, these informal archival practices are located in the digital world, resulting in informality in dealing with the problems that can arise from copyright law[4].

Similarly, Garde-Hansen warns against the problems that come from leaving in the hands of digital companies, such as Facebook, the ability to guard the archives. That is, as guardians, these companies have the power to determine in what way the archive is processed and its respective disclosure, in order to enhance the commercial interests of its activities (Garde-Hansen, 2009, p. 136). On the other hand, there is the consequence of the fact that online archives are located on online servers, from which they are paid, especially in a long-term perspective, namely those archives created and maintained by only one person. Basically, who keeps the projects after the first generation has withdrawn?

Finally, we cannot fail to mention the complex relationships between DIY or informal archives and institutional archives, often marked by some kind of distrust (Cvetkovich, 2003). And this creates very unstable relationships marked by mutual misunderstandings when it exists at all. For example, members of these communities who are dedicated to preserving and disseminating musical archives with strong DIY principles are often hesitant to open their archives to institutional organizations which are perceived as distant and out-of-touch. One of the reasons is related to the concerns by subcultures – such as punk rock – of disclosing compromising or personal information, such as alcohol consumption or illegal concerts, to outsiders (Hamel, Ann, Maher, O'Dwyer, and Coo, 2014). One possibility to overcome this mistrust may be through insider-researchers who also take a subcultural turn. For example, Meriwether talks about the advantages of belonging to both the academy and the subculture of Grateful Dead fans, allowing him to build bridges between spheres deeply suspicious of each other. The reason seems to be simple: it is easier to share this long and costly work to acquaintances than to strangers (Meriwether, 2012). We consider that the explanation of this theoretical contribution - relative to the archives and the (recent) questions of centrality and extension of the notion of archive in contemporaneity - is particularly relevant to understand the various theoretical, methodological, and ethical options we have taken in the KISMIF archive. These questions are addressed below, after an approach to the punk 'movement' in Portugal.

PORTUGAL, PUNK, AND (POST)MODERNISM

Unlike the Anglo-Saxon countries, Portugal is in world-systems theory (Wallerstein, 1980) in a semi-peripheral position (Santos, 1990), with all that this entails in terms of economic, social and cultural development. It is also important to mention that, between 1926 and 1974, Portugal was under a dictatorship. The rural world and its traditional 'modes' were highly acclaimed by the 'New State' regime as the 'true and genuine condition of the Portuguese people', alongside socio-political structures based on low skills, protectionist politics, and closed borders; society was plagued by male dominance, religious oppression, censorship, and low access to information and communication (Barreto, 1996). During those times, the lack of knowledge of what happened 'outside' the country disabled and delayed any attempts to penetrate the imposing unknown; all had been planned so that the population did not muster any desire to change their lives for the better (Guerra and Bennett, 2015).

Although all this has undergone enormous changes after the revolution of 25 April 1974, this remains a past that is difficult to surpass: Portugal still suffers from a chronic economic, social and cultural backwardness with other European countries, the latest positions in indicators advanced by the OECD and Eurostat (Pordata, 2017). As might be expected, culture and its cultural industry in many cases continue to be seen as non-essential, a luxury, and therefore chronically under-invested. We are even faced with low rates of collective and political mobilization (Cabral, 2014). All this explain, in part, the almost nonexistence of programs and practices oriented to the institution of community museums and / or DIY. Apart from the case of some blogs, the very occurrence of 'DIY preservationism practices' (Bennett, 2009) in Portugal can be classified, at best, as tiny and/or scattered (Guerra and Quintela, 2021). Even in musical genres traditionally considered Portuguese, such as *fado*[5], we observed that the Fado Museum[6], inaugurated in 1998, only developed its digital sound archive in 2016.

Despite all this, the April Revolution, ending forty years of fascism and country's isolation, worked certainly as a catalyst for new initiatives and demonstrations. In this sense, the social climate was favourable for the manifestation of youth subcultures and, especially, punk in Portugal. Not yet a unified 'movement', the first punk groups appeared in the late- 1970s as more of an artistic reaction to an aesthetic *status quo*. These first punk groups were somehow linked to the emergence of alternative rock in Portugal, thus taking on a central role in the history of rock music in the country (Guerra, 2010).

It is only from the 1980s, however, during what may be called a 'second wave' of Portuguese punk, that the 'movement' shows signs of major invigoration in Portugal. This was not only a symbol of cultural and musical resistance to a status quo, but also a concrete expression of an urban movement focused on music, fashion and a bohemian lifestyle. Importantly, at this point, punk became more than a music genre: it was a *modus vivendi* for a set of youngsters located in specific residential zones, namely in Lisbon. The local re-appropriations of the punk sonority support Dunn's claim (2008) that punk rock is a clear example of 'cultural hybridism' since it is not the same everywhere; instead, it is locally moulded and redefined according to each space's social and political resources and needs in a process that mixes characteristics of global punk with local elements. Accordingly, Errickson (1999) explains the social-historical specificities of the movement's origin in the USA and in UK showing its plasticity and consequent adaptability to life contexts and agreeing with Bennett's theses about the consolidation of local musical scenes.

In the 1990s, punk expands geographically from the two main Portuguese urban centres, Lisbon and Porto to their peripheries and also to other regions, and also expands politically, with the emergence of new 'causes' and issues such as the veganism and animal rights, the fight against racism and squatting movements. It was a time of great effervescence for hardcore punk and, above all, a time when the 'movement' assumed its presence and took its place according to the actions of its militants (Silva and Guerra, 2015). Nowadays, the importance of punk as a movement, a scene and a lifestyle in the Portuguese context continues to be of a great relevance for two major reasons. First, the recent context of economic crisis and social precariousness (Hespanha and Caleiras, 2017) has been accentuating the recourse to punk both as a word and as a praxis, namely in what concerns everyday forms of livelihood that are linked to a DIY ethos concerning housing, work and urban sociabilities and conviviality. Thus, this is not so much an artistic and musical revival of punk, but rather its affirmation as a lifestyle of resistance to the economic collapses and social turmoil of the Portuguese society. Interestingly, many of these initiatives come from people who usually do not produce or listen to punk music, but who use the word 'punk' as a life *motto* and an active way of demanding dignity. Secondly, and possibly less intensely than in countries like Spain or Greece, there is a strengthening of punk movements that turn towards political struggle and the struggle for a *right to the city*, namely by demanding access to unoccupied or abandoned urban spaces (Leccardi et al, 2012). These (re)emergent dynamics point out to the possibility of concretization of a punk lifestyle of resistance and struggle against the system based on housing, music, organization of common resources and edification of alternative sociability spaces.

THE PORTUGUESE PUNK ARCHIVE: *MORE THAN CARNATIONS AND COCA-COLA*[7]

The Genesis of the KISMIF Archive: *Remember is Living*

Unofficial histories suppressed memories and strategies of resistance all converge in the KISMIF archive. Rather than a nostalgic look at the past, this archive re-activates and repurposes key emblems and stories of punk. The ambition of constructing an archive that connected the diverse expressions of punk in Portugal, throughout an existence of nearly 40 years, is placed in this wide context of discussion that we have been exploring. The discussion gains particular relevance in what concerns the reflection, questioning and redefinition of the notions of archive, heritage and memory in contemporary societies, especially in the social sciences (Samuel, 1994, p.1). One of the central issues of this critical approach on archives and historical-heritage institutions is related to the partial and sectarian treatment of groups, social classes or communities (Hall, 1999) – including popular cultures. In Portugal, this issue is specifically accurate, because systematic approaches of the social sciences (and sociology in particular) to the multiplicity of urban popular cultures, from a social-historic point of view, are still relatively rare in Portugal.

However, the changes in the perception of this field of study have already been felt: the study of popular music has started to gain acceptance as a legitimate area of scholarship within the academy in Portugal. In the same way that many genres and forms of popular music from the twentieth and twenty-first century have become institutionalised and honoured through organisations such as the US's Rock and Roll Hall of Fame[8] or the UK's Beatles Story Museum[9], the study of this topic has developed its own canonic form of key works, lauded authors, conferences and preferred methodologies. If this is generally true for popular music in Portugal, it is less true for the specific case of punk, as we stated above.

The KISMIF Archive (see Figure 1 and 2), which has characteristics of two of Baker and Huber's ideal-types, the 'Online – institutional' and the 'Online – community' (Baker and Huber, 2013), had its beginning in 2012, with the collection of materials linked to the Portuguese punk scene in the scope of the research project "Keep it Simple, Make it Fast". It is an archive under development that aims to make the materials available, especially through its own website, launched by the end of 2013, and also through a set of exhibitions that were carried from 2012 onwards, as we will explain in detail below.

Over the last few years, the project team has been able to collect a variety of materials: about 5000 photographs, 1000 posters, 300 fanzines, 750 newspaper / magazine news, 400 song lyrics, 800 band information, 1200 album covers, audio of 150 records. This documents were mainly collected through (i) the donation or lending of materials for scanning, generally obtained through the interviewees (who, in some way, are or were connected to the punk scene); (ii) online research of materials, and, whenever possible, the downloading of these materials; (iii) the purchase of materials directly from the authors/ editors, or indirectly through concerts, public events, community centers, squads, etc.; and (iv) the permission to access to the personal collections of some KISMIF researchers.

Figure 1. Layout of the punk archive's site

(Punk.pt (http://www.punk.pt))

Figure 2. Layout of the punk archive's site (Punk.pt

(http://www.punk.pt))

With due differences, it is possible to establish parallels between this archive and other international archives focused on punk history, such as the *DC Punk and Indie Fanzine Collection of the University of Maryland*, concerned with documenting the punk and indie scene in Washington from the 1970s. From the same city, we can also speak of the recent, founded in 2014, *DC Punk Archive*, located in the DC Public Library. This archive is of particular interest because the idea came after a documentary about the punk scene and to build a space to conserve the various private archives. Still in the United States of America, the *Punk History Archive*, at Cornell University. In European reality, we can speak, for example, of the projects *Observing the 80s*, of the University of Sussex, the *Mass Observation Project & British Library Oral History*, which proposes to recover a set of voices of the British population in order to obtain a more democratic knowledge of British reality in the 1980s[10]; one the other hand, the *Punk in the East* project, organized by Matthew Worley, who tried to document the history of punk in the city of Norwich, and who was concerned to get a top-down perspective of this reality[11].

As Manoff (2004) argues, the promotion of this interdisciplinary dialog is of a particular relevance in the current context, when, as we have seen, archives have become growingly polysemic and have a wide dominion, in which traditional archivists and librarians work alongside researchers from other disciplinary areas, especially in the field of the social sciences. Another key challenge is how to conceive and develop the databases in which this archive is based, contrasting, and balancing different interests and perspectives: those of the researchers, of the archivists, of the librarians and those of the future users of the archive, be them academics or not[12].

Methodologically, another important challenge has to do with the cataloguing and analysis of this type of documentation. Since it was not possible to find specific guidelines for a content analysis of fanzines in the scientific literature, it was necessary to develop a proper methodology for content analysis of fanzines and e-zines. For this reason, it is useful to present, even in an abbreviated way, the way in which the database was structured that allowed the data processing and the development of this content analysis.

Thus, a database was conceived that includes a total of 18 fields of description and analysis of the various documents on archive. The first level of analysis includes generic characterization aspects of the publication, such as the identification of its name; date of publication; specification of the publisher's name[13]; identification of the geographical origin of the publisher[14]; the cost[15]. On a second level, graphic and editorial aspects are described, such as the total number of pages; the general graphical aspect[16]; the type of print[17]. In a third level, all fanzines included in the database are catalogued according to different formats / typologies[18]. Finally, in a fourth level, the content of each fanzine analysed, including the identification of the type of articles[19]; present images[20]; of topics discussed; of the band names mentioned/discussed[21]; as well as national and international 'scenes' and 'subscenes', which are mentioned / discussed[22].

Another important question that has arisen since the beginning of this research is related to the identification of the best strategy to gather and build up/structure a collection of Portuguese punk fanzines that, as far as possible, was able to cover the broad temporal spectrum of almost forty years which we intended to cover. One of the main difficulties is related to the underground nature of these publications, which generally have very small print runs and restricted circulation to very limited distribution circuits, making access difficult. Note also the only recent character of a patrimonialist conception associated with this type of independent publications, capable of valuing the fanzines as documents of historical relevance, either from the point of view of their remittances or their artistic-cultural value. For this reason, many fanzines have been discarding these objects over time, making it difficult to access and analyse older publications. In fact, in the course of fieldwork, we were often confronted with respondents who expressed regret that they did not have their collection of punk fanzines that they inadvertently destroyed or deposited in uncertain places.

On the other hand, in the case of craft objects, published independently and distributed in underground circuits, fanzines are not obliged to deposit copies in libraries or public archives. In addition, and contrary to what is already being practiced in other countries, there are still rare libraries and archives in Portugal with collections of independent self-published publications - namely, 'artist's books' and fanzines.[23] Exceptionally, one can mention the case of Bedeteca of Lisbon[24], an equipment integrated in the Network of Municipal Libraries of Lisbon and a partner entity of KISMIF. The Bedeteca of Lisbon has an important collection of fanzines and other independent publications, as well as promoting several exhibitions, fairs and exhibitions, events dedicated to independent publishing (particularly those linked to comics and drawing). It is also possible to mention the cases of the Art Libraries of the Calouste Gulbenkian Foundation[25] (Lisbon) and the Serralves Foundation[26] (Porto), whose collections of independent publications are essentially oriented to the visual arts, design and visual poetry. Particularly in the case of the Serralves Foundation, it should be noted that, in recent years, several exhibitions have been regularly held around independent publishing and artist book, mostly curated by Guy Schraenen[27].

Likewise, contrary to the relevance we find in some of the international literature on more informal archival practices and DIY, which, as we have seen, find on the Internet a particularly relevant context for making and preserving documents, information and other artefacts of contemporary popular culture (Bennett, 2009; Baker and Huber, 2013; Collins, 2014), in the Portuguese punk scene are still relatively scarce the examples of this kind of DIY preservation practices. Although there are some weblogs in Portugal – such as *Under Review*[28], *Ephemera*[29], *Rock no Liceu* [Rock In Highschool] [30] or *Rock nas Cadeias* [Rock in Jails] [31], for example – which, on a somewhat regular basis, have been posting online scanned pictures of punk artefacts such as record covers, concert tickets and posters, as well as pictures or press clipping, sometimes including additional information about the context, we could not help but notice the decisive role of personal collections and testimonies, of aficionados of the scene, in the history of punk. While these collectionist practices are related to the preservationist spirit of contemporary DIY, it seems to us that they may not be called archival practices strictly speaking as they hold no value, nor do they have the technical procedures in cataloguing, preserving and promoting the material associated with an archive, even one of a DIY or informal nature. In this way, the constitution of a punk archive in Portugal, which is duly organised in terms of a catalogue, search and access, seems to us to be of the utmost importance in its capacity to lend a more structured and systematic look at the Portuguese punk scene in its whole.

As Derrida argued, an archive is never finished, and is in constant struggle with its contents. It is important to consider how such a collection can be promoted and updated (Derrida, 1996). This in turn leads us to the importance of having the authors, editors and fans as collaborators of the archive, so that they may regularly contribute with new documents, as well as add information to previously analysed material. Huvila proposes a shift in archival practices, defending an 'active archivism', in which the curatorial work is not centralised and there is a sharing of functions between archivists and users (Huvila, 2008). In a context of building an online punk archive, we argue that it is equally important to consider the possibility of users contributing new materials, commentary and observations which can enrich, complete and even rectify the information present in the archive. For this reason, and given its nature as a constantly updated platform striving to be as complete as possible, the KISMIF punk archive assumes the possibility of sharing all sorts of material related to the Portuguese punk scene through an e-mail address.

It is important to note that the scarce financial and human resources, the limited knowledge of archiving by the team (the KISMIF project team, although scientifically well-trained, has no specialized element in archiving practices) and the lack of space capable of housing all these materials make this issue even more difficult to make available to the public. In this sense, in addition to the option to make available most of the materials on an online platform, there was the need, since the beginning, for an articulation between the team of researchers of KISMIF (specialists in the areas of sociology, psychology, anthropology, history, and social communication) and the team of librarians at the Library of the Faculty of Arts and Humanities of the University of Porto[32].

Furthermore, and as we mentioned above, online archives have their own specific challenges. The KISMIF Archive is no exception: the fact that financial resources are scarce requires the team itself to manage the virtual platform, something not easy taking into account the scientific origins of each member of the team. Beyond this, the virtual availability of materials makes the copyright issue even more problematic, often difficult to overcome due to: (i) unclear and insufficient legislation; (ii) the difficulty (and even the impossibility) of contacting the authors: some of them have already died and it was not possible to trace down some of the others or even to identify them, either because nobody knows them, or because they often did not sign their "art-works", or because they adopted nicknames that made it impossible to recognize their identity; and (iii) the lack of human, financial and temporal resources to establish contact with all authors.

Another challenge was (and still is) how to undertake a public promotion of this online archive (see figures 3, 4 and 5), not only opening its use to the specific community, but also considering the various possible strategies of presenting the vast documentation collected. Another issue is related to the communication and public dissemination of this kind of archive, which requires diverse approaches in order to guarantee its effective openness to consultation and participation by the community concerned – a matter that warrants particular attention given that many of the participants in the 'scene' punk are apologists of an independent, autonomous and DIY positioning and, therefore, often refractory to approaches from the academy[33].

Figure 3. God Save The Portuguese Fanzines' exhibition poster by Júlio Dolbeth

(Punk.pt (http://www.punk.pt))

Figure 4. MATTERxANTIMATTER=FRAGMENTS' exhibition poster by Júlio Dolbeth, 2014

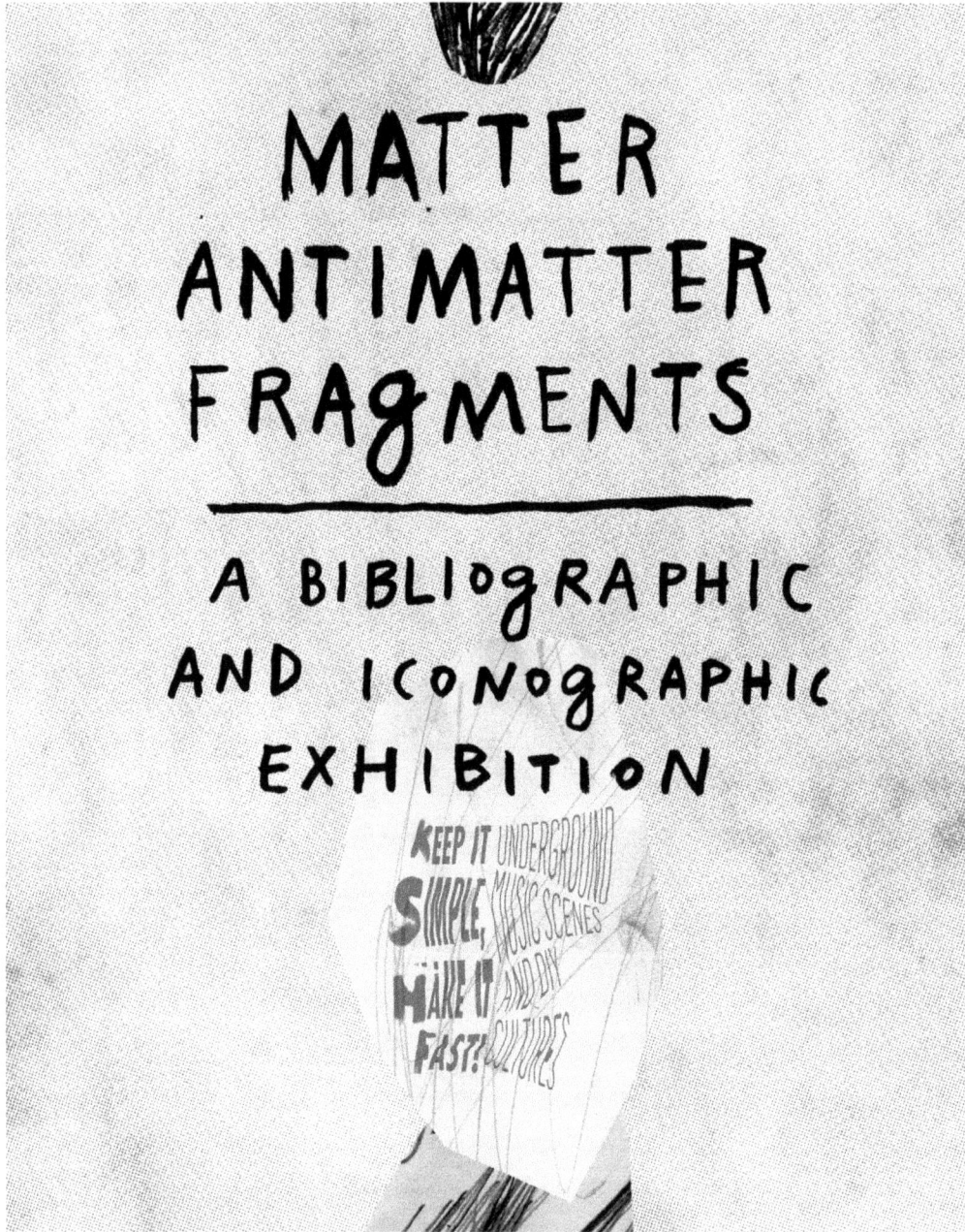

International Conference Keep It Simple, Make It Fast! Underground Music Scenes and DIY Cultures
8 July – 10 September 2014
Library, Faculty of Arts of the University of Porto

(Punk.pt (http://www.punk.pt))

Figure 5. DIY DIY my Darling! Outspace zines & records' exhibition poster by Marcos Farrajota

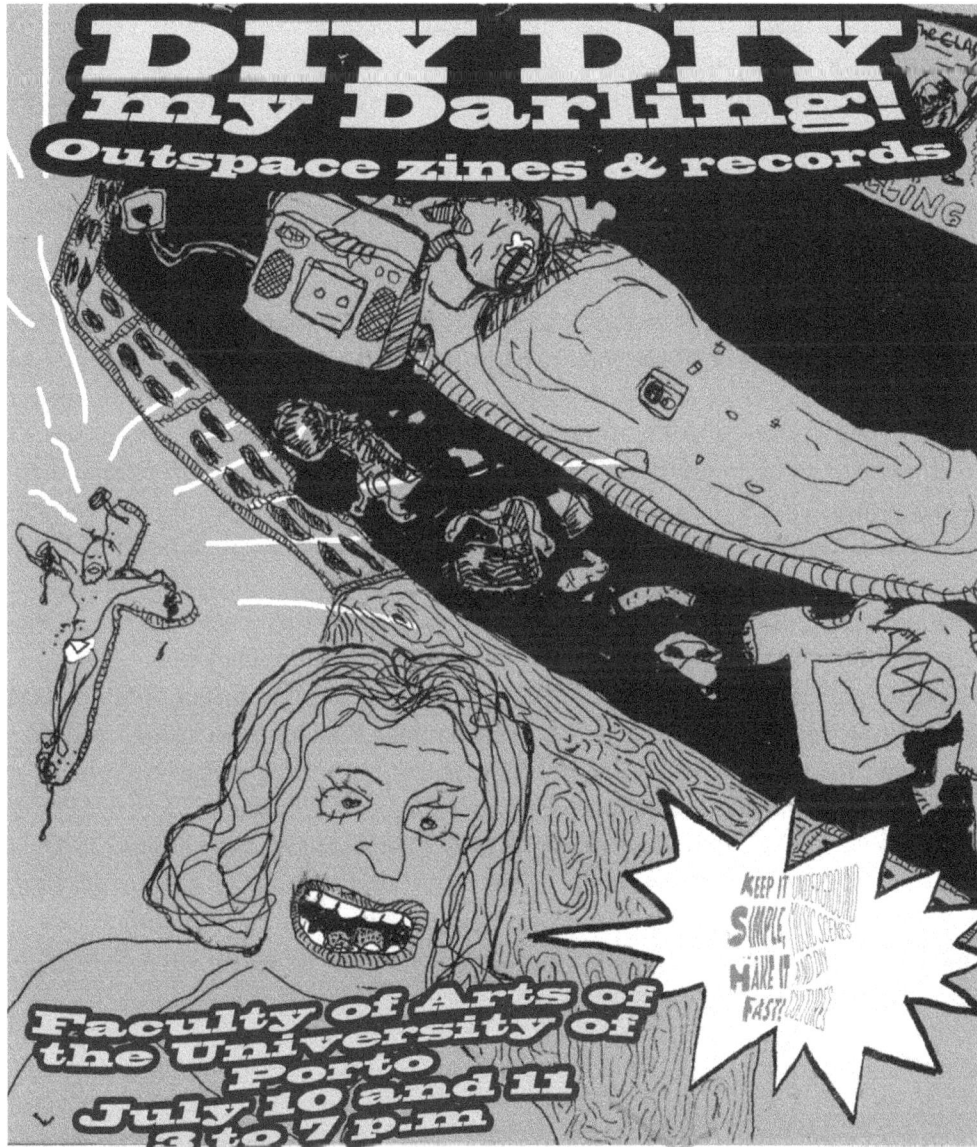

(Marcos Farrajota)

The KISMIF Archive: Remember and Resist

Before we approach the strategies of public dissemination of the KISMIF archive, we must first make a brief analysis of the dilemmas that affect these strategies of public dissemination, namely through curated exhibitions. Although all exhibitions have at their core dilemmas and doubts about what and how to spread and expose, when the theme is punk (or other underground subcultures) the difficulties grow exponentially, since we have to take into account its complex history with the academy and media (Baker, 2015; Baker, Doyle and Shane, 2016; Bennett, 2009; Strong, 2015; van Dijck, 2006).

The introduction of punk in museums, as exhibitions or as museums of and for themselves, can be explained by theories of collective memories, counter memory, cultural memory (Assmann, 2012) or the consecration of a culture by its inclusion in a collective, often national heritage. The change of a public and vivid communication about punk to an institutional preservation in a punk museum could be interpreted as a transfer from a 'functional' communicative memory (with a contemporary meaning and relevance) to a 'storage' cultural memory (archived in storage spaces and obsolete). It has to be examined whether a 'museumification' of pop music/punk is indeed a transformation into a 'dead' storage memory (this implies a certain and normative assessment of museums as conventional high culture institutions). On the contrary, the introduction of punk in museums and exhibition halls might not only include consecration as an important cultural artefact but also a revival of this popular culture as multiplier and booster of collective identities (Kirchberg, 2016). This timely function of museums as an important societal objective has been well received among museum scholars.

The developing of museums of punk culture has been a recent phenomenon. For instance, the *Ramones Museum* in Berlin opened in 2005, the *Los Angeles Punk Rock Museum* in 2012, and the *Icelandic PUNK Museum* in 2016. In addition, also several other museums have staged Punk exhibitions only in the last three years. In Germany these were the exhibitions: 'Geniale Dilletanten' [Great Dilettantes] in the Haus der Kunst München in 2015, 'Story of Punk Rock' in the Spohr Museum Kassel in 2017, and 'Oh Yeah' about Pop and Punk at the Museum for Communication Berlin in 2017/18. In the United States we found recent exhibitions about the 'L.A. Punk band X' at the Grammy Museum in Los Angeles in 2017, about Punk fashion 'PUNK: Chaos to Couture' at the Metropolitan Museum of Art in New York in 2013, and the Ramones exhibition 'Hey! Ho! Let's Go' at the Queens Museum in 2016. Most of these exhibitions received mixed reviews: The New York Daily Beast commented on the opening of the Ramones exhibition in Queens with the header 'A Museum Is the Worst Place to Celebrate Punk and The Ramones'. The New York Times printed the headline 'Punk Rock Doesn't Belong in a Museum' about the idea to convert the defunct CBGB club into a punk-rock museum (Paredes, 2005). The evaluation of the museum institution or a specific exhibition as a 'right' or 'wrong' place for talking publicly about punk and its DIY ethic and culture, is closely linked to the governance of the museum or exhibition. In ethical terms, a DIY culture event needs a DIY organisation, from the bottom up, and not a conventional curatorial authority decision from the top down.

Lucy Robinson, referring to Punk 40th anniversary in London[34], points out that punk aesthetics are especially appealing to exhibitions, but it should not only be a deterrent to a critical reflection of who, how and what should be remembered, but also as a growing popular music that is used to represent a part of national and local history. For, above all, 'There cannot be a right way to present punk because punk is a paradox' (Robinson, 2017, p.8). Hence, with all of these issues in mind, since 2013, we set out to carry a set of events, exhibitions and other strategies for the (partial) public dissemination of the KISMIF punk archive. Because of the lack of space to develop this article which is an extensive analysis of various approaches and strategies, we opt to offer a case-study of only one of these exhibitions– '*God Save The Portuguese Fanzines*'[35].

The exhibition *God Save The Portuguese Fanzines* (see figures 6 and 7), was jointly curated by the authors along with the graphic designer and illustrator Júlio Dolbeth[36]. It seems to us to be paradigmatic of some of the possibilities that this archive offers us. It is an exhibition that is ought to make known to a diverse contemporary public, national and foreign, one of the most emblematic fanzines of punk in Portugal: the *Cadáver Esquisito* [Exquisite corpse, from the original French term '*cadavre exquis*']. Despite its fleeting existence – only two edited issues in 1986 – the *Cadáver Esquisito* translated a unique time in the city of Porto, when it was very possibly responsible for inaugurating the publication of fanzines punk in the Greater Porto area, constituting also a relevant document for the socio-historical analysis of the movements of punk in our country (Guerra and Quintela, 2020). In this exhibition some of the originals and models of this fanzine were publicly presented. It allowed the visitors to observe in detail the overlapping of graphic techniques on which the construction of each number of the *Cadáver Esquisito* was based, as well as make contact with the editorial line, followed by this fanzine which, in our perspective, expresses well a certain subterranean and anarchic style so characteristic of punk fanzines (Atton, 2002).

Figure 6. Inauguration moments from the God Save The Portuguese Fanzines' exhibition, 2014

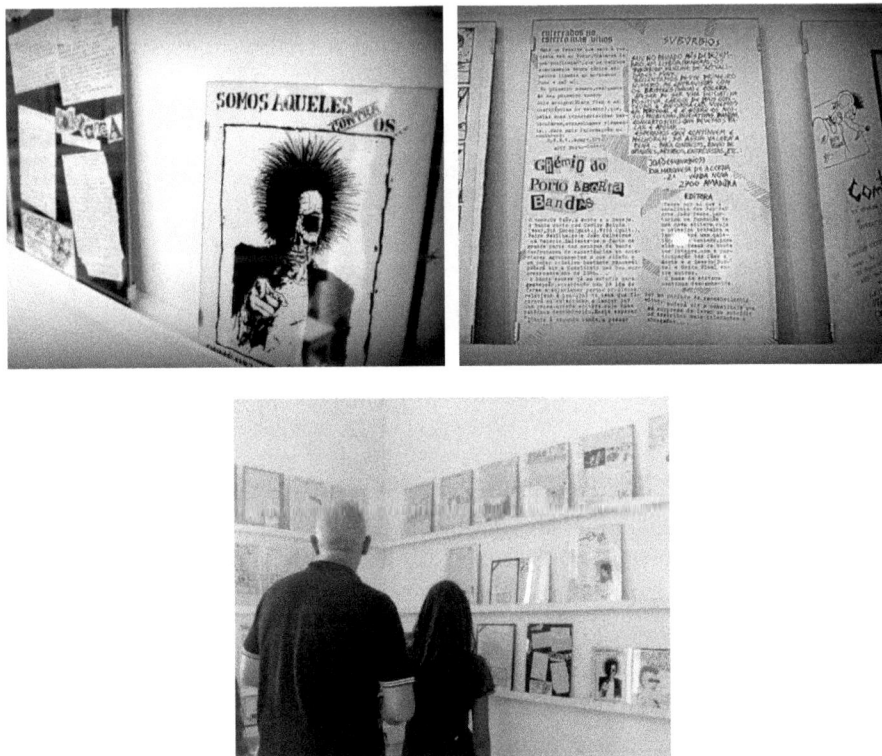

(Punk.pt conference 2014 (http://www.punk.pt/conference-2014-welcome/))

In this process, the welcoming and generous availability of the two elements that integrated the 'core' of the fanzine editorial team – David Pontes and Neno Costa – was essential to collaborate in the research work, reporting in the first person the way they lived that time, detailing the process of designing, producing and distributing *Cadáver Esquisito* (see figures 8). It was also possible to benefit from the inauguration of the exhibition as one of the editors of the fanzine (and former radio broadcaster and musician, linked to one of the most emblematic national punk bands: *Cães Vadios* [Stray Dogs]), journalist David Pontes, who shared with the audience some of his memories of the project and reflected on the impact of the *Cadáver Esquisito* on the cultural life of the city of Porto in the mid-1980s.

Figure 7. Inauguration moments from the MATTERxANTIMATTER=FRAGMENTS' exhibition, 2014 (Punk.pt conference 2014

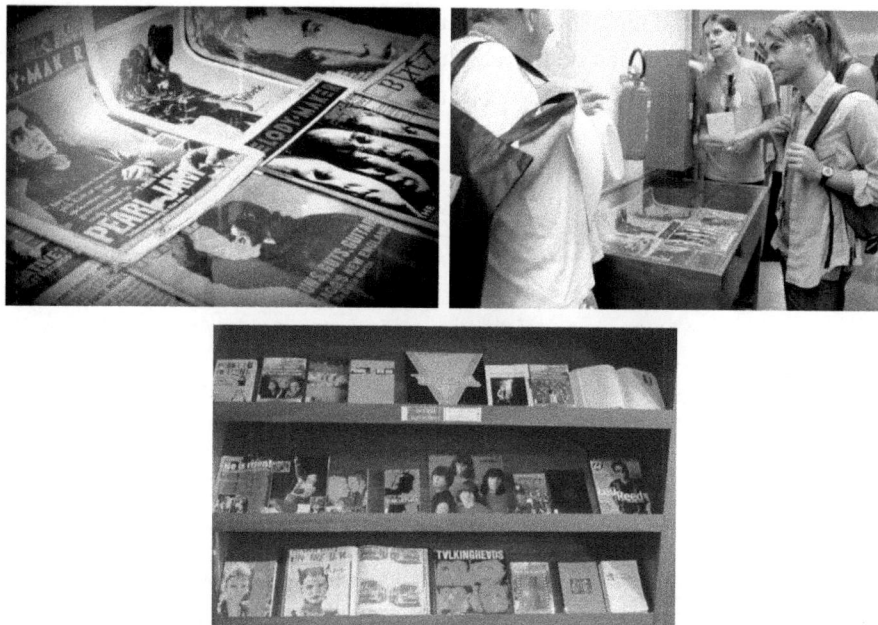

(http://www.punk.pt/conference-2014-welcome/))

We intend to repeat this kind of public event in the future, in other places and formats, focusing on other fanzines, protagonists, temporal periods and territorial contexts. This, in our view is very important in allowing a critical review of these memories and artefacts which are linked to punk demonstrations in Portugal, disseminating, in a more comprehensive way, the contribution of KISMIF to this discussion and, above all, opening research projects and the information and documentation collected to the consultation, discussion and the broad participation of the interested community - scientific community, cultural journalists, and other 'cultural intermediaries', as well as other stakeholders.

These broad-based initiatives can also make an important contribution to a broader reflection on how public (cultural, scientific) policies can support other types of heritage-related projects that focus on a critical analysis and evaluation of cultures and their relevance to the understanding of the processes of transformation of contemporary Portugal. It is therefore necessary to overcome the commercial logic that is prevalent today in the discourses and 'patrimonialist' actions around the popular cultures in general, particularly of rock music, as Roberts argues. In a recent article, in which he criticizes the strongly nostalgic, essentialist and even fetishist approach, connected to a certain cult of 'retro' and 'vintage' that proliferates in contemporary societies.

Figure 8. DIY DIY my Darling! Outspace zines and records exhibition moments

(http://www.punk.pt/conference-2014-welcome/)

BACK TO THE 'OLD HOUSE': CONCLUSION

Throughout this article, we ought to expose the growing interest related to the archiving practices (formal and informal) in the production and distribution of DIY. In which, we were able to find a challenge to academic and cultural institutions to develop new approaches and research methodologies in terms of gathering, analysing, and preserving the sort of productions associated with a more underground culture. In this context, we argued the defence of the heritage of popular cultures as it has grown in importance; we tend to agree with Roberts (2014) that it is (also) the work of the social sciences to contribute, in a critical and rigorous way, to broaden these debates in terms of (sub) cultural expressions in their socio-historical relevance. In this, the effort is to show, through empirical investigation that (sub) cultural expressions are in truth much more diverse and richer than we are often led to believe. We can thus approach all the perspectives that argue the value of memory in the contemporary celebration of heritage, seeking to construct a participative archive which dignifies the productions and artefacts that are stemming from underground, carriers of history, belonging and bonds. In this context of plurality of formats, materials, and a volatility of these same products, it seemed to us an interesting endeavour to develop and promote a form of archivism, cataloguing, exposing, preserving and restoring of a group of artefacts. These, in turn, are to be interpreted symbolically and identified in their importance in the emergence, development and consolidation of the socio-musical and cultural expressions of punk in Portuguese modernity.

We can note that the near absence of investment in archives of popular culture in Portugal – deriving, on the one hand, from the illegitimate nature of these expressions when compared to others in a legitimate (and legitimised) culture, and on the other hand, from a technical and methodological lacking in terms of documentation of an archive destined to function with free-access. However, realising the importance that the process of collective memory preservation has, we sought to mobilise a number of resources towards a community – academic and non-academic – understood as pieces of history of a contemporary expression. More than a reading aid, or a particular look towards the past and present of punk in Portugal, we hope that this archive will allow for the creation of multiple understandings, from a wide range of fragments of the Portuguese cultural heritage and in the process, create for the first time on a Portuguese scale, an archive of memories, heritage, and history. Thus, our future research directions will be focused on activating partnerships with local institutions - collectives, museums, and associations - with a view to creating an archive space with its own programme dedicated to underground popular culture. The work we've been doing at the Museu do Porto is a fuse for this idea and has led to the expansion of the collection of fanzines, posters and discs in a very systematic way since 2021.

Funding: This chapter is part of the Transnational Research Network KISMIF - https://www .kismifconference.com/. For further information, see https://www.kismifcommunity.com. This chapter was supported by FCT – Foundation for Science and Technology within the scope of UIDB/00727/2020.

REFERENCES

Arvidsson, A. (2008). The ethical economy of customer coproduction. *Journal of Macromarketing*, 28(4), 326–338. 10.1177/0276146708326077

Assmann, A. (2012). *Cultural Memory and Western Civilization: Functions, Media, Archives*. Cambridge University Press.

Atton, C. (2002). Alternative Media. *Sage (Atlanta, Ga.)*.

Atton, C. (2006). Sociologie de la presse musicale alternative [Sociology of the alternative music press]. *Volume!5*(1), 7-25. http://volume.revues.org/614

Baker, S. (2014). Saving "Rubbish": Preserving Popular Music's Material. In Cohen, S., Knifton, R., Marion, L., & Roberts, L. (Eds.), *Sites of Popular Music Heritage: Memories, Histories, Places* (pp. 112–124). Routledge.

Baker, S. (Ed.). (2015). *Preserving Popular Music Heritage. Do-it-Yourself, Do-it-Together*. Routledge. 10.4324/9781315769882

Baker, S., Doyle, P., & Homan, S. (2016). Historical Records, National Constructions: The Contemporary Popular Music Archive. *Popular Music and Society*, 39(1), 8–27. 10.1080/03007766.2015.1061336

Baker, S., & Huber, A. (2013). Notes Towards a Typology of the Diy Institution: Identifying Do-It-Yourself Places of Popular Music Preservation. *European Journal of Cultural Studies*, 16(5), 513–530. 10.1177/1367549413491721

Barreto, A. (1996). *Tempo de Incerteza* [Time of Uncertainty]. Relógio d'Água.

Bennett, A. (2009). "Heritage Rock": Rock Music, Representation and Heritage Discourse. *Poetics*, 37(5-6), 474–489. 10.1016/j.poetic.2009.09.006

Bennett, A. (2014) Popular Music and the "Problem" of Heritage. In Sara Cohen, Robert Knifton, Marion Leonard and Les Roberts (Ed,), *Sites of Popular Music Heritage: Memories, Histories, Places*. Routledge.

Cabral, M. V. (2014). *Dimensões da Cidadania: A Mobilização Política em Portugal numa Perspetiva Comparada[Dimensions of Citizenship: Political Mobilisation in Portugal from a Comparative Perspective]*. Afrontamento.

Cohen, S., Knifton, R., Leonard, M., & Roberts, L. (Eds.). (2014). *Sites of Popular Music Heritage: Memories, Histories, Places*. Routledge. 10.4324/9780203514528

Collins, Jez (2012). *Multiple Voices, Multiple Memories: Public History Making and Activist Archivism in Online Popular Music Archives* [Doctoral dissertation, School of Media, Birmingham City University].

Collins, J., & Long, P. (2014). "Fillin in Any Blanks I Can": Online Archival Practice and Virtual Sites of Musical Memory. In Cohen, S., Knifton, R., Leonard, M., & Roberts, L. (Eds.), *Sites of Popular Music Heritage: Memories, Histories, Places* (pp. 81–96). Routledge.

Crown Punks Group. www.facebook.com/groups/108486069179177/> (accessed 5 October 2012)

Cvetkovich, A. (2003). *An Archive of Feelings: Trauma, Sexuality, and Lesbian Public Cultures*. Duke University Press.

Dale, P. (2010). *Anyone Can Do It: Traditions of Punk and the Politics of Empowerment*. [Doctoral dissertation, Newcastle University]. https://theses.ncl.ac.uk/jspui/handle/10443/1101

Derrida, J. (1996). *Archive Fever: A Freudian Impression*. University of Chicago Press.

Dines, M. (2004). *An Investigation into the Emergence of the Anarcho-Punk Scene of the 1980s*. [Doctoral dissertation, University of Salford]. http://usir.salford.ac.uk/id/eprint/2040/

Dowd, T. J. (2014). The Remembering: Heritage-Work at Us Progressive-Rock. In Cohen, S., Knifton, R., Leonard, M., & Roberts, L. (Eds.), *Sites of Popular Music Heritage: Memories, Histories, Places* (pp. 174–191). Routledge.

Duncombe, S. (1997). *Notes from Underground: Zines and the Politics of Alternative Culture*. Verso.

Dunn, K. (2008). Never mind the bollocks: The punk rock politics of global communication. *Review of International Studies*, 34(S1), 193–210. 10.1017/S0260210508007869

Errickson, A. (1999). *A Detailed Journey into the Punk Subculture: Punk Outreach in Public Libraries*. University of North Carolina at Chapel Hill.

Featherstone, M. (2000). Archiving Cultures. *The British Journal of Sociology*, 51(1), 161–184. 10.1111/j.1468-4446.2000.00161.x

Featherstone, M. (2006). Archive. *Theory, Culture & Society*, 23(2/3), 591–596. 10.1177/0263276406023002106

Feixa, C. (2014). *Da geração @geração blockchain: a juventude na era postdigital[From the Genera-tion@ to the #Generation: Youth in the Digital Era]*. Ned Ediciones.

Feldman-Barrett, C. (2015). Archival Research and the Expansion of Popular Music History. In Bennett, A., & Waksman, S. (Eds.), *The Sage Handbook of Popular Music* (pp. 83–98). Sage., 10.4135/9781473910362. n5

Flinn, A. (2007). Community Histories, Community Archives: Some Opportunities and Challenges. *Journal of the Society of Archivists*, 28(2), 151–176. 10.1080/00379810701611936

Flinn, A. (2011). Archival Activism: Independent and Community-led Archives, Radical Public History and the Heritage Professions. *InterActions: UCLA Journal of Education and Information Studies*, 7(2). 10.5070/D472000699

Flinn, A. (2012). Archives and Their Communities: Collecting Histories, Challenging Heritage. In Dawson, G. (Ed.), *Memory, Narrative and Histories: Critical Debates, New Trajectories, Working Papers, 19-35*. University of Brighton.

Force, W. (2005). *No, We Don't Have Any T-Shirts: Identity in a (Self-Consciously)*. Consumerist Punk Subculture. [Doctoral dissertation, University of South Florida]

Garde-Hansen, J. (2009). My Memories?: Personal digital archive fever and Facebook. In Garde-Hansen, Joanne, Andrew Hoskins, and Anna Reading, *Save As . . . Digital Memories* (pp. 135-150). Palgrave MacMillian.

Geiger, T., Moore, N., & Savage, M. (2010). *The Archive in Question.* (CRESC Working Paper 81). https://hummedia.manchester.ac.uk/institutes/cresc/workingpapers/wp81.pdf

Glasgow Apollo Group. www.facebook.com/groups/5586711471/?ref=ts&fref=ts > (accessed 10 October 2013)

Guerra, P. (2010). *A instável leveza do rock: génese, dinâmica e consolidação do rock alternativo em Portugal (1980-2010)* [The Unstable Lightness of Rock: Genesis, Dynamics and Consolidation of Alternative Rock in Portugal (1980-2010)]. [Doctoral thesis, Faculdade de Letras da Universidade do Porto]. http://hdl.handle.net/10216/56304

Guerra, P. (2013). Punk, ação e contradição em Portugal. Uma aproximação às culturas juvenis contemporâneas ['Punk, Action and Contradiction in Portugal: An Approach to Contemporary Youth Cultures]. *Revista Critica de Ciencias Sociais*, 102(102), 111–134. 10.4000/rccs.5486

Guerra, P. (2014). Punk, expectations, breaches and metamorphoses: Portugal, 1977–2012. *Critical Arts*, 28(1), 111–122. 10.1080/02560046.2014.883697

Guerra, P., & Bennett, A. (2015). Never Mind the Pistols? The Legacy and Authenticity of the Sex Pistols in Portugal. *Popular Music and Society*, 38(4), 500–521. 10.1080/03007766.2015.1041748

Guerra, P., & Bennett, A. (2020). Punk Portugal, 1977-2012: A preliminary genealogy. *Popular Music History*, 13(3), 215–234. 10.1558/pomh.39660

Guerra, P., & Quintela, P. (orgs.) (2020). *Punk, Fanzines and DIY Cultures in a Global World. Fast, Furious and Xerox.* London: Palgrave Macmillan.

Guerra, P., & Quintela, P. (orgs.). (2021). *Independent DIY publications and the underground urban cultures.* Porto: University of Porto – Faculty of Arts and Humanities. https://hdl.handle.net/10216/136396

Halbwachs, M. (1992). *On Collective Memory.* University of Chicago Press. 10.7208/chicago/9780226774497.001.0001

Hall, S. (1999). Whose Heritage? Un-Settling "the Heritage", Re-Imagining the Post-Nation. *Third Text*, 13(49), 3–13. 10.1080/09528829908576818

Hamel, Leigh Ann, Tom Maher, Mick O'Dwyer, & Eric Cook (2014). 'Organizing Anarchy: The Forgotten Zine Archive. [Paper presentation]. *iConference 2014 Proceedings*, Berlin. https://doi.org/10.9776/14350

Hespanha, P., & Caleiras, J. (2017). O labirinto das políticas de emprego [The labyrinth of employment policies]. *Cadernos do Observatório*, *10*.https://www.ces.uc.pt/observatorios/crisalt/documentos/cadernos/Caderno10_Labirinto_politicas_emprego.pdf

Hoyle, V. (2017). Editorial: Archives and public history. *Archives and Records (Abingdon, England)*, 38(1), 1–4. 10.1080/23257962.2017.1282348

Huvila, I. (2008). Participatory Archive: Towards Decentralised Curation, Radical User Orientation and Broader Contextualisation of Records *Management.Archival Science*, 8(1), 15–36. 10.1007/s10502-008-9071-0

Ketelaar, E. (2009). Archives as Spaces of Memory. *Journal of the Society of Archivists*, 29(1), 9–27. 10.1080/00379810802499678

Kirchberg, V. (2016). Museum sociology. In Laurie, H., & Savage, M. (Eds.), *Routledge International Handbook of the Sociology of Art and Culture* (pp. 232–244). Routledge.

Kirshenblatt-Gimblett, B. (1998). *Destination Culture: Tourism, Museums and Heritage*. University of California Press.

Kruse, Holly (2010). Local Identity and Independent Music Scenes: Online and Off. *Popular Music and Society33*(5), 625-639. .10.1080/03007760903302145

Leccardi, C., Feixa, C., Kovacheva, S., Reiter, H., & Sekulić, T. (Eds.). (2012). *1989- Young People and social change after the fall of the Berlin Wall*. Council of Europe Publishing.

Lipovetsky, G. (2014). *Capitalismo estético na era da globalização[Aesthetic Capitalism in the Age of Globalization]*. Edições 70.

Loff, M., Piedade, F., & Soutelo, L. C. (2015). *Ditadura e revolução: Democracia e Política da Memória[-Dictatorship and Revolution: Democracy and Memory Politics]*. Almedina.

Manoff, Marlente (2004). Theories of the Archive from across the Disciplines. Portal (Baltimore, Md.), 4(1), 9–25. 10.1353/pla.2004.0015

Marcus, G. (2000). *Traços de batom: Uma História Secreta do Século XX* [Lipstick Traces: A Secret History of the Twentieth Century]. Frenesi.

Mateus, A. (2015). *Três décadas de Portugal europeu: Balanço e Perspectivas* [Three decades of European Portugal: Balance and Perspective. Fundação Francisco Manuel dos Santos. 10.1353/pla.2004.0015

McKee, A. (2011). Youtube Versus the National Film and Sound Archive: Which Is the More Useful Resource for Historians of Australian Television? *Television & New Media*, 12(2), 154–173. 10.1177/1527476410365707

McNeil, B. (2009). *Building Subcultural Community Online and Off: An Ethnographic Analysis of the Cblocals Music Scene*. [Doctoral dissertation, Georgia State University].

Meriwether, N. G. (Ed.). (2012). *Reading the Grateful Dead: A Critical Survey*. Scarecrow Press.

Moore, S., & Pell, S. (2010). Autonomous Archives. *International Journal of Heritage Studies*, 16(4/5), 255–268. 10.1080/13527251003775513

Moran, I. P. (2010). Punk: The Do-It-Yourself Subculture. *The Social Science Journal*, 10(1), 58–65. http://repository.wcsu.edu/ssj/vol10/iss1/13

Muggleton, D., & Weinzierl, R. (2003) (Eds.). *The Post-Subcultural Reader*. Berg.

Paredes, J. (2005). Punk Rock Doesn't Belong in a Museum. *The New York Times*. https://www.nytimes.com/2005/08/14/arts/music/punk-rock-doesnt-belong-in-a-museum.html

Pereira, J. P. (2015). *Aprender com os alemães* ['Learn with the Germans.']. Público. https://www.publico.pt/2015/03/28/mundo/opiniao/aprender-com-os-alemaes-1690586

Pordata (2017). *Portrait of Portugal in Europe 2017*. Fundação Francisco Manuel dos Santos.

Reynolds, S. (2011). *Retromania: Pop Culture's Addiction to Its Own Past*. Faber and Faber.

Roberts, L. (2014). Talkin Bout My Generation: Popular Music and the Culture of Heritage. *International Journal of Heritage Studies*, 20(3), 262–280. 10.1080/13527258.2012.740497

Robinson, L. (2016). Collaboration in, collaboration out: The eighties in the age of digital reproduction. *Cultural and Social History*, 13(3), 403–423. 10.1080/14780038.2016.1202026

Robinson, L. (2017). Exhibition review Punk's 40th anniversary — An itchy sort of heritage. *Twentieth Century British History*, 1–9. 10.1093/tcbh/hwx04729800337

Rosenzweig, R., & Thelen, D. (1998). *The Presence of the Past: Popular Uses of History in American Life*. Columbia University Press.

Samuel, R. (1994). *Theatres of Memory: Past and Present in Contemporary Culture* (Vol. 1). Verso.

Santos, B. (1990). *O Estado e a Sociedade em Portugal (1974-1988)[The State and Society in Portugal (1974-1988)]*. Afrontamento.

Silva, A. S., & Guerra, P. (2015). O mundo do Punk [The Words of Punk]. *Aletheia*.

Strong, C. (2015). Shaping the Past of Popular Music: Memory, Forgetting and Documenting. In *Andy Bennet, & Steve Waksman, The Sage Handbook of Popular Music*. Sage. 10.4135/9781473910362.n24

Terranova, T. (2004). *Network Culture: Politics for the Information Age*. Pluto Press.

van Dijck, J. (2006). Record and Hold: Popular Music between Personal and Collective Memory. *Critical Studies in Media Communication*, 23(5), 357–374. 10.1080/07393180601046121

Wallerstein, I. (1974). *The Modern World-System, vol. I: Capitalist Agriculture and the Origins of the European World-Economy in the Sixteenth Century*. Academic Press.

Wallerstein, I. (1980). *The Modern World-System, vol. II: Mercantilism and the Consolidation of the European World-Economy, 1600-1750*. Academic Press.

Woodbrook, R., & Lazzaro, A. (2013). The Bonds of Organization: Zine Archives and the Archival Tradition. *Journal of Western Archives*4(1), 1-17. URL: https://doi.org/10.26077/e5d9-dec6

Worley, M. (2015). Punk, Politics and British (Fan)Zines, 1976–84: "While the World Was Dying, Did You Wonder Why?". *History Workshop Journal*, 79(1), 76–106. 10.1093/hwj/dbu043

ADDITIONAL READING

Bennett, A., & Guerra, P. (Eds.). (2019). *DIY Cultures and Underground Music Scenes*. Routledge.

Bestley, R., Dines, M., Grimes, M., & Guerra, P. (orgs.). (2021). *Punk identities, punk utopias. Global punk and media*. Bristol: Intellect Books.

Bestley, R., Dines, M., Guerra, P., & Gordon, A. (orgs.) (2021). *Trans-Global Punk Scenes. The Punk Reader Volume 2*. Fishponds, Bristol: Intellect Books.

Dines, M., Gordon, A., Guerra, P., & Bestley, R. (orgs.) (2019). *The Punk Reader. Research Transmissions from the Local and the Globa*l. Bristol: Intellect.

Garrigós, Cristina, Triana, Nuria, & Guerra, Paula (2019). *God Save the Queens. Pioneras del punk*. Barcelona: 66 RPM EDICIONS.

Guerra, P. (2020). Iberian punk, cultural metamorphoses, and artistic differences in the post-Salazar and post-Franco Eras. In McKay, G., & Arnold, G. (Eds.), *The Oxford Handbook of Punk Rock*. Oxford University Press. 10.1093/oxfordhb/9780190859565.013.14

Guerra, P. (2020). Under-Connected: Youth subcultures, resistance and sociability in the internet age. In: Gildart, K., Gough-Yates, A., Lincoln, S., Osgerby, B., Robinson, L., Street, J., Webb, P., & Worley, M. (orgs.). *Hebdige and subculture in the Twenty-First Century*. (pp.207-230). London: Palgrave Macmillan. 10.1007/978-3-030-28475-6_10

Guerra, P. (2021). Leitmotiv: Forgotten women in Portuguese contemporary history I. *ZINES, 2*(2), 70-83. http://strandflat.fr/zines/

Guerra, P. (2023). DIY, fanzines and ecofeminism in the Global South: 'This city is my sister'. *DIY, Alternative Cultures & Society, 1*(3). . 10.1177/27538702231211062

Guerra, P., & Alberto, T. P. (Eds.). (2019). *Keep it Simple Make it Fast! An approach to underground music scenes* (Vol. 4). Universidade do Porto – Faculdade de Letras.

Guerra, P., & López, L. (2021). Peaks and fanzines. *Fuses for a rebellion. ZINES, 2*(2), 4-8. http://strandflat.fr/zines/

Guerra, P., & López, L. (2021). WE @RE the p!nk revolutixn: The breakthrough of queer and feminist fanzines, as places of resistance. *ZINES, 3*(3), 4-8. http://strandflat.fr/zines/

Guerra, P., & Oliveira, A. (Eds.). (2023). *Keep it Simple, Make it Fast! An approach to underground music scenes* (Vol. 6). Universidade do Porto - Faculdade de Letras. [University of Porto. Faculty of Arts and Humanities], 10.21747/9789899082298

Guerra, P., & Pàmpols, F. (2021). 'Not Just Holidays in the Sun'. Mapping, measuring and analysing DIY culture's impact across cities in the Global South. In: Campos, R., & Nofre, J. (orgs.). *Exploring Ibero-American youth cultures in the 21st Century. Creativity, resistance and transgression in the city* (pp. 243-258). Cham, Switzerland: MacMillan Palgrave. DOI 10.1007/978-3-030-83541-5_11

Guerra, P., & Quintela, P. (2021). *(orgs.). Independent DIY Publications and the Underground Urban Cultures.* University of Porto – Faculty of Arts and Humanities. https://ler.letras.up.pt/site/default.aspx ?qry=id022id1768&sum=sim10.21747/9789898969606/ind

KEY TERMS AND DEFINITIONS

Archives: In recent years, there has been a growing academic interest in the subject of archives, both from a theoretical point of view (exploring the polysemic nature of the concept) and from an empirical point of view, arguing for a research practice that today goes beyond the restricted field of history and archives. This critical stance on the way archives are constituted has inevitably challenged the maintenance of the traditional view of the archivist's role as a neutral element, a 'mere' facilitator of historical research. In this context of profound questioning of archives - how they were constituted, who created them and why, which perspectives are represented and which are excluded - another important question arises in relation to access. This is a key aspect for those who study counter-history, and tensions often arise between, on the one hand, archivists and historians who affirm the need to record, preserve and rigorously treat the materials in storage, and, on the other hand, all those who defend the imperative of guaranteeing public access to these archives. It is therefore a question of considering archives as a political issue linked to democratic plurality.

Cultural Heritage, Popular Cultures, and Popular Music: Focusing the discussion on popular cultures, it can be seen that in this field too, the 'value' of this type of cultural and artistic production has been profoundly re-examined, blurring old dichotomies associated with the idea of 'high' and 'low' culture, with consequent implications for its gradual incorporation into heritage discourses. These processes of patrimonialisation are also closely linked to the ageing process of the audiences themselves - i.e. those interested in consuming this type of cultural and artistic manifestation - which has contributed, for example, to the recognition of the 'value' of urban popular music forms such as rock, which are considered to be an integral part of the cultural heritage of the 20th century. In addition, these processes have clearly been stimulated by a group of actors who play a crucial role here as 'consecrators', responsible for making critical judgements about the historical importance and cultural value of certain artistic manifestations that, until a few years ago, were considered 'minor' or even 'despicable' - from rock to graphic design, graffiti or comics.

DYI Cultures: DIY culture, which stands for "do-it-yourself" culture, has evolved from a punk-focused resistance to the mainstream music industry into a widely endorsed aesthetic that underpins a broad sphere of alternative cultural production. It has become a global 'alternative culture' and has developed a degree of professionalism aimed at ensuring aesthetic and economic sustainability. DIY culture provides a space for people with common tastes, perspectives and experiences to come together and build new forms of community, asserting their solidarity and distinctiveness in the late and modern urban context. It has also become the basis for lifestyle projects in which individuals articulate a sense of distance from more mainstream and 'official' discourses of urban transformation underpinned by neoliberal policies.

Fanzines: Fanzines are homemade objects produced in an artisanal manner, either individually or collectively, with limited circulation. They emerged in the 1920s-30s and were initially associated with science fiction fans. They later became popular in the 1950s-60s with comic and music fanzines. The punk phenomenon in the 1970s and 1980s globally increased the production, distribution, and consumption of fanzines, providing an alternative space to conventional media. Punk fanzines are homemade, artisanal objects that emerged as a space for freedom of thought and DIY creation during the punk phenomenon in the 1970s and 1980s in the UK and USA. They functioned as an alternative to mainstream media, providing a platform for expression and discussion for fans of music genres overlooked by traditional music press. These fanzines played a crucial role in creating a sense of community within the punk movement, documenting scenes, enhancing visibility, and fostering a sense of belonging among readers. They were instrumental in shaping the punk culture by encouraging reader participation and actively contributing to the movement's development and dynamics.

Music Scenes: The term "music scene" is used to describe social and cultural environments in which music plays a central role. These environments are characterised by a plurality of socialising spaces, each with different symbolic codes according to different musical genres, youth cultures, social backgrounds, urban contexts and approaches to professional circles. Music scenes can include alternative music production, performance and consumption networks, as well as a proliferation of local, translocal and virtual scenes. Furthermore, they can be regarded as spaces of institutional challenge and resistance, where participants seek authentic artistic expression and unique cultural experiences.

Subculture: Subcultures are groups within a larger culture that have distinct values, norms and practices that distinguish them from the mainstream culture. These subcultures often form around shared interests, such as music, fashion or lifestyle choices, and can be characterised by their own unique language, symbols and rituals. Subcultures can provide a sense of belonging and identity for their members, and often serve as sites of resistance or alternative expression to the dominant culture.

Youth Cultures: The term "youth culture" refers to the diverse and dynamic cultural expressions and practices of young people, particularly in urban settings. These cultures encompass a wide range of subcultures, neotribes, and scenes, and are characterised by heterogeneity, dynamism, and the blurring of boundaries between different youth cultures. The concept of youth cultures emphasises the plurality of youth identities and the exchange of styles, challenging the notion of a singular youth culture. It can be argued that youth cultures play a crucial role in the socialisation and identity construction of young people. This is due to the fact that they are influenced by global trends and the proliferation of subcultures with varied motivations.

ENDNOTES

[1]   For more information, consult the site:https://www.kismifconference.com/pt/

[2]   In other contexts – in seminars and scientific conferences, as well as in articles published in scientific journals – we have been able to present results of the content analysis of this vast documentation, so we will not retrieve the more detailed discussion of the data that results from our analysis (see Guerra & Quintela, 2020, 2021).

[3]   The KISMIF archive can be found from October 2015 onwards, at the website http://arquivo .punk.pt/.

[4]   In Portugal there is the Arquivo.pt website, which has as its objective and concern the preservation of information published on the web since 1997 – the height of the emergence of Internet use in Portugal. For more information, consult the site: https://arquivo.pt/

[5]   Fado is the typical Portuguese musical expression. It is strongly rooted in collective memory and the tastes of the population. It was also the object of much support and ideological foundation on the part of the dictatorship. Since 2011, Fado is inscribed on the UNESCO Representative List of the Intangible Cultural Heritage of Humanity.

[6]   For more information, consult the site: https://www.museudofado.pt/

[7]   The carnations were and are the symbol of the Revolution of 25 April 1974, the revolution that dethroned a 40-year dictatorship – the longest in Europe. Coca-Cola – a mass-produced drink, global and the symbol of cultural Americanization – only arrived in Portugal after the Revolution of April 25, 1974, and this fact is also symptomatic of the closure to which the country was subject. These are metaphorical elements that show that today, after 40 years of democracy, we can finally think about a file of underground popular culture, specifically punk.

[8]   For more information, consult the site: https://www.rockhall.com/

[9]   For more information, consult the site: https://www.beatlesstory.com/

[10]   For more information, consult the website: https://blogs.sussex.ac.uk/observingthe80s/.

[11]   For more information, consult the website: https://www.reading.ac.uk/history/Stories/hist-matthew -worley.aspx.

[12]   It is, however, a work still in progress, since, at the time of writing, we are still organizing the archive. It will therefore be necessary to wait for a few more months – at which time the punk archive will be available for on-site and online consultation – so that we can check if our options were the right ones or if, as is certainly probable, there are aspects to improve.

[13]   Including whether it is an individual or collective fanzine.

[14]   Using the Nomenclature of Territorial Units for Statistical Purposes level 3 (NUTS 3), in order to allow a mapping of punk fanzines in Portugal.

[15]   Whether it is free or paid, in which case the price and currency are specified.

[16]   Colour, black and white.

[17]   Digital, photocopy, etc.

[18]   Fanzine, e-zine, graphzine, etc.

[19]   Interviews, record reviews, DVD / films, concerts, opinion articles / chronicles, advertising, news, letters, cartoons, editorials, others.

[20]   Engraving / drawing / painting, comics, cartoon / caricature, photography, collage, etc.

21   In interviews, concert reports, record reviews, other comments / records, etc.

22   In interviews, concert reports, record reviews, opinion articles, etc.

23   In this regard, one of the greatest archivists of the Portuguese contemporaneity, José Pacheco Pereira, recently stated: "a very conservative conception of history means that many materials have been lost, disappeared, destroyed and dispersed, for example after the [democratic revolution of the] 25 April [1974]. The period before 25 April and even the days of the revolution still have some state collections, such as the *Torre do Tombo* [National Archive], the Mário Soares Foundation [both located in Lisbon], or the 25 April Center [archive located at the Centre for Social Sciences (CES), at the University of Coimbra], in Coimbra, but none of these institutions actively collects the most contemporaries products of our history. (...) This is the question I wanted to draw attention to, since memory work is one of the most significant aspects of civic life, at a time when everything is done to destroy and shorten" (2015: 52).

24   For more information, consult the site: https://blx.cm-lisboa.pt/gca/?id=1394

25   Calouste Gulbenkian Foundation, situated in Lisbon, Portugal, is a Foundation which aims to promote knowledge and raise people's quality of life through the arts, charity, science and, education.

26   Serralves Foundation, situated in Porto, Portugal, is a Foundation which aims to stimulate public awareness and knowledge in relation to Contemporary Art, architecture, the landscape, and critical issues facing society and its future.

27   We must mention here the exhibition 'Déjà-Vu. Repetition and Difference' present at the Serralves Foundation between 26th September 2015 and 3rd January 2016, curated by Guy Schraenen. This exhibition revealed an up until-now untreated theme in the field of artists' publications. A limited section will show the reverse side of the theme. It will point out how designers, advertisers, and aesthetic advisors plagiarize and transform, reedit and remix the aesthetics of historical and contemporary art works into new scenarios of their publications in the culture of visual marketing. For more information, consult the website: https://www.serralves.pt/en/activities/deja-vu-repetition -and-difference/

28   Consult the weblog http://underrrreview.blogspot.pt

29   Consult the weblog http://ephemerajpp.com

30   This blog is associated with the punk fanzine *Alfinete,* with a regular production which continues to this day. Consult the weblog http://rocknoliceu.blogspot.pt

31   Consult the weblog http://rockdascadeias.blogspot.pt/

32   The Library of the Faculty of Arts and Humanities of the University of Porto and its services have a key role in KISMIF archive, namely consulting and scientific support, cataloguing and registration of materials and deposit of materials and objects under conditions of environmental sustainability, as well as to making all the materials collected by the KISMIF team virtually available on the library's own platform.

33   Despite this mistrust, it is noteworthy that in certain cases the people who do fanzines inform us of their most recent publications. However, due to budget constraints, supplanted by a DIY spirit, many of the acquisitions of new editions are made by members of the KISMIF Archive, who bear these costs.

34   For more information, consult the website: http://punk.london/

35   Regarding other initiatives, we can talk about the public presentation of the KISMIF project, on June 20, 2013, at Gallery Hostel, Porto, Portugal. In 2014 we can mention other initiatives, such as the exhibition MATTERxANTIMATTER=FRAGMENTS (see figures 7); the show space DIY DIY my Darling! Outspace zines & records; the exhibition Blitzkrieg Poster: create to destroy!; and the exhibition God Save The Portuguese Fanzines.

36   This exhibition was open to the public for two weeks at the record store Matéria-Prima, in Porto, following the International Conference *Keep It Simple, Make It Fast! Underground Music Scenes and DIY Cultures*, in July 2014. For more information consult the website: http://www.punk.pt/conference-2014-welcome/.

Chapter 15
Anarchist Erotica:
Transmedia and Transmemory in Cyborgraphy

Michael B. MacDonald
MacEwan University, Canada

ABSTRACT

The modern human is performative. If we consider modernity as ritual process, a set of performance technologies that organize the intensive energies of the homo sapien into the extensive coordinates of the modern human, then perhaps altermodern rituals biogram something else. We might see the recent propositions of posthuman, metahuman, transhuman, and ahuman (amongst others) as a confirmation that the modern human is only one set of extensive coordinates for Homo sapien, and perhaps no longer even the most influential. This study folds ethnography, performance studies, and feminist technoscience in a developing cyborgraphic practice called CineWorlding, a mode of cinematic research-creation. The contribution of this chapter is to experiment with a method of transmedia study with emerging xhumans to investigate the role of technologically mobile transmemory in its biogrammatic formation.

THREADING BEYOND THE FLESH OF HOMO SAPIEN SAPIEN[1]

Something in the world forces us to think. This something is an object not of recognition but of a fundamental encounter. What is encountered may be Socrates, a temple or a demon. It may be grasped in a range of affective tones: wonder, love, hatred, suffering. In whichever tone, its primary characteristic is that it can only be sensed. (Gilles Deleuze, Difference and Repetition, 139.)

It is crucial to cyberpunk that virtual or artificial zones are not alternatives to, but additional to, or folds in, the Real. (Mark Fisher, Flatline Constructs, 56).

All that you touch you change. All that you change changes you. The only lasting truth is change. God is change. (Octavia Butler, Parable of the Sower)

Memory prompts an *image of body*. This chapter is concerned with *transmemory*, memory that does not reside in the pink folds of the brain but operates through larger material and technological folds of which the homo sapien sapien body is a component. Transmemory is mobile, performative, and eco-

DOI: 10.4018/979-8-3693-2264-2.ch015

logical. As it moves it threads connections between sensing and recording machines both biological and technological, both organic and inorganic. The Humanist *image of body* and *memory*, the modern Human, is challenged by the threading of the biosphere-technosphere-semiosphere. It is not just a matter of *social* construction, because these threadings make forms that are situated, performative, multiple, and most importantly, they are ecological. They are not accomplished in a free play of signifiers alone, but thread transversally psychic/conceptual, social, technological, and environmental ecologies[2] that are always in motion, always processual, and always of consequence. As transmemory threads, its temporal movements are inscribed in the organization of psyches, bodies, communities, technologies, and environments. This threading and its outcomes challenge assumption that the *modern Human* is the only option for the biological Homo sapien sapien. Bruno Latour and Donna Haraway have separately made the point that *we* have never been modern (Latour 1993) nor human (Gane 2006).

The modern Human is performative. If we consider Modernity as ritual process, a set of performance technologies that organize the intensive energies of the homo sapien sapien into the extensive coordinates of the modern Human, then perhaps altermodern rituals[3] biogram something else. We might see the recent propositions of posthuman, metahuman, transhuman, and ahuman (amongst others) as a confirmation that the modern Human is only one set of extensive coordinates for Homo sapien sapien, and perhaps no longer even the most influential biogram. Recognizing that intensive energies become organized into extensive coordinates[4]--the homo sapien sapien (intensive energy) machined into a collective assemblage of enunciation that carries an xhuman name (extensive coordinates), does not however explain this dynamic. The machinic processes (ritual processes), their biograms, can be investigated using experimental ethnographic research methods. The X is both a placeholder for this variable as well as a negation of the modern Human. This study folds ethnography, performance studies, and feminist technoscience in a developing cyborgraphic practice that I have called *CineWorlding*, a mode of cinematic research-creation (MacDonald 2023). The contribution of this chapter is to experiment with a method of transmedia study with emerging xhumans to investigate the role of technologically mobile transmemory in its biogrammatic formation.

Terraforming Biograms

Anarchist Erotica is a project that attempts to understand *decentralization* as a more-than human force that plays a role in the xhuman rituals of the Decentralized Dance Party. I understand *decentralization* through Erin Manning's concept of *the free radical*, as movement that "cuts across the event to open it to where else it could go" (Manning 2020: 118). Decentralization, understood as a mode of the free radical, encourages an orientation to the DDP as an ritual performance and not a social movement or organization. The DDP is a social ritual/machine that occurs and then, from the perspective of the public, disappears. It is a kind of artwork/ritual/machine that I call an *exstallation*. The DDP is altermodern in the sense that it is not understandable as a social movement attempting to gain recognition, but instead working to terraform alternatives to modernity's worldings. Its performance practice is xhuman ritual that terraforms by creating musical placetime.

I borrow *terraforming* from Donna Haraway's chapter Sowing Worlds from *Staying with the Trouble* (2016; pgs. 117-125). Haraway is thinking with SF and "whole group timeplaces" (pg. 125), of "telling the tale of still possible recuperation" (ibid.), "but only in multispecies alliances, across the killing divisions of nature, culture, and technology and of organism, language, and machine" (pg. 118). Terraforming *biograms* is a way to name the machining of image of body without separating it from its ecological form-taking, and without assuming too quickly the homo sapien sapien as body.

For Erin Manning and Brian Massumi "approaches relying on the concepts of body schema and implicit knowledge fail in their attempted anti-Cartesianism" (2014, pg. 38) because what is implicit in the discourse of embodiment is a mind, "the mental status of the body schema is confirmed by the fact that sequencing can be adequately expressed in logical form: if-then. It has the status of a syllogism" (2014, pg. 38). When the cyborg retains a humanoid shape, it preserves an anthropocentric memory. A non-anthropocentric image of body and its transmemory moves beyond the humanoid, and even perhaps beyond being a geographically and temporally localizable envelope of self-possessive body: "embodiment is the wrong concept. Just 'bodying is better'. Movement goes a-bodying" (Manning and Massumi 2014, pg. 39). Movement, bodying, memory, technology, forming: perception is the "feeling-with of an event forming" (Manning 2012, pg. 80):

> Remembering a feeling involves activating relation by bringing into appearance a feltness in the present passing. A memory is not an unfolding of the bottled past in the neutral present. Remembering is the activation of a contrast that inflects the differential of experience unfolding such that the then is felt as an aspect of the nowness of experience. This is a relational event: it foregrounds the presentness through the past, emphasizing the quality of difference in their contrast. The event of the memory is how it takes form in the present, its hue activated through the contrast past-present, then-now. (Manning 2012, pg. 80)

Manning's *biogram* is "a virtual node out of which a bodyness can be felt. This feltness of a body is an affective experience. It is the tendency of a body to become that the biogram makes palpable. With the appearance of the biogram what is foregrounded is the affective tone of the event rather than a body as such" (2012, pg. 124). Xhumans *biograms* are different to the modern Human biograms. The biogram of the modern Human is so dominant however that it seems to be natural, necessary, and beyond question. I feel *my* body and know where it ends, I have *my* memories, and this makes *me,* the past in contained and accessible. Wherever I participated in the DDP, whenever I returned to those locations, the memories of the DDP were still there, still moving. Events and sensations that were felt and recorded in the DDP returned without warning. This is not a memory that was in my body nor a memory waiting in the environment, not separable from the experience there or from the time spent recording, editing, and screening the films, these were all moving across psychic/conceptual, social, technological, environmental ecologies. This particular urban landscape had the holographic feeling of nowness and virtuality simultaneously, holographically indissociable from any kind of nowness or present-ness. Cinematic events playing over this geography in ways that I cannot separate from *my* memory. The feeling of nowness of that which is no longer now but is also experienced now, that is not recalled by me, but ecologically triggered and that makes a difference in feltness of the present, this is *transmemory*, and its study has required the development of the transmedia performance (cyborgraphy) that this chapter attempts.

Cyborgraphy

Cyborgraphy proposes a method for studying xhumans. What transmemory does as a part of a biogram is part of this question. Therefore the form of this essay is inseparable from its subject. Do transmedia performances cultivate an xhuman *image of body* with the reader/participant having an experience beyond a modern Human biogram. If so, then the method of presentation plays a role in this transformation. An essay is not just the mobilization of information. There is a second-order operation, a kind of post-anthropocentric virus that has the potential for readerly mutation. Cyborgraphy is a proposition for a practice which recognizes that:

> our bodies, ourselves; bodies are maps of power and identity. Cyborgs are no exceptions. A cyborg body is not innocent; it was not born in a garden; it does not seek unitary identity and so generate antagonistic dualisms without end (or until the world ends); it takes irony for granted. One is too few, and two is only one possibility. Intense pleasure in skill, machine skill, ceases to be a sin, but an aspect of embodiment. The machine is not an *it* to be animated, worshipped, and dominated. The machine is us, our processes, an aspect of our embodiment. We can be responsible for machines; *they* do not dominate or threaten us. We are responsible for boundaries; we are they. (Haraway 1991, pg. 180)

This essay is a performance. It is experimental in both subject and form and requires a higher degree of generosity than is usual in an academic essay. It utilizes a variety of registers of writing, linked media, alternative modes of address that will be challenging for those more comfortable with a unified voice as a signifier of scientific rigor. It does not aspire to a scientific ethnographic accounts because "there is no drive in cyborgs to produced total theory, but there is an intimate experience of boundaries, their construction and deconstruction" (Haraway 1991, pg. 181). The degree to which you engage in the performance will influence what it does for you. The QR codes lead off the page into excursions or side quests. They are not separate from the theorizing of the text but essential to it. Transmemory is an experience of media being remembered, often without a subject recalling it. Its arriving alters the texture of experience, adding a synesthetic dimension that is holographic, multidimensional, and multitemporal. This is the sense of transmemory. By the time you reach the end of the essay, transmemory may begin to emerge for you. Sonic and audiovisual experiences will be activated by text, concepts will be activated by audiovision. This experience of threading and transmemory is a sense of movement through a performative threading with the technosphere that operates beyond individual intent, beyond rational action. Transmemory arrives uninvited, the mediated inseparable from the lived. There is no modern Human purity (Shotwell 2016) in transmemory. A QR code calls your attention, tells you to grab your phone, use your camera, select the link, hit play, accept the flow of audio and audiovision. Later sensual and temporal folds begin to occur. Audio or audiovision returning, resuscitated virtualities set off by words or phrases, or conceptual virtualities set off by sounds or audiovision. You begin to have memories of sounds of the DDP inseparable from subject or 'real' experience. This is a performance that is virtually immersive that offers an experience that builds up in ways that seek to shape the texture of the present. In that moment perhaps you will feel this sense of movement, transmemory. If you do, that experience confirms the experimental structure of this essay. It will occur by surprise and in the background. It will be occurring before you notice consciously. Such is the operation of transmemory. Or perhaps you will ignore the QR code, turn your back on the invitation, read the text alone certain that everything needed to understand transmemory is able to be captured by textual concepts. If you do this, you are confirming the dominance of the modern Human and missing what I think is so interesting about the transmedia and perhaps technologies role in transforming xhuman sense.

PART ONE: TRANSMEMORY, CYBORGRAPHY, AND XHUMAN PERFORMATIVITY

Transmedia Performance

This essay is a transmedia performance. Transmedia is an entwining of different media in this case this text, audio recording, and three independent films that you will come upon later in this text. Before (or as) you begin reading this next section grab a set of headphones and listen to this binaural recording made in 2012 about the Calgary, Alberta, Canada Edition of the Decentralized Dance Party. Headphones are best because binaural recording technology creates a 360 degree sound field. I wore earbuds that had small microphones built into them both at the DDP event and spending time with Gary at the DDP-HQ (a secret location) in Vancouver, British Columbia. So you are hearing what I was hearing. This will help us start the discussion of transmedia and transmemory that will follow.

Figure 1. QR code

Transmemory

TransMemory™ is a Toshiba brand-name for a flashdrive. Trans Memory has been described as a Queering of memory, of rethinking the relations between gender, sexuality, and memory:

where marginalized experiences, memories, and identities relating to gender and sexuality can dwell and form unpredictable ties of relatedness to live, thrive, and survive. I argue that the theoretical, methodological, and pedagogical project of studying memory through everyday trans*theorizations/ perspectives as a space of kin and world-making is not about eschewing or forgetting normative kin-ties or codes, such as those that are embedded in normative family life; rather, it is to understand that trans approaches to kin and lineage-making are not defined and exclusively framed by them. (Çaliskan 2023, pg. 1485)

Christa Schönfelder in *Wounds and Words* writes that transmemory "builds, through transmitted or imagined memories, a sense of connectedness with someone who is dead" (2013, pg. 242). In a 2016 anthropology dissertation Siri Schwabe described transmemory as the interworking of memory and spatiality. One might feel this connection of kinship, narrative, and space in anthropologist of music Steven Felds discussion of Bosavi poetics:

the stunning part was that poetic grammar and performance not only involve ecology, but also cosmology. All of these forest names are associated with ancestors: birds are what people become when they are no longer alive. The sounding, images, smells, tastes, sensations of the world of the forest are also the smells, sounds, tastes and visions of the spirit world. So: are cosmology and ecology "inside" grammar, and not simply a *mirror*, on the outside of it? (2020, pg. 89, *italics added*)

The question of the mirror, representation, and the integration of ecology and cosmology is an important one for Karen Barad:

The move toward performative alternatives to representationalism shifts the focus from questions of correspondence between descriptions and reality (e.g., do they mirror nature or culture?) to matters of practices/ doings/actions. I would argue that these approaches also bring to the forefront important questions of ontology, materiality, and agency, while social constructivist approaches get caught up in the geometrical optics of reflection where, much like the infinite play of images between two facing mirrors, the epistemological gets bounced back and forth, but nothing more is seen. Moving away from the representationalist trap of geo- metrical optics, I shift the focus to physical optics, to questions of diffraction rather than reflection. (2003, pgs. 802-803)

Barad's posthuman performative approach (2007) seeks an alternatives to Cartesian common sense, modes of thinking individuals in line feminist posthumanists (Braidotti 2013, 2019; Braidotti and Hlavajova 2018; Braidotti and Simone 2018b) theorizing the productive entanglements between discursive and material regimes: "The asymmetrical faith in our access to representations over thigs is a contingent fact of history and not a logical necessity; that is, it is simply a Cartesian habit of mind. It takes a healthy skepticism towards Cartesian doubt to be able to begin to see an alternative" (Barad 2003, pgs. 806-807).

Thinking cinema beyond representation does indeed require a healthy skepticism. Isn't cinema, especially as part of ethnographic practice fundamentally about representation and authority? *CineWorlding* (2023) began to develop cinematic production within a posthumanographic framework, an entangling of the discursive and material, where the discursive was not reduced to language, and material not limited to what was observed but included the materiality of the camera technology and the bodies that entangle with it. A rich network of relationality rich with agencies of all kinds. Light and sound were activating, so were camera sensors and microphone sensors, visual-images and sound-images, bodies both organic and technological, grain bodies and digital bodies, screens and speakers. CineWorlding was not about representing the world but instead the making of each moment of cinema was adding to it: "it is possible to develop coherent philosophical positions that deny that there are representations on the one hand and ontologically separate entities awaiting representation on the other" (Barad 2003, pg. 807). So when we turn our attention to memory it is important to not fall into the same Cartesian representational trap – that the real event was out there and that a memory is a representation of that event. But how to think through this, when it seems evident that this is indeed the structure? Can we tell the difference between our memories, devices, and information? Is our theory precise enough to disentangle the memory from its provocation, presence from its hauntings? The DDP is not just in a film and no single work describes itself what I think of it. To engage with the DDP required fragmenting across media. It wasn't a planned fragmentation, it was an emergent one and introduced cyborgraphy as research-creation.

Cyborgraphy as/and Research-Creation

As a student of ethnography I was challenged by an Indigenous elder on my very first ethnographic assignment 20 years ago to ask myself why I am doing this and for whom. Neither he nor his community needed the ethnographic work I was doing, they knew what they were doing. The elder said that as ethnographers we are looking for something and when we find it, when we re-find what we forgot, then we will no longer need to ask. I no longer think it is a matter of refinding something but instead that "cyborgs have more to do with regeneration and are suspicious of the reproductive matrix and of most birthing…the regrown limb can be monstrous, duplicated, potent. We have all been injured, profoundly. We require regeneration, not rebirth" (Haraway 1991, pg. 181). Research-creation and cyborgraphy are my practices of regeneration after the Human, or perhaps with xhumans.

Cyborgraphy reads Victor Turner's well-known concept of *liminality,* through Deleuze and Guattari's *geophilosophy* (Bonta and Protevi 2004), and research-creation (Loveless 2019, 2020; Manning 2016). Image of body, what the body is and can be, is of the utmost importance and has significant ramifications for the project formerly-called-ethnography.

From a certain angle, performance space is the definition of liminality "a temporal interface whose properties partially invert those of the already consolidated order which constitutes any specific cultural 'cosmos'" (1982, pg. 41). But from the perspective of the teams of dedicated people who create and run these performances, who designed and developed spaces to elicit experience, who transform (terraform) geographic space into performance space, who understand and apply the histories of performance architecture and technology there is nothing *liminoid* about it. It is an intentional terraforming of previously coded space using performance technology. Turner called these spaces "antistructure" (1969) which can "generate and store a plurality of alternative models for living, from utopias to programs, which are capable of influencing the behavior of those in mainstream social and political roles" (1982, pg. 33). In my research however, there was no single antistructure but a variety of located and proliferating alternatives, operating at a variety of scales, and moving either towards closure and collective assemblies of enunciation or, like the free radical, towards openness and ongoing proliferation that resists named collectives (MacDonald 2016).

Turner suggests that liminoid spaces are "'neutral spaces' or privileged areas set aside from the mainstream of productive or political events" (1982, pg. 33). The binaries of structure and antistructure, liminoid and daily spaces, are binaries that feminist technoscience and science and technology studies have since collapsed. And with my assumption that the modern Human biograms, it seems quite impossible to separate out liminal spaces. Might capitalism be a modern Human ritual that biograms individuality? Instead of thinking liminality as a transition for the modern Human, might we think of it as the transition from the Homo sapien sapien (intensive energy) into the modern Human or xhuman (extensive coordinates) in this case.

Francesca Ferrando observed in *Philosophical Posthumanism* that they "cannot be seen as separated but inherently related" (2020, pg. 26). These Posthuman-isms are also related to Transhumanism, Antihumanism, Metahumanism, Posthumanities, Metahumanities, Object-Oriented Ontology, and the nonhuman turn (pg. 26). We can think with Haraway and recognize these xhumans as "cyborgs. The cyborg is our ontology; it gives us our politics" (Haraway 1985, pg. 50). In all cases they are post-anthropocentric and take as a starting point a technologically extended body that is other than the modern Human. While xhumans and Humanism are different, xhumans are not free of Humanism. Xhumans carry the lineage of modern Humans but are actively developing performative and processual terraforming of timeplace and generating alternative models of transmemory that threads the biosphere-semiosphere-technoshere in alternative arrangements. These biograms are terraforming *altermodern worldings*, some in ways that may be accelerationist and other in critical social justice formations.[5]

Public space in the case of the DDP is terraformed into another placetime. It is not a transitory zone between spaces but an alternative coding that produced not a single liminal space, but a proliferation of alternative spaces at many scales that cannot be contained by any single description or temporal frame. Liminality in this case is the operation of transmemory's infolding as it vectors through performed post-anthropocentric futurity: the directional way that xHumans becoming-futurity is forming in the rituals that it self-designs for the purpose of terraforming heterogenous futurity on a shared planet at risk.[6]

I believe that research-creation practices, like the one proposed in *CineWorlding*, and developed in this chapter, can be an intervention into norms of ethnographic attunement that can help illuminate the developing post-anthropocentric futurity. As Natalie Loveless writes:

> I turn to research-creation to encourage modes of *temporal* and *material* attunement within the academy that require slowing down in a way that does not fetishize the slow but in which slowness comes from the work of defamiliarization and the time it take so ask *questions differently*. Research-creation, at its best, has the capacity to impact our social and material conditions, not by offering more facts, differently figured, but by finding ways, through aesthetic encounters and events, to persuade us to care and to care *differently*. (2019, pg. 107).

A research-creation approach is not an attempt to pin down performance, a body, or transmemory but instead to follow its movement, a

> metamodeling makes felt lines of formation…Metamodeling is against method, active in its refutation of preexisting modes of existence, meta in the sense of mapping abstract formations in conjuctions in continuing variation…whether we call it metamodeling, or whether we think of it as study or call it research-creation or radical empiricism, it is the question of how knowledge is crafted in each singular instance of a practice's elaboration that is key. (Manning 2016, pg. 43)

Anarchist Erotica engages with George Marcus' model of "activist ethnography" (2013), an ethnographic practice dedicated to *cinema-thinking as lived abstraction* that is inseparable from the mobilization of affects (Massumi 2015; 2022) involved in bodying in/with the world: "what is lived abstraction if not thought?"(Massumi 2011, pg. 116). George E. Marcus urges activist ethnography "to make trials or contests of norms and values the basis of forming working collaborations and arguments, with uncertain, often messy outcomes, in the pursuit of ethnographic insights in the field" (2013, pg. 200). Altermodern worldings as ritual performative (liminal) spaces extends the ongoing project of connecting performance studies and ethnography (Keil 1989; Waterman 2019) to deal with contemporary complexity (Marcus 1998). Turner's theory and the performance studies that it contributed to has been enhanced by feminist technoscience and is taking new shape in research-creation. What is perhaps becoming evident is that these ritual/performance/liminal spaces are contributing to terraforming xhuman alternatives just as surely as they are terraforming conservative rituals of modern Human futurity. This reorients ethnography from questions of culture alone to the emergence of modern Humans, xhumans, and more. An xhuman *image of body* and its *transmemory* goes far beyond the flesh of homo sapien sapien and in different directions with different orientations, histories, values, ethics, and dreams for the future. How homo sapein sapien is machined into its extensive coordinates matters.

PART TWO: ANARCHIST EROTICA IN SIX MOVEMENTS

Anarchist Erotica as Cyborgraphy

Anarchist Erotica is partially improvised, scripted, and workshopped with actors who play characters that we made together. One actor – who had never acted before – uses their own name as their character name while the other, who is a professional actor, uses an invented name. The film uses content from a failed documentary. It failed because when the Decentralized Dance Party (DDP) starts, it is difficult to make cinematic sense of it. The film uses a script – the first that I have ever produced - which was written and then workshopped with the two actors Haley and Wren (Georgie) eight times before filming. There is also a philosopher, Prof. Marie-Eve Morin (a third actor) who plays the role of *philosopher* and who responded to the script with an original philosophical text that she performs.

I should say that she *becomes* the philosopher. At first her voice is disembodied and operates as a narrator that introduces the film. It becomes a kind of guide through the film, only sometimes embodied *as philosopher*. Does this sound complicated? Well, I have been working with the DDP, off and on, for more than a decade. In the process I have produced two films, a binaural soundscape recording, and an unpublished ethnography. These have all added up to a small pile of digital artifacts that have produced a kind of digital archive of my time trying to make sense with the DDP.

The DDP is a social machine, with political and ethical dimensions. It hooks bodies to old broadcast technology. In this sense, the DDP are cyber-punk, they use old thrown-away technology for a dance party that shapes anarchist sociality oriented to breaking open the common-sense logic of private capitalist capture of public space under *capitalist realism*. In doing so they illustrate that unlike the totalizing narrative of capitalist realism, there are techniques to terraform capitalist space.

Anarchist Erotica is an experimental cyborgraphic project that co-conspires with the *Decentralized Dance Party*. It is a film project that mixes observational documentary, an original screenplay, and philosophical reflections performed on screen by an unnamed professional philosopher. Anarchist Erotica deals centrally with memory in two dimensions. The first, and most obvious, is when one of the fictional characters in the film has flashbacks. These flashbacks are comprised of documentary footage. Having documentary footage as flashbacks situates the documentary in a particular way, no longer objective and universal but instead personal, situating the viewer as Haley, so you experience the flashbacks together but separately from Georgie. These flashbacks provide momentum for Haley and Georgie's relationship struggles. The flashbacks themselves are motivated by a variety of forces.

The fictional section of the film takes place in a hotel room the morning after Haley and Georgie's anniversary. They spend the morning discussing their lives and relationship as existential projects, dealing with issues that are pressing to them while also trying to figure out what kind of future they are making. The observational documentary footage is not the object of the film but instead Haley's inner world, affects from the DDP motivate her and shape her understanding. This brings us into the experience of memory's moving: transmemory.

There is then a second movement of transmemory through transmedia. The DDP is not isolated to Haley. An earlier film, *Waiting to Connect* (dir. MacDonald 2019), and an accompanying documentary, *Documenting Fiction* (dir. Kuelken 2019), provide other connections to the DDP. In a further experimental move two segments of *Waiting to Connect* are re-composed for *Anarchist Erotica*. This composting, repurposing, or sampling creates another angle on DDP's entanglement. Anna and Francesco from Porto, Portugal arrive from *Waiting to Connect* and join Haley and Georgie in Nanaimo and Vancouver in *Anarchist Erotica*. But Anna and Fran have already shown themselves to be co-conspiratorial improvising social actors in *Documenting Fiction*. Anna narrates her experiences in *Documenting Fiction* and edits a film based on it. Her cinematic sense mingles with other cinematic, textual, and aural sense-making. Transmemory is not bounded by a body, it moves through collectives, operating a threading of biosphere-technosphere. You are now part of this developing seam.

Anarchist Erotica attempts to mobilize the sense of *decentralization* as a more-than human force. Documentary has long participated in and has even been defined by mythologizing capture,[7] even, and most problematically, when in political alignment with movements that resist the centralization of identity.[8] Documentary film as a contributor to machinically enabled and mobile techno-memory or *transmemory* too often (in its most basic understanding as *document*) contributes to the hardening of identity where it could operate against this by emphasizing the free radicals at work in the becoming-imperceptible, in the Deleuzean sense, of anarchist becoming. It is a question of form, of the relations of cinematic form and the techniques operating with the more-than human forces at the interstices of transmemory. Anarchist Erotica is an artwork and it aspires to emphasize the free radical: *erotic submission to the affects of decentralization*, the free radical oriented not to the documentation alone but to the potential for cinema to mobilize minor politics.[9]

Anarchist Erotica, as *Waiting to Connect* (2018)

Join Anna and Fran in Porto, Portugal as they develop a relationship in the days before the first Decentralized Dance Party in Portugal.

Figure 2. QR code

Anarchist Erotica, as Poem

I found a poem titled *anarchist erotica* online in October 2017. I wrote it down in my notes. I found it because having just come up with *anarchist erotica* as a title of my recent experimental *speculative worlding* film, I wanted to see what references I would find.

Anarchist Erotica
I wanna fuck an anarchist
In the hopes that Noam Chomsky
Essays are scribbled
In braille
Across your back

In reading the poem, I was struck by the poetic confluence of anarchist politics and erotics. The body as political, sexual, and literary machines. The drive to simultaneously fuck and fuck the system—fingers stroke the hard curves of bone braille, roughly and wetly protruding from flushing skin. An anarchist body horror erotica.

I am sure that I found this poem online. I am certain of it. Except that I cannot find it now, nor have it found it again. I have transcribed it fully into search engines; a digital incantation. Go ahead, do it now. Tell me what you find. It isn't there is it? Do you believe that I didn't write this anonymous poem of anarchist erotica? I am sure that I did not—mostly sure. But how sure can anyone in the present moment be sure of such things? If it can't be found then it does not exist, it never existed. Except it's here and I remember finding it. Perhaps I wrote it myself and am lying to you. Or my auto-biographical memory has a virus, and by virus I mean trickster. Perhaps I tricked myself into believing that I found it to avoid the responsibility of its parentage. But I have taken it in and have nurtured it. I gave it some space in a word doc and then nested it like a mutating seed at the beginning of the film. Its affective tentacles reached through the screen and across the digital editing timeline to hold us all together, sharpening a critical resistance and cultivating seduction. Maybe you wrote it and being unsure of its illicit lines went and deleated it before someone found out it was you. Perhaps you hated it and were ashamed. Maybe you will read this and write me? It doesn't matter how it got here, it's here now. It is too much of a spell to remain as text. Even if it began life as a late-night bedroom poetic outburst on a now long dead blog, it continues to move through and affect the world, *transmemory*. It brought an edge to *Anarchist Erotica* (2023, dir. MacDonald) that the film would not have had otherwise.

Transmemory names, in part, the sharing/mobility of memory across wetware and hardware, *trans* is the bridge between the relational matrix of my body-worlding happening in psychic/conceptual, social, and environmental ecologies of the biosphere. Second, it names that what is happening in technological psychic/conceptual, social, and environmental ecologies of the technosphere, what Baudrillard called *simulacra* (1994). Third, transmemory blurs the distinction that Baudrillard already weakened and emphasizes the *ecstasy of communications* (2012) while not forgetting or ignoring the consequences (Bauman 2011). It is not a failure of biological memory that causes me to doubt myself, it is something else. Failure is too easy. It is some kind of process where personal experience or biological recordings are coursed through by technological recordings experienced as personal memories. Of course they are personal, but why are we so quick to think that the xhumans doesn't feel their insides. It's just that their sphere of affective possession is stretched out much further than one's biology encapsulates. The Mandela Effect—shared incorrect public memories—and Proustian involuntary memory—are cases of transmemory that shakes the foundations of neurotypicality.

Transmemory is the threading of body-technology. Thinking with Deleuze-Guattari's *free disjunction* where "the differential positions persist in their entirety, they even take on a free quality, but they are all inhabited by a faceless and transpositional subject" (1983:77). *Either* I found anarchist erotica *or* I made it up… "a disjunction that remains disjunctive, and that still affirms the disjointed terms, that affirms them throughout their entire distance, *without restricting one by the other or excluding the one from the other*, is perhaps the greatest paradox" (76). This paradox energizes speculative worldings that mix documentary and fiction, challenging even its creator with problems of telling one from the other. *Either* it's true *or* it's made up. *Either* it's fiction *or* it's ethnography. *Either* it happened *or* it didn't happen. But why choose? It is true *and* it isn't, it is fiction *and* ethnography, it did happen *and* didn't happen. As the body of the earth is wrapped with ever increasingly complex circuits of digital memory, it is necessary to begin to conceive memory that is not, nor perhaps ever really was, only biological. It is biological and it isn't. Transmemory crosses the thresholds of biosphere-semiosphere-technosphere and asks us to reconceive post-anthropos memory, and in the process perhaps the ways that human, more-than human, and non-human interact in distributive cognition.

The poem gave me confidence in my title. That it was both evocative of the subject matter but also not too popular and overused. It does not get lost in the crowd. The poem is the image of the film before any audiovisual images. Cinematic poetics is not the outcome of cinematic images, it is not the piling up of montage, it can work the other way. Cinematic poetics preexists the shots, it is the poetics that moves the cinematic cyborg into action. The cinematic poetics is also not the poem. The poetics resonated with the poem during my search, it emphasized tones and harmonics in the vibrations already in the words that were used to search: *anarchist* and *erotica*. The words fitted like black ultra-lite polyurethane gloves over the worlding resonance bouncing off of the cement and bodies of the Decentralized Dance Party that took over the streets of Vancouver, Nanaimo, Calgary, and Porto. The erotics moving through an anarchist electronic decentralized dance party. The poem activated the erotic thrusting of the DDP that still resides in my body. I tried to get it out with a documentary. But that failed. The refuse of that doc became the hot compost that grew Anarchist Erotica. Then while I was still germinating it, I received a message that the DDP would be in Porto at the same time I was.

Anarchist Erotica, as *Documenting Fiction* (2019)

Join Anna as she unpacks the posthuman performativity inside Waiting to Connect. This is the film that she made as a research assistant to Waiting to Connect and used this as her application film for film school. She graduated and has since become an award winning and sought after filmmaker.

Figure 3. QR code

Anarchist Erotica, DDP as Exstallation, Version 7 (2017), Originally Drafted 2012

In *Aesthetic Theory*, Theodor Adorno (1997) writes: "aesthetics is demanded by the development of artworks" (341), new concepts are needed with the emergence of new forms of art. The *exstallation*—the inverse of the installation—uses information-rich *liquid* culture (Bauman 2011) to produce an aesthetic event outside the confines of recognized or legitimated aesthetic space. The *exstallation*, perhaps related to the 1960s *happening,* is a form of aesthetic social process that draws from the 'cultural environment' for the production of an *aesthetic field* (Berleant 2000), what I will call after Niklas Luhmann (2000) an *aesthetic system,* while holding onto the Deleuzian *assemblage* as a complex dynamic system that both constitutes a dynamic entity that has productive capacity—introduces difference—both internally and externally. As an aesthetic concept that embodies these characteristics, I offer *exstallation*. Related to the work of European contemporary *relational* aesthetics discussed by Nicolas Bourriard (2002), critical to capitalist realism (Fisher 1999; 2009) the *exstallation* is different from *relational aesthetics* in that the exstallation does not operate within gallery walls.

The highway was busy as I exited Edmonton, Alberta. During the 3.5 hour drive south to Calgary, the economic superpower of Alberta, I reflected on my relationship with the Decentralized Dance Party (DDP) and, in particular Gary, one of its founders. It all began over a year ago on Facebook. One of my friends in Ottawa, where I had lived before moving to Alberta, made a comment online about how disappointed she was to have recently missed a DDP. I Googled DDP and, following a YouTube link, watched a trailer. I was blown away. The DDP was two guys, an FM radio transmitter stuffed in a backpack, an iPod, a game glove and a song list made up of party favorites and electronica broadcast to hundreds of available boomboxes tuned to the "party frequency".

Leading up to my trip to the Calgary DDP I had spent a great deal of time reflecting on what the DDP was all about and, in fact, I blogged that it was anarchist musicking taking back the commons (I had just finished reading Michael Hardt and Tony Negri's Trilogy [*Empire* (2000), *Multitude* (2004), *Commonwealth* (2009)]. Soon after my first post I received an email from Gary thanking me for the article and asking to repost it. My blog stats went off the charts. We stayed in touch and in February during the planning for a Vancouver DDP in Vancouver I received an alarmed email from him about a potential legal run-in with the city of Vancouver. Apparently, bureaucrats were trying to insist that the DDP get a permit. Gary insisted that the DDP was not an event but that it was a social gathering in a public space and therefore should not require a permit. The bureaucrat disagreed and threatened the DDP with legal sanctions if the DDP occurred. After a tense few days of emails, discussion, and media, the DDP happened without a hitch.[10]

In August, Gary and I met at the DDP headquarters in Vancouver (an undisclosed location) where I took some photos and conducted my first full-length interview.[11] Again Gary reposted and my stats went through the roof.

I arrived in Calgary just before the scheduled party kickoff. It was pretty easy to find the starting location as Gary had posted the GPS coordinates on a Google Map. The satellite image made it easy to recognize the surrounding area. The gathering point was the largest skate park in Canada.[12] I was pretty excited imagining a DDP taking place on the curvy cement of a skate park.

I parked the car and walked to the skate park a few blocks away. As I approached the park I could hear some chilled jazz in the distance. I began to see employees who looked like extras from *The Office*. The DDP usually has a theme. The theme for this tour was *Taking Care of Business* and everyone was encouraged to wear "business" clothes. I passed small pods of comically attired business-dancers cheerily chattering. This was the first DDP in Calgary; everyone was pretty excited and quite curious. I saw a couple of banana-suited organizers scurrying back and forth. They are part of the DDP's organization. While snapping a few photos of the available boomboxes I caught sight of a small group of Calgary police officers standing off in the distance wearing their iconic Stetson hats. They were talking with

Gary and likely getting the run-down. Gary is always very clear with the city police. He is interested in communication but not asking permission.

I wondered what the cowboy-hatted police thought of the Mexican romance music Gary had collected on his last trip to Mexico, which was now playing through the boomboxes.

The skate park looked quite a bit like I thought it might, thanks to the satellite photos on Google Maps. But the business costumes, the bananas, and the romance music coloured everything in unusual emotional hues. Even the young skaters who were obviously intent on shredding the park were dismounted and casually observing the transformation.

The music flows, morphs, and pulses in unusual shapes, creating unusual densities. The DDP feels different from other events because the sound source is not fixed and focused. Hundreds of boom boxes tuned to the same frequency create distributed-sound forms and a terrain of volume peaks and densities, changeable and chaotic. The sound waves pass through each other in superimposition. Inside the DDP superimposition creates a sound ecology, a sonic rhizome.

Communication within the sound environments first occurred to Tom and Gary years before. They were riding around the city with a group of bicyclists when their iPod—broadcasted through a boombox duct-taped to a bicycle—ran out of batteries. To replace the music they tuned the boombox into a local radio station. A second rider, who also had a boombox, did the same. They rode around within a mobile sound-environment for the first time. It made an impression on them. They soon made the leap that if they had 50 or 100 boomboxes and an FM transmitter—becoming their own radio station—they would have a distributed sound system. Gary soon started collecting boomboxes but it wasn't until 2009 when he decided to take the DDP a bit more seriously.

Gary was inspired by a contradiction between his upbringing in a small Ontario town and the experience of youth people are having in a city like Vancouver, Edmonton, or Calgary. For Gary, he and his friends would hang out in the woods or a local gravel pit and have free space to party and explore. But in the city the parks are closed at night, police patrol and break up groups of young people, and even stores like 7-11 use noise suppression technology to prevent young people from "loitering," the negative word for making community. The city is a sterile environment organized for commerce. Anyone not participating in commercial trade is viewed with suspicion. This includes young people who are either too young to go to a bar or those who choose not to for social, cultural, or economic reasons. The city environment is cold concrete with little opportunity to explore and experiment within the environment in the process that makes it your home.

Gary's voice cuts the air–"It's business time!"–and the deep thrum of electronic music punctuates the crowd penetrating into and synchronizing bodies react with energy only anticipation can create. Released. The DDP begins and the small walled-in space where people were milling, picking out their boombox, was transformed into an outdoor dance club. The sun lies low on the prairie landscape and warms our bodies while it hints at the coming chill of a late autumn Alberta evenings. The staccato of the electronic high-hat ricochets off the concrete wall and the "oooommm" of the tuned electronic kick drum create deep pools of bass that explode upwards in a geyser-like standing wave. The sound sources circle each other and double back painting sound in kaleidoscopic tones, and shades. This music was not composed for this context. Music is being used as communication with space for the production of aesthetic experience.

I am pulled out of my reverie watching Gary flanked by four cowboy-hat-wearing police officers. I snap a picture. I remember Vancouver-based artist Michael Asti Rose once saying: "wilderness and classicism are always in relation to each other." Through the DDP, Gary and Tom orchestrate an experience that leads city youth into the wilderness of experience. Gary often mourns the policing of urban social life that he sees as having lost something essentially human. As Henry Giroux (2009) has noted, poor youth in North American society have become imagined as dangerous and even disposable because they are failed consumers. Participation in social life has been reduced to economic actions. When the relationship to urban space is reversed, that is away from consumption to the production of non-economically mediated social expression, a micropolitics of resistance emerges that Paola Berenstein Jacques has noticed: "A clue of micro-resistance towards the process of urban spectacularization can be found in the everyday use of the city, in particular, in non-planned or in deviating experiences of public spaces; that is, in the quotidian conflictive and non-consensual uses of the city that oppose planned ways of use" (2012). The DDP is Gary's way to confront the control of the city and to enact a rupture to allow for the production of the commons created by ecological communication and the aesthetic experience.

"When I say freeze, you freeze" raps DJ Kool from his 1996 "Let Me Clear My Throat." We gleefully respond to Kool's commands "to make some noise." It doesn't matter that Kool isn't here, after all it's not about him. We are all experiencing the moment that connects us together, the pulse that locks us, the refrain that connects our voices and dissolves space and time. It's this experience when human bodies noisily fill the sanitized urban landscape. To hear dance music fill up a skate park obstacle shaped like a swimming pool, to bounce off the small mountains of cement. Or to see (and hear!) the parade of thousands of us move from the skate park, down the center of the closed off road to… where are we going?

I find myself following along looking at downtown Calgary for what seems like the first time. Certainly, the first time in the center of the street. The red and blue lights of police cars reflect off the tall glass buildings, colour made thinker by the thump of drums off these tall smooth surfaces. From a sonic perspective the urban street of a major city is a canyon. Up ahead we are taking over an empty parking garage!

C+C Music factory is deafening as "everybody dance now" cuts through the garage and the first scratchy pulses of "Gonna Make You Sweat" crash upon the hard cement walls, the smooth cement floors, and the low cement ceiling. We are crammed together like water molecules forced into a hose. Our newly experienced density, such a change from the open spaces of the skate park and the street, seems to propel us to move faster, to rub together more tightly, to feel and smell each other in new ways. I smell the sulfur before I notice the light from a flare. How much of this garage have we filled? I try to move further inside as people flow in and out, creating pools, eddies, and streams pressed by the force of moving bodies. The sound and bodies of the DDP (can they be divided anymore?) fill the space of the parking garage as if the space itself was a mold. What have we now become?

"We're moving!" A banana suit shimmies past me in a blur heading back to the street. Bumping, gliding, swaying, together we flow.

Splashing back into the canyon of the street makes the space feel even larger and more alien. The familiar cocoon of the garage, reminding us of the dance floor, is replaced by the strangeness of a dancing occupation. The lights from fire trucks and police vehicles bounce off the tall glass buildings surrounding us as we approach a downtown park. A familiar horn refrain cuts the air, it mixes with yelps of delight and transforms now tangled timbres. Shadows cut strangely across the few trees, manicured shrubs and standing stones of the city park. People wade into the little stream and play in the fountains; their arms reach together into the sky in the form of a Y.M.C.A.

"Since the dawn of time people would start a fire, maybe imbibe some substances and just dance around," Gary remarked to me last August. I this about this now as I sit in the grass. There is something eternal and natural about sociality. But it is also so bound up with our technology, our customs, education, attitudes, and laws. Gary has traveled a great deal and has seen places where it's still acceptable to party in the street. His experience of social commons was eye opening and inspired him to use the DDP to challenge the North American city.

Flashing red and blue lights silhouette cowboy hats adorned city police who move around the edges of the herd like wolves. We are lucky. We know that the Calgary city police are not going to break this up and that they are here to make sure everyone is safe. But we also keep an eye on them. We know this experience is precious and that ultimately they have the power. Open sociality in the city (an open source city?), while seemingly natural, is very difficult. The city, organized as it is in North America, is engineered to hamper free social life. The city is built for the production and flow of trade, and for silence. Of course this is not a bad thing in itself. Work is just as natural as play. But work and play are out of balance in the urban planning of our cities. Governance through bylaw and zoning impede the formation of spontaneous social groupings. It occurs to me that Canadian cultural studies of music could take this on and work to better understand play in human Canadian urban life.

"This is the biggest crowd we've seen on this tour!" Gary's voice bounces around the urban square and is greeted by human thunder rising into the air column formed by the buildings surrounding the park. "This is fucking awesome!" The textures of the park, the grass, built earth elevations; large stones, fountains and streams create diverse sonic ecosystems. The distributed sound makes its way deeply into the geography of the space in a way that none of us has heard before. This experience is different, and we can hear it. "It's time to sway." The opening acoustic piano arpeggio ripples through the crowd like an electric current. "Grab someone and sway with them!" The energy spikes and nearly everyone begins to sing in unison with Journey: "Just a small town girl, living in a lonely world." I had never really appreciated this song. The park swayed and the chorus thundered:

> Strangers waiting
> Up and down the boulevard
> Their shadows searching in the night
> Streetlight people
> Living just to find emotion
> Hiding somewhere in the night

"Don't Stop Believing" is the meta-anthem for the DDP, everyone screaming the lyrics in an ultra-self-conscious expression of performing Hollywood-belonging with a song already heavily marked by post-modern irony drizzled with a generation of post-irony-irony camp elevated by the made-for-TV Broadway aesthetics of *Glee*. "Don't Stop Believing" might be about the alienation people experience in an isolation deepened by a-social political and economic systems, but the DDP version adds so many levels of recursion that meaning becomes a hall of mirrors. The DDP, using an amalgam of old and new technology, uses what Heinz von Foerster calls "the observation of observation" to reflect virtual life through physical life and aestheticize the aesthetic in a way that produces social life through the sharing of aesthetic information. Tom and Gary found a way to bring the organization power of Facebook and Twitter, the portability of the mp3, the geopositioning of Google Maps, the communication technology of Wordpress, and the crowd-sourced funding potential of Kickstarter, into the physical world. The significance of the DDP is that it functionally couples the virtual world to the physical world to allow for the *exstallation*.

Anarchist Erotica, as Script (2018)

First Page of the Anarchist Erotica Script
CREDITS AGAINST BLACK SCREEN WITH LOUNGE MSIC SOUNDING LIKE IT'S COMING FROM A NEARBY ROOM THROUGH A CLOSED DOOR.
(In black)
PHILOSOPHER
It all started innocently enough.
EXT. BICYLCE FOOTAGE
Gary and his friends were enjoying themselves. They loved riding bicycles together. They also loved music. They noticed that if they attached boomboxes to their bicycles they could listen to music while they roamed around. They soon discovered that if they all tuned their boomboxes to the same channel, they became a mobile sound system.
A steady thrumming beat underscores the philosopher's voice.

.

Years later, Gary built a radio transmitter.
CUT TO:
DDP YOUTUBE CLIP
Electronic dance music with clips from DDP youtube content in multiple screens.
He was soon joined by people committed to decentralization and public parties. Together they collected hundreds of old boomboxes and set out on a mission to show that decentralization and partying can change the world. One party at a time.
They have since put on more that 80 parties around the world and have inspired tens of thousands.
Haley is one of these people.

Anarchist Erotica, as Film (2023)

Figure 4. QR code

CONCLUSION

The Humanist *image of body* as Viverios de Castro (2014) has shown, is narcissistic in its anthropocentrism (concerned with itself), enthralled by its uniqueness, committed to its independence, rationality, and separations. Ethnography was framed by the Anthropos as a Demos observing and reporting back the practices of the Ethnos. Contrary to the claims of universalist Humanism, that it was always oriented to the species as a whole, entry into the category of modern Human was managed. As feminists, decolonial, Queer, critical race, disability theorists, along with anti-humanists and posthumanists have all taught, membership into the Human club was constantly guarded by markers of race, class, gender, neurotypicality, sexuality, and geography. xhumans have no interest in this particular club and are done critiquing it. They have been wounded by the biogram of the modern Human and are moving on to make new xhuman biograms. The Anthropos Regime with its Demos-Ethnos binary is coming to an end.

For Haraway science fiction storytellers and sometimes anthropologists are "exploring what it means to be embodied in high-tech worlds…exploring conceptions of bodily boundaries and social order… helping us to consciousness about how fundamental body imagery is to world view, and so to political language" (1991, pg. 173). Haraway's cyborg is a post-anthropocentric image of body, cyborgraphy is a practice of attachment, experience, immersion, and change. Cyborgraphy has no prohibition against "going native" because there is no learning without change, no experience without transformation, no Other that needs to be separated out from Self. Cyborgraphy is not an address to the center from the peripheries. It is born in the peripheries and is not trying to make a new homeland. It is decentered and usure of its location, it knows its body is a collection of critters and that there are many permeable boundaries and extended connections in its proprioceptive scan. Cyborgraphy is perhaps a kind of *survival* ethnography, or perhaps a cyborgraphy of "wounded flourishing" (Haraway 2016, pg. 120), that may play a role in helping to think with biograms mutating with planetary crisis.

A growing number of xhumans are developing post-anthropos propositions. A post-anthropos *image of body* is an experimental and theory driven practice for critical feminist posthumanists as well as anarchocapitalist transhumanists. Cyborgraphy refuses an a priori biogram (posthuman for instance) from which to do the project-formerly-called-ethnography. Cyborgraphy must be practiced without an xhuman foundation in order to be open to the performativity of xhuman formation of which cyborgraphy is part. If it is indeed a question of how the intensive energies of the Homo sapien sapien are machined into extensive coordinates then it is not just a question of culture although culture remains an orientation.

This is where the proposition for *transmemory* and its *image of body* becomes important for cyborgraphy. In the time I spent with the DDP, in the places that we collaboratively terraformed, I was left haunted by a fledgling biogram that has been growing inside my modern Human body. Over the years it has grown to a size that it can no longer be ignored. It is demanding attention and making it difficult for me to recognize myself in the practice I was trained in. My films projects have changed, my theory has changed, my relational sense of self has both grown and become much less definite. What can the practice formerly-called-ethnography become when the Anthropos is no longer universal, when I do not know what variety of xhuman I am or am becoming. The Human is no longer the only proposition and perhaps there are many other orientations to transmemory that contribute xhuman biograms that we must find a way to understand and theorize. For Rosi Bradiotti:

Theory today is about coming to terms with unprecedented changes and transformations of the basic unit of reference for what counts as human. This affirmative, unprogrammed mutation can help actualize new concepts, affects and planetary subject formations. Just as we do not know what posthuman bodies can do, we cannot even begin to guess what postanthropocentric embodied brains will actually be able to think up. (2013, pg. 104)

The performative aspects of this essay and the challenges that they presents can be read as the difficulty that transmemory, post-anthropos theory, and emergent xhuman biograms present. Cyborgraphy folds performance theory, feminist technoscience, and ethnography into new arrangements that seeks to understand proliferating xhumans. The degree to which this transmedia performance has succeeded hangs on the complexity of your holographic sense of the nowness of the Decentralized Dance Party. The way the transmedia performance called attention to the movement through flesh and technology. What orientations to your biogram are challenged or confirmed?, in what direction do you feel the pull of futurity?, how many placetimes populate and fold through each other as your biogram is taking shape?, how might we share these alternatives to modern Human biograms when our methods too often and too hastily assume the modern Human body as producer and reader?. These are only some of the questions that continue to enrich the development of cyborgraphy.

REFERENCES

Adorno, T. W. (1997). *Aesthetic Theory*. Athlone Press.

Barad, K. (2003). Posthumanist Performativity: Towards an Understanding of How Matter Comes to Matter. *Signs (Chicago, Ill.)*, 28(3), 801–831. 10.1086/345321

Barad, K. (2007). *Meeting the Universe Halfway: quantum physics and the entanglement of matter and meaning*. Duke University Press. 10.2307/j.ctv12101zq

Baudrillard, J. (1994). *Simulacra and Simulation*. University of Michigan Press.

Baudrillard, J. (2012). The Ecstasy of Communication. Los Angeles: Semiotext(e)

Bauman, Z. (2011). *Collateral Damage: Social Inequalities in a Global Age*. Polity Press.

Berleant, A. (2000). *The Aesthetic Field: Phenomenology of Aesthetic Experience*. Cybereditions.

Bonta, M., & Protevi, J. (2004). *Deleuze and Geophilosophy: A Guide and Glossary*. Edinburgh University Press.

Bourriaud, N. (2002). *Relational Aesthetics*. Paris, FR: Les Presses du reel.

Braidotti, R. (2013). *The Posthuman*. Polity.

Braidotti, R. (2019). *Posthuman Knowledge*. Polity Press.

Braidotti, R., & Hlavajova, M. (2018a). *Posthuman Glossary*. Bloomsbury.

Braidotti, R., & Simone, B. (2018b). *Posthuman Ecologies: Complexity and Process after Deleuze*. Roman & Littlefield.

Butler, O. (1993). *Parables of the Sower*. Four Walls Eight Windows.

Caliskan, D. (2023). Tran theoretical approaches to memory and relatedness: Potentials and suggestions at the intersections of transgender studies and queer studies. *Memory Studies*, 16(6), 1484–1499. 10.1177/17506980231204177

Deleuze, G., & Guattari, F. (1983). *Anti-Oedipus: Capitalism and Schizophrenia*. University of Minnesota Press.

Ferrando, F. (2020). *Philosophical Posthumanism*. Bloomsbury.

Fisher, M. (1999). *Flatline Constructs: Gothic Materialism and Cybernetic Theory-Fiction*. New York: exmilitary press.

Fisher, M. (2009). *Capitalist Realism: Is There No Alternative?* Zero Books.

Gane, N. (2006). When We Have Never Been Human, What Is to Be Done?:Interview with Donna Haraway. *Theory, Culture & Society*, 23(7-8), 135–158. 10.1177/0263276406069228

Gangle, R. (2020). *Diagrammatic Immanence: Category Theory and Philosophy*. Edinburgh University Press.

Giroux, H. A. (2009). Hard Lessons: Neoliberalism, Education, and the Politics of Disposability. *Policy Futures in Education*, 7(5), 570–573. 10.2304/pfie.2009.7.5.570

Guattari, F. (1989). *The Three Ecologies*. Bloomsbury Academic.

Haraway, D. J. (1991). *A Cyborg Manifesto: Science, technology, and Socialist-Feminism in the Late Twentieth Century" in Simians, Cyborgs, and Women: The Reinvention of Nature*. Routledge.

Haraway, D. J. (2016). *Staying with the Trouble: Making Kin in the Chthulucene*. Duke University Press.

Keil, C. (1998). Applied Sociomusicology and Performance Studies. *Ethnomusicology, 42*(2), 303-312.

Latour, B. (1993). *We Have Never Been Modern*.

Loveless, N. (2019). How to Make Art at the End of the World: a Manifesto for Research-Creation. Durham, NC: Duke University Press. Cambridge: MA: Harvard University Press.

Loveless, N. (2020). *Knowings & Knots: Methodologies and Ecologies in Research-Creation*.

Luhmann, N. (2000). *The Reality of Mass Media*. Stanford University Press. 10.1515/9781503619227

MacDonald, M. B. (2016). *Playing for Change: Music Festivals as Community Learning and Development*. Peter Lang Press. 10.3726/978-1-4539-1861-6

MacDonald, M. B. (2023). *CineWorlding: Scenes of Cinematic Research-Creation*. Bloomsbury. 10.5040/9781501369421

Manning, E. (2012). *Relationscapes: Movement, Art, Philosophy*. MIT Press.

Manning, E. (2016). *The Minor Gesture*. Duke University Press.

Manning, E. (2020). *For a Pragmatics of the Useless*. Duke University Press.

Manning, E., & Massumi, B. (2014). *Thought in the Act: Passages in the Ecology of Experience*. University of Minnesota Press. 10.5749/minnesota/9780816679669.001.0001

Marcus, G. E. (1998). Ethnography in/of the world system: The emergence of multi-sited ethnography. In *Ethnography through thick & thin* (pp. 105–132). Princeton University Press.

Marcus, G. E. (2013). Experimental forms for the expression of norms in the ethnography of the contemporary. *HAU*, 3(2), 197–217. 10.14318/hau3.2.011

Massumi, B. (2002). *Parables for the Virtual: Movement, Affect, Sensation*. Duke University Press.

Massumi, B. (2011). *Semblance and Event: Activist Philosophy and the Occurrent Arts*. MIT Press. 10.7551/mitpress/7681.001.0001

Massumi, B. (2015). *Politics of Affect*. Polity.

Schönfelder, C. 2013. *Wounds and Words: Childhood and Family Trauma in Romantic and Postmodern Fiction*. Bielefeld, Germany: transcript Verlag.

Shotwell, A. (2016). *Against Purity: Living Ethically in Compromised Times*. Minnesota Press.

Turner, V. (1969). *The Ritual Process: Structure and Anti-Structure*. Cornell University Press.

Turner, V. (1982). *From Ritual to Theatre: The Human Seriousness of Play*. PAJ Publications.

Urion, C. (2023). Some Precepts Taught By Two Cree Elders And Their Implications For Talking About Music. In Stock, J., & Diamond, B. (Eds.), *The Routledge Companion to Ethics and Research in Ethnomusicology* (pp. 21–33).

Vita-More, N. (2018). *Transhumanism: What is it?* Humanity+ publication.

Viverios de Castro, E. (2014). *Cannibal Metaphysics*. University of Minnesota Press.

Waterman, E. (2019). Performance Studies and Critical Improvisation Studies in Ethnomusicology. In *Theory for Ethnomusicology: Histories, Conversations* (pp. 141–175). Insights. 10.4324/9781315408583-7

ENDNOTES

[1]   A very early draft of this paper was given at the Transmemory conference at the University of Porto in the winter of 2022. Subsequent drafts have been read and discussed with Natalie Loveless, Sha Labare, Yelena Gluzman, and Erin Manning. When I wrote *CineWorlding* I was concentrating on cine-ethnomusicology, film theory, and the process philosophy of Manning and Massumi, along with the posthuman theory of Rosi Braidotti. It is only recently that it has been pointed out to me that I am also engaging in performance studies and SF theory. Natalie Loveless invited me to a workshop in the spring of 2024 that she arranged with the performance artist and educator Marilyn Arsem. In the middle of site specific performance art activity I realized that this practice aligned quite exactly with the kind of attunement that I had developed as part of my ethnographic practice. I began to think about the overlapping of ethnography and performance theory and the ways that it produces a kind of holographic ecology. I could conceptually see both separate and together, each contributing to the other without either being dissolved. This aligned quite dramatically with my previous attempts at thinking ecologically (with the concept of ecotone) beyond the dialectic and about Sartre's thinking about scarcity in *The Search for Method* and *Critique of Dialectical Reason*. One of the ways I read Deleuze and Haraway is to think with them about *ontologies* and the with Loveless and Labare about Haraway's SF and what Loveless has called the polydisciplinamory of research-creation. This aspect of my thinking was expanded in Labare's spring 2024 seminar on SF and Haraway hosted by Loveless at CoLABoratory at the University of Alberta. This essay is an attempt to take the next step beyond CineWorlding and beyond posthumanography into something much more unsettling and perhaps much more SF theory. I am deeply grateful for all of the generative conversations that have made this thinking possible.

[2]   As I wrote in CineWorlding: "Deleuze theorized 'a life' as immanence/creativity. A life is the becoming of living, the constant differentiation and change that is the energy of forces that is the in-event of living. Study is folded into 'a life' as Foucault recognized with the techniques of self. Technics, as Bernard Stiegler recognized, are not separate from a life either. Technology is a definitional component of human life. There is no human without technics. Recognizing the cybernetic condition of humanness sees mnemonic technologies like graphic and literary traces – now audio and visual recording – as setting up conditions for the emergence of subjectivation, sociality,

psychology and environmental relational nodes. Guattari proposed thinking transversally along the three ecologies psychic, social, environmental. Stiegler adds technology as a fourth ecology." (2023: 186).

3   The concept of *Altermodern* is a term used by Nicolas Bourriaud, cofounder of *Palais de Tokyo* in Paris, author of *Relational Aesthetics* (1998), and activist curator, who attempts to name "the 'aftershock' of modernism and its mourning, then into the necessary post-colonial reexamination of our cultural frames, 'Altermodern' is a word that intends to define the specific modernity according to the specific context we live in—globalization, and its economic, political and cultural conditions". The two volumes of *capitalism and schizophrenia* course through all of this and have contributed to an immense variety of activist, artistic, and philosophical invention. It is perhaps impossible to consider the development of cine-ethnomusicology without reflecting on the ways these bodyings of Altermodern worldings have impacted Modern worldings. Deleuze and Guattari's *A Thousand Plateaus* is a work of Altermodern worldings, as Brian Massumi writes in the introduction: 'Philosophy, nothing but philosophy.' Of a bastard line The annals of official philosophy are populated by 'bureaucrats of purse reason' who speak in 'the shadow of the despot' and are in historical complicity with the State. They invent' a properly spiritual...absolute State that...effectively functions in the mind.' Theirs is the discourse of sovereign judgement, of stable subjectivity legislated by 'good' sense, of rocklike identity, 'universal' truth, and (white male) justice. 'Thus the exercise of their thought is in conformity with the aims of the real State, with the dominant significations, and with the requirement of the established order (1987: ix). Ritual has been used by contemporary neo-pagan movements, which I have previously written about, which shares with Bourriaud and altermodern orientation. To think Modernity as ritual is to take a very small step, one already considered in terms of Goffman's *everyday performance* and in Butler's *performativity*. To call Modernity a ritual is to already confront Modernity's self-belief in its rationality, what Mark Fisher called 'capitalist realism'.

4   In CineWorlding a great deal of time is spend working through Deleuze and Guattari's concept of the machining of intensive space into extensive coordinates (Guattari 1989; Gangle 2020). This chapter further builds on this concept by thinking homo sapien sapien as the intensive energies that are machines into the collective assemblages of enunciation named modern Humans and the emergent collective assemblages called collectively *xhumans*. In CineWorlding I write: "The value of this view for music and sound studies is that it is possible then to think of machinic assemblages of enunciation at very different scales. The hierarchization of culture and subcultures (what is it a sub of, and are there sub, sub, sub cultures) is no longer a theoretical or methodological problem. Nor is ideology and mediation the only way to theorize culture production.7 In fact, instead of trying to understand how ideology seeps into a citizen through processes of repression, we can follow another path, that is, how does desire (intensive space) get machined to produce collective assemblages of enunciation (extensive space), and then, how are these assemblages captured (capitalism) or defended by practices oriented to the creation and maintenance of autonomous zones (minor). A further value of this approach is that it no longer presents a distinction between media, technology and bodies. A machinic collective assemblage of enunciation can easily accommodate the presence of old and new media machines quite easily, seeing humans, not as a special preserve but as an expanding machinic assemblage. Critical theory can move away from its patriarchal orientation to dispensing cultural truth and demystifying culture from the armchair and instead do cultural research from within mess of machinic processes." (MacDonald 2023, pg. 131).

5   But as I have pointed out in previous essays, post-anthropos does not mean the same thing for each xhuman collective assemblage of enunciation. Transhumans, for instance, amplify modern Humanism by pharmotechnological means, they are often accelerationalist anarchocapitalists where metahumans are collectively generating social justice alternatives to economic and ecological lifeways.

6   It was impressed upon me that learning to work in a good way has eco-existential consequences. During the making of *Pimachihowan* with Chief Conroy Sewepagaham and in conversation with Clan Chief Kwaxsistalla Wathl'thla about cinema production and traditional ecological knowledge, working in a good way requires not only documenting Indigenous worldings but doing so to deconstruct Humanism and its capitalist realism. If ethnomusicology, the field I was trained in, is still considered the ethnographic study of "humanly organized sound" (Blacking) post-anthropocentric theory requires us to ask what a Human is, and as a consequence, relationality makes retaining the *ethnos* as a distinctly observable 'Other' impossible.

7   I'm thinking here with Jill Godmillow's After The Documentary where she writes of the "pornography, imperialism, and … of the real".

8   In my article *Collaborative Projection* I wrote that: "The Body Without Organs (Deleuze and Guattari, 1983: 1987) of capitalist transhumanism, the very framework and foundations of social media and streaming platforms emit a gravitational pull that does not fundamentally liberate, nor determine, but instead orients and shapes mobile desire-producing. It inspires late-night whispering of the natural right of brand self-making and the material luxury awarded to those who are deemed Good, the influencer. In transhumanist capitalism, artfulness is transmuted into the content. In becoming-content, media-becomings are placed in a struggle against each other propelled by potential riches. The economic formula is now well-known even by the very young. Produce yourself in a dominant model, build social and cultural capital (the sweat of the content producer measured in likes, follows, and fans) in the hope that someday this might be exchanged for financial capital. DIY musicians know this model well." (MacDonald 2023, pgs. 154-155).

9   The concept of *anarchive* as it is developing in Erin Manning's writing and in the 3Ecologies project that Manning is seeding with Brian Massumi, is a "feed-forward mechanism" that is not in opposition with the archive but is an "excess energy of the archive" moving with the "traces of past projects towards being reactivatable". The anarchive is not necessarily a location but an impersonal force. This orientation informs speculative worldings because it moves practice away from a *documentation and capture paradigm* and towards *research-creation as worlding*. The focus changes from a cinema of documentation and representation, to a cinema that attempts to mobilize *the energy of events happening* into a speculative future. This work is activist in two senses. First, in the sense that George Marcus suggests when he writes that activism makes "trials or contests of norms and values the basis of forming working collaborations and arguments, with uncertain, often messy outcomes" (2013, pg. 200) and the second, in the activist philosophical sense developed by Erin Manning and Brian Massumi: activism oriented to *events of sense* in artfulness (Manning 2016).

10   Only a few weeks later the Vancouver riots occurred after a hockey game. I bet there wouldn't have been a riot if the city asked the DDP to plan on receiving the post-game revelers and channeled their energy into public dance and positive sociality.

11   The interview was edited into a podcast about the DDP and posted on my Wordpress blog via-SoundCloud.

[12]   For photos and a layout of the skate park please see the website: http://www.spectrum-sk8.com/parks/alberta/millenium2.html (accessed January 15, 2012)

Chapter 16
Memory as a Tool for Choreographic Reenactment:
Gaby Agis' Work as a Case Study

Elisa Frasson
Independent Researcher, Germany

ABSTRACT

This chapter investigates specific case studies of choreographic reenactment through memory considered both as a somatic embodied element and as a tool for reconstruction of choreographic pieces. Focusing primarily on British Gaby Agis, as a somatic movement educator and dancer, the author utilises embodied ethnography in the process of participant-observation and analysis of the case studies. The perspective of the inter-relationships between dancer and choreographer informs fieldwork analysis, delving into the direct and indirect impact of somatics on their works and creative approaches. The enquiry combines theoretical perspectives and fieldwork that acknowledges methodological interactions and parallels in different choreographic narratives.

INTRODUCTION

In this chapter, memory is investigated both as a somatic embodied element and as a tool for reconstruction of choreographic works, where present and past coexist as a manifestation of the creative and physical choreographic gestures. Memory is conceptualised not just as a facilitating instrument through which choreographing is reproduced, but also as a living exercise to embody the actual discourse in some specific dance reconstructions. This chapter stems from my doctoral thesis, entitled *Encounters with Somatics and European Choreography: Discourses, Narratives and Embodied Ethnography between the 1980s and the 2010s* where I addressed how somatic practices, and their relationship to memory, are also able to influence the reconstruction of 1980s choreography in the present day (Frasson, 2022).

DOI: 10.4018/979-8-3693-2264-2.ch016

THEMATIC BACKGROUND

At the time of my doctoral research around 2017, I pursued both theoretical and field work on the re-staging of some European choreographic works from the 1980s from the UK, Belgium and Germany. I followed their rehearsals, observed their training and discussed the dances with the choreographers. For example, two of the reconstructions observed were *Close Streams* (1983, restaged in 2016) and *Shouting Out Loud* (1984, restaged in 2014) by British choreographer Gaby Agis. It was immediately interesting for me to note that one of the tools taken into consideration in the reconstruction process was memory. Although this may seem obvious, it was relevant to see how memory was handled in a transversal and interdisciplinary way. Video footage, when available, certainly provided a useful means of collecting the piece together and reweaving its dramaturgical threads. Nevertheless, the aim was to return to that specific bodily and mental state that certain choreographic passages sought. The choreographers' work seemed to me to be more aimed at reopening the notes, re-practicing the physical/mental exercises that brought back that specific state that the choreography was seeking. Thus began research into the diaries, notes, images, and sketches of the choreographic score. The need was not so much to re-enact a historical piece, but to recreate it in the present time.

As pointed out by dance academic Mark Franko (2018), reenactment handles the dance of the past as something alive in the present time.[1] Moreover, the possibility of considering the practice of dance, which is usually considered ephemeral, as a practice that can be reiterated, i.e. repeated, opens a glimpse into chronological time and offers a possibility of analysing re-enactment as a cultural production in itself. Thus, as Susanne Franco (2024) also points out, our perception as audience members, as of those who witness re-enactments, is somehow unsettled because it is confronted with something that we somehow feel is far away from us, almost lost. This challenges the function of archival sources in dance, as the multiple aspects of dance creation remain complex processes to capture and reproduce. In this light, the dancer as a subject constitutes an archive[2] (Lepecki 2010), and therefore embodies the memory of the choreographic creative processes, where knowledge is preserved "as a result of embodied dance-making (...) experience" (Griffiths, 2014, online). In other words, as Griffiths explains, "the body captures some of the original essences of dance practice and performances that cannot be captured by more traditional materials and modes of archiving in dance" (Griffiths, 2014).

Moreover, besides being a widespread artistic method, reenactment is also forming an anti-positivist and non-temporally linear approach to the history of dance (and art) as Italian scholars Cristina Baldacci and Franco (2022) highlight in their edited anthology *On Reenactment: Concepts, Methodologies*. As indicated, I investigate two reconstructions from the 1980s. It is necessary to bear in mind that reconstructions of historical pieces, or rather pieces that have a historical distance, are a widespread practice. For example, recently in the Biennale Danza 2023, Simone Forti reconstructed *Dance Constructions* (1960, Yoko Ono New York house), re-assembled by long-term collaborator Sarah Swenson and performed by the young dancers of the Biennale College Danza. Or, at the end of February 2024, William Forsythe reconstructed for the Staatsballett Berlin *Approximate Sonata 2016,* a piece from 1996 and re-staged here in the 2016 version for the Paris Opera Ballet.

These represent two diverse typologies of reconstructions: *Dance Constructions* are made for art galleries and are primarily based on improvisation following structures and physical objects, whereas *Approximate Sonata 2016* is a choreography based on duets, where the choreographer leaves some moments for free interpretation by the performers. By reworking the reconstruction approach into a corporeal experience, reenactments engage with the relationship between the archival documentation and the dance work itself. The case studies of Gaby Agis and her two choreographic reenactments of *Shouting Out Loud* (2014) and *Close Streams* (2016) demonstrate this type of process.

RESEARCH QUESTIONS AND CHAPTER OVERVIEW

How can choreographic scores and concepts be re-enacted without losing their original first impact? To what extent does memory, bodily, visual and written, play a role in the choreographic and aesthetic approaches in Agis' reconstruction work? How do dancers react to verbal, written, aural or visual tasks? Can the work of Agis be considered as a possible model for choreographic reconstruction? These are some of the questions from which the research for this chapter starts.

In order to investigate these previous questions, the chapter opens with a brief introduction on the methodology used, before moving onto an overview on what is meant by somatics and the subject of memory in somatic practices. I then focus on the reconstruction of the works *Shouting Out Loud* and *Close Streams* by the British choreographer Gaby Agis, introduced within a brief summary of the artistic biography of the choreographer herself.

The two choreographic works explored below, although from the 1980s, seem young in their reenactments, like the temporal distance was not really perceived because of the 'still fresh' nature of the dances' content. Agis was not working to reconstruct them as the original works; she was more interested in searching for what remained of the past performances and in creating new situations in order to rework the 'old material'. The perspective I am using is the one of embodied memory and somatics.

REMEMBERING THE BODY IN ACTION: SOMATICS AND MEMORY

Methodological Notes

This chapter arises from my research for the doctorate and mainly lies in the meetings: the direct encounters with choreographers, dancers and operators in the form of interviews, informal chats and participation in lessons, combined with bibliographic and theoretical work. Specifically, this chapter focuses on meetings with the British choreographer Gaby Agis and two of her works from the 1980s.

Alongside theoretical and historical research, I pursued a self-reflexive, observational and speculative approach to field research. My investigation has been mainly shaped by observing rehearsal processes and performances of contemporary dance, archival recordings of dances from the 1980s, and ethnographic and qualitative research through discussions and interviews. Finally, I had the opportunity to participate in practical movement research classes led by the choreographer herself. My visits to rehearsals and performances took place mainly between 2014 and 2016. In 2014 I observed the revival of *Shouting Out Loud* by Agis at the University of Roehampton. In 2016 I interviewed Agis and was able to spend a few days with her in the studio for the reconstruction of *Close Streams*.

In the last fifteen years, the theme of reenactment in the field of dance has been very present in the research of academics in the field, starting with the aforementioned scholar, Franko (2018). This study aligns with current research, presented through an overview of recent case studies. In addition to theoretical and historical notes, are taken into consideration those choreographic practices happening in the rehearsal space, observed in person, where embodied practice constitutes a foundational and primary act. I tried in some way to present my experience as an observer and witness. Clearly my perspective has some influence from my personal journey as a practitioner and the precise moment in which I observed. As often happens, field research work occurs in relation to the most personal experiences and the research perspective undertaken. Specifically, during my fieldwork my focus was on researching the connections of somatic practices with the development of some choreographic practices and their reconstructions. I was interested in understanding which mechanisms — corporeal, linguistic, imaginative — were used to bring the dancers into that particular specific psycho-corporeal situation that the choreography required. How do creative possibilities resurface through somatics and related practices? How do somatics act through memory in its bodily, mental, and creative meanings? In order to explore these questions, I introduce the context of the choreographies and how they were reworked, specifying some of the words used and the methods undertaken.

Definition of Somatics

Before delving into the reconstruction of the dance pieces, a brief introduction to the term somatics and its use will underpin analysis of Agis' choreographic practices. When we speak about somatics we should refer to an extended and impacting web of intergenerational and transnational connections (George 2020). Somatics defined a paradigm switch in the approach between external structure (intended as both the overall corporeal structure with bones and muscles, and the choreographic organisation) and personal perception and awareness, shifting the structural focus from the inside to outside, and vice versa.

Etymologically the adjective 'somatic' derives from the Greek word *soma*, which means 'living body' (Hanna 1986). However, the term somatics underpins a particular field constituted by specific body-mind techniques that began to emerge from the beginning of the 20th century. Somatic knowledge, somatic practices, and somatically informed technique/choreography/training demonstrate only a few possible uses of this adjective, but they differentiate in the various contexts in which somatics operates. Practitioner and scholar Thomas Hanna conceived the term 'somatics' in 1976 for its journal *Somatics Magazine - Journal of the Bodily Arts and Sciences* (Bainbridge Cohen, 1995, p. 185). Later, 'somatics' started to be in use in the 1990s, when Michael Murphy, practitioner and founder of Esalen Institute,[3] together with somatic practitioners Bonnie Bainbridge Cohen and Emilie Conrad joined the Somatic Study group initiated by Don Hanlon Johnson, a Rolfing somatic practitioner, scholar, and former editor with Hanna of the journal *Somatics*. During this experience Bainbridge Cohen and Conrad started to use the term 'somatic' and identify themselves with it (Eddy, 2016). Since then, somatics infers a broad field of research where the body is studied "through the personal experiential perspective" (Bainbridge Cohen, 1993, p.1). Interestingly Johnson (2021) explains the origins of somatics as "'somatics' is a fiction constructed by Thomas Hanna in the early 1970s by adding that little 's' onto an adjective that had been variously used before to denote the physical dimension of the self" (Johnson, 2021). Johnson also stresses the extent to which adding that "tiny letter" (the 's') contributed to draw together various approaches, in order to "deepen a collaborative work, with the kinds of dialogue that promote more grounded knowledge and better training of practitioners" (Johnson, 2021).

Somatic practitioner and researcher Martha Eddy (2000) defines somatic disciplines as: "those systems of study that view physical reality and specific bodily or even cellular awareness as a source of knowledge, usually to be gained through touch, movement, and imagery as processes of embodiment" (Eddy, 2000, p. 1). Therefore, Eddy enlarges Hanna's definition of somatics, identifying three key concepts in order to evaluate its parameters: touch, movement and imagery, stressing the concept of embodiment. While for Hanna the predominant approach in explaining the concept of somatics is the body as seen from the 'inside', from the 'first-person perception', Eddy gives these key concepts the expanded possibility of becoming significant elements of a source of knowledge, so the focus is not only the individual and the body as seen through a first person perspective. The focus is also on the relationship between the embodied subject and his/her surroundings through modalities of touch, movement recognized through proprioception, practices with imagery and kinaesthetic sensations. Kinaesthetic derives from 'kinaesthesia' that is "the sense by which motion, weight, and position of various body parts are perceived" (Kent, 2007). Thus, kinaesthesis involves the perception of the body both in motion and in stillness.

As Eddy discusses, even though the field of somatic(s) emerged during the 1960s, the concept of paying attention to physical sensation in order to bring balance to the body and mind is not new. By evaluating the body as a complete entity and not as one divided into specific fragments as in common Western medicine, in somatic practices the body is investigated as an entire body in action, namely in movement.[4]

For instance, somatic practitioner pioneer Mabel E. Todd (1937) in her founding text *The Thinking Body* stated:

> Living, the whole body carries its meaning and tells its own story, standing, sitting, walking, awake or asleep. It pulls all the life up into the face of the philosopher, and sends it all down into the legs of the dancer. (…) Memory likes to recall the whole body. It is not our parents' faces that come back to us, but their bodies, in the accustomed chairs, eating, sewing, smoking, doing all the familiar things. We remember each as a body in action. (p. 1)

Considering the specific movement/dance context, through memory there is an understanding of the bodily capacity to remember specific movement sequence patterns within bones, muscles and so on and at the same time to translate the body into a container of physical pattern and feelings. Furthermore, memory adds another level of understanding the movement as in 'muscular memory'.

The idea of memory is close to key concepts such as empathy and kinaesthesia. Kinaesthesia is that specific body capacity that perceives itself in space and the extension or dimension of its movements, namely the subject perceives its movements in space (Proske and Gandevia, 2009).[5] A dancing body is a body in constant kinaesthetic awareness. According to Susan Leigh Foster (2010, p. 10), the concept of empathy (from the Greek εμπάθεια" (empátheia), itself composed of en-, 'within', and pathos, 'suffering or feeling') as a specific mechanism of identification, originally derives from German aestheticians and philosophers who coined the term *Einfühlung* (feeling with), regarding the experience with artwork as a physical connection to the work of art. Later, it was mainly used by psychologists and considered as a cognitive and epistemological process through which two different individuals could enter a relationship, with movement offering a relevant system to achieve it. Empathy must be recognized as a fully sensorial capability/means, which "entails a kinaesthetic level of recognition" (Foster, 2010, p.10). Recent scientific discoveries such as mirror neurons have provided further supporting evidence (Gallese & Stamenov, 2002).

ON THE RE-MAKING OF A DANCE PIECE

Reconstruction Through Memory

As set out in the introduction, this research derives from fieldwork observations of the re-creation and re-enactment of two dance pieces. Reconstructions of works from the 1980s in the 21st century show the efficacy of those creative pieces, not only for their movement language, but for the strategies used to re-stage them, referring to notes and observing videos, when possible, but above all the corporeal memory of the body which remembers a specific state. In Gaby Agis' work the re-staging processes involved responding to particular types of verbal instructions, connected to visual imagery and physical states rather than following only an original set movement score.

A choreographic work and its process present an internal and external structure: the prior/external/visible structure (that could be of the body, of a movement sequence, of a choreography), and the inside, which means the individual and singular perception and vision of what the body-mind perceives from specific physical movements. For example, Agis in her practice often speaks about internal and external structures, regarding the different layers possible in a movement sequence, and the external movement path and the internal emotional feeling perceived by the mover. The internal affects the external outcome and vice versa. For example, the choreographic structure of both pieces I witnessed were based on a sequence consisting of, for example, running, waiting, and falling. These steps could be considered the external structure of the choreography. In addition to this, one has to consider everything that 'is inside the dancer', what I have previously called the internal structure, i.e. how the dancer's body experiences that run, wait, fall, how it interacts with the other dancers, and how it connects with the music.

Agis' choreographic process is an internal and experiential practice of investigating through imagery and hands-on work, the quality of touch is directly connected to the physical choreographic gestures. Her methodologies of reconstruction include the use of written notes and imagery from the past and present choreographic situations.

Pointing to one of the main topics, "the process is the piece" (Agis, 2016), refers to how the steps towards the creation of the choreography are not only based on an assembly of movement patterns, conceptual ideas and so on, but they become a continuous collective dialogue based on feedback deriving from growing experiences of the dancers and the choreographer. Agis stimulates her dancers to enter deeply into the choreographic material, starting from the preparatory exercises which determine the quality of the choreography (Agis, 2016, 2021). These exercises are release-based movements, partnering sequences, and breath exercises. In the choreography itself, in the rehearsals, and in the movement class and warm up there is a request from the choreographer/teacher to the dancers and students to make choices all the time, taking responsibility: the agency of the dancer/performer/practitioner is always considered. The dancers or students are being challenged and stimulated in each moment, bringing participatory awareness of choreography or in the class, bringing their specific contribution with the physical movement and with concepts/ideas/emotions. This means to be aware of the movement patterns about their own emotions and sensations and to integrate them into the movement (Frasson, 2016). This request to make choices all the time is strictly connected to the necessity of negotiating: during the choreography and/or class the individual is stimulated to not only execute the movements/patterns/sequences, but to act/re-act/re-enact to the diverse stimuli, in order to develop an individual and personal way to 'act' the performance/class. Negotiation is often a prerogative of the improvisation technique, where the dancers are always in relation with non-settled movement sequences, but open to the movement dialogue. Choreography and classes create a specific atmosphere where teachers/practitioners/choreographers strive to shape an ambience. In the class, this necessity derives from the will to realise a specific full sensorial experience for the participants; in the choreography it is part of the process of creating new 'worlds'. For example, Agis uses particular images and words to bring the dancers inside the movement material, such as 'melting' or 'expanding'. This atmosphere or ambience is also obtained by developing images: through imagery and landscapes it is possible to create an atmosphere.

Gaby Agis: Artistic Background

Agis' approach to dance and composition has always been, from a certain sense, multi-disciplinary. Her training and creativity have been influenced strongly by British choreographer Rosemary Butcher's work, after the interrupted experience of study at the London Contemporary Dance School (the professional dance conservatoire of The Place), her experience at Dartington College of Arts, and her study trip to New York and the influence of Skinner Releasing Technique, hereafter named SRT. From the beginning of her career, she was looking for a personal and intuitive way of creating and collecting choreographic movements. Dance critic and historian Judith Mackrell explains how Agis reacted against the discipline of her training at The Place and began to create dances based on improvised and soft movements (Mackrell, 1992, p.79). She also left training at the Place because of a knee ligament injury, and because she found a learning environment with "bullying and mental health problems" (Agis, 2016). In Dartington she had the chance to dance in a different way, thanks to a different awareness of her body, encouraged also by Mary Fulkerson's teaching approach and her two months of travel to New York, where she studied at the Judson Church. The Place and Dartington offered two different approaches to dance: the Place was based upon "Graham-based and Cunningham derived work with a focus on technique, and the softer, more diffuse style introduced largely from Dartington" (Hockey 1988: 27). According to dance historian Stephanie Jordan (1992), in the 1970s Dartington was a point of reference for British dance that later became the independent dance scene. Dartington College of Arts became a significant site of encounter and knowledge regarding new approaches to dance, thanks to the arrival of American Fulkerson in 1973, where she introduced her method as Anatomical Release Technique. Dartington, like the School of New Dance Development (Amsterdam), Laban Centre (London), advanced the new educational somatically informed trend. From the 1970s somatics "reframed the mid-century rejection of modern dance by claiming to train dancers in a way that was unencumbered by aesthetics" (George, 2020, p. 29), and to conceive somatics as reinforcing and positioning the dancer's identity and its role in the artistic process (p. 38). While in modern dance schools (like The Place) the teaching is focused on codified, organised techniques which follow predetermined structures and precepts matching a specific aesthetics, instead a somatic influenced training is looking for various practices that have in common an understanding of the individual body-mind connection.

In a private conversation Agis also explained to me that she studied in "New York with Simone Forti, Trisha Brown company, Joan Skinner, Susan Klein" and she did "lots of improvising with folks". In particular she was practising Contact Improvisation at "PS [Performance Space] 122 especially at the jams (Thursday or Tuesday nights) they were wild and important to me" (Agis, 2016). When she returned, she danced for various British choreographers and groups, creating in 1983 her first work and in 1984 *Shouting Out Loud*, while working as a fashion model and collaborating in various forms with art galleries and music groups. She feels that in those years there was a lot of feminist power between female choreographers. Even though she was working intensively gaining success, she felt "lonely within the dance community" (Agis, 2016), and in 1991 after a decade of intense work, she experienced a burnout.

At this point in her life, Agis started to become even more interested in the work of Joan Skinner (who she followed in New York when she encountered the SRT as a student). The question Agis posed to herself at that point in life was to understand how to age, and the example of Skinner (who was in her sixties) was an illuminating one. Agis considers her work a "big gift". Through Skinner's work, Agis affirms that "you can take people into the process" (Agis, 2016).

Her website explains how "this technique [SRT] has been intrinsic to her creative practice" (Agis, 2021). As explained above, SRT is a somatic approach started during the 1970s by dancer, choreographer and teacher Skinner based on imagery and release of muscular tension through specific guided and improvised movements, alone or with a partner. This kinaesthetic training started from the 'rest position': a position where the body lies down supine, with bent knees and feet on the ground and arms open on the side. In this position, she could present to students diverse kinds of imagery connected to movement and these "proved highly effective in conveying kinaesthetic information in order to re-educate the body without setting up harmful counter-tensions" (Nicholas 2007, p.191).

Skinner (Nicholas, 2007) was a detailed observer of the changes happening in her students' bodies, as she describes:

> The muscles appear to be lengthened and wrapped around the bones rather than contracted or gripped. The joints give the appearance of having space in them and the limbs of being unbound though belonging to the torso. There is a suspended relationship to gravity which can be likened to the suspension of a dust particle in a shaft of light (p. 191).

This description is useful at least from two points of view: first, to understand Skinner's somatic point of view and what she is looking for in the training; and secondly, the specific language used. The use of released muscles together with joints — as the joints release themselves and create more possibility of movements — forms a different dynamic with the environment explicated in the final image proposed. The description of the physical work, with consequent anatomical changes, is conveyed in the final image. This final image — "the suspension of a dust particle in a shaft of light" — is the creation of a poetic metaphor on a kind of effort, which represents one of the specific somatic ways to introduce and present this type of work.

Agis later became an influential teacher of this technique, which led her to coach internationally. She is the first British certified SRT teacher, and she introduced the style for the first time in London in 1993 (Moran, 2010). Later, she helped create the British SRT community, training many independent dancers. Her career as a dancer and choreographer started at the beginning of the 1980s and her voice emerged as one of the leading female choreographers of the New Dance, an influential independent dance movement.

Shouting Out Loud: **Reconstructed**

The first reconstruction I witnessed was *Shouting Out Loud*, a piece from 1984 reconstructed at the University of Roehampton in September 2014. On this occasion the cast was composed of a total of 13 dancers. This corresponded with the original number of performers (including Natasha Beauchamp, Joy Esaya, Rachel Gildea, Jessica Loeb, Jessica Murray, Rosalie Wahlfrid, and Megan Elizabeth Williams), with some dancers from the original cast (Lucy Fawcett, Mary Prestidge) and the live musician and composer Ana Da Silva and The Raincoats. There were extra dancers (Florence Peake, Susanna Recchia) and some Roehampton dance students and staff (Katja Nyqvist, Amaara Raheem). I should stress the differences in the cast's ages and experiences, which ranged from approximately twenty to fifty/sixty years old, from students to professional performers, teachers and retired dancers. In the original version the performers were all in their twenties and Agis demonstrated an ability to turn these differences into a strong positive point instead of a weakness. Each day, before beginning the reconstruction process, Agis gave a SRT class in which I participated along with the dance group. Sensing, feeling, liberating the movement and a complete sense of ease and comfort emerged. Her reconstruction process was in a sense a re-doing of the piece. Dancers acted as if they were doing the piece for the very first time. Interestingly, two of the dancers chosen for this reconstruction, Recchia and Peake, are dancers and practitioners with a strong somatics background.

The idea to remake the piece happened thanks to a conversation taking place at Chisenhale Studios with a collective of dancers in 2013. When she created it, back in 1984, Agis was 24 years old. Agis affirms that she was able to re-enact the piece only in 2014, because her daughter was grown up and living away from home.

Shouting Out Loud derives its title from a song by the band The Raincoats of which Agis was a fan at that time. Their collaboration started when Agis wrote to them asking their permission to use that song for a dance. Then, the collaboration expanded, and Ana Da Silva and The Raincoats wrote the entire soundtrack of the piece (Agis, 2015). Agis remembers that the dance was created on five Saturdays at the Riverside Studios for a performance for Dance Umbrella. This is a piece conceived for 13 female performers to celebrate female power; its main movement language is informed by a physicality that at that time "was radical" and today "maybe less" radical (Agis, 2015), constituted of running, walking, and moving through visual imagery. Within the idea of portraying solitude but also collectivity, expanded on below, this work is contextualized in the political activism of those years, where collective responsibility was a considered issue. In this light this piece is a clear example of the response within dance to the 1980s in the U.K. Agis remembers that in that time you could live in London cheaply, squatting, renting a dance studio for free or for little money, even though it was freezing, there was little emigration and a lot of activism and solidarity against the political economic cuts of Thatcherism (Agis, 2015). As for many dances of that time, there isn't any recording or documentation available; Agis considers the archive material 'in her head', and through the bodies of the performers of the original cast.

The structure of the piece is a container where inside are improvisational sections that depend on mutual arrangement between the performers. Each physical detail is relevant, as for instance in the rolling down of the spine or when two bodies meet each other, keeping awareness in the relationship between people. Agis says that the key point is to "see the person", as each person is important in this piece. For her, one of the questions at the basis of the reconstruction is "how the time you live in impacts your way of creating" (Agis, 2015).

Shouting Out Loud is a piece about collective responsibility (Agis, 2016), understood both as the main theme and the choreographic approach. On the motivation that brought about the recent reconstruction, Agis explains:

> The 1980s were a period of great social and political unrest. Thatcherism was in full swing. The miners' strikes and the gay pride, anti-racist and feminist movements dominated the landscape. This provided the context and backdrop to artists' lives. Again, we live in turbulent and uncertain times.

By reconstructing *Shouting Out Loud,* I am interested in discovering to what degree art reflects the times that we live in. (Agis, 2018a)

Performing *Shouting Out Loud* requires a strong psycho-corporeal connection in order to manifest in a non-didactic way the social and political perspective the piece reflects and imparts. Agis was concerned to transmit and to recreate this perspective with the dancers through the preparatory workshop based on SRT and improvisation exercises on feeling and liberating the body. When I participated in one class, the first attention seemed oriented to the breath and how the breath influenced the spatial position and placement of the dancer's body; the focus on the breath helped to position the bodies in the space because the individual attention to the breath gave an augmented awareness to the dancer's body. Agis was conducting her dancers from the inside of their physical body structure to the outside into the choreographic structure. She was proposing specific somatic movement practices as the SRT to reach a specific released and receptive status (Agis, 2015).

Agis draws attention quite often to perceive the breath as a source of movement. This is an ongoing process, happening during rehearsals and classes. Some of the language which she used in a class held at Independent Dance (2010) and which recurs in her teachings includes: "(…) endless, perpetual motion… …perhaps you can have an image that the breath is like a wave……you can explore different qualities of moving… (Agis, 2010)." After the breath experience, she encourages the dancers to work with a partner, saying: "(…) and I am going to take this one (referring to the hip joint) from my partner; I am going to find the bones and I am going to draw a circle, up to the waist take your time to move to rest…" (Agis 2010). One person was carefully tracing the external body structure path with the hands, starting from the hip joint and moving to the beginning of the rib cage, maintaining a gentle touch. The traced path helps the partner who receives the tactile feedback to increase his/her body's connection awareness.

In working with this new cast in 2014, as the first time that the piece was restaged after thirty years, one of the main concerns was to bring an 'old' performance to life. In explaining this process Agis said: "(…) it's different, it's different, it will be different… how might it be different for me, and when I know … it's something nice in the difference. But, within that difference you will feel the familiarity of this process, and hopefully…" (Agis, 2014). With this concern, Agis shares with the dancers and observer her consciousness of creating a different piece from the one of the 1980s, and she develops a way to make this old piece familiar to new dancers in a new process.

Close Streams: Reconstructed

The second reconstruction I witnessed is *Close Streams* (1983) which was Agis' first choreographic work when she was 23 years old. I observed it at Chisenhale Dance Space in May 2016, where I met Agis and the dancer Eeva-Maria Mutka. In 2016 the curator David Ward invited Agis to reconstruct *Close Streams* at the Turner Contemporary Gallery in Margate, Kent, for a series of performances as part of the summer show *Seeing Round Corners.*

Dance critic Josephine Leask (2016, online) spoke about this reconstruction and the issues of the remaking

Revisiting a piece that you have created back in the past is an emotional and complex undertaking especially in the case of *Close Streams*, which was the first work that Agis made. She describes the challenges of recreating it: peeling back the layers of memory and association in the choreography, meeting the material again as an older woman with a changed body. Consequently, she brings both enormous wisdom and vulnerability to the work.

Interestingly, Leask underlines the extent to which remaking a work from a distance and revisiting it is a self-reflexive work in itself.

In order to reconstruct the piece, Agis used some of the original handwritten choreographic notes from the 1980s, which I was able to access during my fieldwork in 2016 thanks to her availability. These written score notes served as a fundamental track to reconstruct the dance, and Agis and collaborators referred to them in the recreation process. As I explain later, these scores are used both as spatial reminders, as temporal and rhythmic markers, and as indicators of moods and feelings. In addition, there are precise descriptions of the type of movement to be performed (such as running, falling, etc.). I have annotated the movements and actions of the choreographic score observed from my direct observation of the rehearsals in May 2016, in order to collect the memory from the past (the 1980s) to the corporeality work of the present (2016) that enabled the reconstruction. Historical written tasks and recent oral references constituted the basis for it.

At that time there were just the three of us in the Chisenhale space, and I remember the embracing atmosphere that was created. Even though Agis and Mutka were carefully reconstructing the work, they never let me feel like an intruder. On the contrary, we discussed *Close Streams* multiple times and at some point I helped them by starting the soundtrack. In this work, Agis explores different states of feelings and experiments with various levels of energy: quietness, speed, anxiety and so on. The work is a blend of improvised and structured moments (Agis, 2016). *Close Streams* is a duet originally choreographed and performed in 1983, "it is a viscerally intense physical work in which the two performers run for a sustained period of time in circles" (Agis, 2018b, p. 1). It was originally performed by Agis and Helen Rowsell.

As we can read in John Percival's (1983) review in *The Times*, the work was received very positively:

> The most striking work was a solo by Gaby Agis, which actually was meant as a duet but had to be adapted because of her partner's illness. She also chose to perform it not in the studio but on the flat roof, where she danced in a huge shallow pool of water. The capacity of the dance to survive such drastic changes and still look good is evidence of her imagination. Dressed in an old-fashioned underwear and sporty boots, she used a mixture of stomping and skipping, quick energy and stillness, eagerness and reserve, to convey both character and emotion (n.p.).

This description gives an indication of some of the characteristics such as the theatrical presence and costumes and the use of a non-theatrical space. This review also reveals the strength of the piece itself, that was not influenced by the last-minute adaption from a duet to a solo, and the change of setting.

As previously mentioned, Agis was accompanied in the process of reconstruction and on stage by Finnish performer Mutka, who is based in Wales. Mutka has a strong background in body-mind practices such as Mindfulness, Body and Earth, Touch Trust Programme/ Communication through Touch, and she is a collaborator of choreographer and somatic practitioner Miranda Tufnell. Mutka also co-directs the project 'Somatic is...' at Penpynfarch, Carmarthenshire.

In order to reconstruct the piece, Agis and Mutka used some of the original handwritten choreographic notes from the 1980s. They present eight points, where corporeal, spatial, and tempo instructions and tasks are noted. Furthermore, they indicate the sections in which the choreography is set, namely the "running in a circle"; a section "Arms up both lifted by a contact touch"; "This lift slides down to the floor"; "[Helen] goes for a strong march, walk, in very direct pathway"; and "The next […] is very small broken down movement." Other sections included: "We stand up to waltz for a while half"; "…taking it in turns to point out on the other person very small specific contact points only using the hand"; and "End of music and holding of last contact point" (Agis 1983: private notes). I annotated the movements and actions of the choreographic score observed from my direct observation of the rehearsals in May 2016 (see Appendix).

On this skeleton of the dance's physical actions, and observing the rehearsals in May 2016, I noted at least three working points where Agis was focussed. The first is that Agis clearly defined what structure means for her: "essence is the structure — there is a structure and an inside of the structure" (Frasson, 2016). In Agis' work, a defined structure could enable dancers to develop diverse feelings and emotions; with 'structure' she initially refers to the overall/general scheme following specific time/space/move-ment patterns. 'Inside of the structure' refers to specific details of each movement sequence and the subtle subtext of individual dancers' movements. Secondly, the figures of the circles repeat themselves in different moments as if to point out that the choreography presents spatial and movement repetitions. Thirdly, the original diagonal is reconfigured in another circle because of the spatial structure of the gallery exhibiting space which is rounded (Frasson, 2016), showing that the original spatial structure of the choreography is adaptable.

On the same day, after this rehearsal, Agis gave some precise performative feedback to her dance partner. Agis is looking for the person inside-outside, in other words how the person/dancer is connecting her inside movement and feeling patterns to the outside spatial and choreographic indication. With this, Agis refers to the necessity for the dancer to enter in contact with the spatial context in a precise way. Furthermore, Agis is looking for a synchronisation between the two performers, with some movement patterns in or out of sync from the running, namely she refers to the rhythmical approach and working to make it more specific and well-defined. Once the skeletal structure is clear, more work and care are now needed to add and refine elements. This means that, after having reconstructed the overall structure of the dance, Agis now needs to work on specific physical and emotional details.

Considerations About the Reconstructions

During the reconstruction that I witnessed, some concerns came up. For instance, some were spe-cifically spatial connotations, while others were more focused on details regarding the performative gestures. I discuss concerns which Agis was overtly working towards, and aspects that arose from my personal observations, without necessarily being mentioned by Agis.

The following aspects were directly touched on by Agis. First of all, she was striving to maintain a clear overall structure of the piece; once the structure is defined, such as the sections, their length, their spatial organisation, and the work of the emotions/feelings starts. Then, the search occurred for moments of synchronisation between the two dancers, changes in their movement sequences, creating a common pulse, and foot stomps on the ground. Finally, this work was done to adapt the choreography and the spatial structure of the piece to the new gallery space.

Overall, within this choreography, some recurring features emerge. First, there was a search to maintain clear physical intentions, through sound, voice, and breath: when the action became more intense also the body changed its energetic state. Second, as the action increases, tactile feedback between the dancers becomes stronger and more defined. Third, the kind of action was drawn from pedestrian movements such as running in circles, walking in different moments, and raising arms as in protest. Fourth, in the duets dancers were perceiving and giving mutual body weight support. The end of the piece looks as if the two dancers, who were first acting as independent dancers, are reunited in a final moment together. To conclude, the dance presented two women in theatrical costumes which distinguish a western female body. Their bodies are relaxed but at the same time ready to react to different possibilities of relations, actions, and impulses on stage.

During both reconstruction sessions I noticed the following characteristics which relate directly to the previous analysis of somatic practices. These features include: tactile feedback (precise and specific), imagery, journey, agency, perception, consciousness, awareness, encounter, embodied dance practice, trusting the work and the practice, different kinds of layers, and economy of movement.

Agis' choreographic process is an internal and experiential practice of investigating through imagery and hands-on work, this shows her somatics attitude through the use of specific imagery and touch. Her methodologies of reconstruction include the use of written notes and imagery from the past and present choreographic situations. During training sessions for her dancers, she often uses keywords, concepts and practices to develop their perception, awareness, and agency, such as "looking for person inside-outside" meaning that a dancer could project their own inside as well as outside; "preparing the dancers/people to be present;" "being ready to take the responsibility as dancers to make choices all the time." (Frasson, 2016). Furthermore, Agis keeps the attention on movement from the inside to the outside, meaning staying focussed on how the internal physical and emotional states, and consequent emotional feelings, could influence the external/outside choreographic structure, stimulating this process carefully through perception, imagery, journey, layers and encounter. In this way, the process reveals how somatic practices establish mind-body connections, which impact upon qualities of movement. It also highlights the physical engagement that these practices generate through the use of a specific language and key recurring terms.

SOME THOUGHTS FOR A CONCLUSION

This chapter is part of an open research process delving into a discourse in the dance and memory as a part of somatics knowledge methodology. We consider the relationship between choreography and somatics as an expanding field, where the embodied memory of the dancers is one of the primary agents of dramaturgical reconstruction.

This study invites further exploration. This research could be extended and expanded in various directions: in the definition of a more inclusive methodology with more extensive fieldwork, and in the research of the material. Having more time at my disposal would have deepened the relationship from the inside, expanding the project to a practice-based one, for example working with more case studies and thus expanding the subjective sphere. Reconstructions of works from the 1980s in the 21st century show the efficacy of those creative pieces, not only for their movement language, but for the strategies used to restage them: notes, observing videos when possible, but as noted previously, above all the memory of the body. The body is able to carry a specific state and to remember movement patterns and specific perceptions. In Agis the restaging processes involved responding to particular types of verbal instructions, connected to visual imagery and physical states rather than following only an original set movement score. By understanding the choreography as a process of embodied memory, it resulted in a communication and transmission informed by unique somatic practices (comprehending various somatic practices/approach).

ACKNOWLEDGMENTS

I would like to express my sincerest gratitude to choreographer Gaby Agis for her generosity in sharing her time and materials with me and for hosting me during rehearsals. Furthermore, I am very grateful to my dissertation supervisors, Dr. Stacey Prickett and Dr. Larraine Nicholas for their continued support in my doctoral studies.

REFERENCES

Agis, G. (1983). *Private Notes* [Unpublished].

Agis, G. (2010). *Class Description*. Independent Dance. https://www.independentdance.co.uk/author/gaby-agis/

Agis, G. (2014). *Gaby Agis: Shouting Out Loud, Reconstructed 2014*. [Video]. Youtube. https://www.youtube.com/watch?v=B8j6MzyDays

Agis, G. (2015). *Shouting Out Loud Seminar*. [Video]. Youtube. https://www.youtube.com/watch?v=fTxFq6BJOKw&t=2s

Agis, G. (2016). *Interview with The Author* [Unpublished].

Agis, G. (2018a). *Shouting Out Loud*. http://www.gabyagis.com/shouting-oud-loud/

Agis, G. (2018b). *Close Streams*. http://www.gabyagis.com/close-streams-1/

Agis, G. (2021, May 7). *Teaching*. http://www.gabyagis.com/teaching

Bainbridge Cohen, B. (1993). *Sensing, Feeling, and Action: The Experiential Anatomy of Body-Mind Centering*. Contact Editions.

Bainbridge Cohen, B. (1995). Excerpts from Sensing, Feeling, Action. In Johnson, D. H. (Ed.), *Bone* (pp. 185–203). Breath, Gesture. Practices of Embodiment.

Baldacci, C., & Franco, S. (2022). *On Reenactment: Concepts, Methodologies, Tools*. Accademia University Press. 10.4000/books.aaccademia.11990

Bastian, H. C. (1888). The 'muscular sense'; its nature and cortical localisation. *Brain*, 10(1), 1–137. 10.1093/brain/10.1.1

Descartes, R. (2016). *Meditations on First Philosophy/ Meditationes de prima philosophia: A Bilingual Edition* (Heffernan, G., Ed.). University of Notre Dame Press. (Original work published 1685)

Eddy, M. (2000). Access to Somatic Theory and Applications. Sociopolitical Concerns. In *Proceedings from Dancing the Millennium Congress on Research in Dance Conference*. George Washington University.

Eddy, M. (2016). Mindful Movement: The Evolution of the Somatic Arts and Conscious Action. *Intellect*.

Foster, S. L. (2010). *Choreographing Empathy: Kinesthesia in Performance*. Routledge. 10.4324/9780203840702

Franco, S., & Chernitch, G. C. (2024). Reenactment. *Dancing Museums Glossary.*https://www
.dancingmuseums.com/artefacts/reenactment/

Franko, M. (Ed.). (2018). *The Oxford Handbook of Dance and Reenactment.* Oxford University Press.

Frasson, E. (2016). *Personal Notes from the Fieldwork with Gaby Agis* [Unpublished].

Frasson, E. (2022). *Encounters with Somatics and European Choreography: Discourses, Narratives and Embodied Ethnography between the 1980s and the 2010s* [Unpublished doctoral dissertation, University of Roehampton, London].

Gallese, V., & Stamenov, M. (2002). *Mirror Neurons and the Evolution of Brain and Language.* John Benjamins Publishing Company.

George, D. (2020). *The Natural Body in Somatics Dance Training.* Oxford University Press. 10.1093/oso/9780197538739.001.0001

Gibson, J. J. (1979). *The Ecological Approach to Visual Perception.* Houghton Mifflin.

Griffiths, L. E. (2014). *Dance and The Archival Body: Knowledge, Memory and Experience in Dance Revival Processes* (uk.bl.ethos.655236) [Doctoral dissertation, University of Leeds]. White Roses eTheses Online.

Hanna, T. (1986). What is Somatics? *Somatics: Magazine-Journal of the Bodily Arts and Science, 4,* 4. https://somatics.org/library/htl-wis1.html

Hockey, S. (1983). One Man's Writing is another Man's Walrus: An Assessment of Experimental Work in the Early Years of Dance Umbrella (1978, 1983) and attitudes Towards it From the Press and Public. *Dance Theatre Journal*, 6(1), 25–27.

Johnson, D. H. (2021). *Somatics.* Don Hanlon Johnson. https://donhanlonjohnson.com/somatics/

Jordan, S. (1992). *Striding Out: Aspects of Contemporary and New Dance in Britain.* Dance Books.

Kent, M. (2007). *Kinaesthesis. The Oxford Dictionary of Sports Science & Medicine.* Oxford University Press. https://www-oxfordreferencecom.roe.idm.oclc.org/view/10.1093/acref/9780198568506.001.0001/acref-9780198568506-e-3792

Leask, J. (2016). *Close Streams.* http://www.gabyagis.com/close-streams-1/

Lepecki, A. (2010). The Body as Archive: Will to Re-Enact and the Afterlives of Dances. *Dance Research Journal*, 42(2), 28–48. 10.1017/S0149767700001029

Mackrell, J. (1992). *Out of Line. The Story of British New Dance.* Dance Books Ltd.

Merleau-Ponty, M. (2002). *Phenomenology of Perception* (C. Smith, Trans.). Routledge. (Original version published in 1945)

Moran, J. (2010). *Skinner Releasing Technique in Britain.* London Dance. http://londondance.com/articles/features/skinner-releasing-technique-in-britain/

Nicholas, L. (2007). *Dancing in Utopia: Dartington Hall and its Dancers.* Dance Books.

Percival, J. (1983). Review on Gaby Agis. *The Times*.

Proske, U., & Gandevia, S. C. (2009). The kinaesthetic senses. *The Journal of Physiology*, 587(17), 4139–4146. https://physoc.onlinelibrary.wiley.com/doi/10.1113/jphysiol.2009.175372. 10.1113/jphysiol.2009.17537219581378

Todd, M. E. (1937). *The Thinking Body*. Paul Hoeber.

ENDNOTES

1   In this edited volume, Franko collects texts referring both to pieces restaged by their initial creators and as adaptations from other dance artists.

2   Lepecki's *The Body as Archive: Will to Re-Enact and the Afterlives of Dances*, is a relevant essay in the dance studies field, because it clarifies the theoretical problem of the relationship between memory and dance history, and the related archiving processes, which is particularly evident in the creative processes of contemporary dance. The metaphor of the body-archive is based on the idea that the materiality of the body can be conceived as a set of documents capable of preserving traces of a knowledge in continuous transformation.

3   The Esalen Institute is an educational and research centre based in California and founded around the 1960s, devoted to 'exploring and realising human potential through experience, education, and research' (Esalen, 2021). For further information see https://www.esalen.org.

4   The philosopher Descartes believed the body and mind to be separate, i.e. that the material physicality of the body can exist separate from the reasoning and moral judgement of the mind, which is reflected in his 'cogito ergo sum' utterance. Later, in philosophical thought, this dualism is overcome. For example, Maurice Merleau-Ponty (1945, 2002) rejected the mind–body dualism of Descartes by asserting that thinking and feeling are all actions that necessitate embodiment.

5   The term 'kinaesthesia' was coined by Bastian (1888) and refers to the ability to sense the position and movement of our limbs and trunk. According to the perceptual psychologist James J. Gibson "kinesthesia assisted in integrating sensory information from all other systems" (Foster, 2010, p. 7). Recently, neurobiologists investigate how the brain feels the movements of the body.

APPENDIX

I drafted these notes in May 2016, during *Close Streams* rehearsals at Chisenhale Dance Space (London). Compared to the original notes, the movement sequences resulted in the following order:

- the dancers enter walking together, in short feminine dresses in a light material and waterproof boots;
- they run, creating repetitive circular trajectories and staying focused on the intensity of their breath;
- they raise their arms/hands, interlacing them like a protest symbol;
- the dancers look for mutual support: walking on 'all fours', they search for some support points between their bodies; in this way, their bodies became interlaced;
- the physical action of touch between the two dancers became more intense; they start to touch different parts of their bodies with their hands, first very delicate and then in a very intense way;
- the touch intention is more physical, adding sounds, use of the voices, noisy breaths; when the physical action increases, the body also increases in intensity, energy, and sound of the body is getting louder;
- first, they start to walk in circles, then they run, they touch themselves, and after Mutka runs into the circle, while Agis is still;
- they look for some contact points between the two and make them vibrate (hip joint, shoulders, small stomps);
- feet stomps on the ground increase and become more furious — the dancers beat the ground with their boots;
- the two dancers come together again in a moment of reconciliation with *Sunday Morning* by Lou Reed, which is the only music track used in the whole piece;
- the dancers explore different body parts of each other, and they start again to walk in the circle until they become still again, after one precise touch signal;
- after they pass through a range of different emotions, their facial expressions are different now — more relieved — and they go offstage;
- the piece has ended.

Compilation of References

Abril-Gonzalez, P. (2018). *Recuerdos, expresiones y sueños en Nepantla: Identity journeys through spoken, written, and artistic testimonios* (Order No. 10840992). ProQuest Dissertations & Theses Global: The Humanities and Social Sciences Collection. (2113571081).

Acosta, H. L. P. (2020). Kant on Empirical and Transcendental Functions of Memory. *Eidos*, 32, 103–134. 10.14482/eidos.32.193

Adams, J. T. (1931). *The Epic of America*. Little, Brown, and Company.

Adorno, T. W. (1997). *Aesthetic Theory*. Athlone Press.

Adorno, T. W. (2006). *Philosophy of New Music*. University of Minnesota Press.

Agis, G. (1983). *Private Notes* [Unpublished].

Agis, G. (2010). *Class Description*. Independent Dance. https://www.independentdance.co.uk/author/gaby-agis/

Agis, G. (2014). *Gaby Agis: Shouting Out Loud, Reconstructed 2014.* [Video]. Youtube. https://www.youtube.com/watch?v=B8j6MzyDays

Agis, G. (2015). *Shouting Out Loud Seminar*. [Video]. Youtube. https://www.youtube.com/watch?v=fTxFq6BJOKw&t=2s

Agis, G. (2016). *Interview with The Author* [Unpublished].

Agis, G. (2018b). *Close Streams*. http://www.gabyagis.com/close-streams-1/

Agis, G. (2021, May 7). *Teaching*. http://www.gabyagis.com/teaching

Agis, G. (2018a). *Shouting Out Loud*. http://www.gabyagis.com/shouting-oud-loud/

Agnew, V., Lamb, J., & Tomann, J. (2019). *The Routledge handbook of re-enactment studies*. Routledge. 10.4324/9780429445637

Ahmed, S. (2006). *Queer phenomenology: Orientations, objects, others*. Duke University Press.

Akhtar, Z. (2022). Sámi peoples land claims in Norway, Finnmark Act and providing legal title. *The Indigenous Peoples' Journal of Law, Culture & Resistance, 7*(1).

Al-Adeeb, D. (2021). A Letter to My Daughter: An Archive of Future Memories. *Amerasia Journal*, 47(1), 144–149. 10.1080/00447471.2021.1993765

Alanen, L. (1989). Descartes's Dualism and the Philosophy of Mind. *Revue de Metaphysique et de Morale*, 94(3), 391–413.

Alcázar, J. (2014). *Performance: un arte del yo: autobiografía, cuerpo e identidad*. Siglo XXI Editores.

Aldea, A. S. (2013). Husserl's struggle with mental images: Imaging and imagining reconsidered. *Continental Philosophy Review*, 46(3), 371–394. 10.1007/s11007-013-9268-7

Alexander, J. C. (2004). *Cultural Trauma and Collective Identity*. University of California Press.

Aléx, L. (2016). Resilience among old Sámi women. *Ageing and Society*, 36(8), 1738–1756. 10.1017/S0144686X15000719

Aliel, L., Keller, D., & Costa, R. (2018). The Maxwell Demon: Comprovisation in ecologically grounded creative practice. *Musica Hodie*, 18(1), 103–116.

Ali, M. (2003). *Brick Lane*. Black Swan.

Allen, A. S. (2013). Ecomusicology. In Oxford University Press (Hrsg.), *Oxford Music Online*. Oxford University Press. 10.1093/gmo/9781561592630.article.A2240765

Allen, M. T. (2002). *The business of genocide: The SS, slave labour and the concentration camps*. University of North Carolina Press.

Almeder, R. F. (1970). Peirce's Theory of Perception. *Transactions of the Charles S. Peirce Society, 6*(2), 99–110. https://www.jstor.org/stable/40319589

Al-Natour, R. (2017). 'Of Middle Eastern appearance' is a flawed racial profiling descriptor. *Current Issues in Criminal Justice*, 29(2), 107–122. 10.1080/10345329.2017.12036090

Amir, D. (2019). *Bearing Witness to the Witness: A Psychoanalytic Perspective on Four Modes of Traumatic Testimony*. Routledge, Taylor and Francis.

Annas, J. (2003). Aristotle on Memory and the Self. In Nussbaum, M. C., & Rorty, A. O. (Eds.), *Essays on Aristotle's De Anima*. Oxford Academic. 10.1093/019823600X.003.0017

Anzaldúa, G. (1987). *Borderlands la frontera. The new mestiza*. Aunt Lute Book Company.

Anzaldua, G. (1987). *Borderlands: The new mestiza = La frontera* (1st ed.). Spinsters, Aunt Lute.

Ardoin, N. M., Gould, R. K., Wojcik, D., Roth, N. W., & Biggar, M. (2022). Community listening sessions: An approach for facilitating collective reflection on environmental learning and behavior in everyday life. *Ecosystems and People (Abingdon, England)*, 1(18), 469–477. 10.1080/26395916.2022.2101531

Arendt, H. (2006). *Eichmann in Jerusalem: A report on the banality of evil*. Penguin.

Aristotle, . (1907). *De anima* (Hicks, R. D., Trans.). Prometheus Books.

Arlander, A. (2012). *Performing Landscape - Notes on Site-specific Work and Artistic Research (Texts 2001-2011)*. Theatre Academy Helsinki, Performing Arts Research Centre.

Arnold, E. (2009). The Greening of Hip Hop: The Greening of Hip-Hop: Urban Youth Address Climate Change and Sustainability. *Reimagine! Race Poverty and the Environment, 16*(2). https://www.reimaginerpe.org/files/Arnold.Climate.%2016-2-29.pdf

Arns, I., & Horn, G. (Eds.). (2007). *History will repeat itself: Strategies of re-enactment in contemporary (media) art and performance*. Revolver.

Arriva, F. (2008, December 2). *I Fatti di Avola. (C. Muratori, performer)*. Teatro Odeon, Avola. https://youtu.be/tsPhRpzGVCU?si=s5Q4VtnnVMP4VIh8.

Arvidsson, A. (2008). The ethical economy of customer coproduction. *Journal of Macromarketing*, 28(4), 326–338. 10.1177/0276146708326077

Askander, M., Gutowska, A., & Makai, P. K. (2022). Transmedial storyworlds. In Bruhn, J., & Schirrmacher, B. (Eds.), *Intermedial Studies: An introduction to meaning across media* (pp. 265–281). Routledge.

Asquith, N., & Poynting, S. (2011). Anti-cosmopolitanism and 'ethnic cleansing' at Cronulla. In *Ocean to Outback: Cosmopolitanism in Contemporary Australia* (pp. 96–122). UWA Publishing.

Assmann, A. (2012). *Cultural Memory and Western Civilization: Functions, Media, Archives.* Cambridge University Press.

Assmann, J. (2006). *Religion and cultural memory: Ten studies.* Stanford University Press.

Assmann, J. (2011). Communicative and cultural memory. In Meusburger, P., Heffernan, M., & Wunder, E. (Eds.), *Cultural Memories. Knowledge and Space* (Vol. 4). Springer., 10.1007/978-90-481-8945-8_2

Attfield, J. (2005). *Wild things: The material culture of everyday life.* Berg.

Atton, C. (2006). Sociologie de la presse musicale alternative [Sociology of the alternative music press]. *Volume!5*(1), 7-25. http://volume.revues.org/614

Atton, C. (2002). Alternative Media. *Sage (Atlanta, Ga.).*

Augoyard, J.-F. (1995). L'environnement sensible et les ambiances architecturales. *L'Espace Geographique*, 4(4), 302–318. 10.3406/spgeo.1995.3409

Augoyard, J.-F. (1998). Eléments pour une théorie des ambiances architecturales et urbaines. *Les Cahiers de la Recherche Architecturale*, 42/43, 13–23.

Augustine of Hippo. (1841). De Genesi ad litteram. *Patrologia Latina,34*, 245−486. https://catholicgnosis.wordpress.com/2020/02/23/st-augustine-intellectual-vision/

Augustine. (1967). Sense and imagination. In Armstrong, A. H. (Ed.), *The Cambridge History of Later Greek and Early Medieval Philosophy* (pp. 374–379). Cambridge University Press.

Auslander, P. (2006). Musical Personae. *The Drama Review*, 50(1), 100–119. 10.1162/dram.2006.50.1.100

Austin, J. L. (1962). *How to do things with words.* Clarendon Press.

Bäckström, P., Führer, H., & Schirrmacher, B. (2022). The intermediality of performance. In J.

Bainbridge Cohen, B. (1993). *Sensing, Feeling, and Action: The Experiential Anatomy of Body-Mind Centering.* Contact Editions.

Bainbridge Cohen, B. (1995). Excerpts from Sensing, Feeling, Action. In Johnson, D. H. (Ed.), *Bone* (pp. 185–203). Breath, Gesture. Practices of Embodiment.

Baker, S. (2014). Saving "Rubbish": Preserving Popular Music's Material. In Cohen, S., Knifton, R., Marion, L., & Roberts, L. (Eds.), *Sites of Popular Music Heritage: Memories, Histories, Places* (pp. 112–124). Routledge.

Baker, S. (Ed.). (2015). *Preserving Popular Music Heritage. Do-it-Yourself, Do-it-Together.* Routledge. 10.4324/9781315769882

Baker, S., Doyle, P., & Homan, S. (2016). Historical Records, National Constructions: The Contemporary Popular Music Archive. *Popular Music and Society*, 39(1), 8–27. 10.1080/03007766.2015.1061336

Baker, S., & Huber, A. (2013). Notes Towards a Typology of the Diy Institution: Identifying Do-It-Yourself Places of Popular Music Preservation. *European Journal of Cultural Studies*, 16(5), 513–530. 10.1177/1367549413491721

Bala, S., Gluhovic, M., Korsberg, H., & Röttger, K. (2017). *International Performance Research Pedagogies: Towards an Unconditional Discipline?* Palgrave Macmillan. 10.1007/978-3-319-53943-0

Baldacci, C., & Franco, S. (2022). *On Reenactment: Concepts, Methodologies, Tools*. Accademia University Press. 10.4000/books.aaccademia.11990

Bal, M. (2002). *Travelling concepts in the humanities: A rough guide*. University of Toronto.

Bangma, A., Rushton, S., & Wüst, F. (Eds.). (2005). *Experience, memory, re-enactment*. Revolver.

Barad, K. (2003). Posthumanist Performativity: Towards an Understanding of How Matter Comes to Matter. *Signs (Chicago, Ill.)*, 28(3), 801–831. 10.1086/345321

Barad, K. (2007). *Meeting the universe halfway: Quantum physics and the entanglement of matter and meaning*. Duke University Press. 10.2307/j.ctv12101zq

Barakat, S., Milton, S., & Elkahlout, G. (2020). Reconstruction under siege: The Gaza Strip since 2007. *Disasters*, 44(3), 477–498. 10.1111/disa.1239431343753

Barnett, J. T. (2022). Vigilant mourning and the future of earthly coexistence. In C. V. Fletcher (Ed.), Communicating in the Anthropocene: Intimate relations (pp. 13–34). Lanham.

Barney, R. (1992). Appearances and Impressions. *Phronesis (Barcelona, Spain)*, 37(3), 283–313. https://www.jstor.org/stable/4182417

Barreto, A. (1996). *Tempo de Incerteza* [Time of Uncertainty]. Relógio d'Água.

Barrett, E., & Bolt, B. (Eds.). (2007). *Practice as Research: Approaches to Creative Arts Enquiry*. I.B. Tauris. 10.5040/9780755604104

Bartov, O. (2001). *The eastern front, 1941–45, German troops and the barbarisation of warfare*. Springer.

Bastian, H. C. (1888). The 'muscular sense'; its nature and cortical localisation. *Brain*, 10(1), 1–137. 10.1093/brain/10.1.1

Baudrillard, J. (2012). The Ecstasy of Communication. Los Angeles: Semiotext(e)

Baudrillard, J. (1994). *Simulacra and Simulation*. University of Michigan Press.

Bauman, Z. (2011). *Collateral Damage: Social Inequalities in a Global Age*. Polity Press.

Bauman, Z. (2013). *Modernity and the Holocaust*. John Wiley & Sons.

Baumrind, D. (1964). Some thoughts on ethics of research: After reading Milgram's 'Behavioural study of obedience'. *The American Psychologist*, 19(6), 421–423. 10.1037/h0040128

Baxter-Moore, N. (2021). John Prine, 1946–2020. *Rock Music Studies*, 8(1), 92–96. 10.1080/19401159.2020.1852765

Bay-Cheng, S., Parker-Starbuck, J., & Saltz, D. Z. (2015). *Performance and media: Taxonomies for a changing field*. University of Michigan Press. 10.3998/mpub.5582757

Bayle, F. (1993). *Musique acousmatique: propositions... positions*. Buchet/Chastel.

Baysal, S. M. (2020). *Trauma, Survival, and Resistance: Possibilities of Recovery in Monica Ali's Brick Lane and Arundhati Roy's The God of Small Things*. [M.A. Thesis].

BBC News. (2024, May 17). *Gaza war: UN defends casualty tally amid Israeli anger*. BBC. https://www.bbc.co.uk/news/world-middle-east-69025420

Bénhichou, A. (2010). Ces documents qui sont aussi des oeuvres..... In Bénichou, A. (Ed.), *Ouvrir le Document: Enjeux et pratiques de la documentation dans les arts visuels contemporains*. Les Presses du Réel.

Benjamin, W. (1987). O narrador: considerações sobre a obra de Nikolai Leskov. In: Benjamin, W. *Magia e técnica, arte e política: ensaios sobre literatura e história da cultura*. São Paulo: Brasiliense.

Benjamin, L. T.Jr, & Simpson, J. A. (2009). The power of the situation: The impact of Milgram's obedience studies on personality and social psychology. *The American Psychologist*, 64(1), 12–19. 10.1037/a001407719209959

Benjamin, W., Eiland, H., & Jennings, W. (1996). *Selected writings: 1938-1940* (Vol. 4). Harvard University Press.

Bennett, A. (2014) Popular Music and the "Problem" of Heritage. In Sara Cohen, Robert Knifton, Marion Leonard and Les Roberts (Ed,), *Sites of Popular Music Heritage: Memories, Histories, Places*. Routledge.

Bennett, A. (2009). "Heritage Rock": Rock Music, Representation and Heritage Discourse. *Poetics*, 37(5-6), 474–489. 10.1016/j.poetic.2009.09.006

Bering, J. M. (2006). The folk psychology of souls. *Behavioral and Brain Sciences*, 29(5), 453–498. 10.1017/S0140525X0600910117156519

Berleant, A. (2000). *The Aesthetic Field: Phenomenology of Aesthetic Experience*. Cybereditions.

Bernal, D. D. (1998). Using a Chicana feminist epistemology in educational research. *Harvard Educational Review*, 68(4), 555–583. 10.17763/haer.68.4.5wv1034973g22q48

Bernal, D. D., & Villalpando, O. (2002). An apartheid of knowledge in academia: The struggle over the" legitimate" knowledge of faculty of color. *Equity & Excellence in Education*, 35(2), 169–180. 10.1080/713845282

Berry & Rodriguez. (2019). *Latinx Curriculum Theorizing*. Lexington Books.

Beverley, J. (1989). The margin at the center: On testimonio (testimonial narrative). *Modern Fiction Studies*, 35(1), 11–12. 10.1353/mfs.0.0923

Bhabha, H. K. (2004). *The Location of Culture*. Routledge Classics.

Bhattacharya, R. (2021). Negotiating the Trauma of Displacement in Bharati Mukherjee's *Wife* and *Jasmine*. In *Understanding Women's Experiences of Displacement*. Taylors and Francis Group.

Billington, M. (1996). Footage and footlights. The Guardian.

Birkeland, I., Burton, R., Parra, C., & Siivonen, K. (2018). *Cultural Sustainability and the Nature-Culture Interface: Livelihoods, Policies, and Methodologies*. Routledge. 10.4324/9781315625294

Birringer, J. H. (1991). The postmodern body in performance. In *Theater: theory and postmodernism*. Indiana University Press.

Bladow, K. (2019). "Never shut up my native": Indigenous feminist protest art in Sápmi. *Feminist Studies*, 45(2), 312–332. 10.1353/fem.2019.0029

Blass, T. (1999). The Milgram paradigm after 35 years: Some things we now know about Obedience to Authority. *Journal of Applied Social Psychology*, 29(5), 955–978. 10.1111/j.1559-1816.1999.tb00134.x

Blass, T. (2009). *The man who shocked the world: The life and legacy of Stanley Milgram*. Basic Books.

Bloch, M. (1995). *Mémoire autobiographique et mémoire historique du passé éloigné. Enquête*. Archives de la revue Enquête, (2), 59-76.

Bloch, S. (2022). For Autoethnographies of Displacement Beyond Gentrification: The Body as Archive, Memory as Data. *Annals of the American Association of Geographers*, 112(3), 706–714. 10.1080/24694452.2021.1985952

Bobko, A. (2019). Augustinus and Kant – Two Founders of Modern Thinking. *Studies in the History of Philosophy*, 10(3), 27–38. 10.12775/szhf.2019.029

Böhme, G. (1993). Atmosphere as the Fundamental Concept of a New Aesthetics. *Thesis Eleven, 36*, 113-126.

Böhme, G. (1997). Aesthetics Knowledge of Nature. *Issues in Contemporary Culture and Aesthetics*, 5, 27–37.

Böhme, G. (2000). Acoustic Atmospheres. A Contribution to the Study of Ecological Aesthetics, Soundscape. *The Journal of Acoustic Ecology*, I(1), 14–18.

Bonenfent, Y. (2012). A portrait of the current state of PaR: defining an (in)discipline. In Boyce-Tillman, J. (Ed.), *PaR for the Course: issues involved in the development of practice-based doctorates in the Performing Arts*. The Higher Education Academy Arts and Humanities.

Bonta, M., & Protevi, J. (2004). *Deleuze and Geophilosophy: A Guide and Glossary*. Edinburgh University Press.

Book Ban Data. (2024, March 14). Banned & Challenged Books: Advocacy, Legislation & Issues; American Library Association. https://www.ala.org/advocacy/bbooks/book-ban-data

Borelli, M. B. (2022). Choreographing Displacement in Sankofa Danzafro's La Ciudad de los Otros. *Theatre History Studies*, 41(1), 148–165. 10.1353/ths.2022.0009

Bottici, C. (2014). *Imaginal Politics. Images Beyond Imagination and the Imaginary*. Columbia University Press.

Boucher, E. (2019). The dangers of depicting Greta Thunberg as a prophet. *The Conversation*. https://theconversation.com/the-dangers-of-depicting-greta-thunberg-as-a-prophet-128813

Bourdieu, P. (1983). The field of cultural production, or: The economic world reversed. *Poetics*, 12(4), 311–356. 10.1016/0304-422X(83)90012-8

Bourriaud, N. (2002). *Relational Aesthetics*. Paris, FR: Les Presses du reel.

Bowman, N. A. (1966). Investing a Theatrical Ideal: Wagner's Bayreuth "Festspielhaus". *Educational Theatre Journal*, 18(4), 429–438. 10.2307/3205270

Boykoff, M. T. (Ed.). (2010). *The politics of climate change: A survey*. Routledge. 10.4324/9780203819234

Brabeck, K. (2003). IV. Testimonio: A strategy for collective resistance, cultural survival, and building solidarity. *Feminism & Psychology*, 13(2), 252–258. 10.1177/0959353503013002009

Brah, A. (1996). *Cartographies of Diaspora: Contesting Identities*. Routledge.

Braidotti, R. (2013). *The Posthuman*. Polity.

Braidotti, R. (2019). *Posthuman Knowledge*. Polity Press.

Braidotti, R., & Hlavajova, M. (2018a). *Posthuman Glossary*. Bloomsbury.

Braidotti, R., & Simone, B. (2018b). *Posthuman Ecologies: Complexity and Process after Deleuze*. Roman & Littlefield.

Brandt, P. A. (2011). What is cognitive semiotics? A new paradigm in the study of meaning. *Signata*, 2(2), 49–60. 10.4000/signata.526

Brannigan, A., & Perry, G. (2016). Milgram, genocide and bureaucracy: A post-Weberian perspective. *State Crime*, 5(2), 287–305. 10.13169/statecrime.5.2.0287

Braun, E. (1979). *The Theatre of Meyerhold: revolution on the modern stage*. Eyre Methuen.

Braun, J., Lengel, L., & Johnson, J. (2014). Environmental Causes and Campaigns. In Thompson, W. F., Lamont, A., Parncutt, R., & Russo, F. A. (Eds.), *Music in the social and behavioral sciences: An encyclopedia* (pp. 401–406). SAGE.

Brennan, M. (2020). The Environmental Sustainability of the Music Industries. In Oakley, K., & Banks, M. (Eds.), *Cultural industries and the environmental crisis: New approaches for policy* (pp. 37–49). Springer. 10.1007/978-3-030-49384-4_4

Brennan, M. (2021). The infrastructure and environmental consequences of live music. In Devine, K., & Boudreault-Fournier, A. (Eds.), *Oxford scholarship online. Audible infrastructures: Music, Sound, Media*. Oxford University Press. 10.1093/oso/9780190932633.003.0006

Brennan, M., & Devine, K. (2020). The cost of music. *Popular Music*, 39(1), 43–65. 10.1017/S0261143019000552

Brennan, M., Scott, J. C., Connelly, A., & Lawrence, G. (2019). Do music festival communities address environmental sustainability and how? A Scottish case study. *Popular Music*, 38(2), 252–275. 10.1017/S0261143019000035

Broadwurst, S. (1999). *Liminal acts: a critical overview of contemporary performance and theory*. Cassel.

Brooks, L. M. (2005). Testimonio's poetics of performance. *Comparative Literature Studies*, 42(2), 181–202. 10.2307/40247475

Brunow, D. (2018). Naming, shaming, framing? Ambivalence of queer visibility in audiovisual archives. In A. Koivunen, K. Kyrölä & I. Ryberg (Eds.), *The Power of Vulnerability: Mobilizing Affect in Feminist, Queer and Anti-racist Media Cultures* (pp. 174-195). Manchester University Press.

Brunow, D. (2015). *Remediating Transcultural Memory: Documentary Filmmaking as Archival Intervention*. De Gruyter. 10.1515/9783110436372

Brunow, D. (2017). Curating Access to Audiovisual Heritage: Cultural Memory and Diversity in European Film Archives. *Image and Narrative*, 1(18), 97–110.

Brustad, M. (2018). *Sámi health: A summary of published results of population studies in Norway*. Sámi Statistics Speak. https://samilogutmuitalit.no/sites/default/files/publications/3sami_health.pdf

Buckley, D. (2003). *R.E.M. fiction: An alternative biography*. Virgin.

Buell, L. (2001). *Writing for an endangered world: Literature, culture, and environment in the U.S. And beyond*. Harvard University Press. 10.4159/9780674029057

Burger, M. (2009). Replicating Milgram: Would people still obey today? *The American Psychologist*, 64(1), 1–11. 10.1037/a001093219209958

Burgos-Debray, E. (Ed.). (2009). *Yo Rigoberta Menchu: Una mujer india en Guatemala*. Volver.

Burkinshaw, P., & White, K. (2020). Generation, gender, and leadership: Metaphors and images. *Frontiers in Education*, 5, 517497. 10.3389/feduc.2020.517497

Burman, M. (2017). Men's intimate partner violence against Sámi women: A Swedish blind spot. *Nordic Journal on Law and Society, 1*(01-02), 194-215.

Burns, S. (2012). 'Better for haunts': Victorian houses and the modern imagination. *American Art*, 26(3), 2–25. 10.1086/669220

Butler, J. (1999). *Gender Trouble: Feminism and the Subversion of Identity*. Routledge.

Butler, J. (2015). *Problemas de género: feminismo e subversão da identidade*. Civilização Brasileira.

Butler, O. (1993). *Parables of the Sower*. Four Walls Eight Windows.

Butt, K. M., & Butt, A. A. (2016). Blockade on Gaza strip: A living hell on earth. *Journal of Political Studies*, 23(1), 157–182.

Cabral, M. V. (2014). *Dimensões da Cidadania: A Mobilização Política em Portugal numa Perspetiva Comparada[Dimensions of Citizenship: Political Mobilisation in Portugal from a Comparative Perspective]*. Afrontamento.

Caeiro, A. (2020). Beyond the bend in the road. In *The complete works of Alberto Caeiro*. New Directions Publishing. CMÉ. http://www.evora.net/percursos/PercursoAguaPrata.pdf

Caesar, R. (2013). A espessura da sonoridade: entre som e imagem. In: *XXIII Anppom, 2013, Natal*. Anais do XXIII Congresso da Anppom. Natal: UFRN.

Caesar, R. (2012). O som como imagem. In *III SMCT, 2012, São Paulo. Anais do III SMCT*. ECA-USP.

Caesar, R. (2016). *O enigma de lupe*. Zazie Edições.

Caliskan, D. (2023). Tran theoretical approaches to memory and relatedness: Potentials and suggestions at the intersections of transgender studies and queer studies. *Memory Studies*, 16(6), 1484–1499. 10.1177/17506980231204177

Callicott, J. B. (Ed.). (1998). *The great new wilderness debate*. University of Georgia Press.

Cappelletto, F. (2003). Long-term memory of extreme events: From autobiography to history. *Journal of the Royal Anthropological Institute*, 9(2), 241–260. 10.1111/1467-9655.00148

Careri, F. (2017). *Walkscapes: walking as an aesthetic practice*. Culicidae Architectural Press.

Carlson, M. (2004). What is performance? In H. Bial & S. Brady (eds.) *The Performance Studies Reader*. London and New York: Routledge.

Carlson, M. (2004). What is performance? In Bial, H., & Brady, S. (Eds.), *The Performance Studies Reader* (pp. 68–72). Routledge.

Carmona, J. F. (2010). *Transgenerational educación: Latina mothers' everyday pedagogies of cultural citizenship in Salt Lake City*. The University of Utah.

Carson, R. (2000). *Silent spring*. Penguin. (Original work published 1962)

Carstens, M. (2016). Sámi land rights: The Anaya report and the Nordic Sámi Convention. *ECMI Journal of Ethnopolitics and Minority Issues in Europe*, 15(1), 75–116.

Caruth, C. (1996). *Unclaimed Experience: Trauma, Narrative, and History*. The Johns Hopkins University Press. 10.1353/book.20656

Carvalho, J. F. (2021). Arte Litúrgica: criações nas capelas de Braga. In Neto, M.J. & Cunha, J.A. (Coord.), *Arte e Igreja em Portugal - Histórias e protagonistas de diálogos recentes*. Casal de Cambra: Caleidoscópio.

Carvalho, J.F. (2013). *A Capela Árvore da Vida: Arquitectura e Vida. COMMUNIO – Revista Internacional Católica, XXX (2013/2)*, 201-214.

Casale, E. (1998). *Composizione per voce. (B. Guerrera, Performer) Mappe*. Pescheria.

Casale, E. (2010). Conversazioni con Chomsky. (F. Micheli [Zavalloni, E. Ribatto, Icarus Ensemble, & MDI Ensemble, Performers) Teatro Cavallerizza, Reggio Emilia.]. *Director*, C.

Caswell, M. (2021). *Urgent Archives: Enacting Liberatory Memory Work*. Taylor & Francis. 10.4324/9781003001355

Çelikel, M. A. (2022). Traumatized Immigrant: Monica Ali's *Brick Lane*. *CUJHSS, 16*(2), 169-180. 10.47777/canku-jhss.1160709

Cervantes-Soon, C. G. (2012). Testimonios of life and learning in the borderlands: Subaltern Juárez girls speak. *Equity & Excellence in Education*, 45(3), 373–391. 10.1080/10665684.2012.698182

Césaire, A. (1972). *Discourse on colonialism*. Monthly Review Press.

Chahine. (2021). Memory is not about the past. *Journal of Anthropological Films, 5*(1). 10.15845/jaf.v5i01.3189

Chapple, F., & Kattenbelt, C. (2006). Key issues in intermediality in theatre and performance. In F. Chapple & C.L. Kattenbelt (Eds.), *Intermediality in Theatre and Performance* (pp. 11–25). Rodopi.

Chapple, F., & Kattenbelt, C. (Eds.). (2006). *Intermediality in theatre and performance*. Rodopi. 10.1163/9789401210089

Chatman, S. (1974). Genette's analysis of narrative time relations. *L'Esprit Créateur*, 14(4), 353–368.

Chavez-Diaz, M. (2015). *Social justice healing practitioners: Testimonios of transformative praxis and hope*. Academic Press.

Chawla. (2017). The Khalistan Movement of 1984: A Critical Appreciation. *A Research Journal of South Asian Studies, 32*(1), 81-90.

Chion, M. (1999). *The Voice in Cinema. Nova York*. Columbia University Press.

Chion, M. (2002). *Le son: traité d'acoulogie*. Nathan/VUEF.

Chion, M. (2006). Le son et l'image. In Soulages, F. (Ed.), *Les Cahiers du Collège iconique: communications et débats*. INA.

Chion, M. (2011). *A Audiovisão: som e imagem no cinema*. Texto & Grafia.

Clifford, J. (1992). Travelling Cultures. In *Cultural Studies*. Routledge.

Colaço, D. (2022). What counts as a memory? Definitions, hypotheses, and "kinding in progress". *Philosophy of Science*, 89(1), 89–106. 10.1017/psa.2021.14

Collier, Z., & Sutherland, T. (2022). Witnessing, Testimony, and Transformation as Genres of Black Archival Practice. *The Black Scholar*, 52(2), 7–15. 10.1080/00064246.2022.2042666

Collins, J. (1965). The Coming Of The Roads. *Judy Collins' Fifth Album*. Elektra EKS-7300.

Collins, Jez (2012). *Multiple Voices, Multiple Memories: Public History Making and Activist Archivism in Online Popular Music Archives* [Doctoral dissertation, School of Media, Birmingham City University].

Connolly, A. (2011). Healing the Wounds of Our Fathers: Intergenerational Trauma, Memory, Symbolization and Narrative. *The Journal of Analytical Psychology*, 56(5), 607–626. 10.1111/j.1468-5922.2011.01936.x22039944

Cook, N. (2001). Between Process and Product: Music and/as Performance. *Music Theory Online, 7*(2).

Costa, V. F. D. (2016). *Morfologia da obra aberta*. Prismas.

Craig, R. T. (2020). Models of communication in and as metadiscourse. In M. Bergman, K. Kirtiklis & J. Siebers (Eds.), *Models of communication: Philosophical and theoretical approaches* (pp. 11–33). Routledge.

Craps, S. (2013). *Postcolonial Witnessing: Trauma Out of Bounds*. Palgrave Macmillan. 10.1057/9781137292117

Crimp, D. (1995). *Redening Site Specicity in On the Museum's Ruins*. The MIT Press.

Cronon, W. (1996). The Trouble with Wilderness: Or, Getting Back to the Wrong Nature. *Environmental History*, 1(1), 7–28. 10.2307/3985059

Crossley, M. (2021a). A recalibration of theatre's hypermediality. In L. Elleström (Ed.), *Beyond Media Borders, Volume 1: Intermedial relations among multimodal media* (pp. 95–112). Palgrave Macmillan. 10.1007/978-3-030-49679-1_2

Crown Punks Group. www.facebook.com/groups/108486069179177/> (accessed 5 October 2012)

Cvetkovich, A. (2003). *An Archive of Feelings: Trauma, Sexuality, and Lesbian Public Cultures*. Duke University Press.

D'Annunzio, G. (1983). *Contemplazioni della morte {1912}. As quoted in G. Bachelard, Water and Dreams: An Essay on the Imagination of Matter*. The Pegasus Foundation.

D'Orazio, D., De Cesaris, S., Morandi, F., & Garai, M. (2018). The aesthetics of the Bayreuth Festspielhaus explained by means of acoustic measurements and simulations. *Journal of Cultural Heritage*, 34, 151–158. 10.1016/j.culher.2018.03.003

Dale, P. (2010). *Anyone Can Do It: Traditions of Punk and the Politics of Empowerment*. [Doctoral dissertation, Newcastle University]. https://theses.ncl.ac.uk/jspui/handle/10443/1101

Damsgård, E., Thrane, G., Fleten, N., Bagge, J., Sørlie, T., Anke, A., & Broderstad, A. R. (2020). Persistent pain associated with socioeconomic and personal factors in a Sámi and Non-Sámi population in Norway: An analysis of SAMINOR 2 survey data. *International Journal of Circumpolar Health*, 79(1), 1787022. 10.1080/22423982.2020.178702232780007

Dana, K. O. (1997). Sámi literature in the Twentieth Century. *World Literature Today*, 71(1), 22–28. 10.2307/40152555

Data from Form 990s for top 25 US Universities. (2022). Guidestar. https://www.guidestar.org/

Dawe, K., & Allen, A. S. (Eds.). (2016). *Current directions in ecomusicology: Music, culture, nature*. Routledge.

Debord, G. (1958). Theory of the Dérive. *Internationale Situationniste #2*.

Deleuze, G. (1987). Difference and repetition. *Continuum*.

Deleuze, G. (2006). *Nietzsche and philosophy*. Columbia UP.

Deleuze, G., & Guattari, F. (1983). *Anti-Oedipus: Capitalism and Schizophrenia*. University of Minnesota Press.

Delgado Bernal, D. (2018). A testimonio of critical race feminista parenting: Snapshots from my childhood and my parenting. *International Journal of Qualitative Studies in Education : QSE*, 31(1), 25–35. 10.1080/09518398.2017.1379623

Delgado-Bernal, D. (2001). Learning and living pedagogies of the home: The mestiza consciousness of Chicana students. *International Journal of Qualitative Studies in Education : QSE*, 14(5), 623–639. 10.1080/09518390110059838

Delgado-Bernal, D. (2002). Critical race theory, Latino critical theory, and critical raced-gendered epistemologies: Recognizing students of color as holders and creators of knowledge. *Qualitative Inquiry*, 1(8), 105–126. 10.1177/107780040200800107

Delgado-Bernal, D., Huber, L. P., & Malagón, M. C. (2018). Bridging theories to name and claim a critical race feminista methodology. In *Understanding critical race research methods and methodologies* (pp. 109–121). Routledge. 10.4324/9781315100944-10

DeNicolo, C. P., & Gónzalez, M. (2015). Testimoniando en Nepantla: Using testimonio as a pedagogical tool for exploring embodied literacies and bilingualism. *Journal of Language & Literacy Education*, 11(1), 109–126.

DeRocher, P. (2018). *Transnational testimonios: the politics of collective knowledge production*. University of Washington Press.

Derrida, J. (1996). *Archive fever: A Freudian impression* (Prenowitz, E., Trans.). University of Chicago Press.

Derrida, J. (1996). *Archive Fever: A Freudian Impression*. University of Chicago Press.

Descartes, R. (2016). *Meditations on First Philosophy/ Meditationes de prima philosophia: A Bilingual Edition* (Heffernan, G., Ed.). University of Notre Dame Press. (Original work published 1685)

Dettmer, J. (2024, February 2). How the Holocaust shapes Israel's war in Gaza. *Politico*. https://www.politico.eu/article/how-the-holocaust-shapes-israels-war-in-gaza/#:~:text=%E2%80%9CHamas'%20attack%20should%20never%20have,hostages%20alive%2C%E2%80%9D%20he%20added

Deutscher, M. (1998). History of the interest in memory. In Memory. In *The Routledge Encyclopedia of Philosophy*. Routledge. 10.4324/9780415249126-V020-1

Dickens, C. (1853). *Bleak house* (Bradbury, N., Ed.). Penguin.

Dickinson, R. (2024, March 01). *Personal communication [Personal interview]*.

Dickinson, R. (n.d). *The Milgram re-enactment*. R. Dickson. https://www.roddickinson.net/pages/milgram/project-synopsis.php. https://www.roddickinson.net/pages/milgram/project-synopsis.php

Didi-Huberman, G. (2007). Foreword: Knowledge-Movement. In Michaud, P. (Ed.), *Aby Warburg and the image in motion* (pp. 7–19). Zone.

Didi-Huberman, G. (2008). *Images in spite of all: Four photographs from Auschwitz*. University of Chicago Press.

Dines, M. (2004). *An Investigation into the Emergence of the Anarcho-Punk Scene of the 1980s.* [Doctoral dissertation, University of Salford]. http://usir.salford.ac.uk/id/eprint/2040/

Dinis, F. (2020). *Sinuous Sensations Hypnotic Emotions: Contemporary sound and visual performance* [PhD Thesis, Faculty of Arts and Humanities, University of Coimbra. Coimbra: Portugal].

Dinis, F. (2024). *The Production of Effects of Presence in Live Audio-Visual Performances. Springer Series in Design and Innovation.* Springer. 10.1007/978-3-031-47281-7_72

Dinis, F. (2023). Performativity of the Memory of Religious Places through Sound and Image. *Religions*, 14(9), 1137. 10.3390/rel14091137

Dinter, M. T. (2023). *Introduction: what is cultural memory? Cultural Memory in Republican and Augustan Rome.* Cambridge University Press.

Ditty. (2019). Eulogy For A Sparrow. *Poetry Ceylon*. Pagal Haina.

Dixon, S. (2007). *Digital performance: a history of new media in theater, dance, performance art, and installation.* The MIT Press. 10.7551/mitpress/2429.001.0001

Dorsch, F. (2016). Hume. In Kind, A. (Ed.), *The Routledge Handbook of Philosophy of Imagination* (pp. 40–54). Routledge.

Dragojlovic, A. (2018). Politics of Negative Affect: Intergenerational Haunting, Counter-archival Practices and the Queer Memory. *Subjectivity, 11*, 91-107.

Duncombe, S. (1997). *Notes from Underground: Zines and the Politics of Alternative Culture*. Verso.

Dunn, K. (2008). Never mind the bollocks: The punk rock politics of global communication. *Review of International Studies, 34*(S1), 193–210. 10.1017/S0260210508007869

Dussel, E. D., Krauel, J., & Tuma, V. C. (2000). Europe, modernity, and eurocentrism. *Nepantla, 1*(3), 465–478. https://www.muse.jhu.edu/article/23901

Dylan, B. (1979). This Land Is Your Land. *The Hurricane Carter Benefit*. Phoenix Records 44777.

Eddy, M. (2000). Access to Somatic Theory and Applications. Sociopolitical Concerns. In *Proceedings from Dancing the Millennium Congress on Research in Dance Conference*. George Washington University.

Eddy, M. (2016). Mindful Movement: The Evolution of the Somatic Arts and Conscious Action. *Intellect*.

Edmonds, P. (2016). Honourable Colonisation? Australia. In *Honourable Intentions?* (pp. 46-62). Routledge.

Edwards, E. (2016). The colonial archival imaginaire at home. Social Anthropology. *Anthropologie et Sociétés, 24*(1), 52–66.

Eide, Ø., & Schubert, Z. (2021). Seeing the Landscape Through Textual and Graphical Media Products. In L. Elleström (Ed.), *Beyond Media Borders, Volume 2: Intermedial Relations among Multimodal Media* (pp. 175–209). Palgrave Macmillan. 10.1007/978-3-030-49683-8_7

Eidsheim, N. S. (2019). *The race of sound*. Duke University Press.

Eilat, G., & Ilan, R. K. (2013). *Evil to the core*. Israeli Centre for Digital Art.

Elam, K. (1980). *The Semiotics of Theatre and Drama*. Routledge. 10.4324/9780203993309

Elleström, L. (2021a). The modalities of media II: An expanded model for understanding intermedial relations. In L. Elleström (Ed.), *Beyond Media Borders, Volume 1: Intermedial relations among multimodal media* (pp. 3–91). Palgrave Macmillan.

Elleström, L. (2021b). Summary and Elaborations. In L. Elleström (Ed.), *Beyond Media Borders, Volume 2: Intermedial Relations among Multimodal Media* (pp. 213-233). Palgrave Macmillan. 10.1007/978-3-030-49683-8_8

Elleström, L. (2018). A medium-centered model of communication. *Semiotica, 2018*(224), 269–293. 10.1515/sem-2016-0024

Elleström, L. (Ed.). (2010). *Media Borders, Multimodality and Intermediality*. Palgrave MacMillan. 10.1057/9780230275201

Emms, R., & Crossley, N. (2018). Translocality, network structure, and music worlds: Underground metal in the United Kingdom. *Canadian Review of Sociology, 55*(1), 111+. https://link-gale-com.eux.idm.oclc.org/apps/doc/A530106505/AONE?u=ed_itw&sid=bookmark-AONE&xid=247f3b7d

Engstrom, S. (2006). Understanding and Sensibility. *Inquiry (Oslo, Norway), 49*(1), 2–25. 10.1080/00201740500497225

Erickson, R. (2009). The real movie: Re-enactment, spectacle and recovery in Pierre Huyghe's *The Third Memory*. In *Framework 50* (1-2), 107-24.

Eriksen, A. M., Hansen, K. L., Schei, B., Sørlie, T., Stigum, H., Bjertness, E., & Javo, C. (2018). Childhood violence and mental health among indigenous Sámi and non-Sámi populations in Norway: A SAMINOR 2 questionnaire study. *International Journal of Circumpolar Health*, 77(1), 1508320. 10.1080/22423982.2018.150832030112962

Eriksen, A. M., Melhus, M., Jacobsen, B. K., Schei, B., & Broderstad, A. R. (2021). Intimate partner violence and its association with mental health problems: The importance of childhood violence–The SAMINOR 2 Questionnaire Survey. *Scandinavian Journal of Public Health*, 1–3.34192982

Erikson, K. (1976). *Everything in Its Path*. Simon and Schuster.

Errickson, A. (1999). *A Detailed Journey into the Punk Subculture: Punk Outreach in Public Libraries*. University of North Carolina at Chapel Hill.

Escobar, A. (2018). *Designs for the pluriverse: Radical interdependence, autonomy, and the making of world*. Duke University Press. 10.1215/9780822371816

Espino, M. M., Vega, I. I., Rendón, L. I., Ranero, J. J., & Muñiz, M. M. (2017). The Process of Reflexión in Bridging Testimonios Across Lived Experience: Michelle M. Espino Irene I. In *Chicana/Latina testimonios as pedagogical, methodological, and activist approaches to social justice* (pp. 93–108). Routledge.

Facebook. (n.d.). *Areley Kings Windmill and Bleak House*. We love Stourport-on-Severn past and present day. https://www.facebook.com/search/top?q=bleak%20house%20stourport

Farhat, T., Ibrahim, S., Abdul-Sater, Z., & Abu-Sittah, G. (2023). Responding to the humanitarian crisis in Gaza: Damned if you do… damned if you don't! *Annals of Global Health*, 89(1), 1–6. 10.5334/aogh.397537637468

Faulkner, W. (2011). *Requiem for a nun*. Vintage.

Featherstone, M. (2000). Archiving Cultures. *The British Journal of Sociology*, 51(1), 161–184. 10.1111/j.1468-4446.2000.00161.x

Featherstone, M. (2006). Archive. *Theory, Culture & Society*, 23(2/3), 591–596. 10.1177/0263276406023002106

Feixa, C. (2014). *Da geração @ geração blockchain: a juventude na era postdigital[From the Generation@ to the #Generation: Youth in the Digital Era]*. Ned Ediciones.

Feixa, C., & Guerra, P. (2017). Unidos por el mismo sueño en una canción: On music, gangs and flows. *Portuguese Journal of Social Science*, 16(3), 305–322. 10.1386/pjss.16.3.305_1

Feldman-Barrett, C. (2015). Archival Research and the Expansion of Popular Music History. In Bennett, A., & Waksman, S. (Eds.), *The Sage Handbook of Popular Music* (pp. 83–98). Sage., 10.4135/9781473910362.n5

Féral, J. (1992). What is left of performance art? Autpsy of a function. *Birth of a genre. Discourse - Journal for theorical Studies in Media and Culture*. Springer.

Féral, J. (2015). Além dos limites: Teoria e prática do teatro. *São Paulo em Perspectiva*, 2015.

Féral, J., & Bermingham, R. P. (2002). Theatricality: The specificity of theatrical language. *SubStance*, 31(2), 94–108. 10.1353/sub.2002.0026

Fernandes, S. (2011). Teatralidades e performatividade na cena contemporânea. Repertório. *Teatro & Dança, Salvador*, 16, 11–21.

Ferrando, F. (2020). *Philosophical Posthumanism*. Bloomsbury.

Finnegan, R. H. (2007). *The Hidden Musicians: Music-Making in An English Town*. Wesleyan University Press.

Finnmark Act. (2005). Ministry of Justice and Public Security. LOV-2005–06–17–85.

Fischer-Lichte, E. (2013). The Transformative Aesthetics of the Gesamtkunstwerk/Total Work of Art as the Specter Haunting Modernism. *Theatre Journal*, 65(4), 593–603. 10.1353/tj.2013.0104

Fischer-Lichte, E. (2019). *Estética do Performativo*. Orfeu Negro.

Fisher, M. (1999). *Flatline Constructs: Gothic Materialism and Cybernetic Theory-Fiction*. New York: exmilitary press.

Fisher, M. (2009). *Capitalist Realism: Is There No Alternative?* Zero Books.

Flinn, A. (2007). Community Histories, Community Archives: Some Opportunities and Challenges. *Journal of the Society of Archivists*, 28(2), 151–176. 10.1080/00379810701611936

Flinn, A. (2011). Archival Activism: Independent and Community-led Archives, Radical Public History and the Heritage Professions. *InterActions: UCLA Journal of Education and Information Studies*, 7(2). 10.5070/D472000699

Flinn, A. (2012). Archives and Their Communities: Collecting Histories, Challenging Heritage. In Dawson, G. (Ed.), *Memory, Narrative and Histories: Critical Debates, New Trajectories, Working Papers, 19-35*. University of Brighton.

Flores-Carmona, J. (2010). *Transgenerational Education: Latina mothers' everyday pedagogies of cultural citizenship in Salt Lake City, Utah*. [Unpublished dissertation, University of Utah].

Flores-Carmona, J., & Delgado Bernal, D. (2012). Oral histories in the classroom: Home and community pedagogies. In Sleeter, C. E., & Soriano Ayala, E. (Eds.), *Building solidarity between schools and marginalized communities: International perspectives*. Teachers College Press.

Flores-Carmona, J., Hamzeh, M., Bejarano, C. M., Hernandez, S. M., & El Ashmawi, P. Y. (2018). Platicas- Testimonio: Practicing Methodological Borderlands for Solidarity and Resilience in Academia. Chicana. *Latino Studies*, 18(1), 30–52.

Fontes, A. C. (2020). *Conversa com o arquiteto António Cerejeira Fontes*. Junho de 2020.

Force, W. (2005). *No, We Don't Have Any T-Shirts: Identity in a (Self-Consciously)*. Consumerist Punk Subculture. [Doctoral dissertation, University of South Florida]

Foster, C. (1998). The Narrative and the Ambient in Environmental Aesthetics. *The Journal of Aesthetics and Art Criticism*, 56(2), 127–137. 10.1111/1540_6245.jaac56.2.0127

Foster, S. L. (2010). *Choreographing Empathy: Kinesthesia in Performance*. Routledge. 10.4324/9780203840702

Franco, S., & Chernitch, G. C. (2024). Reenactment. *Dancing Museums Glossary*.https://www.dancingmuseums.com/artefacts/reenactment/

Franko, M. (Ed.). (2018). *The Oxford Handbook of Dance and Reenactment*. Oxford University Press.

Franz, N. K. (2011). The unfocused focus group: Benefit or bane? *The Qualitative Report*, 16(5), 1380–1388. 10.46743/2160-3715/2011.1304

Frasson, E. (2016). *Personal Notes from the Fieldwork with Gaby Agis* [Unpublished].

Frasson, E. (2022). *Encounters with Somatics and European Choreography: Discourses, Narratives and Embodied Ethnography between the 1980s and the 2010s* [Unpublished doctoral dissertation, University of Roehampton, London].

Fredericks, B., & Bradfield, A. (2023). Asserting Indigenous Agencies: Constructions and Deconstructions of James Cook in Northern Queensland. In *The Palgrave Handbook on Rethinking Colonial Commemorations* (pp. 351–382). Springer International Publishing. 10.1007/978-3-031-28609-4_19

Freud, S. (2005). *Forgetting things*. Penguin. (Original work published 1901)

Freud, S. (2010). *The Interpretation of Dreams. Translated from the German and* (Strachey, J., Ed.). Basic Books.

Freud, S., & McLintock, D. (2003). *The uncanny*. Penguin. (Original work published 1919)

Friborg, O., Sørlie, T., Schei, B., Javo, C., Sørbye, Ø., & Hansen, K. L. (2020). Do childhood boarding school experiences predict health, well-being and disability pension in adults? A SAMINOR study. *Journal of Cross-Cultural Psychology*, 51(10), 848–875. 10.1177/0022022120962571

Frith, S. (1996). *Performing rites: on the value of popular music*. Havard University Press. 10.1093/oso/9780198163329.001.0001

Fuchs, E. (1985). Presence and the revenge of writing. *Performing Arts Journal*, 9(2/3), 163–173. 10.2307/3245520

Fujak, J. (2011). Comprovisación–Notas para la discusión sobre la validez del concepto. *Oro Molido*, 33, 24–30.

Fuller, M., & Weizman, E. (2021). *Investigative aesthetics: Conflicts and commons in the politics of truth*. Verso Books.

Gaillard, F. (2004). *Watermelon wine: Remembering the golden years of country music*. NewSouth.

Gallanti, F. (2019). Forensic architecture. In *The Routledge Handbook of Re-enactment Studies* (pp. 79–83). Routledge. 10.4324/9780429445637-16

Gallese, V., & Stamenov, M. (2002). *Mirror Neurons and the Evolution of Brain and Language*. John Benjamins Publishing Company.

Ganaie, A. A. (2019). Multicultural Subjectivity and Cosmopolitan Identity: A Reading of Bharati Mukherjee's *Jasmine*. *Advances in Social Sciences Research Journal*, 6(7), 175–180. 10.14738/assrj.67.6175

Gane, N. (2006). When We Have Never Been Human, What Is to Be Done?:Interview with Donna Haraway. *Theory, Culture & Society*, 23(7-8), 135–158. 10.1177/0263276406069228

Gangle, R. (2020). *Diagrammatic Immanence: Category Theory and Philosophy*. Edinburgh University Press.

Ganguly, M. (2002). *Memory (2)*. CSMT. https://csmt.uchicago.edu/glossary2004/memory2.htm

Garagozov, R. (2015). *Collective Memory: How Collective Representations About the Past Are Created, Preserved and Reproduced*. Nova publisher.

Garai, M., Ito, K., D'Orazio, D., De Cesaris, S., & Morandi, F. (2015). The Acoustics of the Bayreuth Festspielhaus. *Proc. ICSV*, 22, 651.

Garcia, A., Neiva, A., Aguiar, D., & e-flux Architecture. (n.d.). *Hydroreflexivity. e-flux Architecture*. e-Flux. https://www.e-flux.com/architecture/hydroreflexivity/535262/editorial/

Garcia-Diaz, M. (in press). Multicultural identity challenge: An exploration of parental involvement in Latinx motherhood. In M. Williams-Johnson & N. P. Rickert (Eds.), *Critical analysis of parental involvement in school: Working with families across sociocultural contexts*. Accademic Press.

Garde-Hansen, J. (2009). My Memories?: Personal digital archive fever and Facebook. In Garde-Hansen, Joanne, Andrew Hoskins, and Anna Reading, *Save As . . . Digital Memories* (pp. 135-150). Palgrave MacMillian.

Garigliano, C. (2009). " *L'Ottava Isola*": Studies on Music, Heritage and Cultural Identity Between Sicily and Sydney [Doctoral dissertation, Macquarie University].

Gaskin, V. (2002). The tenth level. *Rod Dickinson: The power of persuasion*. [Exhibition catalogue]. Glasgow.

Gaskin, V. (2003). Subjects in search of an author. In Rushton, S. (Ed.), *The Milgram re-enactment: Essays on Rod Dickinson's re-enactment of Stanley Milgram's 'Obedience to Authority' experiments* (pp. 5–13). Jan van Eyck Academie.

Geiger, T., Moore, N., & Savage, M. (2010). *The Archive in Question*. (CRESC Working Paper 81). https://hummedia.manchester.ac.uk/institutes/cresc/workingpapers/wp81.pdf

George, D. (2020). *The Natural Body in Somatics Dance Training*. Oxford University Press. 10.1093/oso/9780197538739.001.0001

Giannacopoulos, M. (2006). Terror Australis: white sovereignty and the violence of law. *Borderlands, 5*(1).

Gibson, C., & Warren, A. (2016). Resource-Sensitive Global Production Networks: Reconfigured Geographies of Timber and Acoustic Guitar Manufacturing. *Economic Geography*, 92(4), 430–454. 10.1080/00130095.2016.1178569

Gibson, J. J. (2015). *The Ecological Approach to Visual Perception*. Psychology Press.

Gibson, M. (2004). Melancholy objects. *Mortality*, 9(4), 365–376. 10.1080/13576270412331329812

Gilbert, E. (2021). *The signature of all things*. Bloomsbury Publishing.

Gilbert, S. M., & Gubar, S. (2000). *The Madwoman in the attic: The woman writer and the nineteenth-century literary imagination*. Yale University Press.

Gilman, C. P. (2012). *The yellow wallpaper*. Virago. (Original work published 1892)

Gilmurray, J. (2017). Ecological Sound Art: Steps towards a new field. *Organised Sound*, 22(1), 32–41. 10.1017/S1355771816000315

Giroux, H. A. (2009). Hard Lessons: Neoliberalism, Education, and the Politics of Disposability. *Policy Futures in Education*, 7(5), 570–573. 10.2304/pfie.2009.7.5.570

Glahn, D. (2014). *Music and the skillful listener: American women compose the natural world*. Indiana University Press.

Glasgow Apollo Group. www.facebook.com/groups/5586711471/?ref=ts&fref=ts > (accessed 10 October 2013)

Godlovitch, S. (2008). *Musical performance: a philosophical study*. Routledge.

Goffman, E. (1974). *Frame Analysis: An essay on the organization of experience*. Northeastern University Press.

Goldberg, R. L. (2001). *Performance Art: From Futurism to the Present*. Thames & Hudson.

Grant, A. (1994). Big Yellow Taxi. *House Of Love*. A&M Records.

Graver, H. P., & Ulfstein, G. (2004). The Sámi people's right to land in Norway. *International Journal on Minority and Group Rights*, 11(4), 337–377. 10.1163/1571811042791175

Gray, C. (1996). Inquiry through practice: developing appropriate research strategies. In *No Guru, No Method?* UIAH.

Greiner, C. (2015). "The North chose us": Selected poems by Nils-Aslak Valkeapää as expressions of Sámi cultural ecology and indigenous rights concerns. *IK: Other Ways of Knowing*, 21-32.

Griffiths, L. E. (2014). *Dance and The Archival Body: Knowledge, Memory and Experience in Dance Revival Processes* (uk.bl.ethos.655236) [Doctoral dissertation, University of Leeds]. White Roses eTheses Online.

Gross, A. J. (2021). Archives of the Dispossessed: Mourning, Memory, and Metahistory. *English Language Notes*, 59(1), 219–221. 10.1215/00138282-8815093

Grusin, R. (2015). Radical Mediation. *Critical Inquiry*, 42(1), 124–148. 10.1086/682998

Guattari, F. (1989). *The Three Ecologies*. Bloomsbury Academic.

Guerra, P. (2010). *A instável leveza do rock: génese, dinâmica e consolidação do rock alternativo em Portugal (1980-2010)* [The Unstable Lightness of Rock: Genesis, Dynamics and Consolidation of Alternative Rock in Portugal (1980-2010)]. [Doctoral thesis, Faculdade de Letras da Universidade do Porto]. http://hdl.handle.net/10216/56304

Guerra, P., & Quintela, P. (orgs.) (2020). *Punk, Fanzines and DIY Cultures in a Global World. Fast, Furious and Xerox*. London: Palgrave Macmillan.

Guerra, P., & Quintela, P. (orgs.). (2021). *Independent DIY publications and the underground urban cultures*. Porto: University of Porto – Faculty of Arts and Humanities. https://hdl.handle.net/10216/136396

Guerra, P. (2013). Punk, ação e contradição em Portugal. Uma aproximação às culturas juvenis contemporâneas ['Punk, Action and Contradiction in Portugal: An Approach to Contemporary Youth Cultures]. *Revista Crítica de Ciencias Sociais*, 102(102), 111–134. 10.4000/rccs.5486

Guerra, P. (2014). Punk, expectations, breaches and metamorphoses: Portugal, 1977–2012. *Critical Arts*, 28(1), 111–122. 10.1080/02560046.2014.883697

Guerra, P., & Bennett, A. (2015). Never Mind the Pistols? The Legacy and Authenticity of the Sex Pistols in Portugal. *Popular Music and Society*, 38(4), 500–521. 10.1080/03007766.2015.1041748

Guerra, P., & Bennett, A. (2020). Punk Portugal, 1977-2012: A preliminary genealogy. *Popular Music History*, 13(3), 215–234. 10.1558/pomh.39660

Guesdon, J.-M., & Margotin, P. (2017). *Pink Floyd All the Songs: The Story Behind Every Track*. Running Press.

Guillory, J. (2010). Genesis of the Media Concept. *Critical Inquiry*, 36(2), 321–362. 10.1086/648528

Guilmette, L. (2023). Wayward Fables, Poem-Life Experiments: Foucault and Hartman in the Archives. *The Journal of Speculative Philosophy*, 37(3), 437–446. 10.5325/jspecphil.37.3.0437

Gumbs, A. P. (2019). *Dub: Finding Ceremony*. Duke University Press. 10.1515/9781478007081

Gumbs, A. P., Martens, C., & Williams, M. (Eds.). (2016). *Revolutionary mothering: love on the front lines*. PM Press.

Guttorm, H., Kantonen, L., Kramvig, B., & Pyhälä, A. (2021). Decolonized research-storying: Bringing Indigenous ontologies and care into the practices of research writing. In *Indigenous research methodologies in Sámi and global contexts* (pp. 113–143). Brill. 10.1163/9789004463097_006

Györke, Á. (2022). *From Transnational to Translocal: Space and Emotion in Contemporary Fiction*. [MS. Habilitation Thesis].

Hahn, L. (1950). Spin echoes. *Physical Review*, 80(4), 580–594. 10.1103/PhysRev.80.580

Halbwachs, M. (1992). *On Collective Memory*. University of Chicago Press. 10.7208/chicago/9780226774497.001.0001

Hale, R. (2020). They were just following orders': Relationships between Milgram's obedience experiments and conceptions of Holocaust perpetration. *Holocaust education: Contemporary challenges and controversies*, 74-94.

Hall, S. (1980). Encoding/decoding. In Hall, S. (Ed.), *Culture, media, language: Working papers in cultural studies, 1972–79* (pp. 128–138). Hutchinson.

Hall, S. (1999). Whose Heritage? Un-Settling "the Heritage", Re-Imagining the Post-Nation. *Third Text*, 13(49), 3–13. 10.1080/09528829908576818

Halsaa, B. (2020). The (trans) national mobilisation of Sámi women in Norway. *Le Mouvement Social*, 63, 119–145.

Hamel, Leigh Ann, Tom Maher, Mick O'Dwyer, & Eric Cook (2014). 'Organizing Anarchy: The Forgotten Zine Archive. [Paper presentation]. *iConference 2014 Proceedings,* Berlin. https://doi.org/10.9776/14350

Hammersley, M., & Atkinson, P. (2007). *Ethnography: Principles and practice*. Routledge.

Hanna, T. (1986). What is Somatics? *Somatics: Magazine-Journal of the Bodily Arts and Science, 4*, 4. https://somatics.org/library/htl-wis1.html

Hannan, M. (2006). *Interrogating comprovisation as practice-led research*. Queensland University of Technology.

Haraway, D. J. (1991). *A Cyborg Manifesto: Science, technology, and Socialist-Feminism in the Late Twentieth Century" in Simians, Cyborgs, and Women: The Reinvention of Nature*. Routledge.

Haraway, D. J. (2016). *Staying with the Trouble: Making Kin in the Chthulucene*. Duke University Press.

Harbison, I. (2019). *Performing Image*. The MIT Press. 10.7551/mitpress/10973.001.0001

Harrison, R. P. (2008). *Gardens: An Essay on the Human Condition*. The University of Chicago Press. 10.7208/chicago/9780226317861.001.0001

Harris, V. (2002). The archival sliver: Power, memory, and archives in South Africa. *Archival Science*, 2(1-2), 63–86. 10.1007/BF02435631

Harris, V. (2012). Genres of the trace: Memory, archives and trouble. *Archives & Manuscripts*, 40(3), 147–157. 10.1080/01576895.2012.735825

Hartman, S. (2008). Venus in Two Acts. *Small Axe*, 12(2), 1–14. 10.1215/-12-2-1

Hartman, S. V. (1997). *Scenes of subjection: terror, slavery, and self-making in nineteenth-century America*. Oxford University Press.

Hartman, S. V. (2019). *Wayward lives, beautiful experiments: intimate histories of social upheaval* (1st ed.). W.W. Norton & Company.

Harviainen, T. J. (2008). Kaprow's Scions. In M. Montola & J. Stenros (Eds.), Playground Worlds: Creating and Evaluating Experiences of Role-Playing Games (pp. 216–231). Academic Press.

Haseman, B. (2006). A Manifest for Performative Research. International Australia Incorporating Culture and Policy, theme issue. *Practice-led Research*, 118, 98–106.

Headrick, D. R. (2020). *Humans versus nature: A global environmental history*. Oxford University Press.

Hedgecoe, J. (2006). *The art of digital photography*. Dorling Kindersley.

Heidegger, M. (1971). *Poetry, language, thought*. Harper and Row.

Heller, T. (1997). Textual seductions: Women's reading and writing in Margaret Oliphant's "The library window.". *Victorian Literature and Culture*, 25(1), 23–37. 10.1017/S1060150300004605

Henderson, L., & Stacy, L. (2013). *Encyclopedia of Music in the 20ᵗʰ Century*. Routledge.

Herman, A. (1997). *The idea of decline in Western history*. Free Press.

Hespanha, P., & Caleiras, J. (2017). O labirinto das políticas de emprego [The labyrinth of employment policies]. *Cadernos do Observatório*, *10.*https://www.ces.uc.pt/observatorios/crisalt/documentos/cadernos/Caderno10_Labirinto _politicas_emprego.pdf

Hines, R. (2023). *Kentucky's Green River*. Arcadia.

Hochschild, P. E. (2012). Plato. In P. E. Hochschild (Ed.), *Memory in Augustine's Theological Anthropology* (pp. 9-27). Oxford Academic. 10.1093/acprof:oso/9780199643028.003.0002

Hockey, S. (1983). One Man's Writing is another Man's Walrus: An Assessment of Experimental Work in the Early Years of Dance Umbrella (1978, 1983) and attitudes Towards it From the Press and Public. *Dance Theatre Journal*, 6(1), 25–27.

Hoelscher, S., & Alderman, D. H. (2004). Memory and place: Geographies of a critical Relationship. *Social & Cultural Geography*, 5(3), 347–355. 10.1080/1464936042000252769

hooks, b. (2015 [1981]). *Ain't I a Woman: Black Women and Feminism*. Routledge

Horn, E. (2018). *The future as catastrophe: Imagining disaster in the modern age*. Columbia University Press. 10.7312/ horn18862

Howitt, R., Holt, L., & Locke, M. L. (2022). Challenging the colonial legacy of/at Macquarie. *Geographical Research*, 60(1), 71–85. 10.1111/1745-5871.12496

Hoyle, V. (2017). Editorial: Archives and public history. *Archives and Records (Abingdon, England)*, 38(1), 1–4. 10.1080/23257962.2017.1282348

Huante-Tzintzun, N. (2016). *The problematics of method: Decolonial strategies in education and Chicana/Latina testimonio/Platica*. ProQuest Dissertations. https://collections.lib.utah.edu/ark:/87278/s62n96dz

Huante-Tzintzun. (2020). *The power of testimonio methodology: history, components, and resources*. Sociology Writing Manual.

Huber, P. L. (2009). Challenging racist nativist framing: Acknowledging the community cultural wealth of undocumented Chicana college students to reframe the immigration debate. *Harvard Educational Review*, 79(4), 704–730. 10.17763/ haer.79.4.r7j1xn011965w186

Huber, P. L. (2010). Using Latina/o critical race theory (LatCrit) and racist nativism to explore intersectionality in the educational experiences of undocumented Chicana college students. *Educational Foundations*.

Huber, P. L., Benavides-Lopez, C., Malagon, M., Velez, V., & Solorzano, D. (2008). Getting beyond the 'symptom,' acknowledging the 'disease': Theorizing racist nativism. *Contemporary Justice Review*, 11(1), 39–51. 10.1080/10282580701850397

Huber, P. L., & Cueva, B. M. (2012). Chicana/Latina testimonios on effects and responses to microaggressions. *Equity & Excellence in Education*, 45(3), 392–410. 10.1080/10665684.2012.698193

Huffman, E. (2015). *John Prine: In spite of himself*. University of Texas Press.

Hultin, L. (2019). On becoming a sociomaterial researcher: Exploring epistemological practices grounded in a relational, performative ontology. *Information and Organization*, 29(2), 91–104. 10.1016/j.infoandorg.2019.04.004

Hume, R. D. (1970). Kant and Coleridge on Imagination. *The Journal of Aesthetics and Art Criticism*, 28(4), 485–496. 10.2307/428488

Husserl, E. (2005). *Phantasy, image consciousness, and memory (1898–1925)* (Brough, J., Trans.). Springer.

Huvila, I. (2008). Participatory Archive: Towards Decentralised Curation, Radical User Orientation and Broader Contextualisation of Records *Management.Archival Science*, 8(1), 15–36. 10.1007/s10502-008-9071-0

Ibsen, H. (2010). *The works of Henrik Ibsen.* Kessinger Pub.

Imhoof, D., Menninger, M. E., & Steinhoff, A. J. (Eds.). (2016). *The Total Work of Art: Foundations, Articulations, Inspirations* (Vol. 12). Berghahn Books. 10.3167/9781785331848

Immergluck, D., & Balan, T. (2018). Sustainable for whom? Green urban development, environmental gentrification, and the Atlanta Beltline. *Urban Geography*, 39(4), 546–562. 10.1080/02723638.2017.1360041

Inada, L. F. (1992). *Legends from camp: Poems.* Coffee House Press.

Ingold, T. (2013). *Making: Anthropology, Archaeology, Art and Architecture.* Routledge. 10.4324/9780203559055

Ingram, D. (2008). "My Dirty Stream": Pete Seeger, American Folk Music, and Environmental Protest. *Popular Music and Society*, 31(1), 21–36. 10.1080/03007760601061456

Ingram, D. (2010). *The jukebox in the garden: Ecocriticism and American popular music since 1960. Nature, culture and literature.* Rodopi. 10.1163/9789042032101

International Work Group for Indigenous Affairs (IWGIA). (2022). *Indigenous peoples in Sápmi.* IWGIA. https://www.iwgia.org/en/sapmi.html

Jackson, J. B. (1994). *A sense of place, a sense of time.* Yale University Press.

Jackson, T. A. (2012). *Blowin' the blues away: Performance and meaning on the New York jazz scene* (1st ed., Vol. 16). University of California Press. 10.1525/california/9780520270442.001.0001

Jago, M. (2018). *Live at the cellar: Vancouver's iconic jazz club and the Canadian co-operative jazz scene in the 1950s and '60s.* UBC Press. 10.59962/9780774837705

Jakobson, R. (1960). Closing statement: Linguistics and poetics. In Sebeok, T. (Ed.), *Style in language* (pp. 350–377). Wiley.

James, W. (1891). *Principles of Psychology.* McMillan and Co.

Jamieson, H. V. (2008). Adventures in Cyberformance - Experiments at the interface of theatre and the internet. [Master Theasis, Drama, Creative Industries Faculty, Queensland Universty of Technology].

Janet [Jackson] featuring Q-Tip and Joni Mitchell. (1997). *Got 'Til It's Gone.* Virgin VSTX1666.

Janiak, A. (2022). Kant's Views on Space and Time. In Zalta, E. (Ed.), *The Stanford Encyclopedia of Philosophy* (Summer 2022 Edition). https://plato.stanford.edu/archives/sum2022/entries/kant-spacetime/

Jansen, J. (2013). Imagination, Embodiment and Situatedness: Using Husserl to Dispel (Some) Notions of "Off-Line Thinking." In *Phenomenology of Embodied Subjectivity* (Vol. 71, pp. 63–79). Springer.

Jeanes, E. (2019). Performativity. In *A Dictionary of Organizational Behaviour.* Oxford University Press. https://www.oxfordreference.com/view/10.1093/acref/9780191843273.001.0001/acref-

Jetly, R. (2008). The Khalistan Movement in India: The Interplay of Politics and State Power. *International Review of Modern Sociology*, 34(1), 61–75.

Jim & Jesse. 1974. *Paradise*. Opryland Records P-3842.

Johnny Cash. (1974). Don't Go Near The Water. *Ragged Old Flag*. CBS S80113.

Johnson, D. H. (2021). *Somatics*. Don Hanlon Johnson. https://donhanlonjohnson.com/somatics/

Jokornegay, R. (1993). Hume on the Ordinary Distinction between Objective and Subjective Impressions. *Canadian Journal of Philosophy*, 23(2), 241–269. 10.1080/00455091.1993.10717319

Jordan, S. (1992). *Striding Out: Aspects of Contemporary and New Dance in Britain*. Dance Books.

Jørgensen, D. (2017). Endling, the Power of the Last in an Extinction-Prone World. *Environmental Philosophy*, 14(1), 119–138. 10.5840/envirophil201612542

Joyce, J. (1999). *Finnegans Wake*. Penguin.

Junka-Aikio, L., Nyyssönen, J., & Lehtola, V. P. (Eds.). (2021). *Sámi research in transition: Knowledge, politics and social change*. Routledge. 10.4324/9781003090830

Kabir, N. A. (2015). The Cronulla riots: Muslims' place in the white imaginary spatiality. *Contemporary Islam*, 9(3), 271–290. 10.1007/s11562-015-0347-x

Kagan, C., Burton, M., Duckett, P., Lawthom, R., & Siddiquee, A. (2019). *Critical community psychology: Critical action and social change*. Routledge. 10.4324/9780429431500

Kahn, R. (2013). Environmental Activism in Music. In Edmondson, J. (Ed.), *Music in American life: An encyclopedia of the songs, styles, stars and stories that shaped our culture* (pp. 412–417). Greenwood.

Kant, I. (1998). *Critique of Pure Reason*. Cambridge University Press. 10.1017/CBO9780511804649

Karnes, M. (2011). *Imagination, Meditation, and Cognition in the Middle Ages*. University of Chicago Press. 10.7208/chicago/9780226425337.001.0001

Katyayani, S. (2023). Exploring the Role of Testimonio Method in Shaping Collective Memory of Indenture History: From Empathy to Empowerment. *Rupkatha Journal on Interdisciplinary Studies in Humanities, 15*(2).

Kaye, N. (1996). *Art Into Theatre: Performance Interviews and Documents*. Psychology Press.

Kaye, N. (2000). *Site-specic Art: Performance, Place and Documentation*. Routledge.

Keelaghan, J. (1993). River Run. *My Skies*. JTR 8455-2.

Keil, C. (1998). Applied Sociomusicology and Performance Studies. *Ethnomusicology, 42*(2), 303-312.

Keller, D., Barreiro, D. L., Queiroz, M., & Pimenta, M. S. (2010). Anchoring in ubiquitous musical activities. In ICMC.

Kelly, I. (2008). Wonderful Humans. *Speak Your Mind*. Audiogram ADCD 10225.

Kent, M. (2007). *Kinaesthesis. The Oxford Dictionary of Sports Science & Medicine*. Oxford University Press. https://www-oxfordreferencecom.roe.idm.oclc.org/view/10.1093/acref/9780198568506.001.0001/acref-9780198568506-e-3792

Kershaw, B. B., & Nicholson, H. (Eds.). (2011). *Research Methods in Theatre and Performance*. Edinburgh University Press. 10.1515/9780748646081

Ketelaar, E. (2009). Archives as Spaces of Memory. *Journal of the Society of Archivists*, 29(1), 9–27. 10.1080/00379810802499678

Kierkegaard, S., & Mooney, E. F. (2009). *Repetition and philosophical crumbs*. OUP Oxford.

Kirchberg, V. (2016). Museum sociology. In Laurie, H., & Savage, M. (Eds.), *Routledge International Handbook of the Sociology of Art and Culture* (pp. 232–244). Routledge.

Kirshenblatt-Gimblett, B. (1998). *Destination Culture: Tourism, Museums and Heritage*. University of California Press.

Kitchener, R. F. (1986). *Piaget's Theory of Knowledge: Genetic Epistemology and Scientific Reason*. Yale University Press. 10.2307/j.ctt1xp3sbd

Klein, J., Damm, V., & Giebeler, A. (1983). An Outline of a Theory of Imagination. *Zeitschrift für Allgemeine Wissenschaftstheorie*, 14(1), 15–23. 10.1007/BF01801172

Klöckner, C. A. (2015). *The psychology of pro-environmental communication: Beyond standard information strategies*. Palgrave Macmillan. 10.1057/9781137348326

Koepnick, L. (2014). *On Slowness: Toward na Aesthetic of the Contemporary*. Columbia University Press. 10.7312/koep16832

Korver-Glenn, E. (2015). (Collective) memory of racial violence and the social construction of the Hispanic category among Houston Hispanics. *Sociology of Race and Ethnicity (Thousand Oaks, Calif.)*, 1(3), 424–438. 10.1177/2332649215576757

Kruse, Holly (2010). Local Identity and Independent Music Scenes: Online and Off. *Popular Music and Society33*(5), 625-639. .10.1080/03007760903302145

Kuhn, A. (2002). *Family secrets: Acts of memory and imagination*. Verso.

Kvaløy, K., Melhus, M., Silviken, A., Brustad, M., Sørlie, T., & Broderstad, A. R. (2018). Disordered eating in Sámi and non-Sámi Norwegian populations: The SAMINOR 2 clinical survey. *Public Health Nutrition*, 21(6), 1094–1105. 10.1017/S1368980017003597 29223188

Kwon, M. (2002). *One Place After Another - Site-Specic Art and Location Identity*. The MIT Press. 10.7551/mitpress/5138.001.0001

LaCapra, D. (2011). *History and its limits: Human, animal, violence*. Cornell UP. 10.7591/9780801458927

LaCapra, D. (2019). *History and memory after Auschwitz*. Cornell University Press.

Lacomba, C. (2020). Hispanics and/or Latinos in the United States: The Social Construction of an Identity. *Observational Studies*. Advance online publication. 10.15427/OR065-11/2020EN

Lajosi, K. (2010). *Wagner and the (Re)mediation of Art. Gesamtkunstwerk and Nineteenth-Century Theories of Media. Frame, 23*.

Landy, L. (2010). Rock's Music. In Lane, C. (org.) and Gruenrekorder (eds.) *Playing with Words: An Online Compilation*. Frankfurt: Gruenrekorder.

Langham-Putrow, A., Bakker, C., & Riegelman, A. (2021). Is the open access citation advantage real? A systematic review of the citation of open access and subscription-based articles. *PLoS One*, 16(6), e0253129. 10.1371/journal.pone.025312934161369

Lang, J. (2014). Against obedience: Hannah Arendt's overlooked challenge to social-psychological explanations of mass atrocity. *Theory & Psychology*, 24(5), 649–667. 10.1177/0959354314542368

Larios, S. E. (2020). Digital Testimonios: A personal journey towards healing and empowerment. *Journal of Curriculum and Pedagogy*, 17(3), 318–322. 10.1080/15505170.2020.1808128

Latina Feminist Group. (2001). *Telling to Live: Latina Feminist Testimonios*. Duke University Press.

Latour, B. (1993). *We Have Never Been Modern*.

Latour, B. (2011). Some experiments in art and politics. *e-flux, 23*, 1-7.

Laurel, B. (1993). *Computers as Theatre*. Addison-Wesley.

Lavender, A. (2021a). Multimodal acting and performing. In L. Elleström (Ed.), *Beyond Media Borders, Volume 1: Intermedial relations among multimodal media* (pp. 113–40). Palgrave Macmillan. 10.1007/978-3-030-49679-1_3

Le Goff, J. (1996). *História e Memória*. Editora da UNICAMP.

Leask, J. (2016). *Close Streams*. http://www.gabyagis.com/close-streams-1/

Leavy, P. (2015). *Method meets art: Arts-based research practice*. Guilford Publications.

Leccardi, C., Feixa, C., Kovacheva, S., Reiter, H., & Sekulić, T. (Eds.). (2012). *1989- Young People and social change after the fall of the Berlin Wall*. Council of Europe Publishing.

Leech, N. L., & Onwuegbuzie, A. J. (2008). Recursivity. In *The Sage encyclopedia of qualitative research methods*. SAGE.

Leopold, A. (2013). *A sand county almanac & other writings on ecology and conservation* (Meine, C., Ed.). Library of America. (Original work published 1949)

Lepecki, A. (2010). The Body as Archive: Will to Re-Enact and the Afterlives of Dances. *Dance Research Journal, 42*(2), 28–48. 10.1017/S0149767700001029

Lévinas, E. (2012). *Humanismo do outro homem*. Editora Vozes.

Liao, S., & Gendler, T. (2020). Imagination. In E. N. Zalta (Ed.), *The Stanford Encyclopedia of Philosophy*. https://plato.stanford.edu/archives/sum2020/entries/imagination/

Lima, E., & Caldeira, S. (2006). Em busca de novos paradigmas: concepções inusitadas no teatro europeu. In *Das vanguardas à tradição* (17-34). Rio de Janeiro: 7 Letras.

Lipovetsky, G. (2014). *Capitalismo estético na era da globalização[Aesthetic Capitalism in the Age of Globalization]*. Edições 70.

Lippard, L. (1997). *The Lure of the Local: Senses of Place in a Multicultural Society*. The New Press.

Loff, M., Piedade, F., & Soutelo, L. C. (2015). *Ditadura e revolução: Democracia e Política da Memória[Dictatorship and Revolution: Democracy and Memory Politics]*. Almedina.

Long, P. L., & Gebhardt, N. (2020). Listening again to popular music as history. *Popular Music History, 12*(2), 147–151. 10.1558/pomh.41400

Lopes, R. C. (2018). Índios comunistas? Representações sociais dos imigrantes venezuelanos na cidade brasileira de Pacaraima. *PÓLEMOS–Revista de Estudantes de Filosofia da Universidade de Brasília, 7*(14), 152–171.

Loveless, N. (2019). How to Make Art at the End of the World: a Manifesto for Research-Creation. Durham, NC: Duke University Press. Cambridge: MA: Harvard University Press.

Loveless, N. (2020). *Knowings & Knots: Methodologies and Ecologies in Research-Creation*.

Luhmann, N. (1989). *Ecological communication*. Polity.

Luhmann, N. (2000). *Art as a social system.* Stanford University Press. 10.1515/9781503618763

Luhmann, N. (2000). *The Reality of Mass Media.* Stanford University Press. 10.1515/9781503619227

Lütticken, S. (2005a). *An arena in which to re-enact". Life once more: Forms of re-enactment in contemporary art.* Witte de With.

Lütticken, S. (2005b). *Life once more: Forms of re-enactment in contemporary art.* Witte de With.

Lyons, J. D. (1999). Descartes and Modern Imagination. *Philosophy and Literature*, 23(2), 302–312. 10.1353/phl.1999.0043

MacDonald, M. B. (2016). *Playing for Change: Music Festivals as Community Learning and Development.* Peter Lang Press. 10.3726/978-1-4539-1861-6

MacDonald, M. B. (2023). *CineWorlding: Scenes of Cinematic Research-Creation.* Bloomsbury. 10.5040/9781501369421

Machado, D. L. (2023). History and Latinx Identity: Mapping a Past That Leads to Our Future. *The Wiley Blackwell Companion to Latinoax Theology*, 25-43. Wiley.

Mackrell, J. (1992). *Out of Line. The Story of British New Dance.* Dance Books Ltd.

Macy Gray. 2017. All I Want For Christmas. *Ultimate Chrismas Hits.* Sony 88985430942.

Mahmood, C. K. (2001). Terrorism, Myth, and the Power of Ethnographic Praxis. *Journal of Contemporary Ethnography*, 30(5), 520–545. 10.1177/089124101129024259

Makdisi, S. (2022). *Tolerance is a wasteland: Palestine and the culture of denial.* University of California Press.

Mallick, S. (2016, June 6). *Where We Belong: Artists in the Archive.* South Asian American Digital Archive (SAADA). https://www.saada.org/wherewebelong

Manning, E. (2012). *Relationscapes: Movement, Art, Philosophy.* MIT Press.

Manning, E. (2016). *The Minor Gesture.* Duke University Press.

Manning, E. (2020). *For a Pragmatics of the Useless.* Duke University Press.

Manning, E., & Massumi, B. (2014). *Thought in the Act: Passages in the Ecology of Experience.* University of Minnesota Press. 10.5749/minnesota/9780816679669.001.0001

Manoff, Marlente (2004). Theories of the Archive from across the Disciplines. Portal (Baltimore, Md.), 4(1), 9–25. 10.1353/pla.2004.0015

Marcus, G. (2000). *Traços de batom: Uma História Secreta do Século XX* [Lipstick Traces: A Secret History of the Twentieth Century]. Frenesi.

Marcus, G. E. (1998). Ethnography in/of the world system: The emergence of multi-sited ethnography. In *Ethnography through thick & thin* (pp. 105–132). Princeton University Press.

Marcus, G. E. (2013). Experimental forms for the expression of norms in the ethnography of the contemporary. *HAU*, 3(2), 197–217. 10.14318/hau3.2.011

Marks, L. U. (2000). *The Skin of the Film: Intercultural Cinema, Embodiment.* Duke University Press.

Martinez, T. A. (2005). Making oppositional culture, making standpoints: A journey into Gloria Anzaldua borderlands. *Sociological Spectrum*, 25(5), 539–570. 10.1080/02732170500176021

Masalha, N. (2002). The Palestinian Nakba: Zionism, 'transfer' and the 1948 exodus. *Global Dialogue*, 4(3), 77.

Massé, M. A. (1990). Gothic repetition: Husbands, horrors, and things that go bump in the night. *Signs (Chicago, Ill.)*, 15(4), 679–709. 10.1086/494624

Massumi, B. (2002). *Parables for the Virtual: Movement, Affect, Sensation*. Duke University Press.

Massumi, B. (2011). *Semblance and Event: Activist Philosophy and the Occurrent Arts*. MIT Press. 10.7551/mitpress/7681.001.0001

Massumi, B. (2015). *Politics of Affect*. Polity.

Matherne, S. (2016). Kant's Theory of the Imagination. In Kind, A. (Ed.), *The Routledge Handbook of the Imagination* (1st ed.). Routledge., 10.4324/9781315657905

Mayer, J. (2006). Waiting On The World To Change. *Continuum*. Columbia 8276 79019 1.

Mayer, J. (2019). *Goldness House*. Fine & Country Stourbridge and Kidderminster. https://www.youtube.com/watch?v=duucCoPs8uk/

McDowell, J. H., Borland, K., Dirksen, R., & Tuohy, S. (Eds.). (2021). *Performing environmentalisms: Expressive culture and ecological change*. University of Illinois Press. 10.5622/illinois/9780252044038.001.0001

McGrath, K. (2017). *Riot and revenge: symmetry and the Cronulla riot in Abe Forsythe's Down Under*.

McKay, G. (2007). A soundtrack to the insurrection: Street music, marching bands and popular protest. *Parallax*, 13(1), 20–31. 10.1080/13534640601094817

McKee, A. (2011). Youtube Versus the National Film and Sound Archive: Which Is the More Useful Resource for Historians of Australian Television? *Television & New Media*, 12(2), 154–173. 10.1177/1527476410365707

McKenzie, J. (2006). Is Performance Studies Imperialist? *The Drama Review*, 50(4), 5–8. 10.1162/dram.2006.50.4.5

McKesson. (Host). (2017). *Pod Save the People* [audio podcast]. Crooked Media.

McKittrick, K. (2011). On plantations, prisons, and a black sense of place. *Social & Cultural Geography*, 12(8), 947–963. 10.1080/14649365.2011.624280

McLuhan, M. (1994). *Understanding media: The extensions of man*. MIT Press.

McNeil, B. (2009). *Building Subcultural Community Online and Off: An Ethnographic Analysis of the Cblocals Music Scene*. [Doctoral dissertation, Georgia State University].

Mello, C. (2008). *Extremidades do vídeo*. Editora Senac.

Mellor, K. (2022). Developing a decolonial gaze: Articulating research/er positionality and relationship to colonial power. *Access: Critical explorations of equity in higher education, 10*(1), 26-41.

Meriwether, N. G. (Ed.). (2012). *Reading the Grateful Dead: A Critical Survey*. Scarecrow Press.

Merleau-Ponty, M. (2002). *Phenomenology of Perception* (C. Smith, Trans.). Routledge. (Original version published in 1945)

Mersch, D. (2009). Imagination, Figurality and Creativity Conditions of Cultural Innovation. In Huppauf, B., & Wulf, C. (Eds.), *Dynamics and Performativity of Imagination: The Image between the Visible and the Invisible* (1st ed., pp. 56–64). Routledge.

Mersch, D. (2016). *Meta/dia* two different approaches to the medial. *Cultural Studies*, 30(4), 650–679. 10.1080/09502386.2016.1180751

Messina, M., & Casale, E. (2014). Interview with Emanuele Casale. Síneris. Revista de Musicología, (16).

Messina, M. (2015). Contemporary Music, Unofficial Languages, Subaltern Voices: Composing Musical Pieces on Sicilian Texts. In *PERFORMA'15: Proceedings of the International Conference on Musical Performance.*

Messina, M. (2017). I saw them colours of your flag–A Speech-Based Composition on Aboriginal Sovereignty. *Revista Vórtex*, 5(1), 1–8.

Messina, M., & Aliel, L. (2023). Things, objects, subjects and stuff: IoMuSt and ubimus perspectives on AI. In *2023 IEEE International Conference on Big Data (BigData)* (pp. 4503-4510). IEEE.

Messina, M., Bento da Silva, F., Porto Ribeiro, L., & de Araújo Souza, J. (2023). Towards Amazon-centred memory studies: Borders, dispossessions and massacres. *Memory Studies*, 16(6), 1407–1422.

Messina, M., & Capogreco, S. (2021). "Armato di carnagione": Chromatic Regimes of Racial Profiling in the Italian Press. In *Pesquisa em comunicação: jornalismo, raça e gênero*. Nepan Editora.

Messina, M., Keller, D., Freitas, B., Simurra, I., Gómez, C., & Aliel, L. (2024). Disruptions, technologically convergent factors and creative activities: Defining and delineating musical stuff. *Digital Creativity*. Advance online publication. 10.1080/14626268.2023.2301342

Messina, M., & Mejía, C. M. G. (2020). Contracapas for remote double bass and effects: Creative Semantic Anchoring, Corpus Linguistics and Remote Interaction. In *Proceedings of the 10th Workshop on Ubiquitous Music (UbiMus 2020)* (pp. 173-174).

Meyerhold, V. (2014). *Meyerhold on theatre*. A&C Black.

Meyerhold, V., Gladkov, A., & Law, A. (1996). *Meyerhold speaks/Meyerhold Rehearses (Russian Theatre Archive)*. Routledge.

Mignolo, W. D. (2009). Epistemic disobedience, independent thought and decolonial freedom. *Theory, Culture & Society*, 26(7–8), 159–181. 10.1177/0263276409349275

Mihai, M., & Thaler, M. (2023). Environmental commemoration: Guiding principles and real-world cases. *Memory Studies*, 1–18. 10.1177/17506980231176037

Milgram, S. (1973, December). The perils of obedience. *Harpers Magazine*.

Milgram, S. (2010). *Obedience to authority: An experimental view*. Pinter & Martin. (Original work published 1965.)

Minde, G. (2017). Older Sámi women living in the Arctic: A cultural background that breaks with western conventions. *Journal of Community & Public Health Nursing*, 3(1). 10.4172/2471-9846.1000155

Minton, S. J., & Lile, H. S. (2018, May). A conversation about the proposed truth commission in Norway for the Sámi and Kven peoples: What can be learnt from truth and reconciliation processes elsewhere. In *14th International Congress of Qualitative Inquiry*. University of Illinois in Urbana-Champaign.

Mirski, R., & Bickhard, M. H. (2021). Conventional minds: An interactivist perspective on social cognition and its enculturation. *New Ideas in Psychology*, 62, 100856. 10.1016/j.newideapsych.2021.100856

Mitchell, J. (1970). *Big Yellow Taxi*. Ladies Of The Canyon.

Mitchell, W. T. J. (1994). *Picture Theory: Essays on Verbal and Visual Representation*. The University of Chicago Press.

Moberly, L. G. (1917). Inexplicable. *The Strand*, *54*(319), 572–581. https://lmcc.web.unc.edu/wp-content/uploads/sites/3253/2023/03/Moberly_Inexplicable-Strand-Magazine-1917.pdf

Montoya, M. (2022). An introduction. In *LatCrit from critical legal theory to academic activism*. New York University Press. 10.7551/mitpress/12245.003.0003

Moore, S., & Pell, S. (2010). Autonomous Archives. *International Journal of Heritage Studies*, *16*(4/5), 255–268. 10.1080/13527251003775513

Moraga, C., & Anzaldúa, G. (1981). *This bridge called my back. Writings by radical women of color* (4th ed.). SUNY Press.

Moran, J. (2010). *Skinner Releasing Technique in Britain*. London Dance. http://londondance.com/articles/features/skinner-releasing-technique-in-britain/

Moran, I. P. (2010). Punk: The Do-It-Yourself Subculture. *The Social Science Journal*, *10*(1), 58–65. http://repository.wcsu.edu/ssj/vol10/iss1/13

Mounsey, C. (2023). Frost or Fire? Popular Music Responses to Climate Change, from Woodstock to Glastonbury. In Fosbraey, G. (Ed.), *Coastal environments in popular song: Lost horizons* (pp. 44–57). Routledge.

Muggleton, D., & Weinzierl, R. (2003) (Eds.). *The Post-Subcultural Reader*. Berg.

Mukherjee, B. (1989). *Jasmine*. Grove Press.

Müller, J. E. (1996). *Intermedialität. Formen moderner kultureller Kommunikation*. Nodus Publikationen.

Müller, T., & Durand, A.-P. (2022). Hip Hop Ecologies: Mapping the Field(s). An introduction. *Ecozon@: European Journal of Literature. Culture and Environment*, *13*(1), 1–7.

Munro, T. (1949). *The Arts and their Interrelations*. The Liberal Arts Press.

Murray, J. (n.d.). *History of Kidderminster Medical Society*. Kidderminister Medical Society. https://www.kidderminstermedicalsociety.co.uk/history_of_kms.htm

Nagel, T. (1989). *The View from Nowhere*. Oxford University Press.

Narula, U. (2006). Handbook of Communication: Models, Perspectives, Strategies. Atlantic Publishers & Dist.

Nash, R. F. (2014). *Wilderness and the American mind* (5th ed.). Yale University Press.

Nelson, R. (2013). *Practice as research in the arts: Principles, protocols, pedagogies, resistances*. Springer. 10.1057/9781137282910

Nevanlinna, T. (2002). Is 'Artistic Research' a meaningful concept? In Kiljunen, S., & Hannula, M. (Eds.), *Artistic Research* (pp. 61–71). Fine Art Academy.

Newman, R. (1972). Burn On. *Sail Away*. Reprise Records REP 44185.

Nicholas, L. (2007). *Dancing in Utopia: Dartington Hall and its Dancers*. Dance Books.

Nicholson, I. (2011a). 'Torture at Yale': Experimental subjects, laboratory torment and the 'rehabilitation' of Milgram's *Obedience to Authority.Theory & Psychology*, *21*(6), 737–761. 10.1177/0959354311420199

Nicholson, I. (2011b). "Shocking" masculinity: Stanley Milgram, "obedience to authority," and the "crisis of manhood" in Cold War America. *Isis*, *102*(2), 238–268. 10.1086/66012921874687

Nieland, J.-U. (2008). Politainment. In Donsbach, W. (Ed.), *The international encyclopedia of communication* (pp. 3659–3661). Blackwell. 10.1002/9781405186407.wbiecp047

Nocella, A. J., Parmar, P., Sawyer, D. C., & Cermak, M. (2017). Hip Hop, Food Justice, and Environmental Justice. In Nocella, A. J., Ducre, K. A., & Lupinacci, J. (Eds.), *Addressing Environmental and Food Justice toward Dismantling the School-to-Prison Pipeline: Poisoning and Imprisoning Youth* (pp. 177–192). Palgrave Macmillan. 10.1057/978-1-137-50822-5_10

Nono, L. (2007). La nostalgia del futuro: Scritti scelti. Milan: Il Saggiatore.

Nora, P. (1989). Between memory and history: Les lieux de mémoire. *Representations (Berkeley, Calif.)*, 26, 7–24. 10.2307/2928520

Normann, S. (2019). Constructing dialogues and solidarity through "Radio-Cinema" in the Sámi-Norwegian colonial context. *Community Psychology in Global Perspective*, 5(2), 1–18.

Nöth, W. (2011). From Representation to Thirdness and Representamen to Medium: Evolution of Peircean Key Terms and Topics. *Transactions of The Charles S.Peirce Society*, 47(4), 445–481. 10.2979/trancharpeirsoc.47.4.445

Nystad, K., Ingstad, B., & Spein, A. R. (2020). How academic experiences and educational aspirations relate to well-being and health among Indigenous Sámi youth in Northern Norway: A qualitative approach. *Journal of Northern Studies*, 14(1), 35–61. 10.36368/jns.v14i1.975

O' Connor, S. (1994). *Famine. On: Universal Mother*. Chrysalis Records Limited.

O'Byrne, A. (2023). *The genocide paradox: Democracy and generational Time*. Fordham UP.

O'Doherty, B. (1986). *Inside the White Cube – The Ideology of the Gallery Space. São Francisco*. The Lapis Press.

Okamoto, D., & Mora, G. C. (2014). Panethnicity. *Annual Review of Sociology*, 40(1), 219–239. 10.1146/annurev-soc-071913-043201

Osmon, E. (2021). *John Prine's John Prine*. Bloomsbury.

Otte, M. (1998). Limits of Constructivism: Kant, Piaget and Peirce. *Science & Education*, 7(5), 425–450. 10.1023/A:1008635517122

Otto, U. (2019). History of the field. In V. Agnew, J. Lamb, & J. Tomann (Eds), The Routledge handbook of re-enactment studies (pp. 111–114). Routledge.

Packer, R., & Jordan, K. (2001). *Multimedia: from Wagner to virtual reality*. New York: Norton & Company.

Pallasmaa, J. (2005). *The Eyes of the Skin: Architecture and the Senses*. John Wiley & Sons.

Palmer, M., Larkin, M., de Visser, R., & Fadden, G. (2010). Developing an interpretative phenomenological approach to focus group data. *Qualitative Research in Psychology*, 7(2), 99–121. 10.1080/14780880802513194

Panagia, D. (2016). *Ten theses for an aesthetics of politics*. University of Minnesota Press. 10.5749/9781452958514

Pappe, I. (2007). *The ethnic cleansing of Palestine*. Simon and Schuster.

Paredes, J. (2005). Punk Rock Doesn't Belong in a Museum. *The New York Times*. https://www.nytimes.com/2005/08/14/arts/music/punk-rock-doesnt-belong-in-a-museum.html

Pareyson, L. (1993). *Estética da Formatividade*. Vozes.

Patton Davis, L., & Museus, S. (2019). What is deficit thinking? An analysis conceptualizations of deficit thinking and implications for scholarly research. *Currents*, 1(1), 117–130. 10.3998

Pedelty, M. (2012). *Ecomusicology: Rock, folk, and the environment.* Temple University Press., 10.2307/j.ctt14bt8qd

Pennisi, A., & Falzone, A. (Eds.). (2019). *The Extended Theory of Cognitive Creativity: Interdisciplinary Approaches to Performativity.* Springer Verlag.

Percival, J. (1983). Review on Gaby Agis. *The Times.*

Perdue, K. (2003). *Imagination.* https://csmt.uchicago.edu/glossary2004/imagination.htm

Pereira, J. P. (2015). *Aprender com os alemães* ['Learn with the Germans.']. Público. https://www.publico.pt/2015/03/28/mundo/opiniao/aprender-com-os-alemaes-1690586

Perera, S. (2006). Race Terror, Sydney, December 2005. *borderlands, 5*(1).

Perera, S. (2014). 'Aussie luck': The border politics of citizenship post-Cronulla Beach. *Critical Race & Whiteness Studies, 10*(2).

Perera, S. (2009). A Pogrom on the Beach. In *Australia and the Insular Imagination: Beaches, Borders, Boats, and Bodies* (pp. 137–160). Palgrave Macmillan US. 10.1057/9780230103122_8

Perera, S. (2009b). *Australia and the Insular Imagination: Beaches.* Borders, Boats, and Bodies. New York. 10.1057/9780230103122

Peschel, S. (2020, May 1). *Why Achille Mbembe was accused of anti-Semitism.* DW. https://www.dw.com/en/why-achille-mbembe-was-accused-of-anti-semitism/a-53293797

Peterson, R. A. (1994). Class Unconsciousness in Country Music. In MacLaurin, M. A. (Ed.), *You wrote my life: Lyrical themes in country music* (2nd ed., pp. 35–62). Gordon and Breach.

Phelan, P. (1993). *Unmarked: The Politics of Performance.* Routledge.

Philipp, T. (2023). Simply Longing for Wilderness: Fictions of Nature Preservation in Western Pop Music. *Todas as Artes: Revista Luso-Brasileira De Artes E Cultura, 6*(1), 12–25. 10.21747/21843805/tav6n1a1

Philipp, T. (2019). Popmusikforschung. In Zemanek, E., & Kluwick, U. (Eds.), *Nachhaltigkeit interdisziplinär: Konzepte, Diskurse, Praktiken* (pp. 330–346). Böhlau.

Philipp, T. (2021). Der Sound der Katastrophe. Popmusik als Resonanzraum ökologischer Krisen. *Forschungsjournal Soziale Bewegungen,* 2. https://forschungsjournal.de/fjsb-plus_2021-2_philipp/

Philipp, T. (2022). Spaceship Earth and its Soundscapes: Latency Problems of International Ecological Conflicts in Pop Music. In Flath, B., Jacke, C., & Troike, M. (Eds.), *Transformational POP: Transitions, Breaks, and Crises in Popular Music (Studies)* (pp. 117–134). IASPM. http://www.vibes-theseries.org/philipp-spaceship-earth

Piaget, J. (1999). *Play, Dreams and Imitation in Childhood.* Psychology Press.

Pina e Cunha, M., Rego, A., & Clegg, S. R. (2010). Obedience and evil: From Milgram and Kampuchea to normal organizations. *Journal of Business Ethics*, 97(2), 291–309. 10.1007/s10551-010-0510-5

Pink Floyd. (1987). Sorrow. *A Momentary Lapse Of Reason.* EMI 7 48068 1.

Pitches, J. (2004). *Vsevolod Meyerhold.* Routledge. 10.4324/9780203634172

Polanyi, K. (2010). *The great transformation: The political and economic origins of our time* (2nd ed.). Beacon.

Pooley, J. A., & Cohen, L. (2010). Resilience: A definition in context. *Australian Community Psychologist*, 22(1), 30–37.

Pordata (2017). *Portrait of Portugal in Europe 2017*. Fundação Francisco Manuel dos Santos.

Porsanger, J. (2022). An Indigenous Sámi museum and repatriation on a Sámi drum from the XVII century. *Dutkansearvvi dieđalaš áigečála, 6*(1).

Porsanger, J., Seurujärvi-Kari, I., & Nystad, R. L. (2021). *'Shared remembering' as a relational Indigenous method in conceptualization of Sámi women's leadership. Indigenous research methodologies in Sámi and global contexts.* Brill Sense.

Poulos, C. N. (2021). *Essentials of autoethnography*. American Psychological Association. 10.1037/0000222-000

Prine, J. (1971). *Paradise*. John Prine.

Prior, H. M. (2022). How Can Music Help Us to Address the Climate Crisis? *Music & Science*, 5, 205920432210757. 10.1177/20592043221075725

Proske, U., & Gandevia, S. C. (2009). The kinaesthetic senses. *The Journal of Physiology*, 587(17), 4139–4146. https://physoc.onlinelibrary.wiley.com/doi/10.1113/jphysiol.2009.175372. 10.1113/jphysiol.2009.17537219581378

Prown, J. D. (1982). Mind in matter: An introduction to material culture theory and method. *Winterthur Portfolio*, 17(1), 1–19. 10.1086/496065

Pugliese, J. (2003). The Locus of the non: the racial fault-line of" of Middle-Eastern appearance". *Borderlands e-journal*, 2(3), 1-13.

Pugliese, J. (2006). *Asymmetries of terror: visual regimes of racial profiling and the shooting of Jean Charles de Menezes in the context of the war in Iraq. Borderlands, 5(1).* NA-NA.

Pugliese, J. (2007). Geocorpographies of torture. *Australian Critical Race and Whiteness Studies Association Journal*, 3(1), 1–18.

Pugliese, J. (2009). Compulsory visibility and the infralegality of racial phantasmata. *Social Semiotics*, 19(1), 9–30. 10.1080/10350330802632758

Pugliese, J. (2015). Geopolitics of Aboriginal sovereignty: Colonial law as 'a species of excess of its own authority', aboriginal passport ceremonies and asylum seekers. *Law Text Culture*, 19, 84–115.

Pugliese, J. (2021). More-Than-Human Lifeworlds, Settler Modalities of Geno-ecocide and Border Questions. *Journal of Global Indigeneity*, 5(3), 1–34.

Pujol, E. (2018). *Walking art practice: reflections on socially engaged paths* (1st ed.). Triarchy Press.

Quaranta, D. Caronia, A. & Janža, J. (Eds.). (2013) *RE:akt! Reconstruction, re-enactment, re-reporting.* Lulu.

Quijano, A., Mignolo, W. D., Segato, R., & Walsh, C. E. (2024). *Aníbal Quijano: Foundational essays on the coloniality of power* (1st ed.). Duke University Press., 10.1215/9781478059356

R.E.M. (1986). Cuyahoga. *Lifes Rich Pageant*. I.R.S. Records IRS-5783.

Radkau, J. (2008). *Nature and power: A global history of the environment.* Cambridge University Press.

Radkau, J. (2014). *The Age of Ecology.* Wiley.

Rajewsky, I. O. (2008). Intermedialität und remediation: Überlegungen zu einigen Problemfeldern der jüngeren Intermedialitätsforschung. In Paech, J., & Schröter, J. (Eds.), *Intermedialität Analog/Digital: Theorien—Methoden—Analysen* (pp. 47–60). Wilhelm Fink. 10.30965/9783846743744_005

Ramos, S. L., & Torres-Fernandez, I. (2020). Conociendo los caminos: Testimonios of Latina doctoral students. *Peace and Conflict*, 26(4), 379–389. 10.1037/pac0000450

Ramus, P. (1578). *Scholae in liberates artes. Scholae rhetoricae.* Lib. XIX (ed. of Bale, col. 309).

Rata, A. (2020). Dismantling Cook's legacy: Science, migration, and colonialism in Aotearoa. *New Zealand Science Review*, 76(1-2), 54–58. 10.26686/nzsr.v76i1-2.7834

Ratekin, T. (2005). Allon White tracks down himself: Criticism as autobiography in "too close to the bone.". *CEA Critic*, 67(2), 62–75.

Reddy, M. J. (1979). The conduit metaphor – A case off rame conflict in our language about language. In Ortony, A. (Ed.), *Metaphor and thought* (pp. 284–324). Cambridge University Press.

Redhead, L. (2016). Solo speaking [Album]. Lauren Redhead. https://laurenredhead.bandcamp.com/album/solo-speaking (accessed 15 September 2020).

Rehding, A. (2011). Ecomusicology between Apocalypse and Nostalgia. *Journal of the American Musicological Society*, 64(2), 409–414. 10.1525/jams.2011.64.2.409

Reichling, M. J. (1990). Images of Imagination. *Journal of Research in Music Education*, 38(4), 282–293. 10.2307/3345225

Reid, A., & Petocz, P. (2021). *Educating Musicians for Sustainability.* Routledge., 10.4324/9781003044642

Reinelt, J. (2017). Introduction. *Key Words: A Journal of Cultural Materialism*, 15, 9-22.

Reyes, G. (2011). Latinx curriculum theorizing. *Oxford Research Encyclopedia of Education.* Oxford Press. https://oxfordre.com/education/view/10.1093/acrefore/9780190264093.001.0001/acrefore-9780190264093-e-1598

Reyes, B. K., & Rodríguez, C. J. (2012). Testimonio: Origins, terms, and resources. *Equity & Excellence in Education*, 45(3), 525–538. 10.1080/10665684.2012.698571

Reyes, V. D. (2017). Disparate lessons: Racial climates and identity-formation processes among Latino students. *Du Bois Review*, 14(2), 447–470. 10.1017/S1742058X17000054

Reynolds, S. (2011). *Retromania: Pop Culture's Addiction to Its Own Past.* Faber and Faber.

Richardson, L. (1994).Writing: A method of inquiry. In *Handbook of qualitative research* (pp. 923-948). N. K. Sage Publications, Inc.

Richter, H. (1978). *DADA: Kunst und Antikunst.* Dumont Verlag.

Ricoeur, P. (2004). *Memory, History, Forgetting.* The University of Chicago Press. 10.7208/chicago/9780226713465.001.0001

Riegl, A. ({1901} 1985). Die spätrömische Kunstindustrie (Late Roman Art Industry). Roma: Giorgio Bretschneider

Roberts, D. (2011). *The total work of art in European modernism.* Cornell University Press. 10.7591/cornell/9780801450235.001.0001

Roberts, J. (1995). Between Two 'Darknesses': The Adoptive Condition in *Ceremony* and *Jasmine.Modern Language Studies*, 25(3), 77–97. 10.2307/3195372

Roberts, L. (2014). Talkin Bout My Generation: Popular Music and the Culture of Heritage. *International Journal of Heritage Studies*, 20(3), 262–280. 10.1080/13527258.2012.740497

Robinson, L. (2016). Collaboration in, collaboration out: The eighties in the age of digital reproduction. *Cultural and Social History*, 13(3), 403–423. 10.1080/14780038.2016.1202026

Robinson, L. (2017). Exhibition review Punk's 40th anniversary — An itchy sort of heritage. *Twentieth Century British History*, 1–9. 10.1093/tcbh/hwx04729800337

Rodnitzky, J. L. (1999). The sixties between the microgrooves: Using folk and protest music to understand American history, 1963-1973. *Popular Music and Society*, 23(4), 105–122. 10.1080/03007769908591755

Rodrigo, J. (2019). *Poetry Ceylon: When a girl from Goa fell in love with all that is Sri Lanka.* The Morning. https://www.themorning.lk/articles/40232

Romero, O. (2022). *Why Indigenous people want you to stop labeling them as Latino.* TEDx Talks. https://www.ted.com/tedx

Rosen, C. (1997). *R.E.M. inside out: The stories behind every song.* Thunder's Mouth.

Rosenthal, D. J. (2006). „Hoods and the Woods": Rap Music as Environmental Literature. *Journal of Popular Culture*, 39(4), 661–676. 10.1111/j.1540-5931.2006.00284.x

Rosenzweig, R., & Thelen, D. (1998). *The Presence of the Past: Popular Uses of History in American Life.* Columbia University Press.

Rothberg, M. (2009). *Multidirectional memory: Remembering the Holocaust in the age of decolonization.* Stanford University Press.

Rothberg, M. (2019). *The implicated subject: Beyond victims and perpetrators.* Stanford University Press.

Rothe, E. M., Tzuang, D., & Pumariega, A. J. (2010, October). Acculturation, development, and adaptation. *Child and Adolescent Psychiatric Clinics of North America*, 19(4), 681–696. 10.1016/j.chc.2010.07.00221056341

Rubidge, S. (2005). Artists in the academy: Reflections on artistic practice as research. *Paper presented at Dance Rebooted: Initializing the Grid, Deakin University.* Deakin University.

Russell, B. (1915). Sensation and Imagination. *The Monist*, 25(1), 28–44. 10.5840/monist191525136

Russell, N., & Gregory, R. (2015). The Milgram-Holocaust linkage: Challenging the present consensus. *State Crime*, 4(2), 128–153. 10.13169/statecrime.4.2.0128

Ryle, G. (1975). *The Concept of Mind.* Hutchinsons's University Library.

Saavedra, C. M. (2011). Language and literacy in the borderlands: Acting upon the world through "Testimonios". *Language Arts*, 88(4), 261–269. 10.58680/la201113548

Saha, S., & Potdar, A. (Eds.). (2023). *Performance making and the archive.* Routledge.

Said, E. W. (2000). Invention, Memory, and Place. *Critical Inquiry*, 26(2), 175–192. https://www.jstor.org/stable/1344120. 10.1086/448963

Salomão, W. (2014). *Poesia Total.* Companhia das Letras.

Samuel, R. (1994). *Theatres of Memory: Past and Present in Contemporary Culture* (Vol. 1). Verso.

Santa Cruz, V. (1978). *Me Gritaron Negra* [video]. Youtube. https://www.youtube.com/watch?v=cHr8DTNRZdg

Santos, B. (1990). *O Estado e a Sociedade em Portugal (1974-1988)[The State and Society in Portugal (1974-1988)].* Afrontamento.

Sanyal, D. (2015). *Memory and complicity: Migrations of Holocaust remembrance.* Fordham UP.

Sapienza, Z., Veenstra, A., Kirtiklis, K., & Giannino, S. (2017). The Transmission Model of Communication: Toward a Multidisciplinary explication. *Researchgate.* https://www. researchgate.net/publication/323025486_The_Transmission _Model_of_Communication_

Schafft, G. E. (2019). *Memory research. Sage Research Methods Foundations.* Sage Publications. 10.4135/9781526421036842523

Schechner, R. (1976). Selective Inattention: A Traditional Way of Spectating Now Part of the Avant-Garde. *Performing Arts Journal*, 1(1), 8–19. 10.2307/3245182

Schechner, R. (2002). *Performance Studies: An Introduction.* Routledge.

Schechner, R. (2009). 9/11 as avant-garde art? *PMLA*, 124(5), 1820–1829. 10.1632/pmla.2009.124.5.1820

Schmidt, P. (2014). *Meyerhold at work.* University of Texas Press.

Schneider, R. (2011). *Performing remains: Art and war in times of theatrical re-enactment.* Routledge. 10.4324/9780203852873

Schönfelder, C. 2013. *Wounds and Words: Childhood and Family Trauma in Romantic and Postmodern Fiction.* Bielefeld, Germany: transcript Verlag.

Schramm, W. (1971). The nature of communication between humans. In Schramm, W., & Roberts, D. F. (Eds.), *The process and effects of mass communication* (pp. 3–53). University of Illinois Press.

Scott, H. K., & Cogburn, M. (2023). Piaget. In *StatPearls*. StatPearls Publishing. https://pubmed.ncbi.nlm.nih.gov/28846231/

Scruton, R. (1976). Representation in Music. [Cambridge: Cambridge University Press.]. *Philosophy (London, England)*, 51(197), 197. 10.1017/S0031819100019331

Seeger, P. (1966). My Dirty Stream. *God Bless the Grass.* CBS 62618.

Seeger, P. (1972). This Land Is Your Land. *The World Of Pete Seeger.* Columbia CG 31949.

Segal, S., & Weizman, E. (2003). The Mountain: Principles of building in heights, In Segal and Weizman (Eds.), *A civilian occupation: The politics of Israeli architecture* (pp. 79-99). Verso.

Segaud, M. (2016). *Antropologia do espaço: habitar, fundar, distribuir, transformar.* Edições Sesc São Paulo.

Sepper, D. L. (1996). *Descartes's Imagination: Proportion, Images, and the Activity of Thinking.* University of California Press. http://ark.cdlib.org/ark:/13030/ft0d5n99fd/

Shannon, C. E. (1948). A mathematical theory of communication. *The Bell System Technical Journal*, 27(3), 379–423, 623–656. 10.1002/j.1538-7305.1948.tb01338.x

Shotwell, A. (2016). *Against Purity: Living Ethically in Compromised Times.* Minnesota Press.

Siepmann, D. (2010). A Slight Delay: Agency and Improvisation in, the Ambient Sound World. *Perspectives of New Music*, 48(1), 174. 10.1353/pnm.2010.0011

Siham-Fernández, J. (2022). A Mujerista Liberation Psychology Perspective on Testimonio to Cultivate Decolonial Healing. *Women & Therapy*, 45(2-3), 2–3, 131–156. 10.1080/02703149.2022.2095101

Silva, A. S., & Guerra, P. (2015). O mundo do Punk [The Words of Punk]. *Aletheia*.

Silva, M. J., Fernández, J. S., & Nguyen, A. (2021). Three testimonios on the importance of decoloniality within psychology. *The Journal of Social Issues*, 77(2), 389–390.

Simurra, I., Messina, M., Aliel, L., & Keller, D. (2023). Radical creative semantic anchoring: Creative-action metaphors and timbral interaction. *Organised Sound*, 28(1), 64–77. 10.1017/S1355771822000322

Skrimshire, S. (2014). Climate change and apocalyptic faith. *Wiley Interdisciplinary Reviews: Climate Change*, 5(2), 233–246. 10.1002/wcc.264

Sky News. (2024, March 4). More than 30,500 Palestinians now killed by Israeli strikes, Gaza health ministry says. *Sky News*. https://news.sky.com/story/gaza-hamas-israel-latest-30-000-deaths-sky-news-live-blog-12978800

Sloterdijk, P. (2012). The time of the crime of the monstrous: On the philosophical justification of the artificial. In Elden, S. (Ed.), *Sloterdijk Now* (pp. 166–181). Polity.

Smith, M. W. (2007). *The total work of art: from Bayreuth to cyberspace*. Routledge. 10.4324/9780203963166

Smithson, R. (1996). *Robert Smithson: the collected writings*. University of California Press.

Solnit, R. (2001). *Wanderlust: a history of walking*. Penguin Books.

Solorzano, D. G., & Yosso, T. J. (2001). From racial stereotyping and deficit discourse toward a critical race theory in teacher education. *Multicultural Education*, 9(1), 2–8.

Sonesson, G. (2011). Semiotics Inside-Out and/or Outside-In. How to Understand Everything and (with Luck) Influence People. *Signata*, 2(2), 315–348. 10.4000/signata.742

Sosa-Provencio, M. A., Sheahan, A., Fuentes, R., Muñiz, S., & Prada-Vivas, R. (2019). Reclaiming ourselves through testimonio pedagogy: Reflections on a curriculum design lab in teacher education. *Race, Ethnicity and Education*, 22(2), 211–230. 10.1080/13613324.2017.1376637

Spielmann, Y. (2004). *Video and Computer: The Aesthetics of Steina and Woody Vasulka*. The Daniel Langlois Foundation.

Steinberg, T. (2002). *Down to earth: Nature's role in American history*. Oxford University Press. 10.1093/oso/9780195140095.001.0001

Stern, E. R., & Rotello, C. M. (2000). Memory Characteristics of Recently Imagined Events and Real Events Experienced Previously. *The American Journal of Psychology*, 113(4), 569–590. 10.2307/142347311131743

Stewart, T. J., Throne, R., & Evans, L. A. (2022). Voice dispossession and attributional accommodation for career persistence: A systematic review of gender parity in US higher education leadership. *Policy and Practice Challenges for Equality in Education*, 39-54.

Stewart, S. (2007). *On longing: Narratives of the miniature, the gigantic, the souvenir, the collection*. Duke University Press.

Stockhausen, K. (1964). Music and Speech. *Die Reihe*, 6, 40–64.

Stoianova, I. (1987). Testo-musica-senso. 'Il canto sospeso. In Restagno, E. (Ed.), *Nono* (pp. 126–141). EDT.

Street, J. (2007). *Politics and popular culture*. Polity Press.

Street, J. (2013). *Music and Politics*. John Wiley & Sons.

Street, J., Hague, S., & Savingy, H. (2007). Playing to the crowd: The role of music and musicians in political participation. *British Journal of Politics and International Relations*, 10(2), 269–285. 10.1111/j.1467-856x.2007.00299.x

Strong, C. (2015). Shaping the Past of Popular Music: Memory, Forgetting and Documenting. In *Andy Bennet, & Steve Waksman, The Sage Handbook of Popular Music*. Sage. 10.4135/9781473910362.n24

Styles, H. (2024). *Big Yellow Taxi. Live Sessions Duets And Cover Versions. Not On Label*. Harry Styles.

Suncana, L. (2020). *Performativity*. Elsevier. https://www.unine.ch/files/live/sites/inst_geographie/files/shared/Agenda/Performativity-encyclopedia.pdf

Sykes, C. (Director). (1988, June 23). Exiles: Edward Said (Season 1 Episode 4) [TV series episode]. In A. Yentob (Executive Producer) *Exiles*. BBC.

Tatla, D. S. (2004). Writing Prejudice: The Image of Sikhs in Bharati Mukherjee's Writings. In Singh, P., & Barrier, N. G. (Eds.), *Sikhs in History* (pp. 1–23). Oxford University Press.

Taylor, C. (1985). *Philosophy and the Human Sciences: Collected Papers* (Vol. 2). Cambridge University Press. 10.1017/CBO9781139173490

Taylor, S. M. (2019). *Ecopiety: Green media and the dilemma of environmental virtue*. NYU Press.

ten Kortenaar, N. (2016). Bharati Mukherjee's *Jasmine.Cambridge Journal of Postcolonial Literary Inquiry*, 3(3), 379–385. 10.1017/pli.2016.26

Terranova, T. (2004). *Network Culture: Politics for the Information Age*. Pluto Press.

Thompson, R. L. (2004). The Automatic Hand: Spiritualism, Psychoanalysis, Surrealism. *Invisible Culture*, 7(Spring), 1–14. http://web.mit. edu/allanmc/www/Automatic_Hand.pdf

Throne, R. (2021b). New investigator fidelity: Fostering doctoral practitioner researcher positionality. In *Practice-based and practice-led research for dissertation development* (pp. 165-187). IGI Global.

Throne, R. (2018). The letter: Fidelity in researcher positionality to exhume dispossessed voices for Leavy's concept of coherence in feminist narrative research. *Gender and Women's Studies*, 2(1). 10.31532/GendWomensStud.2.1.003

Throne, R. (2021a). Land as agency: A critical autoethnography of Scandinavian acquisition of dispossessed land in the Iowa Territory. In *Indigenous research of land, self, and spirit* (pp. 118–131). IGI Global.

Tiberghien, G. (2012). Dossiê - Trajetória e interesses: entrevista com Gilles A. Tiberghien. *Revlsiu-Vulise, 2* (3), Porto Alegre.

Timplalexi, E., & Führer, H. (2023). Reconsidering Elleström's medium-centered communication model: a critical inquiry. *EKPHRASIS*, 2, 93-114. https://www.ekphrasisjournal.ro/docs/R1/30e6.pdf

Timplalexi, E. (2022). Theatre Performance through the Intermedial Lens. *Performance Research*, 27(8), 22–34. 10.1080/13528165.2022.2224196

Timplalexi, E. (2023). Challenging key certainties in communication through Elleström's medium- centred model of communication: 'Transfer' and 'medium'. *Explorations in Media Ecology*, 22(4), 399–420. 10.1386/eme_00180_1

Tirino, M. (2017). Mi faccia il piacere! Totò e la sovversione dell'ipocrisia borghese: Un'analisi socioculturale. H-ermes. *Journal of Communication*, 2017(9), 7–36.

Todd, M. E. (1937). *The Thinking Body*. Paul Hoeber.

Toft, T. (2016). *What Urban Media Art Can Do. What Urban Media Art Can Do: Why When Where and How*. Munique: av edition.

Tondo, L. (2024, May 19). UN humanitarian chief delivers 'apocalyptic' warning over Gaza aid. *The Guardian*.https:// www.theguardian.com/world/article/2024/may/19/un-humanitarian-chief-delivers-apocalyptic-warning-over-gaza-aid

Trumbo, D. (dir.). (1971). *Johnny Got His Gun*. Cinemation Industries.

Tseng, C. I. (2021a). Truthfulness and Affect via Digital Mediation in Audiovisual Storytelling. In L. Elleström (Ed.), *Beyond Media Borders, Volume 1: Intermedial relations among multimodal media* (pp. 175–195). Palgrave Macmillan. 10.1007/978-3-030-49679-1_5

Turner, V. (1969). Liminality and Communitas. In *The Ritual Process: Structure and Anti Structure* (pp. 41-49). Cornell University Press.

Turner, V. (1969). *The Ritual Process: Structure and Anti-Structure*. Cornell University Press.

Turner, V. (1982). *From Ritual to Theatre: The Human Seriousness of Play*. PAJ Publications.

UN Office for the Co-ordination of Humanitarian Affairs ReliefWeb. (2023, November 13) *Initial reporting on the ongoing Israeli retaliatory attacks on Gaza: (Reporting Period, 7-28 October 2023) based on preliminary documentation [EN/AR] - occupied Palestinian territory*. Relief Web. https://reliefweb.int/report/occupied-palestinian-territory/initial-reporting -ongoing-israeli-retaliatory-attacks-gaza-reporting-period-7-28-october-2023-based-preliminary-documentation-enar

UN Office for the Co-ordination of Humanitarian Affairs ReliefWeb. (2024, March 14) *Hostilities at the Gaza Strip and Israel – reported humanitarian impact*. ReliefWeb. https://reliefweb.int/report/occupied-palestinian-territory/hostilities -gaza-strip-and-israel-reported-humanitarian-impact-14-march-2024-1500

United Nations Population Fund. (2024, April 2). *'Gaza is at breaking point': Health workers and patients describe an unfolding catastrophe in Rafah*. https://www.unfpa.org/news/%E2%80%9Cgaza-breaking-point%E2%80%9D-health -workers-and-patients-describe-unfolding-catastrophe-rafah

United Nations Population Fund. (2024, April 2). *Crisis in the occupied Palestinian territory*. UNPFA. https://www .unfpa.org/occupied-palestinian-territory

University of Georgia. (2011). *Today's top news from University of Georgia. Obituary, Linda Brooks*. UGA. https:// news.uga.edu/obituary-linda-brooks/

Urguhart, C. (2007, September 20). Israel declares Gaza Strip hostile territory. *The Guardian*. https://www.theguardian .com/world/2007/sep/20/israel1

Urion, C. (2023). Some Precepts Taught By Two Cree Elders And Their Implications For Talking About Music. In Stock, J., & Diamond, B. (Eds.), *The Routledge Companion to Ethics and Research in Ethnomusicology* (pp. 21–33).

Urmson, J. O. (1967). Memory and Imagination. *Mind, New Series*, *76*(301), 83-91. https://www.jstor.org/stable/2252029

Valdes, F. (1999). Afterword - theorizing "OutCrit" theories: Coalitional method and comparative jurisprudential experience - RaceCrits, QueerCrits, and LatCrits'. *University of Miami Law Review*, 1265.

van den Berg, K., & Schmidt-Wulffen, S. (2023). Performative Knowledge. In T. Philipp & T. Schmohl (Eds.), *Handbook Transdisciplinary Learning* (pp. 267–276). transcript. 10.14361/9783839463475-028 van Dijck, J. (2006). Record and Hold: Popular Music between Personal and Collective Memory. *Critical Studies in Media Communication*, 23(5), 357–374. 10.1080/07393180601046121

Vargese, R. (2019). *Ditty's debut album, Poetry Ceylon is a memoir of her life in Sri Lanka.* New Indian Express. https://www.indulgexpress.com/culture/music/2019/jun/07/-15504.html

Vasanthakumar, A. (2021). *The Ethics of Exile: A Political Theory of Diaspora.* 10.1093/oso/9780198828938.001.0001

Vaz-Pinheiro, G. (2005). *Curadoria do local: algumas abordagens da prática e da crítica.* Torres Vedras: ArtinSite.

Vazsonyi, N. (2011). The Total Work of Art: From Bayreuth to Cyberspace, and: Modernism after Wagner. *Modernism/Modernity*, 18(1), 196–199. 10.1353/mod.2011.0021

Versey, H. S., & Throne, R. (2021). A critical review of Gullah Geechee midlife women and heirs' property challenges along the Gullah Geechee Cultural Heritage Corridor. *Examining international land use policies, changes, and conflicts*, 46-64.

Villenas, S. (2001). Latina mothers and small-town racism: Creating narratives of dignity and moral education in North Carolina. *Anthropology & Education Quarterly*, 32(1), 3–28. 10.1525/aeq.2001.32.1.3

Vita-More, N. (2018). *Transhumanism: What is it?* Humanity+ publication.

Viverios de Castro, E. (2014). *Cannibal Metaphysics.* University of Minnesota Press.

Vromen, S. (1993). [Review of *Maurice Halbwachs on Collective Memory.*, by L. A. Coser. *American Journal of Sociology*, 99(2), 510–512. 10.1086/230291

Vygotsky, L. S. (2004). Imagination and Creativity in Childhood. *Journal of Russian & East European Psychology*, 42(1), 7–97. 10.1080/10610405.2004.11059210

Wagner, R. (2001). The artwork of the future. In Packer, R., & Jordan, K. (Eds.), *Multimedia: from Wagner to virtual reality.* Norton & Company. (Original work published 1849)

Wallerstein, I. (1974). *The Modern World-System, vol. I: Capitalist Agriculture and the Origins of the European World-Economy in the Sixteenth Century.* Academic Press.

Wallerstein, I. (1980). *The Modern World-System, vol. II: Mercantilism and the Consolidation of the European World-Economy, 1600-1750.* Academic Press.

Warde, P., Sörlin, S., & Robin, L. (2018). *The Environment: A History of the Idea.* John Hopkins University Press.

Wardrip-Fruin, N. (2006). *Expressive processing: on process intensive literature and digital media.* [PhD Thesis. Brown University, Providence, Rhode Island].

Warnock, M. (1978). *Imagination.* University of California Press.

Waterman, E. (2019). Performance Studies and Critical Improvisation Studies in Ethnomusicology. In *Theory for Ethnomusicology: Histories, Conversations* (pp. 141–175). Insights. 10.4324/9781315408583-7

Watton, C. (2020, April 24). *Using scrapbooks as historical sources.* History Journal. https://historyjournal.org.uk/2019/12/16/using-scrapbooks-as-historical-sources/

Watton, C. (n.d.). The radical history of scrapbooks – and why activists still use them today. *The Conversation.*https://theconversation.com/the-radical-history-of-scrapbooks-and-why-activists-still-use-them-today-172581

Watton, C. (2022). Suffrage scrapbooks and emotional histories of women's activism. *Women's History Review*, 31(6), 1028–1048. 10.1080/09612025.2021.2012343

Weaver, W. (1998). Recent contributions to the mathematical theory of communica tion. In *The mathematical theory of communication* (pp. 1–28). University of Illinois Press.

Webber, T. B. (2021). Creation and relations—A Sámi perspective on Scandinavian creation theology. *Dialog*, 60(2), 155–160. 10.1111/dial.12666

Weissman, A. L. (2017). Repronormativity and the reproduction of the nation-state: The state and sexuality collide. *Journal of GLBT Family Studies*, 13(3), 277–305. 10.1080/1550428X.2016.1210065

Weizman, E. (2012). *The least of all possible evils: Humanitarian violence from Arendt to Gaza*. Verso.

Weizman, E. (2017). *Forensic architecture: Violence at the threshold of detectability*. Princeton UP. 10.2307/j.ctv14gphth

Wenger, E. (1998). *Communities of Practice: Learning, Meaning and Identity*. Cambridge University Press. 10.1017/CBO9780511803932

Wesemann, A. (1997). Mirror Games with New Media: The Story of Dance has Always Been the Story of Technology. *International Ballet Tanz Aktuell*, 8/9.

Westgeest, H. (2008). The Changeability of Photography in Multimedia Artworks. Belfast: Leuven University Press.

Whittington, V. (2023). Memorialisation, Reconciliation and Truth-Speaking: The Role of Explorer and Massacre Memorials in Settler-Colonial Australia. *Journal of Australian Studies*, 1–19.

Wilde, O. (1905). The decay of lying. In *Intentions* (pp. 1–55). Brentano's.

Willie, D. (2015). Testimonio and the discursive politics of feminist epistemology. *Journal of Feminist Scholarship*, 7, 1–15.

Wilson, G. B., & MacDonald, R. A. R. (2005). The meaning of the blues: Musical identities in talk about jazz. *Qualitative Research in Psychology*, 2(4), 341–363. 10.1191/1478088705qp044oa

Winker, M. A. (2004). Measuring race and ethnicity: Why and how? *Journal of the American Medical Association*, 292(13), 1612–1614. 10.1001/jama.292.13.161215467065

Winter, Y. (2016). The siege of Gaza: Spatial violence, humanitarian strategies, and the biopolitics of punishment. *Constellations (Oxford, England)*, 23(2), 308–319. 10.1111/1467-8675.12185

Witkin, S. L. (2011). Why Do We Think Practice Research is a Good Idea? *Social Work & Society*, 9(1), 10–19.

Woodbrook, R., & Lazzaro, A. (2013). The Bonds of Organization: Zine Archives and the Archival Tradition. *Journal of Western Archives*4(1), 1-17. URL: https://doi.org/10.26077/e5d9-dec6

Wood, E. M. (1999). *The origin of capitalism*. Monthly Review Press.

Wood, H. H., & Byatt, A. S. (2008). *Memory an anthology*. Chatto & Windus.

Woolf, V., & Minogue, S. (2012). *A room of one's own & The voyage out*. Wordsworth Classics. (Original work published 1928)

Worley, M. (2015). Punk, Politics and British (Fan)Zines, 1976–84: "While the World Was Dying, Did You Wonder Why?". *History Workshop Journal*, 79(1), 76–106. 10.1093/hwj/dbu043

Yates, F. A. (1984). *Art of memory*.

York House Medical Centre. (n.d.). *A Guide for Patients, Practice History*. My Surgery Website. www.mysurgerywebsite.co.uk. https://www.mysurgerywebsite.co.uk/website/M81040/files/PRACTICE_BOOKLET_13.11.14.pdf

Yosso, T. J. (2005). Whose culture has capital? A critical race theory discussion of community cultural wealth. *Race, Ethnicity and Education*, 8(1), 69–91. 10.1080/1361332052000341006

Yúdice, G. (1991). Testimonio and postmodernism. *Latin American Perspectives*, 18(3), 15–31. 10.1177/0094582X9101800302

Yuval-Davis, N. (1993). Gender and nation. *Ethnic and Racial Studies*, 16(4), 621–632. 10.1080/01419870.1993.9993800

Zamalin, A. (2019). *Black utopia: The history of an idea from black nationalism to Afrofuturism*. Columbia University Press. 10.7312/zama18740

Zemeckis, R. (dir.) (2002). *Cast Away*. 20th Century Fox, DreamWorks Pictures, ImageMovers and Playtone.

Zevon, W. (1989). Run Straight Down. *Transverse City*. Virgin America 210253.

Zuboff, S. (2019). *The age of surveillance capitalism: The fight for a human future at the new frontier of power*. Profile.

Zuliani, A. L. (2022). Imagination in Renaissance Literature. In Sgarbi, M. (Ed.), *Encyclopedia of Renaissance Philosophy*. Springer. 10.1007/978-3-319-14169-5_858

Zulù, O. (2005). *Giuanne Palestina. On: Live in the Al Mukawama Experiment 3*. Novenove.

About the Contributors

Frederico Dinis is a lecturer and artist-researcher at the interface of performance and visual arts, seeking to represent a figurative space-time, combining sound and visual narratives with unusual places, and fostering audio-visual processes that move between past and present, and between individual and collective memory. He holds a PhD in Art Studies - Arts/Drama and Performance Studies from the University of Coimbra, a post-doctorate in Religious Studies from the Portuguese Catholic University and the Research Centre for Theology and Religious Studies and a post-doctorate in Sociology from the University of Porto. He is a researcher at the Research Institute in Design, Media and Culture (ID+) at the Polytechnic University of Cávado and Ave and an affiliated scholar of the Centre for the Study of Storytelling, Experientiality and Memory (SELMA) at the University of Turku. He is the author of several academic articles on theatre and performance studies, research methodologies through artistic practice, memory studies, sociology of art, art and cultural studies, religious studies, and art and technology.

***

Anicka Austin is a mixed media artist who primarily works with experimental movement and archival material. Her work has been supported by Atlanta Downtown Improvement District (2022-2023), Atlanta Contemporary Arts Center (2022-2023), and Fulton County Arts and Culture (2017) and exhibited at Zuckerman Museum of Art's Fine Arts Gallery (2018, GA), the Museum of Contemporary Art of Georgia (2018, ATL) and the Southeastern Center for Contemporary Art (2021). She was an Ansley Park Distinguished Fellow at the Hambidge Center for Creative Arts and Sciences in 2017, a 2015-2018 Lucky Penny Work Room resident artist, and 2021-2022 Art on the Atlanta Beltline Scholar-in-Residence. She works as an archivist at Emory University's Stuart A. Rose Manuscript, Archives, and Rare Book Library (ATL).

Bernadette Buckley is Convenor of the MA in Art & Politics at Goldsmiths, University of London. Her expertise cuts across art, politics, philosophy and cultural studies, in particular exploring the relationship between art, violence, conflict and terrorism. She has published widely in books, exhibition catalogues and journals, considering subjects as varied as the use of guns by women artists, or the evolving role of art in times of war and conflict. She was called as an Expert Witness for an All-Party Parliamentary Committee Evidence Enquiry and Report into building resilience to radicalisation and violent extremism (UK Parliament). She serves on several advisory boards and committees and has worked on funded research projects for AHRC, ACE, En-quire, Heritage Lottery and the Wellcome Foundation.

Beatriz Cantinho is an Assistant Professor at the Theatre Department of the University of Évora (PT). Holds a PhD in Dance and Philosophy from the University of Edinburgh. She was a visiting scholar at TISCH_NYU, performance and film departments_2010/2011. She is an independent choreographer and a researcher at the laboratories of CHAIA – University of Évora and CIAC – University of Algarve. Her recent work has been focused on a critical analysis of movement within its aesthetic/ political dimension, considered as an expanded choreographic practice, which supports her research and artistic creation. Her artistic and research work has been presented both in Portugal, in CCB, Fundação Serralves, MNAC, Acarte, Lisbon Architecture Triennale, and abroad: Galeria Guillotine (FR), SARC, DanceBase, Blue Elephant Theatre (UK), Matadero (SP). Transmedial Festival, Rosa Luxemburg Foundation and TESLA (DE), among others. Her academic research has been presented in several Universities: Surrey, Cambridge, Brunel, Stanford, Berkeley, Chelsea College of Art.

Krina Cayabyab is currently a PhD in Music student at the University of Edinburgh, with a research focus on postcolonial history of jazz in Metro Manila from 1946 to 1986. She works at the Department of Musicology of the University of the Philippines College of Music, where she received her Bachelor of Music in Choral Conducting and Master of Music in Musicology degrees. Krina arranges for and performs with the female vocal trio Baihana (2008), and composes music for theatre, short films, dance, live events, and studio recordings. Her research involves popular music and ethnomusicology in the Philippines.

Shrimoyee Chattopadhyay has completed her PhD from the British Studies programme at the Doctoral School of Literary and Cultural Studies, University of Debrecen, Hungary. She does research in contemporary South Asian diasporic fiction and film, but her interests include gender studies, urban studies, food culture, memory, and trauma studies. Currently, she is working with the literary and cinematic texts of contemporary diaspora female writers and film directors, such as Jhumpa Lahiri, Monica Ali, Bharati Mukherjee, Chitra Divakaruni, Kamila Shamsie, Fatima Bhutto, Tahmima Anam, Sorayya Khan, and Gurinder Chadha. Her main focus lies in the interconnectedness of gender, city space, and memory studies. She has presented her research papers in esteemed universities, such as Oxford and Cambridge, among others. Her scholarly articles have been published in several national and international journals.

Siobhan Davies was brought to England by her mother and English stepfather in 1969. She grew up in the North-West, near Manchester, then studied Fine Art in Newcastle and Birmingham. She moved to London and practiced for ten years, winning awards such as the New Contemporaries and RSA Artists. Working in mixed media, she made site-specific work for projects such as The Berwick Ramparts Project and Salisbury Festival. By the late '90s, she was Henry Moore Fellow and visiting lecturer in London and Norwich and showing in experimental exhibitions. On starting a family, she transitioned into digital design via graphic design and worked in the City of London for many years as an Analyst, keeping her art practice alive through drawing, making and writing in her spare time. In 2018 she began to explore the idea of home as a site, and subsequently returned to further study (2021-23); she now works in the field of interiors and the archive.

Elisa Frasson is an Italian dance researcher currently based in Berlin, with extensive experience in the curatorship of contemporary dance and screendance. Highly interested in creative and collaborative processes, in recent years she has been focused on fieldwork by collaborating with dance companies in Italy and Germany. Her current research areas are dance criticism and fieldwork as relationships creators and the screendance educational potential considered as an expanded genre. Elisa completed a PhD in dance Studies (2022, University of Roehampton, London) with a thesis on the influences of somatic practices into European choreography during 1980s-2010s, a transnational field and archival enquiry study. Her recent projects have been supported by Dachverband Tanz Deutschland and Fonds Darstellende Künst. She is now working with laborgras (DE) on an archive project and as visiting lecturer (Università IUAV, Venice and Dams Roma Tre, Roma, IT). She writes for Dance Context Webzine (CZ) and Stream (DE).

Heidrun Führer works as Associate Professor at the Department of Arts and Cultural Sciences within the Division of Culture Management at Lund University. Her research field is ekphrasis, theatre, performativity, the Total work of Art, popular culture and advertising. To list some of her publications: Heidrun Führer, Anna Kraus, 2019. "Leaving the White Cube of Ekphrasis. Gordon Matta-Clark's Conical Intersection" in Salmose, Niklas and Elleström, Lars (eds) Transmediations: Communication Across Media Borders - Communication Across Media Borders Routledge, pp. 97-117. Heidrun Führer, Cecilia Victoria Muszta, Viktor Kováca, 2023. "The Anchor and the Dolphin: A History of Emblems" in Jörgen Bruhn, Asun López-Varela Azcárate, Miriam De Paiva Viera (eds) The Palgrave Handbook of Intermediality, Palgrave Macmillan, pp. 521–550.

Mayra Garcia-Diaz is a Doctoral Fellow at Georgia Southern University, she has been conducting qualitative research on immigrant Latinxs. Her research interests include Parental Involvement, Critical Race Feminista Methodology, Chicana Feminist Theories, Collective Memory, Testimonio Methodology, and Pedagogies. She also writes and presents on issues of Spanish as a Second Language. Her studies encompass the complex dynamics of foreign language anxiety, a case study in L2, and explore the correlation between effective parental involvement and decreased language anxiety.

Paula Guerra is Associate Professor of Sociology at the University of Porto and Researcher at the Institute of Sociology of the same University. Paula is Adjunct Associate Professor of the Griffith Centre for Social and Cultural Research in Australia. Guerra is a leading international scholar on the topics of sociology of culture, of youth and arts. Based at University of Porto, Portugal, she has consolidated worldwide partnerships and research networks. Guerra has been a visiting professor at numerous international universities. She is founder and coordinator of the scientific network/journal All the Arts. Luso-Brazilian Network of Art and Culture. Paula is the founder/coordinator of the KISMIF (kismifconference.com and kismifcommunity.com). She coordinates several research projects subordinated to the youth cultures, sociology of the arts and culture, co-creation, DIY cultures, among other subjects. She has likewise advised and supervised several Masters, PhD and Post-Doc projects in the aforementioned areas. She is a member of the editorial council of several national and international journals, as well as editor and reviewer of several articles and books.

Michael B. MacDonald is an award-winning cine-ethnomusicologist, Professor of music, and Chancellor's Research Chair at MacEwan University's Faculty of Fine Arts and Communications located in amiskwacâskahikan, what settlers call Edmonton, Alberta, Canada. His ongoing research investigates research-creational posthumanities, digital audiovision, and DIY digital culture. His research-creational intervention works at the interface of music ethnography and cinema production as discussed in "CineWorlding: Scenes of Cinematic Research-Creation" (Bloomsbury 2023). MacDonald's films have screened at more than 80 film festivals winning documentary and experimental film awards. He has published widely on music studies, youth culture, cinematic research-creation, cine-ethnographic and cine-ethnomusicological theory with book chapters included in influential handbooks. He is the author of "Playing for Change" (2016), "Remix and Lifehack in Hip Hop" (2016), and co-editor for "A History of Progressive Music and Youth Culture" (2020).

Susana Mendes Silva is a visual artist, performer, professor and member of the direction of the Portuguese Association of Visual Artists. Her work incorporates elements of research and archival practice that leads to the creation of works whose historical and political references become visible as exhibitions, actions and performances that employ a wide variety of media. Her psychological intimacy and her voice are often the means for the diffusion and reception of poetic and political messages that call upon them. Susana studied Sculpture at FBAUL (Lisbon, PT), and in the Fine Art Studio Based Research PhD at Goldsmiths College with a Calouste Gulbenkian Foundation grant. She has a PhD based in her practice — "Performance as an Intimate Encounter" — by the College of the Arts of the University of Coimbra. Susana is an Assistant Professor at the University of Évora and a Research fellow at CEIS20/Universidade de Coimbra.

Marcello Messina is a Sicilian composer and academic working as Chief Researcher at Southern Federal University (SFEDU). He holds a Ph.D. in composition from the University of Leeds (UK), and is also holding honorary positions as Visiting Professor at the Federal Universities of Paraíba and Acre. He has been the recipient of the Endeavour Research Fellowship at Macquarie University, Sydney, Australia, and of the PNPD/Capes post-doctoral bursary at the Universidade Federal do Acre, Brazil.

Thorsten Philipp studied art history, Romance languages, and political science at the universities of Munich, Vienna, Brescia, and Aix-en-Provence. As an Advisor for Transdisciplinary Learning at TU Berlin, he is in charge of promoting cross-disciplinary and cross-institutional education projects at the intersection of university, business, culture, politics and civil society. Research fellow at the Institute for Language and Communication at TU Berlin, he teaches at several universities, among them Albert-Ludwig-University of Freiburg and Leuphana University Lüneburg. His research focuses environmental communication and pop music.

Pedro Quintela is a sociologist and consultant specialising in planning and development. Pedro has a PhD in Sociology from the University of Coimbra - Faculty of Economics, a Masters in Cities and Urban Cultures from the University of Coimbra - Faculty of Economics, and a degree in Sociology from ISCTE - University Institute of Lisbon. He has published 15 articles in specialised journals. He has one book chapter(s) and five books. Participates and/or has participated as a researcher in 1 project(s). He works in the area(s) of social sciences with an emphasis on sociology. His research interests are: cultural and creative industries; cultural policies; public investment; youth cultures; subcultures; neotribes; scenes; punk culture; fanzines; do-it-yourself (DIY); alternative media; self-publishing; graphic design; illustration; arts management.

Saira Raza is a business librarian at Emory University's Goizueta Business Library. She holds an MSLS from University of North Texas, an MPS in Africana Studies from Cornell University, and a BA in International Studies from Wells College. She has led Emory Libraries DEI Committee since its start as a working group in 2016, witnessing the committee's sustained growth and impact across over the years to nearly 30 highly engaged volunteer members. Prior to working at Emory, Saira worked as a business librarian at Lehman Brothers (now Barclays) and King & Spalding. Saira's interests are in decolonizing libraries and educating future leaders to harness the power of good research skills to make informed, ethical, and equitable decisions.

Robin Throne, PhD, is a human research protections professional and research methodologist. Her research agenda continues to consider doctoral researcher positionality and agency, and voice and land dispossession from various social justice research approaches.

Eleni Timplalexi is a Laboratory Lecturing Staff member, Department of Communication & Media Studies (NTLab), NKUA. She holds a post doc in Digital Media and Theatre, Department of Theatre Studies, NKUA, awarded with an IKY Fellowship of Excellence for postgraduate studies in Greece-Siemens Program (2015-16). She completed her PhD in the same department with an IKY PhD scholarship (2010-14). Also, an Alexander C. Onassis Public Benefit Foundation Scholar in Theatre Practice (2005-07). Recently, a post doc guest researcher with Linnaeus University Centre for Intermedial and Multimodal Studies and in research collaboration with Lund University, Sweden. Awarded playwright, theatre director and artist, currently involved in Magenta Artistic Collaboration and collaborating with Spatial Media Research Group.

Index

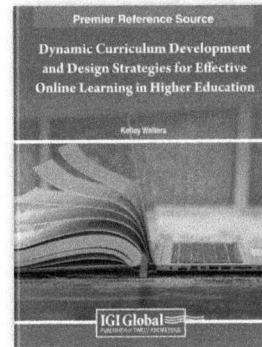

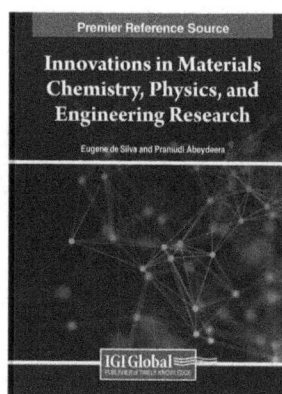

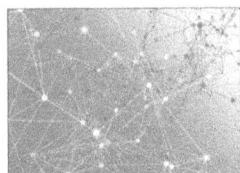

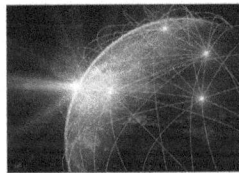

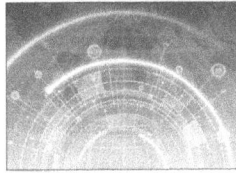